# Structures of Social Life

## The Four Elementary Forms of Human Relations

Communal Sharing
Authority Ranking
Equality Matching
Market Pricing

*With a New Epilogue*

# Alan Page Fiske

THE FREE PRESS
*A Division of Macmillan, Inc.*
NEW YORK

Maxwell Macmillan Canada
TORONTO

Maxwell Macmillan International
NEW YORK   OXFORD   SINGAPORE   SYDNEY

The Free Press
A Division of Macmillan, Inc.
866 Third Avenue, New York, N.Y. 10022

Maxwell Macmillan Canada, Inc.
1200 Eglinton Avenue East
Suite 200
Don Mills, Ontario M3C 3N1

Macmillan, Inc. is part of the Maxwell Communication Group of Companies.

First Free Press Paperback Edition 1993

Printed in the United States of America

printing number

1 2 3 4 5 6 7 8 9 10

Four lines of "The Death of the Hired Man" (p. 352) are excerpted from *The Poetry of Robert Frost* edited by Edward Connery Lathem. Copyright 1930, 1939, ©1969 by Holt, Rinehart and Winston. Copyright © 1958 by Robert Frost. Copyright © 1967 by Lesley Frost Ballantine. Reprinted by permission of Henry Holt and Company, Inc., Jonathan Cape Ltd., and the Estate of Robert Frost.

**Library of Congress Cataloging-in-Publication Data**
Fiske, Alan Page
    Structures of social life: the four elementary forms of human
    relations: communal sharing, authority ranking, equality matching,
    market pricing / Alan Page Fiske.
       p. cm.
    Includes index.
    ISBN 0-02-906687-5
    1. Mossi (African people) Social life and customs. 2. Ethnology
Burkina Faso. 3. Interpersonal relations. 4. Social interaction.
5. Community. 6. Social status. 7. Equality. 8. Value.
9. Exchange theory (Sociology) 1. Title.
HM132.F5728 1991
302-dc20                                 90–40040
                                             CIP

to all those around the world—
beginning with my parents, Barbara and Donald—
who have shown me the meaning and the importance
of the four basic relationships

# Contents

Preface  *ix*

Acknowledgments  *xi*

*Part I: The Relational Models*

Preface to Part I  1
1 Introduction  3
2 The Framework  13

*Part II: Manifestions of the Relational Models*

Preface to Part II  41

3 Things  51
4 Choices  73
5 Orientations  82
6 Judgments  115
 Coda: Discord and Harm  130

*Part III: The Structures of Social Relations*

Preface to Part III  139

7 Generativity and Cross-Cultural Variability
 in the Production of Social Relations  141
8 Defining Features of the Relational Models  169
9 Semiotic Marking and Relational Structures  202

*Part IV:* Ration*al Self-Interest or Solidarity:*
*The Predominance of Noneconomic Motives*
*Among the Moose of Burkina Faso*

Preface to Part IV                                                      231

10 An Egalitarian Motive: The Goal of Even Matching                     243
11 A Communal Solidarity Motive: The Goal of Sharing
   and Unity                                                            258
12 Transferring Women in Marriage: Sharing,
   Not Self-Interested, or *Rational* Exchange                          286
13 Authority Ranking: Precedence and Deference                          309
14 Economic Rationality                                                 324
15 Social Orientations in Neighboring Societies                         346


*Part V:* *Human Nature and Society*

Preface to Part V                                                       369

16 The Multiplicity of Fundamental Social Orientations                  371
17 Sources of Sociability                                               381

   Epilogue to the Paperback Edition                                    409

   Notes                                                                415

   References                                                           438

   Index                                                                469


   Summary table: Manifestations and Features
   of Four Elementary Relational Models                                 42

# Preface

The social sciences have diverged into centrifugal pursuits, and to some extent this is a necessary and appropriate consequence of their diversity of methods and topics (see D. Fiske and Shweder 1986 on the epistemological constraints). But this centrifugal history has also led to a much lamented but little remedied lack of communication among the increasingly far-flung fields of social science. My hope in writing this book is to show that social scientists have independently uncovered bits and pieces of something that can only be understood when we bring the fragments back together and reconstruct the whole from which they come. It is my thesis that whenever human beings relate to each other, they organize their social relations on the basis of four elementary psychological models. If this is so then social psychologists, social and psychological anthropologists, sociologists, political scientists, economists, historians, and other social scientists are all studying manifestations of the same four basic modes of human social interaction.

The same four elementary forms of social relations manifest themselves in diverse social domains in a great many cultures. Communal Sharing is a relation of unity, community, undifferentiated collective identity, and kindness, typically enacted among close kin. Authority Ranking is a relationship of asymmetric differences, commonly exhibited in a hierarchical ordering of statuses and precedence, often accompanied by the exercise of command and complementary displays of deference and respect. Equality Matching is a one-to-one correspondence relationship in which people are distinct but equal, as manifested in balanced reciprocity (or tit-for-tat revenge), equal share distributions or identical contributions, in-kind replacement compensation, and turn taking. Market Pricing is based on an (intermodel) metric of value by which people compare different commodities and calculate exchange and cost/benefit ratios. It is the thesis of this book that people use these four relational models to generate, understand ("parse"), coordinate, and evaluate social relations.

Part I of the book illustrates and describes the models and explains how they have been implicit in earlier social theories in various fields. Part II then shows how the models emerge in diverse domains of social action and thought. Part III shows how four elementary models can produce diverse and complex social forms and analyzes the formal structural congruence among these diverse manifestations. It also presents criteria for distinguishing the class of elementary models from other kinds of rules and schemata. Part IV depicts how the models operate to structure social relations in West Africa, and shows that kindness, equality, deference, and responsibility predominate over cost/benefit orientations in this part of the world, at least. Part V discusses the implications of this theory for the problem of social structure, the question of whether social "systems" are coherently integrated, and the question of the sources of human sociability.

Writing this book has been a great intellectual adventure; I hope reading it will be equally exciting. I do not think that this theory represents the "truth" about human social relations, if there is any such thing. I just hope that it contains interesting errors, stimulating omissions, and fruitful confusions.

# Acknowledgments

$B$arbara Fiske, Donald Fiske, Walter Goldfrank, Nick Haslam, John Lucy, and Kathryn Mason read the manuscript of this book with care and dedication, providing enormous help to me in making it more intelligible and sensible than I could ever have made it without them. Major sections of it have profited greatly from comments by Arjun Appadurai, Sandra Barnes, Jon Baron, Muriel Bell, Donald Campbell, Charles R. Gallistel, Lila Gleitman, Jon Haidt, Michael Kelly, Igor Kopytoff, Mark Lepper, Nicholas Maxwell, Clark R. McCauley, Susan Milmoe, Judson Mills, Pauline Peters, Charlie Piot, David Premack, Rena Repetti, Paul Rozin, John Sabini, Deborah Stearns, and one anonymous reviewer. The work on which it is based has also been fostered and aided by discussions with Assaad Azzi, Mihaly Csikszentmihalyi, John Comaroff, Jean Comaroff, Siri Dulaney, Barbara Fiske, Donald Fiske, Susan Fiske-Emery, Suzanne Gaskins, Lila Gleitman, Lisa Jaycox, Donald Levine, John Lucy, Kathryn Mason, Margaret Meibohm, Paul Rozin, John Sabini, Richard Shweder, Scott Weinstein, and Harold Zullow. In response to talks on this material I have received many valuable ideas and comments from faculty and graduate students at the Psychology Departments of the Universities of Chicago, Pennsylvania, Maryland, Massachusetts at Amherst, and Yale, from participants in Nags Head Conferences, in sessions of the American Anthropological Association, and the Association for the Advancement of Socio-Economics, in the Delaware Valley Faculty Exchange, and the University of Pennsylvania Sloan Cognitive Science Group, as well as by many perceptive undergraduates and graduate students in my classes at the University of Pennsylvania.

The underlying research was supported by a Social Science Research Council International Doctoral Research Fellowship, a National Science Foundation Dissertation Research Grant, a U.S. Office of Education Fulbright-Hays Dissertation Research Abroad Fellowship, a USPHS National Institute of

x                                                               Acknowledgments

Mental Health National Research Service Award, research grants from the University of Pennsylvania, the Threshold IBM program at the University of Pennsylvania, and NIMH grant 1 R29 MH43857-01.

With cheerful alacrity Melissa Barnes and Heidi Dupret tracked down and checked out many of the books cited here and photocopied most of the articles. Ann Fisher carefully checked all the quotations. The Inter-Library Loan staff at Van Pelt Library also provided invaluable assistance. Paul Rozin cheerfully and doggedly prodded me to get the book out of the way so I could write it all up as an article, while Barbara, Donald, and Susan Fiske wisely exhorted and lovingly encouraged me. Throughout the long process of thinking things out and then writing, I was sustained by the patience, encouragement, inspirational ideas, and good humor of Kathryn F. Mason, who was my wife, colleague, fellow fieldworker, and companion. She, Gwendolyn M. Fiske, and Colin B. Fiske all put up with my late returns from the office, groggy mornings, and sometimes worn-out patience, cheering me up and keeping me in touch with the reality of the nicest human relations at times when a theory of human relations was no substitute. With grace and good sense, Susan Milmoe, her assistant Gioia Stevens, and Celia Knight shepherded the book through the transformation from manuscript to published book. Judith Field did the meticulous and sensible copy editing. Michael Drake and his associates expeditiously made innumerable photocopies. Siri Dulaney gave me the courage, faith, reassurance and sense of humor to complete the book, together with the good sense to keep it in perspective. I wholeheartedly thank all these people and institutions, without whose support this work could not have been done.

# Part *I*

# The Relational Models

## PREFACE TO PART I

Part I describes four elementary models that people use (unselfconsciously) to construct, understand, respond to, evaluate, and coordinate social relationships. I begin by illustrating with a hypothetical example how the same four schemata emerge in a variety of domains of social action and thought. In Chapter 2, after defining the four underlying models, I show how the present theory integrates a wide range of antecedent theories in several social science disciplines. Chapters 3 through 6 in Part II then demonstrate systematically how these four models govern social interaction in diverse domains not previously encompassed by social scientists in a single theoretical framework. The framework presented here integrates research on the circulation of things in all kinds of transactions (exchange, distributions and contributions, justice), on the organization of work, and on many of the ways in which people relate socially to objects, land, and time. It seems to underlie marriage systems in traditional societies and major forms of marriage in the industrial world. It also provides an integrated framework for the study of decision processes, social influence, group formation, structure and norms, identity and self, social needs and motivations, moral judgment, political ideology and social legitimation. Further, the framework offers a systematic approach to understanding social emotions, aggression and social conflict, responses to transgression and misfortune, and possibly the psychology of religion. Indeed, this theory encompasses and promises to integrate such a vast range of social phenomena that it suggests there is some reasonable prospect that a unified theory of social relations may eventually emerge.

# 1

# Introduction

My thesis is that people must use some kind of models of and for social relations to guide their own social initiatives and to understand and respond appropriately to the social action of others. People presumably use these models to plan possible actions and anticipate others' future actions, and above all to coordinate action so that dyads and groups act in concert—undertaking complementary actions that mesh with each other in a whole that makes sense as an integrated social relationship. Further, people apparently use such models to evaluate their own and others' actions, to persuade, criticize and sanction others, and to negotiate with them. Taken together, the set of such models should be something like the generative grammar of a language that can yield any number of novel but comprehensible utterances. The models also resemble a grammar in that people use them without generally being able to articulate them as a set of explicit rules. It is my hypothesis that people actually generate most kinds of social relationships out of only four basic models: Communal Sharing, Authority Ranking, Equality Matching, and Market Pricing. These implicit models are the psychological foundations of social relations and society.

## EXAMPLE

To introduce the four generative models and their pervasive role in shaping social relations, let us examine one concrete example of how people might use them in a variety of social domains. Imagine a small town considering the issue of how to provide for fire fighting. How might the townspeople make a decision about their problem? One possibility is for them to mull over and discuss the issue, either informally or at a meeting, until a community consensus emerges. This is, for example, the mechanism used in institutions organized

3

by the Society of Friends (Quakers). Everyone participates, anyone who has an opinion expresses it, and the issue is considered until a sense of the group emerges—a unanimous agreement about the best course of action. If there is no consensus, no decision is reached and the issue has to be dropped. But if the group reaches a decision, it is their collective decision *as a group*, and—ideally—not the result of one faction having overcome another; the community as a unit stands behind the decision. This is decision making in the Communal Sharing mode.

Another mechanism is for a recognized authority to settle the matter unilaterally, by fiat. If a duly constituted leader (or a sufficiently charismatic one) rules on the matter, then that person's word is law, and subordinates comply out of respect, deference, loyalty, or awe. The leader's will is done, within the sphere of her authority, just because it is her will. However, her authority entails the responsibility to make a wise and incisive choice. So in this case the mayor or city manager might be empowered to decide what to do, or a powerful leader of some other sort (the factory owner, the chief, the feudal lord, the charismatic labor leader or preacher) might have the authority to determine what to do. The leader may decide the broad policy and delegate detailed implementation decisions to subordinates at one or more lower levels. This is the Authority Ranking mode of decision making.

A third possibility is to submit the question to a referendum, thereby giving each member of the town (or each adult) a share in the decision that matches every other voter's share at the level of the ballot. Each person's ballot would count equally. Or there could be a two-stage process in which people vote for city council representatives, who in turn vote to decide the fire protection issue. This is decision making according to the Equality Matching model.

Finally, the town could decide what to do about fighting fires through the market. This was the mechanism that many Eastern seaboard towns once followed. Those who wished to do so bought fire insurance and put plaques on their houses to indicate that they were purchasers. In our hypothetical town, fire companies could compete in terms of price and services, allowing each house owner to choose whether to buy insurance and from whom. The existence and quality of fire protection would depend on how much house owners were willing to pay (demand for fire insurance), together with what it cost to provide various levels and kinds of service (supply), as a function of actuarial risk assessments. This is decision making through Market Pricing. Note that deciding through the market means that people will influence the decision in proportion to their wealth and desire for fire protection—unlike Equality Matching, where each person counts equally in the decision (regardless of whether they live in stone or wood houses, are afraid of fire or not, are fire engineers or totally uninformed).

Thus, overall, there are four kinds of decision processes, each with its own distinctive characteristics. Real-life decision mechanisms frequently incorporate more than one of these elementary models, as, for example, when people vote on a general law whose details and implementation are set out in regulations written by officials. On the other hand, people may make no joint, so-cially organized decision at all about fire fighting, and it is worthwhile to keep this anarchic Null relationship case in mind.

Now imagine the kinds of moral and political arguments that townspeople might consider in making the decision about fire fighting. People might have a strong sense of mutual identification and community solidarity, feeling that they should help and protect each other whenever the need arises. They might feel that providing protection from fires is a natural part of belonging to a corporate group of fellow townspeople bound together by kindness, compas-sion, and charity; people in such a community should hang together and look out for one another. It's our town, they might say, we all live in it together, and fire threatens us all, so we should pull together and take care of our own. Anyone's loss is everyone's loss. Here we see moral thinking formulated in terms of Communal Sharing.

Alternatively, townspeople might frame their judgments in terms of the word of some paramount being. They might look to the Bible for guidance, as the revealed word of God and the teachings of Jesus Christ, or to the Koran, as the teachings of the Prophet Muhammad. They might invoke and find direc-tion in the advice of a charismatic guru or a preacher, feeling that he had ex-ceptional insight. Or they might be oriented to some secular authority, whose knowledge and judgment they respected, arguing that her superior wisdom should be their guide about what course to follow. In such a case, they would judge that the right course of action was whatever the paramount being guided them to do; they would obey her out of loyalty or awe. This is moral reasoning in the framework of Authority Ranking.

People also might ground their reflection and discussion about the fire-fighting issue in convictions about human equality, fairness, and reciprocity. They might justify a fire department in terms of rights to equal protection, saying that everyone deserves to be equally safe. It would be unfair, the argu-ment goes, for some to have protection while others go without. They might even decide they should not have a fire department if it could not provide equal service to all, wherever they lived. Or townspeople could formulate es-sentially the same logic in terms of strict reciprocity: "We all vote, we all pay taxes, and we each help out at the fund-raising carnival, so each person should get the same service." Another form of this position grounds arguments in comparisons with other towns: "We're just as good as Neighborville, so if they can have fire protection, so should we—every town should have its own fire department." Or the same basic equality ideal could be expressed in terms of reciprocity: "It's not right that the Neighborville fire department should have to come put out our fires when we can't do the same for them. It's our turn to give them something in return for what they've done for us. If we had our own fire truck, we could help them, and they could help us back. That would be only fair." This is an appeal to moral axioms of the Equality Matching model.

Another possibility is that people might argue in terms of the right to freedom of choice and the moral value of each person's making his or her own rational choices and living with the consequences. Thus they might believe that each individual should be free to choose whether to pay the expense of fire protection, and that no one else is entitled to deprive any person of this freedom of choice. It is up to each person, this argument goes, to make a rational decision about just how much fire protection is worth to him or her, calculating the benefits, costs, risks, and temporal discounts. Implicit in this argument is the belief that contracts voluntarily entered into are morally and legally binding, and that a fire company is bound to actually provide the service to customers with whom it makes contracts. These arguments are couched in terms of Market Pricing. In some unincorporated suburban areas of Cook County, Illinois, for example, individual property owners do in fact make just this choice about whether to purchase fire protection from a neighboring town.[1]

Any actual moral, political, or ideological debate typically includes all of these kinds of arguments, often mixed together in complex ways. In contrast, it may also happen that people try to persuade others through terror, direct physical coercion, or sexual inducements, and people may abandon persuasion in favor of force, threatening, terrorizing, or killing their opponents. In the domain of moral and political debate, these are the Asocial cases, the cases where ethics is abandoned entirely: the Null relationship. Such coercion is not Authority Ranking when those subjected to it do not recognize or acknowledge their hierarchical subjugation in a legitimate social relationship; if they do conceive of their suffering as the appropriate response to their own disobedience, then it becomes a legitimate punishment, not arbitrary violence.

The standards for judging social relations embodied in these four kinds of moral and political arguments correspond with the normative conceptions of social relations underlying the four different decision-making procedures. They correspond in the sense that a preference for one or another form of decision-making procedure would tend to be grounded in the ideology (moral, religious, and political values) that fits, the values that "naturally" form the foundation for each respective decision-making scheme. Furthermore, each decision mechanism corresponds to a specific kind of ideological argument because the four decision procedures and the four social values are based on the same set of four implicit models of how people should, and do, relate to one another. Analytically, this tends to link decision-making schemes with homologous forms of moral reasoning or political debate, although the social forms in the two domains need not always correspond: people may use any form of argument within any particular decision-making process. More important, observe that in each context we find the same four basic kinds of social logic, the same four alternative models: Communal Sharing, Authority Ranking, Equality Matching, and Market Pricing.

People can use each of these relational models to organize the allocation of responsibilities and the organization of work of fire fighting itself. In locations where specialized fire companies do not exist, everyone pitches in and does what they can to put out fires (Communal Sharing). When someone discovers a fire, everyone comes with buckets or whatever they have at hand and all work as hard as they can at whatever needs to be done, contributing according to their various skills, abilities, and strengths. Putting out a fire is a community effort, in which all are jointly involved and individual responsibilities may not be defined and distinguished. "We" do the work together, as a community. Alternatively, people may organize fire fighting as it is done in the military and to a large extent in civilian fire departments, in which there is a hierarchy of officers who direct and control the work (Authority Ranking). Higher ranking people dictate to their subordinates what to do; they delegate tasks, direct the work, and are held responsible for the results. Subordinates must obey commands unhesitatingly and defer to their superiors' decisions, while superior officers are responsible for the safety and protection of those they supervise. Fire fighting can also be organized on an egalitarian basis in a number of ways (Equality Matching). Each adult in the town may take turns being on call a week at a time to respond to fire alarms. Each adult could be drafted to do fire service at a certain age, or the town could hold a lottery to determine who will serve. Or each household may be required to send one able-bodied person who must bring two fire buckets in the event of an alarm. The fourth mode of organizing responsibility for fire fighting is to pay people to do it (Market Pricing). People may choose whether or not to join the fire department, depending on what the pay and benefits are and what effort and risks are entailed. A fire fighters' union could negotiate contracts with the town, trying to get the best possible salary, and fire fighters' contracts would spell out their responsibilities precisely. Fire fighting could be a strictly commercial enterprise, either through fire insurance or, conceivably, by striking deals on the spot. (Salvage and towing of disabled ships at sea by commercial tug boats is often conducted as an ad hoc business enterprise like this.)

There is also a fifth possibility: fire fighting could be completely anarchic, with no true social organization of responsibilities at all. That is, people could try to put out fires without attempting to coordinate with others, without taking into account others' needs, wishes, expectations or standards. Each person could attempt to extinguish his or her own fires, without paying any attention to neighbors' conflagrations. In modern cities this sort of asocial behavior is observable in some domains; in some circumstances, people do not implement any structured social relation at all with respect to a given issue. This is the limiting, Null case (which must be distinguished from the libertarian ethos, whose individual rights ideology is a social construction based on the Market Pricing model). In practice, however, most human behavior is socially oriented to a greater or lesser degree, and these four models for organizing work and responsibilities are often combined in various ways.

The people in our hypothetical town have the same set of four basic alternatives for the distribution of resources (material goods, immaterial benefits, or services) used for fire fighting. Suppose a stock of fire extinguishers were available—say, from a federal grant. They could be kept in a central pool for use as needed, or allocated on a help-yourself basis, so that people took whatever they needed or wanted—and freely passed on extinguishers to others whenever asked (Communal Sharing). In this mode, people think of the extinguishers as belonging to the group as a whole, not as the property of any individual member. Or fire extinguishers could be distributed according to the status of the townspeople, with the mayor getting the most, the biggest and best, and the first choice, the fire commissioner then getting several of the next best, and those of successively lower rank subsequently taking fewer and less desirable extinguishers, with perhaps none available to townspeople of the lowest standing (Authority Ranking). Alternatively, each person or each household could get exactly the same number and type of extinguisher (Equality Matching). Otherwise, the town could sell extinguishers by auction, sealed bids, or at a fixed price, to whoever would pay for them (Market Pricing). Another option would be to distribute extinguishers to households in proportion to real estate taxes paid, to the square footage of houses, or give them to neighborhoods in proportion to votes cast for the winning mayoral candidate, or some other proportional scheme (another form of Market Pricing). Each of these distributional schemes is morally correct according to its own criterion: the four justice principles are need (or kindness, or collective sharing), status, equality, and due proportionality ("equity," or freedom of choice in a market).

The allocation of responsibilities and the organization of work, as well as the distribution of resources, are closely related to another set of options for the townspeople: the kind of transfers (systems of distribution, contribution, exchange, and other transactions) they use to obtain the fire-fighting equipment and supplies, and how rights to their use of it will be structured. Some supplies, like water and sand, may be treated as a commons, freely used by all, with no accountability for use and no counterobligations entailed by use per se (Communal Sharing). In that case, simply belonging to the relevant group or being the right type of person entitles one to free access. Quite probably no one would have to give anything in return for the emergency use of water provided to them—in a crisis, what's mine is yours (if the people involved are close enough). Second, the mayor might expropriate fire-fighting supplies by eminent domain, condemning the property of someone who had a source of sand. Or the lord of a feudal domain might command his subjects to bring him spades and hoes. Conversely, the lord or some great benefactor might supply a fire engine, as an act of seigneurial benevolence in partial fulfillment of his responsibility to protect his people from harm and provide for their general welfare (Authority Ranking). Or the government might provide fire equipment under the same general rubric. In such cases, the townspeople might owe nothing in particular to the authority who provided the fire engine in consequence of that *specific* benefaction. They would, however, be obligated to give respect, deference, loyalty, and possibly obedience to their superior, whose superiority and rank would be considerably buttressed, or even partially constituted in the first place, by giving the fire engine.

As a third alternative, the town might obtain some equipment by reciprocal, quid pro quo exchange (Equality Matching). Suppose one town had purchased two fire trucks of one kind, and over the years another town bought three of another type, and then it was discovered that each kind of fire truck was effective against a different sort of fire. The two towns might trade trucks evenly, one-for-one, so that each town had at least one of each kind. Conceivably, a set of towns might take turns using a single fire engine, say, arranging fireworks displays on different nights so they could each have the fire engine on hand when the risk was greatest, or simply having it in town on alternating months. More likely, they might have reciprocal assistance arrangements, with each coming to the aid of the other and neither required to maintain the entire complement of equipment necessary to extinguish a major fire. "It's a fair system: they come to our alarms; we go to theirs. In the long run it all evens out." And finally, of course, the town (or any individual, family, neighborhood, or corporation within it) could purchase equipment on the open market, asking for bids or comparison shopping, bargaining, and paying for goods received (Market Pricing). Here again we see the same four schemas operating in yet another domain.

Fire fighting according to Market Pricing means that you get what you are willing and able to pay for, and you provide what you have contracted and been paid to provide. People consider what else they could do with their money, resources, and labor, make independent decisions, and voluntarily contract to provide and obtain goods and services. The more you pay for, the more you get, and conversely, you provide goods and services to people in proportion to what they pay you. In contrast, fire fighting according to Equality Matching means that everyone gives the same thing (regardless of ability or interest), and everyone gets the same thing (regardless of need)—or else, in the reciprocal form of Equality Matching, that you give back just what you get.

The pervasiveness of these four fundamental models for social relations is indicated by the fact that victims of a fire in our imaginary town may use each of them to try to make sense of their misfortune. Using the Communal Sharing model, people may act as if the fire were a violation of the unity, solidarity, and wholeness of the community. Americans tend to avoid contact with victims of misfortune, are uncomfortable around them, and avoid talking about the misfortune. Even close friends may stay away, justifying the effective ostracism with such statements as, "I just don't know what to say to her." By this shunning, people implicitly treat the fire as if it breached the unity of the collectivity, effectively separating out victims as if the fire marked them as jinxed or polluted. In some cultures this may take the extreme form of regarding the victims as Jonahs who bring bad fortune on the collectivity, so that people fearfully or angrily outcast them as pariahs. In certain regions of West Africa, for example, villagers may perceive the fire as a sign of adultery within the lineage, a violation that immanently destroys the integrity of the lineage and jeopardizes its continued existence, causing it to die out.

Applying the Authority Ranking model, the house fire victims may try to understand why God would do this to them: What could have provoked His wrath? Why would He bring down such troubles on me, why would He test me like this? This is Job's problem. He asks, in effect, "Have I not loyally worshipped You, have I broken faith, or followed some other God?" This conception of suffering underlies Christ's cry upon the cross, "My God, my God, why hast thou forsaken me?" (Matthew 27:46). Here the underlying conception appears to be that a superior being determines who shall suffer and angrily punishes those who fail to obey and follow him. Those who are devout and follow his commandments need fear no harm, for he will protect his flock. If something bad happens to me, I must have angered my sovereign protector.

Having lost their house in a fire, the victims might try to interpret what had happened to them by invoking Equality Matching concepts: "It isn't fair! Why should this happen to me alone and not to anyone else?" Victims (and non-victims) may be perplexed and disturbed by misfortune that is unevenly distributed, falling on some but leaving others of equal merit unscathed: they want to know why *their* house burned down, and no one else's. In the equality framework, people who lose their house in a fire may search for something they have done wrong that would correspond to the misfortune that has befallen them: What could I have done that would merit the loss of my house in retribution? The implicit idea is that basically everyone deserves the same fortune, together with the idea that each person's good luck and bad luck should even out, so that the good and the bad in a person's life balance, at least over the long run. This may be associated with the implicit conception that people take "turns" having bad luck, or in any case ought to: your time will come. As a result, the victims of the house fire may even have the vague feeling that they are entitled to some compensating good luck, that good things might just come their way. Similarly, other townspeople may try "to help make up for" their loss, attempting to compensate them in various ways.

Finally, people may construe the fire loss as the consequence of a calculated act of choice, or as related to responsibilities inherent in a contract, interpreting the misfortune within a Market Pricing framework. Townspeople might say, "He knew the risks of smoking in bed, and he chose to go ahead and do it. Now he's paid the price of his decision. He could have chosen otherwise, no one made him do it." Even the victim might say, "I wanted to build my own model rockets, and I knew it was risky. But I weighed the risks, and maybe it wasn't such a bad bargain—I got a lot of pleasure out of it. The excitement was almost worth what it's cost me." Here the framework that people are using to think about the misfortune, to render it morally intelligible and coherent, is based on the value of free choice among alternatives, rational comparison of expected costs and benefits, and the corollary that they are bound to accept the consequences. In this framework, people would be especially upset by totally unforeseeable calamities that they could not reasonably have included among the calculated risks of undertaking a course of action.

Thus, depending on the character and culture of the town, its citizens may respond to the fire by using any of the four relational models to make sociomoral sense of the suffering. Now consider people's reactions if a manufacturer knowingly sold the house owner a toaster whose faulty design made it likely to catch on fire. The homeowner would be considered justified in bringing suit for damages, since the vendor has an obligation to provide a safe product and to warn the purchaser of potential hazards. This case brings up yet another set of situations in which the same four models would be invoked: where a human agent is implicated in the fire, and the fire itself is a crime or a manifest transgression of another sort of social rule. The townspeople have the same four fundamental alternatives for defining and responding to transgression. In this first case, the fire is due to a transgression of the laws that govern purchase and sale—it violates the rights of the buyer (Market Pricing). Alternatively, the fire could be a case of arson by a community member, or even a member of the household, in which case it radically violates the community or family relationship, the unity, solidarity, fellowship, mutual caring, kindness and togetherness of the group (Communal Sharing). It betrays the mutual trust of family members or sets the arsonist apart as a traitor to the family. A third possibility is that townspeople regard the arson as a sort of lèse majesté, a sort of treasonous crime against the authority of the town leaders (Authority Ranking). Thus if an important town leader has personally spoken out against arson, if she forbids it, then the act challenges her command and the sovereignty of her will—it is an affront to authority, an act of disdain and disrespect. In the Equality Matching mode, suppose someone sets the fire in the course of an ongoing feud, in retaliation for an earlier perceived wrong against his group. Here each side construes its acts as retaliation for a transgression against itself; the victims treat the fire as a loss which must be made up, either by compensation (e.g., paying compensatory damages) or by being matched with equal harm to the arsonists, an-eye-for-an-eye. Perhaps both the arson itself and the reprisal that the victims carry out "to get even" are acts of revenge which the perpetrators regard as balancing the score.

This last case brings up the matter of both rectifications and sanctions for wrongdoing. The same four models again govern the ways in which people generally punish transgression, think about such punishments, and account for their own and others' punitive actions. Additionally, rectifying the harm done by the fire—meeting the need for rebuilding and replacing lost possessions—could also be organized in accordance with any of these four relational models. The reader may find it interesting to work through the way each of the four models would generate distinct social processes for punishing arsonists and helping a victim recover from a house fire. (For some hints, see the subsection Punishment, Transgressions, Vices, and Excuses in Chapter 6.)

As the fire example illustrates, the same set of four models are available to

frame decision making and moral and political debate; to organize the allocation of work and the distribution of resources; to make sense of misfortunes;
and to respond to transgressions (as well as to recover from them and to redress
and sanction wrongdoing). Of course, this example is simplified by treating the
four models as pure ideal types; people ordinarily use various combinations of
these four modes to structure any social domain. In Part II, I will elaborate on
these observations, and show how combinations of the models also structure
several other domains of social action and social understanding. If these four
models govern most social action, thought, and evaluation, then they must be
the elementary structures of social relations. And if one set of elementary
structures generates such diverse social processes, then perhaps we have the
framework for a unified theory of social life. But before proceeding, we need a
preliminary definition of each of the four types of social relationships, and a
look at the intellectual origins of the current theory and other convergent theories.

# 2

# The Framework

## CHARACTERIZATION

The thesis of this book is that just four elementary relational structures are sufficient to describe an enormous spectrum of forms of human social relations, as well as social motives and emotions, intuitive social thought and moral judgment. While it may be premature to say which are the defining features of the underlying models and which are merely ancillary attributes, we can readily describe a number of features that appear to be characteristic and distinctive of each type. The descriptions that follow are moderately abstract because they are formulated at a level that will permit us to apply them to a great variety of domains of human social action. On the other hand, a statement of the four models totally free of any concrete reference might be difficult to grasp intuitively. So I have incorporated into the definitions below some features of their prototypes in Western society, with the caveat that the substantive implementations of each model vary considerably from culture to culture (see Fiske 1990). Later, Chapter 7, Part III, shows how universal models can generate cultural diversity. In the section Scale Types and Relational Structures in Chapter 9, I present a more formal and totally domain-independent axiomatic definition of the relational structures of the four models.

*Communal Sharing* is a relationship of equivalence in which people are merged (for the purposes at hand) so that the boundaries of individual selves are indistinct. It is characterized by the fact that people attend to group membership and have a sense of common identity, while the individuality of separate persons is not marked. Members of the group are undifferentiated with respect to the dimensions to which people are attending. What is salient is the superordinate group as such, membership in it, and the boundaries with contrasting outsiders. People have a sense of solidarity, unity, and belonging, and identify with the collectivity: they think of themselves as being all the same in some significant respect, not as individuals but as "we."

Five of the important features of Communal Sharing are captured in three English words with a common root: "kind," "kindness," and "kin." "Kind" (type) and "kin" come from an Old English word meaning birth, nature, race, family. "Kind" ("warmhearted") derives from an Old English root meaning natural, innate. All three words are derived from the same Indo-European root, "ginΩ"—meaning to give birth or beget—from which are derived a family of closely linked words: genus, gender, generous, generate, genitor, gentle, genuine, congenital, nation, native, nature, and innate (Morris 1970). This family of words captures the essence of Communal Sharing: it is a relationship based on duties and sentiments generating kindness and generosity among people conceived to be of the same kind, especially kin. Participants think of it as a natural, genuine, and spontaneous form of relationship among people who descend from common genealogical roots and thus share a common nature, an "innate" common substance (e.g., "blood"). However, unrelated people may also have a Communal Sharing relationship. People in such a relationship are oriented toward the group, in direct or implicit contrast to outsiders beyond its boundaries.

*Authority Ranking* is a transitive asymmetrical relationship. It is a relationship of inequality. If the *particular* hierarchy extends to three or more people, they are ordered in a linear hierarchy, although rank is not transitive across different systems of ranks. People in such a relationship construe each other as differing in social importance, or status. Thus rank is associated with the extent or extension of the self: High ranking people control more people, things, or land than others, and may be thought to possess more knowledge and mastery over events. In this sense, the relationship is not only one of linear rank but of hierarchical inclusion, insofar as people in successively higher ranks dominate successively greater numbers of subordinates. Initiative often rests with the highest ranking person or people in a social relationship, and authority typically confers certain related prerogatives involving choice and preference. Attention too is asymmetric, with subordinates less salient than authority figures, who are marked as more prominent and more distinguished the higher their rank. Characteristically, inferiors are deferential, loyal, and obedient, giving obeisance and paying homage to their betters. Followers are entitled to receive protection, aid, and support from their leaders.

Authority Ranking contrasts with purely coercive *power* in which people dominate others primarily by force or threat of harm (on this distinction, cf. Asad 1972:86). Compared to Authority Ranking, pure power in this sense is relatively uncommon in human interaction, but it certainly exists and is important, sometimes devastating, when it does occur. More typically, subordinates believe that their subordination is legitimate (although they may take issue with any given aspect of their subordination).[1]

*Equality Matching* is an egalitarian relationship among peers who are distinct but coequal individuals. People are separate, but equal. The social presence (shares, contributions, influence) of each person balances and corresponds one-to-one. Equality Matching may be manifested in *turn taking,* a cycle in which each person in the relationship performs the same act in temporal sequence. It may also emerge as strict *in-kind reciprocity,* such that people receive and give back what they construe as the "same" thing in return—where "sameness" is a function of the way people frame the actions and categorize the entities involved, regardless of the objective differences in entities involved. In a relationship of this type people do things quid pro quo, so that exchange is narrowly reciprocal: What each person gets matches what he gives up. In conflict or as sanction, this relationship takes the form of *an-eye-for-an-eye retaliatory vengeance* in accordance with lex talionis. When redressing transgressions in this mode, if one person takes away something, she must make up for it, *compensating in equal measure;* this redresses the imbalance, and gets each person even again. Equality Matching as distributive justice takes the form of an *even distribution into equal parts,* such that people are indifferent among the portions, and/or so that what each person receives is the same as what each other person receives. Conversely, Equality Matching entails *matched contributions of the same kind and quantity.* People in an Equality Matching relationship conceive of each other—or the rights, duties, or actions involved in the relationship—as distinct, but as balancing each other, aligning or matching, so they are interchangeable. Persons are inter-substitutable in this sense that they match and correspond on an even basis; it does not matter who gets (or gives) which share or who takes which turn: in short, everyone is equal and things come out even.

*Market Pricing* is a relationship mediated by values determined by a market system. Individuals interact with others when they decide that it is rational to do so in terms of these values. In a Market Pricing relationship people denominate value in a single universal metric, typically price (or "utility"), by which they can compare any two persons or associated commodities, qualitatively alike or unlike. This evaluation of commodities is expressed in terms of a ratio: a price or wage (including interest rates and rent), or an exchange ratio in the case of direct barter. In a Market Pricing relationship people typically value other people's actions, services, and products according to the rates at which they can be exchanged for other commodities. (Indeed, a price is just an exchange ratio against all other commodities, expressed in terms of money, the predominant medium for making such Market Pricing transactions.) More generally, the criterion is proportionality—people structure their interaction with reference to rates whose numerator is a common standard for all Market Pricing social values in the domain (money, time, or utility, as the case may be). People give and get, influence and exert themselves in proportion to the standard.

People in a Market Pricing relationship consider and often explicitly refer to potential substitutes, complements, and temporal conditions in the market in making their choices and in negotiating terms. They may bargain in an adversarial and explicitly self-interested manner, although often there is no explicit negotiation or it is not explicitly adversarial—people may simply make take-it-or-leave-it offers at a fixed price. People may also seek only a just proportion, a fair price and no more. In a Market Pricing relationship, people may or may not try to maximize what they gain and minimize what they give up, and they may or may not be competing with other buyers and sellers. But, like all four types, the relationship is defined by its structure and process from the participants' point of view, not by its objective outcome externally defined. Market Pricing relationships are characteristically and ideally open to all competent and honest participants, in that everyone is eligible to participate if they have something to sell or money to buy.

Because our American ethnosociology and ideology tend to conflate Equality Matching with Market Pricing, it is easy for Americans to confuse the two, although there are manifest differences between them observable in virtually any domain of social activity. To keep the difference in mind, think about bidirectional transfers ("reciprocal exchange"). Under Market Pricing, people exchange unlike commodities in proportion to their market value (or to the work done or the contribution made), while under Equality Matching, each person gives the other the same thing. Compare two systems of taxation that coexisted in Upper Volta. Under the head tax, each adult paid a flat sum, exactly the same for each person. Under the income tax, each person paid a fixed proportion of his or her income—and therefore very different absolute amounts. To state the difference more precisely, Equality Matching is based on the operations of addition and subtraction and the comparison of intervals, while Market Pricing also incorporates division and multiplication with a distributive rule and thus the evaluation of ratios (see Chapter 9). Significantly, this means that within the framework of Market Pricing, you *can* add apples and oranges and exchange them for a third entity, currency. In Equality Matching this is infelicitous; you can exchange "fruit" one-for-one, or just give apples now for the same number of apples in return later. At most, in Equality Matching you can add apples until their value equals one orange and repeat the process for each orange you want to get.[2]

The classic contrast between Market Pricing and Equality Matching is Malinowski's (1961 [1922]) description of the Kula ring, a circuit of reciprocal exchange in Melanesia. Men travel long distances over the sea in canoes to present arm-shell "bracelets" to their partners in return for shell "necklaces," neither of which has any utilitarian value (although anyone may freely borrow them for display). No one keeps either kind of item for more than a few months before passing it on to another exchange partner. The recipient must accept a Kula gift offered to him, and there is no haggling about its value. Yet the recipient must make a return gift of equal value at a later time, to balance the original gift. It is up to the recipient to judge what constitutes a return of equal value. There is no precise metric for comparing arm-shells with necklaces, and neither item has a monetary value—people only exchange arm-shells for necklaces and necklaces for arm-shells. Malinowski stresses that the exchange partners' honor and dignity depend on what they give as much as on what they receive, and that they do not try to obtain an advantage or make a profit on these exchanges. Nor is there any idea that anything other than a single arm-shell of matching value could possibly be given in return for a neck-lace. Equality is the governing principle in the Kula exchanges, and in many other exchanges in this culture.

> Thus, it is quite a usual thing in the Trobriands for a type of transaction to take place in which A gives twenty baskets of yams to B, receiving for it a small polished blade, only to have the whole transaction reversed in a few weeks' time. Again, at a certain stage of mortuary ritual, a present of valuables is given, and on the same day later on, the identical articles are returned to the giver. . . . The view that the native can live in a state of individual search for food, or catering for his own household only, in isolation from any interchange of goods, implies a calculating, cold egotism, the possibility of enjoyment by man of utilities for their sake. This view, and all the previously criticized assumptions [about motives of utilitarian gain], ignore the fundamental human impulse to display, to share, to bestow. They ignore the deep tendency to create social ties through exchange of gifts. Apart from any consideration as to whether the gifts are necessary or even useful, giving for the sake of giving is one of the most important features of Trobriand sociology, and, from its very general and fundamental nature, I submit that it is a universal feature of all primitive societies. (Malinowski 1961:175)

Alongside these exchanges aimed at strict equality, the same people engage in Market Pricing transactions (gimwali), bartering commodities from each other according to their market value. This trade involves haggling over ex-change ratios, trying to get the best bargain one can. Any two people can vol-untarily enter into such a transaction when they perceive it to be advanta-geous, but no one has to accept a deal he does not like. People on each side barter objects that are plentiful and easy to obtain on their island for useful objects that are scarce at home. Trobrianders explicitly contrast this kind of exchange for profit, which they disdain, with the honorable, egalitarian Kula exchanges.

Writing fifty years later, Forge (1972) concludes that egalitarian social rela-tions and evenly balanced exchanges of this Equality Matching kind are the mode throughout the ecologically and demographically varied New Guinea region. Equality Matching predominates both as ideal and as practice. He notes that equality has to be *generated*:

> To be equal and stay equal is an extremely onerous task requiring continual vigilance and effort. . . . The principal mechanism by which

equality is maintained is equal exchange of things of the same class or
of identical things. (Forge 1972:533-534)

Forge explains that there is almost always a delay between a gift and the return
gift that balances it, resulting in a kind of turn taking in which one side always
owes the other. This is true in feuding, where "balance of deaths was con-
ceded as a moral right, to be obtained by compensation if the actual number
of dead were not equal" (p. 538). In marriage, he notes, the direct exchange of
sisters follows the same principle but avoids this temporal imbalance. In these
Melanesian cultures, there is no confusing Equality Matching with Market
Pricing: the people themselves and the anthropologists who study them contrast the two opposed modes of relationship quite explicitly.

Western ideology and much of Western social science also tend to conflate
Market Pricing with seven other concepts that are analytically and empirically
distinct. People engaging in Market Pricing interactions may or may not be
individualistic, selfish, maximizing, competitive; they may or may not be oriented toward the satisfaction of material needs; and they may or may not construe the relationship as based on either voluntary free choice or contractual
obligations. Conversely, people who are trying to meet their subsistence
needs, or who are being competitive, maximizing, selfish, or individualistic, or
who construe their relationship to others as based on free choice or on contractual obligations, may or may not do so in a Market Pricing mode. Market
Pricing in itself does not entail any of these features, although, optionally, they
may occur in conjunction with it in any particular instance of interaction in
any given domain of any specific culture. Nor do any of these features entail
Market Pricing relations, or each other. As we will see, the confusion among
these features runs through much of the theoretical literature, perhaps because of their association in our own culture. Since earlier theorists have rarely
made these distinctions, it is virtually impossible to disentangle individualism,
selfishness, maximization, competitiveness, voluntarism, and contractualism
in any review or analysis of the literature. The one dimension that psychologists have come to distinguish from the rest fairly often is economy as material
subsistence, but economists—the people who study material transactions—
explicitly assume that all eight features go together. Consequently, my synthesis of antecedent work necessarily ignores these important distinctions, although I will take these features apart again in the last chapter.

In thinking about these elementary models, it is important to recognize that
there is only one criterion for determining what kind of social relationship (if
any) it is that people are engaged in: "The trick is to figure out what the devil
they think they are up to" (Geertz 1984:125 [1974]). If we subsume implicit,
unreflective, unreported, and unacknowledged purposes in the term, it is a
matter of the intention of the actors (cf. Parsons 1949). Thus the unit of analysis, the locus of the social relationships, is cognitive (in the broad sense). The
models are goals, ideals, criteria, rules or guidelines that, under certain circum-

stances, conceivably may not correspond closely to what any particular observer sees in the manifest action or its outcome. The standard for determining what kind of social relationship is operative is not the concrete result of the action either in the short run or the long term; the standard is the conception each person has of what the relationship is (or ought to be). Consequently, sometimes different people may reckon that different relationships are in effect. Furthermore, so long as people believe they are interacting with another person, they may apply the models and operate in a social mode even when no other person is really there (e.g., Fridlund 1989).

The *Null* and *Asocial interactions* also exist and should be considered as a point of reference: people sometimes act without regard to any social relationship.[3] People may simply disregard the existence of other people as social partners, acting towards others as if they were merely animate organisms, like ants or rats, or taking no account of them at all. Obviously, any given person has no social relationship at all with most of the people on earth, although people may have a social relationship without ever encountering each other face to face or even communicating directly (Anderson 1983). On the other hand, it is possible for two people to live side by side in a city or a refugee camp or a building, or even in the same room, and adapt their actions to each other socially no more than they would if each lived on separate continents. Using the same bathroom, drinking from the same well, or even occupying the same bed, are not social relationships ipso facto. As I use the term, a social relationship exists only if people structure their interaction with other people or putative beings with reference to conceptions and rules assumed to be shared (or that they believe should be shared) and that they consciously or implicitly use as shared goals, ideals, or standards in guiding their initiatives and responses. This is not intended as a definition, since it does not fully specify what a social relationship is; the fundamental models underlying the basic types of social relationships differ from other sorts of guiding cognitions (see Chapter 8). But it is sufficient to indicate that, for example, colliding with another person in the dark—say, while fleeing from a fire—is not by its nature a social event any more than is the collision of a radioactive decay proton with another proton. Stepping over a body on the street and, reciprocally, being stepped over, is not a social relationship as such—although *ignoring* a panhandler in order not to acknowledge his plea *is* a momentary instantiation of a social relationship. One may even occasionally encounter a gathering of people that is a mere conglomeration of people separately pursuing their individual Asocial goals without regard to their own social models or those of the others around them. These are examples of Null interactions—there is no truly social relationship.

I also exclude from the domain of the social—in this narrow sense—phenomena like armed robbery, invasion, pillage, and simple terrorism in which one party coerces the other with pure force. The world provides appalling numbers of cases of pure power like these in which one party treats the other as a mere impersonal object, a means to an end, and the other submits out of fear, pain, hunger, or the like. But these Asocial phenomena are markedly different in nature from truly social relationships in which the participants coordinate their interaction with reference to a shared directive model defining the meaning of action and specifying how people should act. Thus violence based on simple force is outside the scope of this theory. However, as I argue later, most conflict and aggression is motivated, organized, and judged with reference to the four basic social models. When people jointly organize and orient their interaction in this way, even if the action is harmful or exploitive, it is truly social.

It is easy to confuse Market Pricing with either Asocial egoism (selfishness), individualism, or a maximizing intention. People operating in a Market Pricing mode need not be maximizing—they may simply be seeking a deal that is fair, in proportional cost/benefit or input/return terms. Conversely, people may or may not try to maximize the rewards of any of the four forms of social relations. In the same sense, selfishness need not be associated with Market Pricing interactions, although people *may* act to advance their personal self-interest within the framework of any of the four types of relationships.[4] Many analysts also conflate competition, especially Market Pricing competition, with agonistic behavior or even aggression (or else treat them as adjacent loci on a single continuum: e.g., Sahlins 1965). But the goal of harming another is quite distinct from the goal of profiting from an interaction or coming out ahead on a deal. Competition may or may not involve harm; there is no necessary connection, and the two are often inimical. And competition may occur outside the context of Market Pricing relations, while Market Pricing relationships need not be competitive. Chapter 17 discusses these issues.

These definitions are inductive—they are inferences from the theoretical schemata discussed in the section on Theoretical Roots, below; from the comparative, analytic, and experimental evidence presented in Chapters 3 through 6; and from the ethnographic material summarized in Part IV. As such, it will become apparent that they do not capture, much less predict, all the important distinctions and characteristic features of the models. But they do describe the most consistent, general, and well-established characteristics.

I will have much more to say in Part III about the common features of the four models and what distinguishes them as "social." But before we go on to look at how the models operate in various domains of social action, I shall briefly indicate what sort of entities these relational models are.


## HOW THE FOUR MODELS OPERATE

In the next two chapters I will review the antecedents of the theory and describe the operation of the models in a wide spectrum of domains of social action. To lay the groundwork for this, I will informally preview some of the major points of the theory, and sketch how the models combine to generate social relations at all levels. How do people use the basic models to construct social relationships?

This theory of relational models assumes that people structure their social relationships by drawing from a limited set of basic models. The models are representations, grammars, or script-like social schemata (see S. Fiske and Taylor in press) that guide people in jointly generating meaningful action in coordination with others. Action guided by such models is identifiable in part by the complementarity of the actions of the people involved—their behavior fits together at the level of the relationship, and is fully intelligible only at that level. The relational models do not fully specify behavior in any interaction or situation, but they comprise a set of rules that strongly constrain the possibilities and that organize responses to violations of the rules.

People use these relational models to initiate social action, to understand what other people are up to, and to respond appropriately. That is, people use the relational models prospectively to anticipate, choose, and plan (consciously or otherwise) social action in terms of how others can be expected to respond. And other people generally decode a person's actions with the same model that the actor used to generate the action—or else confusion reigns. Action in accordance with the appropriate model tends to maintain the ongoing pattern of interaction in a more or less homeostatic manner, a pattern that in some sense is the manifest social relationship.[5] People also use the relational models to judge social relationships, including relationships in which they are not direct participants—particularly relationships that their own interaction partners have with others. As third parties, people evaluate others' interactions and sanction them for transgressions. The other side of this is that people know that their conduct in a social relationship is potentially subject to scrutiny and gossip by others, and that their relationships with third parties can be affected by how they behave in any given interaction. For example, Mary goes to Valerie and tells her that Nancy is "borrowing" large sums of money from petty cash and refuses to pay it back; furthermore, she recently went out and bought an expensive fur coat. It is then incumbent on Valerie to modulate her relationship with Nancy in the light of this information, if not by directly confronting Nancy then by spreading the accusation, ostracizing her, or siding against her in factional disputes. The ramifications of the original infraction may continue to spread. If Valerie fails to join in sanctioning Nancy, she in turn is subject to moral criticism and sanction; Mary's other friends may shun *her*. This is typical of the way all four relational models operate: participants' actions within any particular social relationship ramify to affect the participants' relationships with others. Seen from the other side, each relational model is a standard that third parties use in judging and reacting to what people do in a relationship. The models link social relationships into larger systems by making processes in each social relationship contingent on processes in the participants' relationships with other people.

Any actual interpersonal relationship (Jean's relationship with Peter) or pair of roles (customer and client in American business) is typically built out of a combination of these four basic psychological models, linked together in various ways, applied at various levels and in different domains of the interaction. Market Pricing is the dominant model in the customer—client role pair, and the minimal roles may be limited to that. But other models may be added on to the primary one in their own domains, so that, for example, customer and supplier give each other reciprocal Christmas gifts (Equality Matching), or attend parties structured as Communal Sharing. In Jean's interpersonal relationship with Peter, as chairperson of the department where he is a student, she may act primarily as an authority with a subordinate. But when they collaborate on some phase of a joint research project, they may both simply pitch in and do whatever they can and whatever needs doing, without distinguishing between their respective contributions (Communal Sharing). On the other hand, they can take turns being primary author on successive papers, and they might divide up the coding or the literature review, each doing half the work (Equality Matching). Again, Jean may pay Peter as a research assistant in a Market Pricing manner, or he might buy a computer from her.

As we move up from dyads to more complex institutions, groups, and societies the same principle applies: people generally construct large-scale social entities by putting together two or more basic models in various combinations and at different hierarchical levels. For example, people vote (Equality Matching) to elect a mayor who has powers to make unilateral decisions and impose her will in choosing her staff, setting policy, and administering the city (Authority Ranking). Meanwhile the right to vote—only men, or only free men, or only those over age eighteen—is also determined in the Authority Ranking mode. Perhaps the mayor is empowered to request competitive bids and negotiate contracts to get a good price (Market Pricing) for the construction of a public park—a commons—that will be freely available for all to use as they wish, without distinction (Communal Sharing).

These models operate at all social levels, from interactions between individuals to interactions between blocs of nations. For example, each member of a university department may be expected to teach an equal number of courses, get equal sabbaticals, and have one vote each in faculty meetings, and individual faculty members within the department may take turns undertaking the burden of chairing it, in conformity with Equality Matching. In accordance with the same model, a school or university may supply each department with one administrative computer, while each university in a consortium gets an equal voice in determining policies of the consortium. At the same time, all faculty and staff may get unlimited free local telephone service or mainframe computer time (Communal Sharing), while the university bills each person individually for long distance service, for which it has bargained or requested competitive bids to get good prices from various long-distance telephone companies (Market Pricing). A company may have a common meeting hall that is shared by all its divisions for their staff meetings whenever they want the hall and however many meetings they have (Communal Sharing), although the corporation rents or has bought the building or suite that contains the hall (Market Pricing). Corporations and units of government as such engage in Market Pricing transactions all the time when contracting for goods and services. And in an Authority Ranking mode, the U.S. Secretary of State may treat Central American or Caribbean nations as "banana republics," expecting to dominate the affairs of these countries and have them obey the dictates of American foreign policy.

At the United Nations each country has one vote in the General Assembly, while in the Security Council the chairmanship rotates by turns among the nations represented there (Equality Matching). In debates at the UN, the underdeveloped countries often argue that multilateral aid should be allocated on the basis of need and that aid should be increased until it truly meets their needs; or they might argue, for example, that proceeds from undersea mining should be pooled in a fund to be spent on the collective concerns of the world community as a whole, like the control of communicable diseases (Communal Sharing). The historically most powerful nations have permanent seats on the Security Council and each has veto power over its resolutions, while the specialized agencies of the United Nations are organized as hierarchical bureaucracies in which staff are ranked, there is a seniority system, and there is a definite chain of command (Authority Ranking). The United Nations may contract with member countries to provide military units to peace-keeping forces, paying them in proportion to the size of the force and the costs they incur (Market Pricing). In the same mode, one arm of the World Bank makes interest-bearing loans to nations to pay for infrastructure improvements (roads, dams, even schools), assessing the loan-worthiness of such projects—just like any other bank—in terms of the expected rate of return on the investment to the debtor nation and hence the income that will be generated to repay the loan. As these examples illustrate, the models implemented in directing and influencing international relations tend to be the same ones that operate at the interpersonal level.

The same model may look somewhat different in different domains of social action and cognition, and in diverse realizations within any domain. Think of the five kinds of Equality Matching already mentioned: turn taking, one-for-one in-kind reciprocity, equal share distributions and contributions, in-kind compensation to make up for a loss, and an-eye-for-an-eye retaliatory vengeance. All are based on the same concept of balance: people are matched and equally weighted; their opportunities are equal and interchangeable; what they give balances what they get back; people have equally weighted shares; they are obligated to make contributions of equal weight; or they make restitution in equal measure for the harm they have done. While the social logic is the same, as a concrete phenomenon turn taking is phenomenologically different from an-eye-for-an-eye vengeance. As another illustration of the varying realizations of a single model, consider the different bases for according rank to people in an Authority Ranking hierarchy. Rank may be a function of birth order, age, gender, descent, ethnicity, religious observance, knowledge, physical prowess, some form of accomplishment, personality or charisma, appointment to office, or any of a myriad of other criteria. There are considerable differences in the phenomenal appearance of systems of rank ordering based on these different criteria, as well as immensely consequential differences for the lives and experiences of the people in the system. But gerontocracy, meritocracy, theocracy, and so forth may all be based on the same relational logic and have the same formal structure. Any given basic model also looks and feels quite different when it is manifested in different domains. Sharing living space, work, resources, land, and money (as do families among the Moose in Burkina Faso) is phenomenologically different from sharing personal history, plans, information about activities, attitudes, and aspirations (as American families tend to do). More strikingly, Authority Ranking in family relations (where it is linked to Communal Sharing) may be experienced differently from Authority Ranking in the military.

The point here is that there are indefinitely many manifestations of each of the four basic models. This is a function of the domains and subdomains to which people apply them, of the options that people adopt in applying an abstract logic to a given domain, and of the flexibility people have in implementing a model in concrete action. This variability is an important part of what makes different cultures seem—and be—so different and yet comparable and comprehensible. Different cultures realize the same model in distinct and particular ways. For instance, cultures differ in which model they implement in any given domain, and in just how they mark the kind of social relationship that is operative at any given moment (as well as the positions of the people involved). The interaction between spouses in one culture may be governed primarily by Communal Sharing, in another culture by Authority Ranking, in another by Equality Matching, and in yet another by Market Pricing. Moreover, each culture has more or less unique and systematically distinctive—but not arbitrary—ways of operationalizing each model. People in many cultures eat and drink together and kill animals to mark the solidarity and collective identity inherent in Communal Sharing. But different cultures do it differently. We eat turkey and pies at Thanksgiving dinner, a distinctive American ritual. The Moose (pronounced MOH-say)[6] of Burkina Faso, West Africa, mark Communal Sharing in libations and animal sacrifices addressed to the forces of the earth. Specified at a sufficiently precise level of detail, such sacrifices are uniquely Moose rituals, and indeed Moose indicate that, among other things, rituals of this sort mark their distinctive identity. One way of summing up this variability and the indefinitely large number of concrete forms to which any model gives rise is to say that the models are generative, like a grammar (see Chapter 7). Furthermore, it is probably the case that all four of the relationships can operate at any level of intensity.

I should add that people usually are not capable of formulating these models abstractly. People generate social action out of these models without necessarily being able to report the formal properties of the logical structures they are using. The use of the models in action does not require the capacity to describe them reflectively, or even to be aware of the existence of distinct models as such, any more than does the use of a grammar in speaking a language or the use of another person's pupil dilation in assessing his attitude and attractiveness. However, the four models differ in their accessibility to conscious reflexive analysis and verbal report: Communal Sharing is the least accessible to explicit awareness and report, while Market Pricing is the most readily explicated in verbal form.

With some diffidence, for rhetorical purposes I shall state the theory in its radical form. My hypothesis is that these models are *fundamental*, in the sense that they are the lowest or most basic-level "grammars" for social relations. Further, the models are *general*, giving order to most forms of social interaction, thought, and affect. They are *elementary*, in the sense that they are the basic constituents for all higher order social forms. It is also my hypothesis that they are *universal*, being the basis for social relations among all people in all cultures and the essential foundation for cross-cultural understanding and intercultural engagement. This book is a preliminary test of these hypotheses.


## THEORETICAL ROOTS
## AND CONCEPTUAL CONVERGENCE

The theory presented in this book grew out of my discovery of a previously unrecognized convergence in the thinking of three major social theorists, each in a different field. The theory was fertilized by my public health and international development experience in Africa and elsewhere, taking root during my interdisciplinary training at Harvard and the University of Chicago. My fieldwork in West Africa both watered and challenged the seedling. It matured as I wrote up that fieldwork into a dissertation, and then flourished as I taught a course comparing evolutionary, psychological, sociological, and anthropological approaches to social relations. It flowered as I expanded my reading still more broadly across the social sciences during a sabbatical, and bore definite fruit as I wrote this book. Doubtless it will be pruned over the years, and other stock will be grafted on to it. Like any tree it is both old and new, a reembodiment of its ancestors and a unique specimen. My hope is that its seeds will be disseminated and take root far from the parent.

In less florid words, the theory attempts to integrate aspects of a large number of theories that previously were linked to each other only tenuously, if at all. These theories are complementary as well as convergent, each illuminating different facets of human social relations. Assembling them as I do here does not always do justice to the concerns or the elegance of the original work, yet the whole is more than the sum of the parts. Assembled, something new—and often astonishing—emerges from the collection of pieces. They were destined to come together.

Specifically, the relational-models theory builds on my reading of Max Weber, Jean Piaget, and later Paul Ricoeur, together with fieldwork from 1979 to 1982 among the Moose in Burkina Faso. Weber (1975 [1916]; 1978 [1922]) analyzes the orientations of social action, including the legitimation of the social order, most particularly the legitimation of political (and religious) authority but also the legitimation of fate. Piaget (1973 [1932]; see also 1965 [1941-1951]) builds on and argues with Durkheim's discussion (1933 [1893]; 1961 [1925]) of the social sources of individual commitment to norms. Both Weber and Piaget are addressing the problem of social order, framing it in terms of why people regard social rules as obligatory, necessary, or worthy of respect. They both focus on the justifications or grounds that people perceive to be the ultimate bases for social rules, examining the diachronic processes by which one form of rule orientation is transformed into another. Each independently develops a tripartite typology of rule orientations in relation to the perceived source of binding rules. Weber discusses traditional, charismatic, and rational-legal legitimation, (and a related scheme of orientations toward social action in general),[7] while Piaget compares sensorimotor rules (action schemas); rules due to unilateral respect ("heteronomy"); and rules due to mutual respect. It occurred to me that although Piaget and Weber look at very different kinds of material, they each independently recognize essentially the same three forms of rule orientation. Weber's account of traditional legitimation (whether of a social system in general or of "political" authority) is that it is an orientation toward continuity with the past and the perpetuation of forms of action perceived as preexisting, immutable, inherent, and natural, together with belief in the immanent, natural consequences of any deviation from such forms of action. Action in a traditional framework involves the strict, formalistic recapitulation of stereotyped "magical" rituals, performed to remedy wrongs or resolve disputes (or more generally, I might add, to create and mark collective solidarity). Weber says that this orientation is rooted in the experience of childhood dependency in the domestic community, especially the commensal sharing of food and drink. Piaget's corresponding concept is that of motor rules, based on the young child's perception of regularity in nature, in the social practices of her parents, and in her own ritual schemata for repetitive sensorimotor actions. Piaget also shows that the youngest children believe in immanent justice, although he does not associate this conception with motor rules. Piaget regards motor rules as presocial, since he regards the infant as asocial and conceives of the child's awareness of the obligatoriness of rules as emerging from the child's distillation of her social experience. But both Weber and Piaget identify the same basic sense of the immanent necessity of maintaining continuity with the past by replicating patterns of action shared with one's natal primary group. On the basis of my ethnographic research among the Moose, I label this framework for social relationships Communal Sharing (CS).

Weber discusses a second basis for belief in the legitimacy of a social order or political domination, which he considers in two contexts: *patriarchal, patrimonial,* and *feudal* relationships, and *charismatic* leadership (see particularly Weber 1978:954). The common theme is that of a ranked relationship in which people obey the particular commands of a superior out of respect and loyalty for the specific person who commands them. What is right is simply what the master dictates, and disobedience brings down his wrath upon the unfaithful: One must obey the expressed will of a particular superior being. Similarly, Piaget describes *heteronomous authority* based on unilateral respect for a personal authority, initially parents. What is right is obedience to what specific adult authorities reveal and impose. This sense of moral obligation is the expression of the child's experience of coercion and love embodied in parental instructions, constraints, and punishments. The child perceives punishment, Piaget implies, as expiation that restores her social relationship with her parent. Weber and Piaget independently converged on the same conception of people's sense that specific imperatives are obligatory because they are the literal dictates of a personal superior. This orientation, which is quite salient among the Moose, I call Authority Ranking (AR).

The third foundation for social action that Weber describes is *rational-legal* legitimacy. This is based on the idea that people create rules by agreement, in order to achieve pragmatic or ideal ends. The rules are whatever precepts people have duly agreed upon; they are mutually and universally binding because of the "contract" that people have voluntarily entered into in order to advance their joint purposes. Rules are abstract and general statements, applied impartially. Piaget identified a corresponding kind of moral obligation, which he called *mutual respect* and *cooperation.* It is based on reciprocal consent and explicit codification: the group creates whatever rules it chooses to agree on. These rules are rational in the sense that they are elaborated so as to be abstractly formulated, consistent, and universal, and in the sense that they make social life more agreeable, coherent, predictable, and fruitful. People voluntarily consent to enter into such binding agreement because it is objectively rational for them to do so. Weber and Piaget agree in their observation that this kind of rule orientation is based on the idea that people purposefully create abstract, formal, universalistic rules, rules that are binding because they have been properly created in order to improve social coordination and cooperation. Weber's careful historical and cultural analysis demonstrated that this kind of rational-legal legitimation of social relations is closely associated with an entrepreneurial class ethos and connected to the rise of market capitalism in particular (Weber 1958 [1904–1906], 1978). Given the contexts in which this "social contract" orientation toward human interaction is prototypically manifest among the Moose and elsewhere, I call it Market Pricing (MP).

This correspondence between Weber and Piaget is very striking because their levels of analysis are entirely different. The implication is that the basic forms of ideological legitimation of political, economic, and other normative systems at the level of the culture correspond to the basic forms of moral reasoning in individual cognition. Weber focuses on social and cultural transformations from one type to another, while Piaget studies child development, so the parallels between their theories hint at links between history and ontogeny. Furthermore, Weber shows deep connections between the form of ideology and the type of economic system (forms of production, exchange, and planning), and connects the economic system in turn to theology. Piaget shows connections among individuals' conceptions of the source of moral rules, their ideas about the factors that affect culpability, and children's ideas about appropriate forms of punishment and ways to redress transgressions. So the framework that is common to Weber and Piaget encompasses a very wide span indeed.

The main impetus for Piaget's work is Durkheim's (1933 [1893], 1961 [1925]) comparison between *mechanical solidarity* (CS) and *organic solidarity* (MP). This heritage again bridges the gap between the individual and societal levels of analysis, showing a common set of structures at both levels. Durkheim connects systems of production and exchange with the kind of punishment that is prevalent in a society at a given point in history, tying these two domains together again and substantiating the indirect connection achieved by combining Weber with Piaget through the ideology-moral judgment link. Piaget's Durkheimian heritage also reproduces the parallel between history and ontogeny. The difference between Communal Sharing and Market Pricing also corresponds fairly closely to Ferdinand Tönnies' (1988[1887–1935]) analogous contrast between *gemeinschaft* and *gesellschaft*, respectively.

Paul Ricoeur (1967) arrives at a very similar schema in his analysis of the mythology and theology of Western religion, apparently independently. Ricoeur, like Weber (1975), is interested in the varieties of ways in which people have tried to make sense of misfortune in a religious or ethical framework. He shows an historical progression in theodicy beginning with conceptions of evil in terms of *defilement* (dread of the impure and fear of contagion), then in terms of *sin* (rebellion against a personal God), and finally *ethicization* (rationalized analysis of intention, and guilt). The first is a sense of evil as difference from others, being separate and apart. The second is a perception of evil as disobedience to authority. And the third is a conception of evil as breach of abstract, formal, explicit, almost contractual rules. These descriptions correspond with Weber's and Piaget's taxonomy, complementing their emphases and filling out the analysis in another domain. Weber and Piaget delineate the ways in which people define the good, and Ricoeur independently offers a parallel typology of how people define evil. In addition, Weber shows links between ideology and economy, and between economy and religion. The parallel between the results of Ricoeur's investigation of the history of theology and Weber's work on legitimation confirms that the same forms of thought emerge in both theology and political ideology. (For more details on the parallels and differences among the theories of Weber, Piaget, and Ricoeur, see Fiske 1985.)

My own ethnographic research among the Moose of Burkina Faso (West Africa) makes it evident that there is a fourth kind of orientation toward social action, the one I now call Equality Matching (EM). The necessity for formulating this fourth model arises from the fact that many Moose social relationships simply do not correspond at all to any of the other three models. Relationships among cowives (see Mason 1987), agemates, lineage heads, and among members of a cooperative are all fundamentally similar and qualitatively different from Communal Sharing, Authority Ranking, or Market Pricing relations. To account for these and for our observations of the division of gifts, contributions to sacrifices, and the organization of reciprocal labor (see Part IV) requires a fourth model. For example, in the village Moose virtually never work for wages or otherwise structure work in terms of ratios of benefits and costs, but they reciprocate attendance at each other's threshing and cultivating bees, and in these and other contexts there are phases when they match each other's work one-for-one.

Although I did not encounter it among my Moose informants, perhaps the clearest example of Equality Matching relationships are the rotating credit associations (RCAs) that exist in hundreds of cultures around the world (Bascom 1952, Geertz 1962, Ardner 1964, Firth and Yamey 1964, Kramer 1974, Vélez-Ibañez 1983). In contrast to—and often alongside—MP credit institutions like banks, credit unions, money lenders, and coops that make interest-bearing loans, RCAs do not involve any kind of interest or profit (or any sort of ratio calculations at all). All the members of a RCA periodically make equal contributions and take turns receiving the entire amount. No one makes a profit, but everyone can amass a large sum of money for bride price, festival, or other major expenses without having to accumulate cash gradually and face requests for help from needy relatives (or risk theft). RCAs involve four of the five common manifestations of Equality Matching: turn taking, equal distributions, equal contributions, balanced in-kind reciprocity (or matched contributions and receipts), and levelling compensation. None of the other three models can account for RCAs without considerable distortion and ad hoc finagling.

In some culture areas, particularly Melanesia, Equality Matching is the dominant mode of interaction (Forge 1972), and Equality Matching relations emerge in diverse social contexts. For example, Hollnsteiner (1964) describes this relational structure for mortuary contributions in a Philippine fishing village. Everyone in the community contributes an identical sum to the bereaved family. In addition, some people make an additional contribution, which the bereaved family records in a special notebook. When a member of the contributor's family dies, the recipients of the original gift make a return gift of precisely the same sum. Among peers, no other return in any other context is appropriate. This diverse ethnographic material simultaneously helps to show the relevance and the limits of the theoretical typologies worked out by European social scientists using secondary sources. Specifically, it shows the importance and wide distribution of a form of capital accumulation unknown to Weber. Moreover, RCAs and equivalent social forms help demonstrate that the analyses of Durkheim and Piaget often conflate Equality Matching with MP.

Buber (1987 [1923]) emphasizes the fact that not all interactions among humans are sociable—that is, based on true social relationships. Buber contrasts *I—It* interactions, which are based on Null or Asocial orientations, with *I—Thou* relationships which truly take the other into account as a person. Bakan (1966) independently describes a similar contrast between two fundamental modalities of life that he calls *agency* (Asocial interactions) and *communion* (Communal Sharing). The implication that should be drawn from their work is that it is also important not to confuse Null or Asocial interactions with either Authority Ranking or Market Pricing relationships in which the relationship itself (and its corollary moral standards, motives and values) is a good. When people care about the relationship for its own sake and acknowledge the directive legitimacy of shared relational standards, then they are being truly sociable.

Margaret Clark and Judson Mills study a contrast between what they call *communal* and *exchange relationships* (Clark and Mills 1979; Mills and Clark 1982, 1986; Clark 1983, 1984a, 1984b).[8] Clark and Mills's communal relationships resemble Communal Sharing (although they sometimes conflate them with Equality Matching), while the core of their exchange relationships is Equality Matching, although they conflate it with Market Pricing. They do not explicitly cite Weber, Piaget, or Ricoeur (or most of the other convergent schemata discussed here). But Mills and Clark offer direct, experimentally controlled evidence of the distinction between Communal Sharing and both Equality Matching and Market Pricing, showing that the effect of direct immediate in-kind reciprocity, or of a request for direct reciprocity, depends on the type of relationship desired: People prefer not to get or give directly comparable returns, or to get something back that is different from what they gave, if they hope to establish a communal relationship. Mills and Clark find that people keep track of their respective contributions to a task when they seek an exchange relationship, but not when they seek a communal one. People in communal relationships feel obligated to meet each other's needs, and they expect such relationships to endure, in contrast to exchange relationships. They raise an extremely important issue concerning the intensity of social relationships, theorizing that communal relationships vary in strength while exchange relationships do not. The anthropological evidence does not seem to be compatible with this contention about the invariability of the intensity of exchange relationships. For example, the intensity of the potlatch Boas (1966 [1913-14]) describes and the Kula exchanges Malinowski (1961 [1922]) describes exceed the intensity of the Equality Matching exchanges of many other peoples. Again, would we want to say that exchanging sisters in marriage has the same intensity as exchanging friendship bracelets among American children? Furthermore, the intensity issue needs to be distinguished from the question of the number of social domains in which people apply a given model within the scope of any given pair of roles or personal relationships (see Chapter 7), and motivational issues (see Chapter 5) need to be distinguished from ideological issues. But the issue of intensity remains problematic and crucial, thanks to Mills and Clark.

Furthermore, Clark and Mills provide essential controlled experimental evidence for the distinction between Communal Sharing and both Equality Matching and Market Pricing, while showing important qualitative differences in how people feel and how they respond when they are expecting different kinds of relationships. They provide a crucial demonstration that what people expect in one kind of relationship violates the norms of other kinds, and that people feel "exploited" when partners transgress these normative expectations.

There are a number of other theoretical and empirical typologies that are related to this set. Etzioni (1975 [1961]) analyzes the sociological traditions that have been developed to explain social order in terms of (1) the hierarchical distribution of coercive force (typically involving an element of AR),[9] (2) property relations construed from a utilitarian perspective (markets and other economic factors—MP), or (3) normative values (symbolic rewards—in this case often CS). From this more or less Weberian perspective, Etzioni analyzes the literature on compliance in organizations and their recruitment of members (see Social Influence, below). The vital issue that Etzioni raises for consideration concerns the consequences of whether or not the system of social influence (or compliance) that an organization emphasizes corresponds with its system of recruitment. For example, are there social functional or psychological implications of recruiting people in a CS mode and then attempting to organize and control them in a MP mode? Furthermore, Etzioni's work helps fill the gap between the individual judgment Piaget studied and the dyads of Mills and Clark on the one hand, and the sociocultural analyses of the others. It complements the ethnographic work in traditional cultures by bringing the analytic framework back home to modern organizations, and utilizes complementary methodologies as well, particularly survey research.

Blau (1964) independently proposes a theory based in this sociological tradition, in which he argues that social structures are built out of a set of four fundamental modes of social interaction: (1) *Social Attraction*, based on the desire for approval and acceptance in intrinsically rewarding social attachments and associations (e.g., in the family, close friendships, or between lovers; this is CS). (2) *Social Exchange* involving balanced reciprocity in which there is a definite moral obligation to return benefits for benefits received, but no generalized medium of exchange (EM). (Consequently, such exchanges logically must be in-kind, but Blau does not state this.) Social exchange is based on and promotes trust and gratitude, since contingent obligations are not fully specified (or at least not overtly negotiated and explicitly stated; they may be culturally well defined). (3) *Strictly Economic Exchange*, based on a single quantitative unit of exchange, in which people make contracts in instrumental pursuit of extrinsically valued commodities without regard to who in particular supplies them (this is MP; Blau uses this type chiefly as a contrast to social exchange). (4) *Power*, whose differentiation is based on unilateral exchange arising from asymmetrical control over resources (or on brute physical coercion) and leading—via unilateral gratitude and obligation—to differences in status and collective legitimation of authority (AR; note the normative element of obligatory gratitude).[10] (For similar analyses of power as arising from asymmetrical benefaction and unrequited obligation to reciprocate see Davis and Moore [1945] and Athay and Darley [1985].) This analysis was contemporaneous with and remarkably convergent with that of Sahlins (1965, see below).[11] Whether or not we agree with his assumptions or conclusions, the importance of Blau's analysis stems from his attempt to show how all four forms derive from a single process—self-interested transactions.

Economic anthropologists analyzing different types of exchange systems have made very similar distinctions, supported by extensive comparisons among cultures. Karl Polanyi (1957a [1944], 1957b, 1977 [1957], 1966; Polanyi, Arensberg, and Pearson 1957b) develops his ideas out of Malinowski's (1961 [1922], 1966 [1936]) observations on kinship, production, and distribution in the Trobriand islands. (Polanyi makes no reference to Weber, Durkheim, Tönnies, or Piaget; although he must have been aware of their work, he seems not to have considered it apposite.) He describes four different patterns in the transfer of goods among people: householding, redistribution, reciprocity, and marketing. The most ancient, he says, is *householding*, in which production is for the use of the social unit, whether family, village settlement, or the seigneurial manor, however that unit is internally organized (Polanyi 1957a [1944]:53–54, 1966:70–76). While Polanyi says very little about this corporate form of production, we may reasonably impute to it a communal production, resource-sharing organization corresponding to our concept of Communal Sharing within a relatively undifferentiated group.[12] Without specific reference to the concept of householding, Price (1975) shows how sharing is characteristic of production and exchange in such small, intimate, stable communities. Price stresses that people do not calculate returns when they are sharing, but that sharing is limited to a group of defined membership and is specific to the participants; changing the identity of the participants changes the relationship. Polanyi describes *redistribution* as a system characterized by centricity, in which there is a central prominent person, headman, chief, or despot, or else temple priests, lords of the ruling aristocracy, or bureaucracy. These people receive, store, and later redistribute goods to the population. Typically leaders attempt to increase their political power by the manner in which they allocate goods to their followers. They may give much of what they receive to the leisure class, officials, and the military—in other words, to the strata who administer, rule, and enforce their will on the producers. In our terms, this is clearly Authority Ranking in the distribution of goods and services.

According to Polanyi the third form of transferring goods is *reciprocity*, characterized by symmetry, often between established trading partners who engage in a balanced long-run give and take (as in the Kula ring described by Malinowski 1961). Equivalencies are established and typically fixed by custom. This is Equality Matching in the economic domain. *Market exchange*, Polanyi stresses, only became a major form of transaction after the end of feudalism in Western Europe, particularly in the last two centuries. Markets are characterized by rational choice among alternative scarce means to an end. They are based on a price system with money as the medium of exchange, with people bargaining and seeking to maximize their profits. Competition among sellers and among buyers often mediates between supply and demand. Obviously, this is Market Pricing.

In a valuable and influential article Marshall Sahlins (1965) subsequently developed and further schematized this typology from economic anthropology. He provides by far the most extensive and thoughtful existing review of the varieties of exchange systems and their social uses, including an appendix listing brief citations of many ethnographic examples. His comprehensive, ethnographically informed integration of the anthropological material on exchange is also more systematic than anything else in the literature.[13] Yet among other theorists, Sahlins cites only Polanyi, Malinowski, Firth, and Gouldner. Mitchell (1988)—who is still unaware of any of these other convergent schemata we review here—offers a critical revision of Sahlins and a bibliography of other commentaries.

The great anthropological contribution of Polanyi and Sahlins is to show how the transfer of things among people is embedded in human social relations. Exchange is not usually a separate domain set apart from the rest of social life. Giving something to someone always *means* something. It indexes an intention to engage in a social relationship, creates a relationship, sustains it, marks its continued existence and its current status, or modifies it (Mauss 1967 [1925]). Polanyi and Sahlins show how different types of processes and structures of transferring things effect different social relationships, and how people embody different kinds of relationships in different kinds of exchanges. They particularly reinforce and greatly extend Durkheim's and Weber's conclusions in political economy by showing how certain forms of exchange inform political hierarchy.

The fundamental typology emerges again in two cross-cultural studies by Stanley Udy (1959, 1970) on the organization of work in the production of material goods. In the first study Udy examines one randomly chosen production organization in each of 150 nonindustrial cultures, and in the second study

359 work organizations in 125 nonindustrial cultures, in both cases using ethnographic data drawn primarily from the Human Relations Area Files. Although Udy refers to Weber and Blau in other contexts, he neither cites nor is cited by any of these other theorists (not even Polanyi or Etzioni), yet his typology of the modes of recruiting labor and organizing work matches very closely the one that emerges from these other domains. The basic systems of recruitment and production Udy (1959:55–94) describes are familial, custodial, reciprocal, contractual, and voluntary. *Familial* recruitment obtains if the obligation to participate is based on kinship, however extended the group or network (Communal Sharing). *Custodial* recruitment is based on politically defined differences in ascribed power under which people are compelled to work by the legitimate application of punitive force, if necessary (Authority Ranking). *Contractual* recruitment is the determination of participation by voluntarily concluded but binding contract that explicitly specifies terms and periods of future work (MP). *Reciprocal* recruitment is based on an obligation to work "in return for past or anticipated work of a similar nature" (1959:57), assessed in a known but often implicit manner (EM). The residual category in Udy's scheme is *voluntary* recruitment, which contrasts with the other four types in that there is no social obligation to participate or social mechanism for compelling participation or sanctioning nonparticipation. People work when they define it as in their self-interest to do so—this is Null (or sometimes Asocial) interaction. If people do not orient and coordinate their interactions with reference to a shared model that has both motivational and prescriptive dimensions, if, when they associate, they treat each other Asocially as merely objective means to some extrinsic end, then they are using none of the four basic models. As Udy's analysis shows, these Null or Asocial cases do not preclude interaction. But once humans come face to face, the four fundamental social modes usually emerge in subsidiary phases and elements of such an interaction. If people sustain the interaction they tend to adopt one of the four basic forms. Udy finds that in his world sample, voluntary recruitment only occurs when people who happen to be in the area assemble ad hoc, without any social criteria for inclusion or exclusion, to work temporarily on some specific, one-time task. It is unsurprising but significant that Udy reports that voluntary recruitment is never a stable form of organizing work, and in his sample it never forms the nucleus for forming a sustained group dedicated to carrying out a long-term productive activity from beginning to end. All the examples Udy (1959:90–91) cites of voluntary recruitment are hunts on land or sea, or fishing drives.

Udy (1959:98–113) also makes a generally parallel set of distinctions among criteria for the allocation of production "rewards" (although he does not discuss any connection between the two typologies): *gross participation* (mere membership in the group—Communal Sharing), organization *office and proprietorship* (two variants of Authority Ranking), *achievement* (differential performance—typically Market Pricing), and a residual category of status ascribed independently of the production organization. For some reason he leaves out in-kind reciprocity, although Equality Matching is clearly a basis for allocating resources in many of these societies. In his later study Udy (1970:38–40, 66–96) analyzes labor in terms of the same types of work organization, merely changing the term "custodial" to "political" and leaving out of consideration the voluntary case in which there are no normative obligations. In this second study, especially, Udy assumes an economic development perspective in which Market Pricing is the desired and ultimately expected goal. But in both works he uncovers some interesting patterns in the modes of organizing labor that are used for tilling, hunting, collecting, fishing, and construction, and uncovers striking regularities in the ways the four normative modes are combined in the course of production. Guillet (1980) applies Udy's analytic schema to Andean farming and updates it. Although Udy focuses on the development of the modern industrial forms of contractual labor, amazingly, he never cites Karl Marx (1964a, 1973 [1846, 1857–8], Marx and Engels (1959 [1848], 1906 [1867]). As we shall see below in the section on Labor, it appears as though Marx and Udy arrived independently at rather similar conclusions about the basic forms of work, although they label and present them quite differently. This in itself is important, but Udy's data also provide very valuable information about the material constraints and ecological influences on the organization of production: he shows what kinds of labor people organize in which ways. Furthermore, his analysis of production meshes with and completes Polanyi's and Sahlins's work on exchange, showing that people make use of the same set of four forms in each activity. The next step beyond this would be to measure the degree to which the type of exchange correlates with the type of production, at the level of particular products or at the level of the forms that predominate in the society as a whole.

A number of social psychologists who study multiple forms of "justice" report the same basic set of distinctions. Around 1975 several researchers more or less independently concluded that there are three alternative modes of distributing rewards: according to equity (proportionally to contributions—MP), equally (EM), or as a function of need (CS). Separately, some other social psychologists showed that people may distribute benefits according to the status of the recipients (AR). I review this work below in Chapter 3 under Transaction (Exchange). Its importance here is that it is an independent confirmation of the typology of exchange that has been developed in economic anthropology, as well as a demonstration of the normative bases for these four kinds of exchange. It also shows that the fundamental distinctions among modes of exchange manifest themselves at this microsocial level of small groups.

What about the cognitive representation of the universe of social relations? To what extent can subjects make explicit distinctions among the different kinds of social relationships in which they participate? There have been a large number of studies and theoretical integrations that analyze the "spatial" structure of subjects' naive ratings of social relations, using either factor analysis or multidimensional scaling.[14] Basically, this usually involves analyzing people's *conceptions* of similarities and contrasts among kinds of social relations, or people's categorization of relationships. This is a somewhat unnatural task, but despite wide variations in eliciting frames, stimuli, and analytic approaches, there is remarkable stability and convergence in the results. All analyses come up with essentially the same two primary dimensions. One is variously called affection, friendliness, solidarity, affiliation, sociability, or intimacy. Where there are two poles they are labeled cooperative and friendly vs. competitive and hostile; warm–agreeable vs. cold–quarrelsome; or devoted–indulgent/cooperative–helpful/friendly vs. rancorous–sadistic/antagonistic–harmful/hostile. Clearly this dimension has to do with the contrast between Communal Sharing and its exploitatively instrumental opposite, Asocial interactions. The second dimension is labeled control, dominance, power, regulation, individual prominence, or assertiveness. When it is described in bipolar terms it is dominance vs. submission; ambitious–dominant vs. lazy–submissive; control/dominate vs. autonomy, interdependence; dictatorial/controlling/dominant vs. subservient/docile/submissive; equal vs. unequal. This is Authority Ranking, construed as the complementarity between prestige and command on the one hand, and subordination and deference on the other. The "midpoint" can be treated as Equality Matching, but Wish (1976) also reports that in one study he finds a separate "equality" dimension distinct from the AR dimension. Wish and also Bales (1958, 1970) describe another dimension that is task-oriented and formal (or "business") vs. socioemotional and informal (or "family"), which clearly has to do with the contrast between Market Pricing and Communal Sharing. (In addition, some studies find another dimension that has to do with intensity vs. superficiality, or frequency of interaction—showing that any type of relationship can vary in "amplitude," vide Mills and Clark's hypothesis.) Marwell and Hage (1970) refer to Durkheim, Tönnies, and Weber, but otherwise none of the researchers in this tradition refer to Durkheim, Weber, Piaget, Ricoeur, Polanyi, Erasmus, Udy, Blau, or Sahlins, or are cited by students in most of the other paradigms discussed in this book. Adamopoulos (1984) briefly reviews a number of these analyses and attempts to integrate these dimensional analyses with Foa and Foa's (1974) resource-exchange approach, proposing an eight-way taxonomy of "behavior features" in social interaction. Collapsing across his dimension of giving/denying produces four "features": intimacy (CS), superordination-subordination (AR), formality (MP?), and trading (EM).

Geoffrey White (1980, White and Prachaumbmoh 1983) reviews and discusses dimensional analyses of interpersonal language in several widely dispersed cultures that have turned up the same two basic dimensions, solidarity and dominance, suggesting that the structure of the perception of social relations may be pancultural. White points out the correspondence of these two dimensions with the structure of American-English emotion terms as analyzed by Krech and Crutchfield (1965) and the power and solidarity dimensions of sociopolitical role terms that Bailey (1972) reported. These two dimensions also correspond fairly closely to Leary's (1957) system of personality description using a circular representation of interpersonal space. Interpretation of all this work on the spatial structure of social relations hinges on the issue of what kinds of knowledge we suppose subjects can draw on in completing such sorting and rating tasks. The evidence seems to imply that subjects are aware of distinctions in the intensity or amount of CS and AR in different roles and personal relationships, while they do not so readily or consistently differentiate roles and relationships by the degree of EM and MP that the interactions contain. The interpretation of these dimensions and clusters needs further examination, however, since it is contingent on how we resolve a number of tricky methodological issues.

Using pronouns and other forms of address, Brown (1965, Brown and Gilman 1960) also derives power and solidarity as the basic dimensions of relationships (although among these multidimensional analysts he is cited only by White). My own research among the Moose is consistent with Brown's analysis and additionally reveals a widely used etymologically linked nominal suffix (*to* or *taaga*, plurals *taaba* and *taase*) and corresponding verbal noun (*taare*) that clearly mark EM peer relationships.

Coming out of a sociological tradition (Tönnies, Weber—and also Piaget) and making no reference to any of these other dimensional analyses, V. Hamilton (1978, Hamilton and Sanders 1981) independently arrives at a theoretical scheme for judgments of responsibility based on two dimensions; the contrasting poles of the first are precisely equivalent to AR vs. EM, while the second dimension ranges from CS to MP (see Moral Foundations section, Chapter 6). This work is interesting, since it shows that the kinds of obligations to others that people recognize are the same four basic ones that are manifest throughout social life.

Mary Douglas (1978) develops a similar two-dimensional analysis of social forms in an ethnographic mode, again without citing any of the earlier work (except, in passing, Maine).[15] Her dimensions are *grid* and *group*, based on polythetic features that she does not delineate very explicitly. Group clearly corresponds to the strength of CS bonds entailing ingroup—outgroup boundaries. Gross and Rayner (1985) propose operationalizing group strength in terms of such variables as the proportion of available time spent "in" the group, frequency of meeting, permeability of the group boundary, and the extent to which people interact with the interaction partners of their partners ("transitivity"). Grid has to do with role differentiation, rigidity of ascribed social classification, and segregation ("insulation"). One aspect of grid is hierarchy and social power (AR): the more one is controlled by others, the stronger the grid. Highly discriminated rank distinctions also characterize a society as high grid.[16] Gross and Rayner (1985) suggest operationalizing grid strength in terms of the stability of role asymmetry (e.g., masters are unlikely to exchange roles with their servants), proportion of roles that are ascribed, proportion of total roles actually assumed by each individual, and the proportion of roles in which a subordinate is accountable to a dominant other. At the other (low) end of the grid dimension is autonomous, competitive frontier individualism, in which people choose for themselves and freely negotiate their relationships on whatever terms they can obtain (MP)—"Think of people here milling around, occasionally emerging for a time into a society that seems like the ideal of the free market" (Douglas 1978:9). At the low end of the grid dimension,

> The substantive signs of ascribed status are scrapped, one by one, and supplanted by abstract principles. Of these, one is sacred still, that is the holiness of contract itself. As individuals are supposed to transact more and more freely, the rules governing transactions may even multiply. Society turns into a veritable market. (Douglas 1978:8)

In this environment of free individual transactions there is complete mobility of resources and complete knowledge of prices (Douglas 1978:21), as well as rewards for innovation, specialization, and economy of scale. Low-grid societies have an ethics of individual equality (or equality of opportunity, at least). Douglas (1978:17-18, 41-46) also discusses what I am calling the Null interaction, writing about nonassociation and exclusion, especially the withdrawal and voluntary isolation of hermits.

Margaret Mead (1961 [1937]) headed a group of anthropologists who compared 13 cultures and classified them as *competitive* (roughly, MP) or *cooperative* (roughly, CS). Despite the richness of the ethnographic descriptions provided by the anthropologists who collaborated on the project, subsequent theorists writing about the fundamental forms of social relations have largely ignored this valuable study. The finding that competition and cooperation were actually independent dimensions, not opposites, should have guided later research in this area. Significantly, Mead's group finds it necessary to add a third category to their typology, *individualistic* behavior. Behavior is individualistic if "the individual strives toward his goal without reference to others" (Mead 1961[1937]: 16). This is precisely the Null case of interaction in which people do not orient action to any of the three paradigmatic relational models. No society can be generally individualistic and be a society, but some societies are more individualistic than others: Mead's group characterized the Eskimo (hunters in Greenland), Ojibwa (hunters in Canada), Bachiga (mixed farmers, pastoralists, and hunters in East Africa), and Arapesh (root farmers and hunters of New Guinea) as markedly individualistic, and the Ifugao (paddy rice growers of the Philippines) and Maori (farmers, fishers, and gatherers of New Zealand) as moderately individualistic. Note that individualism is not associated with any particular culture area or system of production. Kluckholn and Strodtbeck (1973 [1961]) also independently recognize this Null orientation toward autonomy, calling it "individuality" and contrasting it with MP-like relations.

It is striking that eminent sociologists; economists; economic, social, cul-

tural, and psychological anthropologists; cross-cultural, developmental and social psychologists; sociolinguists; and three theologians have repeatedly rein-
vented more or less the same typology of social relationships.[17] It suggests that
people in many cultures (and many historical periods) use the same four models to structure much of their social action and thought. However, the possibility remains that this convergence results primarily from a reflection in social
theory of our own ethnosociology. In other words, perhaps the convergence of
these independent typologies is not a result of the true nature of human social
relationships in general, but only a consequence of the culturally informed
schema Western peoples all implicitly use in thinking about their own and
others' social relations. Western theorists may conceivably be describing their
own shared—possibly culture-specific—intuitive perceptions of the structures
of social relations, rather than describing the realities of actual social relations.
Of course, our naive folk social psychology may turn out to be a more or less
accurate reflection of our own social structure. That is, it is of considerable
significance if this taxonomy does capture our own intuitive folk concepts of
social relations, since we use our implicit and explicit folk models to generate,
coordinate, understand, assess, and negotiate our social relationships (see Heider 1958). The question is whether non-Western people have a fundamentally
similar set of implicit generative models, and indeed whether the basic underlying models are not only universal but in some degree endogenous.[18] For this
reason, the ethnographic evidence from other cultures and the theories of
non-Western students of society are crucial, and I will highlight such comparative data where I am aware of them. But in the end, the ultimate test of the
universality of this theory should come from a consensus of non-Western
scholars whose ethnocentrisms are independent of my own biases and presuppositions. My hope is that if social scientists from diverse cultures apply this
theory to social relations in a broad range of other cultures, they will find the
theory useful in accounting for the structures and processes they observe.

*Part* **II**

# Manifestations
# of the Relational Models

## PREFACE TO PART II

*I*n sum, my thesis is that there are four fundamental elementary models that
people use (for the most part quite unreflectively) in relating to others. They
are *elementary* in the sense that people combine them to construct complex
and varied personal relationships, roles, groups, institutions, and societies.
They are *fundamental* in the sense that people use them to generate corresponding patterns of action and thought in a great many social domains. Demonstrating these two salient features is the purpose of the following four chapters. In actual fact, however, this theory is largely an inductive inference. In the
next four chapters I will guide the reader through the literature that is half
the evidence; in Part IV will come the rest of the evidence. My point is that
the same four patterns emerge in every domain we examine: we find the same
familiar forms of social relationships almost everywhere. Readers who know
any of these literatures will find I have simplified and left out much, but may
discover that familiar ground looks surprisingly different from the vantage
point of this theory. I hope that most readers will also discover unexpectedly
familiar patterns in those areas that the following chapters reintroduce to
them. If so, this book will achieve its purpose of beginning to reunify the core
of the social sciences.

As a rhetorical heuristic, I divide the material into four chapters, discussing
in turn the ways the four fundamental models govern the creation and interchange of things; the making and imposing of choices; the construction and
integration of social orientations; and the making and legitimation of judgments. I follow these four chapters with a brief coda on how the models give

(Text continued on page 48)

**Table 1** Manifestations and Features of Four Elementary
Relational Models

|  | *Communal Sharing* | *Authority Ranking* |
|---|---|---|
| **DOMAINS** | | |
| *Reciprocal Exchange* | People give what they can and freely take what they need from pooled resources. What you get does not depend on what you contribute, only on belonging to the group. | Superiors appropriate or preempt what they wish, or receive tribute from inferiors. Conversely, superiors have pastoral responsibility to provide for inferiors who are in need and to protect them. |
| *Distribution (Distributive Justice)* | Corporate use of resources regarded as a commons, without regard for how much any one person uses; everything belongs to all together. Individual shares and property are not marked. | The higher a person's rank, the more he or she gets, and the more choice he or she has. Subordinates receive less and get inferior items, often what is left over. |
| *Contribution* | Everyone gives what they have, without keeping track of what individuals contribute. "What's mine is yours." | Noblesse oblige: superiors give beneficently, demonstrating their nobility and largesse. Subordinate recipients of gifts are honored and beholden. |
| *Work* | Everyone pitches in and does what he or she can, without anyone keeping track of inputs. Tasks are treated as collective responsibility of the group, without dividing the job or assigning specific individual duties. | Superiors direct and control the work of subordinates, while often doing less of the arduous or menial labor. Superiors control product of subordinates' labor. |
| *Meaning of Things* | Heirlooms, keepsakes, sacred relicts that are metonymic links to people with whom a person identifies. | Prestige items and emblems of rank. Conspicuous consumption to display superiority. Conversely, sumptuary laws that forbid inferiors to own these items. |
| *Orientations to Land* | Motherland or homeland, defining collective ethnic identity. Natal land received from the ancestors and held in trust for posterity. Land used corporately as a commons. | Domain, sovereign realm, personal dominion, fief, or estate. |

| Equality Matching | Market Pricing |
|---|---|
| Balanced, in-kind reciprocity. Give and get back the same thing in return, with appropriate delay. | Pay (or exchange) for commodities in proportion to what is received, as a function of market prices or utilities. |
| To each the same. Everyone gets identical shares (regardless of need, desire, or usefulness). | "To each in due proportion." Each person is allotted a quota proportionate with some standard (e.g., stock dividends, commissions, royalties, rationing based on a percentage of previous consumption, prorated strike benefits or unemployment compensation). |
| Contributors match each other's donations equally. | People assessed according to a fixed ratio or percentage (e.g., tithing, sales or real estate taxes). |
| Each person does the same thing in each phase of the work, either by working in synchrony, by aligning allotted tasks so they match, or by taking turns. | Work for a wage calculated as a rate per unit of time or output. |
| Tokens of equal, independent status, one for each; e.g., a bicycle, a car, a weapon, a trophy, a set of tools, or a house when each peer must have one to be coequal with the others. | Commodities produced or purchased to sell for profit; or productive capital and inventory. Products developed and presented in terms of marketing considerations. Also, private property valued because of its cost. |
| Equal plots for each family (e.g., U.S. homesteading, 1978–9 Chinese land reform). Land-owning or territorial sovereignty as the basis of equality (e.g., when all property owners are eligible to vote, and when each state or nation gets equal representation). | Investment, treated as capital. Purchased for expected appreciation, for lease or rent, or as a means of production. |

*Continued*

**Table 1** Manifestations and Features of Four Elementary
Relational Models **Continued**

| | *Communal Sharing* | *Authority Ranking* |
|---|---|---|
| **DOMAINS** | | |
| *Significance of Time* | Relationships are idealized as eternal (e.g., solidarity that is based on descent or common origin). Perpetuation of tradition, maintaining corporate continuity by replicating the past. | Sequential precedence marks status by serial ordering of action or attention according to rank. Temporal priority to superiors, often determined by age or seniority. |
| *Decision Making* | Group seeks consensus, unity, the sense of the group (e.g., Quaker meeting, Japanese groups). | By authoritative fiat or decree. Will of the leader is transmitted through the chain of command. Subordinates obey orders. |
| *Social Influence* | Conformity: desire to be similar to others, to agree, maintain unanimity, and not stand out as different. Mutual modeling and imitation. | Obedience to authority or deference to prestigious leaders. Subordinates display loyalty and strive to please superiors. |
| *Constitution of Groups* | Sense of unity, solidarity, shared substance (e.g., "blood," kinship). One-for-all, all-for-one. *Gemeinschaft, mechanical solidarity, primary group.* | Followers of a charismatic or other leader. Hierarchical organization (e.g., military). |
| *Social Identity and the Relational Self* | Membership in a natural kind. Self defined in terms of ancestry, race, ethnicity, common origins, and common fate. Identity derived from closest and most enduring personal relationships. | Self as revered leader or loyal follower; identity defined in terms of superior rank and prerogative, or inferiority and servitude. |
| *Motivation* | Intimacy motivation. Murray's nurturance and succorance. In Japan, *amaeru.* | Power motivation. (Also some items from authoritarian personality F scale.) |

| Equality Matching | Market Pricing |
| --- | --- |
| Oscillation of turns, of hosting, or other reciprocation at appropriate frequency. Synchrony of action or alignment of intervals to equate participants' efforts or opportunities. | Calculus of rates of interest, return, pay, or productivity per unit of time. Concern with efficient use of time, spending it effectively, and with the opportunity cost of wasted time. |
| One-person, one-vote election. Everyone has an equal say. Also rotating offices or lottery. | Market decides, governed by supply and demand or expected utilities. Also rational cost/benefit analysis. |
| Compliance to return a favor ("log rolling"), taking turns deciding, or going along to compensate evenly or keep things balanced. | Cost and benefit incentives—contracts specifying contingent payments, bonuses, and penalties. Bargaining over terms of exchange. Market manipulation. Offering a "special deal" or a bargain. Apparent scarcity and time limitations may move people to act. |
| Equal-status peer groups, e.g., car pool, cooperative, rotating credit association. (A pervasive form of organization in Melanesia.) | Corporations, labor unions, stock markets and commodity associations; *gesellschaft, organic solidarity*. Also, bureaucracy with regulations oriented to pragmatic efficiency: *rational–legal organization*. |
| Self as a separate but co-equal peer, on a par with fellows. Identity dependent on staying even, keeping up with reference group. | Self defined in terms of occupation or economic role: how one earns a living. Identity a product of entrepreneurial success or failure. |
| Desire for equality; insufficiently studied. | Related to achievement motivation. |

*Continued*

**Table 1** Manifestations and Features of Four Elementary
Relational Models **Continued**

| | *Communal Sharing* | *Authority Ranking* |
|---|---|---|
| **DOMAINS** | | |
| *Moral Judgment & Ideology* | Caring, kindness, altruism, selfless generosity. Protecting intimate personal relationships. "Never send to know for whom the bell tolls; it tolls for thee." *Traditional legitimation* in terms of inherent essential nature or karma of group. | What supreme being commands i right. Obedience to will of superiors. *Heteronomy, charismati legitimation.* |
| *Moral Interpretations of Misfortune* | Stigmatization, pollution, contamination. Isolation as pariah. Feeling of being different, set apart, not belonging. Victims seek and join support groups of fellow-sufferers, among whom the misfortune is a source of solidarity. | Have I angered God? Did I disobe the ancestors? (E.g., story of Job.) |
| *Aggression & Conflict* | Racism, genocide to "purify the race." Killing to maintain group honor. Riots based on deindividuation. Equivalence of all "others:" terrorists and rioters indiscriminately kill all members of opposed ethnic group. | Wars to extend political hegemon Execution of people who fail to accept the legitimacy of political authorities or who commit lèse majesté. Also political assassinatic and tyrannicide. |
| **FEATURES** | | |
| *Some of the Features that the Cultural Implementation Rules Must Specify* | Who is "us" and who is "other," including how people acquire and lose corporate membership. What is shared. What kinds of restraint people must exercise in taking from others, and what excuses them from giving. | What are the criteria for accordin rank. What dimensions mark precedence. In what domains ma authority be exercised. |
| *Characteristic Mode of Marking Relationships* | Enactive, kinesthetic, sensorimotor rituals, especially commensal meals, communion, and blood sacrifice. | Spatiotemporal ordered arrays (e. who is in front, who comes first). Differences in magnitude (size of dwelling personal space); plural pronouns for respect. |

| *Equality Matching* | *Market Pricing* |
|---|---|
| Fairness as strict equality, equal treatment, and balanced reciprocity. | Abstract, universal, rational principles based on the utilitarian criterion of the greatest good for the greatest number (since this calculus requires a ratio metric for assessing all costs and benefits). *Rational-legal legitimation.* |
| Feeling that misfortune should be equally distributed: "things even out in the long run." Idea that misfortune balances a corresponding transgression. | Was this a reasonably expectable risk or calculable cost to pay for benefits sought? Is this too high a price to pay? |
| Eye-for-an-eye feuding, tit-for-tat reprisals. Revenge, retaliation in-kind. | Mercantile wars, slaving, exploitation of workers. Killing to protect markets or profits. Robbery and extortion. War strategies based on kill ratios. |
| Who and what counts as equal. What procedures people use for matching and balancing. How people initiate turn taking. What are the appropriate delays before reciprocating. | What entities may be bought and sold (e.g., sex? drugs? votes? people?). What are the ratios of exchange and how do particular attributes affect prices (e.g., how many hours of unskilled weekend labor for one old red bantam hen?). What counts as a cost or a benefit (in either monetary or utility terms). |
| Concrete operations involving physical manipulations of tokens or persons so as to balance, match, synchronize, align, or place them in one-for-one correspondence. | Abstract symbolic representation, especially propositional language and arithmetic, (e.g., verbal negotiations referring to value-relevant features; printed or electronic price lists; symbolically conveyed information about current market conditions). |

*Continued*

**Table 1** Manifestations and Features of Four Elementary
Relational Models **Continued**

| | Communal Sharing | Authority Ranking |
|---|---|---|
| **FEATURES** | | |
| *Corresponding Measurement Scale Type* | Categorical/nominal. | Ordinal. |
| *Relational Structure* | Equivalence relation. | Linear ordering. |
| *Natural Selection Mechanism* | Kin selection according to inclusive fitness. | Adaptive value of submissi and dominance behaviors a linear hierarchy. |
| *Approximate Age when Children First Externalize the Model* | Infancy. | By age three. |

structure to aggression and discord. Not very much rides on this exploratory analytic taxonomy as such, but much of the power of this theory is a consequence of its broad integrative range. However we classify the domains of social action and thought, this theory encompasses most of them. My aim is simply to explore the many situations, tasks, kinds of activities, spheres of action, substantive problems, concerns, attitudes, and content areas in which people use these same four models. The claim that these relational models are fundamental means that people have these four modes available for organizing *any*

| Equality Matching | Market Pricing |
| --- | --- |
| Interval. | Ratio. |
| Ordered Abelian group. | Archimedian ordered field. |
| "Tit-for-tat" in-kind reciprocity (evolutionarily stable strategy, adaptive initially, resistant to invasion). | Adaptive value of specialization and commodity exchange. |
| Soon after fourth birthday. | During ninth year. |

social domain. The fact that so many different domains exhibit the same four relational structures strongly implies that people are using a universal set of psychological schemata to generate these structures. Table 1, pages 42–49, summarizes the manifestations of the four relational models and some other features discussed in Part III. The range of diverse contexts of social action and thought—within and across cultures—that people organize using these four models supports the hypothesis that they are fundamental, general, and universal psychological schemata.

# 3

# Things

This chapter focuses on the exchange and production of things, and in general on how people conceive of things and relate to them. It begins by looking at transactions in which people transfer things in both directions. Then it discusses unilateral distributions and contributions in which people transfer things in only one direction. It then looks at labor: how people organize the production of things. It concludes with a broader analysis of the ways in which people link themselves with things, particularly with land. The chapter concludes by considering the four social meanings of time.

## TRANSACTIONS

Durkheim (1933 [1893]) and Mauss (1967 [1925]) long ago demonstrated that transactions in material objects are often the foundation for social relations and society. People can use each of the four fundamental models to organize transfers of material or nonmaterial goods and services and to provide obligatory or ideal standards for such transactions. For analytic convenience we can categorize transactions into "reciprocal" exchange, distribution, and contribution respectively. In practice these different phases often are so closely linked to each other that it may be impossible to separate out distinct steps in the cycles of circulation.

### "Reciprocal" Exchange

What are the contingencies linking what you give with what you get under each of the four models? In Communal Sharing, people do not truly transfer entities from one person to another, since within the CS framework everything is connected to the collectivity as a whole, not to individual persons. If I catch a fish in the middle of the ocean, no one has transferred anything to me—it was "ours" in the first place, and any of "us" are free to help ourselves to whatever we like. If some entity is for historical, biological, or other reasons associated at some point with a particular person, it is nonetheless at the disposal of any other who belongs to the CS group. So if a mother has milk and her baby is hungry, she gives whatever she has to the baby. If you have the skill, perseverance, and luck to kill an antelope, it still belongs to us all just as much as if anyone else had killed it (Marshall 1961; cf. Rawls's [1971] notion that individual talents belong to everyone collectively). As a form of exchange CS is noncontingent, in that what one person gets from another does not depend on what she has given, and does not create obligations to give anything in particular in return. Of course, the act of giving may help to create a CS relationship in the first place—and failure to be kind and generous may jeopardize the relationship. But sharing pooled resources within such a relationship is contingent only on the supposition of belonging to the collectivity in question, not on any particular previous or future acts. "What's mine is yours, what's yours is mine: it belongs to all of us together." People give and take freely within the boundaries of the CS group as delimited with respect to the issue in question, and ignore those outside the boundaries. Thus inclusion in a CS relationship is binary: either you are in, or you are out. However, on different occasions with regard to different issues people may draw the boundaries so that they include only one other person, or a whole family, a neighborhood, an ethnic group or nation, all humans, or even all sentient beings. W. Hamilton (1963, 1964, 1971) and others analyze a potential evolutionary basis for social relations of this sort.

With Authority Ranking, those of higher rank are entitled to appropriate what they demand, and fealty requires that inferiors pay homage with tributary gifts. The chief is entitled to such tribute by the fact of being chief, and likewise he may take by fiat whatever pleases him. These proprietary rights may be prescribed and delimited in various ways, but they are not contingent on the chief giving anything in particular back in return. However, noblesse oblige: anyone in authority is obligated to protect and look after his dependants. Although it is the prerogative of a chief to be arbitrary and willful in his favors, a pattern of redistributive largess is obligatory. Loyalty should be rewarded, but the boss may do it at his discretion, when and how he chooses and sees fit.[1] Failure to look after his flock and defend it from predation may cost the leader his pastoral following, but he has dominion over them and may choose to exercise it at his will.

Equality Matching is balanced exchange, exchange as equal return. My transfer of something to you entitles me to get back the same thing in return. Analytically, it is crucial to recognize that what counts as a return of the "same thing" is culturally and subjectively defined by the actors, as a function of whatever categories they are using.[2] If you invite me to dinner and I invite you to dinner in return, then we both may feel satisfied that I have returned to you what you gave me, although it would be inappropriate to match the menus of the two dinners precisely, much less the exact quantities. Under EM, if Jean does Mary a favor then Mary owes Jean a favor in return at some point, but anything Mary and Jean construe to be a favor of the same sort will count, however objectively different the favors are. However, as Foa and Foa (1974) point out, people expect EM reciprocity in kind: for Mary to pay Jean back in cash is not acceptable. While bookkeeping in EM is often covert, and although debts may accrue and accounts may even be perpetually unbalanced in one or another direction, the implicit principle is quid pro quo.

Things transferred in exchange transactions under Market Pricing need not be of the same kind—indeed, they usually are unlike (money for labor, grain for machine tools). In many (but not all) such systems, people voluntarily enter into exchange contracts on whatever terms they can obtain or negotiate, and people are free to try to get as much as they can and pay as little as they can. Credit and bookkeeping often are overtly marked, and the contingencies are explicit, often negotiated. You get what you pay for, and people consider their alternatives, choosing a "market basket" of commodities. Market Pricing is quite distinct from anarchy or any asocial exploitation: a market is a socially structured institution, money is the most social of all human products (cf. Marx 1970 [1859]; Polanyi 1957b, 1977 [1957]), and the rules for what constitutes a valid contract and how they are to be enforced are socially generated. A system of prices is a highly social artifice, and indeed each individual act of price setting is socially constructed (Prus 1985).

Reciprocal exchange—that is, social relations involving transfers of objects in both directions—has been the focus of a great deal of anthropological research, and social psychologists have also studied the phenomenon under the rubric of social justice. Let us take a quick look at each in turn.

## Anthropological Perspectives and Ethnographic Accounts

Anthropologists have long stressed the importance of "exchange" in constituting, sustaining, and repairing social relations, and consequently the anthropological work on exchange and reciprocity is vast. On the classic case of the Melanesian Kula system alone there is a large edited book and a bibliographic volume (Leach and Leach 1983; Macintyre 1983), and there is an enormous literature on systems of exchanging women in marriage. We have already discussed the superb theoretical integrations of the literature on transfers of objects written by Polanyi (1957a [1944]) and Sahlins (1965). Since I discuss the anthropological accounts of systems of exchanging women in marriage in the section Social System Functions in Chapter 5, and since I will discuss Moose marriage in Chapter 12, here I will merely skim the surface of this literature to show its general implications.

All four of the basic forms of exchange are probably present in most cultures, although there may perhaps have been cultures in historical times without true Market Pricing, and there are some in which Authority Ranking is very muted and more or less limited to parent-child relations. Lorna Marshall (1961) and Mac Marshall (1977) offer excellent ethnographic accounts of cultural variants of Communal Sharing. Innumerable anthropological accounts of kinship relations and kinship-based production refer to this kind of solidarity, identity, belief in a shared common substance, prescriptive altruism and pooling of collective resources, and collective labor.[3] Of course, kinship systems generally also involve AR differences as well (see Bascom 1942). Blood-brotherhood and bond friendship may involve the same kind of total trust, merging of selves, and unbounded mutual responsibility and concern (Herskovits 1969 [1931–33]; Evans-Pritchard 1933).

Anthropologists often view Equality Matching as the integrating skeleton of social systems. A vast anthropological literature is devoted to showing how this form of exchange constitutes and marks social systems, engendering and solidifying diverse social systems. The seminal work is Mauss (1967[1925]), although he sometimes conflates EM with CS. The classic cases are the Melanesian Kula ring described above in Chapter 2 (Malinowski 1961 [1922]; Leach and Leach 1983; Macintyre 1983; see also Schwimmer 1983) and the analysis of marriage systems involving the "restricted" exchange of wives (Lévi-Strauss 1961 [1949]; see also the discussion of Meillassoux's theory in Chapter 5).

Lebra's (1969, 1976:90–109) description of the Japanese concept of on (reciprocity) demonstrates how Equality Matching contrasts analytically with the other three modes in which objects may circulate among people (even when the medium is money) and yet be connected to them in practice through various social processes. Japanese strive to match gifts with precisely balanced return gifts, if possible by reciprocating in exactly the same circumstances (a funeral gift in return for a funeral gift of the same amount, a counter-present in honor of your son's matriculation to equal your present in honor of the matriculation of my son). A person who has not been able to reciprocate with a precisely matched return gift or service is constrained by a strong sense of obligatory gratitude (giri). On obligations are inherited from one's ancestors and are owed to powerful benefactors, often leading to deferential attitudes of devotion, loyalty, and subordination to traditional authorities (AR), or to an ascribed sense of devoted gratitude toward one's birthplace, group, or society (CS). Further, the EM on obligation extends to the groups to which one belongs, so that the debt and attendant gratitude is collectively shared by one's household, for example (CS)—just like the CS equivalence of all group members with regard to retaliatory vengeance in Western feuds. Lebra also describes Japanese beliefs that filial piety toward parents and services to superiors (AR) will be balanced by matching loyalty from one's own children and subordinates. Moreover, the on benefaction and resultant obligation to reciprocate is easily transformed into an Authority Ranking relationship if the benefaction takes the form of something that is intrinsically impossible to repay, as in a fief granted to a feudal vassal, parental care and self-sacrificing nurturance, or the political and religious leadership of the emperor. Indeed, Lebra notes that as a principle of reciprocity in Japanese culture, *on* is normally asymmetric: the superior exhibits his grace and nobility in bestowing a favor on a subordinate, who is eternally beholden, and hence loyal. Thus the *on* concept encompasses three distinct modes of reciprocity, together with the normative obligations and feelings of debt and gratitude that are linked to them.

Communal Sharing is the typical within-group form of transaction, especially in primary kin groups, while exchanges between groups commonly take an Equality Matching form. However, EM is common within more extended groups as well. In many societies there are reciprocal labor arrangements like those of the Moose, in which the men in a village work together threshing each man's grain in turn. Attendance at these bees is reciprocal, and the men structure most of the work so as to match each other's labor stroke for stroke (cf. Udy 1959, 1970, discussed below; Skinner 1964a, 1964b; see also Part IV). Freeman (1987) demonstrates the antiquity and pervasiveness of turn-taking rotations and some other EM forms in the political and social systems of Iberia.

Schieffelin (1976) sensitively captures the contrast between Equality Matching and Communal Sharing transactions among the Kaluli of Papua New Guinea. First, CS: "The giving and sharing of food among the Kaluli communicates sentiment; it conveys affection, familiarity, and good will" (pp. 48-9). From the day of birth, close relatives give food to the newborn, and within the communal longhouse where everyone in the community resides, nuclear families share freely with each other when anyone is in need (see need-based justice norms, below). Anyone who gets a major gift of food or brings back game or fish must share it with others in the longhouse. Kinsmen or friends may mark an especially close relationship by addressing each other by the name of a food they have eaten together. People share sago shoots even more widely, so that they can always get whatever they need for planting. Although not all kin realize the potential for active CS, among kinsmen—and others—CS relations can always be actualized by giving and sharing fresh meat and other food and also by visiting, helping with work or contributions to bride wealth, or inviting people to hunt. These forms of kindness and affection do not require any specific quid pro quo.

In direct contrast, affines (in-laws) exchange cooked meat and other goods according to strict Equality Matching. The Kaluli term *wel* means exact equivalent, something given as an in kind return for something received, like a pig for an identical pig. To be *wel*, the entities must be of the same kind and number. For example, Kaluli mark the consummation of marriage by the husband giving his affines, say, 18 smoked game animals, for which they later return exactly 18 smoked animals. Although a group that wishes to resolve a dispute peacefully will settle for compensation (*su*) in valuables to indemnify them for an injury, strict in-kind *wel* is more apt and far more satisfying, and Kaluli make EM into a fine art. In battle when a man is struck by an enemy, the victim's side tries to strike a blow of equal severity against any of the enemy.[4] Thus when group G killed a man of group W and sank his body in a river upstream from the W territory, W men killed a man of G and sank his body in a river upstream from G territory. Schieffelin says nothing about AR relations among the Kaluli, but with regard to Market Pricing he does say (pp. 12–14, 16, 58) that they have always actively engaged in "trade" and other sorts of "business transactions."

Ethnographic reports of Market Pricing are less numerous than accounts of other forms of transactions, perhaps because anthropologists take them for granted as banal and obvious. Welsch (1981) provides diverting accounts of horse trading in this mode a century ago in Nebraska, and Makower's (1988) advice book offers a detailed ethnography of contemporary American used car sales; see also Polanyi (1966) and Skinner (1962, 1964b). Some of the work on "spheres of exchange" makes manifest the contrast between MP, EM, and CS transactions. For example, Bohannan (1955) shows that the language and practices of the Tiv of northern Nigeria delimit three distinct spheres of exchange. One involves food and subsistence items bought and sold in the market, over which people bargain to gain advantageous terms (MP). The second sphere involves slaves, cattle, white cloth, and metal bars, whose principal significance is the prestige they confer on their possessor (AR). The third category involves only rights in human beings who are not slaves, particularly rights to give away women in marriage in return for receiving a wife (primarily EM, it appears). Tiv rank these three categories hierarchically as having very different values and thus accord considerable moral significance to transactions that involve conversions across disparate categories. They are, therefore, strongly motivated to undertake some kinds of conversions and avoid others. Tiv exclude CS transactions that involve freely giving land and labor from any of these three other spheres, because such transactions are acts of generosity or obligations that are due to kin or age-mates, not matters of crassly contingent accounting.

Obviously, transactions take an enormous variety of culture-specific forms,[5] but it appears that most can be generated out of the four basic models. There is more anthropological evidence on this in the section Systems of Exchanging Women in Chapter 5. Note that the entities people transfer to each other under any of the models need not be desirable: people conduct transactions in liabilities, risks, or hazardous wastes, for example, using the same models.

All four forms of exchange involve "exchange" and "reciprocity" in the sense that each side gives something to the other, or at least is motivated (or obligated) to do so. As many social scientists use the terms "exchange" and "reciprocity," they are too indefinite to be of much analytic use. What differentiates among the four forms of bidirectional transfer is the kind of contingency linking the transfers in each direction and the ways in which people work out what they will transfer. It should be apparent even in this snapshot of the vast anthropological literature on "exchange" that there are four different conditional principles at work: people may give to other members of the group unconditionally; they may reverently give to superiors in the hierarchy to please and satisfy them and graciously give to inferiors in the hierarchy to display dominance; people may give just in return for getting the same thing back to balance the transfer, or people may exchange commodities at market rates determined by their exchange ratios (prices). The anthropological literature exhibits these same four distinct alternatives in innumerable cultures around the world, suggesting that these are the four basic modes of transfer that people intuitively initiate, understand, and desire.

### Social Psychology: Principles of Social Justice

A number of social psychologists working within the framework of concepts of "justice" have advanced the idea that there are three distinct normative principles that people use in distributing "rewards:" need (CS), equality (EM), and equity (proportionality to contributions—MP). Some of this work compares the three justice principles as procedural rules, and some considers them in terms of substantive distributional outcomes. This work was inspired in part by Adams's (1965; see also Walster, Walster, and Berscheid 1978) work on equity, which assumed that in seeking maximization of benefits and minimization of costs, people arrive at what they regard as a fair market distribution of rewards in proportion to inputs. Following this up, researchers found that proportional equity is not the only principle people regard as just; sometimes people prefer strict equality, and sometimes they want to give people what they need. Unfortunately this work on social justice has been conducted in isolation from the other theoretical traditions described here. But the research covers a wide range of dimensions, comparing the equity and equality principles with each other and in many cases with need as well.[6]

Mikula (1980; Mikula and Schwinger 1978) and Schwinger (1980) summarize experimental literature revealing that in these situations subjects choose a justice principle on the basis of "politeness," modestly proposing the option which confers the greatest benefits on the other and the least for the subject. However, in some cases subjects then readily agree to the other person's proposal of an alternative principle that benefits the subject more. This is a significant finding, since I think it hints at the operation of a metaprinciple of nonselfishness and a principle of seeking consensual agreement that people use as criteria for proposing principles like equity and equality in ambiguous situations. If the operation of such metaprinciples could be shown in other contexts, it would be of great interest, not least because both of these seem to be CS metaprinciples that appear to determine the use of MP and EM rules.[7]

For the most part social justice researchers do not consider Authority Ranking as a meaningful justice principle in its own right. But Austin and Hatfield (1980) do bring AR into the discussion. They build on Walster and Walster (1975), generating hypotheses about when people implement principles of equity, equality, or legitimated power in distributing resources. In essence, they argue that people use equity (MP: rewards proportional to contributions) when the matter is important, and equality (EM) only as a sort of heuristic when it is too difficult to decide on the value of contributions. (They do not really consider the possibility that people would prefer EM for its own sake.) Austin and Hatfield argue further that people in power generally succeed in promulgating self-serving ideologies that overvalue their own contributions (AR). This amounts to a false-consciousness theory, disregarding the possibility that reflective subordinates might really prefer AR as a social justice principle. Most researchers in this tradition (see for example the papers in Bierhoff, Cohen, and Greenberg 1986) assume that distributions ranked by the status of the recipients (which all concede to be ubiquitous) are ipso facto illegitimate from the point of view of the participants. These researchers assume that such ranked differentials must be the result of brute "power"—an assumption that would have amazed the people of the Moose village where I did my fieldwork. I once asked the village chief when it is proper to divide things according to rank (*pui natende*) and when one should divide equally (*pui tι zemse*). He replied with emphatic astonishment that it is never suitable to divide things equally—rank must always be taken into account. Like social justice researchers' assumption that all rank favoritism is illicit in the West, the chief's statement is a slight exaggeration of the local norms.

Virtually all of the rest of the social justice work ignores the universal existence of substantive and procedural Authority Ranking norms that prescribe differential treatment by rank, according to which superiors (as a function of seniority, office, prestige, gender, caste, estate, or other status system) are entitled to more than their inferiors.[8] One wonders whether social justice researchers would think it legitimate to restructure academic salaries, for example, according to equity, equality, or need, without regard to seniority of rank. The only researcher in this tradition who treats status as a valid distributional criterion compared to the equity, equality, and need principles is Azzi (1988), who studies hypothetical political configurations. Weber (1978 [1922]) shows that social authority is often based on people's belief in the legitimacy of that authority. French and Raven (1959) picked up this theme again, arguing that power commonly is based on legitimacy with respect to some internalized norm or value—a sense of entitlement—or identification, not just brute coercion or ability to reward others. But most researchers in the justice paradigm neglect this fact.

Approaching the problem from the sociological paradigm, however, Berger, Cohen, and Zelditch (1972) show that prior status differences among members of small decision-making groups determine power and prestige within the group, as well as members' chances to perform task-related activity ("action opportunities") and their opportunities to make contributions to task performance ("outputs"). Prior status also determines the magnitude and likelihood of a member's receiving benefits ("rewards") in the final distribution. Berger et al. explain this behavior in equity terms as a result of group members' expectation that status and task performance are related, even when there is no manifest link. However, it is more plausible to infer that the AR model per se is the source of such differentiation; in fact, subjects distributed rewards according to rank. The most parsimonious interpretation of their results is that people use a justice conception of social hierarchy—of legitimate status differences—to confer authority and allocate rewards. This interpretation is supported by the fact that Berger et al.'s subjects combined disparate sources of information about each other to order all members in a unique linear ranking. Sampson (1963) independently argues that people typically do combine status criteria into a single system of rank. Sampson draws on consistency and dissonance theory to argue that incongruence among the various dimensions or indices of status produces conflicting expectations that are socially and cognitively dysfunctional. The result, he says, is a tendency toward status congruence. More simply, we might just say that people tend to order themselves into a single rank hierarchy, with a unique and complete ordering.

Equity theorists (Adams 1965; Walster, Berscheid, and Walster 1973; Berkowitz and Walster 1976; Walster, Walster, Berscheid, et al. 1978) have taken postulates about rational maximization of self-interest and argued that all social behavior takes the form of what amounts to a market equilibrium in which people allocate "rewards" (pay prices) in proportion to each person's contributions or inputs. While this extreme position is clearly not tenable, it does remind us that not all market pricing distributions involve money as the medium of exchange.

This small-group psychological literature on social justice demonstrates that the choice of a mode of transferring "rewards" is a function not only of culture and product, but of various details of the specific situation and the personal relationships of the interactants. Researchers have still explored only a small part of the total range of social situations and have only begun to consider the effects of the nature of the entity actually being transferred. Perhaps most interestingly, this literature does not indicate that people commonly use intermediate forms of the models—a group tends to use one pure principle in a given transfer.

The complementary anthropological literature on systems of exchange and the social psychological literature on justice principles confirm that people use these four models to organize most of their giving and taking. No other distinct types seem to be needed to account for the observed patterns, as the systematic comparisons of Lévi-Strauss (1961 [1949]), Polanyi (1957a [1944], 1957b, 1966, 1968) and Sahlins (1965) demonstrate (see Chapter 2). The anthropological literature has focused on the manner in which bidirectional transfers ("reciprocal exchange") of all four kinds constitute and sustain integrated social groups (see the section Constitution of Groups and Social Identity, below). At the end of Chapter 7, I summarize social justice research that independently concludes that people use each justice principle to create and sustain social relationships. The experimental social justice literature discussed above makes more controlled and systematic comparisons, showing that people follow the principle that corresponds to the kind of social relationship they actually have or intend to have, but offers no clear conception of what a "social relationship" is. The broader scope and more holistic anthropological approach gives a qualitative account of the local flavors of social relationships, driving home the fact that there are innumerable phenomenological variations on each justice principle. Since the same four modes of interchange emerge from the research in these two independent paradigms, there is some reason to believe that they represent the basic types of mutual contingencies between giving and getting objects. In this light let us see what we can make of unilateral, unidirectional transfers (that is, transactions that involve no return in the opposite direction).

## Distribution and Contribution

The same four models generally govern the allocation of fixed and renewable resources among persons. People may apply Communal Sharing by treating a resource as a shared commons, corporately held for collective use. The actors may define collective either as free access by individual members, or as use by the corporate group as a whole in some group activity. The contributors to McCay and Acheson (1987) describe many ethnographic examples of communal use of resources. Pandya (1988) describes such a pattern today among the hunting and gathering Ongees of the Andaman Islands, writing that all resources on the island are available to all; there is no private ownership of any kind of food source.

> Each evening when the men return to camp with the kill of the hunt and women return with what they have gathered, all the food is placed in the middle of the camp ground at the communal cooking place. All Ongees are expected to just go and pick up a portion of whatever food is there, [it is] irrelevant who brought it and who is related to the person who hunted or gathered it. As the Ongees explain, "No one gives food and tools since they are never taken away. They are always there for use." (Pandya 1988:4)

The only privately owned things are ancestor jaw bones and related ceremonial objects, and Ongees never hesitate to ask for or lend them whenever anyone wants to use them. Except for these, "every other thing is and can be given away but may not be expected or demanded back" (Pandya 1988:6). So within the tribe, people freely share all resources. On the other hand, they ordinarily kill, dismember, and burn the bodies of visitors to the islands.

As Hardin (1968) points out, a shared commons (a CS situation by its structural definition) may deteriorate if people put their selfish individual maximizing interests ahead of the collective interest, making it necessary to prioritize access (AR), divide the commons into equal shares or allocate access by lottery (EM), or to sell the commons or access to it (MP). The crucial point is that such social dilemmas (Dawes 1980) arise only when the distribution system does not coincide with the social motives of the participants. In the prisoners' dilemma for example, the mutually optimal outcome will be reached only when neither player is selfish and both put the collective interest ahead of personal interest. The bind in such social dilemmas is that the payoffs reward CS, while the people involved have individual maximizing MP motives (see Motivation, below). In effect, such dilemmas are situations in which, ironically, everyone is individually better off if all or most put the collective interests of the group ahead of their personal interests. On the other hand, the negative or inverse side of CS as a distributional principle is that it involves favoritism toward the we-group and ignoring and discriminating against outsiders—ethnocentrism. It seems to be characteristic of CS groups that they are based on radical contrast of an oppositional sort; all that is good is We, all that is bad is Other (Sherif et al. 1988 [1961]; Sherif and Sherif 1964; Le Vine and Campbell 1972). Tajfel (1978, 1982) strikingly demonstrates how readily people bias distributions toward we-group members even when the groups—actually social categories—are constituted on the most frivolous and ephemeral bases. These are artificial categories, but there is hardly any need to demonstrate experimentally the radical biases in everyday life brought about by truly strong and enduring Communal Sharing loyalties.

In distributions conducted according to Authority Ranking, participants receive portions that are ordered in size or quality according to their rank. In any given distribution, subordinates below some rank may get nothing. In contrast, distributive justice under Equality Matching means exactly identical shares. The classic way to achieve this is to have one person divide things up, and then give him or her the last pick among the shares. Alternatively, everyone may participate in dividing up the entity into shares until all agree that they are indifferent as to which share each person gets. This corresponds roughly to what Rawls (1971) calls "the veil of ignorance," and he argues that in such a situation people would maximize the welfare of those who would be worst off.[9] When the entity in question is more or less indivisible among the people participating, people may opt to implement EM by taking turns. Or they may conduct a fair lottery, as the Pennsylvania state parks do to allocate cheap cabins each season. In EM, people divide each distinct kind of entity separately and independently, since there is no common metric for comparing entities of different kinds.[10] (What people construe as entities of the "same kind" depends on the cultural and situational taxonomies they are using.) Morgan and Sawyer (1967), Leventhal (1976a), and O'Malley and Schubarth (1984) address some of the factors that may result in a norm of even distribution within a group.

In Market Pricing, Adam Smith's (1976 [1776]) invisible hand allocates the entities in question. Given their budget constraints, people get what they choose to pay for. People need not pay with money; teaching assistants may be allotted to courses in proportion to class enrollments (which are roughly proportional to tuition revenues). Or produce may be distributed to coop members according to the number of hours each worked during the year. In contrast to the period when Smith writes, in the West we now take the market so much for granted that, until we consider the quotas and rationing of a centralized economy, for example, we sometimes forget that it is the distributive mechanism par excellence. But Smith was not merely describing a procedure—he was justifying MP as a normative rule. As I hypothesized earlier, people use the same model to structure, to understand, and to judge social interactions.

Elsewhere (Fiske 1985) I give more ethnographic detail on how the Moose of Burkina Faso use all of these distributive schemes in dividing up kola nuts, wives, and many other things. Here we shall briefly consider the "input" side of transactions: how do people organize donations to collective projects?

The inverse of distribution is contribution, in which people give something to some social collection. The most obvious examples for us are taxation and donations to charities, but one could consider also bringing food to a feast or a potluck supper, or contributions to bride wealth or funeral rituals. Guided by Communal Sharing, people give whatever they have, but without marking, recording, or otherwise attending to how much each person gives (Clark 1983, 1984b). Collections at church illustrate this mode. Under Authority Ranking, people may be expected to donate amounts ordered by social rank. This is the practice in my department, where the suggested assessments for voluntary contributions to department parties and to the fund to subsidize graduate student attendance at colloquium dinners are graded ordinally by faculty rank, followed by lesser amounts for staff and then students. In Equality Matching, people are assessed categorically identical contributions, however the category is defined. Membership dues are sometimes identical for all members (see Kramer 1974 on burial societies in Soweto) and sometimes serially ordered by social status, as in some professional societies. Among the Moose when the ritual leader of the village conducts a sacrifice on behalf of the entire village, he assesses each independent cultivator a flat amount (say, 25 francs CFA) regardless of each person's wealth or the size of his household. Student activity and athletic fees at universities are usually the same for all contributors.

In the framework of Market Pricing, people pay in proportion to some socially relevant attribute, prototypically money. Sales taxes, custom duties, social security, and income taxes are classic examples. In Philadelphia, for example, the system is simple: All wage earners pay a flat percentage of their total income to the city. Similarly, many cities and school districts assess real and intangible property taxes as a flat percentage of the value of the property. Tithing is another example, when people adhere strictly to the payment of

one-tenth of their income to a church. In more complicated systems of progressive taxation, the ratio principle is iterated at two successive levels so that
the rate of taxation is more or less proportional to the amount of income, for
example, quintuple your income, and you pay twice as high a proportion in
taxes.[11] Under another extension of this MP principle, the market determines
what people pay in: people choose what to contribute as a function of their
resources and their payoff expectations. Consequently, people's payments
into a money market fund or any other joint venture depend on the expected
rate of return it pays and the perceived risk and convenience of the investment. This is more usefully seen as a bidirectional transaction rather than a
pure contribution, however.

It is obvious that a given social phenomenon may often be more or less
equally amenable to analysis as a system of exchange transactions, or distribution, or contributions: sometimes the distinctions among these analytic domains are merely matters of focus and perspective. But the distinction can be
important: in bidirectional transfers the analysis hinges on the precise manner
in which giving something is conditional on receiving something, while in unilateral transfers there is some other external criterion that guides the unidirectional transfers. Logically, any number of patterns of transfer of either kind are
possible, and the patterns of unidirectional transfers need not correspond to
those of bidirectional exchanges. Yet the evidence is that most observations of
both kinds of transfers fall nicely into just four categories. Neither logic nor
nature requires this—people make the forms. There appear to be only four
widespread forms of human transactions, which implies that people are constructing and constraining their material transactions with reference to only
four implicit ideas or models.

The entities transferred need not be tangible, but may include services or
any sort of labor. For example, Udy (1959) and Polanyi (1966) describe contribution structures used for organizing labor that are congruent with our typology. Although labor systems are almost invariably embedded in systems of
transfers of material goods, since work is so intrinsically important and has
some distinctive qualities, we will consider it separately.

## LABOR

The most important work on the organization of labor is that of Karl Marx
(1964a, 1964b, 1973 [1845-6, 1857-8], Marx and Engels 1959 [1848], 1906
[1867]),[12] along with that of Emile Durkheim (1933 [1893]). Erasmus (1956) and
Udy (1959, 1970) are the modern classics in this field. Although all aim to explain the emergence of modern industrial contractual wage labor, neither
Erasmus nor Udy make any reference to Marx or to Durkheim, each apparently having developed his own schema independently.[13] Marx and Durkheim
based their historical analysis on the limited sources then available, while Eras-

mus and especially Udy developed their analyses from surveys of a rich array of ethnographic primary sources on contemporary societies. This makes it very striking to find a considerable degree of correspondence between Marx's and Durkheim's historical accounts and Erasmus's and Udy's cross-cultural syntheses. All four arrive at very similar schemata, although neither Marx nor Durkheim discuss Equality Matching and Durkheim neglects Authority Ranking.[14]

Marx links presumed historical stages in the division of labor to distinct forms of property, each involving a particular kind of control over the labor of others. Throughout, Marx's analysis focuses on the necessary precursors for the development of wage labor and capitalism, so for the most part he considers earlier forms of labor and property only as antecedents of capitalism, not for themselves. In *The German Ideology* (1964a [1845–6]) he and Engels outline four forms of ownership. The first is tribal (or clan) collective ownership, in which there is very little division of labor except that which emerges from the family; this is Communal Sharing (see also 1964b [1867, 1853]:119–21). However, patriarchal power—partly in conjunction with the family head's role as military chieftain—extends itself over the family, other members of the tribe, and slaves (AR). The second stage is based on communal ownership in which people are vested in the property of the state (including its slaves and their labor) only as citizens (still CS). The third form is feudal ownership or estate (*ständisch*) property, in which the rural nobility controlled serfs[15] while urban guild masters dominated filial apprentices and journeymen, and monarchs ruled over all. Craftsmen had an immutable form of estate capital in their house, tools, and customers. At this stage the only division of labor that appears is a sharply separated hierarchy of ranks and hierarchically structured rights in land; this is clearly a system of production governed by Authority Ranking. Merchants were the first possessors of true movable capital, and as manufacturing began to develop, workers were forced into a strictly monetary relationship with capitalists, accompanied by international competition in the form of mercantilism, thus arriving at modern Market Pricing.

Twelve years later Marx (1964a, 1971, 1973) carried his analysis further in the *Grundrisse*. Here he describes three kinds of production that preceded capitalism. In the first, *Asiatic*, form of production there is a natural tie between a person and the land from which he secures what he uses to live. Moreover, people relate to each other in a spontaneous natural community which is presupposed in the collective clan ownership of the land they use (CS), without their having any sense of any subdivision of it into private property. People may utilize much of the land as individuals, but they pool some resources for the needs of the community as such, either through communal labor or by contributing the surplus from separate production. An individual with paternal responsibility for holding the land and the harvest or coordinating work embodies this unity at the level of a number of communes, thus giving rise to Authority Ranking. (As is happens, this "Asiatic" form is in fact a fairly good description of contemporary Moose rural society and much of traditional West

Africa; see Chapter 13 and also Suret-Canale [1964] and Coquery-Vidrovitch [1969].) The second, *ancient* form of production also presupposes the community, but is based on the city. Private property exists, but individuals are proprietors only by virtue of their historically defined membership in the commune and the state, through which they defend and preserve their territorial rights against outside groups. There is also a jointly utilized commons (continued CS). In the third, *Germanic,* form there is also common land used for hunting, grazing, and timber, but families live separately on their own private property. The commune exists as a relation among isolated, independent households by virtue of periodic gatherings of people with a common ancestry, language, and history. People express their membership when they assemble for mutual security, dispute settlement, or religion. In all these forms, Marx writes, people are proprietors as members of a community, and their labor presupposes this relation to the means of production: they are essentially collective, communal beings, and by virtue of this fact also intrinsically "working owners" (CS).

*Slavery* and bondage, in which the worker does not control the objective conditions for his or her own labor, are derivative forms of property that arise from communal property and labor; serfs, in particular, are attached to the fief they cultivate and their lord owns them along with it. The defining feature of such domination is that the superior appropriates the will of the subordinate (AR). In *capitalism* (MP), others appropriate the labor of workers via exchange, but not their will or their persons as such (although the persistence of indirect domination is one factor in the eventual dissolution of capitalism, Marx asserts).

Marx's project is to explain the necessary conditions for capitalism—Market Pricing—in terms of the contrasting systems that gave rise to it. Only when the worker is separated from the land or the necessary tools of artisan production, as well as from the means for his own sustenance during the period until production is completed, can labor enter the market. Further, a labor market can arise only when workers as slaves or serfs are no longer controlled by others. Such freed workers uprooted from any property confront the land and tools necessary for production as alien capital, capital owned by others. The transition to capitalism occurs when labor, land, and tools, as well as the food, clothing and shelter necessary for sustenance and human reproduction, become interconvertible through money, which circulates and mediates among them. The labor of a worker becomes functionally equivalent and monetarily interchangeable with machines. Previously, people worked to produce what they themselves used; under capitalism they must work to produce things specifically to exchange them for what they can use. Individuality is a consequence of this pattern of exchange that occurs when CS breaks down so that the individual is set against the community, rather than embedded in it. Marx anticipated that the ultimate form of labor and property would be a form of communism in which, instead of being directed at making something to exchange, work would be a form of participation in the collective production and consumption (1971:75). When this day comes, each person will contribute to the collectivity whatever she is able to give and take whatever she needs. In other words, people will produce and conduct their transactions according to Communal Sharing. It is an irony of history that the states created by the Communist revolutionaries quickly became centralized economic and social systems under AR dictatorships and authoritarian bureaucracies, and are now rapidly transforming themselves into MP entrepreneurial capitalist economies.

Marx neglects Equality Matching, although in later letters he cites Tacitus and subsequent law codes as reporting that the early Germans exchanged fields every year by lottery (1964b [1868, 1881]:141, 144). In a sense this neglect is justified by Udy's (1959) later analysis of a sample of work groups in 150 contemporary societies (although Udy does not link his research to Marx). Udy finds that "reciprocity" (EM) is never the basis for recruitment of the "basic," core group of workers who carry out a particular productive process from beginning to end. However, "reciprocity" is commonly used for recruiting occasional auxiliary labor at some phase of production, sometimes at crucial points (for more on Udy, see the section Theoretical Roots, above).

As this precis makes evident, the forms of labor and property Marx distinguishes are more distinctive—and correspond more closely to our types—than the stages he describes as though they were distinct historical epochs. CS, AR, and MP overlap in each one of Marx's historical stages, although typically one is dominant while another remains emergent. Furthermore, as the relational theory presented in this book argues, in most societies more than one mode of production exists at any one point in history (Rey 1975).

Udy's (1959, 1970) survey demonstrates that in contemporary societies people continue to use the four basic relational models to organize most work. Part IV provides a more detailed description of how these forms operate among the Moose. In the CS form of work everyone pitches in and does whatever they can until the job is done. There is no task assignment and no specification of individual responsibilities. Any given job is "our work" and it does not matter how much or how little each person does, merely that everyone is doing something, working together. This is the way Moose cultivate their principal fields. Durkheim's (1933 [1893]) description of mechanical solidarity as a system in which everyone produces the same things captures one aspect of CS. Authority Ranking in labor means that superiors direct the work of subordinates, controlling the manner in which it is done while not necessarily engaging in the productive activities per se. It may also mean that the lower one's rank, the more one must work and the more onerous the tasks one is assigned (as reportedly obtains in some academic departments). High rank may bring entitlement to prestigious, "cushy," or otherwise desirable tasks and roles. Typically, high-ranking people control the product of their subordinates' labor. Durkheim (1933) regarded forced division of labor as abnormal; the division of labor should occur without constraint, so that everyone does what suits him or her. Moose would regard this as an odd idea. In particular, they regard it as entirely legitimate that men should exercise control over much of the labor of their wives (compare Llewelyn-Davies 1981 for a sensitive analysis of women's acceptance of the legitimacy of patriarchal control among the Maasai on the other side of Africa).

People implement Equality Matching by matching each other's work one-for-one. For example, at a cultivating bee Moose line up side by side at one end of a field and hoe until they reach the other end, so that each person cultivates a strip the same length as every other person. At a threshing bee, men line up and strike the sorghum heads with flails in synchrony, beating in time to drums, with the result that each person makes the same number of strokes. Since there are usually more workers than space on the threshing ground, men rotate through the threshing line in turn, resting and then reentering the line. Moose also structure the threshing bees on an implicitly reciprocal basis, so that people go (or send their juniors) only to the threshing bees of men who have come to their last bee. Moose women hold very similar bees to thresh the sorghum they cultivate in their personal fields (*beolse*), inviting other women and attending their bees in turn. Erasmus (1956) describes similar systems elsewhere, as does Udy (1970:67–71), who distinguishes three types of EM: discrete and rotational reciprocity, and mutual associations.

Market Pricing usually takes the form of wage labor (or piece work) in a labor market. People work at the highest paying jobs they can obtain (given their other utilities), while employers seek the cheapest forms and sources of labor for the work they want done. Workers are employees whose responsibilities are strictly delimited by contract, often with prior negotiation. Employers pay employees at a specified rate per unit of time or work. Durkheim (1933) uses the analogy of the functional integration of the organs of vertebrates to describe MP as organic solidarity, based on specialization and the division of labor. He describes contractual relations as a particular variety of organic solidarity, one that should be based on strict "equality," so that contracts involve the exchange of social values that are equal in terms of the amount of useful labor entailed.

Quite independently of almost all of the other theoretical formulations we have reviewed here,[16] Erasmus (1956) analyzes the decline of reciprocal labor in Western South America and elsewhere in the world. In an article that is a neglected gem, Erasmus contrasts two systems of "reciprocal" farm labor. Exchange arrangements are based on strictly obligatory in-kind reciprocity, mostly among social equals, either all men or all women, who help each other in rotation for a fixed period of time at a given task (EM). If a participant is unable to attend, a substitute must be sent. Participants may also take turns using corporately owned equipment none could afford individually. This differs from festive labor in which the host provides a lavish feast to workers and may or may not attend the work parties of the people in attendance (CS). In such festive systems the host may take pride in the abundance and quality of the food he provides. Indeed such generosity may be a source of prestige and is common in hacienda or feudal contexts, in which case it may assume the AR character of hierarchical "redistributive" (Polanyi 1957a, 1966) systems. The festive form usually involves larger numbers of people than in-kind reciprocity, and the host may be of higher status than the workers. Erasmus then hypothesizes that wage labor (MP) replaces these forms of work as land becomes scarce, labor diversifies and specializes, people begin to grow crops for sale, cash and credit become available, the overall economy becomes commoditized, and consumption aspirations rise. Guillet (1980) builds on Erasmus (1956) and Udy (1959) to offer a rational cost-benefit decision flow model to explain peasants' choice of what forms of labor to use. But he demonstrates that, in actual fact, reciprocal labor is not declining. Guillet shows that reciprocal, festival, familial, and custodial labor coexist in the Andes with cash crops, commercial agriculture, the commoditization of labor, and full monetization.[17] The same situation occurs in West Africa, where Moose men all go and work as wage laborers in the Ivory Coast for much of their adult lives, yet return to their natal villages where wage labor is almost nonexistent and labor organized in terms of CS, AR, or EM is the norm. Similarly, rotating credit associations coexist with modern banks and other interest-bearing MP investment instruments (see Recursion section in Chapter 7).

There is no a priori basis in ecology or technology that would limit the organization of human labor to just four systems, and a priori there is no reason why the four predominant ways in which people organize labor should correspond to the four modes of transferring material objects. If that is what we find across continents and historical eras, it is a human artifact. It is an artifact of social cognition.

Marx regarded the social relations of production as the basis for social relations in general and indeed as the wellspring of a people's entire mode of life, including the superstructure of politics, ideology, consciousness, and culture. So he would not have been surprised at the parallels outlined in this book among the small set of principles that people use to organize so many social and psychological domains. The present theory diverges from Marx, however, in proposing that it is a set of fundamental shared human models for social relations that gives shape to production and exchange transactions, while simultaneously informing all other domains of human sociality. No domain has causal primacy, since all are products of the same set of basic grammars. Nonetheless we can still fruitfully follow Marx in passing from the study of work to a brief examination of people's orientations toward objects and land.

## LINKS BETWEEN PEOPLE AND THINGS

Within and outside the frameworks of production, consumption, transfers, and labor, the four relational models orient people in different ways to material objects, places, animals, plants, and such. In a Market Pricing context, as

Marx and Engels (Marx and Engels 1959 [1848], 1906 [1867], Marx 1959 [1859])
pointed out, things are commodities, whose value to the producer is controlled
by what she gets paid for them; think of the assembly line worker putting left
front-door handle gaskets on automobiles. For consumers, too, the denominator of value is market cost; consider people purchasing things just because
they are nominally "on sale." Under Equality Matching, things again mark the
relationship, but in this case they are tokens of the balance or imbalance, of
reciprocity initiated, compensated, or reversed (Malinowski 1961 [1922],
Mauss 1967 [1925]). Often the items in question can be aligned, weighed, or
otherwise directly compared so as to achieve equality by a concrete operation
of matching, as Mason (1987) describes in Moose salt distributions. In Authority Ranking, differences among things mark and constitute differences in rank
among people. Only Moose chiefs may display ostrich eggs at their roof peaks,
and formerly only chiefs could build rectangular houses. The Moose leather
hassocks and the Ashante stools are chiefly emblems of office, like the scepter
and crown of European royalty. Out of this ranked use of things come medieval sumptuary laws about who could wear velvet or furs, as well as modern
Western displays of status (see Veblen 1934 [1899]). Within the context of
Communal Sharing, things associated with the core relationship may have the
character of heirlooms, sacred relics, or keepsakes. What is important about
the object is who wore it or used it, and thus to whom it metonymically connects you—the wedding dress to your grandmother, the piece of the cross to
Christ, the ring or sweater to your lover (Nemeroff 1988). (Csikszentmihalyi
and Rochberg-Halton [1981] and Appadurai [1986] provide illustrations of the
varieties of the social meanings of things.)

Some of the same kinds of distinctions can be made with regard to the social
orientations toward land. Again Marx (1959, 1973; Marx and Engels 1906) is
the seminal thinker here, although he focuses primarily on the alienation of
workers from the products of their labor under MP. Tönnies (1988 [1887]) also
discusses the contrasting kinds of property entailed in CS and MP. Within CS,
land may be our commons, the family farm, a homeland or motherland, or
simply home (see Part IV). Moose and many other peoples treat the earth as a
nurturant (sometimes maternal) being that feeds them and that needs human
feeding. As Marx (1973:492) said, a person may relate to the earth as his own
"inorganic body," or, as Australian aboriginals do, relate to the landscape as
the geographic imprint of mythological ancestor totems; for them, geographic
features are transformed ancestors. Place of residence may be an important
part of people's social identity (Schieffelin 1976:41–45).

The land is a spiritual value, a beneficent Source—the home of the
ancestors, "the plain of one's bones," Hawaiians say. And the things a
man makes and habitually uses are expressions of himself, perhaps so
imbued with his genius that their ultimate disposition can be only his
own grave. (Sahlins 1968:80)

From the attitude of AR, land is a dominion, a realm, a sovereign territory or a jurisdiction. The characteristic attitude is one of control, appropriation, and exclusionary defense. From the perspective of EM, land can be the token of coequal status among peers, as when the Homestead Act gave every American family the right to a deed for an equal-sized plot of land if they lived on it and farmed it. In the scheme of MP, it is real estate, private property, an investment, collateral, a leasehold or tenancy, mineral rights, or air rights. People buy or rent land and "develop" it, or use it as an instrument of rational production like any other commodity. In China every form of orientation toward land has been visible within recent history. Feudal land-tenure systems (predominantly AR) were abolished after the Communist revolution, and people worked communally on enormous collective farms (CS in ideological principle). Under a 1978 and 1979 land reform, every family in each province received an equal allotment of land (EM). Now in the name of efficiency the authorities have allowed the sale of land and the development of larger entrepreneurially organized farms that contract with the state for equipment loans, sell futures contracts, and sell produce on the free market; wage labor is now being legalized as well (MP; Gargan 1988). It would be interesting to study the correlates and consequences of such abrupt mandatory restructuring, whether it involves land or other socially meaningful entities.

In sum, there are four pervasive modalities of social perception of objects and land. People seem to have just four primary ways of dealing socially with material things, whether they are making them, transferring them, or associating with them. Is this a matter of physics? If people persistently construe things in the same four ways, then people must have four primary ways of making sense of things. It is a matter of meaning, psychologically endowed, socially generated, and culturally formulated.

## Time

Time has four kinds of social meaning, depending on which of the four models people use as a frame of reference. In the context of Communal Sharing, relationships are often oriented toward the past and are ideally eternal, or at least enduring. For example, the sense of primordial unity that is based on descent or common origin typically involves the idea that these ties have existed "from the beginning." As Weber (1978 [1922]) and Piaget (1973 [1932]) observed, people implicitly or explicitly validate CS relationships in terms of their continuity with the past: This is our tradition, it is what we have always done. People perceive these reproductions of primordial rituals as deriving from and marking their collective nature: Moose *are* the people who collectively reproduce certain ritual performances. CS rituals (e.g., American Thanksgiving or anniversaries, Moose sacrifices and calendrical rituals) are what they are just because each enactment is a reiteration of past enactments, a reprise in perpetuity of countless putatively identical reenactments. The obverse of this is that calendrical ritual enactments of corporate solidarity segment time de facto, marking cycles or repetitions of the same events. Thus, ironically, people constitute the constancy of CS relationships partly by the repetition of ritual enactments at fixed temporal intervals (see Whorf 1956 [1941, 1950]). The inverse of this continuity orientation is that people are reluctant to imagine the end of intense, core CS relationships, or any substantial change in them—consider being deeply in love. The loss of such a CS relationship is deeply disturbing (Bowlby 1980). Continuity is the essence of the Communal Sharing orientation toward time: past, present, and future should be the same.

In contrast, what counts in Authority Ranking is just the asymmetry of time; people mark hierarchy in temporal precedence. Among Moose, a person who is senior to others comes before them in starting to eat, in beginning to harvest, in receipt of shares in a distribution, and in the order in which a visitor pays his respects. This serial ordering of similar events in a sequence is a principal mode for the social representation and acknowledgment of rank (see Chapter 9). In Moose society and many others, birth order—age—is the principal determinant of rank within gender. Ancestors' ranks are similarly a function of their ordinal position in time (according to their seniority of office) and even clans and ethnic groups may assert rank by referring to temporal precedence in occupation of a unit of social space. In general, AR time is an asymmetric linear sequence of discrete events.

In Equality Matching relationships people construe time in terms of the wave length of oscillatory cycles of reciprocal interchange, manifested in synchronism, appropriate delay, and interval correspondence or turn matching. Moose, for example, often implement EM in labor through the medium of working in rhythm to drum beats or songs, keeping time while matching each other stroke-for-stroke. Other examples of simultaneity as the medium for coordinating EM relationships include people handing over hostages at the same time, or all starting a race at once. In some circumstances this translates as both beginning and ending together at the same time, which is one form of interval correspondence. The timing of many team athletic events takes this form, and also sometimes takes the form of alternation of equal interval periods (halves, quarters). Many other kinds of turn taking do not involve matching durations, but simply alternating opportunities or privileges among two or more sides. So people may host each other back and forth, or speak by turns, so that the interchange alternates directions. A feature of such symmetrical oscillations is some kind of social standard for appropriate delay in reciprocation; people must not return a gift or an invitation to dinner too soon or too late. In order to sustain the EM relationship, people seek to reciprocate with suitable delays, maintaining a proper tension of outstanding obligations in alternating directions. As anthropological observers have noted, returning a favor or gift too soon is unseemly because it suggests a desire to acquit oneself of one's obligations and terminate the relationship. Delay too long, and it appears one is trying to take advantage of others' trust and duck one's obligations. Hence people structure EM relationships in most domains around some kind of culturally defined norms for the correct oscillation frequencies. This enables people to compare and match durations.

With respect to Market Pricing, people are concerned about rates and efficiency. The socially significant concerns have to do with the ratio of events, items, or actions per unit of time. MP revolves around rates of pay, rent, interest, and rates of return on investment. One dimension of efficiency is the proportion of things "done" or produced per unit of time. Time is money, and "wasted," unproductive time is lost time and missed opportunity (see Weber 1958 [1904–1906] quoting Benjamin Franklin). Hence MP-oriented societies value time as a commodity in itself ("how much time did you spend on that?"), and have concepts and mechanisms for keeping track of time very precisely. This goes along with a tendency to value the future over the past, expressed in the ideas of progress and advancement (Kluckhohn and Strodtbeck 1973 [1961]).

In sum, while CS relationships operate in a constant mode emphasizing continuity and perpetuity, the concept of time embedded in AR relationships is discrete and sequential. EM time is an oscillatory wave whose frequency is socially significant and which generates matched durations, while MP time is a ratio variable over which people calculate the integral of some output function (the area under the curve representing productivity or rate of return).

Up to now we have been considering the organization of transfers, of work, of people's links to material things, and their perceptions of time, as if these were simply given facts about society. But people are not automatons who simply enact norms. Often they have to decide together what to do and how to do it. What are the social mechanisms available for people to influence each other and to reach decisions in a group?

# 4

# Choices

$T$his short chapter is about how people make collective choices together and how choices are affected by others. That is, the topic is
the making and exchanging of ideas about action, together with the selection and changing of attitudes and actions. The first section considers how groups make decisions, the second part how people influence
and persuade others.

## DECISION MAKING

Each of the four models can serve as the basis for a decision scheme. Decision
as Communal Sharing is a collective process resulting in consensus. This is the
mode preferred by my own Psychology Department, and the one traditionally
used by the Fox Indians (Miller 1955:284). Everyone should participate and
contribute ideas, comments, and convictions, taking careful account of what
others say and the emerging sense of the group. People generally defer to the
wisdom of the group as a whole, unless someone has a fundamental objection
of conscience, in which case the group will try to respect that position by not
making the decision in question. The decisions jointly arrived at are decisions
of the group, and everyone stands behind them. Janis (1982 [1972]) examines
the conditions under which a group makes a rapid decision by this kind of
unanimous consensus, sometimes failing to fully consider objections and alternatives—the phenomenon of *groupthink*. McCauley (1989) reexamines Janis's
historical case studies and the experimental evidence. He points out that unanimity may be the result of group members' internalization (personal commitment to the decision) and/or compliance (public conformity in the presence of
unexpressed private doubts). High group cohesion promotes both internalization and compliance. McCauley also points out that rapidly developed concur-

rence among decision makers is useful for trivial decisions (and, I might add, in situations where almost any consensus is better than continued disagreement or no decision). McCauley concludes that group insulation and group homogeneity (and perhaps external threat) are conducive to groupthink. In other words, this kind of decision by collective consensus without marking any of the distinct or disparate judgments of individuals is a manifestation of Communal Sharing.[1]

Americans tend to condemn this CS approach to decision making as a subversion of individual judgment and responsibility, but some subgroups value it highly, including the Religious Society of Friends. Sheeran[2] (1983) makes a number of valuable points about Quaker processes that probably apply to CS decision making in general. One is that total unanimity of opinion is not as essential as universal participation in the process, including the fact that every Friend in the meeting is expected to attend and join in the decision making. Thus while a few participants may hold to divergent views, and even place their objections on the record, yet—having participated in the decision and the group having considered and respected their points—they finally stand aside and support the consensus to which they object. (An apt analogy is an individual who, while initially ambivalent, still needs to come to a decision and adopts it wholeheartedly.) A second of Sheeran's observations is that this mode of making decisions among Friends is a function of their belief that the meeting is collectively seeking to find divine truth, that the "Spirit of Truth" is in everyone, and that unity is a sign of divine guidance. Consequently, rational argument and verbal rhetoric is sometimes superceded by a kind of communal inspiration that produces a strong sense of collective conviction. This is particularly evident in the patience with which Friends meetings approach major decision making, waiting however long it takes until a sense of the meeting emerges. This attitude is also evident in the meditative silences that a meeting observes at the beginning and end of the session and whenever they have a very difficult dilemma to resolve, or simply reach an impasse. Finally, Sheeran notes that Friends (like my own department) simply make no effort to resolve abstract questions of doctrine or creed, focusing instead on pragmatic issues together with matters of religious witness and acts of conscience. A corollary of this is that Friends meetings tend not to be dependent on a written constitution that specifies the precise criteria for making a legitimate decision, often relying more on continuity, tradition, and mutual trust. In sum, the essence of Friends decision making is their commitment to unity, without seeking oppressive uniformity.

L. T. Doi (1981 [1971]) describes the Japanese desire for *tatemae*: unanimous agreement or consensus as the basis for collective decisions (see also Kerlinger 1951). Japanese nearly always seek this kind of consensus and regard it as essential in public discussions, where it is a token of CS mutuality. They recognize that people's private positions may differ, but they hate to contradict or be contradicted. Disagreements are expressed by hesitation or ambiguity in response, facilitated by a verb-final grammatical structure that prolongs ambiguity and permits changing one's stance at the very end of a sentence, after reading the other's initial response. Subtlety in speech permits the Japanese to express, accommodate to, and resolve implicit differences without confrontation, and indeed without explicitly acknowledging that there are any disagreements. Doi reports that when it is appropriate, Japanese will speak gracefully for hours without ever coming to the point or taking a definite, clear position. The CS mechanism as well as the objective, it seems, is an empathically derived sense of interdependent solidarity and unity of outlook.

Decision making in Authority Ranking is a hierarchical chain of command, like most military systems, in which command and obedience are the basic operating principles. Each person has the prerogative to decide for and direct subordinates, or to delegate decisions to them (while still being held responsible for the consequences). The charismatic leadership Weber (1978 [1922]) analyzes involves this mode of making decisions. In more institutionalized forms of AR, subordinates or specialized staff may collect information for the decisions of commanders and then transmit these decisions down the chain. In bureaucracies or "feudal" political systems like those of the Moose, superiors will not judge a case unless it is processed through the proper channels along the hierarchy.

The paradigmatic Equality Matching scheme for deciding is the one-person, one-vote ballot. Each person's expression of his or her judgment and interest has equal weight. It is also possible to take turns deciding (e.g., what game to play next), and to both match and trade votes, as is common in the U.S. Congress. Sometimes, as in the United Nations Security Council, a key decision role like that of chair rotates at regular intervals among the members. A fair lottery is another logically congruent method of deciding (and sometimes of allocating at the same time).

With Market Pricing, the market decides. What kinds of computers, restaurant meals, or house paints should be available and who should use them? The market is the major middle-level, middle-term mediator of such decisions. How much wheat and how many tires should people produce? The market decides. Who shall be professors and what shall they be paid? The market is a major determinant. These decision schemes have been described by anthropologists, sociologists, students of small groups, political scientists, economists, and specialists in decision science, but I have not yet come across any systematic analysis of the range of possible forms. There are innumerable schemes that are logically available for making decisions—simply consider the mechanisms in a complex computer program. But people almost always settle issues and make collective plans in one of four ways: Communal Sharing, Authority Ranking, Equality Matching, or Market Pricing. Where do these alternatives come from, if not the human mind?

## SOCIAL INFLUENCE

It is only a short step from a group making a decision to an individual's acceding to a request as a result of social influence. If you like, one involves choosing a course of action for a group whereas the other is choosing a course of action for an individual; the underlying mechanisms are similar.

One of the first systematic analyses of social influence was Cooley's (1922 [1902]) tripartite analysis of forms of emulation. He contrasts conformity, based on the motivation to do as others in one's group do, to act the same (CS); rivalry, based on the ambitious desire to strive, win, succeed, and impress others (MP); and hero-worship, based on idealistic loyal admiration—particularly in youth—which Cooley equates with religion (AR; see section on religion below). In each case, people orient their behavior to others (who may or may not intend them to do so) and modify their behavior accordingly. For example, rivalrous competition may influence people to be efficient and to maximize their gain assiduously in order to outshine some reference group, say by buying an expensive car for display purposes (Veblen 1934 [1899, 1918]).

Communal Sharing is operating when people imitate the actions of others whom they perceive to be similar, or whom they want to resemble (e.g., Asch 1955, 1956; Krech, Crutchfield, and Ballachey 1962). The more similar the people, the stronger their influence (Festinger 1954). The other side of the same CS orientation is that people may go along with others when they fear the derision and embarrassment of standing out as disparate or opposed to the group. That is, conformity may result from identification and the desire to belong (Allport 1962). People exhibit the effects of Authority Ranking when they obey a superior who has legitimate authority, charisma, prestige , or simply the requisite situational role (Milgram 1974).[3] Such influence is a consequence of the subordinate's sense of awe, duty, loyalty, respect, or deference. As Weber (1978 [1922]) points out, charismatic authority derives from the perception that the authority is unique, extraordinary, and absolutely different from ordinary people, that she has special powers and insight—almost precisely the opposite of the mechanism of CS influence. The bureaucratic authority of an officeholder is also based indirectly on the special qualifications and expertise that set her apart from ordinary people, together with the commission or election that sets her apart from the people under her jursidiction. There are societies in which AR influences are extremely muted, where it is almost always inappropriate for one person to give orders to another or to try to control another person (even a child), and where people hardly ever obey or defer to others (e.g., the Fox Indians as Miller [1955] describes them, and the Religious Society of Friends). But it appears that even in such societies people probably understand this mode of relating to others—they just think that it is wrong.

People often adhere to Equality Matching when they agree to do something to reciprocate a favor the requester has done for them (Homans 1958, Gouldner 1978a [1960], Blau 1964, Clark 1983, Cook 1987). People take this course out of a sense of fairness, a desire to appear—and to be—just and reasonable. The desire and anticipation of receiving the same aid in the future also may motivate compliance with such requests. People also may comply with a request to undertake an onerous task because they acknowledge it is their turn to do so. And people will comply to make up for harm they have done to another with a compensating good that balances or offsets the harm with a corresponding good and thus restores the relationship to equilibrium.

Market Pricing is manifest in what Americans all take for granted: People will generally do something for you if you pay them enough, or if you offer them sufficient compensation in some other form—"everyone has his price." In the United States there are moral and legal constraints on what may be purchased. It is illegal to buy or sell political influence, sexual services, or slaves (including yourself). While there are a number of domains where we regard monetary influence as unseemly, the efficacy and appropriateness in the United States of asking people to do something for financial compensation is so taken for granted that, although social psychologists frequently pay subjects, they rarely direct explicit attention to the social forces involved in their subjects' cooperation, or focus on MP as a mechanism of social influence per se (although of course economists do). Another factor operating in many experiments that has been extensively discussed is subjects' implicit desire to do what the experimenter expects or wishes them to do, in part simply out of obedient respect for his status as experimenter (Orne 1962, 1969). Other factors are also involved in demand effects, but subjects' confidence that the experimenter knows what she is up to and is taking responsibility for the situation appear to be crucial. It is notable that normal subjects are virtually indistinguishable from hypnotized subjects; both obediently do what they are told, especially if the experimenter acts as if he expected compliance (Orne and Evans 1965). This, of course, is AR, defined as Weber (1978) stated it— doing something just because it is the will of a person perceived to have legitimate authority over the subject. As Sabini (in press) observes, this kind of experimenter effect confirms the validity and pervasiveness of Milgram's (1974) results on obedience. Rosenthal (1969:242) cites unpublished studies by Bootzin showing that the more dominant the experimenter, the greater the effects he or she induces.

Cialdini (1988) discusses how people are influenced to make a purchase by the perception of scarcity of goods or limited time, together with supposed competition from other buyers—all MP criteria manipulated by the marketer. In addition he reviews research showing that Americans often rebel strongly against perceived constraints on their freedom of choice by doing what they think someone is trying to prevent them from doing. This, too, is an effective marketing tool. Reactance (Brehm and Brehm 1981) of this kind may result either from the MP ideal of autonomous individual freedom or from the strong American sense of the limitations of AR, which we frequently regard as illegitimate and hence have a tradition of rebelling against.[4] (It would be interesting to design experiments to distinguish the circumstances in which MP and AR reactance operate.) Cialdini also discusses the efficacy of what he calls "commitment," the Market Pricing contractual principle that people are bound to keep promises, especially explicit, public, intentional ones. He devotes much of his book to techniques salespeople use with potential customers, so at a meta-analytic level, Market Pricing is the focus of his entire book.

Cialdini also discusses three other major social relational influence mechanisms. One is authority (AR), especially when marked by titles and official uniforms, and another is reciprocation (EM). The third influence technique Cialdini calls social proof or imitation, in which people model their behavior on others similar to themselves: "We view a behavior as correct in a situation to the degree that we see others performing it" (Cialdini 1988:110–111). This is CS, as his example of the contagious effects of canned laughter (and paid claquing) illustrates—despite the fact that people are modeling their behavior on what they know is not a genuine response. People laugh more and rate jokes as funnier when they hear recorded laughter and applaud more when others are applauding, just as they donate more when a street musician's hat is seeded with "contributions." Cialdini shows that the same imitative, assimilative principle works in treating phobias, fear of dentists, and shyness and social withdrawal in children, and that in another form it accounts for the unresponsive bystander, and for waves of imitative suicide and suicidal accidents. What social proof comes down to is copying (and "incorporating") the behavior of other people, especially people like us. The principles Cialdini calls liking and similarity are also forms of CS; they often involve praise, mutual and successful cooperation, familiarity through repeated contact, and one form of identification. The effects are strongest when there is perceived unanimity, or the possibility of unanimity if the subject conforms; then everyone will be alike (Allen 1975). Even one dissenter breaks the hold of this fear of being different (Asch 1955, 1956). People's sense of belonging or a desire to belong to a corporate group that transcends their individuality tends to yield a consensus of value and belief. Indeed, Sabini (in press) summarizes the social influence literature as a whole with the conclusion that, "When people interact the usual consequence is a convergence of opinion. . . . We find people believing that there is one world, one moral order, one virtuous way of living." Cialdini also cites Razran's (1938, 1940) talks reporting discovery of the lunchroom effect that makes people give higher ratings of photographs and political slogans they view while eating; in the anthropological literature, eating and drinking together and the sharing of stimulants (tobacco, betel leaf, kola nuts) are widely recognized as marking and constituting what we are calling Communal Sharing.[5] Although he does not organize his material in just this way,

Cialdini's overview of the influence literature is clearly compatible with the present theory. Others who have studied the same sorts of problems formulated in other terms have also arrived at distinctions that correspond closely to our analysis.

Although Cialdini does not cite him, Etzioni (1975 [1961]) defines his central concern, power, as "an actor's ability to induce or influence another actor to carry out his directives or any other norm he supports." Footnoting similar approaches by Boulding (1953:xxxi), Niebuhr (1953), Neuman (1950:168), Commons (1957:47–64), Janowitz (1960:258), and Deutsch (1953:218ff.), Etzioni bases his book on a differentiation among three means actors use to obtain compliance: coercion (actual or threatened physical sanctions—not a true social relationship in our terms here), remuneration (salaries and other payments in services or commodities—MP), and the allocation and manipulation of symbolic normative rewards. Normative power comes in two forms.

> One is based on the manipulation of **esteem, prestige,** and ritualistic symbols (such as a flag or a benediction); the other, on allocation and manipulation of **acceptance and positive response** (Parsons, 1951, p. 108). Although both powers are found both in vertical and in horizontal relationships, the first is more frequent in vertical relations, between actors who have different ranks, while the second is more common in horizontal relations, among actors equal in rank—in particular, in the power of an "informal" or primary group over its members. (Etzioni 1975:6; his emphasis)

While the correspondence is not exact, this distinction roughly amounts to the contrast between AR and CS (somewhat conflated with EM). Etzioni (1975) constructs his analysis of organizations using a second axis as well, the form of involvement that is the organization's means for recruiting members and orienting them toward the organization (or any other entity): alienative (a negative, hostile orientation—Asocial interaction); calculative (a business-like, utilitarian attitude typical of entrepreneurs in modern rational capitalism—MP); and moral, which involves intensive commitment. Then there are two subtypes of moral involvement, pure moral commitment based on identification with authority and internalization of norms, characteristic of vertical relationships (AR), and social commitment based on sensitivity to pressures of primary groups and similar horizontal relationships, in which—unlike all the other orientations—people are ends to each other (CS).[6] (He has nothing to say about anything resembling EM.) Etzioni reports that organizations are empirically likely to have power (i.e., influence) and involvement relations that are congruent, and his book is a test of the core hypothesis that such congruence exists because it is a functional equilibrium state that enhances organizational effectiveness. In effect, Etzioni shows that members (especially in lower echelons) are susceptible to persuasion that takes the form of the particular model that is constitutive of that organization. There is a long history of theorizing about how groups are formed and about their fundamental relational structures, a literature we will consider shortly.

But first a word about the issue of compliance (merely going along with an idea because it is expedient) versus internalization (belief in an idea or emotional commitment to it).[7] The thrust of this relational perspective on social influence is that choosing a course of action for oneself or for a group is often a social process. When the decision is embedded in a stable social relationship or otherwise framed with reference to one of the four basic models, the distinction between compliance and internalization is often moot. Think about a person who cheerfully is going along with your choice of a restaurant because, he agrees, it is your turn to choose, even though he does not particularly like the restaurant: what use would it be to distinguish between compliance and internalization? What about someone who wholeheartedly goes along with the majority vote on a referendum because she believes the mechanism was legitimate, although she cast her vote against the winning issue and still believes another alternative would be better? Or consider a Quaker in a worshipful meeting who, although she has voiced objections, has faith that the unity of the group is a sign of Divine Truth (or at least believes that the group as a collectivity is wiser than she, and that consensual solidarity is a paramount good). If, as often occurs in the meetings of the Society of Friends (Sheeran 1983), she puts aside her reservations and supports the consensus (without "changing her mind" about the problems she foresees), is this internalization or compliance? If a soldier is convinced his commanding officer has made a terrible misjudgment, yet willingly goes into battle expecting to die because he believes that his superior officer should be obeyed, right or wrong, what shall we make of the internal-external distinction? If, in order to make a profit, a jeweler decides to make a fast-selling style of earrings she would not choose to make on purely esthetic grounds, is her choice internally or externally controlled? Or is this another case of mistaking the internal-external metaphor for an analysis of causes (Sabini and Silver 1987)?

From this overview, the conclusion emerges that people are susceptible to four sorts of influence. People are moved to do things for four social reasons: they want to belong and be the same; they want to obey; they want to balance and make things even; or they want to choose, get a bargain, and abide by their contractual commitments. (In fact, they may well want to pay a fair price, too, so they feel they haven't cheated anyone.) Actually, the relational theory suggests another motive. People can be influenced by the desire to acquire power or demonstrate high status, and of course there is ample evidence that people frequently do this (e.g., automobile commercials). In the first part of this chapter, we saw that the way of making a collective decision is often an embodiment of a social relationship, and in the second part we saw that people are often influenced to do things because they want to sustain, repair, or create social relationships. In sum, there are four principal modes for people to coordinate their actions and impinge on each other. Neither students of decision making nor students of social influence have generally recognized that the processes fall into just these four preeminent categories, but the taxonomy seems apt.

In order to understand this better, we need to know how people form groups and interact within and between groups. We also need to know what social motives move people—what do people want in social relations? So in the next chapter we will begin by taking up the literature on the mechanisms for constituting groups and considering the ways in which the four relational models can produce groups and inform social identity.

Four pervasive patterns are manifest wherever we look in social relations. The modalities of organizing labor could conceivably be a function of technical or ecological constraints on production as such. But the same material constraints do not exist in decision making. Conceivably there are only four ways of thinking about objects because there are four natural categories of objects or of object use. But if the ways that people influence each other correspond to the ways that people orient to things, land, and time, then it must be a consequence of the ways that people are capable of relating. The patterns transcend the particulars of diverse domains of social activity and thought. So they must be patterns that reflect the basic set of human relational capacities and proclivities.

# 5

# Orientations

$T$his chapter is about how and why people establish the bonds that connect them with each other. The first part concerns how people organize themselves into groups and how they develop a sense of identity or self in relation to these groups. This continues with a discussion of systems of exchanging women in marriage in traditional societies and ways of structuring marriage in the West. The first part of the chapter concludes with an account of the system-maintaining functions of different norms. The second part analyzes the kinds of social motivations that entail seeking out relationships of different kinds and structuring relationships in different ways.

## THE CONSTITUTION OF GROUPS
## AND SOCIAL IDENTITY

The four models give form to collectivities as well as to dyadic interpersonal relationships; social groups may implicitly constitute themselves on the basis of any of the four models. Similarly, each of the four models provides the basis for a distinct kind of identity or self for group members (or other people who associate themselves with a group). Typically the form of people's social identity corresponds to the type of reference group that they use as the basis for their identity, so I will treat group structure and social identity together here. I will also ignore here the important distinction between the origin of a group and its functional maintenance and perpetuation, although obviously a group can come into being in one form, and then transform itself into another (Weber 1978 [1922]).[1] My assumption is that a person defines her self largely in terms of the most focally meaningful social relationships in which she engages, or seeks to engage. Thus the self is the person who relates to others in specified ways, and for us to understand a person's self we need to know the nature of the relationships that the person assumes to be most valid: What kinds of social relationships reflect the ultimate reality of human nature and one's personal character? What relationships do people regard as revealing the meaning of a life? In general this is a parameter specified by a person's culture (see Chapter 7), but there is a limited repertoire of basic types of relationships from which cultures may draw: CS, AR, EM, MP. Although most of what I will discuss here are the ways in which people construct groups with each model, the same principles apply to the generation of self characterized as the person who participates in dyadic interactions or networks.

## Communal Sharing

Consider first how Communal Sharing shapes groups. People may constitute a group because they have a sense of common substance (flesh and blood), a feeling of being the same kind, of unity, and of belonging—whether to a family, town, college, club, team, gang, ethnic group, or nation. Members' identities (and the identities of those who intend to associate themselves with the group) involve a merging of self into the greater whole that is the group, often conveyed by emblematic clothing, jewelry, hair styles, facial or bodily scarification, or dialect. The Amish are a clear example of the marking of identity in these ways, and their CS ethos is beautifully captured in a television interview with an Amish man who said, "Being Amish to me is belonging and being needed, in the community, the neighborhood, the family, and the church." Another man said,

> When we join the church, when we are baptized into the church, we lose our individual individuality, and we become, we join one body, we form one body, same as if someone should make a loaf of bread: they take a lot of different grains of wheat, and grind them together, and they lose their individual shape, they form one body, they form one loaf of bread, and I think that's the way the church is. (from Larimore 1985; see also Hostetler 1970)

Note, in this example, the way in which the informant represents CS as identity of personal substance and in terms of food (see Chapter 9).

Tönnies 1988 [1887, 1935] described this kind of community as *gemeinschaft*, a relationship based on *wesenwille*, the judgment of the intrinsic value of acts. Tönnies wrote that *gemeinschaft* is an intimate, private, exclusive relationship of total communion, characteristic of a bridal couple, family, or religious community, but which may extend to the community of mankind. It is often based on common language, folkways, mores, and beliefs, and on occupational or other similarities, as well as harmony of character and dispositions. People feel that *gemeinschaft* relations are old, lasting, strong and genuine, intrinsic, and inherently necessary. They are based on a sense of unity of being, mutual coherence, and continuity of substance in blood ties (or marriage). In short *gemeinschaft* involves empathy, identification, unity of will. It expresses itself in the sharing of food, drink, possessions and pleasures.

Independently of Tönnies the anarchist Kropotkin (1972 [1890–1914]) wrote persuasively about the human tendency to organize social relations around the recognition of mutual dependency and of solidarity born of respect for the rights of others of one's kind. Kropotkin traces *mutual aid* up through the animal phyla and human history, including kin and tribal groups based on belief in common descent, through village groups based on common territory (including common lands—see Marx, above). He further traces mutual aid through medieval cities and their guilds based on common trades and occupations, to later communitarian societies and contemporary mutual assistance groups, cooperatives, brotherhoods, and labor unions. Kropotkin documents how guilds, common lands, cooperatives and unions were forcibly suppressed by the modern state, and sprang up again wherever they were permitted.[2]

Without ever mentioning Kropotkin or Tönnies, Durkheim (1933 [1893]) develops an extremely similar account of what he called *mechanical solidarity*, based on similarities in what people produce and associated with other social resemblances. Cooley (1962 [1909]) delineates the well-known concept of *primary group*, a formulation very close to Communal Sharing as defined here. (He cites Kropotkin but gives few other sources.) Primary groups are small, face-to-face groups that are the fundamental source of all human sociality.

> The result of intimate association, psychologically, is a certain fusion of individualities in a common whole, so that one's very self, for many purposes at least, is the common life and purpose of the group. Perhaps the simplest way of describing this wholeness is by saying that it is a "we"; it involves the sort of sympathy and mutual identification for which "we" is the natural expression. One lives in the feeling of the whole and finds the chief aims of his will in that feeling. (Cooley 1962:23)

This passage could easily have been taken straight out of T. Doi's (1981) account of how Japanese derive their most fundamental sense of identity from belonging to a bounded ingroup in which the self is immersed (see Motivation, below; see also Lebra 1976). It also corresponds to Sampson's (1988) psychological conception of fluidly inclusive *ensembled individualism*, which he advocates as an alternative to the separateness, exclusionary boundedness, and personal control of self-contained individualism. The key distinction is in the extent to which other persons are incorporated in the self and the person's embedment in an assimilating social milieu.

Cooley (1962 [1909]) writes that people identify with their primary groups so that their individual minds are merged into the whole, into a moral unity based on mutual empathy that engenders kindness and a submergence of the self in the purposes of the collectivity as a whole. From this experience in primary groups, Cooley asserts, three other social impulses naturally arise as the individual widens his or her social horizons: respect for authority (AR), commitment to rules of turn taking (EM), and an ideal of individuality and freedom of choice, limited only by social contracts necessary to keep the peace in larger associations (MP). Although Cooley is not always entirely systematic in his delineation of these social modalities, he is clear in asserting that each of these forms is an expression of a fundamental (motivational) facet of human nature.

George H. Mead (1934 [1900, 1930]) discusses two universal social relationships, one of which he calls the *religious attitude* of kindness, helpfulness, universal neighborliness, and sympathetic assistance to those in distress.[3] It is expressed in patriotism and team work. But Mead says that this (and the economic attitude; see below) both can transcend local groups and extend to anyone, and in a sense do extend to everyone, creating the potential for the highest level of universal world society. When this religious attitude exists,

> everyone is at one with each other in so far as all belong to the same community. . . . In such a situation as this, the religious situation, all seem to be lifted into the attitude of accepting everyone as belonging to the same group. One's interest is the interest of all. There is complete identification of individuals. Within the individual there is a fusion of the "me" with the "I." (Mead 1934:274)

In this attitude of mutual identification, Mead says, people attain a special sense of self since the reaction one elicits in others (internalized as the "me") is identical to the person's own creative response (the "I")—we might call it a feeling of communion.

Writing in a theological and psychoanalytic genre without reference to any of these earlier theorists, Bakan (1966) describes one of the two fundamental modes of human existence as *"communion,"* which he characterizes (p. 15) as "the sense of being as one with other organisms. . . . lack of separations. . . . contact, openness, and union. . . . noncontractual cooperation." Gilligan (n.d.) mentions empathic emotional fusion like this in which a person does not discriminate between her own and another's feelings, but focuses more on engagement and mutually affecting, responsive relationships in which people feel sympathy for each other. Gilligan derives this kind of loving "co-feeling" from attachment, showing how it is related to themes of inclusion and exclusion, fear of isolation and abandonment. While this is a common orientation in her female American subjects, it is rare in her U.S. males. Gilligan shows that this kind of relationship is the source of a fundamental CS moral orientation oriented to the needs of people with whom one has personal relationships.

Victor Turner (1969, 1973, 1975; see also Bilu 1988) gives ethnographic descriptions of an intense socioemotional form of CS, an experience that he calls *"communitas."*

> Communitas is a nonstructured relationship, or, better, a spontaneously structured relationship which often develops among liminaries,

individuals in passage between social statuses and cultural states that have been cognitively defined, logically articulated, and endowed with jural rights and obligations. . . . The social experience . . . of communitas [is] the corporate identity between unique identities, the loss of the sense of number. (Turner 1975:22)

Turner regards communitas as a paradigmatically liminal[4] state achieved in rituals of passage, opposed to "social structure" and yet the ultimate source of structure. He equates it (1969:126-7, 136-7) to Ludwig Feurbach's and Martin Buber's (1987 [1923]) "I—Thou" relationship, and compares it (1973:216) with Tönnies' *gemeinschaft*. Communitas involves the experience of the deep, generative, nonrational undifferentiated unity underlying all apparent social differences, hierarchical and otherwise. It is the spontaneous, direct, immediate, and concrete homogenizing relationship of oneness, typified for Turner by his experience of the mutuality of village life in Central Africa and the solidarity of a wartime bomb-disposal unit. He gives other examples of communitas manifested in the fraternal ideals of St. Francis and the erotic community of Vaisnavas in Bengal, in the universal fellowship of pilgrims, and by African earth and fertility shrines that stress inclusiveness and collective responsibility. In such a relationship people's individual identities and social statuses are unmarked, so they are a homogeneous whole.[5] Turner contrasts communitas with "structural" social forms in general, but particularly with hierarchical rank (AR) and commercial concerns (MP) and the segmented system of jural statuses and differentiated roles they involve. He distinguishes (1969:132ff., 1973:193-4) among existential or spontaneous communitas, normative communitas (routinized, in Weber's terminology), and utopian ideological forms of communitas. Turner concludes that there is a human need to participate in communitas relationships, as well as in a structured modality (see Motivation, below), so that society tends to move back and forth between the two.

Communitas in the strong form Turner delineates can be evoked by appeals to potent symbols of shared contrastive identity (Trosset 1988; cf. G. H. Mead [1934 {1900-1930}] on patriotism), but group boundaries and biases indicative of weaker forms of CS crystallize quickly in other contexts as well. Calling them reference groups, the Sherifs have shown experimentally how rapidly such groups actually do form among preadolescent boys and how hostile they will be to outsiders if their interaction with other groups is given a competitive form (Sherif et al. 1988 [1961], Sherif and Sherif 1964). Tajfel (1978, 1982) forcefully exhibits people's proclivity to form an identification with a minimal we-group constituted on the most arbitrary distinctions, and to bias rewards accordingly. Heider (1946, 1958) makes *liking* and *unit* relations the core of his theory, and shows how they tend to coincide. Unit relations are relationships based on membership, similarity, proximity, interaction, causality, or ownership. Liking relations are those that involve affection or admiration, and they tend to be symmetrical; we like those who like us. This reflects the tendency, noted earlier, to be kind to those of one's own kind, especially kin. A considerable body of subsequent research has confirmed that people are attracted to people whom they perceive as similar to themselves (e.g., Huston 1974).

In her discussion of *group* Douglas (1978) develops a very similar characterization of bounded CS relationships which, in their strongest form, entail the sharing of residence, work, resources, and recreation (she does not cite any of these earlier characterizations).

Without reference to any of this earlier work, Meeker, Barlow, and Lipset (1986) build on Mauss and Lévi-Strauss to show that there is a strong ethos of communality and community in the islands of Southeast Asia, Australia, and Oceania. In the stateless, food-harvesting societies of this culture area, "the self is oriented toward the help, care, and love of others" (p. 22):

> The figure of an autonomous self apart from others is weakly developed. This means that individuals are more emphatically oriented toward intimate and close relationships with others within a face-to-face community. (Meeker, Barlow, and Lipset 1986:22)

Assertive individualism exists in these cultures, but it is muted. When people express this aspect of the self, they do so in ostentatious benefaction, for example by feeding dependent community members and rivals at great feasts. Confirming what Gilligan (n.d.) notes among Americans, in this culture area too this relational orientation goes along with an emotional fear of isolation, abandonment, and loneliness. Since nurturance, interdependency, and care are manifestly displayed in maternal physiology, Meeker, Barlow, and Lipset argue that in these cultures in which communal solidarity is the dominant relational value, men find women's birthing, nursing, and sexuality threatening to their own authority, identity, and relationships. This in turn reinforces a masculine ethos of food giving.[6]

An important feature of social relationships constituted by CS (and often by the other models) is that the people who are included in the relationship vary contextually. CS is an idea, an idea of unity and identity, and in varying contexts people may opt to mark the unity between themselves and any given subset of others, contrasting "we" and "they" by drawing the exclusionary boundaries where they wish. However, people often fail to recognize this and think of the "group" as a definite, concrete, enumerable set of people. Galaty (1982) shows how the ethnic identity term *Maasai* in East Africa is a "shifter" of this kind, and the term *Moose* works the same way. For example, "*Moose*" may mark the royal Nakomse in contrast to other clans, or the Nakomse and the Yĩyõose and Sãaba in contrast to Yarse. Yĩyõose also use it to refer to themselves in contrast to the Nakomse! Alternatively, "*Moose*" may be used to mean all these people of the Maane area, excluding Gurunsi to the south and Yadse to the north, or it may include Gurunsi and Yadse but exclude Bobose and Silimiisi. And the people whom the Moose of Maane sometimes call

Gurunsi often call themselves "*Moose*" and may refer to the people of Maane as Yadse. In a sense, "*Moose*" means "we."

As this example shows, attenuated forms of CS may extend very widely; the intense, paradigmatic form is a sort of core "primary group," but people may assert unity and solidarity at any level, however remote.

In a sense, Communal Sharing is the simplest and most primitive basis for group formation, and it is ubiquitous. Apparently it can vary in intensity, although that variable is difficult to define very precisely. Certainly it varies in extent, in the range of people it encompasses. Arguably, all groups are founded on the equivalence relation and the binary contrast between in and out that is the essence of CS (see Chapter 9). What is clear is that CS groups contrast with groups whose structure is more differentiated.

## Authority Ranking and Equality Matching

An orientation toward Communal Sharing relations generates and grows out of a sense of self that contrasts with the sense of self that is coordinate with an orientation toward Authority Ranking relationships. McAdams (1988) illustrates this in his research exploring the ways in which intimacy (CS) and power (related to AR) themes shape life history narratives and inform personal identity. Using TAT (Thematic Apperception Test) and other personological measures together with interviews or open-ended questionnaires, he shows how subjects high in intimacy motivation recount life histories in terms of their closest and warmest relationships. In contrast, subjects high in power motivation describe their lives with reference to social themes of impact and physical strength. People high in power motivation report pursuing careers in which they can exert influence over others, report taking extreme risks for the sake of notoriety, and report collecting prestigious possessions. To examine this link in more depth, McAdams offers the interpretive construct of imagoes: focal, motivated, characters with well-delineated personalities, goals, and attitudes that appear in people's life stories as personified images of the self. His research shows that imagoes reflect people's key motivations. Power imagoes emerge most often in the life stories of people high in power motivation, while intimacy imagoes are most frequent in people high on intimacy motivation. In other words, TAT story themes correlate with the kinds of characters that are central in people's life history narratives. This indicates that CS and AR orientations are two independent relational concerns at the core of the sense of identity that people represent in narrating their lives.

Authority Ranking gives rise to a group when it forms around a charismatic or duly appointed leader, so that the group consists of his or her followers. In that case people may identify with the leader, wishing to emulate or simply obey the leader, so that a member defines her social self as a loyal follower (see Freud 1959 [1921], 1967 [1937]:136–41). G. H. Mead (1934:256–7, 284–6, 311–17) also describes the ways in which a social relationship of dominance, or leadership through force of personality, involves the realization of the self in superiority over others (AR), with or without becoming the basis of administering a community. And he also describes the ways in which AR allegiance to a common monarch forms a link among people otherwise unconnected, and hence in some cases permits the organization of large communities. P. Brown (1951) describes how authorities exercise control and maintain social order through lineages and other kinship groups, associations, and states in West Africa. Of course, dominance hierarchies are a well-known organizing principle in social groups of birds, mammals, and other vertebrates (e.g., Guhl 1956, Sade 1967, Wade 1978).

Peer groups may form in accordance with Equality Matching among people who reciprocate favors or gifts or take turns, or among other sorts of exchange partners (EM). A person's social identity, and hence his standards of fairness and justice expectations, may derive from such a reference group to which he is oriented, whether or not he is strictly a participant member. That is, a person may think of himself as one of a set of equals who reciprocate fairly, share and contribute equally, a partner on a par with his fellows. Further, Sampson (1975) illustrates how people choose a distributive justice rule in order to present a particular self-identity to others.

Axelrod and Hamilton (1981), Kurland and Beckerman (1985), and Axelrod and Dion (1988) have discussed potential evolutionary bases for EM reciprocity, showing that precise tit-for-tat reciprocity is an evolutionarily stable strategy under reasonable assumptions, provided that interchanges are sustained and have no definite foreseeable end point. In order for tit-for-tat reciprocity to be selected over other strategies, it is also necessary that most interactions be dyadic, or else that it be possible to exclude nonreciprocators from further exchanges—which requires that individuals be able to recognize each other and remember what others have done in the past. If such reputational knowledge about the behavior of third parties diffuses widely, cooperative reciprocity is strongly favored. Clearly Homo sapiens meets these conditions better than any other species.

## Market Pricing

The idea that civil society in general and the state in particular is the product of a voluntary contract between autonomous individuals who bind themselves to a circumscribed compact to further their individual self-interest goes back to Locke (1952 [1690]) and before that Hobbes (1958 [1651]), although Hobbes derives absolute authority from such a contract. Indeed some writers still try to explain all social interaction in such "economic" terms (Homans 1958, 1974 [1961]; Thibaut and Kelley 1959, Kelley and Thibaut 1978, Kelley 1979; Becker 1976; and the equity theorists mentioned above). Market Pricing certainly is the manifest catalyst for the formation of many kinds of groups, including corporations, partnerships, franchise chains and other business enterprises, labor unions, trade associations, chambers of commerce, and cartels, as well as stock, commodity, and futures exchanges. In these contexts and others, contracts or other interactions based on prices frequently create social groups linking buyers to sellers, or grouping either buyers or sellers separately. Not all such linkages construct face-to-face groups or ones that interact directly, however, or even give people any sense of common identity. Indeed, one of the central issues in the work of Karl Marx (1959 [1859], Marx and Engels 1959 [1848]) is the question of when a social class with common economic interests will recognize their joint interests and unite behind them. Interestingly, to some extent Marx's predictions about economic class consciousness were a self-fulfilling prophecy, fueling a social movement that built on and promoted such an awareness of common identity, and hence potentiated joint action.

Influenced by Maine's (1963 [1861]) concept of contract law (see below), Tönnies (1988 [1887]) was the most influential theorist since Marx to make a systematic contrast among modes of organizing a society. Tönnies used the famous term *gesellschaft* to characterize MP relations. They are based on *kürwille*, the conscious, rational choice of means to an end by autonomous individual wills. *Gesellschaft* is typified by the relations among independent strangers in a commercial interaction, urban business associates, merchants in a market, or people linked by joint stockholding. It is a product of occupational specialization that is entailed by the division of labor. *Gesellschaft* relations— often transitory—are commonly based on enforceable contracts, and entail a sense of competition, tension, and hostility against others. They involve only self-interested exchange of commodities among independent individuals who work for their own separate interests, which tend to be defined in materialist terms. In contrast to *gemeinschaft*, *gesellschaft* relations are public, out in the world, and people feel them to be new, mechanical, and artificial (or at least they did a century ago in Europe). The orientation toward property (as Marx also observed) is isolating and exclusionary (see Links Between People and Things, above). Durkheim (1933 [1893]) never cites Tönnies, but develops a somewhat similar account of organic solidarity based on specialization in the division of labor, together with exchange of commodities.[7] Durkheim does briefly cite Maine's (1963 [1861]) work contrasting societies built around status law and those organized around contract law, but Durkheim goes beyond Maine in explaining the nature of punishment by the mode of organizing labor in the society (see Moral Foundations, below). Durkheim and Tönnies are important for two reasons: because they pioneered the systematic contrastive study of different kinds of social systems, and because they showed that the modes of organizing various domains of social life are interdependent. Durkheim discovered a connection between the societal structure of work and the preferred form of punishment, and Tönnies demonstrated the correlations among systems of production, types of exchange, and the qualitative aspects of social relations.

G. H. Mead (1934) describes the tendency of *economic relations* to link people together through trade and money, frequently even despite political antagonisms, drawing communities and their members into ever closer relationships with each other. Thus MP orientations are also universalizing, since one may enter into MP with any human with whom one can communicate (or anyone else). With regard to MP relations Mead once again shows how closely the constitution of social groups is related to the psychological question of individual social identities.[8] The important point for Mead is that such relations

> represent an interrelationship of communication in which the
> individual in his own process of production is identifying himself with
> the individual who has something to exchange with him. He has to put
> himself in the place of the other or he could not produce that which
> the other wants. If he starts off on that process he is, of course,
> identifying himself with any possible customer, any possible producer;
> and if his mechanism is of this very abstract sort, then the web of
> commerce can go anywhere and the form of society may take in
> anybody who is willing to enter in this process of communication. Such
> an attitude in society does tend to build up the structure of a universal
> social organism. (Mead 1934:292)

In this benign view of the impact of MP relations on the self Mead is in accord with Durkheim (1933, especially pp. 372–73), but of course dramatically at odds with Marx, who argued that capitalism results in the alienation of the worker from his work and the product of that work. Mead (1934:300–302) explains that in this economic process people produce things that have no value to them personally because they are able to call out in themselves the attitude of the people with whom they will exchange their products. Mead says that the economic process is not possible in species that lack this capacity to recognize others' needs by identification with each other through the medium of the language of money. However, sociobiologists have lately been attempting to explain all animal behavior in game theory terms as a kind of rational "economic" maximizing. In an influential, misleadingly entitled paper on "reciprocal altruism," for example, Trivers (1971) offers a theory of the natural selection of these social capacities for MP relationships.

People may also have a Null orientation toward others, as Buber's (1987 [1923]) *I* illustrates. Without reference to Buber's *I-Thou* contrast, Bakan (1966:15) defined a corresponding *agentic* mode of life (in contrast with communion) as manifested in "self-protection, self-assertion, and self-expansion. . . . the formation of separations. . . . isolation, alienation, and aloneness. . . . the urge to master. . . . the repression of thought, feeling, and impulse." This theological perspective clearly converges with the sociological classics in its characterization of this exploitive, means-ends mode of relation to others. This sort of assertive, aggressively autonomous self is manifest in some domains in the pastoral cultures of East and North Africa (Abu-Lughod 1985, Meeker, Barlow, and Lipset 1986) as well as in modern cultures.

In relating the individual self to various sorts of reference groups I have neglected the concept of identification that is entailed, but the same kind of analysis could be done for that process. Identification may take different forms, depending on which model governs it. If identification means wishing to resemble another person in some respect or be wholly identical to that person, the process should differ according to whether that wish operates in the framework of CS, AR, EM, or MP. Compare, for example, Freud's (1962 [1923]) AR concept of identification and introjection of the will of the powerful and dangerous authoritarian father with Mead's MP concept of the producer's identification with the purchaser of her product, quoted above. Again, consider the kind of identification entailed in CS mother–child attachment (cf. Bowlby 1969, 1988 and Freud's concept of narcissistic identification), and compare it with the kind of reciprocal identification that Turiel (1983)—and to some degree Piaget (1973 [1932])—effectively imputes to the child who experiences harm and recognizes that it is wrong to harm others, giving rise to a commitment to the universality of moral rules.

If groups tend to assume just these four universal forms, what engenders these structures? What is the proximate mechanism that consistently generates just these four forms of sociality under all kinds of demographic and ecological conditions in all sorts of cultures? My inference is that social organization is informed by shared psychological models that people use to initiate, coordinate, understand, and evaluate social interaction. Groups form and continue to exist as a consequence of people's interacting with others in any of the four modes. Moreover, the same models provide the structure for whole societies—people use the same set of four alternatives to organize relations between groups that they use to organize dyadic relations and interaction within small groups. The best way to demonstrate this is to show how the same models regulate the exchange of women in traditional societies, and family relations in all kinds of societies.

## Marriage and Sexual Relationships

Anthropology has demonstrated that the framework integrating many societies consists of their system of marriage, the process and pattern in which women become transformed from daughters and sisters of one group of men to wives and mothers of other men.[9] The transfer of women in marriage links kinship groups into alliances (as the etymology of "alliance" shows) that connect primary groups with each other to form the integrating framework of the social system as a whole in many traditional societies. The transfer of women among groups may be organized much like the transfer of other entities. In a previous work (Fiske 1985) and in Chapter 12 here I show that Moose use all four relational models in this transfer of women.

In the West we no longer regard marriage as a transfer of women between groups. But American marriage also exhibits each of the four relational models in the form of the relationship between spouses. The romantic ideal in the West makes marriage a prototype of Communal Sharing, based on love that involves a merging of selves, a desire for intimacy, and sharing of body, time, space, interests, and values, together with indefinite and potentially unlimited obligations, desire to serve, and selfless mutual caring. The romantic ideal, in short, is that two people become one, forever. The practice to varying degrees in most American and European marriages has tended to be based on Authority Ranking, with the husband having proprietary control over and pastoral responsibility for his wife and family. Men have made the fundamental decisions, exercised broad powers, and had much higher status than their wives. Many contemporary marriages in principle are based on Equality Matching ideals, in which each spouse should have equal rights and equal say in decisions, take turns with onerous tasks, do equal amounts of child care and housework, and have distinct, coequal personalities (Stapelton and Bright (1976). Among the wealthy, marriage reputedly has major elements of Market Pricing, structured by prenuptial contracts, insurance policies, and financial considerations related to taxation. It is MP insofar as the prospective partners (or their lawyers) treat the financial component of marriage as a negotiated contract in which both sides engage in "horse trading" to give as few concessions as possible in return for the most advantageous possible terms. In such negotiations, everything has its price and is commensurable with everything else in terms of potential or actual exchange ratios. Moreover, such contracts follow MP if the parties conceive of marriage as an exchange of sex, companionship, entertainment, and/or status in return for money and financial security, according to the going rates of exchange for such commodities.

There is a popular perception of the process of match-making as a "marriage market" or a "meet market," which depends on salesmanship, rationally calculated negotiation over valued commodity elements in the relationship, and attractiveness as a scalable numeric value (perhaps 1 to 10). Becker (1976) and F. Blau and Ferber (1986) formalize this analysis of marital choice, although they do not demonstrate that their macromodels correspond to the mental models of "singles" making real choices. Some feminists seem to have the perception that only contractual monetary payments for childcare and housework can provide the ultimate social validation of the value of women's work: Only when people pay for work do they recognize its true value. As yet, few marriages have reached the point captured in the New Yorker cartoon in which a man is saying to his wife, "Look, all I'm asking is that we let market forces bring a greater degree of efficiency into our marriage" (Mankoff 1988). Burgess, Locke, and Thomas (1971) examine the evolution of the family from an *institution* (an economic unit governed by status relations under patriarchal authority—AR) to the family as *companionship* (a unit of affection, mutual love and companionship—CS). Wood (1985) contrasts two distinct dimensions of family interconnectedness: parent-child *hierarchy* (typically AR, although Wood reports that this asymmetry may break down into egalitarian peer relationships—EM) and *proximity* (involving permeability and sharing of personal and emotional space and information, conversing and spending a lot of time together, and making decisions collectively—CS).

It is easy to see that sexual relations within or outside of marriage tend to take one of the four basic forms. Communal Sharing sex is mutual, nurturant, empathic, and responsive. Sex as CS is a merging of selves, an expression and realization of unity, a shared experience of caring and closeness. This is indexed in the invitation to disregard the normal boundaries of personal space and enter the body of another.[10] Authority Ranking sex is domination and submission, command and obedience. It is sex as docile service at the whim of the superordinate person, who controls a submissive partner. Another form of AR sex is copulation as conquest, overcoming and vanquishing to demonstrate superiority—superiority over the partner, or superiority of status over others who failed. Equality Matching sex is taking turns pleasing each other, as when a woman brings her partner to orgasm in return for his bringing her to orgasm. Additionally, EM is manifest in sex in which partners try to keep each other stimulated at equal levels in order to be fair, because each partner should get equal satisfaction: If one person climaxes and the other does not, the second feels jealous, or more likely, deprived. (In polygynous societies, EM also emerges in a husband's sleeping in rotation with each wife on consecutive nights.) The paradigmatic form of Market Pricing sex is sex for money, prostitution. More broadly, MP sex includes any sexual relationship in which the partners calculatingly take advantage of each other, each giving up as little as possible in order to get the most they can. In MP sex, each individual remains apart, seeking personal satisfaction and giving satisfaction to the other only as means to selfish ends. Another variant of MP sex is sex as achievement, "scoring" as often and as quickly as possible—often connected with sex as conquest. In general, MP sexual relations may be based on any intermodal calculus of the ratios of benefits to costs. Between any two people, sex may take different forms at different times, of course. Bakan (1966) discusses the CS mode of sexuality under the rubric of "communion," which he says is typically feminine and which he contrasts with the typically masculine "agentic" (Null or Asocial) orientation.

Thus we find the same four universal models whether we look at the systems by which men in traditional societies transfer women in marriage, at interpersonal relations within the Western family, or at sexual relations. This is doubly significant, since it suggests that people are using the same set of alternatives to structure within-group relations that they use to organize between-group relations. What I have been saying is that you can make a social relationship, a group, or a whole society using any of these four models (typically but not necessarily in combination). Sociologists have tended to take the inverse perspective on social structure, exploring the question of how various norms contribute to the functional stability of social systems. What norms have they regarded as fundamental?

## Social System Functions of the Basic Norms

The sociological question of the functional requirements of a social system, including the basic norms maintaining the system, is closely related to the matters of group formation and identity. Social system theorists who adopt this view of norms describe the system-maintaining functions of each of the four universal models. Some describe only a single norm or structural principle, while others compare two or more of them.[11]

In a seminal work on kinship and marriage systems, Lévi-Strauss (1961 [1949]) contends that the incest taboo is a functional prerequisite for society, since the taboo requires men to give up their own sisters and daughters to other men in exchange for wives that other men give them. Two forms of exchange result from the incest taboo, depending in principle on whether postmarital residence and the descent rule are "harmonic" (coincide) or not. If both rules coincide (patrilocal marriage with patrilineal descent, or matrilocal marriage with matrilineal descent) this should yield *generalized (indirect) exchange*. In contrast, if the residence and descent rules are disharmonic, this leads to *restricted (direct) exchange*.[12] All societies construct themselves out of these two elementary forms of marriage exchange, but with contrasting results, Lévi-Strauss argues. Restricted exchange—Equality Matching—is simply giving a woman to another group in direct return for a woman from the receiving group. The reciprocity is immediate and assured, but it only links groups in pairs and thus cannot readily tie together a complex system. Generalized exchange—Communal Sharing—means giving up a woman to others without getting a woman back from them, so that the wife-givers are dependent on some other group to give them a woman to marry. This is a greater risk, but it has a greater potential. Generalized exchange can link together any number of groups in a vast, coherent network, bonding men in alliances that effectively create whole societies. Like language, exchange is a communicative sign system that constitutes society as a logical product of the human mind.

Lévi-Strauss postulates that these two elementary systems of exchange are capable of generating all the very complex and diverse marriage systems that cultures actually realize around the world. There has been an extended debate about this, but most anthropologists agree that both noncontingent unilateral transfers ("gifts") and bidirectional transfers ("reciprocal exchange") are essential to sustaining and integrating traditional social systems. The structural-functional school of Radcliffe-Brown (1965c) has been particularly emphatic about this, but the tradition goes back to Malinowski (1961 [1922]) and Mauss (1967 [1925]). Interestingly, in an earlier work Lévi-Strauss (1967 [1945]:47) proposes that there were *four* basic relational attitudes underlying all kinship systems: mutuality, affection, kindness, and spontaneity (CS); reciprocity (EM?); debt obligations; and creditor rights (MP??).[13] He observes that in many actual social systems, the relationship between any two individuals expresses a "bundle" of these attitudes, but he does not elaborate on the nature of these attitudes.

Meillassoux (1981 [1975]) argues that the elementary, logically or historically original form of the exchange of women in marriage is one-for-one, one child-bearer for one child-bearer. He asserts that in this elementary form of exchange people treat women as categorically identical, all their individual qualities being ignored—in this context women are simply potential procreative partners. This exchange of identicals develops into the exchange of equivalents when delayed reciprocity and enlargement of the circuits of wife exchange lead people to use durable bride wealth as a sort of fiduciary, conventional IOU—the bride wealth is a kind of place-keeping reminder about who owes what. As such, the amount of bride wealth given is of no significance: you get only one wife, however little or much bride wealth you give. He goes on to project how bride wealth becomes commoditized in various ways, so that it transforms from bride equivalent to bride price in a market sense. Although as a sequence this is purely hypothetical, Meillasoux draws clear and important conceptual distinctions among EM and MP transfers. In addition, he describes how the AR control of brides and bride wealth by wife-giving elders complements the egalitarian EM exchange among elders.

Coming out of sociology, Alvin Gouldner has proposed more or less Lévi-Strauss' same two norms as functional prerequisites of any stable social system: the *norm of reciprocity* (Gouldner 1973a [1960]) and the *norm of beneficence* (Gouldner 1973b). Gouldner (1973a) builds on Marx and Durkheim—both of whom, as we noted above, neglected Equality Matching—but incorporates the work of Malinowski (1961 [1922], 1966 [1936]) to propose that a norm of reciprocity is essential in order to reduce exploitation and reinforce status (role) obligations. Actors define what constitutes an exchange as equivalent in either of two ways: as a return of "the same thing" (*homeomorphic reciprocity*—EM) or as a return of entities that have equal value (*heteromorphic reciprocity*—MP). In a follow-up paper Gouldner (1973b) argues that stable social systems also require provision for indulgent relationships that involve neither complementarity nor reciprocity. Thus he shows that a *norm of beneficence or goodness* (CS) that prescribes altruism, charity, or hospitality is another functional requirement for a stable social system. This norm obligates people to give others what they need, to offer "something for nothing." Gouldner writes that the reciprocity norm constitutes a contingent, striving, entified self based on the utility of what one does for someone else, while the norm of beneficence constitutes a noncontingent, passive, dependent self. He also discusses the special duty of beneficence (noblesse oblige) associated with elites, since leaders must be perceived as taking responsibility for subordinates (AR). Leadership elites legitimate their hegemony by giving something for nothing, which elicits gratitude, respect, and deference. Gouldner's approach derives AR from either an EM norm of gratitude, or from people's MP need for a scarce but essential production resource—people who corner the market become able to command.

Giving the justification for AR a different twist, Niebuhr (1953) offers a view of the interplay, limitations and hazards of three types of social relations. He argues for the necessity and therefore legitimacy of state coercion (AR), writing that we cannot rely on the market (MP) alone to bring people closer to a loving community (CS). Again preceding Gouldner, Davis and Moore (1970 [1945]) also consider AR to be a functional necessity of social systems, arguing that any social system must have rewards that it distributes differentially. This differential distribution is necessary in order to place qualified individuals in critical, demanding roles that are essential to the system, and to motivate people in these roles to perform their arduous duties. This results in a socially functional stratification of rank and prestige—Authority Ranking. Without referring to any of these theories, Lebra (1969, 1976:103) explains the process in Japan by which hierarchical deference arises out of the inability to meet obligations to match a benefaction with a precisely equal repayment. Many Japanese folktales revolve around the unanticipated opportunity for precisely matched in-kind reciprocation (cf. the European tale of the lion and the mouse). Komorita (1984) later independently developed a complementary MP-based argument about the derivation of power from bargaining leverage. Komorita states that people who control scarce resources needed for achievement of group goals can exert pressure by threatening to defect, thus exacting a share of group resources that is disproportionate to their contributions. He also extends the analysis to coalitions. Athay and Darley (1985), again independently, make a very similar argument about the "positional power" of individuals with scarce and motivationally important "production competencies" that are essential for the operation of the social system, again basing their approach on essentially MP axioms. Basically they propose a Marxist reduction of modern AR relations to MP exploitation in personal relations. Writing before these theorists, Hollnsteiner (1964) describes such a process in a Philippine fishing community. A continuing series of acts of unilateral benevolent assistance often creates indefinite obligations of gratitude. This leaves the recipient perpetually beholden to the donor, frequently creating and reinforcing status asymmetry.[14] Mauss (1967 [1925]:72) was one of the first to bring this process to the attention of anthropologists.

While these analyses highlight the important fact that authorities and others in positions of prestige necessarily have a responsibility to give, and not just take, these theorists neglect the qualitative differences between transfers in basically different modes. Nonetheless, they offer an important conception of how relationships of one type may transmute into other types of relations. What is missing from this approach is filled in by many ethnographic descriptions of the qualitative flavor of social relations of the different types, as well as by the research on motivation that we shall come to very shortly.

There are innumerable statements of the functional utility of markets and prices for social systems, but the classic is Adam Smith (1976b [1776]). He demonstrates that the *invisible hand* of the market adjusts prices and hence allocates resources, producing not only economic growth, but an orderly society. Smith's thesis is that, given freedom to operate, people's inherent competitive acquisitiveness and their natural proclivity to trade generate an ordered society with efficiently coordinated processes of production and exchange. The best known modern academic spokesmen for this point of view are Friedman (1982 [1962] and Friedman and Friedman 1981) and Nozick (1975). The key economic theorem about the functions of MP for a social system states that MP produces an optimal distribution of resources. Provided that each individual's satisfaction is unaffected by any other's satisfaction, a competitive market equilibrium results in a Pareto optimum in which no consumer's satisfaction can increase without decreasing at least one other consumer's satisfaction (Koopmans 1957). Note, however, that this conclusion about the efficiency of the market assumes that satisfaction is solely determined by the individual's work (sold in a labor market) and his or her consumption of commodities obtained through transactions in the market. In other words, it holds only within the framework of MP relations and values. Yet, as we will shortly see, it is not at all true that people's satisfaction is solely determined by their transactions in market commodities and wage labor.

These functional analyses describe the system-maintaining consequences of each of the four kinds of norms. From Lévi-Strauss to Gouldner, sociologists have demonstrated that these four norms sustain and stabilize social groups. Indeed, they are arguably *the* four potent frameworks for building human social organizations and societies. To call something a norm is to say both that it is an ideal standard, and that people impose it on their associates and even enforce it on third parties (see Chapter 8). Why do people have these goals for social interaction and insist on these particular standards? The only answer that seems to me consistent with all the evidence is that in some form these directive models are endogenous facets of the human mind.

Finally, a considerable body of work demonstrates that it is highly *dys*functional for the operation of a social system if people structure a domain in the form of Communal Sharing when there is no operative CS relationship among them and their predominant motivations in that domain are those of Market Pricing. The consequence of this mismatch between collective structure and personal motivation can be described as the tragedy of the commons (Hardin 1968), the prisoners' dilemma (Luce and Raiffa 1957), or other related kinds of social dilemmas (Dawes 1980). Frank (1988) offers an intriguing theory of how evolution may have solved such social dilemmas: Natural selection for moral

emotions occurs due to the increased fitness of individuals whose commitment can be trusted, who will not accept unfair transactions that are in their
own self-interest, and who can be expected to retaliate even when it is not
actually cost effective to do so. So selection will favor individuals with these
irrational emotional tendencies. This raises the key issue of the connections
between human motives, social relations, and social systems. Adam Smith
(1976a [1759]) and others have identified additional basic social sentiments beyond acquisitiveness and a tendency to competitive exchange: What are these
social motives and how are they linked to the four relational models?


## MOTIVATION


Above we considered the system-centered sociological perspective on the
functions of norms for social systems, but here I would like to take the individual-
centered psychological perspective. People have both a subjective desire and
an objectively observable proclivity to associate with other people and interact
in each of the four basic modes. In other words, the models are not just system
norms and they are more than abstract cognitive structures, they are also social motives.

As I try to portray in Part IV, people seek to relate to others in each of the
four ways and pursue these social goals assiduously when they are blocked. In
social relations of each type one primary, ultimate, irreducible goal is the specific form of sociality for its own sake. People may have other subsidiary or
concurrent goals when they engage in any social interaction, but the crucial
point is that people commonly relate to other people in any of these modes
primarily for the sake of relating in that mode, for the sake of experiencing the
relationship itself. The strengths of these four basic social motives vary among
individuals and between societies, as well as from situation to situation. But
there is evidence to suggest that nearly everyone has each of these motives to
some degree, in some culturally shaped expression. The evidence includes a
considerable psychological literature, as well as a number of good ethnographic case studies of these motives and the attitudes and institutions they
generate in specific cultures. Sociopathy is the exception to the universality of
these motives, since sociopaths apparently have the normal cognitive component of the basic models but lack the motivations; they have no commitment
to their social relationships (McCord and McCord 1964, Hare 1970, Cleckley
1988). In this motivational sense, the antisocial personality of sociopaths is a
striking motivational form of Null or Asocial orientation in which people act
with cognitive reference to one or more models but are not emotionally bound
or even oriented to any of them. It would be interesting to know whether there
are distinct forms of sociopathy corresponding to separate motivational deficits for each of the four models.

What are the fundamental social goals and the classes of actions and feelings that these goals entail? One of the earliest systematic modern explorations of social motivations is Cooley's (1922 [1902]) discussion of emulation and its instinctive foundations (CS, AR, and MP), discussed above. Although there is little agreement among psychologists on the taxonomy of animal or human motives, there is general agreement that there are a great many autonomous motivational states. As long ago as 1938, Murray (1938) listed 41 basic human needs (some social, some asocial), and many of these are now thought to be divisible into more than one independent motive. No psychologist would attempt to reduce the drives or need states of any organism to a single paramount motivation.[15] In social psychology the story is similar, although the lists of potentially fundamental motives may be shorter. For example, Buss (1983, 1986) reanalyzes Foa and Foa's (1974) schema of the cognitive structure of social relationships in terms of the different kinds of rewards involved in social interaction of different types. He contrasts "social" rewards (love and status) with material or economic incentives (money, goods, services, information), recasting Foa and Foa's six-part typology into these two primary types. In our terms, this approximates a contrast between Communal Sharing and Authority Ranking motives on the one hand, and Market Pricing motivation on the other. In either Foa and Foa's or Buss's formulation, the essential point is that there are a number of distinct, more or less incommensurable goods—i.e., rewards that are not interchangeable and thus not exchangeable.

The primary focus in this motivational research has been on measuring differences among individuals in the strengths of the motives, together with the conditions that arouse them. Since Pittman and Heller (1987) offer a recent review of the literature on social motives (see also Walters and Park 1964), and since much of that literature is irrelevant to our present purposes, I will focus here on a limited body of research that directly ties in to the approach developed here. What is important for the present discussion is that the social psychological research identifies a set of independent and disparate kinds of social motivation corresponding to the four models we have been considering. Most modern work on human motives (or needs) descends more or less directly from the work of Murray (1938) and his colleagues, who emphasized the multiplicity of motives. So let us begin there.

## Affiliation or Intimacy (Communal Sharing)

Murray's analysis (1938:83, 173–177) categorizes affiliative motives in a loosely delineated set with *succorant* and *nurturant* motives (as well as an opposed motive, rejection). According to Murray, *need for affiliation* is a desire to draw near other people who resemble or like the person, to please others and win their affection, join groups and cooperate. It involves trust, good will, affection, sympathetic empathy, and love. It leads people to seek to be in the proximity of the others and to make physical contact with them, to communicate and share confidences, be receptive and harmonize sentiments. Murray stresses that affiliativeness involves what he calls "similance," a desire "to feel and act like an allied object, to imitate and agree with, to be 'as one with'" (p. 174). Murray notes that need for affiliation may be subordinated to most other motives, and conversely that on any given occasion many other motives may be subordinated to it, as means to an end. For example, one may be motivated to be affiliative toward voters, acting in a friendly manner in order to satisfy a superordinate need for dominance (an example of Murray's). Or one may be motivated to work rationally and efficiently on a joint project (need for achievement) as a means of fulfilling the affiliative need to strengthen one's group membership and mutual solidarity feelings (my example, based on Japanese and Hawaiian culture; see Gallimore 1981, further discussed below).

Murray also discusses two mutually complementary motivations of succorance and nurturance (Murray 1938:83, 181-187). Need for succorance involves seeking to be cared for, and need for nurturance involves need to care for others. Succorance needs are manifested in seeking love, tenderness, sympathy, nurturance, aid, or protection; it is a dependent attitude. It comprises desires to be indulged, supported, consoled, and have a secure haven. Need for nurturance is the motivation to give such succorance to others, to "mother" the needy and helpless. Nurturance includes desires to feed, nurse, help and support others, based on feelings of compassion or pity. In the United States there has been little research on succorance and nurturance, but L. T. Doi (1962, 1981) has written extensively on succorance in Japan; see below.

Shipley and Veroff (1952) and Atkinson, Heyns, and Veroff (1954) pioneered the experimental measurement of need for affiliation. French and Chadwick (1956) built on this work, defining affiliation motive as a desire to establish and/or maintain warm and friendly interpersonal relations and to avoid rejection. Schachter (1959) then initiated an influential line of research on the effects of anxiety (fear of a very painful electrical shock) on affiliativeness; subjects expecting the shocks chose to wait with other subjects expecting shocks, whether or not they were allowed to talk with them. But in effect, his research restricts the much more complex construct of Murray to an operational definition of simple proximity seeking. This misses the essence of the concept, which is unity seeking.[16]

McAdams (1980) argues that studies of affiliation that include tendencies to seek and perpetuate all social relationships regardless of type have defined the motivation too broadly. (Schachter's operationalization of affiliation as mere proximity seeking is a case in point.) McAdams rightly insists on the importance of considering the quality of relationships people are seeking, and he has pursued a line of inquiry focusing on intimacy relationships "characterized by openness, contact, and union, in which there is reciprocal dialogue among peers, in which there is caring and concern for the welfare of the [other], and which are experienced by the participants as convivial and enjoyable . . . in and of themselves" (1980:416). He relates *intimacy motivation* to other theorists' conceptions of warmth, love, and communion (McAdams 1988, 1989). McAdams has projective TAT (Thematic Apperception Test) measures of intimacy motivation, and validated those measures (as well as measures of affiliative and power motives) against time-sampled self reports, descriptions of friendship episodes, and psychodrama enactments (McAdams 1982, McAdams and Constantian 1983, McAdams, Healy, and Krause 1984, McAdams and Powers 1981). Both intimacy and affiliative motives correlate with frequency of conversations and letter writing in real life. When they are alone, subjects high on affiliative motives frequently wish to be interacting with others. Intimacy motives correlate with frequency of thinking about relations with others and with positive feelings when actually engaged in interaction. Intimacy motives also correlate with more concern for the well-being of friends, more listening, more self-disclosure, more frequent friendly interactions, more "we" and "us" references in the psychodrama, and the enactment of more positive and mutual relationships in the psychodrama. People perceive subjects whose scores indicate high levels of intimacy motivation as more loving, sincere, and natural and as less dominant than subjects scoring low on intimacy motivation.

Without reference to McAdams, Hill (1987) independently explored dimensions of affiliation motivation, coming up with a dimension involving "positive affect or stimulation associated with interpersonal closeness and communion," as well as dimensions of emotional support, social comparison, and attention or praise. Hill's research suggests that in his Interpersonal Orientation Scale there are four distinct factors that he considers subtypes of affiliation motive, one of which is the desire for positive affect associated with interpersonal closeness.[17] Clark et al. (1987) offer a third measure of CS orientation.

Although he does not make the connection himself, McAdams's conception of intimacy motivation is very close to a combination of Murray's (1938) nurturance and succorance needs. It is this combination of motivations to give and receive noncontingently that corresponds to Communal Sharing as I have described it above. The CS motive, in other words, is the desire to merge selves, to be one with others. The goal of the motive is unity of thought, feeling, and activity. People may express this in attentive, empathic concern, in extensive, honest and revealing communication, in speech that refers to their mutual identification, in seeking out others' informal companionship, and in the expression of pleasure in such companionship.

Part of the significance of this research in social psychology is that—as the ethnographic data discussed below and in Part IV also indicates—the desire to give and receive "kindness" and to share work, resources, living space, and a common social identity is entirely distinct from material acquisitiveness or profit-making motives. It is not inherently calculated and expediential, it has no extrinsic purpose, it is simply the joy of Turner's (1969) communitas or Buber's (1987 [1923] "I and Thou" relationship.


## Power (Authority Ranking)

Murray (1938:82, 151–156) identifies needs for *dominance* and for *deference*. In dominance, the need is "to influence or control others; to persuade, prohibit, dictate; to lead and direct; to restrain; to organize the behavior of a group" and to shape the sentiments of its members (p. 82). The complement of this is deference, the motivation to admire, follow, and gladly serve a leader. (Murray contrasts these motivations with autonomy, the need to go one's own way.) Dominance is characterized by the desire "to influence or direct the behavior of [others] by suggestion, seduction, persuasion, or command" (p. 152). Among corresponding behaviors he includes ruling, judging (rendering decisions), restraining, punishing, the establishment of principles and standards. Dominance also involves needs to be attended and listened to, be followed, and be an admired exemplar (cf. Weber's 1978 [1922] concept of charisma). The aim is to prevail over others or to govern. Deference is the inverse of this; it involves feelings of "respect, admiration, wonder, reverence" toward a superior (p. 154). It is expressed by willingly behaving in conformity with the wishes of a leader, obeying, serving, and emulating (again, cf. Weber 1978:946 on domination).

A number of psychologists have carried out studies related to Murray's concepts of needs for dominance and deference. The seminal work is that of Adorno et al. (1950), who examine the personality factors that make people susceptible to fascist propaganda. Their work, conducted just after World War II, is part of a larger program of research into prejudice and anti-Semitism in particular. They seek to determine what kinds of psychological needs (goals or drives) increase some people's readiness to "exhibit anti-democratic tendencies" and respond to authoritarian ideologies. Their method is to ask people how much they agree or disagree with ideological and moral statements on a questionnaire (which is validated in part by in-depth interviews). The most important of the classic scales that they develop, the F-scale, contains nine subscales, three of which are related to an orientation toward social relations structured in terms of power, loyalty, and discipline (clusters b., Authoritarian Submission; c., Authoritarian Aggression; and f., Power and "Toughness"). In all, six of thirty questions on the scale have to do with power, respect and authority,[18] while five others are fairly closely related to this theme.[19] While most Americans disapprove of the *authoritarian* orientation that this scale taps, in many other societies these attitudes and motives are entirely congruent with the culture. For example, Ho and Lee (1974) show the connection between authoritarianism and the Chinese ideal of filial piety.

Adorno et al. also show that their A–S (anti-Semitism) and E (ethnocentrism) scales correlate with a view of social relationships as fundamentally authoritarian, although none of the items on these scales explicitly deals with issues of rank or authority. They compare subjects with high scores on ethnocentrism (most of whom were also high scorers on the correlated A-S and F scales) with low scorers. The most ethnocentric subjects tend to idealize the manifest, external qualities and status of their parents in global, undifferentiated terms (Adorno et al. 1950:239ff.). They glorify their parents using superlatives like "best in the world," "excellent man in every way," "Father—he is wonderful; couldn't make him better." Highly ethnocentric subjects also have a submissive attitude toward their parents, reporting that they treated their parents with respect based on fear. Ethnocentric subjects report having been subject to strict discipline and often harsh corporal punishment, and these subjects approve of such punishment. They regard their parents as the absolute arbiters of right and wrong, considering parental will as law. More generally, subjects with the highest E scores exhibit a hierarchical conception of human relations, in contrast to the egalitarian mutuality view of social relations that low scorers held (Adorno et al. 1950:413-14). The typical ethnocentric subject has a

> conception of people as seeking only power and material benefits, . . .
> [together with the] assumption that . . . the more ruthless must
> necessarily win out. His orientation in interpersonal relationships is
> thus toward getting power by associating with the powerful and
> influential, or at least toward participating in the power of those who
> have it. Admiration for the strong and contempt for the weak
> accompany this attitude. (Adorno et al. 1950:413)

Projective tests confirm the results of the questionnaire studies, showing that subjects high on these scales are concerned with power and submission to authority (Adorno et al. 1950:599-600). Authoritarian subjects express deference to authority, while what they "admire most in others is power, strength, authority, and rugged masculinity" (p. 600).

In short, authoritarian subjects conceive of human relations as structured vertically, speaking often of "the bottom and the top" or of "moving upwards" in power and influence (p. 414). Adorno et al. conclude that this orientation is very general, extending from sexual partners to God. (It contrasts with low-scorers' orientation toward social relations as "affectionate, basically equalitarian, and permissive" [p. 971].) Why should ethnocentrism, which is the negative side of CS, correlate with AR orientations? The best guess is culture and social class. Analytically CS and AR are entirely distinct, but both were salient among blue-collar workers and immigrants of this period, and both were muted among more educated people of higher socioeconomic status (see R. Brown 1965 for a discussion of this and other methodological issues in this work).

Following up the work on the authoritarian personality, Veroff (1957) explored the measurement of *power motivation* per se, using projective techniques similar to those used for measuring other motives (see Veroff and Veroff 1972). Based on earlier dissertation research, Uleman (1972) and Winter (1973) offer somewhat different projective measures of power motivation. These and other studies are reviewed in Winter (1973), who defines social power as "the ability or capacity of O to produce (consciously or unconsciously) intended effects on the behavior or emotions of another person P" (p. 5). Measures of power motivation are based on the specific TAT themes that increase under conditions conceived of as power arousing: candidacy for student office, playing the role of experimenter, observing hypnosis, seeing a film of the Kennedy inauguration (after his assassination). McClelland (1975) and Winter (1973) each review their own and other experimenters' findings indicating that such measures of the power motive are associated with a relational style involving drawing attention to oneself and attracting followers, as well as seeking prestige (acquiring symbols of prestige) and seeking control over information flow. Young male Americans high in need for power tend to participate in and read about competitive sports and watch more violent television programs and, like older men high in need for power, join and hold office in more organizations than those low in power motive. Winter presents codings correlating 12 U.S. presidents' need for power with their political style (i.e., assertion of authority). Among graduate and undergraduate students in India, a TAT measure of power motivation also correlates with leadership activities (Kureshi and Fatima 1984).[20]

Taken together, this research demonstrates a distinct, discriminable Authority Ranking motivation that varies between individuals and varies within each individual over time and circumstances. In any given context, people vary in their responses as a function of the intensity of their need for power and, presumably, the recency of their other opportunities to satisfy this need. Some people intensively seek out opportunities to create and exercise power—they attempt to structure social relationships in the form of AR, and vigorously attempt to enter into positions of high rank and authority. Others do so much less actively, or are even averse to participating in relationships structured according to this model. People motivated to seek power approve of others who enact the complementary subordinate role. (For example, in an industrial simulation experiment, "supervisors" with high need for power evaluate the performance of "subordinates" more highly when the subordinates behave ingratiatingly [Fodor and Farrow 1979].)[21]

This research also shows that the need for power is expressed in a great variety of ways, in part as a function of cultures. But the forms in which the motive can be expressed are circumscribed. It is not that every human social action is an expression of need for power—far from it. Need for power can be distinguished from other social motives, and indeed an important purpose in psychological research on this topic has been to refine that discrimination and work out the limits of the range of forms in which people manifest this type of motivation. Winter (1973:1) starts off his book by stating that "I do not believe that the power motive is the only important human motive, or that all of a person's behavior can be understood by studying only his strivings for power." McClelland's work using TAT projective tests clearly shows that the power motive is only one among at least three major social motives, including affiliation and achievement. Harrell and Stahl (1981) describe another technique for measuring these three motives, based on choices among hypothetical jobs, and further validate the trichotomy against the actual occupations of their subjects. McAdams (1984 and earlier work) demonstrates that there is a contrast in social relationships between power motivation and intimacy motivation (and distinguishes both from achievement motivation).

Independently of this motivational tradition (and not cited by them), Schutz (1958) proposes a theory of basic human social needs supported by numerous experiments that show that the *need for affection* is distinct from the *need for control* over others. Both are independent of the motivation to receive social attention and participate in social interaction in general (*need for inclusion*), a need whose negative pole corresponds to the Null orientation of being ignored, alone and not relating, without any social significance. Schutz defines need for affection as a motivation to establish and maintain close, personal, loving dyadic relationships. Emotional closeness is the hallmark of relationships resulting from this need, whether in close friendship, dating, marriage, or parenting. Such emotional attachments involve confiding intimate feelings, fears, and hopes. In contrast, need for control is manifest in efforts to influence, lead, exercise authority, be respected, and take responsibility; it is the need to have power over others. Schutz shows that there are individual personality differences in the strength of these social needs, and demonstrates that group functioning and productivity depend on the compatibility of the social needs of the group members. It is striking how closely the later studies on power and intimacy motivation replicate Schutz's findings, although they do not cite him. Moreover, unlike most of his successors, Schutz explicitly considers the Null case under the rubric of "undersocial" people with very low need for inclusion, one of his three basic dimensions. However, Schutz has virtually nothing to say about achievement motivation, a major focus of the subsequent research on human social motives to which we will now turn.

## Achievement (Market Pricing)

The motivation most closely linked to Market Pricing is *need for achievement*, although Murray did not define achievement motivation with specific reference to economic activities. Murray's (1938:80–81, 164–66) classic definition of need for achievement is in terms of effort and exertion, the desire "to strive to do something difficult as well and as quickly as possible" (pp. 80–81). In its essence Murray's concept is a formulation of a utilitarian orientation toward efficiency and the effective mobilization of resources. Murray's definition focuses on mastery, exercise of talent, and success. He describes the actions which manifest this need:

> To make intense, prolonged, and repeated efforts to accomplish something difficult. To work with singleness of purpose towards a high and distant goal. To have the determination to win. To try to do everything well. To be stimulated to excel by the presence of others, to enjoy competition. To exert will power; to overcome boredom and fatigue. (Murray 1938:164)

Building on this foundation, McClelland and Atkinson (McClelland et al. 1953, McClelland 1955, Atkinson 1958, Atkinson and Feather 1966, McClelland 1976) develop and validate a TAT measure of need for achievement. People with high need for achievement scores choose experts in preference to friends as working partners in an experimental task situation, have better memory for uncompleted tasks, and learn difficult tasks (but not boring, routine ones) faster than others. These subjects seem to set goals for themselves and use concrete external rewards only as measures of achievement in terms of their personal standards.

Winterbottom (1958; cited in McClelland 1976) measured the achievement motives of eight-year-old boys. Mothers of boys who were high in their need for achievement encouraged their sons to be energetic, competitive, self-reliant, and determined. Stimulated by this study, McClelland (1976) proposes that what Weber called "the spirit of capitalism" was in fact based on the need for achievement. In a variety of historical and cross-national studies, he showed that rapid economic development is often preceded by increases in achievement motivation, variously measured. Also, in the United States and Germany, boys with strong achievement motivation are more likely than others to prefer the occupations of stock broker, real estate salesman, advertiser, merchandise buyer, and factory manager (McClelland 1976:55–56). In the United States and Turkey, successful young executives have greater need for achievement than less successful ones. In general, achievement motivation appears to be associated with taking rationally calculated, moderate risks—not gambling, and not pursuing the sure thing with a low payoff.

Roger Brown sums up and assesses the measurement of achievement motivation:

> It was to be a measure of generalized motivation for achievement. The scoring categories specified a concern with excellence but this excellence could be in any field—poetry, wrestling, inventing, or in dentistry. It is surprising, therefore, to find that the measure has turned out to be chiefly a measure of motivation for business or economic achievement. This gradual shift in emphasis has been an unanticipated outcome of the efforts made at validating the original measure. . . . The scores are higher for managers than for other sorts of professional men;

they are related to economic growth; they go with a taste for moderate
risks, long range planning, and tasks that involve clear criteria of
success and failure. The process of validation has turned into a process
of reconceptualization. The measure now seems to be primarily
concerned with motivation for economic achievement rather than
with achievement motivation in general. (Brown 1965:473-4)

In short, achievement motivation is above all the proclivity to engage in social
relations mediated by markets, prices, money and other pan-modal construc-
tions of ratio value. As Weber (1958 [1904–1906], 1975 [1916, 1920–21]) demonstrated through historical and sociocultural comparisons, profit maximization,
savings and investment, and concern with rational efficiency are orientations
that are meaningful primarily within a particular type of social relationship.
Probably this is because global maximization is only possible with respect
to some intermodal ratio scale of value; efficiency and "achievement" can
be assessed only in terms of ratios of benefits to costs (including expected
risks).

Murray's formulation and subsequent psychological research make it clear
that achievement motivation is not grounded in biological subsistence needs
as such. Need for achievement is need to be efficient and productive for the
sake of the intrinsic rewards of the calculus of utility maximization itself. Need
for achievement is need for economic rationality for its own sake, for the satisfaction of making decisions and mobilizing resources in the most effective way
possible under the circumstances; that is, for maximizing outcome ratios.
Profit making, material returns, wealth, status and success are important for
someone with strong achievement motivation as measures for assessing his
performance, not as ends in themselves. As Weber (1958) shows, the orientation toward frugality, economizing, weighing alternatives rationally according
to their expected utilities, making sound investments that pay off well, using
time efficiently, avoiding waste, and concentration of effort that was at the
origins of modern market capitalism was not a consequence of increased desire for material consumption. The Calvinists did not spend their money, they
reinvested it while living very austere lives. Motivation to achieve is not derivative from hunger drives or any other organic homeostatic mechanism, it is an
autonomous social motive. We will consider this point further in Part IV, but
the point in brief is that need for achievement is a social motive because it is
inherently a need to interact with others in a particular mode: to bargain, compete, make (adversarial) contracts, outwit competitors, corner the market,
treat others as commodities and extract a profit from them, and so on. The
game is a social game whose means and ends are socially constructed, and
whose audience is the achiever's reference group. The points you score are
social (Veblen 1934 [1899, 1918]), and you can't be a golf champion in a
country where they've never heard of golf. You can not be selfish by yourself.

For the present discussion, there are two important conclusions that come out of the extensive body of research on achievement motivation that I have summarily reviewed here. First, the same types of measures (TAT stories, coding of school primers, career preferences) differentiate among at least three basic social motives: intimacy motivation (Communal Sharing), power motivation and some subscales of authoritarianism (Authority Ranking), and achievement motivation (Market Pricing). Second, achievement motivation is related to only certain delineated kinds of social behavior and not to others. People high in need for achievement do not perform better at dull and routine tasks, do not perform better in order to be able to leave the experiment sooner or get a cash bonus (McClelland 1976:44–45), are less likely to be nominated by peers as probable future leaders (McClelland 1976:55), and so on. People with high need for achievement do not perform better when the experimenter appeals to them to cooperate to help him, while subjects high in need for affiliation do perform better. We will see from the Moose ethnography in Part IV that achievement motivation is only one of four ways of organizing work, as Polanyi (1947, 1957b) emphatically demonstrated with historical data. As Gallimore (1981) observes about Japan and Hawaii and other cultures, people may be energetic, dedicated, and motivated to do well out of a sentiment of solidarity and inclusive belonging (CS; see also Salisbury 1973:90). Thus there are a number of motives for working hard, of which achievement motivation is only one. K. Doi (1982) makes a statistical and cultural argument that in Japan people may be motivated to achieve (economically) out of affiliative motives (e.g., working hard to advance collective corporate goals). L. T. Doi (1981 [1971]) makes the same point independently on the basis of psychodynamic inferences. Hence the same surface behavior may be the outcome of diverse motives.

Need for achievement per se is defined by peoples' responsiveness to particular kinds of social challenges, and by a tendency to give a distinctive kind of social orientation to the structure of work. Different kinds of motives lead people to respond differently to the same situation; different situations stimulate different people, according to the relative strengths of their motives. In laboratory games, subjects assessed as high on individualism or competitiveness take more for themselves, while cooperative and altruistic subjects give more away (Liebrand and Van-Run 1985). In another study, subjects high in achievement motivation allocated rewards "equitably"—proportionately to success at a mental task—while subjects who scored high on affiliative motivation were equitable (proportional) with a computer-generated "partner" oriented toward input/output ratios, and divided equally with an egalitarian "partner" (O'Malley and Schubarth 1984).

In short, the motivation to structure social relationships in Market Pricing form and to seek out and engage in such relationships is quite distinct from the motivation to organize social relationships in the form of Authority Ranking. Both of these are distinct from the motivation to constitute and participate in

Communal Sharing relationships. The strength of each of these motives varies across individuals, so that there are more or less stable trait-like differences between individuals in their tendencies to engage in each type of social relationship. What about Equality Matching motives?

## Equality

Murray (1938) identifies 20 basic "manifest needs," and describes a number of others. We have discussed only six of these, grouped in three categories. Several other social motives have been proposed that were not on his list. I will discuss just one: the motive for fairness, equality of outcome, balanced reciprocity, and distributive justice. This motive has been explored much less thoroughly than the other three, but it has been studied with a much more direct methodology: observing the actual distribution of rewards in various experimental conditions. Lerner (1974) shows that children often distribute rewards equally, regardless of the relative amounts of work done. Kindergarten and first-grade children tend to prefer equality ("*parity*") over proportional *equity*. This is generally true regardless of whether the kindergartners are "supervisors" allocating rewards to others, or whether the child is a participant dividing the reward between herself and a putative other. First-graders' preference for equality is strengthened by instructions referring to the participants as partners and as a team. Among fifth-graders who are not told they were partners or a team, about half divide a reward equally and half allocate proportionally to the work done. At none of these age levels do the children show evidence of self-interest biases in their allocation of rewards, at least in front of the experimenter. Morgan and Sawyer (1967) describe a bargaining experiment in which fifth- and sixth-grade boys prefer equality to equity (but the "equity" alternative may not have been very salient to them). These studies indicate that in many situations fairness and equality in social relations is an important goal of young children especially. Lowenstein, Thompson, and Bazerman (1989) have shown that adults want equal shares in many situations (not maximization). (We will discuss a developmental illustration of the orientation toward EM and other models in Part IV.) This developmental research complements the findings of the social justice research discussed earlier showing that people choose among AR, EM, and MP principles to distribute joint rewards as a function of the sort of social relationship the participants have or desire. It should now be clear that in part this must be the result of social motives oriented toward the rewards intrinsic to engaging in each kind of social relationship.

Lerner (1977) offers a theoretical framework for understanding "parity" (equality) and other kinds of "*justice*" *motivation*, in which he cites experimental evidence contradicting the idea that people merely try to maximize their self-interest. Presumably the projective tests and other techniques used to assess other kinds of social motives could be used equally effectively to measure levels of need for EM, but Murray does not list such a need and it appears that no one has attempted to develop and validate such measures. To demonstrate the existence of EM motives in the psychological paradigm would require convergent evidence of other kinds (evidence that I do not have for the Moose). Ideally, one would wish to have fantasy materials of the kind used to study achievement motivation (Atkinson and Feather 1966), and conduct interviews with reflective informants about their ultimate hopes, aspirations and ideals, together with experimental studies of what people do in situations in which factors predicted to affect the strength of different kinds of motives were controlled (McClelland 1976:39–46). Much more remains to be done here.

It is often assumed that, deep down, the most fundamental, superordinate motive is maximization of self-interest. That, theorists presuppose, is human nature. Yet any review of the psychological research on human social motivation must lead to the conclusion that there are a number of distinct, independent motives. As Murray (1938) notes and Gallimore (1981) and K. Doi (1982) illustrate, on any given occasion any motive may be subordinated to any other end. But generally all four of the needs I have discussed above are hierarchically autonomous. That is, none of them is necessarily subordinated as a means to any of the others. Furthermore, for any individual on any given occasion, any of the four motives may take precedence. In particular, other motives are often stronger than need for achievement, even among Americans (e.g., Harrell and Stahl 1981, McAdams 1984 and earlier work). And need for achievement is generally much weaker in non-Western societies than it is in the U.S. and has been much weaker in other historical periods than it is today (McClelland 1976). Thus in general it is misguided to assume that people's sole or primary or paramount need is maximizing their individual self-interest. Hard-driving ambition, competitive striving, rational bargaining, and calculating efficient trade-offs among alternative choices are characteristic of people with high achievement motivation (when that motive is aroused), but not characteristic of most people most of the time.

## The Social Motives of Non-Western People

Although some of this motivational research has collected data from subjects outside the United States, much of that data is about people in more or less Westernized societies or populations. Do people in other cultures have the same set of basic social motives? In Part IV I use ethnographic evidence from the Moose of Burkina Faso to argue that each of the four relational models can be construed as a fundamental, autonomous type of motivation. The ethnographic evidence from the Moose is based on inferences from the ways in which they organize their actions in pursuit of their most valued goals. In particular, Moose men want wives and children, there is a severe shortage of arable land, and often insufficient or precarious supplies of food and water. Yet Communal Sharing is the dominant mode in which they obtain and distribute women, land, food, and water. Authority Ranking is an important subsidiary mode for Moose transactions in such entities, followed by Equality Matching. In these contexts they organize some activities according to Market Pricing, but to the present day MP remains a minor structural alternative in the village.

Rosaldo (1980) gives a superbly rich, "thick" description of the social motives and sense of self of the Ilongot headhunters of the Philippines. She intends her ethnography to be quite idiographic, yet her account clearly shows that Ilongot manifest culturally recognized motives corresponding to at least three of the four basic models, as well as social norms related to these three motives. Their most powerful—or at least most culturally salient—motive is an envious desire ('apet) to equal their peers and not to be outdone. Much of Ilongot culture revolves around the focused energy (liget) that such jealousy evokes when a peer has something special that another lacks. This envy is based on their norm of distributive equality (bēret) among peers—EM. The Ilongot norm of bēret prescribes that individual shares should be equal and that one should revenge oneself if necessary to achieve parity, retaliating in kind (tubrat) to balance any evil one suffers. One can get even by taking any other person's head, or by magically taking another's garden yield for one's own garden, or by receiving indemnifying compensation ('aked) (Rosaldo 1980:46–53, 57, 76–84, 88–96, 204–10). Among young, unmarried Ilongot men jealous energy takes the form of morose belligerence, energetic focused activity, or violent aggression. In its mature form this liget motivation is tempered by the bēret norm into mutual respect and giving honor where it is due, giving equal return for gifts received, taking turns and making equal contributions (pp. 134, 180, 186–88). Ilongot also have a well-defined conception of an AR motive that applies to children's relations with adults: children and other immature persons should fear (kayub) their elders, and show bētang—respect, humility, and deferential shame. People should follow ('unud) their seniors and be commanded (tuydek) and directed (bukur) by them (pp. 69–71, 84–88). Rosaldo also repeatedly describes definite Ilongot CS motives and norms of sharing and generosity (especially regarding cooked food), giving help freely, and being tolerant and forgiving with kin and neighbors (pp. 77, 96–97, 133, 182–87, 206, 215, 219).[22]

Although cultural anthropologists tend to focus on structures and norms rather than motives, there are other descriptions of culture-specific forms of each of these social motives from other cultures as well. Independently of the American motivational paradigm, L. T. Doi (Doi 1962, 1981, Morsbach and Tyler 1987) has brought to the attention of Western social scientists the core CS concepts of amae (dependence) and the desire to amaeru (be dependent) in Japan. Building on and modifying a psychoanalytic foundation, Doi describes a need which corresponds almost precisely to Murray's (1938) need for succorance, although he makes no reference to Murray. Doi shows that this motivation to depend on and get indulgent, prescient, nurturant care from others is fundamental to Japanese personality, and indeed to Japanese culture as a whole. Inability to *amaeru* or to develop relationships that allow *amae* are major complaints of patients seeking psychotherapy in Japan, where psychotherapists regard helping patients to *amaeru* as a basic and natural goal of therapy. Doi demonstrates beyond any doubt that *amaeru* is a highly valued pivotal motive in Japanese society, exploring *amae* psychodynamically and showing how it operates as a basic social need in individuals while it is at the same time the foundation for highly elaborated and specifically Japanese forms of social relations.[23] Caudill (1962) reports that CS is the primary orientation of both Japanese values and emotions. Lebra (1976) confirms the importance of belonging and of dependency needs in Japan, emphasizing the ways in which the group is paramount over the individual.

Doi's (1962, 1981) superb analysis of the elaboration of the CS motive of need for succorance in Japanese culture has rich implications for understanding CS in cultures where it is not so clearly delineated, recognized, elaborated, and accorded such great importance. To *amaeru* is to passively depend on someone for indulgence of one's needs and wishes, to desire to be nurtured and cared for. It is a wish, conscious or unconscious, to be so close as to be inseparable. To *amae* is to be trustingly, presumptuously, willfully dependent, confident that one will be given whatever one desires, without needing to assert oneself to get it, to be "spoiled."[24] There is a strong assimilative flavor to *amae*, and it often involves a kind of identification with another person or group in which ego boundaries partially dissolve. *Amaeru* is a desire to merge the self with a nurturant maternal person or persons, overcoming all separation and boundaries. With *amae* there is no privacy, independence, or exclusive personal realm—one is incorporated into the whole that is the relationship. People in an *amae* relationship do not even express gratitude, since gratitude is an EM debt to a separate, coequal person. Doi relates *amae* to the Platonic idea of "love" and intimate friendship. He notes that it tends to entail a high degree of conformity and submergence of personal wishes in favor of the group's goals, although there is also an element of willful self-indulgence. Japanese experience great distress if they let people down who depended on and trusted them, even if they have done so merely by expressing autonomy or acting independently. *Amae* means a sense of belonging. What in the West would be personality is submerged in the group consensus, so that one's most basic identity is defined by membership—and the greatest fear is isolation, being left out. Doi goes into considerable detail about the feelings people experience when their *amaeru* is frustrated, including the feelings of resentful victimization people experience at losing someone who indulged them. The contrasting Japanese terms are *tanin*, outsider, unconnected or unrelated person, and *enro*, to hold back, to be ill at ease with someone, feeling constraint and lack of relaxed, intimate trust.

Gallimore (1981) reviews studies showing how "achievement motivation" may motivate people to work hard and efficiently and to do well when they are working as a group on a collective project, as people often do in Hawaii, Japan, and elsewhere. That is, people exert themselves in order to contribute to the group, to strengthen its solidarity and cohesiveness together with their sense of belonging to it. Doi (1981) makes the same point. Here productivity and efficiency are subsidiary goals—they are primarily means to uniting the group.

Other descriptions of social motives in non-Western cultures also support the hypothesis that the four models constitute the basic repertoire. Kracke (1979) offers an ethnographic account of varieties of leadership style and differences in disposition to exercise authority in an Amazonian culture. Kaut (1961) and Hollnsteiner (1964) both explain the motivational importance of the *utang-la-loób* EM obligation to reciprocate in-kind in Tagalog culture (Philippines). Lebra (1976) describes the very similar Japanese social motivation of *on*, which is the sense of gratitude or moral obligation to reciprocate, the humility one feels toward a benefactor to whom one owes a debt (see also Ho 1982). In sum, the available evidence suggests that just four models may inform the basic and universal motives of social relations, although there are enormous cultural differences in the settings and manner in which people realize these motives (see Implementation in Chapter 7). Part IV focuses on assessing the social motives of the Moose of Burkina Faso to see which of their motives are paramount.

From what we have seen already, it is evident that each of the four fundamental models entails not only a structure but also a goal-seeking process. People seek out relationships of each of the four kinds and try to shape their interactions to be congruent with the models. I interpret this as strong evidence for the psychological status of the models as templates or guidelines for action. Furthermore, in this chapter we have seen that the same models comprise congruent motives and norms together: people desire the social relations, and they require others to conform to them. This means that failure to realize the requisite forms of these social relations is a fault: it is wrongdoing. Whereas the preceding section shows that each of the four models is an ideal that people strive to realize, the next chapter shows that people abhor actions that contravene or negate the model. Each model is a standard for the good and the desirable, which means that it also defines what is evil. The next chapter also discusses how people seek to rectify deviations from the models, responding to disturbances by taking steps to restore the social equilibrium.

# 6

# Judgments

$T$his chapter is about the jural and ideological standards the four models engender. The issue concerns the nature of the standards people use to make evaluations, how people pass judgment on each other, and the consequences of such judgments. I begin by considering the jural (moral and legal) and ideological frameworks the models entail. The focus of the rest of the chapter is on what makes something wrong, what factors affect culpability, and what people do to rectify a wrong. The second part of the chapter looks at what people think when things go wrong—how people make sense of suffering. It concludes with a brief speculation about religion.

## MORALITY, LEGITIMATION, LAW, AND IDEOLOGY

> The problem of ethics does not lie in the consciousness of an isolated individual but in *the relationship between man and man*. It would be impossible to reach a real understanding of what distinguishes a good from a bad action, or what comprises a duty, responsibility, or virtue, unless considered as a problem of the relationship between man and man. (Watsuji 1962:12, quoted in translation by Lebra 1976:12; italics in original quotation)

There is something more to the directive force of these models than people's proclivity to implement them in their social relations, something that sets them off from sexual and other quasi-social motives. To understand the operation of the four models, we need to recognize that it is not only that people have shared cognitive conceptions which they are commonly motivated to enact. Nor is it merely that people fear sanctions if they violate norms derived from these models. People also feel that it is right and necessary to structure social relations in each of these four ways—which is why they enforce these models on each other in the first place. Trivers (1971) and Frank (1988) offer theories of how natural selection produces moral emotions, including both altruistic commitment and the desire for righteous retribution. Quite simply, each model entails a basic, irreducible intuitive moral ideal and a moral standard of evaluation, as I have previously shown (Fiske 1990).[1] These four folk moral presuppositions are "irreducible" because each derives from a distinct, autonomous model. The culture, of course, specifies which model must be applied in defined circumstances (see Implementation in Chapter 7).

Communal Sharing as a moral ideal is the axiom that people should be altruistic, sharing generously with others of their kind, and placing the needs of the community ahead of their own personal needs. Gilligan (1982, Gilligan and Wiggins 1987) and Noddings (1984) suggest that this kind of compassionate, caring morality is characteristically feminine in our own culture, but they would not argue that it is exclusively feminine. Gilligan (n.d., Gilligan and Wiggins 1987) discusses the sources of this morality of love and care in personal relationships, showing how responsiveness to the needs of others grows out of attachment to the mother. The sympathetic emotional "co-feeling" of this moral emotion is a product of the infant's experience of engagement in this nurturant relationship. This reasoning is effectively extended by Fortes's (1970 [1963], 1983) demonstration that the norm of prescriptive altruism in personal relations is the essence of kinship in Africa (e.g., Marshall 1961) and elsewhere. In Africa, this moral orientation is not specific to women, of course, although its strength seems to vary among individuals and cultures.

However, Blum points out that altruism is a term that presupposes the separation between egoistic self and other:

> The notion of altruism, for instance, conveys the notion that one's giving to others is entirely cut off from any concern for oneself, or even that it is at the expense of the self. In contrast to altruism, the notions, for example, of 'community' and 'friendship' are relationships in which concern for others, while not reduced to self-interest, is not separable from concern for self. To be concerned for a friend, or for a community with which one closely identifies and of which one is a member, is not to reach out to someone or something which is 'wholly other' than oneself, but to that which shares a part of one's own self and is implicated in one's sense of one's own identity. (Blum 1987:317–18)

This captures elegantly the essence of Communal Sharing: self and other are not opposed or even marked alternatives, they are one. Blum goes on to argue persuasively for the view that responsiveness (concern for others) is present from early childhood, belying the assumption of most current theories that moral development starts from an initial state of childish egoism. Furthermore, Blum contrasts two moral orientations: the self-conscious, rational application of an abstract, universal MP principle like Blum's concept of "justice," understood as an impartial standard, and the compassionate responsiveness that involves caring and responsible concern for a particular person or community, in what I am calling the CS mode. Our concept of the moral should not be limited to the MP conception of impartial and deductively universal rules.

Another way of thinking about this is that people may act morally because they feel concern for others, or because they feel an obligation to be concerned. L. T. Doi (1981:33–35) describes this contrast between traditional Japanese Communal Sharing ethical concepts of *giri*, a sense of social obligation to serve others, and *ninjo*, human compassion or kindness. He notes (pp. 42–43) that such moral obligations are strictly limited to one's own closed primary group. While CS morality often emerges in, and defines, close relationships, it is also widely manifest as a morality of service to the community, in which the good is defined as that which fosters the collectivity and sustains the corporate group. This ethical standard of cooperation and contribution to the common good has been the predominant moral framework in many cultures, including classical Greece (Wong 1984). As a political ideology, CS has been the core of much thought and action, from the anarchist Diggers through Gandhi's influence on modern Indian village ideology (e.g., Kropotkin 1972 [1890–1914]).

The morality of Authority Ranking consists in an attitude of respect, deference, loyalty, and obedience by subordinates, complemented by the pastoral responsibility of the authority to exercise his or her strength to provide security and protection for subordinates and to give wise directive guidance. Distributionally, it is also an ethic of privilege and perquisites. In our own society, particularly among middle-class intellectuals, this dual moral principle is often devalued—and sometimes even regarded as immoral—but it is the backbone of the moral systems of cultures in Africa and Asia. As filial piety (and responsible stewardship) this is the pivot of Chinese Confucian ethics, as set out in the ancient *Hsiao Ching* (Makra and Sih 1961;[2] Fung 1952:360–61, 411, 413), and the foundation of Chinese society ever since (Ho and Lee 1974, Ho 1982, Wong 1984). According to Mo Tzu, founder of the Mohist school of Chinese philosophy and in other respects a critic of Confucius, each new ruler, once established, should issue an edict ordering, "Upon hearing good or evil, one shall report it to one's superior. What the superior thinks to be right, all shall think to be right. What the superior thinks to be wrong, all shall think to be wrong" (quoted in Fung 1947:59).[3] The morality of Authority Ranking was also fundamental to ancient Japanese society and salient in medieval Europe. In many African societies it is a cornerstone of contemporary as well as traditional ethics (e.g., Brown 1951, Fortes 1965, Llewelyn-Davies 1981) as it is in the lowland Philippines (Bulatao 1964). In our own philosophical ancestry, Machiavelli (1963 [1513]) offers one of the earliest modern philosophies of AR. One interpretation of Nietzsche's formulations of superpersons and the will to power is that they represent a philosophy of AR.

The precepts of equality, of justice as equal treatment, in-kind compensation, or the righteousness of strictly reciprocal revenge, together with fairness as even distribution and uniform contributions, comprise the ethics of Equality Matching. Rawls's (1971) theory elegantly captures one aspect of this morality, when Rawls gives what amounts to a formal elaboration of the widespread egalitarian folk practice of letting the person who divides up something into shares get the last pick. I am reminded of two brothers who had to mow the lawn every week. Each week, one person divided up the lawn into two parts, the other chose which half he wanted to mow. (They took turns by week being divider.) The veil of ignorance is egalitarian for the same reason: if you don't know which is going to be your lot, you make sure you are indifferent among them—which means that they are the same to you.[4] In the EM framework what is right is everyone concerned getting the same thing—once people are included in the relationship in the first place, differences among people are irrelevant. As a moral principle, EM entails the autonomy of domains and kinds of transactions: each distinct distribution, transaction, or turn-taking rotation should be kept entirely independent of all others, without intermodal trade-offs or adjustments.[5] This is a consequence of the absence in EM of any universal currency for comparing, lumping, and trading-off unlike things; ratios and the distributive principle are simply undefined (see Chapter 9). Vlastos (1962) attempts to reduce all distributive justice principles to EM, arguing that the five competing principles of need (CS), worth and merit (AR), work and agreements (MP) actually all come down to a single underlying principle of equal natural rights.

On the other hand, some attempts have been made to reduce all other moral principles to MP proportionality. The morality of Market Pricing is represented in the libertarian ideology of absolute freedom of rational choice, together with the sanctity of voluntarily negotiated contracts or promises: people should be trusted and entitled to calculate their own utilities, costs and benefits, and maximize them as best they can (Boulding 1953, Friedman and Friedman 1981, Nozick 1975). Dumont (1977) provides an incisive history of the rise of the ideology of economic self-interest in the West. In this ethical framework, each person should be autonomous and should enter into transactions with others only when it increases his or her individual utility to do so. The only legitimate, enforceable obligations are those commitments people freely undertake when they voluntarily bind themselves in return for profitable considerations. There are no a priori obligations per se, only "natural" rights to personal freedoms. Sandel (1982) offers a clear and sympathetic statement of the individualism of MP liberal moralities, explaining how, in consequence, contract is the basis for moral commitments in this frame. He also shows that such an MP morality alone is inadequate because it only takes into account those affections and attachments that can be described as personal preferences: the CS morality that grows out of people's historically situated identity as members of a transcendent community has its own independent validity, quite apart from any MP morality. We can confirm this, for example, with reference to L. T. Doi's (1981:42, 84–95, 174–75) description of the rich cultural elaboration of such CS norms—and psychological desires—in Japan; *amaeru* is the ideal of a passively dependent envelopment in which there is no place for freedom as individuality or autonomous expression of personal choice.

Outside the Western tradition, MP contractual individualism has rarely been an ideological and philosophical keystone, and one or another of the other three models generally has occupied that place. Even in the Western tradition, some modern philosophers have incorporated diverse models into their ethical schemata. Notably, Rawls (1971) proposes a hypothetical distributional procedure that is essentially EM as his standard for justice, yet he justifies this standard with a CS argument that actual differences in individual endowments must be regarded as communal assets that belong to the collectivity as a whole. However, he moves to an MP framework in treating this hypothetical distributional procedure as a contractual legitimation of the principle of justice that maximizes the welfare of those who are worst off. Like other social contract theorists, Rawls faces the historical problem that in point of fact the members of actual social systems never have made a voluntary choice to bind themselves to any such contract. The best that can be said is that perhaps people sometimes act *as if* they had done so.

As mentioned earlier, V. Hamilton (1978, Hamilton and Sanders 1981) hypothesizes that people make moral judgments with reference to two dimensions of social roles. The first is hierarchy, ranging from *authority* (AR) at one pole to *equality* (EM) at the other. The second dimension is solidarity, ranging from *status* relations involving collective identity (like a family—CS) to *contract* (relations that are voluntary, temporary, limited, and impersonal—MP). Unfortunately, Hamilton offers only a tantalizingly sketchy theoretical analysis of these relations and the dimensional structure in which she places them.

Cultures differ in the domains to which they apply each model (implementation rules), and differ also in the ways that they realize each model by setting specific parameters that have to be specified to make empty rules substantive guides to conduct (e.g., what counts as "the same" in Equality Matching?). But there seem to be few, if any, cultures in which people do not recognize each of these foundational moral principles in culturally appropriate contexts. And there seem to be few moral axioms that are not in one way or another derivative from the four ethical models.

In a seminal analysis of the principles embodied in legal precepts, Maine (1963 [1861]) showed how Roman and then European law has tended to evolve from status law to contract law (see also Gluckman 1955). Maine's concept of *status law*—like Weber's 1978 [1922] traditional authority—conflates CS and AR, with the emphasis on the latter. It is based on the corporate integrity of the family or local kin group, belief in their descent from a common ancestor, collective responsibility,[6] and the personal authority (and ultimate responsibility) of the father within the family and for the family. Contract law is based on individuality, freedom, and the precept of voluntary commitments to binding agreements (MP). Maine (1963:296ff.) derides the idea of a primitive social contract as the source of society, demonstrating that while universally present, the idea of contract has only a small, unelaborated place in ancient law (compare Polanyi 1957a [1944]). A long line of theoretical schemata contrasting MP with other forms of society springs from Maine's early analysis. Morgan (1877) builds on Maine's distinction to compare societas and civetas, and Redfield (1955) also develops Maine's contrast in formulating his folk-urban continuum.

We have already reviewed Piaget's (1973 [1932]) use of a small set of ideal types of individual moral reasoning to analyze ontogenetic progression, focusing on AR and EM and touching briefly on CS. Weber (1978 [1922]) explores the ideology of political and economic legitimation, focusing on MP and contrasting it with charismatic AR and with traditional authority, again a conflation of AR with CS (see Fiske 1985 for a fuller analysis and comparison). One of the remarkable points of convergence between Weber and Piaget is in their account of the perceived grounds to which people appeal in order to justify the morality of particular systems of social relations. People tend to perceive the rituals of CS as having always existed, as having been carried on since time immemorial—this is the way our parents and our ancestors acted, so we continue the traditions, perpetuating them and reenacting the old ways. The source of right in AR is the will of a personal superior, particularistic commandments taken as an end just because they are the dictates of a superior being. In MP what is right is what serves the interest of all the participants who choose to participate—people voluntarily enact whatever rules rational considerations of efficiency and utilitarian calculus lead them to agree to include in the social contract. Thus Weber and Piaget point out that people legitimate each different kind of morality with respect to a distinct ultimate source. In this approach they are in basic accord with Marx and Engels (1906 [1867]), who regard different political ideologies as derivatives of specific types of social relations, although Marx makes each type of social relations in turn the result of a particular mode of production.

## Punishment, Transgressions, Vices, and Excuses

Durkheim (1933 [1893], 1901) proposes a method of determining the fundamental kind of social relationship that structures a society by analyzing the predominant form of punishment (retributive or restitutive). Adopting Durkheim's approach and applying it to individual cognition about hypothetical cases, Piaget (1973 [1932]) interviewed children to determine what form of punishment they considered appropriate in the event of transgressions. He found that children thinking in terms of each particular kind of morality tend to believe in corresponding types of sanctions. Let us reduce his subtle account to a set of ideal types. Very young children who construe morality in terms of the uniform practice of motor regularities (CS) expect immanent justice; they do not distinguish between natural causality (physical dangers) and social sanctions. Retributive punishment based on a harsh notion of expiation is distinctive of heteronomous (AR) morality [perhaps including corporal punishment?]. Punishment is the painful consequence of the righteous anger of a personal authority, and should instill a fear of wrongdoing. Later, children become concerned with equality and acquire the idea that the transgressor should repair the harm she did. In effect, what is required is restitution (EM), and sanctions should bring about (balanced) reciprocity. This initial concern with distributive justice as equality becomes tempered by considerations of relativistic personal circumstances and evolves into a conception of justice as equity (MP). The point of this rather schematized rendition of Piaget's findings is that there appear to be distinctive conceptions of how to resolve transgressions of each of the four respective types of social relationship. The kind of punishment (if any) required for the rectification of a wrong, and more broadly the particular form of redress people consider appropriate to restore social equilibrium after a violation, is a function of the relational model people apply to the transgression. For a group based primarily on CS like the Amish, the appropriate sanction is shunning, avoidance, and excommunication, as Hostetler (1970:62–65) describes, although people may also expect immanent punishment for attempting to diverge from the traditional communal ways and seeking to be different (two informants interviewed in Larimore 1985).

Thus each model establishes a different kind of action as transgression; what is a violation depends on what the social relationship is. Ricoeur (1967) independently demonstrates this most cogently in his study of the historical development of religious perspectives on evil in the West. The earliest representation of fault, he says, was a dread of the impure. People saw misfortune as a sign of defilement and treated it as magically contagious (CS). Later people represented evil as disobedient sin that violated the sinner's personal relationship with God (AR). God responds with indignant wrath to rebellious pride or lack of faith from those who should offer only their loyal devotion—and woe betide the object of His wrath. Ricoeur reports that Westerners ultimately have come to conceptualize evil in terms of responsibility and guilt in an ethicized, rationalized system of justice (MP). Abstract reflection leads to the explicit formulation, enumeration, and systematization of rules, so that juridical sanctions are meted out in proportion to the harm caused by an infraction. Ricoeur leaves out an EM perspective that construes evil in terms of imbalance, unequal distribution of fate and benefits.[7]

Piaget (1973 [1932]) and Kohlberg (1984, Kohlberg, Levine, and Hewer 1983) also focus on the fact that what constitutes a transgression differs according to the moral framework, while Piaget in particular places moral thinking in its social context. For Piaget, the origin of the idea of moral constraint and moral necessity is in the regularities children experience in being cared for—the habits and routines of daily life and natural regularities (CS). What is wrong is what is different and unprecedented. Later children recognize their parents as powerful law givers—what is wrong is whatever parents forbid (AR). Subsequently children come to perceive wrong as inequality, lack of distributive justice or failures of reciprocity (EM). Finally they arrive at a mature conception which takes into account individual circumstances, in which what is wrong is any violation of proportional equity (MP). For Piaget, each form of moral judgment is the cognitive distillate of the experience of a particular form of social relations. That is, a model of becomes a model for. This differs from the present theory that posits relational models as endogenous models both for and of social relations, since according to our theory the abstract, empty forms of the models are prior to any social experience—they are unlearned. But surely Piaget is correct that any specific conception of right and wrong is shaped to an enormous degree by social experience (see the section Implementation in Chapter 7).

For at least two and probably three of the models, there is a particular kind of action which is the moral antithesis of the social relationship in question. Other sorts of violations represent deviations from the norms: failure to observe the prescriptions, or doing the right thing to the wrong degree or in the wrong way. But the focal taboo of a social relationship defines the relationship by contrastive opposition. That is, people predicate the relationship on the observance of a particular constitutive taboo and implicitly represent the relationship as the opposite of this taboo behavior. For example, consider the incest taboo in the United States: the very existence of the family seems to us to depend on family members' observing this taboo. Transgressing the incest taboo violates the essence of the family and makes it cease to be a family. Incest does not simply diverge from the prescriptions and ideals of Communal Sharing, it pollutes, nullifies, and destroys CS. More generally, ethnographic evidence from the Moose of Burkina Faso combined with comparative material from elsewhere in Africa suggest that the paradigmatic transgression of CS among men often entails sexual relations with some definite, culturally delineated category of prohibited woman (Fiske n.d.). The observance of some particular taboo of this sort may be necessary for the continued existence of the CS relationship; indeed adherence to the particular taboo defines the relationship, in part. Lesser transgressions like stinginess or sloth diminish CS, but they do not desecrate and invert it—they are not abominations. To see the difference, compare a man's failing to support his family with a man's having sexual relations with his daughter. Often linked with such a sexual taboo is some prohibition on eating. As Arens's (1979) research demonstrates, cannibalism is one such focal CS transgression. Like incest, people often attribute cannibalism to the totally Other, to nonhuman people who are opposed to the inclusive "We" of CS. Labeling some outside group as cannibals or committers of incest is a performative act that defines them as nonhuman, as beings who, as polar opposites, define what CS is among us.[8] Food and sex taboos seem to be focal to CS because people perceive violations as contaminating the shared substance that indexes CS: violations of these taboos all seem to involve breaches of body boundaries that corrupt the essential purity of the CS group (see Fiske n.d.).

The Moose ethnography and other comparative evidence indicates that the antithesis of Authority Ranking is probably assassination (parricide, regicide, mutinous murder). Disobedience, minor cases of lèse majesté, and other lesser offenses impair AR, but they do not necessarily destroy it, and are not generally perceived as threatening the entire system of AR as such. If social order is defined as obedience and hierarchy, so that what is good and what is necessary is doing the will of the supreme leader, then assassination annihilates order. Regarding Market Pricing, it appears that, while price gouging and profiteering, false advertising and misrepresentation, bargaining in bad faith and breach of contract all distort and infringe on MP, it is perhaps theft (piracy) that is absolutely antithetical to it. Stealing denies the validity of voluntary choice, property, and price. I do not know the focal transgression of Equality Matching. If each social relationship has a focal transgression as its polar antithesis, the taboo of EM would have to be something that fundamentally— perhaps irrevocably—inverted or perverted the relationship, something that desecrated and destroyed it utterly.

Jonathan Baron has pointed out to me in conversation that each type of social relationship depends on different virtues. Conversely, it also seems to me that each type of social relationship is uniquely susceptible to being undermined by different kinds of vices and temptations, or disrupted by particular sorts of "deviance." For example, Communal Sharing is vulnerable to greed and covetousness, Authority Ranking to tyranny on the one hand and blind obedience on the other (cf. Arendt 1977). Equality Matching is vulnerable to defection, to jealousy—immoderately wishing one had the same thing another has—and to envy—wishing the other would lose what he has that one does not. The vices of Market Pricing are deceit, avarice, and exploitation. As a balanced mode of reciprocity or taking turns, EM transfers also fail unless some are initially willing to risk an unreciprocated benefaction, although given an indefinitely continued series of interactions it is a stable morality under natural selection (Axelrod and W. Hamilton 1981, Axelrod and Dion 1988).

Douglas (1978) argues for a method of social analysis focusing on how people justify, legitimate, and excuse their behavior in relation to the constraints they perceive (and follows up Durkheim's hypothesis that the kind of punishment a society favors depends on its fundamental relational principles). Austin (1961), as well as Piaget (1973 [1932]), Much and Shweder (1978) and Kohlberg (1984, Kohlberg, Levine, and Hewer 1983) have demonstrated empirically that much can be learned from the study of excuses, justifications, and the whole range of factors people consider in assessing how responsibility for transgressions is mitigated or aggravated by the particular circumstances of the event.

A great deal of what people consider to mitigate and aggravate transgressions can be gleaned from gossip (e.g., Haviland 1977), indictments, and the like. As Lloyd-Bostock (1983) points out, even the description of "the facts" of a moral event is a choice from innumerable possible accounts, a choice that reveals what people consider to be socially relevant factors. Some of this work and my own observations suggest that the factors people take into account in judging the mitigation and aggravation of culpability differ as a function of the model people employ in making a moral judgment.

Although this is a complex, uncultivated topic, it is possible to make some ideal type distinctions that may apply to focal transgressions, at least. In CS, for example, the transgressor's intention and even her sincerity or belief may be irrelevant in judging whether she is defiled or immanently dangerous. For example, traditional Bedouins might kill a daughter who dishonored the band by being raped, even if she resisted the rape and was not personally at fault in any way. Under AR people appear to judge behavior with respect to pure outcome, assessed in terms of the absolute amount of benefit or harm (damage) done, regardless of whether or not it was foreseeable or controllable (Piaget 1973 [1932]). Governmental leaders are effectively held accountable for the economy, or for success in war, regardless of whether they have any control over events. Conformity to the letter of the law is also important. In contrast, for MP the actual harm done may sometimes be irrelevant, if people judge only on the "rational" basis of intent, due care, and foreseeability. MP excuses may thus focus on procedural issues, and justifications should focus on the legitimacy of the goals given the means. When MP excuses and justifications are consequentialist, they should compare the (incidental) costs with the (significant) benefits of the action. These are preliminary speculations, not conclusions, but this is a crucial problem that requires attention. (For one thing, the qualifying factors that affect EM culpability remain to be analyzed.) Understanding what mitigates and what aggravates responsibility for transgression and what counts as a justification is important, since it reveals just what transgression is for each kind of model, and by contrast, just what probity is.


## INTERPRETATIONS OF MISFORTUNE

Many observers have noted that people try to make moral sense of their own and others' misfortunes: Weber (1975), Evans-Pritchard (1937), Mitchell (1965), Horton (1967), Ricoeur (1967), Lerner and Mathews (1967), Ryan (1971), Geertz (1973a), Gillies (1976), Guimera (1978), Kiernan (1982). People may judge themselves guilty and try to understand what they have done to deserve their suffering—they want to know how they have transgressed and against whom. People may hold others responsible and look for another person to accuse of committing a wrong against them. Or they may consult diviners to determine who is morally responsible, what moral breach has occurred, and what the social, ritual, or religious remedy is. This is the inverse of the issue we considered above in the discussion of transgressions. In the case of transgressions people start with wrongdoing and find an appropriate sanction, while here people start with a presumed "punishment" and find a corresponding wrongdoing (their own or someone else's against them).

When people search for a disrupted relationship that might explain the misfortune, the relationship may be an imputed one that people carry on with immaterial or intangible social beings; it need not be a relationship among living persons. So long as people construe their actions in social terms, a "relationship" exists, even if the skeptical observer perceives it to be unilateral. In Africa, for example, people very often make the inference that illness, death, drought, and major setbacks are the ancestors' punishment for some offense against them, or else the work of malevolent, greedy witches acting wrongfully against the victims. Unpublished interview research by my students indicates that although Americans lack the same kind of cultural channels and institutional provisions for pursuing such inferences, they usually share this concern for finding moral sense in suffering. There are four principal socio-moral frameworks in which people can interpret misfortune:

People can regard misfortune as marking the victims as different and opposed to members of the group. Here, misfortune is an index of defilement, so that people outcast victims (CS; see Ricoeur 1967). In this CS frame people may also treat victims as jinxed, unlucky, and hence dangerous, and avoid all contact with them. Although Americans do not consciously hold this attitude, it is remarkable that victims of grave misfortunes, as well as their relatives and friends, find that, in effect, they are shunned. Even when people do approach such victims they carefully avoid raising the topic of the death or suffering. This is the experience of people who have lost a child to sudden infant death syndrome, and of accident and cancer victims—never mind people infected with AIDS (for AIDS, see Nemeroff 1988; Rozin, Markwith, and McCauley n.d.). Sometimes people suffer more from the social isolation than from the loss or pain itself. L. T. Doi (1981) perceptively probes the resentful feeling of abandonment Japanese and others feel when death or other loss deprives them of the nurturant CS dependence they long for (amaeru).

People may also interpret their own or other's misfortune as a sign of abandonment by God or the ancestors, as the Moose do (AR; see also Ricoeur 1967, Kiernan 1982). Suffering may be due to the righteous wrath of higher beings like ancestors, as a consequence of disobedience, disloyalty, or lèse majesté (see Fortes 1959, 1965; Guimera 1978). Where people believe in witchcraft and sorcery, they may construe misfortune as the social result of envy on the part of jealous neighbors or associates who act as if the victim had more than his share of good things (EM). In another Equality Matching belief, Moose, like many other peoples, fear that sorcerers will attack anyone who appears to be better off than his neighbors and kinspeople, out of spite: sorcerers make others lose the good things they have so as to bring them down to their own level (see Evans-Pritchard 1937). Sorcerers and other beings may also harm humans in tit-for-tat retribution for people's offenses against them. People sometimes rail against the unevenness of fate, complaining that "It's not fair!" when they suffer some calamity that makes them worse off than those who escape the same fate—but who should be on a level with them. In yet another EM outlook on misfortune, people often take the attitude that, "Things even out in the long run," or anxiously anticipate that something bad will happen to counterbalance some good fortune ("knock on wood"). This suggests an implicit expectation of offsetting fortunes, also exhibited when people act as if "the odds" even out, so that a string of lost bets makes a win more likely.

Finally, people sometimes treat adversity or catastrophe as a "price to pay" for taking a calculated risk and making an "expensive" mistake (MP). "You got off cheap!" they say, or "That was more than I bargained for." Bulman and Wortman (1977) found that victims of permanent spinal injury were able to cope better if they could make sense of it by interpreting it as a known risk they took after voluntarily making a rational choice in return for specific benefits they actually had enjoyed. In essence we might say that they felt that although their choice really "cost" them a lot because they got a "bad deal," they had "bought into" a known risk and "paid the price," so the paralysis was intelligible in Market Pricing quasi-contractual terms. Then again, people would feel that the cost was all out of proportion with the fault if in a moment's carelessness a soldier "bought it" by tripping a mine. And they would be outraged at this disproportion.

One might be inclined to ask why people make such "superstitious" attributions about their misfortunes. The answer may be that it is only because they have a proclivity to interpret sanctions as sociomoral signs that they are able to function in society. If children and adults were not predisposed to recognize suffering as misfortune and to seek out an antecedent transgression, it would be impossible to socialize anyone, or to regulate social behavior and enforce norms effectively. Although the culture-specific parameters have to be learned, it is not a matter of "internalization" of norms. People are prepared to appreciate punishments as such, and intrinsically motivated to respond so as to redress the social relationship that has been jeopardized. Only sociopaths do not distinguish between "punishment" in the S–R learning theory sense and "punishment" in the sociomoral and legal sense. That is what makes them incorrigible and impossible to "socialize." Jural (moral or legal) punishment—or the possibility of punishment—is only effective to the extent that the recipient regards it as a sign of the disruption of a social relationship that he wants to sustain. Otherwise it is only a risk factor to take into account and avoid. Consider trying to discipline a child who did not care about disapproval and cared nothing for pleasing authorities, who never felt humiliation, guilt, or regret, and who did not distinguish between the social significance of being spanked and the causal consequences of putting his hand in the fire. If the child had no endogenous proclivity to interpret suffering as the sign of disequilibrium in social relationships, then he would never acquire any commitment to doing right in social relations. He would be amoral.

Normal people commonly interpret misfortune by putting it into a sociomoral framework in which suffering is either wrongdoing against the victim (for which the perpetrator may merit punishment) or a punishment for the victim's wrongdoing. If people regard suffering as an index of disequilibrium in their social relations and are motivated to try to work out what has gone wrong in their social relations, then they will try to set them right again. This is appropriate when the suffering is administered at the hands of some human agent, and leads to redress and/or punishment that tends to restore the disrupted social relationship. When there is no human agent, as when lightning strikes or cancer kills someone, interpreting misfortune in moral terms is overgeneralization, and is irrational. However, as Evans-Pritchard (1937) and others have pointed out, the fear that you will be suspected and eventually accused of witchcraft if you are rude, selfish, or otherwise antisocial can be a potent mechanism of social control. And, as has often been stated, the belief that gods, spirits, and ancestors strike down—or fail to protect from other malevolent beings—violators of the social order is likewise a powerful support to that order. So these sociomoral interpretations of misfortune as punishments or attacks by nonhuman beings have substantial functional consequences for the maintenance of social relations between human beings.

My hypothesis is that normal people tend to use just the basic set of four relational models to do this. Often people regard the form of the misfortune as indicative of the particular kind of relationship that has been transgressed (e.g., Gillies 1976, Guimera 1978). But whether they make this connection or not, people do seek to understand misfortune in sociomoral terms, and they use each of the four fundamental models to interpret suffering. We are currently exploring the conditions that lead people to do this, and trying to discover when people resort to each particular model.

## Religion

Lebra's (1976:234–47) study of spirit possession in Japan reveals how three of the basic models emerge in the Salvation Cult. Some ancestral and guardian spirits may punish the person whom they possess, indicating displeasure for the devotee's lack of discipline and devotion (AR). Possession by high status spirits gives prestige to devotees, elevating their status in the cult. When the possessed person serves the possessing spirit with offerings and prayers, the spirit incurs a reciprocal *on* obligation to repay the person (and others who have participated) with corresponding benefactions (EM). In general, however, spirits possess people because the spirit itself is suffering as a result of having committed some *tsumi* (sin or blood/water pollution) like suicide, homicide, adultery, rape, abortion, or miscarriage while it was a living person, or having died a violent—hence polluting—death. The spirit is afflicting the human sufferer to appeal for sympathy for its own suffering. The spirit, isolated from other spirits and lonely, neglected and abandoned by human survivors, seeks to be saved by joining its own ancestors or a group of spirits of its own kind (CS). The supplicant spirit is asking for empathic indulgence (*amaeru?*) from a responsive, dependable human, preferably one with whom it has blood ties. The possessed cult member cares for the spirit by repetitive penitent acts and prayers, apologizing to appropriate deities on the spirit's behalf. Above all, the possessed person nurtures the hungry spirit in a maternal manner, making the spirit offerings of its favorite food and drink (especially milk and baby food). This nurturance also includes repetitive mantras and the pouring of sacred, purifying hydrangea tea over the spot where the spirit resides. Spirit possessions occur when a member of the cult suffers a misfortune, and the possession explains misfortune as a consequence of the spirit's need for a CS relationship with the sufferer, in consequence of a polluting event that is antithetical to the spirit's CS relations with others.[9]

It is not only in situations of suffering that people posit the existence of intangible beings and interact with them socially. Lorenz (1970 [1932–1937]) describes various animals' spontaneous performance of fixed action patterns. The behavior runs off, more or less fully formed, in the absence of its usual object, especially when the animal has been deprived of the releasing stimulus for a long time. For example, a caged bird fed an artificial diet picks nonexistent insects out of the air, using the same motions it would use if it encountered real insects. From the perspective of the present theory we can construe a great part of religion as a "vacuum activity" of this kind in which people interact with nonhuman beings to whom they impute social motives. Generalizing and refining what Horton (1967) observes for Africa, the essence of this aspect of religion is the projection of one or more of the basic relational models outside the human realm, so that people relate socially to beings who may be perceived as lacking other human features, or endowed with extrahuman features. In effect, people collaboratively implement one of the fundamental models in the absence of any actual living human partner in one or more of the key positions—carrying out a social relationship in a partial vacuum.

Pace Freud (1975 [1928], 1967 [1937]) and Durkheim (1965 [1912]), religion is not simply an extension of childhood experience[10] or an apperception of the transcendent nature of society. Rather, both social relationships with humans and religous relations with gods and other beings have a common source. Each derives its forms from these endogenous relational models, basic forms that cultures elaborate in unique and distinctive directions. African and Western religions include phases of both CS and AR relations with religious beings. In African religions, Turner (1973:206–7) describes the mutuality of earth and fertility cults (CS), in contrast to the hierarchically differentiated structure of ancestral and political religious practices (AR). This contrast is quite evident in Moose religion. In Western religion, one has only to think of the patriarchal Old Testament God (AR), in contrast to the self-sacrifice of Christ embodied in the rite of communion (CS) and the maternally loving Virgin Mary (see Parsons [1969] on South Italy, and also L. T. Doi [1981:16, 92–3]). L. T. Doi (1981:62–3) describes the ancestors and the emperor whom Japanese worship as beings whose desire for passive dependence (*amaeru*) is totally fulfilled. In the institutional organization of churches, consider the parallel contrast between papal authority and the collectivist consensualism of the Society of Friends (Quakers). EM and MP relations with noncorporeal beings probably are more common around the world than the Judaic, Christian, and Islamic traditions would lead us to expect (consider Greek mythology). The comparative study of religious beliefs and practices and mythology and folktales from this perspective offers a potentially interesting way to explore the nature of the underlying social models. There are many important cultural determinants of religion, mythology, and folk tales, but the point is that these forms of social relations and social cognition have significant degrees of freedom because there is no actual human interactant out there, only the believers' imputations. These conceptions and actions are not constrained by the same kind of biological and social facts that may limit the realization of some aspects of the models in interactions with corporal, motivated, responding human beings. So religion, mythology and folktales may be interpretable as projections that reveal facets of the models that are not readily apparent in social relations among humans.

People make moral interpretations of misfortune with reference to the four fundamental models, and they realize the models in religion. Globally, the chief significance of this for our relational theory is that these phenomena are "projective" manifestations of psychological proclivities. In these interpretations of misfortune people often are imputing social purpose to events and states that are not the product of human action. In religion, people are generating social relationships with nonexistent beings, and treating natural events as social communications. There is nothing in the physics of a lightning bolt or the biology of high voltage currents in the human body that requires people to interpret death by lightning as a punishment for angering a superior being. If people decide that a man has died as a moral consequence of angering the ancestors, it is not the ancestors themselves who suggest that interpretation. There is no ecological reason why people have to attribute the uneven distribution of locust damage to the jealousy of sorcerers aggravated by some other inequality. Such inferences have to be the product of human minds—acting individually or in social concert, whether Moose victims following cultural recipes to make sense of their concerns, or American victims struggling with unintelligible emotions. Of course, it makes a lot of difference to the victim to have a culturally formulated question, a defined set of alternative answers, and a specified mechanism for finding the right answer. But the need to find moral meaning in misfortune and to believe that there is social order in the natural world is a psychological need; although culture directs and modulates it, culture does not create the need. This interpretive need indicates the operation of the four fundamental models in the absence of the relevant relational partners. These imputations of social intent in natural phenomena demonstrate dramatically how potent the models are, and how much they permeate human social perceptions.

# CODA—DISCORD AND HARM

To balance an impression that may have been created by the preceding four chapters, this codicil considers mayhem and anguish. The topic is the ways people harm each other in the name of the four fundamental models, how the models produce distress, and how they can go wrong.

## Conflict and Aggression

It may seem that the theory of relational models can explain social harmony better than it can account for conflict, but it is not a functionalist theory. It is perfectly possible for people to have discordant assumptions about which model applies to a particular situation, and it is common to have conflict over who will assume particular roles (e.g., who will be duly constituted as the authority) and who is included in the scope of a given social relationship (e.g., who is included in the equal shares of a distribution under Equality Matching). Also, it is important to note that the present theory postulates that people consider themselves to have moral obligations only if and when they construe themselves as having one of these types of social relationships with the people concerned, that is, when they are applying one of these models to the issue. For example, while people give freely and merge their identities under Communal Sharing, if there are people who are not included in the CS relation in any domain at any time, then such people are no different from bugs, bushes, or stones. Sabini (in press) points out that the atrocities performed in the Nazi concentration camps were made possible in part by the systematic degradation of the victims (see Haney, Banks, and Zimbardo 1988 [1973]). That is, extreme brutality is facilitated by breaking down people's sense (if any) of common humanity, destroying the residual generalized sense of Communal Sharing people tend to feel toward any other human. Without any of the four basic bonds of social relationship to give moral meaning to interactions, people operate in the Asocial mode, treating others as merely instrumental means or impediments to their ends—no different from rocks or weeds. The slaughter of the native populations of the New World and Tasmania by many groups of European settlers and their descendants, continuing up to the present in parts of Brazil, is only one example of how people may treat others with whom they do not recognize any CS commonality, any shared corporate substance, origin, collective identity, or any other social relationship. Conversely, deindividuation among actors (a form of CS) may lead to mob violence (Diener 1980).

Moreover, conflict may be caused by or justified in the name of any of these models. People may commit violence in outrage when they hold that someone has wronged and harmed them in violating any of the four models. As Pastore

(1952) shows and Sabini and Silver (1982) explain, anger is the result of people's perceiving an injustice, the violation of an important social norm. The same can be said of envy, shame, embarrassment, the sense of wounded honor, the righteous thirst for revenge, and other moral emotions. They represent people's social construction of a situation as not in accord with the applicable model. These emotions, of course, are closely associated with aggression. Trivers (1971) and Frank (1988) analyze the evolutionary basis for moral emotional reactions to transgression, showing that such emotions may be essential for the maintenance of sociable relations. So while the four models shape social relations, not all social relations are amicable. Aggression and strife may be just as socially coherent as solidarity, and they have some of the same sources.

The Communal Sharing relationship is capable of generating great bloodshed. In many traditional societies in the Mediterranean culture area, patrilineal kin groups were so dishonored by extramarital or premarital sexual relations of their wives or daughters that the offended group might well kill the woman (even if she were raped) and kill her despoiler, starting a blood feud (Peristiany 1966). On the basis of the same model, people may fight a war to incorporate others like them into the motherland, feeling that people who are alike in language, culture, and race naturally and inevitably belong together (whatever the cost). Conversely, people may be exterminated because their killers regard them as polluting the purity of shared substance of the breeding stock of the ancestral race.

To see the agonistic side of Communal Sharing, one has only to look at the ethnic and racial conflicts, wars, atrocities, or genocide in the last 30 years in the United States, the Soviet Union, Zaire, Uganda, Burundi, Soudan, Nigeria, Bangladesh, India, Kashmir, Sri Lanka, the Middle East, and many other parts of the world, as well as religious conflicts and wars. An element of many such conflicts is that people feel injured and threatened by harm to members of their own ethnic group or religion, and consequently strike out at the perpetrating group. This is based on a sense of identity: harming any of us harms me. Furthermore, desecrating any of the symbols of a CS group's collective identity (flags, shrines, sacred books, mascots) often leads to angry violence against the offending group. Conversely, CS categorization applied to hostile groups typically leads the avengers to hold all the members of the offending group collectively responsible, and thus proper targets for retribution—killing any member of the enemy is equivalent to killing those who committed the original act. All such violence is based on the nominal equivalence of all the members of a salient social category.

There have been innumerable murders, coups, and wars over accession to leadership, and other wars when rulers attempted to extend their authority over people who did not accept their subjugation. European history exhibits many such wars over royal succession and dominion. On a smaller scale, people may kill or maim those whom they perceive to be violating the limits of Authority Ranking relations: Lèse majesté, whether actual harm or simple affront to the dignity of the sovereign, has been regarded as a treasonous capital offense. People may be tortured or suffer other corporal punishment for sedition—that is, merely for holding an authority in contempt. In parts of Latin America, Africa, and elsewhere around the world, people are executed or "disappeared" for refusal to accept the legitimacy of political authorities or their edicts. And mutiny or failure to obey orders is often a capital offense in wartime military forces. The other side of this is that rebellions, coups d'état, assassination and tyrannicide often result from subjects' judgment that sovereigns have abused their authority. Either success or failure in such attempts to overthrow leaders may lead to the slaughter of thousands.

Remember also that at Nuremberg and Jerusalem the Nazis who tried to exterminate the Jews and Gypsies explained their actions as simple obedience to authority (Arendt 1977). Milgram (1974) showed that most ordinary Americans would torture strangers if calmly and firmly told to do so by another stranger. Any military force in wartime (or war-like conditions) offers appalling evidence of the violence that men will commit if ordered to do so by authorities they perceive to be legitimate. In all these cases, people consider their killing or mayhem to be justified and even required by the dicta of AR. People may also kill themselves if commanded to do so, as the events of Jonestown, Guyana prove (Ulman and Abse 1983).

Adherence to Equality Matching may produce endless reciprocal bloodshed in feuds, or lead to tit-for-tat reprisals between groups or nations. For example, Schieffelin (1976) describes how the Kaluli of New Guinea balance violence for violence very precisely, based on their explicitly elaborated cultural sense of evenly matched reciprocation. Reagan held Libya responsible for bombing Americans, so he bombed them in retaliation, as the Israeli air force bombs "Palestinian guerilla bases" in revenge for terrorist attacks. The principle of equal retaliation has been elaborated by sophisticated philosophers; see Dworkin's (1985) rationalization of a "bounce-back device" and Kavka's (1987:40–42) critique. In addition, politicians and military planners argue for the creation of nuclear arsenals with reference to the moral or political "necessity" to maintain balance, that is, equality in the number of machines for wiping out human kind. An-eye-for-an-eye, a-tooth-for-a-tooth, a-life-for-a-life, people match harm for harm—and believe it is right.

EM can be grounds for violence in other ways. Sabini (in press) observes that in the Milgram experiments, subjects felt that it was fair to shock the learner, apparently because they believed that the respective roles of teacher and learner had been decided by a fair lottery—an EM device. People seem to have considered the injury and death that occurred in duels to be excusable so long as the duel was fair, so that both parties had an equal chance of death. Many feel the same way about injury in boxing matches. Shirley Jackson (1949) gives a compelling fictional account of the thinking underlying aggression legitimated by EM in her short story, "The Lottery."

Market Pricing (as opposed to mere competition) is the source of conflict when nations battle to open or preserve markets, whether under mercantilism or modern capitalism. The conquistadors searched for gold with bloody swords, and some contemporary gold seekers in Brazil carry on the tradition of murdering indigenous peoples. People operating in an MP mentality generated appalling bloodshed, atrocities, and misery when they enslaved people, sold them as commodities, and forced them to work and breed for their owners' profit. We do not call this war, but it was worse than war. Later, the leaders and administrators for European nations were again impelled by an MP rationale when they attempted to convert the economies of African colonies to comprehensive Market Pricing, for example by introducing a per capita tax and obliging people to grow cash crops. This wreaked havoc on the indigenous people, and labor recruitment and migration in search of wage labor continue to split and destroy innumerable families. The miseries wrought by the commoditization of land (the enclosure movement) and labor in the industrial revolution are also well documented. Today, the improvident borrowing and unwise expenditures (and corruption) of business and political leaders in many developing nations have effectively bankrupted many nations, forcing them to adopt austerity measures and free market price systems imposed by the International Monetary Fund and other creditors. This austerity and the abrupt shift to a market economy often mean hunger and suffering among the poor.

Just as people may argue in EM terms for evenly balanced nuclear deterrence, American planning for nuclear war also appears to be organized with reference to the MP terms of efficient expenditure on weapons, and their "rational" design and use. Decisions are based on a calculus of "benefit" to cost ratios—where the benefits are death and destruction. Similarly, American military leaders in the Vietnam war devised and justified operations in terms of favorable "kill ratios," as if deaths were commodities on which one could make a profit. These are not examples of people justifying anger or aggression after the fact in order to exonerate themselves; they are instances of an MP mentality guiding people to plan to kill millions and wipe out civilization.

Most aggression thus has the same basic sources as compassion and morality. Our relational-models theory depicts people as naturally aggressive in the same four ways that they are naturally sociable. Aggression and conflict are the obverse of kindness, respect and responsibility, equality, and market rationality. People also harm others when they fail to apply any of the models and do not engage the other in any of the basic forms of human relationships; in such Null or Asocial cases, people are just things, to which one has no obligations. And people initiate or justify injurious acts in the name of principles—like equality or rational efficiency—derived from each of the four models. But more often, people attack when they feel wronged, punishing someone whom they perceive to have transgressed against one of the four fundamental social relationships.

## Dysfunction and "Clinical" Implications

These models can also generate other kinds of stress and strife short of physical injury. Unstated—or even explicit but unreconciled—discrepancies between the models that people use in structuring their relationships may result in both sides repeatedly feeling betrayed. For example, in a marriage or any other relationship, actions concordant with Authority Ranking offend a partner who expects Equality Matching, just as adherence to Market Pricing principles violates a partner's Communal Sharing assumptions (see Fiske 1990). Some models may be unsuitable for some domains, so that they never work smoothly, break down constantly, or are doomed to failure (Fiske and Baron n.d.; see also Schwinger 1980). Imagine organizing decision making in an army or a battleship in action by CS consensus, or structuring a university along the lines of EM so that everyone performs equal amounts of each and every institutional task in turn. Reflect on Udy's (1959, 1970) finding that in the societies he studied people never organized the entire cycle of core productive activities in the form of EM. Consider the fact that China and the Soviet Union have tried moving away from centralized state direction of their economies as they faced the limitations of AR in organizing large-scale production and exchange. On the other hand, think of using MP to organize all the tasks within the nuclear family; to my knowledge there is no culture in which this has ever been done. But Wood (1985) discusses clinical literature arguing that many families require more autonomy and individuation, and cites a survey showing that this is the goal of 87 percent of family therapists. In other words, American therapists believe that too much familial CS is pathological. L. T. Doi (1981:101–41) discusses a number of pathologies of CS in Japan, but he states that a major aim of much Japanese psychotherapy is to enable people to become more dependent.

Delineation of the elementary forms of social relationships is the first step toward an inventory of the set of potential interpersonal problems. Horowitz (1979, Horowitz and Vitkus 1986) finds that the interpersonal problems that psychiatric patients present at intake interviews ("I can't . . .") have a semantic structure described by the two basic dimensions—affiliation (love, friendship) and control (power, status). Horowitz and Vitkus (1986) show that this kind of analysis of the underlying forms of social relations can contribute to developing a systematic theory of how to interact with people therapeutically to help them deal with such problems. Furthermore, the implication of the findings discussed earlier about individual differences in relationship-specific motivations is that people vary in the kinds of relationships in which they are most comfortable and fulfilled. Conversely, it may be that some people are so strongly motivated to interact in a particular mode that they attempt to oblige others to interact with them in just that modality, with sometimes unfortunate consequences. Other people may be unhappy if constrained to engage in even normal levels of some modes of interaction.

The more we understand about how social relationships operate in ideal equilibrium, the more we will know about how they can malfunction. Perhaps it is the malfunctioning of these models or their misimplementation that is the cause of what are called "personality" disorders (Millon 1981). Personality disorders (see American Psychiatric Association 1987) appear to be either hypersocial or hypo-social malfunctions of normal relational models. Some, like borderline personality (Knight 1953, Gunderson and Singer 1975, Hartocollis 1977, Soloff and Milward 1983), antisocial personality (McCord and McCord 1964, Hare 1970, Cleckley 1988) and histrionic, narcissistic, dependent, and avoidant personality disorders, involve intensified expectations, concerns, demands, needs, and valuations of normal models. Schizoid personality disorder and possibly some others may be characterized by a lack of motivation to participate in—and undervaluation of—the normal forms of relationship. In other words, they appear to be motivational excesses or deficits of normal social models. The present theory of relational models may elucidate the nature of these disorders by suggesting a typology of the elementary modes of relationship that may malfunction and specifying the structures of the underlying social models that are dysfunctional. Conversely, the study of people with such personality disorders may reveal a great deal about the structure of normal social relationships and the ways in which ordinary people apply them in moderation and with culturally appropriate modulation. A better understanding of normal moral evaluations, emotions and intrinsic social motivations may also result from the study of paranoid disorder (persistent, unrealistic fear that others intend illegitimate harm), as well as depression (feelings of excessive guilt, self-reproach, and worthlessness accompanied by social withdrawal), and dysthymic disorder (depressive symptoms accompanied by excessive irritability and anger, together with an inability to respond to praise or social rewards) (see American Psychiatric Association 1987). It is conceivable that autism represents the more or less complete lack of the capacity to use any of the basic models for social relations: if so, then it reveals a great deal about just what these elementary forms of social relations consist of. In all these disorders, it would be valuable to investigate the hypothesis that there are specific disorders resulting from the dysfunction of each of the four models separately.

None of the social relationships is uniformly benign merely by virtue of functioning in a clinically "normal" manner as a stable system. The fact that people are well integrated into such a relationship in equilibrium by no means guarantees that the participants are ipso facto happy, or that they are contributing to the larger social system. Beyond the abuses and pathologies to which each type of model is vulnerable when it is distorted, there are intrinsic drawbacks, risks, and possibilities for extrinsic harm even in the prototypical equilibrium functioning of each. The study of these dangers must be placed high on the agenda of the social sciences.

# CONCLUSION TO PART II

I have focused here on the comparison of social relationships across these diverse domains to demonstrate the parallels and thus begin to characterize the elementary relational models that may produce the common relational structures. I have had two purposes in discussing this wide range of social domains. First, it is important for people in each of these fields to be aware of parallel work in other disciplines. Second, the discovery of the same four structures in so many disparate domains that people have independently studied with diverse methods and distinct biases reveals something fundamental about the common structures. It shows that the structures are not products of the specific conditions of each kind of interaction or thought. Demonstrating that the same four forms of social relationships cut across all these domains proves that they are generated by something that operates in all of the domains. These forms of relationship are products of something that transcends and encompasses all social processes, something that gives order—the same order—to all of them: the human mind. The discovery of congruent structures in such diverse domains is strong evidence that in each case people are using the same four blueprints to produce the structures. People desire, feel obligated, and know how to relate to each other in just four basic ways.

Some readers familiar with the original sources may feel that I have lumped together social relations that ought to be split: for example, does Turner's account of communitas really correspond to Ricoeur's description of evil as sin? Is either of these equivalent to distributive justice defined according to a principle of need? Are the Japanese desire to *amaeru* that L. T. Doi describes and the !Kung sharing that Marshall describes also culture-specific manifestations of the same CS model? My hypothesis is that all of these social forms are actually generated out of the same underlying model, expressed in different social domains in different cultural traditions, analyzed from the perspectives of five different academic disciplines. (In the next chapter, 7, I show how this phenomenological diversity of manifestations arises, and in Chapter 9 I show, conversely, that these different manifestations of a given model have the same formal relational properties.) Indeed, the congruences among the manifestations of the same model in different domains are such that in composing this book I was often struck by the rather arbitrary rhetorical choices I had to make in presenting a particular theoretical or empirical description in one section rather than describing it under the rubric of some other domain. Frequently the choice was dictated by the stance taken by the author, rather than the substance of the account: Lévi-Strauss's analysis of the exchange of women would have fit equally well in the sections on marriage systems, on transactions, or on moral systems. Hence any catalog of social domains is to some degree merely heuristic—and mine is far from complete. As I shall explain in

136

the next chapter, any actual, sustained social interaction and every complex role and institution almost invariably involves combinations of the basic models, intercalated in various ways. For this reason, empirical descriptions of social relations in the literature often conflate two or more basic models, and some previously proposed theoretical types have been mixtures of distinct models. Some researchers ignore one or two models, some conflate certain pairs (especially EM and MP, or EM and CS). But the evidence converges on just four basic types, and wherever we examine the structure of social relations the same four basic types of relational models emerge again and again. Table 1 summarizes these four chapters and some other aspects of the theory.

The relational models theory makes many empirically testable predictions. Perhaps the most direct deduction from the theory is the hypothesis that these four models are salient schemas in naive, intuitive social cognition. Fiske et al. (n.d.) tested this prediction in five studies examining the pattern of substitutions in naturally occurring social errors when people confuse one person with another. Two studies investigated instances in which people called a familiar person by the wrong name, one examined memory errors in which people misremembered with whom they had interacted on some occasion, one looked at actions that were mistakenly directed to an inappropriate person, and one encompassed all three kinds of errors. All five studies provide support for the theory, revealing a strong tendency to confuse two people with whom the subject interacts in the same basic relationship mode. The effects of basic relationship mode were independent of most of the effects of the attributes inhering in the person, and remain significant after partialling out the effects of the correlated confusions among individuals with similar personal attributes.

Once we establish the existence of these four basic relational models and their constitutive role in giving form to all the dimensions of social relations, we can proceed in four possible directions. One is to try to address the question of who uses which model in what domains, and when. My belief is that history and culture are by far the major determinants, and that to decipher these determinants we will need to follow the lead of Marx, Durkheim, Weber, and more recent ethnohistorical initiatives. While studying the nature of the models is a social psychological task, the primary factors that affect the selective application of the models are not themselves psychological: most of the variance is at the level of culture. One of my intentions in Part IV is to illustrate this fact. Nevertheless, the present synchronic theory lacks some of the integrative power of the more specific theories of Maine, Marx, Durkheim, Weber, Ricoeur, Piaget, Erasmus, Udy, Blau, Sahlins, Turner, Guillet, and Douglas, since it is not yet a dynamic account of the conditions for each of the forms of social relationships or of the kinetic processes of transformations and diachronic transitions among them. The theory needs to be developed in the direction of understanding process, stability, transformation and change. If it has value in its present state, it is because it promises to integrate much of the fundamental work in social science by providing a common taxonomy of fundamental forms and illuminating the psychological sources of these forms. Thus it may provide a foundation for transcending our current understanding.

The second possible direction in which to proceed is to try to work out the "syntax" of these relational models, the patterns of combination and exclusion among them. This is to pursue the goal of analyzing the *langue*, the grammatical system that constrains how the elementary relational models can be put together. Preliminary exploration in this direction is a major objective of Part III. The third possible direction is to explore the *parole*, the tactics and practice of social relations. This is the study (possibly idiographic) of people's daily implementations of the shared models for their more or less idiosyncratically convergent or cross purposes. People presumably can manipulate the models and exploit cultural ambiguities in order to pursue ulterior objectives (whether individual or corporate). In this book I do not follow up this avenue.

The fourth course of action is to attempt to discover additional new elementary relational models through some combination of ethnography, cultural comparison, and formal analysis. There are a few forms of interaction that need further consideration as possible basic forms, although they are probably qualitatively different from the basic four. In particular, are joking relations (see Radcliffe-Brown 1965a, 1965b; Kennedy 1970; Howell 1973) and sexual bonding pure types, or are they each built out of mixtures and compromises among the elementary forms? By the criteria set out in Chapter 8, neither sex nor joking are elementary models. The evidence to date does not suggest that there are any other fundamental forms of sociability that consistently emerge out of well-grounded observations in more than one domain. But Part IV scouts some ethnographic terrain to begin checking on the ethnocentrism or adequacy outside our own culture area of our inductive derivation of these four models.

# Part *III*

# The Structures of Social Relations

PREFACE TO PART III

A general theory of social relations ought to explain the complexity and diversity of social relations in terms of a few elementary principles. Within and across cultures, social relations are strikingly intricate and varied—and a general theory has to encompass all this.

Chapter 7 shows how the set of four simple models can generate complex social relationships, roles, groups, institutions, and societies. People produce complex social relations by applying the models at a variety of levels (lower levels embedded—nested—within higher levels) and concatenating the models together in various combinations. Chapter 7 also answers the question of how a few universal models can generate the great cultural diversity of social systems that we see around the world and through history. The general principles involved in producing diversity from a small set of elements are quite simple. First, there are diverse implementation rules that determine the domains and persons to which people apply each model (rules that specify when a model is applicable). The rules for selecting which model to apply to a given domain of social activity, and indeed the cultural construction of domains themselves, vary greatly across cultures. For example, what "marriage" is and which models govern which phases of marriage depend on the culture. Second, there is great latitude about how to set the parameters necessary for implementing the abstract, "empty" models. Different cultures implement the same fundamental model differently, according to how they specify the free, arbitrary parameters for a given model in each domain. For example, given that two cultures both organize labor exchanges among "friends" according to Equality Matching, they may still differ greatly in what they define as constituting quid pro quo reciprocity, and what sorts of delays are appropriate in reciprocating. Third, there are semiotic variations: cultures differ in the signs people use to mark the existence and status of each type of relationship (e.g., Ashanti chiefs sit on carved stools; European monarchs sit on thrones). Finally, there are major ideological differences in cultural precepts about what kinds of social relationship are good, what kinds are real or "natural," and what are possible.

To evaluate the claim that the four models are elementary and fundamental, we need to specify criteria for inclusion in this analytic category. Hence Chapter 8 considers the general nature of the set of four models people use to generate social relations. What kind of "models" of social relations and for social relations are we talking about? How are they similar to, or distinct from, other sorts of rules, grammars, precepts, and standards? To make explicit the nature of the theoretical claim that people use these models to generate social relations, Chapter 8 addresses the nature of the category such models comprise. What are the definitive or characteristic features of these shared moral-legal models that set them apart from other cultural models and cognitive representations? To address this question, I advance claims about the sociological, cultural, psychological, and evolutionary status of these models. This provides a foundation for future searches for any additional elementary models that may exist.

Then in Chapter 9, I propose the hypothesis that people use a distinctive sign type to communicate about each model. That is, I suggest that there is a distinctive primary mode of representation that people characteristically use to mark and coordinate each kind of social relationship. Then I offer an outline (developed with Scott Weinstein) of the formal relational mathematics of the four models. We show that the relational structures of the models can be constructed axiomatically. This approach facilitates the analysis of what kinds of distinctions and associations operate in each model and how the four models are related as a set. Results from measurement theory suggest that the four basic relational models belong to a very small set of fundamental relational structures characterized by special mathematical properties, and that fact may help explain why there are so few elementary forms of relationships.

I provide only theoretical suggestions and illustrations here; hard evidence about the adequacy of the proposals I offer here will have to come from future ethnographic, historical, economic, political, sociological, and social psychological research. The focus in Part III is pure theory, and the reader who wishes to get a better feel for the concrete manifestations of these models might well read Part IV first, taking on faith for the time being my grand claim that the four basic models are tools powerful enough to build most components of almost any society. But for those who want to delve into the problem of just what these models are and how they operate, who want to explore the nature of the models as such, Part III is the next step.[1]

# 7

# Generativity and Cross-Cultural Variability in the Production of Social Relations

*I*s it really conceivable that the incredible variety of forms of social interaction in any society, let alone the range of patterns known from the thousands of varied cultures in the world, could be generated by four basic structures? Yes. A little exploration will demonstrate how these four elementary models can generate a myriad of complex and culturally diverse personal relationships, social roles, groups, institutions, social systems, and international relations.

There are three aspects of the construction of social relationships that result in a limitless variety of surface manifestations of a limited set of relatively simple underlying models. First, the models are in one sense "empty" principles, which can be realized in behavior only within the context of certain arbitrary cultural rules. These indefinitely varied conventions result in a phenomenological multiformity of realizations of each fundamental structure. Second, the recursive application of the same model at successive embedded levels results in a limitless potential for elaboration of any one model. Thus any given model may operate at many levels within the same institution, group, or interpersonal relationship. Third, the four models are ordinarily combined in various ways to yield complex structures, which, though analytically reducible to the four fundamental structures, nevertheless may have emergent properties as a combination. This compositional aspect of social organization raises a further question, since it means that disparate rules and incompatible standards operate side-by-side in the same social system (personal relationship, set of roles, group, institution, or society). The question is whether such a complex social entity can be said to be a "system" with functional integration or logical coherence. Let us look at each of these issues in turn.

I should issue one caveat before launching into this discussion of the nature of the principles that result in variation and diversity in the manifestations of the elementary models. It is difficult enough to describe the structures of social relationships without trying to predict in what particular surface form the structure will be realized, or trying to predict when people will use each structure and how they will combine them. In this book I do not attempt to explain the uses to which people put the models. For the most part, use is a function of historical processes, cultural transmission, and enculturation. People rarely make an explicit choice among models or implementations of models, because they take their cultural application rules for granted. Guided by their culture, adults unreflectively do what people around them do. Where the cultural rules for realizing the models come from and how they change is an important question, but this book is devoted to the logically prior question of characterizing the fundamental models and their transformations.

## IMPLEMENTATION

The four fundamental models, as I have pointed out, are "empty" of specific content and cannot be realized or used to organize any particular action until the culture (or, rarely, ad hoc agreement) specifies five kinds of implementation rules: (1) the domains to which each model applies, (2) the persons who are eligible to relate in each way, (3) the parameter settings that specify the actual values and categories defining the applied meaning of each model, (4) the particular code that people use to mark the existence and quality of any type of social relationship, and (5) the ideological variables defining what is real, what is good, and what is possible.[1]

### Domain Application Rules

Any of the structures I have discussed can be used to organize action in many domains of social interaction. A great deal of what distinguishes different cultural systems can be understood as different application rules for the utilization of the respective models. It appears that all cultures may share the same limited set of fundamental models but apply them to different domains. For example, in some American subcultures marriage is constituted primarily as a relationship of Communal Sharing, in others primarily as Authority Ranking, and in others as Equality Matching or Market Pricing. Coming from one sys-

tem, we may be surprised or even offended to discover that the "same" relationship is so differently constituted in another subculture. Yet it may not be
the structure as such that disconcerts us, only its application to this domain.
The possible distribution of models over domains of activity is virtually infinite, and each culture represents a uniquely variegated patchwork of structures. Cultures also differ in how widely they use each model and in their ideological and explanatory use of the models. Clearly diverse social structures will
be produced by such different patterns of application of the four structures
across the myriad domains of social life. Very simply, the point is that any
given activity can be organized using any of the four basic modes. Sampson
(1969, 1975, 1988) illustrates this, for example, when he shows how the justice
principle people use is a sociohistorical function of the culturally shaped social
character and personality of the allocators (see Chapter 3).

The realization of any of these structures in action requires that certain essential categories, dimensions, procedures, or parameters be established. For
example, Communal Sharing involves a sense of unity and identity. But there
are many forms this can take, with different results in the manifest quality of
social relations. For example, Communal Sharing relationships often involve
the sharing of resources. But exactly what is to be shared? Phenomenologically
different social relations emerge depending on whether a group of people
share the use of a park, fishing rights in the ocean or grazing rights on a commons, the responsibilities and dangers of a hazardous war patrol, Thanksgiving dinner, a joint bank account, or conjugal rights in a polygamous marriage.
What you share determines the quality of the relationship—having a totem in
common is not the same as having a surname in common, nor is sharing a
frying pan the same as sharing a toothbrush. The Moose of Burkina Faso treat
land on which to build homes as communal property (like most of their resources), not something any individual owns privately: anyone may have land
to build a home on just for the asking, regardless of who is currently farming it.
On the other hand, knowledge about recent deaths, upcoming marriages, personal travel plans, or the pursuit of public office is closely held and absolutely
private information: individuals who "own" such knowledge have the right to
control to whom it is revealed and the prerogative to decide when it is made
public. Differences such as these between sharing land and sharing attitudes
make a Moose kingdom and the contemporary United States dissimilar societies. Implementation rules can be quite complex, so that, for example people
may use the same object in all four kinds of relationships in a short span of
time (Appadurai 1986, Fiske 1990).

Kluckhohn and Strodtbeck's (1973 [1961]) research offers a straightforward
illustration of the importance of domain implementation rules. Their pioneering work compares social relational values and expected practices among Texans, Mormons, Spanish-Americans, Zunis, and Navahos in the U.S. Southwest. Although they did not study actual behavior, their systematic
comparative data on norms demonstrates the differences in the models that

cultures apply to various key domains. Furthermore, we can readily adapt their framework to serve our purposes here. In their brief sketch of a theoretical framework they define the *lineal* principle in a way that conflates AR with CS, but in the options they asked informants to choose among, lineality generally comes out as AR. Although Kluckhohn and Strodtbeck's short definition of the *collateral* orientation focuses on CS features without clearly distinguishing them from EM, in the interview questions the CS form is usually most salient. They define *individualistic*[2] values in terms of autonomy to pursue personal goals at the expense of enduring loyalties to associates or corporate groups: so far as the definition goes, this is the Asocial orientation, but the questions they use to assess individualism, although somewhat underspecified, tend to implement it as Market Pricing. They present informants from each of the five cultures with choices among these three orientations in various briefly specified hypothetical situations. The significance of their research lies in their clear recognition that societies and individuals differ in ideological values and expectations but each recognizes and uses all of the basic forms: "It is, we maintain, in the nature of the case that all societies and all subgroups within societies must give heed to all three of the relational principles" (p. 17). Moreover, they also implicitly recognize that the same relational principles emerge in such varied domains as the organization of work, making group decisions, getting help, and managing inherited livestock or land.

Kluckhohn and Strodtbeck (1973 [1961]) asked three questions that are relevant to the domain of transactions, specifically contribution and distribution. Their question 7, for example, asked informants to choose which of three alternative sources of help in the event of a crop failure was best and next best, to state what they would actually do, and also what other community members would do. The choices were to ask siblings and other relatives to help out "as much as each one could" (collateral orientation—CS), to raise money on one's own outside the community (individualism—probably MP), or to "go to a boss or senior relative who is used to managing things" (lineality—AR). They did not present the EM option of asking a peer for help that would later be returned in kind. Informants from the five Southwestern cultures gave different answers to these questions; that is, they used different implementation rules in this domain. Kluckholn and Strodtbeck also asked two questions about preferences and practices in the organization of work in the five communities in the American Southwest. Their question 12 asked about labor decisions, offering individualistic (MP), collateral (CS), and lineal (AR) alternatives. Item 8 inquired about family work, again asking informants to choose among MP, CS, and AR options. (Had they known about related work in anthropological economics, they would surely have included an EM option.) Again, they found different application rules in the different cultures.

The dividing line between human links to objects and object transactions is arbitrary. Kluckhohn and Strodtbeck's questions about values and expected behavior in the inheritance of livestock (16) and land (17) illustrate this point. However, their questions on this topic conflate the basic types of social relationships, since in this instance their lineal option combines AR and CS, while their collateral option is largely but not purely CS, and the individualism option, apparently MP, is not described in a way that would unequivocally exclude EM. Their work systematically shows that people's orientations to the same kind of object vary as a function of their culture. In addition, three of Kluckhohn and Strodtbeck's questions (2, 9, and 12) compare decision-making values. They asked informants to choose among consulting an authority (lineal orientation—AR); everyone discussing an issue until they reach consensus (collateral orientation—CS), and voting by majority rule (individualism—one-person, one-vote EM). They also asked informants what they thought others would do. The five Southwestern cultures differed in their preferences for the three approaches to decision making, and informants also expressed major cultural differences on which mode of making decisions they valued in particular domains within each culture. The essential point is that at an abstract level the CS, AR, EM, and MP principles that people use are essentially the same in the five cultures, while there are major cultural differences in the implementation rules for applying them to situations. For example, Navaho who prefer collaterality in other domains nonetheless prefer to seek help from an elder in the event of crop failure; Zuni value collaterality most highly in three domains and place individuality first in three other domains, but believe that a group of siblings who inherit livestock should entrust its management to the most senior sibling (lineality). In other words, the cultural differences have to do with when and where people use a few universal relational models.

## Ascription and Acquisition of Roles

One of the important variables in the ways any abstract relational structure can be embodied in a concrete social structure is in the assignment of persons to roles. This aspect of social relationships is perhaps the one people fight over the most: they assume that a given structure applies to the domain they are contesting but argue over who is to play what roles. For example, citizenship in the United States confers rights in civic relationships of all four kinds (CS, AR, EM, MP), but on whom is citizenship to be bestowed? Or, granted that a husband and wife should pool resources and share a home, a great deal still hinges on who is to marry whom. The President has legitimate authority to execute the laws and command the armed forces, but elections are hard fought. We are ready to accord all students in the college the same access to courses and grade them by the same standards, but whom shall we admit to the college? Market Pricing is generally more fluid and open to diverse participants but is still not without limits: minors and mental incompetents may not make a binding contract, while convicted felons may be excluded from jobs with armored car services. Foreign corporations may be excluded from buying American high technology companies or bidding for defense contracts.

In general, the factors that determine who enters into what kinds of relationships with whom shape the society in very pervasive ways. For the most part, Moose accord authority to men strictly according to priority of birth order—that is, relative age.[3] We would think it odd to make distinctions on the basis of a few days' difference in age, but among an ad hoc group of military officers of equal rank the precise date of promotion to that rank determines who commands. Anthropologists have studied in depth the differences in social organization that result from reciprocal exchanges of brides among different combinations of groups: all may involve reciprocity (often Equality Matching), but the patterns in the network of bonds that result from different pairings of wife givers and wife receivers vary widely, with far-reaching social implications. For example, a society divided into six groups that each exchange wives reciprocally with all the other groups has quite a different character from one in which each group exchanges wives with only one other group, even though the individual exchanges assume precisely the same EM form (see Lévi-Strauss 1961 [1949]). Similarly, patrilineal, matrilineal, and bilateral descent groups all are based largely on the equivalence relations of Communal Sharing, and hence have important common properties. But they are each different manifestations of that one structure, since they group different people together.

Again, anthropologists since Malinowski have been interested in the ramifications of diverse cycles of reciprocal "gift" giving. In such systems of exchange, Equality Matching can be maintained by balanced, one-for-one exchange with anyone, but the patterns of alliance that people seek may require difficult and dangerous journeys to find trading partners among distant people. In many traditional cultures, the very fabric of society is woven on the warp of EM exchanges. The same is true of Market Pricing in modern societies: who buys and sells from whom, where people purchase their textiles, steel, automobiles, and computer chips, is the subject of considerable interest in contemporary political economy. Different patterns in the flow of trade— all within the framework of Market Pricing—affect economic development, and changes in the flow determine the incidence of economic boom and prosperity, recession, inflation, war and revolution.

Furthermore, the very system of determining how people are distributed among roles is of considerable consequence. Whether people are born into their roles, as is more or less the case in a kinship or caste system, or whether they come into them by voluntary choice, by administrative procedures of one sort or another, through individual combat or war, or in some other manner makes a great deal of difference for the nature of the society and the human experience in it. Just consider the implications of racial, ethnic, and gender bias in marriage or admission to clubs or housing, in promotions and elections, in the distribution of resources, or in business opportunities and contracting. Moose become village chiefs by currying favor with the paramount chief; in the U.S., people become mayors by being elected. The form of recruitment makes a considerable difference in who actually exercises authority and in the way people exercise it. Moose men become hereditary diviners by surviving until no older man in the lineage is left alive, and then experiencing a seizure-like possession fit. Americans become psychotherapists through a somewhat different procedure, and therein lies an important component of the difference between the authority of diviners and of psychotherapists. Who enters into what social relationships is a major determinant of the shape and substance of society, and of the quality of human social experience.


## Constitutive Parameters:
## Social Action Is Not Fully Specified by Any Model

Specifying the domain- and person-application rules is not sufficient. Communal Sharing is the application to human relations of the structure of equivalence relations. But this leaves open what aspects of the participants' identities are merged and how they operationalize the equivalence principle with people who are biologically, psychologically, circumstantially, and historically manifestly heterogeneous. Similarly, for Equality Matching to operate, people have to have an implicit (or explicit) consensus about the taxonomy of the relevant actions and things.[4] Suppose that under Equality Matching you invite me to a dinner party, and some time later I reciprocate by inviting you to a dinner party in return. This presupposes the cultural category of "dinner party," and within that a finely detailed understanding of what sorts of dinner parties there are. Of course, my dinner party will not be exactly the same as yours—and indeed attempting to make it identical in every respect would be regarded as gauche, tacky, and rather incredible. On the other hand, peanut butter and jelly sandwiches with plastic flatware would not do in return for an eight-course, haute-cuisine candlelight dinner. Making any implementation of Equality Matching work requires a subtle cultural understanding of what counts as "the same."

To take another example, if shares are to be divided equally, in principle (that is, with respect to the structure of the Equality Matching model) any procedure or mechanism for balancing the shares will do as long as it exhibits the necessary formal properties. Yet in practice, the method of comparison used may have appreciable social consequences. Structurally, a lottery to draft conscripts in which all the eligible people have a two percent chance of serving 50 years is equivalent to a draft in which all serve one year. Formally, the EM model is indifferent. Politically and ethically, however, we are not indifferent. The same would be true of a land reform scheme which gave every family 100 acres of land. At the level of "families" and "land," such a scheme observes distributive justice and meets the formal criteria of Equality Matching. But if some land is underwater in a swamp, some is desert, some is fertile farm land, and some is downtown in the capital city, or if some families are childless couples and some are extended families with many children, while another is a family of cats in the governor's mansion, then we might well feel that the categories had not been fairly defined in any substantive sense.

Similarly, the realization of Market Pricing in any particular case involves establishing particular ratios of exchange for all pairs of commodities (including units of the currency, if any). That is, prices have to be set. There is nothing about the structure of Market Pricing that requires any particular rate of exchange for any specific goods or services, but some price must be assigned to everything on the market. This assignment of prices to items is arbitrary with respect to the structural properties of MP, but, in phenomenologically crucial respects, the actual prices nonetheless limit the transactions that do take place, with momentous pragmatic significance for the nature of the resulting society. In other words, there are constitutive rules that must be culturally specified (or, rarely, invented ad hoc) in order to implement any of the models.[5]

## Marking Social Relationships

Another source of surface variation in the manifestations of the universal models is the way in which people communicate the existence and status of each relationship. In order to convey that a given social relationship is operative and to display how it is going, people need to use some kind of semiotic code, some kind of sign system. Although there seems to be a characteristic mode of encoding each model that people prefer to use (see Chapter 9), within each type of code there are indefinitely many particular signs or symbols that people can use. Different cultures have different ways of marking each kind of social relationship, and within any culture different instances of, say, Authority Ranking can be indicated in many different ways. Abstractly, anything that can be linearly ordered can serve to mark the social relationship of Authority Ranking. Suppose that people find it natural and intuitive to use temporal precedence and magnitude to mark rank. To operationalize AR in any concrete relationship, people must have shared understandings of what kinds of precedence and what kinds of magnitude will be used (e.g., one's body size or the size of one's automobile). Cultures differ considerably in this respect. It is also necessary to choose what dimensions will be used on what occasions to mark social hierarchies, and to pick starting points for the linear sequences that indicate rank: which end is the head of the table at a diplomatic reception? Among Moose, the eldest person should take the first drink in a round; but just what counts as starting a new round of drinking? More generally, even if going ahead of someone or having more of something indicates higher rank, it is just not empirically feasible for superiors to precede and exceed their inferiors in literally all respects in the physical world.

High-ranking Americans often mark their rank with large homes and offices, frequently on the upper floors of high buildings or the summits of hills. Nothing about the size or elevation of the homes in most Moose villages distinguishes the rank of their occupants. The Moose (like many others) address superiors with the plural "you" to express their relative social magnitude; modern English uses the plural "you" for everyone, having dropped "thou" over two hundred years ago. Moose men show extreme deference by lying down on their left side with elbows to the ground and swinging both closed fists up and down, or putting their foreheads in the dust. We usually stand upright in greeting all and sit in chairs whose elevation reveals nothing of our ranks. Again, when eating or drinking, the eldest man present will first spill a little beer or toss a bite of food on the ground before beginning to eat, giving precedence to the ancestors. All of this is intelligible to us, but does not correspond to our normal practice. But, unlike Westerners in military and diplomatic circles, the Moose do not worry themselves about precedence in the seating order within an eating group, the order of arrival and departure at a ceremonial meal, or who leads off a formal dance. For a final example, consider the vagaries of the contextual rules specifying when rank is marked by order of procession, including the confusing exceptions (motorcycle escorts, women before men, guests before hosts, crew before captain abandoning ship). Obviously there are an enormous number of dimensions in the physical world that can be used to order people by rank and authority, but each culture (and institution) uses only a few, and these only in delimited contexts.

In the section Representation, Marking, and Accessibility in Chapter 9 I argue that there appears to be a different characteristic, natural, and primary mode of marking each type of social relationship. But specifying the primary kind of code does not determine the specific form of the code. All the examples of AR marking in the preceding paragraph involve the semiotic use of space, time, and magnitude, but different cultures develop this same semiotic mode in very different directions. An enterprise in which status is spatially marked by the floor where a person's office is located seems quite different from one in which status is spatially marked by subordinates' prostrating themselves on the ground in front of their superiors.

## Ideology

Finally, an individual applies a model in an ideological environment. As Therborn (1980:18) argues, in a given culture people share implicit or explicit conceptions of what is real, what is possible (and how it is possible), and what is good (in various senses of each of the words). Compared to many African and Asian cultures, my own American culture tends to derogate Authority Ranking relations as generally undesirable and as relatively unimportant and uncommon. We also have a cultural conviction that a Market Pricing system of production and exchange is fair, is feasible, and makes possible all kinds of individual success and collective progress. Many other cultures at many times in history have had different ideals and beliefs about Market Pricing; the !Kung and the Trobriand Islanders, for example, greatly disparage MP (Marshall 1961:242; Malinowski 1961:191). We believe, more or less, that an Equality Matching system for selecting political leaders minimizes corruption and makes political leaders responsive to the popular will—which we think is a good thing. As Godelier (1986b:171–75) points out, in virtually any culture people are aware that other forms of social relations are possible—although they may be abominable, ridiculous, or unwise. Such ideological factors have pervasive influences on what models people use and how they use them.

The universal, precultural, abstract forms of the models leave unspecified five kinds of implementation rules: the domain and person application rules, parameter settings, social marking, and ideology. Each model may be implemented in innumerable diverse realizations. Thus much of the variation in social relations between cultures and within societies can be explained in terms of these five kinds of implementation rules: people can use a small number of universal models to generate any number of actual roles, personal relationships, institutions, and groups. However, the existence of this range of possible implementation rules raises two crucial, linked questions. First, what are the limitations of each kind of implementation rule: what logically conceivable realizations of each model are humanly impossible in the face of constraints of a biological, psychological, social, cultural, or technical nature? For example, modern communications might make communal decision making increasingly feasible in groups previously too large to use the process. But CS decision making appears functionally ill-adapted to the coordinative problems of rapid, large-scale warfare. The second question is, are there default values of the implementation rules, values that people prefer (other things being equal)?[6] For example, there is a general tendency to apply Communal Sharing among close biological kin, especially in the mother-child dyad, and drinks, cooked food, tobacco, and other stimulants seem to lend themselves naturally to Communal Sharing distribution and consumption. Future research should explore these major issues concerning the limitations and proclivities of humans applying models that are logically free of content.

## RECURSION

In addition to variability, a general theory of social relations has to account for complexity. How can simple elementary models underlie the intricacies of everyday social relations? Complexity in the implementation of the basic models, together with flexibility and functional adaptability, results partly from the recursive application of the structures. Social relations manifest a system of nested layers in which the same structure is hierarchically embedded within higher order structures of the same type. People generate these structures by applying the same relational model repeatedly, often applying it to the component units generated by the hierarchically higher level application of the model.

## Communal Sharing at Various Levels of Inclusion

The simplest example of this nesting of structures is the existence of Communal Sharing groups embedded within other communal groups. Among the Moose, a polygamous "nuclear family," a *zaka,* lives together and cultivates together, sharing stocks of food and eating together on a daily basis. Such a group is part of a compound (also *zaka*) that pools labor and food intermittently, occupying an enclosed living unit composed of one or more polygamous families. These compounds are grouped in larger unnamed communal groups that share a common grinding platform (*neere*) and greet outsiders ("*yeela*") when they first enter the area each day. People in this CS group routinely help each other with housebuilding, floor and yard pounding, beer brewing, and the like. These units are grouped in a named lineage neighborhood (*saka*) that is a communal group for other purposes, including giving and receiving wives, and making collective sacrifices to the ancestors. A set of neighborhoods comprise a village, which makes collective sacrifices to the earth for community fertility, rain, and protection from epidemics. The village (or sometimes a neighborhood) often pools labor to dig water catchment basins or wells. A set of villages makes up a named section with a loose sense of identity, and a few sections comprise a chieftainship under a paramount chief (*kombere*). The chieftainships together make up the Moose region. Together with other ethnic regions, they form a country. In another, related sequence, each *zaka* belongs to a sublineage, which belongs to a lineage, which belongs to an exogamous totemic group, which is part of an ethnic subgroup, which belongs to the Moose "tribe." The tribe is in turn one of a number of kinds of humans. Interestingly, each of these levels is called *buudu,* and each represents—in ever-decreasing intensity and a more limited range of domains as they expand—a Communal Sharing relationship. So the innermost group shares most of their labor and food, while intermediate groups share food and labor only occasionally, still larger groups intermarry and help each other out in time of war, and so on to the community of all humans, who—for example—share water with each other. While this kind of nesting is particularly prominent among the Moose, for whom Communal Sharing is the predominant and most highly valued form of social relationship, this same kind of embedded series of communal relationships is observable to some degree in any society.

## Ranks: Orders of Orderings

It is possible for multiple rankings of the same persons to coexist "side-by-side," just as a person can belong to several nested and overlapping Communal Sharing groups. In the United States, people can be ranked by the number of years of education completed, prestige of the college or university attended or prestige of their occupation, rank achieved in that occupation, political or institutional office, income, wealth, family name and heritage, associates (whom you know), neighborhood and housing, and, unfortunately, by gender and ethnicity. Although scales of social class attempt to combine these correlated factors into a single ranking, the fact is that rankings on these various scales do not coincide precisely. However, when people interact hierarchically they tend to orient to only one of these hierarchies at a time, acting as if relative rank were a property of the person. In this sense, relative rank is a relational shifter like CS solidarity.

There are also situations in which systems of rank and authority are themselves ranked on a scale. In the framework of the inclusive, overarching ordering, people at a given rank are equivalent. Within a given rank there may be an ordering significant only internally within that setting relative to others at that rank, while disregarded in the inclusive order. So for most laymen a professor is a professor, and academic ranks are not recognized, understood, or taken into consideration: outside of academic circles, they just don't count. The same is true of sanitation workers and congressmen: for most outsiders, a representative is a representative and a garbage collector is a garbage collector. At another level of inclusion, in much of the African bush a Euro-American is just that and, aside from age and gender, people make no further distinctions among strangers: Euro-American senators, professors, and sanitation workers are all one. Outside of the species, for all but a few humans a Rhode Island Red is just a chicken, and a macaque is just a monkey. At Colonel Sanders or in the zoo, they all get treated alike: pecking orders, alpha males, and the inheritance of maternal ranks are of no account to the lords of the earth. From the point of view of a medieval scholar ranking God's creatures, distinctions of rank within a species of bird may be unknown, but for the hens involved it may be of considerable consequence. While for the hens, the great chain of being matters little.

Among other things this means that in dealing with categories of others who are relatively distant, people respond according to the rank of the category as such. Yet those within each category may make much of the distinctions of rank internal to the category. Thus in some contexts people treat nationalities as ranked, while within nations ethnicities may be ranked and within ethnic groups people order themselves hierarchically according to yet other factors.

## Equality Matching: Rotating Credit Associations

One of the clearest examples of how a complex and functional institution can be constructed by the recursive application of a single model is the rotating credit association, an institution known from diverse and widely distributed societies (Bascom 1952, Geertz 1962, Ardner 1964, Firth and Yamey 1964, Kramer 1974, Vélez-Ibañez 1983; see also Chapter 2 here). In these associations, a number of people each make contributions of money in a fixed amount at regular intervals. At each occasion in turn, the entire sum goes to a different member. During the course of a complete round, each member pays out an amount exactly equal to what she or he receives. But once in each rotation each member is able to amass capital in an amount she typically would have been unable to accumulate on her own, especially in the absence of banks.

This simple Equality Matching principle can be elaborated by embedding so that at the top level, instead of individual shares, the association is composed of several groups, each of which makes identical contributions to the pot at each round and each of which receives the entire pot in its turn. Large associations of this kind exist in which members never meet face to face, and in which no member knows the identity of all the others. The head of each subgroup knows all the members in her subgroup and knows the heads of the other subgroups and can easily verify that the contributions of each of the other subgroups matches her own. The same one-to-one equal shares principle can be applied at the level of the individual share. This makes it possible to include people who are unable to contribute a full share on their own. The group as a whole need only know who is responsible for producing each share. But that share may be made up by two, three, or even more shareholders who make equal contributions to make up the one full share. When this occurs, it is notable that the joint holders of the individual share divide it equally, matching each other's contributions and dividing up their pot into equal parts. Similarly, any member can hold more than one share, contributing two or more allotments at each round and receiving the corresponding number of pots in each rotation. Another variant involves equal probability shares, in which there is a fair lottery in each round.

Further elaboration is possible. If a member drops out part way through a round, she can be reimbursed for her contributions by each person who has already received a pot. If she has already won the pot, she can reimburse the contributions of the other members. More often—and more feasibly—a dropout is replaced by a new member. The dropout and the new member divide the pot that one of them receives, splitting it to correspond with the number of contributions each made.

These associations are logically equivalent to a series of interest-free reciprocal loans among each pair of members, in which each member matches what she gives with what she receives in return. What is gained by institutionalizing EM in a rotating credit association is a regular schedule and structure, together with mutual peer pressure on the members, making default unlikely. The rotating credit associations accomplish such a fruitful and diverse combination of valuable social and economic functions that they coexist with modern credit institutions (which of course have the drawback that they charge interest for loans) and thrive all over the world, apparently as independent inventions. They are remarkably similar, and in each instance the governing principle generating the social structure is Equality Matching. At each turn, every share contributed is equal to all the others. The only calculations required to assure the fair operation of a rotating credit association are addition and subtraction, or—equivalently—a record-keeping scheme (that may be as simple as a pile of mnemonic tokens or a series of notches or knots), which assures one-to-one correspondence between contributions made and contributions received. All the relations and procedures used in these rotating credit associations conform to EM, recursively applied.

The same principle can be seen in a system in which one group collectively pays a fine to compensate another, and then the individual members of the group pay each other back. For example, if people in one tribe were to make a collection to compensate another tribe for the death of their pig, the EM principle is operating between groups. Within the group, people may (or may not) then apply EM so that the individual wrongdoer pays back each of his fellows for their contributions to the fine they collectively paid. The same kind of EM arrangements might be made between and within groups in making bride-price payments, although in both cases people may also use other models (cf. Meillassoux 1981 [1975]).

## Market Pricing: Trading in Contracts and Markets

When people operate within a Market Pricing framework they negotiate and bargain with reference to the relative prices of different items, and people can do this at several different, hierarchically nested levels. In many sophisticated large-scale markets, there are also futures markets in which traders buy, sell, and maintain a market in contracts to buy or sell various commodities at various times in the future. Some traders buy or sell only futures—they never actually buy or sell the commodities, use them, or even see them. There are also money markets in which money is traded—that is, people buy from each other the right to use money, which the buyer then uses to buy commodities and services. And there are currency futures markets in which people negotiate rights to exchange currencies at specified rates at fixed times in the future. People also buy options: they contract for the future right (not the obligation) to buy airplanes, grains, metals, or other commodities at some specified time.

Companies may bid for construction or weapons contracts and then invite subcontractors to bid for segments of the job. Subcontractors may further subcontract, and the lowest level firms may deal with individual employees in the labor market in more or less the same way.

In the sports world, a team may buy the contract of a player from another team, just as they may bargain over and trade player draft rights: the right to negotiate a contract with the player. Moreover, people may buy and sell whole markets. A corporation may buy a sports or food franchise, which is the right to sell a given product to individual consumers in a given market. Franchises for the entrepreneurial rights to sell a given kind of commodity (hamburgers, baseball games, or computers) are exchanged in a market mode, and on a larger scale individuals and companies bid to buy other companies in "takeovers." This is trade in trade, a market in markets. Even whole countries haggle over tariffs, quotas, and access rights to each others' markets, trading off access to textile markets for access to automobile markets. At the same time, there is a market in shares of the company that purchases the franchise, and a market in shares in the banks that lend money to the corporation to buy the franchise. At another level up, there is the market in stock exchange seats to sell the shares of banks. In general, a person may sell and purchase seats on these stock exchanges, and on futures and commodities exchanges. It is possible to buy a seat on the Lloyd's of London insurance brokerage exchange that entitles one to buy and sell portions of the risk in insurance contracts, and there are enough such sales to make it possible to specify the current price of such a seat. Meanwhile, people pay lawyers, bankers, and various kinds of formal and informal brokers to work out deals to purchase such seats. These firms in turn pay their employees, who in turn. . . .

All of these are examples of the recursive application of the Market Pricing structure, in which complex institutions are constructed by a kind of nesting of structures within other structures of the same genre. Only in terms of this kind of recursion is it intelligible to hire a lawyer (who hires assistants) to negotiate a deal to buy a seat on a currency futures market where people buy the right to buy a currency that may be used to sell bonds to buy a franchise to sell equipment to people who sell hamburgers to people who hire lawyers.

More generally it is apparent that the same model may operate at a number of levels, so that a given structure is embedded within the framework of a social relationship that may have the same structure at a higher level. The embedding of structures within structures is one of the principal features of these models, enabling a limited set of basic structures to generate complex and diverse social relationships. Moreover, this kind of embedding is not limited to the embedding of a given structure within another of the same type, as we shall now see.

## COMPOSITION: COMBINATIONS OF THE FOUR TYPES

In practice it is rare to find a social interaction governed by only one of the structures I have described. Rather than pure types, what we typically observe are relationships, roles, institutions, and societies that are composites of the four fundamental models. This is increasingly true as we go up to the level of large-scale social entities, but even at the lowest level of the interaction within any dyad, it is still the rule. More than anything else it is this compositional aspect of the production of social relations that makes for the observed complexity and the experienced variety of social life. Nevertheless, in the variegated array of any actual social interaction or social organization it is possible to discern distinct phases, issues, modules, and aspects of the interaction that can be characterized as one or another of the four elementary types. Let me illustrate.

## Personal Relations Between Particular Individuals

Consider the interaction between any two particular people, analytically isolated for a moment from the social environment. Take an American husband and wife; the reader might want to think about a specific pair familiar to her and follow along with an analysis parallel to ours. The couple organize much of their personal relationship as Communal Sharing. They pool their money in joint accounts, and spend it on both individual and collective purchases without regard to who contributed what to the account and without any accounting of how much each one spent. They share a house in more or less the same way, including perhaps some aspects of its upkeep. They have a common identity as "the Robertsons," and they give each other emotional support and affection, time, energy, and help noncontingently, as needed and as they feel moved to do. But in some other matters they may follow an Authority Ranking model. Perhaps the wife has arbitrary personal authority over some domains of the household and unilaterally makes some decisions that affect them both. For example, she may decide to accept a promotion or a job offer in a new location, and this determines where the couple will live; perhaps she selects a particular house without consulting her mate. He respects her and defers to her decisions "because she is the head of the family—she's the boss, it's my duty to love, honor, and obey." Still other kinds of activities are governed by a principle of fairness, under Equality Matching. They take turns doing the dishes, and each vacuums half the house. He cooks her something he specially likes one night, and she cooks her favorite meal the next. He agrees to arrange the living room the way she wants and in return she agrees to accept his preferences in the arrangement of the den. He does her a favor by helping her fix the car, and she reciprocates by doing him a favor with the laundry. Other important spheres of joint concern are controlled by Market Pricing. Perhaps they negotiated a marriage contract specifying who owns what in the event of divorce, with the help of lawyers who bargained as their agents. They first met when he sold her his Jaguar, and now she employs him as a research assistant on her consulting jobs. Her business makes him a business loan to start up a new software company.

This couple constructs their marriage out of the four elementary kinds of constituent units. While the marriage as a whole is a melange of the four models, each of the fundamental structures is discernible in various distinct, delimited aspects of the total relationship. Of course, in any particular marriage or in any other pattern of interaction between two individuals, all four models need not be salient, and one or two may dominate to the point that they obscure most manifestations of the other types.

## Sets of Roles

What is true of the personal relationship of two people is also true of any interlocking set of social roles. Think about the complementary roles of professor and graduate student. In large part (especially in some European and third-world universities) this is certainly defined as an Authority Ranking relationship in which professors direct their students, instructing students what to read, how to carry out research, and sometimes what research to conduct. The students more or less obediently carry out much of what they are told to do and avoid confronting professors with instructions they fail to carry out. The students owe and show respect and deference to professors, listening politely to what they are told and avoiding direct challenges to professors' authority. Professors set requirements and examination topics, grade students, determine who gets fellowships, and influence their prospects for employment in critical ways. But there are also market aspects of the relationship: students may pay tuition, part of which is indirectly channeled to professors' salaries (although students no longer hire professors directly, as they did in the days of the earliest universities). Professors may hire students as research assistants, negotiating rates of pay established in part on the basis of the employment market. The university may pay students for working as teaching assistants to professors or for teaching evening or summer school courses. Professors and students also share a communal identity as members of a department, school, university, and academic discipline, and they share certain pooled resources like the library, bathrooms, and drinking fountains, and perhaps athletic facilities. They may also write and publish joint papers, to which each more or less freely contributes ideas, analyses, and perhaps research work without any explicit accounting of who does what or how much; the paper may be their collective project as a collaborative team, and their respective contributions are not separately identified. Elements of Equality Matching may be rare to nonexistent in the defining features of these roles but conceivably enter in to such things as buying each other coffee alternately, or perhaps dividing up equally the articles to read for a review paper or the undergraduate exam questions to grade.

It should be clear now that a "social relationship" is typically a composite. This is true for the personal relationship between two or more particular people, as well as for reciprocally defined roles like professor, student, departmental secretary, and chairman. Most personal relationships and most sets of social roles are constituted of components of more than one structural type: the participants structure each interaction, or the aspects, issues, phases and concerns in an interaction, with implicit reference to one of the four basic models. However, one model may predominate and determine the general configuration of the relationship. So sometimes it is an adequate shorthand to speak of a "social relationship" of a given type, as I do at times in this book.


## Organizations and Institutions

It will be apparent that in the same manner, virtually any concrete organization (e.g., the University of Chicago) or cultural institution (e.g., the ideal conception of and prescriptions for "family," "university," "factory," or "municipal government") is a composite of many organized sets of roles, each with the kind of structural heterogeneity described above. Bradach and Eccles (1989) show how business firms operate using a combination of three control mechanisms: price (MP), authority (AR), and trust (a concept which they do not analyze precisely), because the three together are more effective than any one alone. Beyond this, the larger scale, higher level patterns of interaction within an organization or institution are also composites of modules, phases, and aspects generated out of multiple relational structures. For instance, look at a university department. Faculty members share some facilities communally, with no marking or accounting of individual usage: lounges, lobbies, local telephone calls, office supplies, utilities, shop facilities, administrative services, perhaps photocopying or postage. Faculty members may have a sense of collective identity as a department (and as members together of superordinate communal groups like the university), and many kinds of decision making may be made by communal consensus. At the same time, there is a definite Authority Ranking hierarchy from chairperson to other departmental officeholders, to other faculty, students, staff and technicians, janitors and cleaning people. (Faculty members are also ranked among themselves, as are staff and janitors.) These ranks can be manifested in office size and furnishings, access to some facilities, salaries and benefits, job security, and control over own and others' activities. Some decisions are handed down by the authority of the chairperson, whose prerogative it is (within a circumscribed domain and traditional limits) to make unilateral decisions about some aspects of departmental policy, temporary appointments, and budgets.

Members of a university department also organize some phases of their interaction according to Equality Matching. Egalitarian distributive justice (to each the same) may be observed among faculty in the allocation of a lump sum for discretionary long-distance telephone calls or photocopying, in conference travel money, microcomputer equipment, and course teaching load. The faculty may vote to make important decisions, one person—one vote. They may more or less take turns at teaching onerous courses, at taking on committee assignments, or with burdensome administrative duties. And faculty may return favors reciprocally, giving help for help in reading each other's papers, giving guest lectures, or taking each other out to lunch. Among students, degree requirements, fellowship stipends, and teaching assistantships may be uniformly distributed, the same for each student. Staff at each rank have identical work hours, benefits, and vacation days. Market Pricing also enters into the life of the department, governing to a greater or lesser extent salary offers to faculty with competing offers at other universities, wages for staff, and certainly the purchase of supplies and equipment. Some journals require payment by the word for the publication of articles, and faculty commonly enter into market relations with book publishers and as consultants with business and government. Faculty may buy time off with grants, and their ability to generate revenue through competitive grant applications is a major factor in the ultimate economic viability of both department and university.

Different departments present different mixes and arrangements of the four basic structures, and other types of institutions differ still more in their relative utilization of the models. This is part of what gives different organizations and kinds of corporations, associations, and communities their distinctive characters. For example, one distinctive feature of the Basque industrial cooperatives that Greenwood (1988) describes is their use of EM as a decision-making scheme, voting on all major policy matters and rules. At the same time, like other corporations they employ AR in their hierarchical management structure, and the corporations as institutions are very much oriented toward MP investment and profit making. But they operate in a CS mode in their emphatic goal of generating and maintaining social solidarity and mutuality, their policy of sharing of all information about coop management and operations, their commitment to permanent employment of their members, and in their expectation of universal participation in the annual general assembly.

## Societies

Like groups and institutions, different societies differ greatly in the relative empirical prevalence of the four fundamental structures, and cultures differ in their ideological valuation of them. How much of social life do people organize as CS, and how much as MP—and what do people think is the right way to organize social relations? These differences between cultures in the weightings of and preferences for each of the models are striking and important, but most cultures probably exhibit all four of the models in significant degree. In some hunting and gathering societies Market Pricing may be limited to interaction with outsiders, and even then play a very restricted role (e.g., Marshall 1961). So perhaps historically there have been a few small, isolated societies in which Market Pricing was virtually absent, or at least given little cultural recognition and elaboration. Karl Polanyi (1947, 1968) emphasizes the relatively minor role played by markets and Market Pricing in most societies outside the postmedieval West, but he does not describe any society in which MP is known to be totally absent. Other writers have shown that relations of authority and rank are much less elaborated and less extensively implemented in other societies than they are even in our own nominally egalitarian society (e.g., Miller 1955). Yet given the human life cycle with prolonged childhood dependency and a long life span, together with the apparent universality of some sort of dominance hierarchies in primate bands and among many other social mammals, it is doubtful whether Authority Ranking is entirely absent from any human society. Communal Sharing and Equality Matching are almost certainly operative in all societies.

While any type of social relationship may be restricted and downplayed to a considerable extent, it may be asked whether it is even possible, in social functional terms, to operate and maintain any society without a combination of at least three of these structures; and for a large and intricate society, all four may be necessary (see the subsection Social System Functions of the Basic Norms in Chapter 5). Imagine a society operating without any Communal Sharing, or without any hint of Equality Matching—would it endure? Each mode has distinct benefits under certain conditions (see Fiske and Baron, n.d.), and the specific advantages of each respective type may be necessary for the performance of some essential social functions. Looked at obversely, it may be that the potential to engage in social relationships of each type is built into the human genotype and the operation of the brain in such a way that it is practically impossible to block completely its phenotypic expression in human interaction. I will come back to this issue below.

It should be obvious by now that an entire society will ordinarily comprise structures of all four of the fundamental types. This is true in two senses. Of course, the personal relationships, sets of complementary roles, particular organizations, and variety of institutions that a society contains are themselves heterogeneous compounds, as illustrated above. Then, too, a society is a composite of larger scale patterns of social intercourse exhibiting the fundamental structures on that scale as well. Each of the four structures emerges at every level of social organization.

At the level of the society as a whole (or the entire social universe), each of the four social relationship types is typically manifest in the macrostructures of group-to-group relations. Groups, as collectivities, engage in interactions with other groups, and these interactions can be governed by any of the basic models. The United States federal government has authority over the states, since federal law preempts state and local law in any domains in which the federal government has constitutional authority, and the federal Constitution directly limits the legislative and administrative powers of local governments. Similarly, a government may tax, regulate, or outlaw private organizations of various kinds. Or the Mafia may dominate a municipal government, while a parents' association wins effective control over a school. In certain matters the governing body of a religious denomination (as a body and not as individual persons) may have powers to control and impose its will on church congregations, and the national labor union may exercise some such powers over member unions. In some countries and some periods of history, the Catholic church may dominate a separately constituted civic organization or foundation, effectively—and with cultural legitimacy—dictating what they may and may not do. The CIA or a Communist Party might have full authority over a resistance movement, or a resistance movement could conceivably command a publishing corporation or a local debating club.

Equality Matching also enters into the panoply of structures that organize the relations among groups. Every state in the United States has two senators, and in many other organizations every local chapter sends the same number of delegates to national conventions. (In others, of course, representation is proportional to membership, which is MP.) In sports, opponents take turns hosting games, kicking off, leading off, or serving; teams alternate at bats or defending ends of the field or rink; and each team is allowed the same number of players on the field and on the roster, the same number of at bats or downs, the same amount of time per down or per shot at the basket, and each pair of teams has identical, matched goals or nets. In order to make it a fair contest, both sides have to have this equal start—otherwise it isn't a game. National conventions of professional organizations may rotate among countries, regions of the country, states or cities, giving each a turn (and the chair may rotate in like fashion). Every store on a block might agree to put out one potted tree to decorate the sidewalk, or an association of shopkeepers might erect a directory board or publish a joint flyer, with each entitled to equal space and each putting up the same amount of money. Universities undertake joint projects, like the Human Relations Area Files, to which all participants of a given kind make equal annual contributions and each receives identical materials.

Like individuals, corporations may engage in Market Pricing commercial transactions, and industry associations engage in collective bargaining with labor unions about the rates of exchange at which individuals will sell their labor. All kinds of groups and organizations bargain, make contracts and buy and sell services to each other in the mode of Market Pricing. Relations among groups are generated out of the four basic models, and the overall fabric of interaction between two groups is commonly an intricate weave in which several of the fundamental structures can be discerned.

Even at the international level, relations among nations may be governed by combinations of the models. Nations enter into communal undertakings. Good examples are the international campaign to eradicate smallpox or the West African onchocerciasis project, to which countries voluntarily contributed funds, personnel, and supplies as they wished and were able and from which all benefited collectively. Treaties have declared outer space, the Antarctic, and the oceans as commons for all to frequent and use freely, without limit, coercion, reciprocity, balance, or payment. Nations provide disaster relief and some foreign aid grants to each other according to donors' willingness to give and recipients' need, without explicit obligations or conditions. Distinct political units may even merge to form a single, less differentiated political entity, like the federation of the thirteen colonies into the United States of America, or the partial political union of Tanganyika and Zanzibar to form Tanzania, the failed union of Tanzania, Uganda, and Kenya, or the European Economic Community. Military alliances like NATO are common between countries of quite unequal power and capability, in which all agree to come to the aid of any other, with no formal ordering or authority of one over another, without any balance among the several contributions or reciprocity for services rendered, and without purchase or payment for such services. And "voluntary" contributions to various United Nations organizations are assessed according to ability to contribute, while, in principle, services are freely distributed according to need.

Authority among nations has often been salient in history when nations conquered and coerced others, exacted tribute, controlled the political and military policies of subordinate states, named their heads of state, or simply ruled over them directly. The colonial epoch is not entirely finished, and protectorates and Bantu "homelands" still exist in which the colonial power exercises absolute political control over the affairs of the colony. The United States, the Soviet Union, China, Great Britain, and France are permanent members of the Security Council of the United Nations, and they alone among nations have veto power over its resolutions. Much of the rhetoric of international relations takes the form of bitter denunciation of systems of postcolonial rank and authority among nations that operate despite nominally communal, egalitarian, or market surface forms.

There is perhaps more Equality Matching in the theory of international relations than in the practice, but certainly there are many organizations which conduct voting on the basis of one nation, one vote. The chairmanship of the Security Council of the United Nations and a few other similar international offices rotates among all the members in turn. Countries may trade scientific and cultural delegations reciprocally, as well as visits by heads of state, airline landing rights, on site inspections of nuclear test facilities, arms reductions— or military provocations. Nations may exchange prisoners of war, each releasing all they have captured. Nations also retaliate according to lex talionis by expelling each other's diplomats on an exact person-for-person basis, or bombing the other to revenge a raid.

Market Pricing, too, has long operated among nations. The United States purchased the Louisiana Territory from France and Alaska from Russia. Nations and international organizations lend money at interest to other nations, sell bonds on the open market, enter into commercial agreements state to state or state to corporation for the sale of weapons, water, and grain. Nations may undertake joint economic ventures like the St. Lawrence Seaway or dams on international rivers, or negotiate and effectively purchase what amounts to a lease for military bases. Socialist nations form, purchase, and operate national corporations, and nearly every country attempts to market its tourist attractions. Market Pricing among nations is also apparent in the efforts of central banks to influence exchange rates by buying or selling currency from their reserves.

Thus, all four of the elementary kinds of relationships are intertwined in the ties among groups and even among nations. The interaction between any pair or among any set of organizations is often, like the interaction among individuals, a composite built up out of more than one fundamental type of structure. This is part of what makes it possible for four simple elementary models to generate a profusion of observable forms. Just these four models exhibit a limitless combinatorial potential for operating at different levels among social entities of every scale. These models are concatenated and embedded across a range of uniquely defined cultural domains of activity, in the context of the more or less arbitrarily specified implementation rules that are required to realize them in practice. Their elaboration in these ways yields much of the phenomenological multiformity of empirical social relations.

This theory builds on the work of many theorists who offer dynamic conceptions of how one mode of relationship succeeds another in ontogeny or history (especially Maine, Marx, Durkheim, Weber, Ricoeur, Piaget, Kohlberg, Erasmus, Udy, Blau, Sahlins, Turner, and Guillet). Several of these theorists hypothesize a temporal order that includes some or all of the following sequence: Communal Sharing evolves into Authority Ranking, which transforms into Equality Matching, which ultimately develops into Market Pricing. The last section of Chapter 9 offers the germ of an idea of why both individual and societal changes might tend to exhibit this order of progression over the long run more often than other sequences. My suggestion there converges with the hypotheses of some of these dynamic theorists, who argue that there is a unique order of increasing span, comprehensiveness, logical elaboration, and complexity. Regardless, it would be exciting to explore the short- and medium-term sequential constraints and possibilities.[7]

## Combinations, Choices, Changes, and Integration

Throughout this book I write as if people make choices among models, since only one model can be applied at a time to any given activity or issue. This is not strictly true. The models are relational criteria, constraints, and ideals, and occasionally a single action may be congruent with more than one model. That is, two or more models may converge by simultaneously generating the "same" concrete behavior. From the point of view of the actor(s) concerned, there may be two or more social events going on, each linked to a distinct kind of social relationship, so that a single course of action "is,"—or at least means—two different things. In the sense that people are generating, understanding, coordinating, or evaluating behavior with reference to more than one model, then one "behavior" constitutes as many distinct "actions" as there are models to which it is oriented. As evaluative standards, it is easy to see that multiple models could lead by different paths to the "same" moral condemnation of an action (although the kinds of morality concerned and therefore the kinds of moral judgments made remain distinct). For example, suppose that your relationship with your younger brother makes it appropriate to share freely some candy you have received at a birthday party. Furthermore, your father *told* you to give your brother some. Your younger brother missed the party and he asked you to give him some of your candy, reminding you that he gave you four candy bars last time *he* went to a party. So you bargained with him and negotiated a payment of three candy bars if he would mow the lawn and walk the dog in your place, which he did. All in all, it would be disobedient (violating AR), inegalitarian (violating EM), ungenerous (violating CS), and a breach of a ratio-based contract (violating MP) to fail to give your little brother some of your birthday candy. Hence, giving him the candy would be "overdetermined" in the sense of being required by all four models. It is not clear just how often behavior is congruent with more than one model simultaneously, much less actually motivated and governed by two or more models.[8] Surely such convergence occurs. More commonly, the actions required by the separate models are incompatible and so the models are mutually exclusive. But the cases in which the same social action is overdetermined by multiple models are especially important (compare Freud's 1955 [1893] conception of the overdetermination of hysterical symptoms and other psychological products). Since overdetermined behavior is multiply constrained and therefore inflexible, overdetermination may cause such behavior to become frozen in form and frequently reiterated—in other words, ritualized.

The combinatorial aspect of the construction of social relations raises a further set of four issues for social theory. The *first* question is, how does it come about that people implement a given structure in any given domain of activity? The answer to this issue of selection must involve evolutionary, ontogenetic, historical, cultural, and other factors best addressed by longitudinal case studies and temporal elaborations of the present theory. There are also a large number of pragmatic considerations that must affect both conscious choice and other kinds of selection; Fiske and Baron (n.d.) address these and some of the social contextual and personality issues, as well. Leventhal (1976a) discusses task performance and productivity consequences of adopting different principles of social justice in exchange. Leventhal (1976b, Leventhal, Karuza, and Fry 1980) integrates individual preference and social system perspectives by explaining people's choices among alternative rules as the purposeful, instrumentally rational pursuit of their individual and collective goals. He offers a formal theory of such a decision process that reflects people's awareness of the system-functional and social-relational consequences of their choice, as well as other value and motivational factors. (It is also possible to make esthetic evaluations of the qualities of the various types of relationships, and these also must play a small part in people's choices among them.)

Schwinger (1980) and Mikula (1980) review the empirical literature on the issue of how people decide among the three social justice principles of need (CS), equality (EM), and proportional equity (MP) in distributing benefits, emphasizing that the key factor in people's choice of an allocation principle is the nature of the social relationship among them (see also Leventhal 1979).[9] And Schwinger concludes that the choice of a distributional principle reflects the kind of relationship the actors seek (cf. Clark 1984b, Mills and Clark 1982). Most of the empirical research that Schwinger and Mikula review concerns choices between equality and "equity" (rewards distributed in proportion to inputs) in situations involving the distribution of rewards for work, but Schwinger (1986) emphasizes the significance of the need principle. Deutsch (1985) also discusses how people choose a particular justice principle as a function of the kind of social relationship that exists among them, and (1985, 1987) looks at how that choice in turn affects the form of their future relationship. From the perspective of the current theory, saying that people have or seek a particular type of social relationship means that they apply a particular model broadly and persistently, using it as the preferred, criterion, or default mode of organizing their interaction. Hence the implication of these reviews by Schwinger and Mikula is that, as we would expect, there is some generality and stability in people's use of the models: confronted with a novel experimental task situation in which they have to choose how to transfer things among themselves, people tend to use their preferred, criterion, or default model.

Komorita (1984) makes the very important point that the principle of reward allocation people use is likely to depend on the manner in which individual inputs determine the outcome of a group task. He suggests that people are most likely to apply an MP equity principle where the joint task divides neatly into independent individual subtasks and the collective outcome depends on the performance of the most competent (actually, he means productive) members. People may also apply the equity principle when group outcome is an additive result of individual performances. In contrast, when the group's outcome depends on the performance of the least competent participants, Komorita hypothesizes that people are more likely to apply the equality principle. Extending this observation, we might hypothesize that people would either share rewards communally or divide them equally when group performance is some multiplicative function of individual performances, so that people are maximally interdependent. The crucial point is that task structure, not simply relative inputs, is a decisive factor in determining how groups distribute rewards. By implication, some technological ecological factors will affect the mode people use for organizing work and transfers.

It might be imagined that the central problem for research ought to be this issue of what models people select to organize the activities of each domain. But the analogy of language should at least give us pause here. Although it is enormously difficult to understand the principles that give structure to a particular language and that unite phenomenally disparate languages, it seems like a reasonable goal. It is not clear whether it is even possible to predict the actual utterances or the particular grammatical rules that a speaker will employ in any specific sentence. In the same spirit, my goal for the time being is to understand the *langue* of human social relations, not the *parole*.[10]

The *second* combinatorial issue is how people actually manage the pragmatics of switching among modes, and how they coordinate their selections and switches so that all the participants in a complex interaction activate corresponding models at each moment in each domain. Participant observation quickly reveals the remarkable fact that people almost always smoothly and unobtrusively maintain complementarity of expectations in social interaction, despite the intricate embedding and concatenation of structures in a complex social relationship. People typically agree about what mode they are using in virtually every case, except where there are ongoing disputes of certain special kinds.[11] Understanding just how people within a culture maintain correspondence so precisely will require, above all, appropriately focused studies of socialization, together with study of the cues people use to frame interactions (on framing interactions, see Bateson 1972a,b [1953, 1955], and Goffman 1971, 1974). At another level, this issue of the changes among modes of organizing any social activity (or thought) goes back to the central sociohistorical problem that occupied Marx, Maine, Durkheim, Weber, and Ricoeur: is there any orderly process to the transformations from one to another dominant mode of organizing relationships in society? Is Marx correct that the successor to Market Pricing is another, deeper form of Communal Sharing? This problem brings us to the third set of questions that emerges as a consequence of the combinatorial construction of social relations.

The *third* constellation of questions is, how does a society operate if it is not structurally homogeneous and hence neither uniform in its fundamental logic nor functionally integrated? Most social theorists have assumed that societies have some kind of organic integrity or ideal coherence that makes them unitary "systems." But the picture of social organization that emerges from my analysis is fundamentally polymorphous, and hence potentially inchoate. Each of the models I have described is an autonomous source for the formation of social relations and organizations, an intrinsically valid functional alternative form of structuring any activity. Each structure provides a fundamentally disparate model for organizing work, exchange, consumption and distribution, social influence and decision making, moral judgment and ideology, and so forth. What coordinates or integrates this jumble of four models more or less arbitrarily applied to each domain? So far, no master principle has come to light that mediates among them, and there is no reason to believe that there has to be such an integrative principle. The formal, axiomatic characterizations of the models in Chapter 9 only confirm this conclusion.

The four models predominate in the structure of different phases, aspects, and domains of life in any society, and in any given molecular social action people usually follow one model and disregard the others. Social order is not a crystal with a unique, uniform, endlessly reiterated structure: society is a conglomerate of related but distinct structures. And there is no evidence to suggest the existence of any matrix determining the arrangement of all the components and giving society an overall form. Unlike some theories of human society, this one provides no single determinate focus, no single source or unitary final form, and hence no definite prognosis of eventual homeostatic equilibrium. Disparate principles may coexist peacefully, or they may not—we need to understand how and when they fit together, and what happens if they do not (see the section Construction of Emergent Entities in the next chapter). But where there is stability, it is not a consequence of monistic structural coherence. *Sociability has no unique ultimate source or essence.*

One result of this may be the omnipresent potential for social flux. If there are always three other ways any aspect of any activity in any domain could be organized, then there may always come a time when chance or circumstances transform the way the activity is organized. Once again we face the question of searching for patterns in the changes, a question that future research should pursue. The only further suggestion I would make is that if overdetermination of the sort hypothesized above does occur, it should be a stabilizing condition.

The *fourth* and final issue about the composition of social relations concerns the *combinatorial syntax* of these models. There must be some constraints on how the four models can be put together in different phases of one personal relationship, set of roles, group, institution, or society. There are two somewhat different aspects of this question, one much studied, the other not. Many of the most influential scholars have worked on the problem of the connections between the mode of organization of one social domain and the mode of organization of another domain in the same society or group: Marx and Engels (1906 [1867]) and Weber (1958 [1904–1906], 1978 [1922]) studied the relationships between systems of production, political structure, and political ideology and religion; Durkheim (1933 [1893, 1926]) explored the link between the predominant mode of production and exchange in a society and the prevalent type of legal sanctions. Etzioni (1975 [1961]) initiated a major line of research on the links between the mode of recruitment to complex organizations and the predominant mode of social influence by which people run the organization. But the other aspect of relational syntax has been less extensively analyzed, apparently because the combinatorial nature of social relations has not been fully appreciated. This is the problem of the syntactical constraints on—and propensities for—combinations and sequences of the elementary models within a single activity or domain. This issue is related to the second question above of how people make transitions from operating in one mode to operating under a second model. And it is intimately connected with the sequence issue I raised at the end of the previous section. Less linear than the utterances of an individual speaker, however, social relations involve several things going on at the same time on different levels. We do not know very much about how various types of decision making go together in a single dyad or group, for example. Again, we still know only a little about how people can combine various modes of recruiting and organizing labor in the process of producing a single crop, operating a farm, or sustaining a regional system of agricultural production and exchange (see Erasmus 1956; Udy 1959, 1970; Şaul 1983). In various domains there must be relevant studies I have not yet discovered. But without any doubt the whole problem of social-relational syntax is open for exploration.

How does an individual choose what combinations of models to use in what situations? As I indicated at the start of this chapter, I think the answer is that individuals rarely choose at all. People acquire cultural implementation rules and syntax during enculturation, and then take them for granted (unless they encounter entirely novel situations). Indeed, socialization can be described as just that: learning the culture-specific implementation rules needed to realize endogenous models. So we must seek historical and cultural explanations of most use of the models, rather than looking at the matter as an individual decision process.

The conclusion is straightforward: four simple models can generate complex and diverse social relations. And why not? After all, how many kinds of bases are there in the genetic code of DNA?

# 8

## Defining Features of the Relational Models

Social behavior is inherently relational in nature: Individual behavior
assumes social meaning only in the context of human relations. . . .
The basic unit of analysis is therefore not individual behavior, but
behavior-in-a-relational-context. Accordingly, relational concepts lend
themselves most aptly for the representation and analysis of social
behavior. (Ho 1982:33)

*U*p to this point I have discussed the four models that structure social relations without characterizing the category of "elementary" and "fundamental" social models to which they all belong. What distinguishes these four
models from other kinds of concepts or prescriptions? I have said that there is
a small and limited set of fundamental models—perhaps only four—for the
construction of social relationships, but I have not yet specified what it is
about the four models that distinguishes them from any other rules about (or
constraints on) social behavior. If we are to search for other fundamental and
elementary types of social relationships, we need to stipulate what qualifies a
structure as a member of this class. Can we identify the unique features of
these models, features that (taken together) would enable us to recognize new
candidate members of the category of elementary relational models? What are
the distinctive qualities shared by all of the models as elementary models, beyond their manifestations in particular social domains?

In this chapter I will argue that all four models do share many features that
collectively set them apart from other concepts, precepts, guides, or rules for
behavior. Some of the defining features are sociological qualities having to do
with the structure of social networks. Some are cultural properties concerning
how people use the models in collectively making up a world of social meanings. And some are psychological attributes of the way individuals function,

assimilating, accommodating to, and acting on their social worlds. Many of the features I will describe are almost entirely hypothetical, since there is not yet sufficient evidence to demonstrate what I will assert about them. At a minimum, however, defining the possible distinctive features of these models will help to delineate a domain of discourse and give direction to our explorations.

The characteristic features are not binary, they are matters of degree, and some other kinds of models may approximate Communal Sharing, Authority Ranking, Equality Matching, and Market Pricing on one or another of these features. But I know of no other models that exhibit all these features to the same degree. If there are other models that do, then they belong in this class of fundamental elementary forms of social relations.

## SOCIOLOGICAL STRUCTURES: RELATIONS AMONG RELATIONSHIPS

### What Distinguishes Jural Models from Others?

The most important distinctive feature of this class of structures is that they are jural, or normative, models. That is, the models have intrinsic imperative force and are the source of moral, legal, religious, customary, and traditional rules and practices. Norms always exist in a social context, with reference to some social relationship (see Fiske 1990), and these models are the basic structures that give rise to norms. Specific rules and practices are held to be obligatory and legitimate because they are derived from these fundamental models. Simply, every social relationship entails moral obligations, and every moral obligation derives from the imputation of a social relationsip.

What this means from a social point of view is that the four basic models are essentially quadratic in form. The operation of the models can only be fully specified with reference to the interaction of four social positions: two or more participants in the social relationship proper, third parties who have relationships with the participants, and others who relate to the third parties. This is because recognition of the jural relevance of any of the models entails an obligation to "enforce" the model on others. Third parties are legitimately concerned with the performance of dyads with whom they have some social link, and other people interacting with such third parties take account of whether they have properly carried out their enforcement obligations (cf. Goode 1960:250, 255; Gibbs 1981:77–109.[1] The behavior of people in the social relationships generated out of these models is everyone's business; people are entitled to concern themselves with the performance of others in these relationships. Moreover, it is reprehensible not to concern oneself with the performance of others in these social relationships: there is an obligation to monitor, intervene, and sanction where appropriate. Simply put, there are imperative obligations at three levels: First, the parties immediately and directly participating in the primary relationship have a duty to conform to the model. Second, people with social links to the primary parties have a duty to react when the primary parties fail to meet their obligations—they must modify their social relationships with the primary parties in suitable ways. Third, it is the duty of others with social links to the secondary parties to appropriately modulate *their* social relationships with the secondary parties if the latter fail to react to the primary parties' breaches of duty. In other words, people get sanctioned for failing to sanction.[2]

Heider (1946, 1958) describes the related but more general fact that social relationships in a triad are interdependent: people take account of others' relationships with their own social partners. People are distressed if their relationships with each of two people are discordant with the relationship between these two people. (For example, if you hate your best friend's wife.) As a result, the three people involved tend to adjust their relationships in order to make them mesh.[3] Brown (1965) builds on Heider and integrates later work on cognitive consistency and balance to show how this works. However, what all these theorists fail to recognize is that the interdependence among social relationships operates very weakly insofar as the issues in the relationships concern matters of personal taste, esthetic judgments, or prudential and expediential prescriptions. In contrast, congruence and balance are extremely powerful processes when the issues are moral (including the institutionalized moral rules that we call law). That is, people are not obliged, and often do not bother, to reconcile differences with their associates in judgment about esthetics, or discrepant personal preferences and opinions. Even impractical or incompetent behavior in nonessential domains does not absolutely require admonishment and correction—it may be none of your business. When there is no moral flavor to these orientations and actions, associates may or may not take any substantial account of them.[4] But people "must" and typically do concern themselves with the jural (moral and legal) status of their partners in each of the four basic types of relationships.

For example, if I am your friend and we all know that I have borrowed a lot of money from a mutual friend under false pretenses and failed to pay her back, you must either censure me or jeopardize your friendship with her. If I am your boss and another employee is publicly known to be molesting your child, I had better take action against him, or lose your loyalty. On the other hand, if I like to tell my brother silly, tasteless jokes (which do not harm him in any way), though our sister considers this to be foolish and puerile, she need not rebuke me or attenuate her communal solidarity with either of us.

Neither the consistency and balance theorists nor most game theoreticians have adequately taken into account this feature of the contingencies among social relationships. When people construe someone's action as problematic in purely nonmoral terms, they may (or may not) modify their own relationship with the deviant person accordingly. But they do not sanction others for failing to sanction a third person's violations of standards of prudence, esthetics, or personal preference. So, for example, if I enjoy making and trying out new kinds of parachutes, it's up to my friends whether they want to associate with someone who might die any day. Unless they think such risk taking is immoral, no one would sanction my friends for either maintaining or ending our friendship, or for trying or not trying to get me to desist. But if I enjoyed making new kinds of parachutes and secretly putting them in other skydivers' packs to test them, anyone who knew and failed to take steps to stop me would be subject to punishment. Anyone who knowingly continued our friendship regardless of my actions, without trying to influence me to stop, would be morally (and legally) culpable. Consequently, others would be obliged to sanction my friends for failing to sanction me.

When it is discovered that a Moose woman is a witch who has killed someone in the village, her husband must either repudiate her and join in driving her out to permanent exile and ostracism, or else must flee with her and be perceived as her accomplice. There is no neutral ground. Other kinds of moral issues are not always so clear-cut, and indeed there may be moral failings that people construe as failures of supererogation rather than as actual moral transgressions: people may fail to live up to the ideal of a model without others regarding them as wrongdoers. In this regard, not every divergence from exemplary behavior impinges on every linked relationship. But major transgressions do.

If I were a Jew and you knowingly chose to finance the pharmacy of a man who experimented on poison gases in concentration camps, I would rebuke you and, if you continued, break off my association with you. This is because I have a (strong or weak) Communal Sharing relationship with other Jews. Thus the social relationships between the third and fourth parties (you and me) is to some degree dependent on how the third party (you) modulates his or her relationship with the second person (the pharmacist) as a function of the state of the social relationship between the first and second parties (concentration camp victims and the pharmacist). That is, I must not tolerate your financing his pharmacy, because by financing it you are implicitly condoning the fact that the pharmacist willfully killed people with whom I have a relationship of caring and identity. In this way, people's adherence to the moral rules embedded in each of the four types of social relationships links social relationships in complex, interdependent webs.

In some of the examples I have given, in Heider's theory, and in later consistency and balance theories the relationships involved form a closed loop. In such a structure, the component relationships are very strongly contingent, but they may also affect each other considerably even when the linked relationships are concatenated in other kinds of open-loop chains. Suppose Bartholomew robs the bank of his (AR) boss, Archibald, and Clarissa disregards this crime and maintains her love (CS) for Bartholomew undiminished, going off on vacation with him to Bulgaria as planned. Clarissa's friend (CS)

Delphinia has a duty to modify her friendship with Clarissa (criticizing the action and distancing herself in some way) as a consequence of Clarissa's failure to condemn Bartholomew's theft from Archibald. This assumes, of course, that everyone regards the bank robbery as a transgression of Bartholomew's legitimate AR relationship with Archibald. If, on the other hand, they all regard Bartholomew's daring guerrilla raid as a necessary and politically justified part of the righteous revolutionary struggle of the downtrodden proletariat against the capitalist oppressor, then Delphinia should give admiring praise to Clarissa, and their friendship will be strengthened and deepened. What Delphinia (and Clarissa) cannot do is to acknowledge the act and its moral significance and yet say, "What do I care? It's none of my concern!" On the other hand, if Bartholomew had taken eggs away from Attie the frog (an Asocial or Null interaction) or picked apples from a wild apple tree, then no one need pay it any mind: the difference is that Bartholomew has no fundamentally social relationship with Attie the frog or a wild apple tree. So taking frog's eggs and picking apples is not theft (unless people attribute social rights to animals or the environment). His actions in such a case have no necessary implications for others who relate to him, and they can perfectly well disregard what he does if it has no relevance to one of the basic types of social relationship.

These things work in all directions, of course: Archibald should modulate his relationship with Bartholomew if Bartholomew, unconcerned about the fact that Clarissa has murdered Delphinia, were to maintain his love affair with her unabated. If Bartholomew ackowledges a legitimate friendship between Clarissa and Delphina, or any other kind of social relation between the two, then he must abhor and condemn Clarissa's murdering her. Likewise, in relating to Bartholomew, Archibald should take into consideration whether Bartholomew does so. Of course, considerations of love and friendship may mitigate against doing what other jural obligations require one to do. But that is merely to say that sociomoral obligations conflict, sometimes irreconcilably (see Fiske 1990).

Note that there the "victim" need not be physically present, or aware of the violation, or even be materially existent. So a person may die in ignorance of the fact that her bankers in Switzerland (whom she never met) defrauded her; others still take account of the transgression. For those who regard pornography as exploitation of the categories of people depicted, pornography is a violation of a social norm of mutual respect and reciprocity not fundamentally different from violations of personal relationships with particular victims. Furthermore, if I blaspheme against a god, that god need not objectively exist in order for others to react violently to my transgression of the AR relationship that they impute and prescribe for me.

Other factors affect the degree and form of this mutual dependency among the four basic social relationships. There are always issues concerning how people frame a transgression: different accounts of the same actions suggest very different moral implications and thus have different consequences for the social relationships linked to the one in which the transgression occurs. Furthermore, the consequences for linked social relationships are always modulated by the relevant mitigating and aggravating factors. Linked to MP in American culture there is a very powerful norm of freedom of personal choice, with corollaries of noninterference and nonjudgmental relativism: there is virtually unlimited "room for opinion" and respect for others' right to disagree. This autonomy norm goes so far in some American subcultures that there is a folk confusion between morality and opinions or attitudes: no one wants to be seen as imposing a judgment on anyone else or insisting on the objectivity of obligations. This militates against the kind of mutual contingency and interdependence of social relationships that I am describing. Americans are inclined to say, "It's awful! But if that's the way he wants to lead his life, who am I to interfere?" Americans take this MP ideology to an extreme, with the consequence that often no one feels that he has standing to sanction overtly. However, this should not disguise the basic fact that even our social relationships are contingent on each other; what we do in any one of them has implications that radiate out and resonate far into the web of social relations surrounding us. These resonances depend on awareness, of course, and we also insist on an extraordinary degree of privacy, which our architecture and urban anonymity permits. But gossip has an insidious reach.

The point is that the four elementary models each govern more than simple dyadic relationships. These models also organize the contingent links *among* social relationships. That is their key sociological feature, and therein lies the crucial difference between these jural models and other prescriptive guides for action. It is what enables the models to generate higher order social groups. This kind of quadratic intercontingency is unique to the normative or jural social relationships that people generate out of the four fundamental models. Judgments about pragmatic, esthetic, and preferential features of social interaction do not ramify to other interactions in this strong manner. So it is of little necessary consequence to my relationship with you, my colleague, if I play a bad game of tennis, enjoy motorcycling with my wife, refuse to buy bubble gum for my children, am an effective bargainer in negotiating for African art, sew badly, or read a map well. None of these things need concern you in your relationship with me, because none are intrinsically relevant to any of the four fundamental types of social relationships. Of course, in hiring a typist you may well look into how well he types, as you may consider how someone dresses in deciding whether to go out on a date with him. But it's none of my business if you hire a poor typist or go out with a sloppy date. The one is inefficient and inexpedient, the other tasteless and lacking in sensibility, but neither is immoral, illegal, or sinful. And that means that we have neither the right nor the obligation to enforce our judgments or our preferences on you.

The consequence is that in a network of social relationships governed by the fundamental models, relationships are interdependent and mutually contingent. The actions of any person in a social relationship have potential ramifications for all the relationships linked to the primary relationship. Transgressions in particular ramify through the network and may be reflected back on the transgressor in an onslaught of sanctions through all of his or her social relationships. Thus the state of every relationship is to some degree a function of the moral or jural state of all the other normative social relationships directly or indirectly linked to it in the same region of the network. This is what yields the stability of social structures and also their potential for abrupt collapse.

## Construction of Emergent Entities

It is also characteristic of the four basic models that they produce high level emergent social phenomena. The production of emergent collective phenomena is evident in two respects, both of which I have already pointed out. As I discussed in Chapters 2 and 7, these models may govern the modes of interaction between groups. Another example of this is the "restricted" marriage exchange systems of the kind Lévi-Strauss describes (1961 [1949]) that may be generated out of Equality Matching even though no individual exchanges a wife for a wife; reciprocal matching is at the level of groups. The other, more complex, aspect of the construction of emergent social patterns is the result of the interdependence of linked dyadic interactions. Collective social entities like families, lineages, villages, departments, universities, and corporations are the products of this kind of interdependence. Consider what an American family is: a social unit based in large part on Communal Sharing in which the state of each component dyadic relation and of the family unit itself is a function of the state of each of the other component dyads. One essential constitutive rule of the American family is the incest taboo. Sexual relations are limited to the husband-wife dyad. Their occurrence in any other dyad throws all dyads into disequilibrium. In a sense (as the courts recognize), extramarital sexual relations within the family are antithetical to the triadic (or higher order) CS relationship that is the family. Among Moose in Burkina Faso, core CS relationships also have triadic and quadratic structures like this. Focal sexual taboos define mutual contingencies among three or four social relationships, and sexual relations in one dyad are antithetical to continued Communal Sharing relationships in other dyads, and vice versa (Fiske n.d.). For a more commonplace and less drastic instance of the interdependence of relations within the family, consider divorce. If the husband-wife dyad falls apart, all the other family dyads are seriously disturbed. Or suppose that one pair of siblings are feuding, and won't talk to each other: what happens to Thanksgiving reunions? All the other family dyads are disrupted to greater or lesser degree, as is the whole unit. In other words, the social world is a web whose strands are social relationships. If one strand breaks, the whole web trembles and its shape changes.

Now think about a company of any kind. Its operation, and in fact the very idea of a company, is predicated on suppositions about the interdependence of its constituent relations. This is true, for example, of the Authority Ranking relations within it. A manager can direct and control her subordinates effectively only as long as she has the backing of her superiors; without it, her authority generally evaporates. She exercises authority only if she has in fact been hired and installed by her superiors, and until she is transferred or fired. At the same time, she retains her role as trusted subordinate to the company executives only so long as she does in fact mobilize, oversee, and direct her subordinates effectively. If she fails in this, she loses the trust and support of her superiors (along with praise, recognition, bonuses, promotions), and ultimately perhaps her job with the company. The better she is at managing her subordinates, the better off she is in relation to her bosses, of course. Equality Matching relations in the company are interdependent on each other and dependent on the other three types of basic social relationships in similar ways. For example, imagine an employee who repeatedly fails to do his fair share, to take a turn at unpleasant jobs, or to reciprocate with help when others have helped him. His fellow workers will regard him as selfish, untrustworthy, and dishonest. Co-workers, including those who have not been victims of this behavior, will tend to avoid him and refuse to cooperate with him. This disequilibrium in his peer relationships is also very likely to affect his status as a good employee, his salary, assignments, and opportunities—in short, his relations with his supervisors. In general, the qualitative state of any fundamental social relationship is a function of the moral and legal status of all the social relationships linked to it through any person. Any group or organization is made up of such a web of mutually contingent social relationships. This is a consequence of the triadic (and higher order) jural nature of these four fundamental types of social models. They are the constituent pieces out of which higher order social entities emerge. In essence, I am suggesting that an appropriately directed analysis of any social system will reveal that the models are the structures that give order to social relations. Moreover, the component social relationships are not loose filaments in a pile, they are a mutually supporting, mutually contingent web. In sum, a defining feature of the four elementary relational models is that the dyadic cores interconnect so as to generate emergent social structures that are far more complex and interdependent.

The mutual contingency and emergent constructive aspects of the fundamental forms of social relationships are two aspects of the same sociological feature. The four basic modes of relationship are mutually implicating, interdependent linkages that combine like molecular bonds to form higher order structures: indeed, it is just because they are mutually conditional that the basic relationships can combine to form larger wholes. If there are any other elementary models, they must also possess this characteristic feature. In addition to this sociological dimension of these models, there are cultural and psychological qualities that, taken together, help set the basic models apart from other kinds of models and guidelines for social behavior.

## CULTURAL MEANINGS

The social models are important elements of culture. That is, they take on culture-specific but recognizable symbolic relational values, and enter into the construction of shared systems of social meaning. A culture is a system of symbols and meanings, in which the meaning of any symbol derives from its links to other symbols on various planes together with its referential functions (if any). Generally, all of the fundamental models for the construction of social relationships are adopted, applied, modified in detail and substance, phenomenologically transformed, and incorporated into the matrix of symbols and meanings constituting the particularities of a unique culture. Thus incorporated into a particular culture, the models assume unfamiliar shapes and take on idiosyncratic accretions the way hermit crabs disguise the shells they appropriate. But the four elementary models are still analytically discernible. Their status as cultural entities is a characteristic and important distinctive quality of the models.

Geertz (1973a) demonstrates that cultural meaning systems have mutually reinforcing representational, constitutive (constructive), motivation- and mood-inducing, ontological-interpretive, and moral dimensions. D'Andrade (1984) distinguishes analytically among constructive (constitutive), representational, directive (motivational), and evocative (affective) aspects and functions of culture. I will address all of these, but since these features have both cultural and psychological sides, I will divide the discussion between this section and the one following, where I discuss the psychological reality and status of the basic models. As both Geertz and D'Andrade emphasize, however, the collective, cultural dimensions of such models and their psychological dimensions are intimately connected, and the distinction between the models' cultural and psychological features is more heuristic than phenomenological.

### Cultural Constitution of Social Relations

The models which I have been discussing provide foundations for the cultural constitution of social relations and statuses. That is, they provide the basic set of frameworks available for the cultural construction of the social world. Each culture extends, elaborates, combines and applies them in distinctive ways to make up what we call kinship systems, alliances, peer groups and age sets, marriage systems, political and economic systems, and other social relationships, networks, and groups. These fundamental models provide the matrix within which a culture defines what it is to be a mother, an employee, a prostitute, a friend or a thief, a *tēngsoba* (the Moose custodian of the earth), *naaba* (chief), a *zoa* (friend), or a *sõea* (witch), or any other kind of person, as well as judgments about the jural and esthetic quality of a person's performance in such roles. The four models also provide a foundation for the cultural construction of such "performative" actions as getting married, making a contract, apologizing, executing a criminal, or committing incest.

The American middle class cultural construct, "father," will illustrate this (cf. Schneider 1980). The idea of father is essentially based on Communal Sharing and Authority Ranking. A father is a man who has children whom he cares for uncontingently—and who will care for him when he needs it. A man and his children are a basic component of the social unit that is the family, an entity quintessentially communal. The family pools resources, shares living space, income, transportation, name, and commensally consumed food, while (ideally) spending a great deal of working, playing, talking, and resting time together. Physical contact and affection embody the sense of identity and solidarity of father and children. At the same time, a father is a person who has authority over his children while they are young, and who takes responsibility for them. He (in many subcultures along with his wife) makes decisions about his children's education, activities, and associates, and he instructs them in manners and morals. His children owe him obedience and respect, at least in certain contexts, and young children ultimately must defer to his wishes and expressed decisions.

In some American subcultures there are also minor elements of Equality Matching involved in the father role, for example in playing and competing on an equal basis with teenage and adult children, or in taking turns in some domains. Market Pricing is a negligible component, for the most part, although a father may pay his children for certain chores or hire them as employees to work their way up the ladder in the family business. To see that CS is essential to the American definition of "father," imagine a man who did not live, eat, or frequently talk and play with the other members of the family when he was able to do so, who did not feel any kind of sense of identity with them or they with him, did not share living space and food or was not believed to share any "biological substance" (e.g., "blood") with them, who did not care for them or have any intrinsic responsibility to do so, who could not be called on to help without compensation in time of need, and who did not share a name or social identity with them. Would he be a true and complete "father?" Regarding Authority Ranking, imagine a man who did not direct, oversee, supervise, or otherwise bring up children, who was not older, wiser, or more powerful than the children, who took no responsibility for any children, who made no decisions regarding young children's current life or future, and in no other ways commanded, instructed, directed, supervised, protected, represented to others, stood up for, or took responsibility for children. Would he be fully a "father?" I submit that the American cultural construct "father" depends on the fundamental ideational structure of CS and AR and that its implicit definition, its very meaning, requires these concepts of equivalence and rank order. Of course, the American construct "father" is much more than the combination of the ideas of equivalence and order, but these two conceptual structures are necessary foundations for the culturally formulated definition.

In the same sense, all the core social roles in any culture are built up around an armature composed of these fundamental models. How could the idea of "client" have any meaning without the underlying conceptual structure of Market Pricing? What would "boss" mean without the idea of a rank ordering and the notion of authority, together with the MP concept of employment? What would a "colleague" or "friend" be without the basic models of Equality Matching and Communal Sharing? Is it possible to define or express the implicit definition of "lover" without some ideational construct congruent with CS? Of course, Communal Sharing isn't all there is to "mother," or else mothers and lovers would be the same thing. Although these two cultural roles are defined in part as opposites, they both depend on, they both presuppose and take form out of the basic concept of CS equivalence relations.

In brief, my assertion is that the fundamental models are essential to the definition of the core social roles of any culture. The cultural meaning of the major social roles and relations in any society is partly derived from these underlying models—however much it may be developed and transformed in any particular culture. That is, these models underlie the prescriptive representations for social relations shared by the members of any given culture. Like any such theory of universals, this theory cannot be proved. But it can easily be disproved if anyone can come up with a few important social roles and relations in any culture that can be adequately defined and articulated without using anything corresponding to the structures I have described, or any others demonstrably belonging to the same genus. The central point is that a defining feature of these fundamental models is that they are the elementary constituents with which cultures define major roles and relationships (and therefore also persons). Any other candidate for inclusion in the category of fundamental relational models must share this feature.

## Directive Entailments of the Fundamental Models

As D'Andrade (1984) points out, the constructs in a cultural meaning system have directive entailments of two kinds. Both needs and obligations are attached to the constitutive aspects of social constructs. As I argued in the example above, to be a father is to have a set of obligations toward one's children, and typically it is also to experience a subjective need to do many (perhaps most) of the things one is socially obliged to do. There are a great many intrinsic rewards in fatherhood. This combination of external obligation and constraint (including the threat of sanctions) together with internal motives is characteristic of these models. This is Geertz's (1973a:93–95 [1966]) notion of prescriptive models *for* reality. As I showed above, much of the immediate feedback acting to induce role conformity operates in terms of triadic jural interdependence of social relations. To maintain one's good standing in other linked relationships, one must perform each focal role adequately. Most moral precepts, legal rules, and ideological values are in some degree derivative from the fundamental underlying models. To the extent that people take such rules and values as axiomatically governing their own behavior, and as requirements which they must necessarily impose and enforce on others, the basic models are directive ideals. Overall, these models require and imply congruently structured social action. A father is not just someone who essentially is some constellation of qualities, but a person who must do the right things.[5] So the models not only provide the basic terms to define social roles, they also have directive force obligating and motivating people to perform these roles. A major facet of this is that the models provide the basic ideals and standards that people use to evaluate social action. Just as people in a linguistic community have reliable and highly congruent grammatical standards for judging whether an utterance is well-formed, so people in any stable community use the culture-specific forms of these social models to assess each other's behavior. This evaluative use of the models is an integral part of their directive role in governing social relations.

In Chapter 5 I reviewed research on the distinctive motivational qualities of the four models, and most of Part IV is devoted to demonstrating the distinct motivational force that each exhibits among Moose. So there is no need to elaborate on this aspect of the models here. Suffice it to say here that one of the distinctive features of these models is that they have dual directive force as major obligations and as basic social motivations. If there are other fundamental models, they too must have this dual character of entailing both needs and obligations.

## Making Sense of Social Reality

A culture does not only generate meanings, it provides a framework for making sense of the experienced world: people use the constructs their culture provides to understand the world. In particular, people utilize the social constructs in a culture (which are built on the foundation of the basic models) to make social relations intelligible. I argued above that people draw on the models to generate appropriate action, but they also draw on the models to understand what other people are doing (and in turn to respond appropriately). Just as in language, where the same grammar may be used to generate speech and to decode it, or as in cognition where the same algorithm may possibly be used to encode something perceived and to reconstruct it, so in social relations the same models may underlie action and the understanding of action. This seems to operate at two levels. For example, as naive entrants to any new sociocultural world, whether as children or adults, we can quickly learn who's in charge, where they are entitled to precedence, how to show respect, and what constitutes a command—because as humans we all share the same basic model of Authority Ranking, and the same sense of the natural ways to mark AR. Coming into a new culture as children, immigrants, in-marrying spouses, or partic- ipant observers, we use the AR model in its empty, generic form as a potential matrix for learning the particular culture-specific forms. Expert members of a culture all know how the Authority Ranking model is elaborated, expanded or reduced, recognized or suppressed, applied and transformed into the subtle- ties of a particular system of rank and authority. So cultural adepts recognize a polite request as an imperative, distinguish fine gradations in the hierarchy, and discern when nominal deference is actually insulting disrespect. All this is built on the foundation of the Authority Ranking model which we draw on to figure out what people are doing.

Thus these models are like scientific "models," which can be used to ex- plain, predict, or give a retrospective account of events. They may also be ap- plied outside the domain of interaction with concrete human organisms, for example in prayer or accounting for misfortune in terms of gods or witches (cf. Horton 1967). This use of the models corresponds to Geertz's (1973a [1966]) notion of interpretive models *of* reality, and to the concept of social schemata developed by social psychologists (S. Fiske and Taylor in press). In any case, the third cultural feature that characterizes these models is that people use each of them to make sense of their social worlds—not only to respond appro- priately, but simply to understand, to make their experience coherent. We should search for other basic models that people use in the same way.

## Coordination

Since people in a given culture tend to share the same cultural tokens of the four basic types of models of and for social relations, another characteristic of the models is that they coordinate action. They are the source of much of the complementarily of action; under their governance the actions of interacting individuals and interacting groups fit together. We take this so much for granted that it is difficult to recognize either how pervasive or how important it is in social relations. At the level of dyadic interaction, it is the shared knowl- edge and joint adoption of Equality Matching that makes it possible to orgin- ate and sustain a friendship, a collegial, or a peer relationship. Suppose that you and I live next to each other and we both commute a long way in to work at the same office. Given that we both understand Equality Matching and rec- ognize its applicability, we can easily take turns driving together in each other's car. And either of us can readily propose such a one-to-one exchange because we both recognize what is involved. Each of us has a corresponding representation of the turn taking. I do not just show up at your door every day expecting you to drive, nor do you get in your car and drive off without me. Neither of us resents driving and paying for the gas on the alternate days when it is our turn. Adjustments are easy to make; if my car is in the shop for a week so that I miss my turns, when I get it back I offer to drive all the next week. If we had different models or no model at all for what was going on (as may happen in cross-cultural interaction), confusion, resentment, dissension, and conflict might well result. Or we might simply adopt the Null social arrangement and each drive our own cars separately. As it is, we both know what to expect, we (and our spouses) know when the car will be free for our spouses to take, and we can readily adapt to contingencies like having another office mate moving in to our neighborhood.

Higher orders of coordination also are commonplace. I know how to distribute ice cream to my children, because I know that in such matters they operate in a strict Equality Matching mode. Thus my knowledge of the model they apply to this situation results in the avoidance of bitterness, jealousy, and conflict between the children, as well as avoiding any misunderstandings about implications of favoritism in uneven distributions. If this example seems trivial, just reflect on debates over unfair distributions of wages, taxes, or contributions to the United Nations.

Consider the mutual comprehension required for the operation of Communal Sharing relationships. Among the !Kung of the Kalahari, anyone in a band can ask anyone for virtually anything, and almost always get it (L. Marshall 1961). Among the Moose, people in joking relationships may come into your compound in your absence and take a tool, a chicken, or a pot without asking or telling you in advance. In some American families, any family member may be able to use the car, eat the food in the refrigerator, or take a swim in the pool without prior arrangement, notification, or compensation. In all of these cases, if their need (or desire?) is sufficient people can count on asking for and receiving help even when such help represents a considerable imposition or hardship on those giving it. In contrast, imagine a stranger trying to do any of these things. The prerogatives of a family member are predicated on the presupposition of a particular type of social relationship. People with whom a person has a Communal Sharing relationship not only permit and encourage, they also plan on their joking partners' or family members' taking such actions, just because they have this joint understanding of the social relationship. That is to say, people coordinate their actions within this framework by each referring to a common model, the model of Communal Sharing.

Beyond the group itself, outsiders also take account of the model and organize their action with reference to it, even when not themselves participants. Thus is some societies people can suitably take revenge for a murder by killing any member of the kin group of the murderer, and this may be accepted by the original murderer's group as just and equitable (e.g., Schieffelin 1976). This is possible because all recognize that every member of the kin group is equivalent, and taking the life of any of them is equivalent to taking the life of any other. At the same time, this kind of coordinated action "works" because all concerned recognize that the violent death of a person can be canceled out by the compensating death of a member of the killer's kin group. By implicit reference to their shared model based on Equality Matching, such revenge may end a feud (although nothing need actually be said about what motivates or structures the action). Or people may continue a feud indefinitely, back and forth: just like other organized social relations, violence may be coordinated with respect to these structures. War and cooperation are both structured, and it is the common reference to these models by the respective parties to the interaction that makes for something other than anarchy and chaos.[6]

This kind of coordination may exist on any scale, at any level. The phenomenon of rotating credit associations, described in Chapter 7, illustrates this for Equality Matching. Similarly, it is the shared understanding and common implementation of Market Pricing by each of the different individuals in a social field that permits the operation of markets. Think about the stock exchange. My broker can call me and say that she has just heard that the Organization of African Unity has made a joint declaration of war against the government of South Africa, so she anticipates a drop in the market—but suspects that a few select defense companies will immediately go up. I can then tell her to sell some stocks and buy others, and she will execute these trades, holding the shares for me, and billing me of course.[7] We do this because we have a joint understanding of our social relationship as a Market Pricing relation, and I know that not only does she probably believe that her future earnings depend on her honest execution of this oral agreement, her company and the stock exchange will to some degree oversee her actions and enforce the verbal contract. She gives me this information partly in the hope of generating brokerage fees, as well as because if she is correct, she anticipates that I will take her advice in the future and possibly entrust more of my future assets to her account. Beyond this, the whole discussion is predicated on our joint expectations about how other people owning stocks, oriented toward Market Pricing, will act in the face of the declaration of war. So our actions are oriented toward our application of Market Pricing to the prediction of the effect on the price of stocks of the behavior of other sellers and buyers. These other stockholders' actions, in turn, are based on their understanding of the actions of individuals and firms operating primarily under the same model. Will the demand for a given commodity change under the expected condition of an African war, and how will changes in the supply curves of certain commodities (due to shortages of materials from South African mines) affect the prices of other commodities, and hence the anticipated profitability of various publicly held corporations, and hence the price of their stocks?

In cases like these, people may be applying a model on four different levels simultaneously, coordinating their actions accordingly. We take for granted the intricately complex complementarity of the actions of all the people involved. Yet this fit is precise and dependable, both in the way the actions of diverse direct and indirect interactants mesh at any moment in time, and in the anticipatory alignment of present decisions with the future actions of others far removed. This complementarity is dependent on the fact that all of the parties concerned are referring to a single model they share in common, and also dependent on the fact that the parties all implicitly take into account others' implementation (under known conditions) of the jointly understood model. Thus the fourth cultural feature is also a sociological and psychological feature: people coordinate their action by each referring to a model that they all know everyone knows, and know that everyone takes into account. This coordinative function grows out of the constitutive function of the fundamental models, their directive force, and the ways people use them to understand their social experience.[8] Any other social models that we might propose as fundamental models must be shown to have a similar coordinative function in social relations.

Altogether, the four basic models are an essential foundation for the construction of cultural meaning in social relations. The models are distinctive in providing the basic framework for the cultural constitution of social roles and relations. The models are characterized by their inherently directive nature, both as individual motivations and as collectively enforced obligations. The models are the foundation on which people base the cultural representation of social relations, which is to say that the models mediate peoples' understanding of their social worlds. The models also make up the framework linking social action into locally more or less integrated, coherent wholes: where people in fact manage to coordinate their social relationships to fit together and interlock systematically they do so using these models as their common template.[9] Hence the models are the foundation for the shared ideas providing much of the structure underlying the collective construction of systems of relational and referential meaning in social affairs. In effect, the other side of my assertion is that a cultural analysis of social relations in any society will reveal some particular instantiation of at least some subset, and usually all, of the models. The elementary models in this set are not just observers' etic descriptive formulations or analytic theories, they are the raw material on which each culture builds its own emic categories.[10] Indeed, the models are useful analytic and interpretive tools only to the degree they do correspond with the models people actually use to constitute, direct, understand, and coordinate their social relations.

## PSYCHOLOGICAL REALITY AND FEATURES

In proposing a characterization of the category of fundamental models for social relationships, I first considered their sociological features, particularly their quadratic jural nature as contingent links among dyadic social relationships. Then I discussed their cultural features, focusing on their constitutive, directive, representative, and coordinative roles in the construction of meaning systems. Now I will look at their psychological status and psychological characteristics. I will discuss in turn the ontogeny and spontaneous emergence of the models, the human capacity to recognize them, their motivational and emotional components, the need to punish transgressions and the recognition of the validity of punishment. The sociological, cultural, and psychological features that characterize the fundamental models turn out to be homologous.[11] Indeed, to a large degree, most of the sociological, cultural, and psychological features are merely alternative descriptions of the same phenomenon from the perspectives of three different kinds of analysis. But the languages of analysis are sufficiently different to make it useful to complement the sociological and cultural descriptions with an account of the characteristic features of these models in psychological terms. Most of the accounts of the psychological features I propose here are even more speculative than the hypothesized social and cultural defining features, but it is nonetheless important to attempt to delineate the sorts of features all elementary and fundamental relational models should have.

## Ontogeny and Spontaneous Emergence

Informal observations and interviews with a few informants suggest that each of the fundamental types of social relationships emerges spontaneously in American children in a definite sequence: CS, AR, EM, MP (see Chapter 17 for more details). For example, Equality Matching appears rather abruptly around age four, and immediately becomes a dominant mode of social interaction. At this point, children become intensely interested in distributive justice, taking great care to be sure everyone has the same number of cookies, for example—regardless of who likes or wants the cookies, and despite the child's own desire for the cookies. Turn taking is suddenly very important, so that the child wants everyone to have a turn at everything, regardless of the person's interest or the cultural suitability of the activity for that person. And everything is seen as reciprocal, including for example being sent to one's room or other punishments. Fairness becomes the paramount moral value. What is striking about the emergence of this mode of social interaction is that it appears to crystallize at about this age without regard for the kind of socialization the child has been receiving; the child organizes her social relationships this way at her own instigation, even if she has not been specifically taught to do so. Any earlier training in distributive justice and turn taking fell on deaf ears and had little result, until at this point EM comes out all over the place, even where it is culturally inappropriate and socially deviant, and even when the need for EM overrides many of the child's other significant motives and desires. I have repeatedly been struck by the observation that beginning at age four it makes a child (and often an adult) less happy to give her something if you give a sibling or peer more of the same thing, or just something different. As a parent I find that if I cannot give virtually equal presents, generally we are all happier if I do not give anything to either child. This means that the child's distress at the inequality between gifts often outweighs and even negates completely the child's pleasure at receiving the gift.[12]

The converse of this is an age-specific readiness to accept relevant kinds of instruction and example. There seem to be periods of unique sensitivity in the child's adoption of each mode of social relationship, during which he is prepared to acquire culture- or family-specific realizations of these fundamental modes, realizations that are very easily learned and subsequently very persistently retained.

It also seems that the particular persons with whom the child forms relationships of each type may retain a certain primacy over later ties. For example, a person often permanently retains a unique sharing relationship with his mother, in part because of the developmental stage at which they formed the communal relationship. And it is conceivable that vicissitudes in the development of object relations of the different kinds find their origins in specific ontogenetic windows (cf. Ainsworth 1967, Bowlby 1969, 1988). The postulation of a sensitive (if not "critical") period for the emergence and formation of social relationships of the four basic kinds is for the most part a speculative hypothesis, but of considerable importance if correct (cf. Erikson 1980 [1959]).

There are complex epistemological and methodological issues to be resolved before it would be possible to validate the claim that the cognitive and motivational features of each model emerge spontaneously as a consequence of maturation, like walking and talking, at distinct periods in development. I will develop this point further in Chapter 17. Pursuing this approach would also mean a complete rethinking of the question of "moral development" and "socialization." Comparative evidence from cultures that differ greatly in their social organization and child-rearing practices would be crucial. For the moment, I simply want to propose that a fundamental model for social relations should be endogenous and emerge maturationally, as a structure that children impose on their social world and not simply as a form learned or "internalized"[13] from raw experience. Children will at the same time "project" the model on their social relations and be especially receptive to cues about the application rules that are needed to implement the model.

### Spontaneous Generation

Fundamental relational models should also appear in the spontaneously generated social relations of adults. It happens among both children and adults that an ad hoc aggregation of two or more people comes together in circumstances in which there is neither a clear social precedent nor a well defined cultural recipe for organizing group relations. The structure that then emerges is partly a function of the nature of the immediate situation, and in part indicative of the endogenous models people bring to the situation. I maintain that the fundamental relational structures I have described are ones that "naturally" emerge in a wide variety of such circumstances. Lacking definitely prescribed modes for organizing social relations in novel domains and contexts in which the prescriptive rules are, if not irrelevant, at least ambiguous, people fall back on these basic models. Old structures of social relationships decay, fall apart, and sometimes collapse abruptly, and what arises out of their ruin may reveal something about the human psychic repertoire of basic social forms. We would expect to get similar information when disparate cultures come in contact ("creolization"), and especially when people from extremely heterogeneous cultures are isolated and required to function as a corporate group. Extremely prolonged lifeboat and desert island experiences may approximate the necessary conditions. What we need to investigate are a variety of situations of the kind William Golding (1955) imagines in *Lord of the Flies*.

This characteristic of the category of fundamental models is a sort of "projective test" in social practice. Like other kinds of projective tests, the idea is that in the absence of extrinsic structure, people collectively produce the forms that are natural and intelligible to them and that reflect their underlying cognitive social dispositions. If people consistently generate the four basic types of social relations without prompting, without external constraints or extrinsic pressures, then it seems appropriate to speak of endogenously generated organizing principles for social relations. This might be interpretable as evidence for their psychological reality, although of course people import, adapt, and apply cultural norms for situations they deem similar to any novel domain. Thus it will be extremely difficult to distinguish the cultural and psychological components of the way in which people structure a novel situation. However in personnel selection, unstructured situation tests of this kind have proved to be potent tools (U.S. Office of Strategic Services 1948). With proper experimental controls or the analysis of sufficiently diverse cases of natural experiments, however, such "projective" evidence about how people organize initially undefined, ambiguous, and unstructured social relations could be quite compelling.

## Recognition

Another psychological quality characterizing these fundamental models is that children, immigrants, fieldworkers and other neophytes recognize them easily and reliably, even when they have had no prior experience with the specific realization of the model they encounter. People are able to discern the existence of such models even when the data at hand are not extensive or redundant enough to permit a rigorously logical inductive derivation of the structures involved. This recognition also occurs despite the fact that the manifestations of the underlying model a person observes may be very complex and intermingled (in the ways described in Chapter 7). My hypothesis is that these elementary models resemble in this respect the grammatical knowledge that Chomsky (e.g., 1981, 1986) claims humans universally share at birth, and without which they could not learn any particular human language. This robust—almost irrepressible—ability to pick up these patterns in social interaction, however inadequate the information and however great the "noise," is a distinctive feature of these models and an indication of their psychological reality. As is the case for the first distinctive psychological feature, natural emergence, the human preparedness to recognize the local representations of the elementary models is observable both ontogenetically and in culture contact.

### Learnability

Certainly the most salient phenomenon of this type is the socialization of children. I submit that children are able to learn the culturally appropriate forms of social interaction because the task they face is limited to recognizing how to apply models which they already in some sense "know." From the point of view of the learner, socialization then consists of discovering five kinds of things (see Implementation in Chapter 7): (1) How are people assigned to roles in each structure? (2) Which structure applies in which domains of activity, with respect to what empirical dimensions, and with what substantive content? (3) What are the parametric conventions that set the specific values and taxonomies that people use to apply the generic models to real life? (4) What are the local implementations of the characteristic semiotic codes people use to mark and coordinate social relations? (5) What are the ideological precepts about what sorts of relations are good, true, and possible? That is, the child has to learn how to fit what she observes into the limited set of incompletely specified fundamental models with which she is equipped. It is these models that, as templates or heuristics, make it possible for the child to understand what is going on and to learn to act appropriately herself. She does not have to construct the culture-specific forms of the models by some kind of pure inductive empiricism, and indeed she could not do so (again, cf. Chomsky 1959, 1981, 1986). That is, the models underlying CS, AR, EM, MP relations probably could not be learned from ordinary social experience by a generalized behaviorist machine that lacked prior knowledge of the particular structures. Nor would the widely varying experiences of different children converge on such a small set of shared models without the elementary structures as a common psychological foundation.

This implies that social ontogeny involves a combination of two processes. First, there is the maturation of the cognitive capacities and the motivational proclivities to engage in each kind of social relationship; this may take place over nine or ten years. Second, there is the concomitant process of discovering the five sorts of implementation rules, and this is where social learning—socialization—takes place, within the context of a small set of highly constrained relational frameworks.

### Fieldwork, Understanding, and Cultural Translation

The same logic applies to the experience of crossing cultures. How is it that an anthropologist (or any other person) doing participant observation is ever able to understand and participate properly in the social relations of a new culture? The mechanism is essentially the same as in primary socialization, although an ethnographer has more sophisticated analytic tools and more breadth of comparative background material to use in developing her understanding of experiences in a new culture. But what makes ethnography possible is again the fact that the ethnographer only needs to discover how CS equivalence relations operate in the particular culture; there is no need to learn the structure of equivalence relations in the first place. An anthropologist doing fieldwork does not need to inductively derive from her observations the structure of Authority Ranking relations, she just needs to see how and when that structure is realized in the particular culture. Similarly, an immigrant immersed in a new culture does not need to make observations and carry out an analysis sophisticated enough to discover the fact that there are social relationships organized according to the structure of ordered Abelian groups (see Chapter 9)—"all" he has to do is recognize which relationship are the Equality Matching relationships and learn the manner in which people implement and mark them. Learning such things is not easy, as anyone who has been a child or raised one—or tried to learn to live as a participant in a new culture—can attest. But it is possible, whereas it is doubtful that the inductive task of discovering de novo the structures necessary to generate everyday social relationships would be readily or reliably accomplished ex nihilo.

## Motivation and Emotions

Another quality that characterizes the fundamental structural models for social relationships is that there are probably definite, discrete, identifiable motivational states corresponding to each type of social relationship, and perhaps distinct emotions as well. If a motivation is a potential for organizing behavior according to a particular structure (Gallistel 1980a, b, 1981), then the motivation for a type of social relationship is a potential to seek out relationships of that kind and to structure ongoing relationships in that mode. As Geertz (1973a) and D'Andrade (1984) point out, such motivations, emotions, and moods inform and in turn are informed by the constitutive, directive, interpretive, and ontological aspects of models with cultural dimensions. I have discussed these aspects above. Since I have considered motivation in Chapter 5 and will consider it again at length in Part IV, here I will just mention the related issue of social emotions.

That there are specific emotional states corresponding to each type of social relationship has not yet been clearly established and so should be treated as a speculative proposal. What I suggest is that there may be distinct positive subjective states associated with equilibrium participation in social relationships of each type, and distinct negative subjective states associated with the loss or threatened loss of engagement in social relationships of each type. Fridlund

(1989, 1990) argues that emotions are essentially social intention states, and I believe that in that ethological sense there are probably different intention states corresponding to readiness to engage in social relationships of each type. Beyond this, I show elsewhere in this book that there are type-specific appetites for relationships of each sort. Hence people have needs to participate in each kind of relationship, and will seek out specific types of social relationships as an inverse function of how recently and intensively they have been engaged in relationships of that type. Furthermore, I would hypothesize that people may experience these specific appetites directly as subjective needs for participation in each kind of relationship. This ethological hypothesis thus suggests that there may be distinct emotions associated with seeking out and anticipation of each type of social relationship, as well as emotions related to the equilibrium states, emotions connected to the violation of each, and emotions linked to the disturbance or dissolution of each type. We can call these respective categories of emotions the emotions of need or appetite for CS, AR, EM, and MP relationships, the transgression emotions of outrage, shame, guilt, envy, disgust, and so forth[14] (see Levy 1973, 1985; Sabini and Silver 1982), the emotions of satisfaction or enjoyment of each type of relationship, and then the emotions of loss—or fear of loss—of each type (on the latter, see Bowlby 1969; Baumeister and Tice 1989). Certainly there are important individual and cultural differences in the experience and conscious formulation of the experience of emotions. But across the species, the motivational quality and potential to give rise to distinctive social emotions probably distinguish the elementary models from other kinds of cognitions, schemata, and precepts.

## Transgression and Punishment

One of the most striking sets of collectively distinctive features of this category of fundamental models for social relationships is that they each define distinct and salient forms of evil. This characteristic is the psycho-cultural side of the quadratic jural social nature of these models, discussed earlier. While each model provides a basis for constructing a specific relational structure, the converse of this is that each model marks certain forms of social action as violations of that relationship. Each model specifies some things as right and some things as wrong. Each model lays the foundation for the designation of what constitutes an ordinary deviation from the social relationship, and beyond that each model is the basis for constituting certain focal taboos that people conceive as antitheses and inversions of that type of social relationship. These go together with the definition of the relevant sanctions and forms of redress for either deviations or violations of constitutive taboos (Piaget 1973 [1932], Ricoeur 1967, Kohlberg 1984, Kohlberg, Levine, and Hewer 1983).

## Constitution of Definite Transgressions

As we saw in Chapter 6, each model designates some forms of social action as transgressions of the social relationship. Transgressions may be mere quasi-moral faults, or they may be focal moral transgressions. Failing to fully conform to the relational ideal defines a social shortcoming, deficiency, inadequacy, or imperfection. A lord may be too haughty or his vassal insufficiently obsequious; a mother may be thoughtless or ungenerous. These deviations grade into more serious breaches that are fully moral, like wanton rapacity, or child neglect and abuse.

Beyond these faults and failings, it appears that each kind of social relationship is constituted, in part, by refraining from violating certain focal taboos. For example, anthropologists have advanced a variety of arguments that all arrive at the conclusion that an incest taboo (in some form or other) is the basis for the formation and perpetuation of the family or other primary kin groups. These primary kin groups, which in this context can be construed as essentially strong Communal Sharing relationships, are marked by certain positive actions like the sharing of living space, pooling of labor or resources, intensive interaction, and eating together. At the same time the focal CS relationships are marked and constituted by the observance of certain sexual taboos prohibiting sexual relations with persons defined with respect to the primary communal relationship. Violating this focal taboo potentially destroys the Communal Sharing relationship (Fiske n.d.).

Probably each type of fundamental social relationship has as its converse a fundamental prohibition of this sort, the violation of which is literally antithetical to the relationship. The observance of this prohibition is a necessary condition of the relationship (although not a sufficient condition) while its transgression inverts and destroys it. Transgression of the focal taboo entailed by these social relationships does not simply terminate the relationship, it "violates" the relationship in a way that is felt to be horrible and unthinkable. For example in the case of Authority Ranking the focal taboo seems to be physical assault. Imagine a subordinate attacking and beating up his boss, and consider the public reaction to the assassination of John Kennedy or the attempted assassination of Pope John Paul II. And think about the great importance the French Algerian right wing attached to their attempts to assassinate Charles DeGaulle.

Not only is the observance of such focal taboos conceptually essential to the maintenance of these fundamental types of social relationships, but people also have strong feelings about the prohibitions. One of the many links between culture and psychology that these models entail is their directive force. Compare how Americans feel about incest as compared with divorce or other ways of dissolving the family unit. It is not just that incest disrupts or jeopardizes the relationship; transgressions of these taboos are inherently abhorrent, even beyond their consequences. Nor are these taboos simply a matter of

means–ends expediency: people do not avoid incest and find it disgusting because of their awareness of its pragmatic consequences. People feel that incest
is intrinsically evil and "gross" in the same way that Communal Sharing is
intrinsically good.

Like the implementation of the models themselves, focal taboos assume
phenomenally different forms in different cultures. For example, consider
three examples of the sexual taboo that is focal to male Communal Sharing
groups in different parts of Africa. Moose taboo sexual relations between a
man and the man's lineage-mate's wife. Maasai regard it as appropriate for a
man to ask his wife to sleep with his age-mate but are horrified at the idea that
a man might sleep with his age-mate's daughter. Many North Africa people
regard it as an appalling dishonor if the mother, wife, sister, or daughter of any
member of the band has any extramarital sexual relations (especially with outsiders?). In contrast, in the U.S. the focal taboo is on sexual relations among
any two members of the same family other than husband and wife. The specific taboo is different in each of these cases, but each variant is a sexual transgression which must be avoided to sustain the Communal Sharing group intact.

Overall, it is characteristic of these models that they not only define what is
right, they define what is wrong—including what is absolutely intolerable.
However, to some degree cultural implementation rules fill in the actual substance of focal taboos, and other implementation rules define what constitutes
a venial fault.

Furthermore, Durkheim (1933 [1893, 1926], 1901) and Piaget (1973 [1932])
observed that the kind of punishment people regard as appropriate is a function of the kind of rule people perceive to be transgressed (see Punishment,
Transgressions, Vices, and Excuses in Chapter 6). For example, civil restitutive sanctions contrast with repressive criminal sanctions. More generally, any
fundamental model for social relations may entail a distinctive sense of the
specific sort of action that should follow transgression, including the kinds of
acts that effectively redress a wrong.

## Desire to Punish Others for Violations

A central feature of these focal taboos is that people have a strong subjective
desire to see major violators punished and are often inclined to apply sanctions
directly. This corresponds to what I said earlier about the quadratic jural interdependence of social relationships. People undertake to punish others when
they have no concrete or immediate "interest" in doing do—when they have
nothing directly to gain by punishing, and there may be some risk or cost in
doing so. Yet people want transgressors to be punished, and they often want to
be involved in inflicting the punishment, or at least participate as observers in
the event (see Durkheim 1933 [1893, 1926]; Foucault 1977). This sensibility is
deeply ingrained in human nature, and (despite Western norms of charity, forgiveness, privacy, and noninvolvement) quite widespread in regard to viola-

tions of the taboos entailed in the basic models. This characteristic of the four jural models distinguishes them from many other prescriptions and constraints on behavior whose transgression does not evoke this desire for retribution.

### Recognition of the Legitimacy of Punishment

Closely related to this is the fact that people tend to accept punishment for violations of the prohibitions derived from the fundamental social structures. Of course, people often dispute accusations, deny that they have committed such a violation, or attempt to excuse or justify their actions. But in cases where people acknowledge their guilt, they often accept their punishment. Sometimes punishment may actually be received with relief for the welcome absolution it implies. But even when people avoid punishment for admitted transgressions, they typically accept the legitimacy of the punishment meted out, or at least appreciate that it is meaningful. That is, they recognize that what they are undergoing is punishment and not just random violence imposed on them by pure power. If people recognize that they participate in a legitimate social relationship, then they acknowledge society's right to apprehend, judge, and punish them in accordance with the norms of the relationship. They may not like it, but they understand that it is right. It can be extremely threatening to the legitimacy of the establishment if people who transgress its norms repeatedly ignore or sneer at their punishment—a punishment cheerfully laughed off has not been received.

Moreover, as a function of their engagement in social relationships people are susceptible to the relevant social sanctions (cf. Spiro 1961). A reprimand from an acknowledged superior acting within his realm of authority is felt as a punishment. The subordinate is sensitive to the reprimand just because it occurs within the framework of the Authority Ranking relationship. From someone outside an authority relationship such criticism would be quite another thing—meddling, or perhaps an intolerable insult to one's honor. Superiors are entitled to rebuke (in appropriate ways) their subordinates, who—by virtue of the authority relationship—have to accept it or else leave the relationship. Again, exclusion from a Communal Sharing relationship (say on account of selfishness and refusal to extend help when needed) is a punishment only in so far as the person excluded was or wishes to be included as a participant in the communal social relationship. Of course, people are not amenable or accepting of punishment for "transgressions" of norms they do not recognize, or at the hands of agents whose legitimacy or standing they deny. So members of a gang may deny the validity of middle-class norms and law and regard police and the courts simply as enemies, not legitimate enforcers of valid rules. In that event, they would not accept the jural validity of legal sanctions.

More generally, people's concern about potential sanctions—and thus the efficacy of most everyday social sanctions—is consequent to the existence of the social relationships in question. If potential customers refuse to do business with you because you are known to have cheated other customers, that only matters to you because you have lost the possibility of engaging in those lost Market Pricing relationships. So avoiding a cheat is a sanction only within the framework of the MP relationship that the cheater violated; the cheater is susceptible to the sanction because the sanction is the loss (or diminishment) of a desired and expected social relationship. If a child hogs a computer game, taking so long that his peers threaten to make him lose his next turn, the threat is effective not just because he is trying to maximize his game playing for its own sake, but because (and insofar as) he wants to be a friend, a peer, a turntaker. Hence to understand sanctions, to understand why people punish, and why punishments and the prospect of punishment influence social behavior, we have to understand the prohibitions, transgressions, and punishments in the framework of these fundamental social relationships. It is characteristic of the fundamental models that they define focal taboos, that they motivate people to punish violators of these taboos and other rules derived from the basic models, and that participants in the basic types of social relationships are susceptible to and tend to recognize the legitimacy of such punishments as a function of their participation in the social relationships.

A corollary of this is that people use the models to make sense of suffering, in searching for the moral meaning of misfortune. People make sense of misfortune in terms of the transgression of one or more of the models, seeking to understand whether the misfortune is a punishment for their own transgressions, or is an offense against them in violation of one of the models. Thus Job wanted to know how he had offended his Lord and Master—why else would He make Job suffer so?

For the present I may sum up by noting that in addition to definite sociological and cultural features, the four known fundamental types of social relationships share several characteristic psychological attributes, apparently including their spontaneous emergence in the ways that adults structure novel social situations. The four elementary models are also notable for the facility with which children and adults learn the culture-specific application rules that enable them to function as enculturated participants in society. Further, the four basic models encompass characteristic motivations and probably distinct emotions. Related to this are their characteristic entailments concerning deviations and focal taboos, together with the desire to sanction others and the tendency to recognize the legitimacy of punishment. I also suggested that the four models emerge in a definite ontogentic sequence (CS, AR, EM, then MP), which I sketch in Chapter 17 from two informal case studies.

Several of these psychological features of the models correspond to the sociological quality of jural interdependence—that is, the mutual relevance of the state of each core social relationship for the equilibria of the other linked relationships. These psychological and sociological features in turn both correspond to the key cultural features of the models: their constitutive, directive, interpretive and coordinative properties. The sociological, psychological, and cultural definitions of the category are restatements of essentially the same properties in different languages. Once again, we see the convergence of multiple paradigms, each of which independently arrives at the same point. It all comes down to the fact that people generate, interpret, and judge social relationships with reference to the models, enforce them on others, sanction transgressors, and adjust their relationships with others to take account of whether these third parties conform to the models. The motivational and directive quality of the models can be seen as the human proclivity to relate to people in these modes, also reflected in the emergence of the models and people's facility at recognizing them and learning their implementation rules. People are "prepared" and attuned to find and participate in these forms of social relations, to create them, and to insist on them. Taken together, the gist of this chapter is that people search out relationships based on these models and impose these models on their social world.

## EVOLUTIONARY BIOLOGY AND PHYLOGENY

Something very like Communal Sharing structures social relations in many other species besides our own. As W. Hamilton (1963, 1964, 1971) has demonstrated in the theory of inclusive fitness, closely related or inbred groups of animals have a high probability of sharing any given gene in common, and natural selection will be indifferent as to which individual happens to carry the gene. Organisms will be selected to maximize the representation in succeeding generations of copies of their own genes, regardless of which particular individual passes them on. Hence it will be adaptive for genetically identical individuals to be absolutely altruistic toward each other, maximizing their collective fitness, not the individual fitness of the individual actor. Genetically identical individuals will be selected to maximize their aggregate fitness, regardless of the consequences to any individual. Individuals having only some of their genes in common will be less than perfectly altruistic (unless they can detect in some deterministic way which other individuals share the altruism gene), and will modify their altruism as a function of the probability that they share any given gene with the other animal(s) concerned. Hence organisms will be selected to act altruistically whenever the mean proportion of genes shared (r) with other affected organisms is greater than or equal to the ratio of expected fitness costs to self (c), divided by the total expected fitness gain to the kin (b):

$$r > \frac{c}{b}$$

Observations of a number of species in nature suggest that this kind of altruism is common. Many social insects demonstrate a mode of social organization that appears to be based on genetic identity ($r = 1$) (Hamilton 1963, 1964, 1971; Wilson 1971). The best example of this besides the social insects is the cells in a multicellular organism, all of which collaborate on behalf of the gametes, which are the only cells whose actual concrete genes are passed on to the next generation, although these genes are identical replicas of the genes in all the other cells. In more attenuated form, CS operates in many species between parent and offspring and among siblings, who share genes in a proportion equal to at least[15] 0.5 (e.g., African wild dogs [H. and J. von Lawick-Goodall 1970], and other animals [Trivers 1974]). Of course, CS in humans is not restricted to groups that share a high proportion of their genes, and the degree of altruism and self-sacrifice is not well predicted by the proportion of genes shared (for a detailed critique see Sahlins 1976b). Nevertheless, it is important to consider the fact that natural selection might produce a proclivity for the kind of unity, merging of individuality, and pooling of resources that occurs in Communal Sharing, even if there is no known proximate mechanism in humans. What about natural selection of the other modes of relating?

A form of behavior congruent with Authority Ranking is also widely represented among social animals, particularly birds and mammals, in the familiar form of dominance hierarchies (e.g., Packer 1979). Linear dominance hierarchies (transitive "pecking orders") are common among social primates and other social mammals and birds (Cheney and Seyfarth in press). As Wade (1978:126ff.) carefully proves, linearly ordered dominance hierarchies do not arise in groups of any size simply from random differences in size, strength, aggressiveness, number of agonistic encounters experienced, or any other quality of individuals per se. He demonstrates that a linear dominance hierarchy must result from some triadic (or higher order) features of social interaction. This proof that linearity is a result of individuals' taking into account interactions among other members of a social group is consistent with the triadic sociological nature of the four elementary models. Species that have linear dominance hierarchies must have the ability to "understand" the transitivity of linear orderings. That at least some primates can make the logical distinctions involved—even with nonsocial problems—is apparent from laboratory experiments with squirrel monkeys and chimpanzees (McGonigle and Chalmers 1977, Gillan 1981) and field studies reviewed by Cheney and Seyfarth (in press). Humans are quite good at reasoning about some kinds of linear structures, apparently using a spatial representation of social orderings (De Soto, London, and Handel 1965).

There is ample evidence from field observations of Cheney and Seyfarth (Cheney, Seyfarth, and Smuts 1986, Cheney and Seyfarth 1985, 1990, in press; see also Byrne and Whiten 1988), and the sources they cite, to show that many primates regularly take into account the state of the relationships between other animals and adjust their behavior to them accordingly. Most strikingly, there is evidence suggesting that vervets are more likely to threaten an animal if there has been a recent fight between the close kin of the two animals (Cheney and Seyfarth 1986, 1990). Vervets are also more likely to engage in reconciliative affinitive interactions if their respective kin have recently fought. Seyfarth and Cheney make the important point that we might expect to see considerable domain specificity in the ability to use such relational knowledge, and that the strongest natural selection on cognitive performance might well be for competence in social relations. Hence primates might regularly display the ability to use a linear ordering principle in social relations, even where such an ability is not readily evident in regard to nonsocial stimuli.

There is no good evidence for Equality Matching relations in any other species besides Homo sapiens. A number of observers have described "reciprocity" in interactions among primates (see Packer 1977, Cheney and Seyfarth 1985, Seyfarth and Cheney 1984, Taylor and McGuire 1988 and the rest of the special issue of *Ethology and Sociobiology* 9 [1]). But there have been no reports of evidence suggesting that an animal intends to match the behavior of another so that the "reciprocal" actions correspond one-for-one. There are no reports of turn taking, of distributive equality or distributions that balance contributions, or of measured retribution or compensation that aims at "evening the score" in any other species. Nor is their any evidence yet of animals keeping accounts in a way that would require addition and subtraction. Perhaps close observation directed specifically to determining the kinds of tit-for-tat occurring in nature will yield instances of behavior in some primates congruent with the full structure of EM, but no one has yet searched for just this structure. The lack of this type of social relationship in species other than our own—if indeed it does not occur—may be explained in part by limitations in the cognitive capacity of other species. There seems to be no evidence of any nonhuman animal being able to do addition and subtraction, for example, which would be required if animals were to keep track of what they owed under EM.[16] Indeed, Kurland and Beckerman (1985) suggest that the natural selection of human cognitive capacities may have evolved just as a result of the benefits of "reciprocal" sharing of food source information among foragers. Humphrey (1976) makes a similar argument about nonhuman primates (see also Trivers 1971), and Byrne and Whiten (1988) have collected a number of other proposals about the special nature and evolution of primate social intelligence.

Of course, the question that follows from this is how natural selection produced this cognitive ability in some social species and not in others. Addressing this issue requires (among other knowledge) an understanding of the benefits and costs of Equality Matching and each of the other forms of social organization; Fiske and Baron (n.d.) propose a framework for such an analysis. However, there is another possibility: that among the major constraints on the application of these structures to the social domain is the requirement for certain "commitment devices" that will solve the social dilemmas reviewed by Dawes (1980). Frank (1988) advances this game theoretic evolutionary argument. He shows how natural selection might produce human emotions that induce behavior that is irrational because it reduces the fitness of the individual who actually carries it out; these emotions would be selected because the contingent potential to act in these emotional ways almost always obviates the necessity for actually doing so. The individual with these emotional potentials gains the fitness benefits of participating in social relationships that require trust and cooperation, for example, where individuals without these emotions would have lower fitness due to the defection of their partners. This account confirms the close functional and phylogenetic link between the fundamental models and the corresponding social emotions.

Only Homo sapiens has ever been observed to use money, to exchange un-like commodities at a fixed ratio, to make distributions in proportion to contri-butions, to bargain with reference to a market, or to pay wages according to a determined rate. Yet paradoxically, evolutionary theory in its modern form is in many respects a Market Pricing theory and is based on the supposition that in the long run natural selection operates just like a market in which fitness is profit. This is not just an historical coincidence, since evolutionary biology and economics developed in part from common sources and have continued to influence each other. The issue that our current theory raises, however, is whether social interaction among nonhuman animals could really operate as an implicit "market" with "economic" trade-offs among qualitatively unlike benefits and costs. Certainly, modern evolutionary theory argues only that natural selection operates *as if* organisms were competing for resources to pro-duce genetic profits *in the long run*, and this implies that the apparent paradox can be resolved by recognizing that two different levels of analysis are in-volved. (Doubtless this also rescues an MP form of evolutionary theory from any simple confrontation with the everyday, short-term market "irrationality" that is readily observable in any organism.) But it is crucial to recognize that such long-run transgenerational processes are entirely different qualitatively from the social cognition in the mind of any single organism. It would be ex-tremely problematic to suppose that any nonhuman organism does anything closely resembling rational calculation of budget trade-offs, costs and benefits, given the apparent cognitive limitations of nonhuman species and the ab-sence of any real manifestations of Market Pricing in their social behavior.[17]

We have been taught in modern times that it is basic human "nature" to analyze opportunities in terms of the ratio of benefits to costs, to maximize, to compete for scarce resources, and to exchange only to make a "profit"—in short, that we are market animals like all other organisms. But we have some-times lost track of the distinction between the processes of natural selection over evolutionary time and the processes of social interaction between partic-ular individuals. There is no doubt that, as forms of social relations, fully elab-orated Equality Matching and Market Pricing are distinctive of our own spe-cies. We are also Authority Ranking and Communal Sharing animals as well, and if we share a social nature with other species, social interactions that look like CS and AR are one thing that we have in common. However, it remains for us to determine the degree to which human CS and AR relations are phy-logenetically homologous with the apparently corresponding modes of social organization in other branches of the phylogenetic tree—or whether they are examples of convergent evolution, or merely superficially analogous. In any case, any model that is fundamental, elementary, and universal in human social relationships has to be phylogenetically situated, and we must ultimately account for it as a product of natural selection, among other levels of explanation.

My hypothesis is that, in the empty, generic form described in Chapters 7 and 9, the four basic models are represented in the human genome. These models are much simpler than the universal grammar posited by generative linguists, and perhaps no more complex than the courtship rituals or other fixed action patterns described by ethologists. If this seems implausible, consider the alternative. If you believed that the four relational structures were some kind of emergent result "drawn out of nonspecific genetic potentials by the exigencies of social life and the natural environment,"[18] then you would have to explain how the four structures emerge in so few and such consistent forms. What kind of social and ecological constraints would produce just the same four forms of relationship in decision making, transactions (exchange, distributions and contributions), ideas of justice, the organization of work, the ways in which people relate socially to objects, land and time, in systems of bestowing brides in traditional societies, forms of marriage in the industrial world, sexual relations, decision processes, social influence, group formation, identity and self, social needs and motivations, moral judgment, political ideology and social legitimation, social conflict, responses to transgression and misfortune, and the psychology of religion? What constraints on everyday interaction and thought could generate the same basic forms in so many diverse cultures around the world? Does any one have any substantive proposals for such constraints? By far the most parsimonious account is the nativism hypothesis that the models are endogenous.[19]

One likely prediction of the innateness hypothesis is that the capacity and the motivation for each type of social relationship emerge at a specific "stage" of maturation, and in a specific order. If the understanding of each mode of relating and the orientation toward it emerge in a fixed order and at predictable times in a variety of diverse cultures with varied child-rearing practices, then it is hard to see what kind of theory of learning or environment would be tenable. In Chapter 17, I sketch an example of the kind of observations that illustrate the sort of data that would confirm this hypothesis, if they were rigorously replicated.


## GENERALITY

In this chapter I have suggested that a structure belonging to the category of fundamental models should entail a definite kind of focal transgression—the antithesis of the relational ideal—which is probably associated with each model. The model should be demonstrable as a motivational construct in a great many individuals, be very widely dispersed across societies, and be represented in many distinct cultural meaning systems. In individual ontogeny, it should tend to emerge "spontaneously" under a wide variety of conditions and over a range of environments. It should take shape frequently among new, ad hoc aggregations of people and regularly crystallize in historically novel social situations. It need not have wide phylogenetic distribution, but the discovery of a type of social relationship in a number of species (and in multiple ecological niches) will tend to confirm the identification of the underlying model as a fundamental evolved structure.

Alongside these sociological, cultural, psychological, and evolutionary features, there is one final attribute of the elementary models that sets them apart from many other cognitive and social structures. To qualify as a fundamental and universal relational structure, a model should exhibit considerable generality. It should be manifest in diverse domains of social activity, at different levels, and be realized in conjunction with a great variety of cultural implementation rules. It should also appear in many combinations with other models and be applied recursively in the construction of complex systems of relationships. If a form of social relations appears only among some subset of individuals and is defined in only some cultures, while it may be of considerable interest in its own right, it is not universal and therefore may not be fundamental in the same sense as the basic four. The implication of the material in Part II is that if other elementary models that are fundamental forms of social relationships exist, then they should emerge in all of the social domains discussed there. To the degree that a mode of interacting with other people is specific to some particular domain or to a small subset of these important domains, then it is probably not an elementary model in the same sense as Communal Sharing, Authority Ranking, Equality Matching, or Market Pricing. This should be the first test of any other model that we propose to add to the first four relational models: is it manifest in every major sphere of human relations?

I have proposed in this chapter that there may be a discrete, delimited, uniquely bounded category of elementary, fundamental, and universal models definable by a list of necessary and sufficient sociological, cultural, psychological, and evolutionary features. However, it may turn out that the category of basic relational models is a well delimited but polythetically defined class. That is, the category may not be characterized by sharing any single necessary feature in common, but nevertheless unambiguously be identifiable with reference to a (possibly weighted) list of defining features like those I propose. Or it may turn out that what exists is a diffuse cluster of such basic models exhibiting varying numbers and combinations of these features, a fuzzy set: there could perfectly well be types of social relationships meeting some but not all of these criteria. I claim that the four models I have described meet all the criteria, but there is no a priori reason to believe that every model that people use for the construction of social relationships exhibits all of the characteristic features. It would be pointlessly dogmatic to insist on arbitrarily stipulating a definition of "basic relational models" a priori. We should leave it to empirical investigation to determine what kinds of models actually do structure the social relations of our own and other species.

In the next chapter I describe features of the models that suggest two more criteria for a fundamental model. First, a structure that belongs to the category of fundamental models should have a natural form of mental representation, together with a characteristic semiotic mode of cultural marking that is consistent across contexts and cultures. The second section of the following chapter offers another, qualitatively very different criterion for inclusion in this set of fundamental elementary models: such models should map onto tractable mathematical structures of certain kinds.

# 9

# Semiotic Marking and Relational Structures

Any social relation contains a mental element, an element of thought, of representations which are not merely the form that this relation assumes in our consciousness, but are part of its content. . . . Not all representations present pre-existing realities to the mind "after-the-event" as it were (where these realities are conceived as having been born independently of and unaided by these representations). Ideas are not an instance separate from social relations; they are not merely appearances, nor are they deformed and deforming reflections in social consciousness. Rather, they are an integral part of social relations as soon as the latter begin to take shape, and they are one of the conditions for their formation. (Godelier 1986b:129)

The mental part of a social relation consists, first of all, in the set of representations, principles and rules which must be "acted upon" to engender that relation between the individuals and groups which constitute a society needed to make it into a concrete mode of organization of their social life. . . . The mental part of a social relation also consists of the values, both positive and negative, which are associated with this relation, and of the rules and ideal principles which enable it to be generated. By "values" I mean here both principles and judgments, and representations charged with a force of attraction or repulsion. . . .

None of this implies that the mental part of social reality can be reduced to its conscious part. I deliberately use the term "thought," and it goes without saying that for me thought considerably exceeds consciousness (and language). . . .

In spite of what certain sociologists and psychologists still maintain, the social formation of individuals cannot be reduced to the child's interiorization of external norms of behaviour which then increasingly become all but unquestioned habits. Even for the child, the social relations into which it is born never exist entirely outside its own self. (Godelier 1986b:169–77)

What sort of "models" are these, after all? I have compared them to grammars, rules, and templates, saying that they guide, direct, structure, or govern social relations. The focus of this book is on the fundamental, elementary, universal forms of social relations themselves, but I have persisted in stating that people use shared mental representations to generate these social relationships. And I suggest that people use certain shared semiotic codes to mark these social relationships and thus to coordinate, negotiate, and interpret them. What are these mental representations and these semiotic codes? The phonemics of any given language is based on contrasts in which some of the differences in sounds are meaningful features, while people do not attend to other objective variations. Similarly, in any social relationship in any given culture, people use some subset of the objectively available distinctions among people and objects to make social distinctions, and ignore other attributes of social entities. Can we state precisely and formally what characterizes the particular patterns of social distinctions made and empirical distinctions ignored that we call Communal Sharing, Authority Ranking, Equality Matching, and Market Pricing? This chapter poses the problem as directly as possible, and proposes the outline of some possible solutions. First we will look at the semiotic codes people use to mark relationships, and then we will attempt to axiomatize the relational structures of the four fundamental models.

## REPRESENTATION, MARKING, AND ACCESSIBILITY

To say that people actually construct their social relationships out of the four basic relational models is to claim that the structures have psychological reality. This implies that these models must have some definite cognitive representation, while the social relations they generate also must be publicly marked in some definite cultural code. Of course, any kind of knowledge, motivation, or guide for social behavior must be represented and marked in these senses, but the four models seem to be semiotically distinguished by people's proclivity for encoding each in a different characteristic system of social signs. The semiotic specificity may also correspond with a distinctive mode of mental representation that is "natural" or primary for each model.[1]

Communal Sharing is characteristically encoded in *enactive* form, as sensorimotor rituals. Among the Moose, these seem to include animal sacrifice ceremonies and shared meals in which the meaning and significance of the event are embodied in motor actions themselves, performed for their own sake as reenactments of rites that have "always" been performed in the same stereotyped manner. For example, Moose make sacrifices to feed the ancestors and then share the libation beer and eat the roasted sacrificial animal together. It is this very act of drinking and eating together that marks and reinforces the CS relationship among the people and that constitutes the CS phase of the relationship with the ancestors. Think what it means in our culture to invite a boyfriend home for dinner with the family—or to refuse to eat your mother's cooking. The code is in the action itself—not in the meaning of the words, but in what people do, or don't do. Many rituals have this character: their point is to reenact and perpetuate timeless forms, and they stand or fall on whether the actions are performed the "same" way as they have always been done. Think of a birthday party: what makes it a birthday party is doing certain things with certain props. Why do you eat cake and ice cream, light and then blow out candles, conceal presents in paper and then unwrap them again? Because the communal solidarity that a birthday party conveys and sustains is conveyed and sustained by doing the traditional things, by carrying out just these stereotyped acts. The same is true of a wedding—what makes it a wedding and makes the bride and groom married is that people have "gone through all the motions" in the proper sequence, replicating the standard script. The encoding of CS is based on "knowing how," without necessarily having the reflective, declarative perspective which Ryle (1949) calls "knowing that." Knowledge of CS relations is more kinesthetic than propositional. Under appropriate circumstances people may use many other forms of representation to mark CS relationships, but an enactive, kinesthetic system of marking seems to be characteristic and natural to CS relationships.

In contrast, Authority Ranking is encoded predominantly in visual or *iconic* form, as *spatio-temporal* orderings. For example, the Moose mark rank by the order of persons in processions, by having leaders take positions in front of followers at major ceremonies, by giving people major items of information and material gifts in sequential order according to rank, and by distributing shares that are ordinally ranked in magnitude according to the social hierarchy. Thus they represent authority in terms of precedence, magnitude, and other spatio-temporal sequences. People speak of "high-" ranking people as being above, in front, and first—indeed, at least in English, French, and Moore it is difficult to speak about AR at all without using these dimensions. In all three languages people use plural pronouns to mark preeminence (e.g., the royal "we"), as if superiors (note the vertical metaphor) were more numerous than inferiors. In innumerable ways, people display and assert rank by being above others and show deference by lowering themselves. Over and over again, positions in space and time and relative magnitude are the dimensional signs of rank. As this account predicts, humans show considerable facility with spatial representations of social relations (De Soto, London, and Handel 1965). People are perfectly capable of using other modes of representation for AR relations, but spatiotemporal representations seem to be the primary, preferred mode of marking them.

People have a proclivity for representing Equality Matching relations in *concrete operational* form, as manipulations of indexical tokens. This is observable in the concrete balancing of shares in a distribution, the synchronous matching of labor stroke-for-stroke at a work bee, in the one-to-one correspondence of turn taking and quid pro quo reciprocity among peers, or in the cooking rotations among co-wives. The representation of justice as a blindfolded woman holding a balance is apt. She does not need to see the things she weighs or the people to whom she is handing out justice; she needs only to balance them evenly. So too for the Moose, equality among people in a distribution is marked and accomplished by taking lumps of a kind of meat and weighing with one's hands to be sure they match, or of counting out kola nuts so that each person gets one, then each person gets another one, and so on. When people at a Moose cultivating bee work across a field cultivating parallel strips of the same length, they demonstrably match each other, doing equal work. In all such marking of EM, people attend to only one dimension, and typically divide or exchange only one item at a time. (In this sense, in Piaget's terms these are often actually "preoperational" measures of equality.) People convey and create equality by concrete actions of comparing, aligning, balancing and matching some indexical token of their social relations.

People most readily represent Market Pricing in *abstract symbolic* form, as language-like "propositions." The clearest case is the structure of prices, which abstractly encodes the innumerable ratios of exchange of all commodities exchanged. A system of market prices is revealed in competitive propositional bargaining, and in the verbal (or written) exchange of comparative information about transactions that constitute a "market." That is, people use propositional language to inform each other about prices and to negotiate a deal. "Here's a red two-door Mustang with a supercharged V-eight, racing slicks, and quad sound that was owned by a little old lady who only used it to drive to church—you can't beat the price." If you have read the propositionally formulated want ads to judge the market you know whether you can beat the price. And then you have to do some abstract analytic thinking, which may be expressed in your bargaining: "Well, I saw a pink '86 Corvette with racing cams and fur seat covers I can get for less than that—how about taking $500 off?" This use of language represents true abstract symbolic marking of MP relations, a form which entails a certain kind of declarative "knowing that" perspective (Ryle 1949). It may be that only primates are capable of using truly abstract codes of this sort (Premack 1983, Cheney and Seyfarth in press).

The differences among these four forms of mental representation result in differing degrees of accessibility to abstract self- reflective analysis and verbal report. The culture-specific implementation of the MP model is more or less readily accessible to awareness in linguistic form: people can easily talk about how they go about things in an MP relationship, and generally can say something about "why" they are doing it in a particular way. For example, Quinn (1978) found that Mfantse fish sellers in Ghana could readily verbalize and discuss the criteria they used in deciding when to take their fish to market in the capital. Perhaps this facility for verbalizing MP relations is one of the factors that has led modern social science to develop the MP model so fully and attempt to apply it so widely—it is naturally stated in abstract form, so every adult can fairly readily give a verbal account of his or her own MP behavior, and for the MP behavior of others. Equality Matching behavior is less easy for naive informants (that is, untrained in social science or abstract scholastic thinking) to translate into propositional form. Although people can certainly think about what EM involves by imagining the concrete manipulations involved, typically people cannot so easily "explain" it propositionally to themselves or others. At most, people can describe the procedures by which one-to-one correspondence is pragmatically achieved with some particular kind of item. But there is a long way to go from unreflectively using the practical recipe for dividing things equitably or implementing turn taking to stating the abstract principles in a formal description.

Action organized by the Authority Ranking model may be still less intuitively available to natives' formal linguistic explication. The program for executing hierarchical relations can be difficult for unreflective actors to translate into a form that they can analyze or discuss. When people do discuss AR, they generally use spatiotemporal "metaphors" or express the relations in terms of magnitudes or force: "the higher ups," "leaders" and "followers," "big" people and "little" people, the "powerful" and the "weak"—terms that reflect the underlying dimensional representation.

People sometimes have the most difficulty giving an abstract account of their Communal Sharing; the typical answer people give to questions about why they do communal things the way they do is simply, "That's our tradition, that's just the way we do things," or sometimes, "That's the Moose (or American, or whatever) way." Which of course is exactly correct—action in the CS mode represents a motoric reiteration of things as they have always been done, a kind of kinesthetic reenactment that yields a timeless continuity with the past.

The close correspondence that I hypothesize between mental representations and the preferred cultural mode of marking of social relations is not fortuitous: for many reasons, the codes people predominantly use to mark relationships and communicate about them are likely to correspond to the natural, intuitive mental codes individuals characteristically use to represent and process the same relationships. This correspondence of public and private codes may lead to semiotic specialization and "speciation." Over evolutionary or cultural scales of time as well as in individual ontogeny, a distinctive semiotic code may emerge for any fundamental relational model. Such differences in characteristic modes of encoding would have strong implications for the modes of transmission and acquisition of the culture-specific application rules of each type of social relationship. Hence in considering any elementary and fundamental model it is appropriate to ask four questions: How are the relational properties of the particular model encoded in the mind? What are the semiotic codes people collectively use to mark social relations of this kind? How closely do the form of mental representation and the system of collective marking of the relational model correspond—is there a common sign system for mental representation and collective marking that is distinctive to this particular model? Through what channel do people transmit to children the culture-specific application rules for this model?

I have hypothesized that there is one "fundamental" mode of mental representation that is characteristic of each model, corresponding to a distinctive semiotic sign type that is the "natural" mode of marking that type of social relationship. People have the capacity to represent any type of social relationship in any mode, but people seem to prefer a different sign medium for marking each of the four basic types of relationships: a different form seems to be inherently appropriate for constituting and displaying each kind of relationship. If this proves to be true, it constitutes a previously unrecognized link between psychology, culture, and social relations.

But all this still leaves unaddressed the problem of defining the patterns of social interaction that constitute Communal Sharing, Authority Ranking, Equality Matching, or Market Pricing. The issue we have yet to resolve is, exactly what are each of these relational configurations? What is the common pattern inherent in every realization of, say, EM? What we want to know is, If people have models they jointly use to generate social relations, what are the relational properties and operations that compose each model? So let us now turn from mental representation and cultural encoding to relational structures, formally defined.

## SCALE TYPES AND RELATIONAL STRUCTURES

In Chapter 1, I offered qualitative definitions of each type of social relationship, as well as a hypothetical example of people's use of the four models in organizing various aspects of fire fighting in a small town. Now let us define and describe the four models in more formal terms. The point of this is not mere formalism for formalism's sake. We need to specify just what kinds of social distinctions are important in what types of relationships. Formal statements of the structures of the four models will help us to formulate explicitly the social dimensions people take account of and those they ignore; that is, what empirical differences make a social difference in each kind of social relationship.

These features can be analyzed by considering what kinds of transformations of the structure preserve the defining relations and operations (Stevens 1946, 1951:23–25, 1958:384–85). For example, the structure of Communal Sharing is unique (preserved with no socially significant change) under various mappings that would seriously distort the structures of the other models, including various one-to-one mappings. For example, it would make little difference to the CS relationships among team members or the insider-outsider relationships between members of different teams if all the Chicago Cubs were transferred to the Philadelphia Phillies team at once, and all the members of each other team were similarly transferred as a group to some other team. It would simply amount to a change in names. But the hierarchical rankings of each team would be completely changed by such a switch: the players who had been at the bottom of the standings might be at the top, and so forth. Consider making all sergeants into generals and all generals into sergeants: the Authority Ranking relationships among the people would be transformed. Such one-to-one mappings of groups distort AR relations but not CS relations.

Or, to take another example, suppose that some Equality Matching relationship were transformed by adding a constant increment to everyone's lot, so that each child in a rotation got two additional turns on the swing, each side in a feud killed one more person from the other group, or each person in a Moose distribution received one additional kola nut. The balance or equality in the relationship would be undisturbed (although the relationships might in an important sense be intensified). In contract, adding a constant to each transaction in Market Pricing would alter the nature of the relationship in socially significant ways. Imagine if the prices of all the things related to some MP relation (including all hourly wages) were increased by $10.00; while the number of houses that could be purchased per hour of unskilled labor would not be greatly affected, the number of candy bars per hour would be radically altered. Or imagine that everyone's taxes next year were increased by a flat $20,000; the social burden would be distributed in a very disproportionate manner. Thus adding a constant to both numerator and denominator changes the proportions on which MP relations are based. Different kinds of transformations leave different kinds of social relations intact and more or less unaffected. So, for example, if the two currencies are freely convertible, nothing fundamental to MP is changed if people denominate prices in German marks or Japanese yen: the transformation from one to the other is achieved by multiplying prices by some constant, and it leaves the nature of MP relations unaffected (e.g., the exchange ratios of various commodities, debts, interest rates, profits, economical substitutes). The specific transformations that preserve the structure of each type of social relationship reveal the properties of that structure. (This idea of invariance of relational structure under specific transformations parallels in interesting respects Piaget's concept of conservation.)

In this and some other respects the present project resembles the construction of scales in measurement theory (Narens and Luce 1986). Indeed, the four elementary models correspond rather well to the four classical scale types that Stevens (1946, 1951) describes. Roughly speaking, Communal Sharing is a kind of *categorical* (nominal) scaling, in that the only distinction that people make is of type or class: are two people of the same kind, or different? Within the framework of a CS relationship, if two people belong to the same category (say, a family or ethnic group) then, with regard to the dimension that is communally organized, the people in that relationship are equivalent and undifferentiated. So, if people at each table in an Indian restaurant are sharing all the dishes at their particular table communally, to know whether you can help yourself to some food, you only need to know what table you are at. But you cannot switch people at random from one table to another without disrupting the relationship (see Price 1975:4).

Authority Ranking takes the form of an *ordinal* scale, in that people are ranked in a linear hierarchy. (Linearity means that there are no loops or incomparable ranks: any person can be ranked against any other person.) Within any one particular system of rank (say, line officers in the Navy) the asymmetry of rank is transitive: if a captain outranks a commander and a commander outranks a lieutenant, then the captain outranks the lieutenant. But in comparing two people with different ranks there is no metrically specifiable distance between them: one person is greater than another, but there is no systematically meaningful measure of how much greater. If the admiral has started to eat, it is of no consequence to the AR relationship whether a lieutenant at the table starts his meal ten seconds later or ten minutes later.

In contrast, Equality Matching relationships resemble an *interval* scale in that people can not only specify who owes what to whom, but also how much they owe. In order to determine whether they are even, people match or balance what each person has given and/or received, and they can assess how great the imbalance is. In EM, order is represented by the fact that owing someone two big favors is a greater debt (a greater asymmetry) than owing the person one small favor. But unlike an ordinal scale, in EM people take implicit account of how much they have coming to them. So if I am behind in my driving turns, I owe you a definite number of car pool rides. If you lecture three times to fill in for me while I am away and I lecture for you once, I owe you two lectures.

One step beyond this is Market Pricing, in which not only order and intervals but also ratios are meaningful, so that we have a relational structure corresponding to a *ratio* scale. In an EM relationship, there is no meaningful sense in which people consider the ratio of the imbalance in dinner party invitations on the one hand, with child care hours owed in a baby sitting coop on the other hand. But in MP relations, the price of a dinner of a specified kind at a particular restaurant has a definite, socially meaningful ratio to the cost of an hour of child-care by a baby sitter who charges a specific rate. The MP ratio scale of prices entails categorical distinctions (there are different kinds of workers, and everyone in a certain category may receive the same benefits), ordinal distinctions (welders get paid more than sweepers and two hour's work is worth more than one hour's work), and interval discriminations (a week of missed work can be made up by working five Saturdays).

There are two significant kinds of features of the four models that this preliminary formalization highlights. First, it makes plain what qualities of each kind of relationship people attend to (like price ratios in MP) and what relational features are undefined, meaningless and irrelevant in each type (like intervals between groups in CS). Second, this formalization displays an intriguing feature of the set of four models taken together: each successive structure incorporates all the relational distinctions and operations defined under the previous model and adds new ones. That is, the four structures are uniquely ordered by hierarchical inclusion such that each model is formed by adding relations or properties to a structurally simpler one. Like CS, AR entails a conception of differences among types of people, but only in AR are the differences ordered. EM also explicitly involves categories of entities that are compared and matched—e.g., an-eye-for-an-eye. Like AR, EM also requires a conception of transitive linear order; owing someone three turns is more than owing two turns, which is more than owing one turn. MP incorporates all of these concepts. Prices, for example, are defined with respect to categories of commodities ("Oranges, 3 for $1.00"). An essential part of the meaning of prices is their linear ordering and transitivity. (What could it mean to assert the contrary, that A is cheaper than B, B is cheaper than C, but C is cheaper than A?) And MP definitely encompasses the idea of additive intervals: it makes sense to add the price of three oranges to the price of two apples and say how much the total costs. But the concept of ratios that makes MP distinctive is undefined in EM, AR, and CS; the intervals of EM are unintelligible in an AR or CS mode; and the rank ordering of AR is incoherent within CS.

This Guttman scaling[2] of the structures is exciting in its own right, but it also has vital implications about the nature of the category of fundamental relational models as a whole. In fact, it begins to address the question of how the four models are connected to each other and suggests possible constraints on the forms that any other fundamental relational models might take. Before we take this up, however, it will help to give a formal definition of each of the four structures.

## AXIOMATIC DEFINITIONS OF THE FOUR RELATIONAL STRUCTURES[3] (With Scott Weinstein)

It is possible to describe the relational structures of each of the four models in a more formal, axiomatic system. Based on work done jointly with Scott Weinstein, this section proposes simple formal representations for the four fundamental types of social relationships. The properties of Communal Sharing correspond to the structure of equivalence relations; Authority Ranking is formally defined as a linear ordering; Equality Matching has the structure of ordered Abelian groups, and Market Pricing is axiomatically formalized in terms of Archimedean ordered fields. We will use the notation of relational mathematics to represent the four structures.

Readers who are not comfortable with this sort of algebra may be guided by knowledge of the related types of measurement scales and by the illustrative exegesis in each subsection. Basically the formalization amounts to the claim that CS is like a category or set, each of whose elements are equivalent (or undifferentiable with respect to a given property). AR is a linear ordering in which everyone's rank can be compared to everyone else's: in an AR relationship you can always determine whether one person has a rank at least as high as any other given person. EM is a relational structure in which people can compare amounts with addition and subtraction (I did two favors for you and you did me one favor, so you owe me one), and the order in which people have done the favors (e.g.) is irrelevant. MP is structured like the rational numbers; you can multiply and divide costs, for example.

In reading the axioms we propose, the relevant question is, is this relation or operation meaningful in this kind of social relationship? If so, the axiom appropriately represents the relationship. To make it easier for the reader to make this analysis, a qualitative prose formulation of the principles of each relational structure precedes each axiomatic definition. At the end of each section there are additional brief examples, and following all the formal definitions is a more detailed illustration of the similarities and differences among the models as they are manifest in the allocation of space in corporations.

## Communal Sharing is an Equivalence Relation

Imagine a Moose community, call it C, in which there are a number of men, whom we represent here by letters of the alphabet. Suppose we call the relationship of eating the main daily meal together, R. Any person x in community C obviously eats with herself; this property is called *reflexivity*. We know that if x eats with y, then y eats with x; this property is *symmetry*. Furthermore, since we are thinking of the one main daily meal, if x eats with y and y eats with z, then x eats with z; this is *transitivity*. A relation that is reflexive, symmetric, and transitive is called an *equivalence relation*. These are the properties of the social categorization of people into discrete groups or classes that is the foundation for Communal Sharing. Let us state the definition in formal, symbolic notation:

An equivalence relation, R, on a set C has the following three properties:

   (i)   for every $x \in C$, $R(x,x)$   [R is *reflexive*];
   (ii)  for every $x, y \in C$, if $R(x,y)$, then $R(y,x)$   [R is *symmetric*];
   (iii) for every $x, y, z \in C$, if $R(x,y)$ and $R(y,z)$, then $R(x,z)$   [R is *transitive*].

In brief, the thesis is that Communal Sharing is a kind of equivalence relation. In the community, C, there are groups of people who have the relationship R of eating together. A class of people who share their food is a subset of the larger community, a subset defined by this food-sharing relationship R. A larger group of people eats together at certain rituals. Let's call the relationship of eating a certain kind of festival meal together, R. If we are talking about equivalence relations like sharing cooked food at meals, distinguishing a group of people who eat their daily meal together is a *finer* distinction than distinguishing people who eat ritual meals, since the group of festival meal sharers includes all of the members of at least one daily food sharing group, and others as well. The finest distinction we can draw by the relationship eating together is a solitary individual who eats alone: in this case the relationship of those who eat together is *identity* (the people who eat together are the same person). We can state this formally:

> Associated with any equivalence relation R on a set C is a partition of C into equivalence classes. For each $x \in C$, the *R-equivalence class* of x (written [x], where R is understood from the context) is $\{y \in C \mid R(x,y)\}$. One equivalence relation R is *finer than* another R just in case each R-equivalence class is contained in some R-equivalence class and one of these containments is proper. Note that identity is the finest equivalence relation since each of its equivalence classes contains exactly one element of C.

Ethnographic investigations might well turn up other properties shared by people who eat a given type of meal together. For example, Moose who eat the daily meal together also cultivate a collective field together, harvest together, share a granary, and are all protected by a particular altar to which they sacrifice together. Let's call this kind of collection of properties universally and exclusively shared by precisely the same group of people a *congruence*. If an equivalence relation like eating together is a congruence with respect to properties like sacrificing, it means that we know that if two people, x and y, eat together, then a person x sacrifices to a certain altar if and only if person y also sacrifices to it. Formally, this is:

> An equivalence R on C is *a congruence with respect to collection of properties* W just in case
> (∗) for every $P \in W$ and for every $x,y \in C$, if R(x,y) then, P(x) if and only if P(y).[4]

In social relations, CS equivalence relations obtain where, for example, there is no differentiation among members of a given group with respect to access to given resources. The collection of properties with respect to which differentiations among the members of a given group fail to be made will be those properties with respect to which the equivalence relation will be a congruence. For example, if a given group pools their food, their labor, and their corporate responsibility for harm done by any member of the group to outside groups, then food sharing, labor sharing, and harm responsibility form a congruence together.

It is important to remember that people participate in a number of CS equivalence relations. Properties like transitivity and congruence only obtain within each particular equivalence relation.

### Authority Ranking is a Linear Ordering

In a Moose community, C, people are hierarchically ordered according to their authority and prerogatives. Let's take an ordering, O, which is defined by being served food no later than another person. Obviously, a person can be served food no later than himself, so the ordering O is reflexive. It is also transitive: if x can be served food no later than y, and y can be served food no later than z, then x can be served food no later than z. Two people can each be served no later than the other if and only if they are equivalent (technically this is called *antisymmetry*). That is, in any given context some group of people may be accorded equivalent rank. For example, it often happens that a group of people receives a pot of beer to drink together, so that for the purpose of that beer distribution, they are equivalent. Hence Authority Ranking incorporates and preserves in its own structure the prior relation of equivalence (although with a different social sense in this new relational context). An ordering that has all these properties is called a *quasi-ordering respecting the equivalence relation E*. Let us give the formal definitions:

Let E be an equivalence relation on a set C. A relation O on C is said to be a *quasi-ordering respecting E* if it satisfies the following properties:

(iv) for every x, $O(x,x)$   [O is *reflexive*];
(v) for every x, y, z $\epsilon$ C, if $O(x,y)$ and $O(y,z)$, then $O(x,z)$   [O is *transitive*];
(vi) for every x, y $\epsilon$ C, $O(x,y)$ and $O(y,x)$ if and only if $E(x,y)$
[O is *antisymmetric up to E*].

Suppose that the quasi-ordering is such that if person x must be served no later than person y and y also must be served no later than x, then they must be the same person. In such a case we say that the ordering *respects the identity relation* and we call O a *partial ordering*. A partial ordering means that it is not possible for each of two different people to have a rank that is at least as great as the other; in a partial ordering symmetry implies identity. For example, when the ordering is such that if person x may succeed to the lineage headship while person y is still alive and y also may succeed to the lineage headship while person x is still alive, then x and y must be the same person.

The fact that a partial ordering respects identity simply states that two distinct people cannot each be superior to the other, but it does not require that any definite relationship exist between two people in a given ordered set: it allows for the possibility that x is not relationally superior to y nor is y superior to x. So in the relational structure of quasi-orderings and partial orderings, it is still possible that between some particular pairs of people in a given structure there is no specification of who should be served first—precedence between them is simply undefined. But in actuality, when Authority Ranking relationships obtain among a set of people, then precedence is always defined (although people may not mark it in every context). In this case, that means that for any two people x and y in an AR ordering, either x must be served no later than y, or y must be served no later than x. There must be some rank ordering of two people in the same AR hierarchy. For example, when we look at order of succession to lineage headship or some other social context in which Moose make fine distinctions, we find that Moose always do discriminate between the ranks of any two men—they never treat two people as if their relative rank were undefined. To say that rank is defined among *all* pairs of people in the hierarchy means that the relation is *connected.* This makes AR a *linear quasi-ordering respecting E.* Since AR also respects the identity principle, Authority Ranking meets the definition of a *linear ordering.* Let us define the terms abstractly:

> O is called a *partial ordering* if O is a quasi-ordering respecting the identity relation $(x = y)$. If in addition to properties (iv)–(vi) above, the partial ordering O satisfies
>
> (vii) for every x, y $\epsilon$ C, either O(x,y) or O(y,x)   [O is *connected*],
>
> then O is called a *linear quasi-ordering respecting E.* A linear quasi-ordering respecting the identity relation is called a *linear ordering.*

Most Authority Ranking relations are linear orderings, in the sense that, for example, every officer in the U.S. Navy has a rank that is ultimately distinct from every other officer (officers can always distinguish among themselves by dates of commission and, if necessary, by their unique numbers in the naval list). Similarly, Moose men in a village in principle can always sort themselves by rank according to their birth order.

Remember that two people who frequently relate to each other in AR terms may also relate to each other in non-AR terms some of the time. Not all of their interaction will conform to the linear ordering structure, but when they are relating to each other in an AR framework, the linear ordering principles will be observed with respect to the actions that mark or constitute that relationship. Ancillary, incidental, and socially irrelevant actions that the participants do not generate out of the AR model, that they do not understand or evaluate or coordinate with respect to the AR model, need not have this structure. So while in a given context in a particular culture people may be served in AR linear order, the order in which they cough, or go off and urinate, need not be so structured.

Again, remember that people commonly participate in several AR linear orderings. The fact that person x must be served food no later than person y and that person y gives orders to person z need not mean that person x may speak harshly to person z, if serving food, giving orders, and speaking harshly are distinct linear orderings. It may even be that person x commands person y in one linear AR relationship (say, at work), and person y commands person z in a completely different AR ordering (say, coaching a Little League team), so that person x does not command person z, or have any AR relationship with him at all. Reflexivity, transitivity, antisymmetry, connectivity, and so forth obtain only *with respect to each particular linear AR ordering.* The same is true of the properties of EM and MP relations that we will now describe.

## Equality Matching is an Ordered Abelian Group

Suppose that people in a given community, C, give each other wives and keep track of the exchange balance.[5] If we give you two wives this year and then none next year, the total gift to you obviously is two wives. Not giving a wife leaves the balance unchanged; more technically, zero is the *additive identity.* If one man in our community gives you two wives and then one more, while another gives you four, the balance (seven wives) is the same as if the first man give you two, while the second gave you one and four. It does not matter how the brides are grouped by individual giver, all that counts is the total sum. In other words, wife-giving is *associative.* If you give us three wives and then receive three wives from us, we have evened up the exchange. That is, x wives received cancels x wives given, or receiving wives is the *inverse* of giving wives. If these are the rules for wife-giving, then in mathematical terms wife-giving is a *group.* Formally:

Let C be a set, + be a binary operation on C, − be a unary operation on C and 0 (zero) be an element of C.[6] The structure $\langle C, +, -, 0 \rangle$ is a *group* just in case it satisfies the following properties:

(viii) for every x $\epsilon$ C,   x + 0 = x   [*zero is the identity* for +].
(ix) for every x, y, z $\epsilon$ C,   (x + y) + z = x + (y + z)   [+ is *associative*].
(x) for every x $\epsilon$ C,   x + (−x) = 0   [−x is the *inverse* of x].

In wife-giving exchanges, the order in which we give women is of no significance for the current balance: if we give one wife this year and four next year, the balance is the same as if we gave four this year and one the next. That is to say, wife-giving is *commutative.* If the wife-giving relationship is a group and commutative, then it is known mathematically as an *Abelian group.* Formally,

If in addition to properties (viii)–(x), the structure satisfies

(xi) for every x, y $\epsilon$ C,   x + y = y + x,   [the operation is *commutative*],

it is called an *Abelian group.*

Such a wife-giving relationship necessarily entails a conception of the linear ordering of number of wives given, since the gift of any given number of brides can be compared with any other number, and it is always possible to say whether a specified number exceeds another number—and that issue is socially significant. It makes a difference whether you owe three wives or two. So the Abelian group structure of EM encompasses the linear-ordering structure that is the basis of AR. But how does this linear-ordering structure combine with the operation of addition? Specifically, what happens when there is a particular asymmetrical balance in the exchange of wives, and then both sides give each other an identical number of brides? In fact, the asymmetry in the balance—the debt—remains the same: Wife giving is *order preserving*. Suppose you have given us four wives and we have only given you two. Clearly, four is more than two, and the debt is in your favor. If you give three more to us and we give three more to you, the direction of the imbalance, the asymmetry, is unchanged.[7] Naturally, an Abelian group that preserves order is called an *ordered Abelian group*. Abstractly, we can state this as follows:

If $\geq$ is a linear ordering of C then the structure $\langle C, +, -, 0, \rangle$ is called an *ordered Abelian group* just in case it satisfies properties (viii)–(xi) and

(xii) for every x, y, z $\epsilon$ C, if x $\geq$ y, then x + z $\geq$ y + z [*order preserving*].

Equality Matching relationships have all of these properties, and therefore are *ordered Abelian groups*. Consider a baby sitting cooperative. Doing no hours of baby sitting leaves a member's obligations unchanged (zero is the additive identity). Sitting for the Jones family for 4 hours one night and 2 hours another night, plus sitting 3 hours for the Smiths, gives one coop credits exactly equal to sitting 4 hours for the Joneses, together with 2 hours for the Smiths one night and 3 hours for the Smiths another night (EM is associative). When the Smiths baby sit for the Joneses for 3 hours and then the Joneses sit for the Smiths for 3 hours, the Smiths' and the Joneses' obligations are cancelled out (negative x is the additive inverse). The order in which people sit for others is irrelevant to their obligations: sitting for the Smiths for an hour and then for the Joneses for 4 hours is the same as sitting for the Joneses for 4 hours followed by sitting for the Smiths for an hour (commutativity). Finally, if the Smiths owe more baby-sitting hours than the Joneses and then each family separately sits for the Blacks for 2 hours, the Smiths still owe more baby-sitting hours than the Joneses (addition of baby sitting is order preserving). Note that the starting point in such a relationship is irrelevant to the balance: it does not matter whether the Jones family has sat 10,006 hours for the Smiths, and the Smiths 10,003 hours for the Joneses, or the Jones family 6 hours and the Smiths 3 hours; in either case, the Smiths owe exactly 3 hours. In that sense, all that matters for the relationship is the current "debt:" the baby-sitting interval or distance between the two families.

## Market Pricing Is an Archimedean Ordered Field

Let's take the same Moose community, C, and consider how people sell and buy things. Clearly people use addition and subtraction in buying and selling; zero is the additive identity in the market, subtraction is the inverse of addition, and such addition obeys the associative and commutative principles. So the operation of addition in Market Pricing is an Abelian group. People also use multiplication when they buy and sell: 8 kola nuts at 3 *wakiri* per kola equals 24 *wakiri*. What is the relational structure of this MP multiplication operation? The price of 6 kolas at 2 *wakiri* each is the same as 2 kolas at 6 *wakiri* each, so MP is commutative. If someone is selling kolas at 3 *wakiri* each, the price of one kola equals just 3 *wakiri*, so 1 is the multiplicative identity. A *wakiri* is a conceptual unit of currency that equals 5 francs CFA. To figure the price of an item in CFA currency, you can multiply the number of items by the price in *wakiri*, and multiply the total by five. Or you get the same answer if you multiply the price in *wakiri* by five, and multiply that total by the number of items, so price calculations are associative. There is also a multiplicative inverse for every number, its reciprocal. If a handful of kolas costs 7 *wakiri* all together and you divide the handful into seven equal parts, each part is worth 1 *wakiri*. (This multiplicative inverse can be written exponentially, $x^{-1}$, or as a fraction, $\frac{1}{x}$.) Hence this MP multiplication operation in market transactions, like addition in MP, is also an Abelian group.

How do the two operations of addition and multiplication combine? By the *distributive* principle. If you buy 3 hand spans of cloth at 2 *wakiri* per span and then 4 more spans at 2 *wakiri* per span, the price is the same as if you had bought a single 7-span length at 2 *wakiri* per span. A relational structure composed of two Abelian groups linked by the distributive principle is called a field, so MP relations are structured as a field. Specifically, in MP relations we have a structure in which the two operations, addition and multiplication (represented as + and •), with their inverses (represented as − and $^{-1}$) and the identity elements (0 for addition and 1 for multiplication) are each Abelian, and the two operations are linked by the distributive principle. The distributive principle means that you can multiply each of two elements by the same multiplier separately and then add them together, or you can add them together first and then multiply by the multiplier; either way, you get the same result. To formalize:

Let C be a set and let + and • be binary operations on C, $^{-1}$ and − be unary operations on C − {0} and C, respectively, and 0 and 1 be elements of C. The structure $\langle C, +, \bullet, -, ^{-1}, 0, 1 \rangle$ is called a *field* just in case it satisfies the following three properties:

(xiii) $\langle C, +, -, 0 \rangle$ is an Abelian group;
(xiv) $\langle C - \{0\}, \bullet, ^{-1}, 1 \rangle$ is an Abelian group;[8]
(xv) for every x,y,z є C,  $x \bullet (y + z) = x \bullet y + x \bullet z$   [*distributivity*].

The distributive law seems "obvious," but it is not defined and need not obtain in CS, AR, or EM.

Naturally, some prices are more than others, and everyone would agree about the linear ordering of prices. This means that MP is not just a field, it is an *ordered field*. Technically:

> If $\geq$ is an ordering on C, the structure $\langle C, +, \bullet, -, ^{-1}, 0, 1 \rangle$ is called an *ordered field* just in case its associated additive structure is an ordered Abelian group and for every x, y, z $\epsilon$ C, if x $\geq$ y, and z > 0, then x $\bullet$ z $\geq$ y $\bullet$ z  [multiplication by a positive number is *order preserving*].

There is one final issue to address—are all prices comparable? If you want to buy some commodity, you want to know if you can sell another commodity to get the money for it, and how much of your commodity you would have to sell. In fact, no matter what the prices of the two commodities, there is always some number of one commodity whose total price exceeds the unit price of any other commodity on the market. So any commodity can be exchanged on the market for any other commodity, provided you have enough of them. That means that Market Pricing has the structure known in mathematics as an *Archimedean ordered field*. There is always some specifiable finite number of any marketable item whose price comes to the price of any other marketable item. In formal equations:

> If in addition the ordered field satisfies
>
> (xvi) for every x $\epsilon$ C, there is a natural number n such that x $\leq$ n1 [*Archimedean property*],
>
> then the structure is called an *Archimedean ordered field*, where n x is the *n-fold sum* of x with itself.

In sum, Market Pricing is an Archimedean ordered field, since prices, wages, rents, interest, and price-like utilities exhibit these properties (at least over some ranges). For example, the price of two acres of land at $800 per acre is $800 (1 + 1) = $800 + $800 (MP obeys the distributive principle). MP is Archimedean because no matter how low any actual price for an item, there is always some number of such items whose total cost exceeds any given quantity, say $1.00. That is, everything has its price—there are no free lunches.

The distinction between Equality Matching and Market Pricing is the contrast between being limited to the relation of balance (with the operation of concatenation) on the one hand, and having a concept of proportion, on the other hand. When people are applying Equality Matching, they usually use operations that involve one-to-one correspondence or side-by-side alignment, with concatenation. One paradigm is the pan balance like the one in the hand of the blindfolded figure of Justice: the two pans should be even. (Note that this balancing or one-to-one correspondence makes sense only if the entities on the two sides are categorically the same in the sense of their qualitative social significance.) When the balance is even, adding the same weight to both sides leaves the balance even. Market Pricing transactions can not be conducted with this kind of balancing (or one-to-one matching equivalence) and concatenation alone: MP transactions entail the more abstract idea of proportions. A salary, for example, is a rate; to calculate what wage a person has earned for a job requires multiplying the units of work times the rate of pay, a problem logically equivalent to finding the area of a rectangle.[9]

The wage earner can figure out how many commodities of a given type her salary is worth by dividing this sum by the price of the given commodity (monetary units per entity). The distributive law means that she can first add the number of units of work (say, days) she has done and then multiply the sum by the rate of pay, getting the same result as if she had first multiplied her pay rate times each of the units separately, and then taken the sum. Inflation in the value of the currency, or even changing the unit of currency, do not affect these calculations, and have no social significance as long as all prices are modified by this same transform (multiplication by a positive number). But adding the same amount, say 10 *wakiri*, to the daily wage and to the unit price of all commodities would change their relative prices and exchange rates, and would thus change the relationships involved in socially significant ways.

Observe that the axioms of an Archimedean ordered field in no way imply anything that translates into social relations entailing individualism, selfishness, maximization, or competitiveness, and of course there is nothing in this structure that need connect it to material subsistence activities. None of these four relational structures intrinsically entail individualism, selfishness, maximization, competitiveness, or concern with material subsistence. Any of these separate features could operate in conjunction with any of the four elementary structures, and they would all operate differently in relation to each of them.

The reflective reader may have noted some apparent notational inconsistency between the formal definitions of the different structures. In the discussion of CS and AR, x, y, and z are treated as people, while in EM and MP they are treated as obligations and prices. But the inconsistency is only apparent. In each case, the entities whose properties we are discussing are not persons as total selves, but the aspect of the person that enters into a specific relation. In a CS relationship, the equivalence is not among, say, members of a lineage in all their facets and qualities, it is equivalence of membership, equivalence of labor responsibilities, equivalence of rights to eat cooked food, and so forth. In many other features irrelevant to the CS relationship, people are not at all equivalent—they have different temperaments, different fates, different physiognomies. In an AR relationship, what is linearly ordered is not physical bodies, ear size, or order of urination, it is social precedence, initiative, command, and so forth. Similarly, in an EM relationship, people do not weigh their life histories in a balance or measure and match their respective libidos, they mark and keep track of specific kinds of work or certain transfers of objects or rights in marriage. In just the same way, the aspect of the person that is implicated in an MP interaction is the price of the commodity they are offering or paying, their salary, their rent, or their interest rate. You do not relate to a bank as a total person, but (in an MP frame) only as a seller of services. So in our notation, the set C and its elements x, y, and z are always the socially relevant features of people with respect to the particular kind of relationship. In general, in any kind of social relationship it is not the total person or associated objects per se that are structured according to these relational properties, only certain socially constituted, marked attributes of them.

## An Illustration of the Properties of the Four Structures

The theory outlined here is a theory about ordinary everyday social interaction, so it will be useful to have a familiar concrete case to illustrate the abstract structures above. Consider the allocation of offices. One possibility is for a delimited group of people to share a work space, using it freely according to their needs without assigning particular areas to the exclusive use of any individual. The Japanese reportedly (Pfeiffer 1986) make considerable use of this mode, so that even people who work in separate "offices" regard themselves as occupants of space belonging to the business as a whole. All users of a collective work area are equivalent in terms of their rights to use of the pooled work area, and, inversely, all parts of their joint work area are equivalent with regard to their use by the occupants of the space. Even in institutions and countries where primary work space is not pooled like this, meeting rooms, corridors, bathrooms, lobbies, and elevators are typically used freely in this way, with no accounting of who uses how much, no attempt to balance use, few if any rules of precedence or priorities, and no compensation demanded as a function of usage. Other office amenities like water from the water fountain, paper towels, local telephone calls, photocopying, or desk supplies may be similarly distributed on a "help yourself freely according to your needs" basis. In such systems there are boundaries, which may vary for different items—it is not that anyone in the world may come in and use anything: these resources are more or less reserved for the collective use of members of the organization in question, and others connected with them.

This form of allocating space according to CS exhibits the structure of an equivalence relation. A person shares space with herself (reflexivity), and if Peter shares space with another member of his work group, Mary, then Mary shares space with Peter (symmetry). If Peter shares a space with Mary and Mary shares the same work space with George, then Peter and George share the common work space (transitivity).

Alternatively, people may be assigned individual offices, with the largest offices going to those of highest rank and greatest authority, as is common in American and particularly German businesses. Indeed, the size of one's office, together with the size and expense of its furnishings, depth of carpet—and often the number of the floor it is on—commonly are the most prominent markers of rank in the organization. Interestingly, it is doubtful whether most occupants, however keenly aware of their status, know the actual area of their office in square feet, the depth of the carpet in millimeters, or the height of their office off the ground. What they know is what they each have, compared to others in the system: who has more and who has less. They know and care little about the absolute quantities or the precise quantitative differences among themselves, but they typically know precisely how these factors are ordered. There is no exact formula that anyone can state that gives the precise area of offices as a function of rank in a business, but the ordering of offices by size typically corresponds quite closely with the ranking of occupants by corporate status (i.e., corporate rank is not an interval scale for most social purposes). The "big" men and women at the "top" have the biggest space, and so on down the line. In the same way, officers of a business may be entirely ignorant of just how much money someone else makes, but they often know who makes more and who makes less than each other individual. Groups of people at a given rank may have identical starting salaries, expense accounts, and other privileges, but in every Western business, at least, people at different levels of authority have different amenities.

This Authority Ranking system of allocating office space is a linear ordering. Each person's space is at least as great as her own space (reflexivity). If Jubin has more space than Lamusa and Lamusa has more space than Pierre, then Jubin has more space than Pierre (transitivity). If Maria has at least as much space as Yuri and Yuri has at least as much space as Maria, then they have the same amount of space (space is antisymmetric up to equivalence). For any two people in a corporate building, one must have at least as much space as the other (the ordering is connected).

A third way of structuring office space has recently come into vogue in the United States, Pfeiffer (1986) reports. Union Carbide and some other firms have recently moved into office buildings designed so that many employees, if not all, have precisely the same size office. This equitable distribution of office sizes has been the mode for some time in Scandinavia. Such buildings may be designed so that all employees—or all those of a given broad category—are on a single floor, each at the same elevation. Each person may have an identical choice among furnishings of a fixed cost, or even among status-equivalent works of art. Generally, but not always, a few high-ranking officers have more spacious and elegant accommodations, and nothing is said in these descriptions of janitorial and other service personnel, who may have no individual offices at all. But within larger or smaller subgroups, the principle is maintained: equal but separate space and furnishings for each one. Often all the members of a specified subgroup have the same number of vacation days, the same kind of personal computer equipment, the same class of airplane ticket, the same company-financed life insurance, and the same photocopying allowance. Perhaps each has one secretary. This kind of egalitarian distributive justice in the allocation of space according to Equality Matching has the structure of an ordered Abelian group. Giving anyone zero additional space keeps that person's space allocation unchanged (zero is the additive identity). Assigning a person rooms A and B, and later giving her room C as well leaves her with the same amount of space as giving her room A, and then giving her rooms B and C together (space assignment is associative). Assigning space and then taking the same space away leaves the person no space (additive inverse). Getting room A and then room B gives you the same amount of space as getting room B first and then room A. Furthermore, if Muhango has more space than Mvula, and they each get an identical additional increment in space, Muhango still has more space than Mvula (space allocation is order preserving).

Finally, of course, office space is commonly bought and sold, generally across organizations or between an organization and an individual. Space in buildings is often sold at a price per square foot, as a function of the location, the floor, the view, the furnishings (if any), and as a function of other relevant amenities. Price per square foot also depends on the amount of space leased, together with the length of the lease. There is a market for office space, and at any time, in any location, sellers are competing with other sellers of comparable facilities and buyers are potentially competing with other buyers who might make an offer for the same space. The prices which organize the purchase and sale of office space reflect not only the kinds of substitutes available for office space, but the alternative uses of the money; a price is a ratio of exchange and a ratio of trade-off among other commodities that the buyer could use the money to obtain. Although zoning or prejudice may restrict who enters into such a transaction, space like other commodities is typically offered for sale to anyone who will pay, and the buyer who is willing to pay the highest price chooses freely among sellers. All the other items mentioned above are also available on the market, including carpets, photocopying, insurance, and secretarial services. In each category, better qualities and higher quantities can be obtained at higher costs, while buyer and seller may bargain and negotiate to get the most for what they are offering. To a first order of approximation, this sort of Market Pricing transaction in space manifestly displays the properties of Archimedean ordered fields. In particular, buying and leasing typically obey the distributive law. If you sign one contract to lease a 1,000 square foot suite and another 2,000 square foot suite at $14 per square foot for the total, the price is the same as if you signed two simultaneous leases, again paying $14 per square foot for the 1,000 square foot suite and $14 per square foot for the 2,000 square foot suite. Further, no matter how cheap the space, it is not free: if you buy enough square feet, its price will exceed any given total price.

The hypothesized properties and operations are axioms about social psychology, however, not the natural world. They are only correct if they capture the psychological facts about social relations. That is, we are trying to represent human intentions, perceptions, and judgments. So these axioms can be falsified. For example, in assessing how much space people have, to the extent that the order in which people received the space is socially significant, the commutative axiom of EM and MP fails to capture the structure of the relationship. Indeed, in MP there are some interesting apparent exceptions to the commutative and distributive principles. These exceptions have to do with discounts for quantity purchases and for long term contracts with options for additional purchases. For example, the price of leasing 100 rooms separately usually is more than the price of one lease for 100 rooms together. And leasing 100 rooms first and then an additional room may be cheaper than leasing one room and then later leasing 100 rooms. Thus there may be some MP-like transactions that involve mathematical structures that are not Archimedean ordered fields. These structures need further analysis to determine whether they can be axiomatically defined and to discover whether they have the characteristic features of fundamental models described in Chapter 8.

An important part of these formal definitions of the four models for social relationships is that we are hypothesizing that various properties and operations are *not* defined in some of the relational structures. Thus we are asserting that multiplication and the distributive principle are not socially meaningful or even intelligible within the framework of EM, that AR entails no sense of intervals or addition, and that linear orderings are not a part of the social phenomenon of CS. What does it mean to say that a property or operation is undefined? It means that we should expect a lack of regularity, consistency, or consensus with regard to that aspect of the structure. So, for example, stating that CS involves no intrinsic idea of linear order implies we should be able to observe social relationships in which people attend to equivalence properties without marking or attending to order. More precisely, the hypothesis is that people create and sustain CS relationships based on equivalence and the related congruences, relationships in which they do not intentionally create or attend to linear social orderings, much less to additive intervals or multiplicative operations. This hypothesis can be tested by observation, interview, and experiment, and in the future it should be tested in all these ways.


## THE USES AND CONSEQUENCES
## OF AXIOMATIC FORMALIZATION


Providing abstract, axiomatically constructed formal representations of social relationships clarifies the basic nature of each type of social relationship, particularly the structural similarities of apparently diverse forms of social interaction within and across cultures. That is, the hypothesis is that Equality Matching interactions always conform to this structure of ordered Abelian groups, whether they take the form of children dividing up cookies and taking turns with a toy or assume the lex talionis form of terrorist reprisals. This axiomatization shows the formal relational congruence among the merging of selves in the communitas of a ritual, pooling land in a commons, treating a group decision as a matter of finding consensus, regarding another's needs as equivalent to one's own, and reacting to rape as a polluting defilement. This suggests that it is plausible to hypothesize that these kinds of human interaction might all be based on the same psychological structure: the equivalence relation of Communal Sharing. I suggest that this isomorphism exists because these structures correspond to real mental models: people actually generate, understand, coordinate, and evaluate social relations using structures formally equivalent to these. That is not to say that people can report anything about the structure of the models or are aware of how they use them, however. Like natural language grammars, people usually use the models without analysis or insight into what they are doing. The problem of self-reflective consciousness is quite separate from the issue of the cognitive basis for the collaborative construction of social relations. What this axiomatic formalization explicates is the kinds of relational distinctions people are making and the differences they ignore, in each kind of relationship.

The proposed axiomatic construction indicates that the four fundamental types of social relationships comprise a series in which each relationship in turn is built on the structure of the previous type, with the addition of new mathematical relations or operations at each step. Thus the four structures make a kind of Guttman scale, in which each successive model makes all the distinctions and includes all the procedures of the models it encompasses, along with some others. This global pattern of successive inclusion has broad implications for the pattern of emergence of the fundamental types of relationships during childhood, since it gives a strong reason why they should emerge in a specific order. Note that the prediction of this unique order of emergence of the cognitive capacity to understand and implement the four models is consistent with either a view that children are learning the relational structures involved or that the capacity to understand the relational structures and operations is a function of brain maturation. In either case children would be expected to manifest CS, then add AR, then grasp EM, and finally fathom MP.[10] Indeed this order corresponds with my informal observations (see Chapter 17). Having mastered a relational structure in no way entails abandoning the preceding ones, however: people do not give up CS and AR relations when they acquire the ability to implement EM. What is more, when people come to understand MP relations they generally do not reinterpret their EM relationships as degenerate or special cases of MP; the EM relations retain their proper qualities. Having discovered the sense of AR, we do not ipso facto convert all current CS relationships into AR relationships, nor do we lose the capacity or inclination to engage in new CS relationships in which rank order is meaningless. Each type of social relationship retains the qualities proper to it, despite the emergence of new structures that encompass—and in that sense transcend—it. This appears to be true historically and phylogenetically as well as ontogenetically. Thus close kinship relations ("the family") more or less resist being commoditized or being reduced to quid pro quo matching. Personal relationships change and social roles do evolve, of course, but this is not because the logically "simpler" (and ontogenetically earlier) modes of relating are superceded or supplanted once a person learns to make additional distinctions and master new operations.

There are also predictions about social structure that follow from this Guttman scaling of relational structures in which each successive form builds on the previous ones and defines new properties. This axiomatic analysis of the relational structures shows that if people or other organisms have the capacity to relate in an MP mode, then they also have the capacity to relate in EM, AR, and CS modes. Similarly, if an animal is capable of implementing and understanding EM relationships, then it is logically capable of relating in AR and CS modes. And of course if an animal can engage in AR relationships, it ought to be able to participate in CS relationships. Capacity does not imply necessity: there may be exogenous constraints that prevent organisms from realizing social relationships they are cognitively capable of engaging in. So in principle it is possible to organize a society utilizing MP relations in which there are no manifestations of EM or AR. But if the more complex forms of social relationships are adaptive (in either the natural selection sense or the social functional sense) and cognition is the principal constraint, then it should be rare to find a social system in which the more complex forms are evident and the logically simpler relational structures are not in evidence.

Note, however, that the relevant psychological constraint on adaptation may be on the capacity of the organism to apply the structure in the social domain. Gallistel (1990) shows that even invertebrates perform feats of navigation that require cognitive representations based on structures at least as complex as any of the four defined above. Yet only one species seems to apply structures like ordered fields to social relations.

Each relational structure is built on a set of defined properties and operations. Hence, like atoms, the models are not formally elementary, but are themselves composites. This poses a problem: in what sense can the social relations that people generate with these models be decomposed into these distinct properties and operations? A closely related question is, do people combine these properties in other relational structures based on other subsets of the fourteen properties and operations? Of course, some subsets cannot logically be combined: certain properties and operations (e.g., distributivity) are defined just in terms of certain others, and cannot be included without their logical antecedents. But there are many other possible collections of axioms besides the four proposed here. Are there social relations whose structure corresponds to a mathematical group that does not obey the commutative principle, or social relationships whose relational structure corresponds to a mathematical group that is commutative but whose basic operation is not order preserving? The thesis is that people order most of their social relations with reference to just the four specified relational structures, but this hypothesis remains to be rigorously tested.

This formalization is vital in directing the search for other congruences between mathematical structures and basic patterns of social relationships, for it suggests that we should look at relational structures that fall between these four, or that continue the Guttman scale by the addition of further properties and operations beyond those of Archimedean ordered fields. In effect, this provides an additional potential criterion to add to the features defining the models that we may call fundamental and elementary. If anyone proposes a new model that is mathematically unrelated to these four, or that is not part of this Guttman series, then it is ipso facto a less plausible candidate. This formal structural criterion could be a strict one if we choose to apply it narrowly, but perhaps it should be given relatively low weight until this relational axiomatization is rigorously validated.

A prediction from this account is that in the appropriate social domains every socially functional adult in every culture ought to demonstrate the functional ability to use each of the four relational structures. This should be true regardless of whether or not people have attended Western schools and been taught mathematics. Indeed, if presented with appropriate content, children of the right ages should find the properties included in each of these structures relatively intuitive, obvious, and necessary. In contrast, people may find that properties and operations other than the fourteen that are included in the four elementary structures seem arbitrary, hard to grasp, and difficult to use.

At the same time, specifying precisely how these types of social relationships differ, while demonstrating that they are distinct and discrete but related structures, provides an analytic basis for approaching the problem of the logical coherence and functional integration of social "systems," discussed above in Chapter 7. That is, the possibilities for reconciling and integrating the four models within a single social system depend on the kinds of relations that are defined and undefined in each. So it is of considerable significance that the Archimedean ordered fields of MP relations encompass all the relations and operations of the other three models. But we should bear in mind the crucial point that the fact that a relation or operation is undefined in the structure of a given model is an essential characteristic of that model—defining the relation or operation transforms the essential nature of the social relations concerned. For example, converting a CS system of discrete social identities into an AR hierarchical ordering transforms the social identities absolutely. Adding the MP ratio metric based on the operation of multiplication and the distributive principle to the additive intervals of EM qualitatively changes the social meaning of those intervals: it is the difference between giving a dinner party and opening a restaurant.

This axiomatization is also useful for sorting out the qualitative similarities and differences among the four models. For example, is EM simply the special case of AR in which people do not differ in rank? No, because EM entails operations and properties that are undefined in AR—addition and subtraction. Therefore in EM the magnitude of differences between the aspects of the people in the relationship are defined and socially meaningful, but such intervals have no meaning in AR. Again, is EM simply a degenerate case of MP? Yes, in the same sense that each model is a special case of all the succeeding relational structures since they encompass all of its properties, but No, in the sense that the fact that a property or operation is undefined and so does not have any social significance in a given structure radically changes the nature of the social relations built on it (cf. Stine 1989:346). So in this case, the fact that EM is composed of only one operation, addition, (with its inverse, subtraction) means that using EM you can add apples, and you can figure out how many apples you still owe after returning two. But since multiplication with its relation to addition is undefined in EM, you cannot intelligibly combine the two operations.

Suppose that people are structuring wife-giving transactions as EM, and that the people receiving the bride give a cow and get back three goats as a balancing equivalent, and then give a spear and again receive in return three goats, again to match their gift. Everyone agrees that in marital exchanges one cow equals three goats, and one spear equals three goats. Imagine that the standard bride-price is 12 cows and 40 spears and suppose the wife receivers have ample herds of goats, but no cows or spears, and they want to pay the bride-price in goats. Can they multiply 12 cows times 3 goats per cow, and multiply 40 spears times 3 goats per spear, and give 156 goats as bride-price? Not at all—since the distributive law is undefined within the framework of the relational structure of EM, there is no way to know how the value of cows and goats united as they are in bride-price relates to the value of cows and goats separately.[11] Even though all the exchanges take place within the same EM structure, the goat-value of cows and the goat-value of spears cannot necessarily be combined in any predictable manner.

Take a simpler example of the implications of the lack of the distributive law in EM. Suppose we are operating in a strict EM framework, and I take you twice to a supper club where we have dinner and listen to folk music (2 • [dinner + music]). Then you take me to dinner two other nights, and a third night you take me to hear Judy Collins ([2 • dinner] + music). Now, do you owe me a concert? There is no definite answer provided within the relational axioms of EM—the social obligations are ambiguous, just because EM encompasses only the operations of addition and subtraction, leaving the distributive principle undefined.

Any procedure for solving such equations involves a combination of addition and multiplication that is undefined in the structure of EM. In effect, the usual social result of this is that there are no fixed, definite, context-free exchange values: exchange equivalents depend on how the entities in question are combined. Consequently, people tend to limit EM transactions to the give and take of the "same thing" back and forth (although sometimes people do exchange two categories of things whose values are conventionally matched—see Malinowski 1961 [1922]).

The models are composed of a succession of independent relational axioms. The distributive law, which is an essential property of the Archimedean ordered fields of Market Pricing, cannot be derived from the Equality Matching relations and operations of an ordered Abelian group. But there is no ultimate "justification" for postulating the distributive law and imposing that restriction on the properties of any particular system: EM systems function just fine without the distributive axiom. Similarly, each of the basic structures differs from the others by the inclusion or exclusion of one or more independent axioms. I have suggested only that there is a unique order in which these axioms are combined to yield progressively differentiated systems. The four models are not like a family of mutually implied theorems within a single axiomatic system—they are four related but distinct axiomatic systems. Hence society as a whole is not reducible to any one primary, natural, or fundamental system but is based on at least four disparate ones. Since each relational structure differs from all the others by at least one arbitrary, independent axiom, they are in that sense incommensurable: there is no single principle or set of principles that is necessary and sufficient for them all.

And there is no internal axiom that specifies when each of the other axioms "should" be adopted. Whether a given axiom applies to the organization of a particular social activity is not a question with any a priori or formally deducible answer. And there may be no systematic, coherent, principled mechanism for arbitrating or selecting among them in situations where the choice among models becomes problematic. In its present form the theory provides no basis for supposing that societies must exhibit the functional coherence that many functionalists assume or the ideal–logical coherence that cultural anthropologists tend to assume. Furthermore, the illustrative examples in Chapter 7 and in Part IV suggest that there is little ground for the inference that societies actually do exhibit either functional coherence or coherence of meaning based on relational monism: in most societies there are at least four separate relational structures operative. Generally the four relational structures operate alongside each other without generating social conflict, and they are often concatenated in complex combinations. But there is nothing to suggest that the four modes of relationship can be reconciled with each other when people do see them as alternatives. And they cannot be reduced to any unitary relational principle that encompasses and subsumes them all (see Fiske 1990).

Hypothesizing that the empirical structure of a social relationship is congruent with the formal structure of a mathematical system implies that the relevant properties of the relationship are reflected in the mathematical structure, as well as vice versa. The value of validating such a mapping would be that manipulating the mathematical model may permit us to deduce properties of the systems that were not immediately apparent from observation of the empirical social relations, and which could not be tested by any feasible or ethical empirical manipulations. The power of such an approach is amply demonstrated by the field of economics. But economics either attempts to reduce all human social interaction to one basic mathematical structure—Archimedean ordered fields—(e.g., look at Becker 1976, 1981), or ignores social interaction which does not display that specific structure.[12] There are a few exceptions, like Etzioni (1988), who recognize the limitations of the MP model and the consequent limitations of economic theory, but they do not offer a systematic or formal account of the non-MP forms. My proposal here is that different relational structures underlie distinct types of social interaction, which consequently have correspondingly different social properties. Specifically, I have argued in this chapter that there are important types of noneconomic social relationships whose formally-defined structures comprise proper subsets of the relations and operations involved in "economic" interaction. This formalization offers the ultimate prospect of a quantitative theory in which economics can be seen as just one of a set of four fundamental models. In Chapter 7, I showed that people can construct a diversity of functional and complex social institutions on the basis of each of these structures. Next, in Part IV I will show that the Market Pricing economic model has no special primacy over the other three models.

Perhaps the most important potential value of the kind of formal axiomatic treatment presented in this chapter is that it may provide one answer to the question of why people use just these particular social models, and not others. Recent research in measurement theory has shown that the structures of categorical, ordinal, interval, and ratio scales have interesting properties that are not widely shared by other relational structures (Narens 1981a, 1981b, Alper 1985, Narens and Luce 1986, Stine 1989, Suppes et al. 1989).[13] These properties have to do with the degree of *homogeneity* (the extent to which all elements have the same properties) and the degree of *uniqueness* (redundancy under transformations) of the structures. Although much work remains to be done to develop the concept of meaningfulness in measurement theory, it is already clear that all known scale types are reducible to only a few fundamental relational structures. Anything that can be measured in any known scale type can be measured by one of the basic types. Since no new, additional information is captured in any other scale type that is not represented in the basic types, all other measurement structures are redundant with the basic types. Aside from *absolute* measurement (the extreme case under which any transformation loses meaningful relational information) and the four scale types discussed here, the only other basic measurement structure is the *discrete interval* scale, which is unique up to transformations of the form x goes into $k^n x + a$, where k is a fixed positive constant, n is an integer, and a is a real number. In the Guttman sequence of relational structures, this scale fits in between interval and ratio scales. It would be interesting to search for social relationships with this structure, since one deduction from this axiomatic treatment of social relations is that such social relationships ought to exist.

In addition, more work needs to be done to understand how the distinctive properties of all of these basic relational structures are related to the kinds of relations and operations that are socially meaningful in the corresponding types of human relationships. For the moment, however, it is sufficient to note that measurement theory suggests that the basic relational models belong to a very small set of fundamental relational structures. The uniqueness and homogeneity of these structures make them distinctive and fundamental from a measurement point of view; quite possibly these characteristics also make them singularly suitable for organizing social relations. If so, then this may explain why people structure their social relations with reference to just these few elementary models.

# Part IV

# Rational Self-Interest or Solidarity:
# *The Predominance of Noneconomic Motives Among the Moose of Burkina Faso*

PREFACE TO PART IV

Pour l'observateur européen, les échanges mobiliers extra-familiaux se caractérisent chez les Mossi par un étrange manque d'âpreté au gain et par une confiance à l'égard du co-contractant qui paraît souvent excessive: c'est que le contrat est rarement senti comme un simple échange de choses ou de prestations économiques. (Pageard 1969:414)

(For the European observer the exchange of goods [movable property] outside the family is characterized among Moose by a strange lack of ruthless profit-seeking [lack of drive to get ahead] and by a trust in the other party which often appears excessive; this is because contracts are rarely regarded as simple exchanges of things or of economic payments.)

A theory is interesting to the extent that it provides a clear account of significant phenomena. Of two alternative theories, the better is the one providing the clearest, most elegant account encompassing the broadest range of phenomena. By these standards, the most influential general alternative to the present relational-models theory is the approach that attempts to explain human behavior as the product of a calculus of benefits and costs. Generally this approach assumes that people aim to maximize their individual utility in a selfish, competitive manner. This broad self-interest "theory" takes the individual as the basic unit of analysis and treats people's social relations as more or less *rationally* calculated means to their individualistic ends. That is, people are assumed to strive to maximize the *ratio* of expected benefits to costs, risks, or effort incurred. In this framework, all apparently sociable behavior is seen as merely a means to the ultimate goal of long-run maximization of individual self-interest.

Is it valid to assume that people are generally *"rational"* in the original sense of being concerned with the *ratio* of benefits to costs? Can we also assume that people are primarily oriented toward maximizing their individual self-interest? Does each person seek to maximize his or her own individual advantage, competing, striving, and using others only as means to material gain or personal utility? That is, do people treat most social interactions like the sale of commodities, calculating the "price" they pay and the "profits" they make? Economists have taken these assumptions as their core axioms, and most other social scientists have taken them for granted as implicit assumptions. In the following chapters I want to use ethnographic materials on the Moose of Burkina Faso to examine these presuppositions.

In a trivial sense, the theory of personal utility maximization is a tautology. Whatever mix of outcomes people actually do seek can be assumed to maximize their nominal utility, by definition. But does this mean anything? Of course, we already know that there are constraints on human reasoning, information-processing capacity, and other aspects of *rationality* that impede effective maximization (e.g., Simon 1965 [1947], Kahneman, Slovic, and Tversky 1982). But the deeper question is whether or not people's goal actually is selfish utility maximization. Never mind the constraints—is selfishness the necessary, universal, or preeminent motive in human social relations?

In the chapters that follow, I advocate the position that selfish utility maximization is not the unique or paramount motive in human social relations. I argue that the monistic *rational* selfishness axiom is an ethnocentric, historically peculiar conception of human nature, a conception that would appear bizarre or even perverse to people of many other times and places. The relational-models theory treats shared cognitive models for social relationships as the basic structures of social life. The present theory posits the existence of four autonomous modes of interacting, only one of which—Market Pricing—is concerned with cost/benefit ratios. There is nothing uniquely natural, primary, or privileged about MP "economic" behavior or motives.

It is important to note again that the relational-models theory defines Market Pricing as a form of social relations oriented toward social ratios and *ratio-*

nality, and as such it does not entail individualism, egoism, competition, or maximizing goals. The ideas of free choice and obligations based on voluntary contracts are also not inherent features of Market Pricing. However, as we have seen, theorists presupposing rational individualism usually conflate these seven features explicitly or—more often—implicitly. So I will continue to treat them together in the ensuing analysis of the Moose, in order to address all of these aspects of the *rational* individualism approach.

Now in Part IV I show that while Moose at times structure their social relations with reference to a *rational* calculus of benefits and costs, this is not the mode of interaction that usually prevails. In their social relations, Moose only occasionally exhibit individualism, egoism, competition, maximizing intentions, or operate in a framework of free choice and contractually based obligations. *Rational* selfish individualism is the least important of the four distinct, autonomous social orientations that Moose exhibit in their social relations. Furthermore, by investigating how Moose utilize their most valued scarce resources, we can draw inferences about the ultimate ends of Moose social life. When we do so, we always discover that Moose prefer to share crucial resources, or offer them in tribute to authorities, or divide them equally—they rarely implement a Market Pricing calculus of cost/benefit ratios, much less one that is individualistic, egoist, competitive, maximizing, voluntaristic, or contractual. Moose do interact in a Market Pricing mode at times, but the ethnographic evidence from the Moose and five other African societies show MP to be only one of four modes of relating to other people and no more basic than the other three. Indeed, among the basic, irreducible social motives of these villagers, Market Pricing is the least pervasive orientation; Communal Sharing predominates, along with Authority Ranking and some Equality Matching.

In this sense, Part IV is about the cultural implementation rules discussed in Chapter 7. The relational-models theory posits that in principle people can apply any of the four models to any domain (and to interaction with any person in any given context). Implementation rules differ substantially from culture to culture. So does the ideological valuation of each model: people evaluate each mode of relationship differently, as a function of their culture and the domain in question. The ethnographic materials in the following chapters illustrate the importance of application rules and ideology; differences in the implementation of the four universal models constitute a large part of what makes Moose society so different from Western society. Consequently, one way of phrasing my critique of the selfish individualism approach is to say that a central problem in sociocultural analysis is to determine the implementation rules that operate in a given context. We cannot merely assume that people always apply the Market Pricing model, because there are three other models, equally basic, that people may apply instead.

In the following analysis, I build on the psychological research on motives reviewed in Chapter 5 and discuss the evidence that Moose—and other people—seek out and participate in all four kinds of social relationships for their own sake, not simply as ulterior means to achieve external utilities. The explanatory perspective that I adopt is that people find each type of social relationship intrinsically satisfying, not merely as an expedient, but as an experience.

The ethnographic material in Part IV has another aim: to show that this relational theory provides good tools for anthropological "thick description." I do not offer the kind of ethnographic detail that would show how the four models might provide a comprehensive account of Moose social life, encompassing all major domains of interaction and shared thought. But Part IV does give some sense of how this might be done, and adumbrates what such a comprehensive ethnography would look like. For the time being, the reader may judge from this preliminary sketch whether it appears feasible to encompass the social life of the Moose—or any other people—within the theory developed in the first three parts of this book.

At the end of Chapter 2, I raised the issue of whether the four relational models might be "merely" an explicit formalization of our own implicit folk models of social relations—folk models that are ethnocentrically Western. Since I hypothesize that these are the four models that people actually use to generate, coordinate, and evaluate social action, the problem is not whether they are tacit folk models—if they do guide behavior, they are. The question is whether people in other cultures use the same four models to generate their social relationships. Since social relations in other societies are manifestly different from our own, sometimes strikingly different, this is a crucial issue. In Chapter 3 and elsewhere I have cited evidence of corresponding structures and processes from a number of cultures. And indeed, the convergent theories that I compared in Chapters 2 and 3 are the work of social scientists from a wide range of Western subcultures, spanning a century of history. Collectively, they analyze material from hundreds of widely distributed cultures. Yet among the many analyses on which the relational-models theory builds there are no immediate, detailed accounts of individual cultures that employ precisely these four models—although it is just such detail and "experience-near" immediacy that would reveal whether people in other cultures do in fact construct their social relations using just these particular models. It is essential to know whether this theory applies universally, or whether its apparently universal applicability is merely my own ethnocentric misreading of other cultures. So Part IV is a modest step in the direction of such an extracultural test of the theory with ethnographic "thick description" based on first-person participant observation.[1]

In sum, Part IV has three simultaneous purposes: to make an initial test of the universality of the theory (in response to the challenge that it is only an expression of Western ethnosociology); to indicate how the four elementary models could guide a deeper, thicker ethnographic description of an entire society; and to demonstrate that Market Pricing is just one of four sides of human social nature.

*Chapter 10* shows the importance of Equality Matching in Moose social relations. In many contexts Moose aim to make equal contributions or divide things into equal shares, or they seek an even balance of give and take, organizing transactions so that each person gets the same thing. Many descriptions of such behavior in other societies conclude with facile explanations of how each individual supposedly maximizes his or her individual self-interest by adhering to norms of equality and participating in egalitarian social relationships. But the Moose evidence does not support this conclusion. Moose seem to make even trades, distribute or contribute equally, and reciprocate in-kind for the sake of being equal. Their aim is simply to create, sustain and participate in Equality Matching relationships for their own sake. And why not? Equality Matching motives are autonomous, not hierarchically subordinate means to ulterior selfish or material ends.

*Chapter 11* explores a motive that is even more pervasive and important in Moose social relations: the Communal Sharing desire to share, belong, and be one with others. The scarcest material resources on which Moose survival depends are labor, water, and land. Moose pool these resources and share them freely within communal groups at various levels extending from the inner lineage out to total strangers. In the village, people virtually never work for wages, nor do they sell water or land or selfishly restrict access to them. Furthermore, they share together or give away most of the food they produce, using much of it to feed participants in communal rituals and collective religious sacrifices. *Chapter 12* demonstrates that this collectivist Communal Sharing orientation encompasses what Moose lineages value above all else: women to bear them children who will be kin and descendants. Moose do give women to chiefs as an act of fealty in an Authority Ranking framework, and chiefs give wives to some subjects as an act of noble largesse. In certain very limited respects, Moose transfer brides using the Equality Matching model. Also, formerly Moose men sometimes purchased slaves as wives, obtaining them in the Market Pricing mode. But Communal Sharing is the mode of transferring women in marriage that Moose overwhelmingly prefer and that empirically predominates. Moose elders give brides to men who are friends and have shown them great kindness. Giving a woman is an act of affection, not an obligation or a quid pro quo: no amount of help, no quantity of gifts, ever gives a man the right to receive a wife. Moose wife giving is almost always an act of generosity, rarely an obligation or an entitlement. Chapters 11 and 12 thus show that CS is the predominant mode of relationship among Moose: Moose prefer it, and it is the most prevalent. Moreover, the fact that Moose communally share their scarcest, most materially important and most culturally valued resources indicates that Communal Sharing is an autonomous value-motive at the highest level of the motivational-value hierarchy. Moose do *not* share communally in order to advance their individual self-interest.

*Chapter 13* deals with the place of Authority Ranking in Moose social relations. Although it is hierarchically autonomous and not a means to any other end, AR is subsidiary to CS in both ideological valuation and empirical prevalence. Many Moose roles and institutions connect the two models in various combinations, but when circumstances juxtapose CS and AR in such a way that they are potentially opposed, Moose consistently choose Communal Sharing.

Similarly, Moose subordinate Market Pricing to all of the other three models. *Chapter 14* shows how insufficiency of land, late marriage, and extreme poverty force Moose men to work as wage laborers in the Ivory Coast for most of their early adult years. Working for a salary is clearly Market Pricing. But close examination of this labor migration indicates that Moose men are simply obliged by force of circumstances to eke out their subsistence in this way, and labor migration is not based on a cost/benefit calculus. Migrants are not trying to maximize their material self-interest, they are simply trying to survive.

In *Chapter 15* we see that comparable ethnographic material from four other societies in the same culture area and one elsewhere in Africa confirms this inference. The Tallensi to the south, the Bambara to the west, the Dogon to the north, and the Gouro to the southeast, as well as the matrilineal Bemba of Zambia, exhibit the same noneconomic, communal orientation.

Taken together, the evidence indicates that the "economic" model of selfish individualism does not apply to a vast range of social life in many societies. On the whole, these West African villagers simply do not organize most of their social relations with reference to a Market Pricing calculus of personal costs and benefits, they do not typically seek to maximize their individual material or utilitarian self-interest, they ordinarily are not competitive, and they usually do not focus on free choice in human relations or conceive their major social obligations to be contractual. Of course, these villagers sometimes adopt *ratio*nal, individualistic, egoistic, competitive, maximizing, voluntaristic, and contractual social orientations, but these are not the predominant features of social relations in these societies.

The bulk of the evidence about human motives that I analyze here is ethnographic. I hope that this material, together with the anthropological evidence cited earlier in this book, will challenge many psychologists, economists, sociologists, political scientists, and philosophers, provoking them to reexamine the standard presuppositions of much of modern social science. Except for the material on marriage systems, my description of Moose mores will not surprise anthropologists, however, since every anthropologist is familar with many cultures whose social organization is more or less similar to the Moose (e.g., Firth 1965 [1938], Fortes 1945, 1969 [1949], Meillassoux 1971). What I hope will challenge at least some anthropologists is the inference that I draw about fundamental human motives from this account of Moose Communal Sharing, Authority Ranking, and Equality Matching. Polanyi (1966, 1968), Sahlins (1965, 1976a) and many others have analyzed institutions much like those of the Moose and pointed in the right direction, showing that values are culturally variable and in part culturally constructed. But they have not gone all the way to the *motivational* inferences that I want to induce from these patterns of social behavior. In brief, my inference from the ethnographic evidence is that some people, at least, are fundamentally sociable.

## THE PRESUPPOSITIONS OF *RATIONAL* COST/BENEFIT CALCULATION AND MAXIMIZATION OF INDIVIDUAL SELF-INTEREST[2]

D'Andrade (1990, in press) recently reminded us that to understand human action we need to understand its motivation. We need to know how cultural schemata move people and mobilize action: What sorts of high level social goals do people have? The usual assumption is that people are selfish, more or less *rationally* calculating individualists. In a review of the recent history of anthropology, Sherry Ortner concludes with a discussion of the contemporary idea of "practice." She notes that

A theory of practice requires some sort of theory of motivation. At the moment, the dominant theory of motivation in practice anthropology is derived from interest theory. The model is that of an essentially individualistic, and somewhat aggressive, actor, self-interested, rational, pragmatic, and perhaps with a maximizing orientation as well. What actors do, it is assumed, is rationally go after what they want, and what they want is what is materially and politically useful for them within the context of their cultural and historical situations. (Ortner 1984:151)

Practice theory is neither unique nor original in this restricted conception of human motivation. Much of social science since Adam Smith is based on similar assumptions. The individual "reward" maximization axiom is implicit in much of the work in the social sciences, and quite explicit in virtually all formal theories, especially those based on Hullian or other learning theory paradigms, economic and game theory models, especially the social exchange and equity theory approaches.[3] Burling (1964) and H. Schneider (1974) both argue that analyses in economic anthropology should be based on the axiom that people make choices so as to maximize utility. In his influential analyses of African political economy Bates (1983, 1989) explicitly advocates a theoretical stance based on the assumption of selfishly rational individualistic maximization. In his seminal anthropological analysis of Swat political organization, Barth (1959) explicitly assumes selfishly rational motives, analyzing Pathan politics as a series of individual voluntary choices among political contracts, choices aimed at maximizing personal advantage. Asad (1972) criticizes Barth's assumptions from a Marxist perspective, demonstrating their Hobbesian character. Indeed, in moral and political philosophy since at least Hobbes the predominant view has been that people are aggressively selfish; Kavka (1986), for example, argues in his cogent reanalysis of Hobbes that egoism (but not full rational maximization) does actually predominate in human motives, especially in conditions of insecurity. Wellar (1986) points out that the field of political economy still suffers from this sort of limited and inadequate view of human motives. As Palmer (1988) shows, philosophers have refuted this universal selfishness assumption many times, yet (Western?) people have a pernicious cynical tendency to discount altruistic anecdotal accounts of the behavior of people whom they don't know personally. Schwartz (1986) explains how this selfish individualism axiom in fact pervades contemporary thinking in economics, sociobiology, and behavior theory as well. Schwartz reviews the relevant literature and rejects this view of human nature on empirical grounds and condemns its impact on our ideology, regarding it as a major threat to morality and compassion. Wallach and Wallach (1983) show the insidious effects of the egoism assumption in clinical psychology. Westen (1984) and Peters (1989) in anthropology, Etzioni (1986, 1988) in sociology, Frank (1988), and many others have demonstrated the inadequacies of these models based on the axiom of calculatingly *rational*, selfishly individualistic economic people.

Although the axiom that people are fundamentally selfish, assertive, individual utility maximizers concerned with cost/benefit *rationality* is very widespread in contemporary social science, we have seen in Chapter 5 that it is not supported by psychological research on motivation, even in the U.S., where we might expect such motives to be strongest. More generally, Karl Polanyi (1947, 1957a, 1957b, Polanyi, Arensberg, and Pearson 1957b) has emphatically demonstrated that our pervasive orientation toward economic rationalization in a market framework is a feature unique to the modern West. Asserting that people are maximizing symbolic or other utilities (e.g., Becker 1976, Bourdieu 1977) rather than material values ultimately still fails to rescue the selfish *rationality* assumption. Sometimes added to and sometimes conflated with this economic axiom is the axiom that people are power or rank maximizers. This assumption that selfish maximization of control over others is a unique or invariably preeminent motive for human social behavior is also inadequate, as we shall see.

Ironically, anthropologists in particular—who are in the best position to know better—have somehow ceased to regard systematic *rational* utility tradeoffs, selfishness, and maximization as problematic issues. What has happened is that ethnographers who recognize the tremendous relativity in the *means* people use, nonetheless take the ultimate *ends* of social action—individual wealth, prestige and power—as universal and given. For some reason anthropologists, like many other social scientists, assume a fundamentally entrepreneurial and power-seeking orientation to action, rather than focusing research on determining just what high level, autonomously activated motivational schemata do operate in any given society.

As Dumont (1977) shows, social thought in the West has increasingly been pervaded by the economic individualism ideology that humans are and ought to be more or less rational, autonomous maximizers of their individual material self-interest. Yet, as we saw in Chapter 2, this assumption about the inherently egoistic nature of the human actor goes against some of the classic, foundational analyses of human social relations. A century ago Emile Durkheim (1933 [1893]) analyzed the historical evolution of society in terms of the shift from mechanical solidarity based on parallel production of similar goods (CS) to organic solidarity based on the division of labor and commodity exchange (MP). Subsequently, Max Weber (1958 [1904–5, 1920], 1978 [1922]) demonstrated that competitive, pragmatic economic rationality is only one of at least three ultimate orientations of human action. He regarded the dominance of economic rationality as a form of social organization and as a legitimating ideology for the exercise of political power as a problematic issue to be explained in socio-historical and cultural terms—not as an assumption.[4] For Karl Marx (Marx and Engels 1906 [1867]) too, the constitution of social relations in a market framework was problematic—indeed the central problem of social science. Marx maintained that the values or goals to which people orient, human motives, were a product of the system of production—and thus variable. Anthropologists have been aware of the great diversity across cultures in modes of organizing the social relations of production, distribution, and consumption since Malinowski's (1921, 1922, 1935) fieldwork, a diversity which Polanyi (1947, 1957a, 1966, 1977, Polanyi, Arensberg, and Pearson 1957) forcefully presented and Sahlins (1965) elegantly summarized. As they showed, the anthropological literature abounds with descriptions of societies in which gift giving, selfless sharing, wholesale appropriation, offerings of tribute, reciprocity and turn taking, and other such "noneconomic" forms of interaction are common, while overt selfish maximization and *rational* concern with profit making are rare.

But when considering the *sources* of such modes of social relations, Western analyses of other societies (and of our own) have generally assumed that people act in this way in order to advance their covertly selfish personal interests. It is assumed that people are sociable, kind, helpful, generous, just, fair, respectful, deferential, or loyal essentially because such behavior is the most effective means toward *rationally* maximizing the actors' individual utilitarian ends, their material interests, or their desire for power. In other words the common assumption is that, given social sanctions and related constraints, the selfish maximizer or power seeker will act like a kind and generous, or loyal and respectful, or responsible, considerate and protective, or fair and just person, according to the social circumstances. But why should we assume that when people act, say, protectively, they are really doing so out of selfish motives? We need to consider more seriously the possibility that people who act generously are often impelled by truly generous motives, that the respectful subordinate may be motivated by true loyalty, that a person being fair may actually be attempting to see justice done, and simply that. That is, people often engage in Communal Sharing, Authority Ranking, Equality Matching—or Market Pricing—purely for the sake of the relationship itself. Each type of social relationship is intrinsically rewarding.

Others before me have criticized the axiom that humans are inherently self-interested rational economic (or personal utility) maximizers. But they have generally done so by noting that people's natural "economic" motives are offset by "social" motives, or that self-interested materialism is channeled and constrained by "norms" or "culture." For example, Etzioni (1986, 1988) points out the inadequacy of a purely economic model of value, but like many other writers he tentatively collapses all other social motives into a single "moral" dimension. This kind of critique misses the point that economic self-interest is a culturally formulated and socially realized motive. Contrasting "individual" self-interest with "culturally shaped" motives and "social" controls conceals the intrinsically cultural and social nature of striving for success, of orientations toward individual achievement, of economic competition, and of rational decision making. Furthermore, it is not enough to show that, in addition to individual utility maximizing, there are counterbalancing social and cultural motives. We need to know just what the other motives are, and describe them explicitly. In this book, of course, I am offering formulations of three other distinct kinds of social motivation, showing how they operate and how they can be studied.

I use the terms "motives" and "motivations" instead of writing about "values" in order to emphasize that the directive force (see D'Andrade 1984, in press) of each of the four basic models has psychological sources, along with cultural dimensions. Both psychological and cultural factors determine the kinds of social relationships that people seek to create and participate in. But social scientists, including many anthropologists, have tended to assume that there is an endogenous psychological basis for individualistic, calculatingly rational Market Pricing social orientations. In contrast, social scientists have tended to assume that people's orientations toward Equality Matching and especially Communal Sharing are cultural artifacts that result from socialization, the force of norms, and imposed "external" sanctions. Social scientists sometimes also treat Authority Ranking as a basic psychological predisposition, and sometimes as a cultural corollary of Market Pricing drives. In contrast, my position is that people find all four types of social relationships inherently satisfying: each is the expression of endogenous motives that are culturally enhanced or suppressed, elaborated or ignored, valued or denigrated. These four endogenous social motives can only be realized in particular, culture-specific forms of the basic types of social relationships (see Chapter 7). And cultural experience and context certainly affect the relative strength of the four motives. Indeed, one of the chief aims of Part IV is to show that among Moose these motives have different relative strengths than they do among Americans. But each kind of social motivation ordinarily stands on its own as an autonomous intrinsic goal. In the following chapters I show that Communal Sharing and Equality Matching behaviors are not social means to accomplish covert Market Pricing ends: they are ends in themselves, just like Authority Ranking and Market Pricing. So I use the terminology of "motives" to stress that there is a distinct and unique psychological basis for people's seeking out, constructing, and participating in each of the four fundamental types of social relationships.

In Part IV, then, I will explore the fundamental orientations of social action in one West African culture, considering the issue of how one might characterize the relative priorities of social motives within a particular culture, or the comparative force of social models in different cultures. Do Moose constantly calculate the ratios of their benefits to their costs? And do selfish, competitive individual material or utilitarian motives really predominate? Let me begin by sketching for you some scenes from the Moose* of Burkina Faso, scenes which, since they concern their utilization of their scarcest and most critical resources, may help us to delineate their highest level goals and deepest motivations.

---

*Unless explicitly indicated, the focal reference of terms like "the Moose" or "the villagers" is to the people of Habra, one village in the Maane district, and to what we know of practices in neighboring villages; the observations may or may not generalize to other regions or individuals among the 4,000,000 or so people who call themselves Moose.

# 10

# An Egalitarian Motive: *The Goal of Even Matching*

D o Moose try to get ahead, to win, to achieve? Is their paramount goal in social relations to maximize personal gain and minimize personal effort and costs? Or is such a presupposition an ethnocentric imposition on a culture where other orientations predominate? If so, what are the paramount motives Moose pursue in their social relationships? Do any of our other three relational models elucidate the core patterns of Moose sociality? This chapter explores these issues by considering cases in which Moose try to make things even, to match what others do and be equal to their peers.

## GALLOPING HORSES

Imagine the following scene. It is a festival market associated with some ritual day in the West African sahelian land of the Moose, and a crowd of a few thousand people is gathered, drinking, eating, socializing, and buying meat. Some horsemen approach, dressed in embroidered flowing robes and decorated leather shoes. Their horses are decked out in elaborate multicolored leather tack with brass trim. At intervals, a pair of horsemen go off some distance from the crowd, and then suddenly gallop side by side at full tilt toward the crowd, reining in their horses in a cloud of dust at the last possible moment as people at the edge of the crowd scatter out of their path. It is an impressive show of horsemanship. Although the onlookers know that the riders will be able to control their horses, it is an intimidating display of horsemanship as they gallop over the rough fields and stop their mounts just before they trample the onlookers. The exhibition is reminiscent of the fact that cavalry like this once conquered the indigenous inhabitants of the land (Yĩyõose) and ransacked Timbuktu 650 years ago. The descendants of these conquering horsemen, the Nakomse, maintained tight political control over the region for many centuries, and still exert considerable authority as traditional chiefs.

To a Western observer, these displays look at first very much like horse races. But closer observation reveals them to be something else. In each case, the pair of riders stay so close together that their stirrups touch, yet they are not trying to ride each other off the course, to gain an advantage over the other, or interfere with each other at all. Indeed, their arms are wrapped around each other's shoulders! While riding at a full gallop over uneven ground, they keep pace with each other exactly, riding side by side start to finish. It appears that the objective of each rider is not to beat the other, but to equal him; the pair coordinate their horses perfectly so that their progress over the course matches each other's precisely. It is reminiscent of the games cited by Lévi-Strauss (1966:30-32), including the Gahuku-Gama form of soccer matches, in which the two teams play for days, as long as is necessary to reach a draw (Read 1959). Like the American Blue Angels or Thunderbirds precision flying teams, the point in these displays of horsemanship is to stay in formation, to keep even with one another. But this is just an occasional event at a few annual festivals. What about more common and important productive activities?

## SISOAAGA: A CULTIVATING BEE

> The data from nonliterate societies make it clear that considerations
> other than those of economic best advantage dictate labor and thus
> production. (Herskovitz 1952:111)

Now picture a Moose work party, called a *sɩsoaaga*. A man has invited his neighbors and friends to help him catch up on his cultivating; or the ritual leader (*tĕngsoba*) is holding the annual growing season ritual at which, among other things, all the young men come and cultivate his sorghum. We see people bent over their short hoes, scraping the soil between the sorghum or millet stalks to dig out the weeds. Everyone works incredibly hard for long hours in the hot season sun, often going without a break or a drink of water until the work is done. People seem to work even harder and more persistently at these cultivating bees than they do when they are working alone, and it seems that people take pride in how hard they work. The young men cultivate faster than the women and older men, and get ahead of them as they work across the field. In the literature on West Africa there are accounts of cultivating "contests" among young people, and certainly at these Moose events everyone seems to be cultivating as hard and fast as they can. But is this actually a contest that individuals are trying to "win"?

If you watch closely what you often can see is a line of the youngest men and adolescents, flanked on one side by a line of somewhat older men and perhaps on the other side by a line of women. All three groups start out at one side of the field, cultivating a wide swath to the other side, going back and forth until the field is done. The young men's line cultivates faster, going ahead until they reach the opposite side, then stopping and waiting for the other lines. Each group, however, cultivates more or less in line abreast, despite a little straggling here and there.

Now imagine me in the line; I am pretty slow at cultivating, particularly early in the season when I can not yet distinguish the young sorghum or millet from the weed grasses. But I don't get left behind—the people on either side of me catch me up by moving over and helping me cultivate my strip, or tacitly leaving me only a very narrow strip to cultivate myself. So each line moves together across the field, as a line. People are working in parallel, side by side: they are actually trying to stay even with each other, not trying to get ahead.

Often the line is followed by a pair of drummers who beat out the time and encourage the workers, and everyone enjoys working to the drum beat. The drumming tends to synchronize the cultivating strokes and set the pace. The goal of the cultivators here is indeed to work hard and get the work done soon, but to do so together, in unison. They match their efforts, aiming at an even balance, at one-to-one correspondence in the work each one does: each cultivates a parallel strip of the same length as all the others.[1]

## ZAIIGA: A THRESHING BEE

Imagine another Moose scene. This time we are at a threshing bee, a *zauga*. During the course of the dry season people invite their neighbors to help them thresh their finger millet. A particular "official," the telling chief (*tog naaba*) announces the event the preceding evening from a central location, and typically 30 or 40 men come to thresh and then drink beer. Often they eat food provided by the host; the host often provides kola nuts to chew as well. The group threshes in a line, often to the beat of drums, with synchronized strokes of the wooden flails, so that people in the odd-numbered positions beat together, alternating with people in the even-numbered positions.[2] The line of threshers keeps together, beating in unison. Since there are fewer flails and less space on the threshing ground than there are people in attendance, the men rotate through the line, coming in at the left end, and passing off each flail from right to left across the line—without missing a stroke—so that as each person comes in to the line on the left, the flails shift hands until someone drops off the line at the right. After a short break each person comes into the line at the left again. If someone should come late to a threshing bee, his age-mates happily toss him in the itchy chaff, and the late-comer cheerfully pitches in and works especially hard, apparently to make up the work he missed (cf. Lewis 1981:67 on similar sanctions in a Bambara [Bamana] village in central Mali). The threshers work very hard, but no one attempts to excel or in any way outdo the others. On the contrary, they try to match their efforts with one another so that their contributions correspond blow for blow. Moreover, attendance at both these kinds of bees (*zause* and *sɪsoose*) is reciprocal, and contingent on the host's having attended the previous bee of each worker (see Kawada 1979:217 on Moose of Tenkodogo region).[3]

On certain other occasions groups of villagers act in parallel like this, each person doing just what the others do. For example, each independent cultivation group head (*kod a menga*) brews beer for the annual *Kiuugu* festival. Each such cultivator may be asked to contribute 25 francs CFA in cash toward an offering for rain, or the head of each lineage neighborhood (*sak kasma*) may contribute one chicken toward the annual sacrifice for the welfare of the entire village. Or again, when a wife-seeking group makes a gift of salt, the women in the receiving lineage divide it so that all the women (i.e., wives) in the lineage receive equal shares.[4] In these and various other contexts the Moose make equal, matched contributions, including subscriptions for collective projects, or divide things into equal shares.

In all these cases the relationship is structured in such a way as to have each person's actions match the others; there is concrete balancing of shares or contributions to make them interchangeable. In other words, it is an Equality Matching relationship.

The egalitarian ethos of such work is captured in an experience I had toward the end of our fieldwork. Digging out large water catchment basins, the members of the youth group (*Jeunesse*) dig the hard soil with small sharp planting hoes (like short-handled mattocks), working in a line to the beat of drummers behind them. They work in the same synchronized manner as they do in *sɪsoaaga* and *zauga* bees. After the men break up the ground, they stop and use broad weeding hoes to load the dirt into baskets, which women and girls haul away. It is very arduous, slow work. After working with them on a few such occasions, when I went to the capital I bought them some picks and shovels (which they already knew how to use). I demonstrated that using a shovel, they could remove the damp earth at the edge of the water in a single operation at a rate that was certainly at least one order of magnitude greater than what they were accomplishing by picking at the hard dry soil. People observed what I was doing, and from a time, motion, energy, and efficiency point of view, it was obvious to everyone that the technique represented a vast improvement. But digging along the edge of the water, with the irregular and somewhat slow strokes necessitated by variations in the soil, did not lend itself in any obvious way to the pattern of a synchronized line of workers, matching each other's blows stroke for stroke. So they were not interested, and ignored the innovation. It was more important to work side by side, with each person doing just the same work as each other person, than it was to dig a deep pond that would hold water later into the dry season—despite the fact that this meant the continuation of a severe shortage of water for house construction, watering livestock, and drinking. The essence of these collective work parties is not efficiency or maximization of the cubic meters of soil removed per hour or per calorie of work. It is the joy of laboring in synchrony, in unison side by side, matching each other in one-for-one correspondence, working together. People would rather have Equality Matching than ample water.

But nevertheless, you may suspect, surely when it comes to money, even the Moose must get down to business and be rational profit seekers. Not so. People who know each other may make purchases on credit (samde). The Moose generally can be counted on to pay their debts, and they very readily accord credit to purchasers (see Pageard 1969:417). Similarly Moose occasionally ask to borrow (pēge, which also means to lend) money, particularly from their peers (redētaase, rogētaase). It is considered shameful to borrow money, so Moose solicit loans with considerable secrecy, and are very concerned lest anyone discover they have done so. They are generally quite reliable about paying back loans—I never made one that was not repaid. The crucial point here is that ordinarily people pay no interest on loans or purchases on credit, nor is any remunerative gift required (see Pageard 1969:421–22). Informants say that occasionally, if one had kept the funds for an especially long time—say, a year—the borrower has the courteous option of expressing his appreciation for the lender's forbearance by adding something to the repayment. But the ordinary expectation is that the debtor will simply pay back the exact sum of money lent. In the village context, the only interest-bearing loans I know of were made for the purchase of plows, donkeys, horses, oxen, and donkey carts, through a village cooperative recently established by the Dutch Association pour le Developpement de la Region de Kaya (ADRK). The officers of the cooperative also made interest-bearing loans from its funds to members. But this is a recent innovation; there are no money lenders in the markets, nor do people borrow from strangers. The fact that Moose choose to borrow from co-equal peers and the lack of interest on loans show that Moose usually borrow and lend money in the framework of Equality Matching.

Unlike Market Pricing transactions, yōodo (profit) and nafre (gain, positive results) are not involved in traditional loans. In the Moore language to pay back, make up, or compensate is role: to return is lebse. Role and lebse denote even matching, returning something precisely equal to make up for what one received, and they are the terms people use to describe repayment of loans. There is another Moore term, zemse, meaning "to be even," that also has an EM sense. For example, to divide into equal shares so that people are indifferent about which share they each receive is pui tı zemse. These Moose concepts, along with the practices of reciprocal attendance at bees and the even matching of labor at these bees, clearly suggest that the idea of Equality Matching is a salient element in the culture, and not merely an exogenous theoretical imposition.

## TEKRE: EQUAL-QUANTITY TRADES

Despite these examples, it may seem to the Western reader that Moose participate in these Equality Matching exchanges simply because the norms require such behavior, not because they would choose to do so if they had any other option. So let us look at a final case where Moose do have a clear and perfectly appropriate alternative to Equality Matching. Suppose a woman has sorghum but needs millet for an offering, or red sorghum to brew beer. She may, of course, sell (*koose*) sorghum or something else, take the money and buy (*ra*) the millet in the local market. Millet, sorghum, and all kinds of other locally produced goods are bought and sold there on market day, every third day, and it is perfectly suitable to sell grain. But Moose also have another option, making a trade, *tekre*, with a neighbor. *Tekre* works as follows. A person finds someone who agrees to make a trade. The first person brings sorghum in a large calabash to the second person, empties her sorghum out, and then the second person fills the same calabash with exactly the same quantity of millet, which she or he gives back to the first person. It is a quantitatively even trade, measure for measure. In such a trade, the market prices of the millet and sorghum need not be precisely the same, although they are rarely very different. So, from a strictly economic point of view, typically someone is losing out on these trades. But the same is true, for example, in the exchange of dinner parties—if I invite you to dinner in implicit return for a dinner at your house, our costs surely differ somewhat, so one of us has "suffered" an economic loss. But we do not concern ourselves with that matter—we consider the exchange balanced, and continue from there. The Market Pricing, economic perspective is simply irrelevant to Equality Matching reciprocity.

Moose also make such trades when they only have millet seed that will mature in 110 days, but they want a kind of seed grain that will mature in 90 days. Again, the two parties exchange exactly the same quantity of grain, measured out in turn in the same container. They do this regardless of the fact that late in the planting season, 90-day seed is in much greater demand than 110-day seed. Sometimes Moose exchange other commodities in even trades like this, for example trading a man's bicycle plus 500 CFA for a woman's bicycle, or seeking a black chicken (needed for a sacrifice) in return for one of another color. The value of the items transferred in such a trade may be substantial by any measure.

Why do people make these *tekre* trades? Are the time and trouble of going to the market prohibitive, so that people "resort to " EM because MP exchange is too inconvenient? Although such considerations may enter in to the decision to seek or agree to a trade, people sometimes do take the trouble to go to the market and sell fairly small quantities of sorghum or other goods and buy quite small amounts of other items. So evidently people *could* perfectly well sell and buy on the market in place of making a *tekre* trade if they were so inclined. Are people obligated to make these even trades if asked, and do people ask to make such a trade only when what they want to obtain has a higher market value than what they have to exchange for it? No, apparently not. In fact the Moose have a proverb, "If a trade is like a gift, let each person keep his/her own [goods]" (*Tekre sã n wend kũuni, bι ned fãa tall a renda*). Yet people do make such trades even when the market value of the two kinds of goods are appreciably different.

So why do the Moose sometimes trade even-up instead of buying and selling in the market? Well, why not? Why not structure a social relationship with the aim of fair matching, of even reciprocity and equality? Why should the Moose always maximize their profits from exchange (and the devil take the hindmost), or be concerned with profit at all? Should we assume that it is only "natural" or *rational* to shop around, compare, bargain, and always seek out the best deal you can in every exchange? Unless we want to define "rationality" technically in just that sense (as Weber did, and as is done in decision theory), or unless we can demonstrate that people always do maximize their rate of return—compared to their alternatives—on such interactions, there is no reason to assume a priori that this kind of market maximization is everywhere and always people's predominant goal. Economists attempt to use the utility model to account for all kinds of social behavior (e.g., Becker 1976), but is economic "utility" the only concern of human beings, or even the most general and fundamental orientation of human action? Skinner (1962:262–63) describes such even-volume exchanges of peanuts for rice or cotton among Moose, which perplexed him since, in MP economic terms, one side was incurring a very substantial loss. He discovered that Moose were well aware of this fact and readily acknowledged it. "I then suggested that it would be possible to manipulate the system to one's [MP] advantage, and was again greeted with a show of indifference by most of my auditors." In terms of volume, such exchanges are even, and in the framework of EM, often that is enough. Even when Market Pricing is a perfectly acceptable, culturally defined and approved alternative, Moose sometimes prefer equality to profit. Meillassoux (1971:27, 68) notes that such forms of "immediate exchange" without regard for market profit have long prevailed in West Africa. People exchanged, for example, a head-load of one item in direct return for a head-load of another item (the porters of each perhaps being included in the deal). This means that if we do not recognize the possibility of Equality Matching and appreciate its legitimacy as a culturally defined mode of organizing social relations, we will not understand Moose social relationships.

## THE "ECONOMIC" ALTERNATIVES

In all of the above cases we see Moose aiming to match or balance each other in one-for-one correspondence. Their manifest goal in these interactions is equality or evenness (*zemsgo*) with each other—not profiting, exceeding, defeating, winning, or maximizing. Is this because they have no other alternative? Do Moose only engage in Equality Matching when they are unable to organize their social relations in Market Pricing form? In principle, motivation might have little to do with the prevalence of Equality Matching. It might be that the Moose do all of this Equality Matching simply because there are constraints that make Market Pricing impossible—for example, either wage labor is unavailable, or there exists no culturally delineated or acceptable form of working in a Market Pricing mode. We need to consider these possibilities carefully, so the rest of the chapter explores the two issues. First we will consider the availability of wage labor, and then the question of whether there exists a culturally formulated form of Market Pricing work. Other possible constraints that we will then consider are the availability of cash to pay laborers, and technical considerations that might require massed labor for cultivating or threshing. In fact, none of these factors explains the Moose preference for Equality Matching over Market Pricing. They just prefer Equality Matching for its own sake.

Mahir Şaul (1983) studied the kinds of work bees described above; he concludes that

> Wage labor is cheaper for an employer than work-party labor, and this
> is largely due to the inefficiency of party labor, where volunteers are
> careless, cannot be pushed, and try to combine work with diversion.
> (1983:85)

So if people want to maximize the ratio of their farm production over their costs, they should hire laborers to work in an MP mode rather than work reciprocally for each other in an EM mode. Indeed Şaul claims (1983:90) that "all farmers preferred wage labor" to work parties, but he does not provide any data to support this assertion. What he reports is that even in the comparatively market-oriented Manga region, where soils are relatively good and the population density relatively low, wage labor is little used. Only 19 percent of the families in his survey used wage labor at *any* point during the year, and wage labor represented less than 9 percent of the total estimated hours of farm labor. In contrast, 94 percent used work party labor, and work party labor hours outnumbered wage labor hours 14.6 to 1. Yet Remy (1973:81) singles out the situation in the Manga region as one in which a wage-labor force has recently emerged, in contrast to other Moose regions where wage labor is still less evident. Şaul attributes this lack of utilization of wage labor in Manga to a "scarcity of paid labor at the going wage rate." (It is notable that Şaul subsequently [1988] reports that the use of wage labor was also rare in his 1978–79 samples among the Bisa, without saying anything about availability of different kinds of labor.)

In some periods of the dry season there were *zause* (plural of *zauga*) bees nearly every day in our village, except on the days when a major funeral was

scheduled. And although not everyone is expected to attend each *zauga*, people had to plan their bees weeks in advance and the elders had to set up a
schedule to fit them all in without too much overlap. In the area where we did
our field work alternative opportunities for wage employment were much
more limited, and wages substantially lower than those Şaul cites for a year
earlier on the Manga plateau 150 kilometers to the south. And many men go
to the Ivory Coast in search of wage labor. So whatever the case in Manga, in
our Maane fieldwork area people presumably could readily find willing workers if they wanted to hire them. In fact, villagers occasionally asked us if we
had paying work (although we unfortunately did not keep records on this),
with the labor supply far exceeding our limited demand. Moreover, at any one
time the great majority of village men between the ages of 18 and 40 are absent
in the Ivory Coast for years at a time, where they go to seek wage labor, typically on plantations.

Virtually all Moose men spend much of their adult lives working abroad to
earn money.[5] That is, the core of the male labor force actually has to go abroad
in order to find wage labor. While there are a variety of reasons for working
away from the village, there are also incentives for being able to earn money
without leaving home.

I should say that my impression of work bees in the Maane area is not so
jaundiced as Şaul's—people work hard and assiduously at bees, as they generally do when working in other contexts. Moose are known throughout West
Africa as hard workers, and generally keep themselves well occupied; in the
rainy season men work dawn to dusk, while women work considerably longer.
In the dry season after the harvest (when the *zause* are held), men build and
repair houses, animal huts, walls, and roofs; they make unfired bricks, weave
mats and baskets, and weave and sew cloth. Some men do indigo dying, some
are leather workers, and others engage in small-scale commerce limited to the
dry season. Women spin cotton, build or repair grinding platforms, mud-plas-
ter walls, spread special mud on floors and courtyards and beat it to compact
it, build clay granaries, collect firewood, prepare karité (shea nut) oil, brew
beer, plait each other's hair, and continue year-round to grind millet, haul
water, collect firewood, prepare food, and care for children. Sāaba (Blacksmith) men make blades for tools and weapons, manufacture tool handles,
doors, locks, and bowls, while a subgroup of Sāaba (Kinda) make jewelry; Sāaba
women make clay pots. Most of these products the Sāaba sell. Everyone attends various rituals and ceremonies, especially funerals—which last for three
days. But men, especially, do have some time on their hands; it is not unusual
in the dry season to see men just sitting around in the heat of the day, dozing
and chatting for a few hours.

Further, some of the work that men, and sometimes women, do in the dry
season they undertake specifically in order to earn money: they sell the bricks,
mats, and cloth they make, sell livestock or buy and resell innumerable commodities. Women brew beer to sell, and both women and men sell foods they

have collected or grown.[6] This tends to suggest that even among the Moose who do not migrate to the Ivory Coast in search of work, the aggregate person-hours of wage labor potential is by no means insignificant. There is definitely no stigma attached to working for money as such. So probably if Moose wanted to hire laborers to cultivate or thresh for pay, and if Moose men (and to some extent women) wanted to work for pay, they could readily do so—the time and energy is available.

Certain craft specialists are paid for their work. This includes bicycle and moped repair and welding, as well as tailoring with or without a sewing machine, all of which are commonly available in bush markets as well as towns. Such artisans set a price and are paid directly for their services. Besides hand sewing, the other traditional crafts in which people are paid for their work are leather working and dyeing. A person who acquires a sacred amulet (*Tẽnga, Tẽese,* or *Tubo*), medicine or magic (*Tum*) will take the object to a leather worker to have it bound up in leather in the form of a bracelet or pendant. A man or woman who has a piece of cloth and wishes to have it dyed takes it to a dyer who dyes it in a pit with indigo. Neither leather workers nor dyers are castes, and anyone may take up either craft, although Marense, an ethnic subgroup with their own language, are dyers by tradition. Except for some urban repairmen and welders, artisans of all these kinds are also farmers, practicing their crafts primarily in the dry season.

This evidence indicates that the availability of human labor cannot be the factor that constrains the use of wage labor. Given that people were able to attend work parties in Manga and in the Maane region of our own fieldwork, and that people do undertake other kinds of craft work to earn money, the shortage of *wage* laborers, if it exists, seems to reflect Moose preferences for participating in agricultural bees over working for pay at the going rate. The point to keep in mind is that the kind of labor "available" depends on what kind of "labor relations" people want. Clearly people are available to *work*: the question is, what *kind* of work? Although *zauga* and *sısoaaga* work parties (bees) are common in villages in the Maane area, wage labor arrangements are extremely rare. In the village context the Moose almost never pay anyone for any kind of work, or work directly for a wage (see Pageard 1969:385, who cites Tauxier 1917).[7] Thus the prevalence of EM labor arrangements and the lack of MP arrangements can only indicate a preference for the EM form of work.

This is not because Moose cannot conceive of an MP form of agricultural labor. There is an indigenous culturally formulated model of doing agricultural work for money, although it does not involve either bargaining or making a contract. Hammond (1966:92) writes that "the Mossi also work individually on a contractual basis," particularly at specialized tasks but also in agriculture. But he makes it clear that this represents only a very small proportion of total labor. A very few of our informants reported doing such work in the village context. This activity is called either *yi yan waore* (go out east "bagging" [with a leather sack]) or *yi koo n bõosgo* (go out to cultivate begging/requesting).[8]

When they do this, Moose men or youths in need of food or money seek out a wealthy man (rakãagre) (generally in another village) and simply begin cultivating his field—at their own initiative, without informing him. In return, they expect a meal and either millet or money. I do not know how the amount of the payment is fixed. This arrangement is uncommon—I never observed it or heard a report of it immediately after the fact; one set of young informants described doing it, particularly with a Fulani man in another chiefdom. It is significant that people reported working in this fashion for a man from a different ethnic group, the one Moose use to define by antithesis their own ethos and identity. I heard of one other instance in which two men from the village went off to a distant village to work for a few weeks. Similarly, Fortes (1970:247) describes how in the 1930s Tallensi paid youths from other ethnic groups a daily wage (and food) for agricultural work, while

> if the same work were undertaken for a sick clansman, matrilateral
> kinsman, affine [in-law], or neighbor by a Tallensi, he would be
> offended if he were offered monetary payment for it. (Fortes 1970:247)

The conclusion is that Moose culture definitely includes the concept of pay for work, but that Moose work in an MP mode only with strangers and outsiders. They do not want to interact with kin and neighbors in terms of pay per hour, profit and loss, efficiency and maximizing rationality.

There is one seeming exception to this general principle, but as they say, the exception proves the rule. There were two associations made up of age-mates from Habra and the neighboring villages, one composed of adolescents and one composed of young unmarried or recently married men. The elder group, which had dealings with the agricultural extension agent, was called the Jeunesse (French: youth). On at least two occasions it arranged to dig out communal water catchment basins in different village neighborhoods, and compensation was expected, but I do not know the details. Apparently these were "fund raising" activities to raise money for parties. Hammond (1966:91–94) describes work groups like this, composed of the adolescent "age sets" of both sexes, who contract with farmers to cultivate for cash.[9] When a price is agreed upon,

> The young people then set to work without supervision and are paid
> when the job is done. Because the work is performed collectively and
> the profits are shared equally by all participants, the laggard worker is
> quickly noticed and pressured by ridicule to do his share .... [When
> the work is done] they are paid and go marching and singing home.
> The leader keeps the cash payments received until harvesttime when
> they are used to purchase millet cakes and beer at the festivals that
> follow. At this time some of the money is also often used to buy
> clothing for the work group members—head cloths and skirt material
> for the girls, shirts and caps for the boys. (Hammond 1966:92)

Hammond offers no more details on how the money is spent or on what contingency rules link the labor contributed to the clothing and food ultimately received. But if the groups he describes are like the Jeunesse groups in Maane, the group buys identical outfits for all members. In other words, in the one kind of occasion in which people hire others to work for pay, Moose work as a group, splitting some of the money equally according to the EM model, and spending some of it on food for joint consumption in a Communal Sharing mode.

In principle again, people could invite their neighbors to work at bees and incur the obligation to attend their neighbors' bees reciprocally just because they have no other way to recruit labor, lacking money to pay anyone. But in fact choosing to hold a *zauga* or *sɩsoaaga* instead of either hiring labor or doing all the work within the cultivating group is probably not the result of an inability to obtain cash to pay for labor. Throughout Moose territory there are well-frequented local markets every three days at which any locally produced commodity can be bought or sold in virtually any quantity. The Moose regularly sell food, livestock, and other items in the markets and villages. The traditional cash economy is well established and is not a recent introduction from outside the culture (see Skinner 1962, 1964b), although the currency has gradually changed from cowrie shells (*ligidi*; now *ligidi peelga* to distinguish it from modern currency) to West African CFA bills and coins. Virtually everyone participates regularly in the market economy for tangible commodities—although for only a very small proportion of what they produce and consume. Hence the food and beer provided to bee workers could be sold, and if it were profitable to do so and if profit were a dominant motive, money could probably be found to pay wage laborers. In other words, people could easily sell part of their grain for wages to increase their net profits if they wanted to. But they do not want to.

There is one final consideration that might make people hold cultivating and threshing bees instead of hiring laborers. Are there decisive technical factors that necessitate massed labor that would be difficult to organize dependably in an MP frame? Ordinarily, I think there are not. The finger millet that Moose ordinarily thresh in bees they sometimes thresh in small quantities, bit by bit, like the sorghum that they thresh individually or in small groups as they use it. Sometimes, it is true, a person gets behind in his weeding for some reason and holds a *sɩsoaaga* bee to cultivate his field before the weeds take over. But there is no logical reason why a person could not hire laborers to cultivate or to thresh. Quite simply, it seems that Moose enjoy working for each other, taking turns helping each other out.

But what about the people who come to these work parties—what are their motives? Why do the Moose attend these work bees? Is it simply because there is no local opportunity to work for monetary pay? Or that the value of the beer provided (together with the kola nuts and food, if any) is greater than the return on the alternative forms of labor? Certainly for the older men, who may do relatively little work but get the most beer and kola nuts, bees hold definite attractions. This is especially true of the chief (*naaba*), earth priest—ritual leader (*tĕngsoba*), and the heads of lineage neighborhoods (*kasmdãmba*), who may do hardly any work at all, drinking beer and giving occasional directions—that are often ignored—while the others work. But, interestingly, the Moose see attending as a kind of favor to the host and feel that they have an obligation to attend the bees of prospective or past wife-givers. Wife-receivers are expected—obligated—to attend wife-givers' bees, but I do not recall anyone ever mentioning that they had a duty to invite their wife-receivers (although they often did so). I never heard anyone complain or blame anyone, even privately, for coming uninvited—on the contrary, people appreciate the work of those who attend. Passers-by are expected to stop and lend a hand, and I occasionally heard praises for people who did so and worked especially hard. Furthermore, I never heard anyone criticized or blamed for not holding any kind of work bee, although Moose are quite sensitive about their neighbors' or lineage-mates' failures to attend.[10] Nonattendance is a slight. The Moose (without discussing it publicly) keep track of who attends a bee, and if someone fails to show up, the host may not go to that man's next bee: attendance is reciprocally matched and balanced in Equality Matching mode. Thus the Moose evidently regard attendance as something of a duty or at least a favor. Why? Because to attend a work bee is to pitch in and help, to make your work my work in a rather communal sense. But above all, attending links people together in a network of bilateral bonds, in which you help with my work and I help with your work. I count on you, you count on me. I can depend on you, and you can depend on me. As even reciprocators, we are equals.

All of this leads to the conclusion that the Moose neither hold nor attend working bees for strictly economic or utilitarian reasons. Hosts might get more work done by hiring laborers than by inviting their neighbors and in-laws to do the work at a bee, and they would achieve economic savings if they used wage labor. Wage labor is available, but no one directly sells or pays fellow-villagers for labor.[11] On the other hand, there is nothing to suggest that Moose gain any prestige, honor, or power by holding bees; rank and authority are simply not involved (except marginally in the order of precedence in which they may be scheduled). Why should people hold such bees if it is not to their material advantage to do so, and on the other side why should they treat attendance as a *duty* if participation is economically advantageous? Moreover, why do they never discuss or seem to consider the economic costs and benefits on either side? The Moose frequently discuss the prices and publicly evaluate the factors involved in exchanges which they think of in Market Pricing terms (that is, in terms of maximizination of the ratio of benefits to costs with respect to alternative choices). But I never heard anyone consider bees in this fashion.

The way the Moose organize agricultural labor makes sense if we realize that people's goal in conducting and participating in these work parties involves Equality Matching *for its own sake*. Moose are not merely covert entrepreneurs and politicians—there is much more to life than simply making money and getting ahead. Of course, the Moose sometimes are oriented toward entrepreneurial or political objectives, but these are by no means their only, their principal, or their most fundamental goals. For the Moose (and others) there is an intrinsic value in working all together, in synchrony, side by side. Moose like to trade off working for each other. They find it rewarding to work alongside their friends, neighbors and peers, matching and equalling their contributions—in my personal experience, it is just plain satisfying comradeship, and often fun. All these examples, including running horses side by side and one-for-one quantity-matching trades, suggest that "winning," exceeding others, economically *rational* maximizing of returns, and competitive "success" are definitely not the only goals underlying Moose social interaction—and probably not the primary ones. Instead, Moose often orient toward balance, synchrony, coordination and correspondence in social interaction, trying not to beat each other but to match each other, one-for-one. This is just the structure that I have labeled Equality Matching. It also emerges in a variety of other contexts beyond those that I have mentioned here. In sum, Moose generally value social relations structured according to Equality Matching more highly and engage in them more often than they do relationships organized according to Market Pricing.

In short, Equality Matching is a form of social relations indigenous to Moose (but not limited to them). The Equality Matching model underlies many prominent, culturally important kinds of social interaction, including much of the organization of Moose labor and exchange. Market Pricing is present in Moose society (see Chapter 14) but it does not subsume, dominate, or in any other way account for relationships involving turn taking, balanced in-kind reciprocity, equal-share distributions, identical contributions, or other forms in which people match what they do with others on one-for-one correspondence. Moose generated these social relationships with reference to Equality Matching.

Furthermore, it would be difficult to understand, much less explain, the structure and process of Moose social relations without recourse to this relational structure. Indeed, it was the lack of fit between either Communal Sharing or Market Pricing and these Moose phenomena of egalitarian distribution, even contributions, turn taking, in-kind reciprocity and matching work one-for-one that led me to formulate the Equality Matching model in the first place. It was not an ethnocentric framework I imposed on Moose social relations from outside—I derived the model inductively from a distillation of these major forms of Moose interaction. Then I found it in reports of research in American culture and elsewhere around the world.

Moose are not the only people who orient a wide range of behavior to Equality Matching. In his Malinowski lecture, Forge (1972) reviews the literature on New Guinea and concludes that societies in this region are "dedicated to equality and the expression of equality in exchange" (p. 538), especially balanced, symmetrical, in-kind exchange. Equality Matching is the predominant orientation in marriage, blood feud revenge, labor, and ceremonial giving in New Guinea. In the section Recursion in Chapter 8 we saw that rotating credit associations based almost exclusively on Equality Matching are prominent in many African, Asian, and New World cultures. Udy (1959) reports results from a world sample of 150 societies indicating that Equality Matching reciprocity is by far the most common mechanism for supplementing the core of the productive labor force. So when we look more closely at balanced egalitarian behavior around the world, the concept of Equality Matching appears essential for describing and understanding many aspects of diverse social relations all over the world.

The material in this chapter makes a prima facie case that for Moose, at least, Equality Matching is an end in itself. That is, it suggests that Moose (and other people) aim to balance and match social relationships and maintain egalitarian relationships with peers primarily for the sake of the EM social relationships. Experimental research shows that Americans, too, often prefer equality to maximization of self-interest (Lowenstein, Thompson, and Bazerman 1989). But the evidence presented so far does not conclusively prove that Moose value Equality Matching for its own sake. In the next five chapters we will explore the issue of how to determine when a social goal is hierarchically autonomous and when a goal is a means to a superordinate end. At the same time, we will explore the question of the relative importance for Moose of the basic, autonomous social motives. That is, when goals are independent but to some degree mutually exclusive alternatives, which predominates? I will show that among Moose each of the four basic models is an autonomous high level social motive, none of which is (ordinarily) a hierarchically subordinate means to any of the others. But Moose do not value all four modes of relationship equally, and Equality Matching is neither the most prevalent nor the most preferred of the four modes.

# 11

# A Communal Solidarity Motive:
## *The Goal of Sharing and Unity*

People have ulterior motives. That is, people may organize action according to a particular model because they are overtly or covertly using that model as a means to some other, superordinate end. As Charles R. Gallistel (1980a, 1980b) and Roy D'Andrade (in press) point out, goals are hierarchically organized so that lower level goals often are means to higher ones, and the motivational force of a goal may come from its being embedded in an inclusive higher order schema. Thus it could be that, in some obscure manner, the Moose (and others) match their contributions precisely, observe egalitarian distributive justice, take turns, make even trades, and reciprocate according to Equality Matching, just as a pragmatic, indirect means of achieving their selfish long-run material (or political) individual ends. Social theorists often assert—but rarely demonstrate—that a surface concern with equality and balance, or a show of kindness and generosity, is merely a strategy for maximizing personal self-interest. Perhaps personal economic advancement or power are indeed the paramount goals of Moose, despite their surface concern with Equality Matching. How would we decide whether EM motivation, or any of the other basic motives, is actually autonomous in the sense of being a hierarchically independent motive at the highest level? More generally, how can we discriminate between goals that are autonomous and goals that are subordinated to another, higher level goal?

There are two kinds of evidence that can indicate when the directive force of a model is autonomously activated. First, it is often possible to demonstrate that people are choosing to devote time, effort, and resources to one goal to the detriment of a second. If this is so consistently and in the long run and the people concerned are aware of the results of their action, then the goal taking precedence cannot be subordinate to the second; it must be either on the same or a higher level with respect to the existing organization of behavior in that domain.

Second, a special case of the above is that we can get evidence about people's highest level goals by looking at how they use their most valuable resources, especially their priorities for resources in short supply. When critical resources can be used to advance more than one high level goal, then how people choose to use such resources is likely to reveal their ranking of goals. If we know that people consistently allocate scarce and highly valued resources to a particular social end in preference to another, then we can rank their relative importance. We have already suggested that in the village, Moose choose to work in the mode of Equality Matching at bees in preference to selling their labor for a wage, and that people who need help threshing or cultivating choose to invite their neighbors to attend bees (and thereby commit themselves to attending their neighbors' bees) in preference to hiring wage laborers. Let us now consider what else we can determine about Moose motivational priorities from their commitments of labor and three other essential resources: food, water, land.

This chapter begins with a broader look at the organization of Moose agricultural labor, including the disposition of the harvest. Moose share the production and consumption of food communally. Moreover, Moose share a great deal of the food they produce in festival rituals where hundreds of guests are fed. They also distribute water and access to land communally. The essentials of Moose society could be described and understood without any reference to Market Pricing or self-interested maximization. In contrast, Communal Sharing captures the essence of their own implicit models and motives. CS is more than an etic category derived from a comparative framework, it is the distillation of an emic idea that permeates Moose thought and directs the construction of their most important social relationships. Altogether, this chapter and the next intend to establish that Communal Sharing is the core of Moose social relations, their focal motive, and their highest good.

## COMMUNAL CULTIVATION
## AND COMMENSAL CONSUMPTION

In every aspect of the organization of work within the patriclan the individual economic activity and personal economic interest of every member is subordinated to the interests of his elders and to the kin group as a corporate entity. (Hammond 1966:87 on the Yatēnga Moose)

Although I began by describing Moose social relationships which take the form of Equality Matching, there is another model that is more prevalent and that they value more highly as a structure for agricultural labor and other social relations. Since Moose subsistence depends on farming, and their farming is dependent on labor and land, let us begin by taking a look at how the Moose organize farm labor. As indicated above, Moose work very long hours during the cultivating season. Particularly during planting and harvesting, which have to be done rapidly, my impression is that most Moose are working at somewhere near the limits of what is physically sustainable by the human body, especially given their health and nutritional status. Women, especially, grind, cook, haul water, collect wood, and tend children as well as farm, working late into the night and rising before first light in the rainy season. But even Moose men farm perhaps 12 or 13 hours a day—hours of vigorous, sustained labor in the hot sun with relatively few breaks. Under these circumstances, labor seems to be a major resource limiting production, so we can learn quite a bit about Moose motives by seeing how they allocate their labor.

The Moose typically work their fields communally.[1] A small group of people led by a senior man jointly cultivates a collective field (*puugo*). A cultivating group typically consists of the senior man and his wives and children, often with his younger brothers and their wives and children. They pool their labor, working together, and they pool the harvest: during the rainy season the people who belong to the corporate field group eat their meals together in the field, drawing grain from the previous years' harvest. Of course, some people work harder than others, and some eat more than others. Inevitably in such a collective work group, what people get out is not in proportion to what they put in. But this is not an issue for the Moose. Nor do people in such a farming group attempt to match their labor so that they make equal contributions, and they are not concerned to divide up the harvest equally—in fact they do not divide it up at all. The orientation of Moose in their collective farming corresponds to the communist maxim, "From each according to his abilities; to each according to his needs."

In these cultivating groups, what really matters is participation, even token participation—if a member is making an effort, people do not assess the amount. Complete failure to participate in the collective farming, however, produces tension and results in critical gossip, although the group in fact continues to feed a member who does not work. For example, a cultivating group often supports one or more old people who do little work, but I do not recall hearing any criticisms of old people for their inability to produce "their share" of food as long as they did something. One blind man of perhaps 60 years (our immediate neighbor) gropingly persisted, almost entirely by feel, to plant, cultivate, and collect his own firewood to heat his hut in the cold season. He produced very little grain, but the people in his compound fed him without demur. During the period of our fieldwork, one close friend and informant in his mid- to late-eighties ceased cultivating, and was widely criticized for it (although he continued to guard fields against birds and animals, to weave and to sew). His wife, infirm and nearly as old, continued to cultivate as well as she could, collected wood and water, and sometimes prepared food. No one commented on the issue of the relation between what she consumed and what she produced. These people and another blind man in his late eighties who did no work at all were all supported by their families without any hint of complaint that I ever heard. In contrast, a nearly blind man in his late nineties (who was a friend and excellent informant) repeatedly felt that he had to offer excuses for why he was no longer able to do any cultivation, and from time to time expressed to me his distress about not being able to contribute. A younger married woman in the village who was totally blind also did not cultivate, although she fetched water from the well a kilometer away, ground millet, and did whatever chores she could. She was tolerated, but widely disparaged for her inability to farm, apparently since she did not participate at all in the communal cultivation. Making a contribution, any contribution, is what counts, and not the size of that contribution.[2]

Conversely, such a farming group frequently includes one or more people who work but eat little or nothing of the grain they produce. In fact, young men leaving for the Ivory Coast commonly depart just after harvest, taking nothing with them from the work they have put in on the fields. On the other hand, if a young man from the group returns after the harvest, having spent several years in the Ivory Coast, he is fed just as if he had worked along with the others, and he bears no onus—people are glad to have him rejoin them, even if temporarily. All this shows that Communal Sharing is an all-or-none relationship in which people attend to the issue of participation but do not compare "inputs" to "benefits."

The people who spend the bulk of the day cultivating the joint corporate field (*puugo*) of the extended family together also cultivate separate fields (*beolse*). They cultivate these other fields very early in the morning and in the late afternoon and evening. The corporate field takes precedence over the separate field, so that work on the separate fields may have to be put off while the corporate field is planted or harvested. Such a separate field may be cultivated by a junior man with his wives and children (if any), or by a wife of the senior man together with her children (if any[3]); sometimes older children have separate fields. A new co-wife initially cultivates a separate field with a senior wife, and later receives her own. In addition, each woman plants her own *zẽedo* (sauce, vegetable) plots, which she tends along with her children. Sometimes a separate field is cultivated alone by an adolescent, by a young man not yet married, by a widower with no surviving children at home, by a young wife with no children yet, or by a wife with no surviving children. But often the separate field, like the corporate field, is cultivated collectively. Postmenopausal women, especially women whose husbands have died, are the only peo-

ple who break off from the group and cultivate as individuals without participating at all in the communal work on the corporate field and without regularly sharing its grain. And even they often cultivate collectively with their
children or the children they are raising, typically with the occasional assistance of their younger co-wives.[4]

The harvest of the separate field feeds the members of the separate field
group during the dry season, as well as the head of the corporate field (who
does not have a private field of his own). In the dry season after a good harvest,
people also eat a second daily meal made from grain from the corporate field.
Otherwise, the harvest from the separate field is at the disposal of the head of
the separate field group to use as he or she sees fit; as with the corporate field
grain, the senior person responsible for the field and its harvest may sell part of
it and use the money for personal ends, if there is enough. Thus there are two
levels of pooling of everyday agricultural labor and grain, one nested under the
other. McMillan (1986) reports that in a village in the Kaya region (in the district of our own field site) the corporate fields compose 62 percent of the cultivated land, and these corporate fields consumed 59 percent of the labor hours
reported in 1979. Another 14 percent of the land is in separate fields cultivated
by subhousehold family groups, and only 24 percent was cultivated by individuals. Thus most land and agricultural labor is organized as Communal Sharing.

On various occasions the Moose also pool labor beyond the group that cultivates together, including men's collective village labor on wells and water
catchments. Delobsom (1929:426) notes that if someone falls ill during the
farming season, his *"comarades"* [age-mates?] will get together and cultivate
his fields. Male compound members and often neighbors work together to
build a house or animal shelter. No man ever builds a house or animal shelter
by himself; he always invites his lineage mages from the compound and the
neighborhood (*saka*), who come together, pitch in, and work until the job is
done. On certain occasions, all the men in a compound (*zaka*) may collect firewood while the women in the compound collect water for brewing beer for a
ritual or festival. Women from a compound all work together to haul water and
mud plaster the walls of a house, or to mud and pound a floor or yard, and
women from outside the compound may come over and pitch in. Women
come together from all over the village to pound the ritual courtyard of the
chief. Moose organize many aspects of this work communally. So Communal
Sharing is also the predominant Moose mode of organizing much nonagricultural work. In both agricultural and nonagricultural communal work, Moose
do not allocate individual responsibilities or assess quotas, do not keep track of
the separate contributions of each participant and do not link consumption
rights to contributions. Moose share the responsibilities and the effort communally, thinking of the work as "ours," as something to do together as a
whole group.

## Sharing Food Communally

Most of the food that Moose produce communally in their collective fields they consume together, and they also share much of the food they produce separately or individually. In the rainy season, the women who cultivate a corporate field together routinely take turns cooking for the whole group out of their common granary, taking the food out to the group in the field where all the men in the group eat together out of common bowls, and all the women eat together. This kind of Equality Matching cooking rotation is thus embedded in the overall scheme of communal cultivation. While the women take turns cooking the food and carrying it out to the fields, all the women in the group pitch in and collectively help to grind the grain the night before; each takes grain from the pile and grinds until the grinding is done. Thus while the cooking is done in turn, the work of grinding is pooled communally (see Delobsom 1929:423). Though they eat food prepared in the same cooking pot from grain drawn from the same granary at the same time, the Moose serve men and women separately and the two genders eat separately.

In the dry season, each woman in the compound (*zaka*)[5] group may prepare food separately every day from her own respective separate field granary and her own stock of sauce (*zẽedo*). Then all the women bring their food together to eat with their children, all of them dipping into the bowls and eating all of the food together without marking who provided what or who gets what. Sometimes two or more wives of the same man who have separate fields may take turns (EM) providing the grain and sauce and preparing the meal for the two or more separate field groups to eat together and for the men. Women tend to do this only when the number of people in each of their separate fields—or more precisely, the amount of grain needed to feed each of their respective separate field groups—is about the same; that is, when their contributions match one-for-one.

In most compounds, all or most of the men eat together even in the dry season, along with all but the youngest male children, regardless of whether or not their wives share food from their separate fields. The wives of each of the men bring out the food they have separately cooked from their respective granaries and stocks of sauce, and the husbands pool the food and eat it together, everyone helping himself to whatever food he likes. Food sharing may also occur at higher levels. Even the men from a whole neighborhood (*saka*) may eat their daily meal together, sharing food that has been separately cultivated, stored, and prepared.[6] So most of the food the Moose eat has either been produced by communally organized labor or is shared with people who do not produce it. In these collective meals Moose exercise some restraint, particularly when it comes to special meat sauces, making sure that everyone partakes and —if there are guests—encouraging everyone to eat heartily, but they do not distinguish individual portions or comment on how much anyone eats. The group eats as a group, without regard to the source of the food or to any other concept of individual entitlement.

When women prepare a special dish (e.g., *wehela*) they typically bring bowls of it to some of their neighbors and kinsmen—we often shared in such delicacies. On a variety of ritual and ceremonial occasions I have not described here, especially commemorative funerals, Moose also share beer even more widely, pooling the beer produced by many different women and distributing it to hundreds, sometimes thousands, of people. And of course Moose, like other Africans, are very hospitable. They always feed guests generously, without wanting any explicit quid pro quo, and any chance visitor is always urged to join in any meal or beer that is served.[7] When Moose buy food, beer, kola nuts, or tobacco they never consume them in public without sharing. People ask and receive tobacco from anyone who gets out his or her tobacco tin, and anyone who gets out a piece of kola to chew generally shares it with those present.

Besides the staple grains, Moose eat an assortment of other foods. Moose grow a variety of vegetables, including beans (whose leaves they also eat), okra, and sesame. Further, wild leaves, fruits, roots, mushrooms, insects, and fish make up an important part of their diet, especially from the point of view of vitamins and proteins. Women collect most of these foods, generally in the latter part of the wet season. Women dry both cultivated and collected foods in the sun, and store them in stacked pots in their houses. They use these dried foods as condiments all year round. Women also keep stores of the potash they make and salt they buy. Every meal is composed of the staple doughy paste (*sagbo*) made from finger millet or white sorghum flour together with sauce (*zẽedo*). If a woman does not have some ingredient she needs for the sauce, she simply asks a co-wife in the compound, or a neighbor, to give her some. When asked, women apparently almost always give what they have. No specific repayment is expected or appropriate. Moose say that they share because a woman who refuses to share what she actually has would find herself unable to get anything she needed from others if she ran short. One informant, discovering that my wife had not come to ask for an ingredient she needed, expressed indignation and reproved her with the rhetorical question, "I come ask you when I need something, don't I?!" In other words, we give each other what we need—you just have to ask. Here again we see this pervasive pattern of sharing and giving, especially in relation to food. It is important to observe that people get something out of their generosity and selflessness beyond "insurance" against times when they need help—they participate in a communal relationship that is secure and emotionally satisfying.[8]

McMillan (1986:260) concludes from her survey of Moose farm expenditures and income that a relatively small proportion of the harvest reaches the market, the bulk being given away, used to feed neighbors at work bees, or "bartered" [often in an EM mode?]. More generally, in most rural areas of Africa ... the majority of productive resources and most of the food eaten by farm families and their neighbors are acquired through nonmonetary exchanges or as part of the set of transactions characterizing social life. (McMillan 1986:260)

Thus a major share of the total production of the Moose goes into non-economic activities whose goals involve communion with ancestors and other religious beings, food-sharing solidarity, gestures of support and sympathy, as well as fealty and obeisance. All this is above and beyond the basic fact that, as we have seen, most of Moose labor goes into communanl production of food that they consume together. Most of what Moose produce they consume without ever transferring it outside the compound. Calculations based on Sherman's (1984) work around Manga show that, even in this relatively market-oriented area, families sell an average of only about 11 percent of the sorghum, millet, and rice they grow; on average, they buy grain equivalent to about 6 percent of what they produce. Even the "cash crops" (peanuts, beans, cotton, condiments, fruit, and grasses) they produce are not primarily destined for the market: they sell only 31 percent of these. Presumably these figures would be lower in the Maane area where we did our research. Kawada (1979:219) observes that in the Tenkodogo region as well, cash crops represent only a very small fraction of the total agricultural production. Although data on livestock owned or produced are very unreliable—livestock are taxed, and cattle especially are often concealed savings, so livestock are grossly underre-ported—all indications are that only a small percentage of the goats, sheep, pigs, cattle, horses, and donkeys that Moose raise are sold. A very large proportion of the maize that men produce they give to the wives of their neighbors and friends. McMillan (1986) reports that in a resettlement village, individual women receive about 100 to 200 kilograms of maize this way. Furthermore, many families in the resettlement villages "sponsor" newly arriving families, often giving them 30 percent to 50 percent of their harvest—despite the fact that the resettlement administration provides new settlers with food aid:

By far the major motivation to become sponsors is the desire to affirm, strengthen, and in many cases to create ties between older and newer settler families. Typically, new settlers claim some form of prior lineage or affinal tie with their sponsor. (McMillan 1986:270)

The food sharing and the collective agricultural and construction work de-scribed above sometimes involves Equality Matching. In most kinds of work, however, everyone in the group simply pitches in and does whatever needs to be done, without any allocation of responsibilities or marking of personal in-puts. There is no division of labor: people are not assigned distinct individual tasks in the work. Nor do the Moose divide the product of the work into dis-

tinct individual shares. What characterizes this production and consumption
is that everyone contributes whatever they are able to give and takes whatever
they need. People give no explicit attention to what each separate person gives
or gets, and make no attempt to see that what anyone gets corresponds to what
he or she individually gave. The group as a whole is thought of as the unit of
production and consumption, without differentiating among its constituent
members.

## Why Do Moose Produce and Consume Communally?

For certain of these agricultural and other activities, economies of scale or
the available technology may require massed labor, but such factors do not
appear to dictate the communal organization of that labor. Much of the pooling of labor seems unrelated to such technical constraints and appears to be
organized as it is simply for the sake of working communally. In such cases the
younger and stronger members of a communal group apparently would be
much better off from a material standpoint if they worked alone, retaining
personal control over the products of their labor, and selling or investing their
surplus. Of course, cultivating alone would require taking some risk in the
event of illness or injury and might entail social sanctions. But I think that
these considerations do not fully account for why the Moose use this communal schema to organize their labor. Phenomenally, it appears that Moose enjoy
working, eating, and living together for its own sake. The communal organization of work and the sharing of food is not a means to the ulterior end of maximizing each individual's personal self-interest. Moose engage in Communal
Sharing because this kind of social relationship has unique intrinsic rewards,
and because Moose value Communal Sharing very highly as an activity and an
end in itself.

Of course, people nearly everywhere enjoy communal work, eating together, and collective living in at least some contexts. The solidarity, unity,
coherence, and integrity of CS groups and participants' sense of common
identity is typically marked by working together or, especially, eating together.
One has only to think of rituals like Thanksgiving, where people share a meal
(to which they have often contributed dishes), without worrying about getting
equal shares—and without contracts or direct payment for what is received.
Beyond the evident differences in the particular ways in which people of different cultures realize the Communal Sharing schema, what differs between
cultures is the relative preponderance of this schema as compared to others,
its ideological valuation, and the assumptions people make about what really
motivates people (see Chapter 7). The Moose practices contrast with what we
take for granted in the modern West in that their basic productive activity,
millet and sorghum cultivation, is organized communally, as is another basic
productive activity, construction work.[9] At the level of the separate field and

at the level of the collective main field, Moose produce collectively and pool their food. The compound or group of compounds sharing a grinding platform often pools food as well. The Moose are extremely poor, and theirs is truly a marginal subsistence economy—food stores run out in some years and people may have to fall back on selling their very limited reserves of livestock. So the ways in which they organize the production and consumption of their staple crops is indicative of their priorities among alternative modes for structuring social relationships. In such precarious circumstances where hunger is normal and starvation looms close, if Moose communally produce the food essential for their survival and share it with each other, what higher goal can they have but Communal Sharing itself?

Communal or affiliative motives related to pooling labor and sharing resources sometimes conflict with material achievement motives related to individual economic maximization. As indicated above, when a strong young Moose man or woman pools his or her labor with older and younger people who are less productive, the person is choosing Communal Sharing over material self-interest. There is very little evidence of such people attempting to break away and avoid pooling their labor, nor does one hear complaints or resentment from these people (many of whom were close friends and frank informants). Corporate-field cultivating groups do fission (*welege*) occasionally. This tends to occur, however, when a male elder dies and his sons decide to cultivate independently, each with his own family, or when a separate field group breaks off as a group, often including children and old people. We will explore in some depth this choice between Communal Sharing and selfish Market Pricing in Chapter 14, but here I merely want to state that Moose prefer to farm communally and eat together—they work and consume this way willingly and happily, not merely because they have to do so.

Furthermore, as we will see in Chapter 13, the Moose prefer Communal Sharing to Authority Ranking when the two are mutually exclusive. Furthermore, when the self-interest of the compound head conflicts with the collective interests of the group, the corporate interests of the group prevail. On behalf of the group as whole, the senior male head (*kasma*) of the collective cultivating group controls the grain from the corporate field that he holds in trust in his granary. It is his responsibility to feed everyone in the group from the corporate field granary during the following rainy season (when everyone is cultivating again). Subject to his responsibilities to feed the group, the head of the corporate field may also sell the grain for his own personal purposes, without consultation with the others who have jointly produced it. Thus there is a potential conflict between his own selfish personal ends and the collective interests of the group. The Moose are well aware of this issue; for example, men sell grain to buy beer and kola nuts for themselves.[10] Men may also buy cattle—sometimes secretly—which they may entrust (mistrustingly) to Fulani to herd. (The nomadic Fulani tend to keep apart from the Moose.) And they often spend money on a lover (*rolle*). Unfortunately we have very little detailed information on how these collective and individual interests are balanced, and it would probably be somewhat difficult to obtain good data, since people may be unwilling to disclose such expenditures. But there does not appear to be much friction or dissatisfaction on this account—I do not recall hearing much complaint, nor is this an issue which is culturally defined as problematic.[11] One does not hear either worry, gossip, cautionary folk tales or myths about profligate elders who squander the harvest of their dependents' labor. This tends to suggest, albeit inconclusively, that the heads of such communal cultivation groups take their responsibilities toward the collectivity seriously, and do not greatly abuse their trust.[12]

In sum, the Moose organize their most important activity (cultivation of millet and sorghum) in the form of Communal Sharing, pooling their labor in two nested levels: people working together on a corporate field, and subgroups working together on separate fields. While in most years Moose produce barely enough to get by, they routinely share their food together, not only at the level of the two cultivating groups, but commonly at higher levels as well. In this crucial domain and in many others, the Moose emphasize cooperative, group-oriented behavior. Very similar systems of production and consumption are common in West Africa (e.g., Arnould 1984:139–40 for Hausa in Zinder, Niger; see Pollet and Winter 1968 for a review). Nor is it unusual in other parts of the world: six of the thirteen traditional cultures that Margaret Mead's (1937) group studied were characterized by cooperative social relationships, "in terms of the motives of the participants" (Mead 1937:16). Furthermore, in a world sample of the organization of production in 150 societies, Udy (1959) found that the most common form of organizing people into a permanent work force is along the lines of kinship: the family works together as the core work group.[13]

The Moose preference for Communal Sharing does not appear to be driven by technological and utility-maximization constraints. This conclusion is supported by the fact that Margaret Mead (1937:463–67, 506, 511) and her colleagues also found that whether any culture emphasizes "cooperative" (as opposed to competitive) motives and behavior is independent of either technology or environment. That Moose pool their labor collectively and share their food, often in the face of material incentives to do otherwise, demonstrates that their primary motivational orientation is toward corporate participation and belonging, and that their paramount goals concern mutual solidarity, a sense of common identity and belonging, unity, and kindness. This mode of production is common in Africa and elsewhere. Hyden (1980) calls it the "economy of affection," noting that it is quite resistant to intrusion or subversion by the world market economy.[14] In short, like many other traditional people (Sahlins 1968:75, 77, 78), Moose are not trying to maximize production or make a profit, they are simply trying to produce what they need to feed themselves and share with their kin and neighbors.

## Water

In the central and northern parts of the Moose plateau, water is a critical resource, often limiting the number of people and livestock that the land can sustain. Not only is drinking water frequently limited, but water is often in short supply for brewing beer and for building and mud-plastering houses and floors, as well as for washing clothes and bathing. Due to overgrazing, deforestation, the deterioration of traditional water-retaining dikes and the failure to build new ones, rain water infiltration is decreasing. The result is that wells used for generations have gone dry in the last 15 years, so that new wells must be dug—and often have to be deepened as much as a meter every year or two. Digging or deepening a well this deep in the hard, rock-like soil is slow, arduous, moderately dangerous work: sometimes a gang of 10 to 20 men may be able to dig only 10 or 15 centimeters a day. Although the villagers of Habra had dug numerous wells over the previous 15 or so years, until we left there was only one with water. It was 37 meters deep. From December until May or June it was the only local source of water for about 600 people and their livestock. People had to haul water up out of this well by hand in rubber buckets and then carry it on their heads hundreds of meters to their homes. When the lower wall of the well collapsed, the well went dry and required laborious repairs both years we were in the village. Even after these repairs it still went dry by the end of the dry season each year, so people had to haul all their water, (including water for most livestock) two to three miles on their heads, on bicycles, or in a couple of donkey carts (when fodder could be found for the donkeys).[15]

This shortage usually does not lead to overt competition between individuals over water, or to any system of rationing. For the most part, there is no prioritizing of users or uses. For the most part, access to the village well is free to all comers, including outsiders, strangers, and even Fulani, whom Moose disdainfully regard as embodying the antithesis of the Moose ethos and cultural identity.[16] Anyone who comes by the well may ask for a drink, and anyone who is drawing water will give the passerby a drink from her bucket. In the village, outsiders, even Fulani, can always have water to drink for the asking. (Within the compound, however, a woman may decline requests from other members of the compound if her water storage pot is running low or if she has to travel a long way to get the water, telling the requester to go to her own pot.)

Generally, everyone is free to draw as much water from the well as they like for any purpose, although when the well is running dry some restraint is expected. From June until the water runs out in November or December, the water in the three catchment basins around the village is freely used by everyone for whatever purpose they wish. When water ran out at the village well, most of the village shifted to using a well in a neighboring village. When the water in that well began to run out, the people of that village asked the people of our village to stop using their water for bathing and other nonessential purposes, and eventually—perhaps when they judged their water was finally running out—they told the people of our village to go elsewhere. That meant that all of us had to get all our water from wells in two other villages five or more kilometers away. Although I do not think anyone in our village had helped dig any of these other wells, they were free to use them.

Briefly, Moose share wells and water. In extremely severe shortages they constrict the group with whom they share, but they generally share widely and rather freely even under moderate scarcity. Wells and especially drinking water are a kind of commons (cf. Hardin 1968), freely used by whoever has a need, even when the user has had no hand in digging the well or hauling the water and will not be able to reciprocate the favor. When a well threatens to run dry, villagers may restrict outsiders' access to it, but they continue to share the water communally within the village—they do not allocate water according to any Authority Ranking, Equality Matching, or Market Pricing scheme. The sharing group may be confined to a core membership, but the form of allocation within the group is still communal.

It should be noted that digging the well was not quite so communal or so free from friction as using it. The people of Habra had considerable difficulties in organizing themselves to make the needed repairs to the village well, primarily because of a long-standing conflict over proprietorship (*so*, to own, control, be responsible for) of the adjacent traditional well (*Kibs bʋlga*), which had been dry for some years. Two related lineages of Yīyõose (indigenous people, people of the earth: pronounced approximately nyi-NYOOSÉ) in the village each claimed to be ritual proprietors of the traditional well. One of them was believed to have cursed the well to make it go dry, in order to conclusively demonstrate their proprietorship. However the proprietorship claims of the two Yīyõose groups were communally defined—in terms of corporate ownership by the lineage. And their dispute over ritual proprietorship did not involve limiting access; neither group ever sought to exclude the other from using the well.

This was the background to frictions over who showed up—and who failed to show up—to do the heavy labor involved in the repairs of the modern well, a tedious job that went on for weeks. Each year after a couple of weeks of hard labor, too few people were showing up to work, and the equipment and technical support that had been provided by *ADRK*, the regional development program, was withdrawn. In disgust and frustration, in successive years two ethnic subgroups in the village, the Yarse (Moslem traders and weavers) and the Sāaba (an ethnic subgroup whose men are blacksmiths and woodworkers; women are potters) each eventually undertook to dig their own wells, independent of the rest of the village.[17] Although the fact that the Yarse split off to dig a well of their own represented a division within the village, the Yarse maintained complete solidarity and pooled their labor at the lineage (*buudu*) and neighborhood (*saka*) level. That is, they dug collectively as a neighborhood, aiming to have a well available for all of them to use together. (I presume the same was true of the work of the Sãaba after we left the village.) In all of these cases, the labor on the wells was organized essentially in a Communal Sharing mode (with some aspects of Authority Ranking and of Equality Matching—see below). People came and simply pitched in, doing whatever needed to be done. And access to the village well was in no way restricted to people who had helped to dig or repair the well. [18]

The giving and sharing of water is a core act in the Moose enactment of hospitality, communion, and solidarity. When a visitor or a villager returning from afar arrives, Moose give the guest a drink before beginning the preliminary greetings, often even before saying a word to them. Then the host prepares and serves the guest water with flour mixed in and flavored with honey (or sugar) and sometimes hot pepper flakes (zom koom). Then the hosts go through the full initial greetings. When Moose conduct a sacrifice, they pour libations of water, flour water, and beer, and then share the beer around. The Moslem Yarse, who do not sacrifice, share flour water in their rituals. And when an adult dies, everyone makes offerings of coins so the deceased may buy water to drink (ra koom n yũ).

As the death rituals suggest, it is possible to purchase water—girls sometimes sell drinking water in markets at festivals. But the overwhelmingly predominant mode for the distribution of water is as a commons, where everyone helps themselves freely. So the Moose share communally two essentials for sustaining life, food and water. They work collectively to obtain these essentials, and they consume them together, without attending to who gets how much, and certainly without concern for the ratio of contributions to benefits (pace Burline 1964, H. Schneider 1974, Becker 1976, Walster, Walster, and Berscheid 1978). It is not each man for himself or each woman for herself, it is "one for all and all for one."

Labor, food, and water are three of the five most important "resources" among the Moose. All are in short supply, and typically all are communally shared. The fourth vital resource, one that limits the productivity, welfare, and resident population of the Moose, is arable land. According to economic theory, individuals should "economize" such a scarce, critical resource as efficiently as they are able, and it should command a high price. Economic theory predicts that individuals should compete fiercely for a resource like land under the conditions of scarcity that Moose face, each person maximizing what he or she can get. But how do Moose actually distribute and use their limited arable land?

## Sharing Land

"I conceive that land belongs to a vast family of which many are dead, few are living, and countless members are unborn." (Anonymous Nigerian chief speaking in 1912, cited by Elias [1956:162])

When we began our rural fieldwork among the Moose I requested research permission from the Ministry of Higher Education and Scientific Research, which they generously gave me, without restriction. I obtained clearance from the Ministry of the Interior and then visited the Préfet of Kaya and the Sous-Préfet of Maane to notify them of my desire to work in the area of their jurisdiction. Both were hospitable and made me welcome, leaving me free rein to do as I pleased. I then went to the Paramount Chief (*Kombere*) of Maane, Naaba Tegre, and asked his permission. Again I was welcomed and told I could work wherever I chose. At no point did any of these authorities indicate the slightest resistance to my plans, show any reluctance to have me working in their jurisdiction, or attempt to limit me in any way; they were all quite cordial. Then I spent three weeks reconnoitering the region we had chosen, and went to see the Chief of the village that seemed like the best prospect for us. I asked him if we could come to live and work in his village for two years; again I rather expected that obtaining permission might require lengthy meetings with the elders of the village and a more extended explanation of our purposes than the brief one I had already given. Instead, the Chief said, "Of course!" It seemed that there was no question about it, no decision to be made: if we wanted to come live there, we could do so.

Next we discussed housing, and where we would build our mud huts and set up our compound. The Chief said it was up to us, we could live wherever we wished. I asked to have a look around, and we did. I picked a central site near the shade of one of the few unoccupied trees, and asked if that would be OK. The Chief said, "Fine, let's go ask the person who cultivates here." So we went in to the nearest compound and spoke to a very old man, who could not have been more surprised to hear that a Euro-American (*Nasaara*) had come to see him. He was even more astonished to hear from the Chief that we were proposing to move in next to him, but he agreed immediately, without giving it a moment's thought.

I assumed at the time that the readily granted permission was the result of our Euro-American status, but it turned out to be irrelevant in this case. What we ultimately learned is that anyone and everyone is welcome to move into a Moose village. The community is always eager to add to its numbers and will always take people in.[19] Moreover, land on which to build a compound (*zaka*) is always given for the asking (see Pageard 1969:405). This is a notable fact because the land around the central village area is exceptionally fertile and productive, since it is constantly fertilized by the dung of goats, sheep, and donkeys. This is the land where the Moose grow corn, in contrast to their larger sorghum and millet fields in areas farther out from the compounds. But the proprietor of the land I chose did not hesitate to give us this land, and when it became evident that in order to get our tiny car in and out we needed a right of way much wider than the old path, he did not begrudge giving up still more of his field. In the end, we occupied a considerable piece of his corn field.

We made careful inquiries to determine what we owed in return for this land, and the answer was, nothing! The Chief and others freely told us what our obligations were and what people expected of us in various circumstances, but it turned out that we owed nothing to our host in return for the land he gave up to us, nor was there any hint of resentment or frustration at the loss. Our host and his son and daughters-in-law became close friends and were among our best informants. But the gifts that we gave to them in the course of our fieldwork, particularly to the old man, made them feel beholden to us. They did not feel that they had anything coming to them in return for giving us their land.

Indeed, Moose would be insulted to have someone offer to pay them for their land, or make any explicit quid pro quo. It would be rather like being invited to Thanksgiving dinner and then asking for the check. It simply is not appropriate—land is not for sale. More generally, Moose villagers never sell or rent land. Any land that is fallow is freely available to whoever wants to cultivate it.[20] Should that person later cease to work the land, cultivation rights revert to the giver, that is, the original cultivator.[21] But village land is never bought or sold, it is simply used by whoever needs it. People respect each other's boundaries, and if they try to cultivate land someone else has been farming without asking permission the prior user will take a case before the chief. But land that is not in use can be cultivated by anyone—even outsiders from other villages. All that is necessary is to ask.

It is considered appropriate, I believe, for the cultivator to make a gift of millet to the person from whom farming rights were acquired, but the amount is not fixed, nor, I believe, does it represent a burden on the cultivator. Unfortunately I do not have detailed data on this point, but Hammond (1966:75) states that such gifts serve to mark the continued existence of the lender's prior rights. McMillan (1986:263) reports that in another village in the Kaya area where land is scarce, 56 percent of the cultivated land was borrowed. She writes, "No rent money is paid nor is any interest charged." Similar free-lending arrangements are common in Africa, for example among the Embu of Kenya, where three-fourths of one sample participate in land-lending arrangements (involving both kin and nonkin) that are not based on monetary payments or obligatory gifts (Haugerud 1989).

The Moose are among the poorest people in the world, and their life is fairly precarious. The land is overpopulated, the soil is overgrazed, and erosion is becoming a severe problem. So next to rain and water, land is one of the most valuable things Moose have. Land is very unevenly distributed, with the Nakomse (descendants of chiefs—the royal clan) and Yīyōose (descendants of the indigenous people) of the village having more than others, and descendants of the earliest inhabitants having more than late comers. But if they cannot use what they have, Moose allow others to use it. People share what land there is, in the sense that people do not benefit in any direct or substantial way from any land other than that which they are currently cultivating. As far as I know, there is almost no unused land that anyone wishes to cultivate—nearly every square meter of arable land in the village is under cultivation every year.[22] Indeed the shortage of arable land is a major impetus for the migration of Moose men to seek work in the Ivory Coast, and some emigrants acquire land there and establish cocoa or coffee plantations (see Chapter 14). The carrying capacity of the land has been exceeded, and arable land within reach of water is truly the limiting constraint on the population. So there is also an appreciable exodus of Moose who emigrate from the Maane area (and elsewhere) to more sparsely populated lands to the south and west of the Moose plateau (see Benoit 1982). It is notable that on their arrival, their new hosts treat these Moose as they treated others back in their natal village. The Bobo, at least, ordinarily freely give immigrants whatever land they need to cultivate.

The original cultivator may reclaim rights to the land whenever he or she wishes, and in principle, the borrower should request permission annually before planting, but I think these principles are not often implemented; land once lent tends to remain in the hands of its current cultivators. If the borrower dies or moves away, the lender may be able to reclaim the land at that point, unless his or her rights have remained unacknowledged for many years. In practice it seems that land probably would not revert to the original proprietor automatically; the residual rights of an earlier user would have to be exercised to be validated. It appears that after a generation or so it would be virtually impossible for the "original" proprietor to reclaim land that has been cultivated by someone else.[23] People do remember from whom they acquired permission to cultivate land, even after several generations. (Although it is not publicly discussed, in response to my inquiries in several cases both parties were willing to say from whom the current cultivators acquired the land.) For example, most of the land the Sāaba (Blacksmiths) cultivate seems to have come from the Nakomse (royal/chiefly clan) some generations ago when the Sāaba established themselves in Habra.

Ṣaul's (1988) data on Bisa and Bobo villagers and his review of the literature on land tenure among other groups show that Communal Sharing of land is the mode throughout Burkina Faso.[24] Indeed, Ṣaul cites some evidence (1988:247–48) that Moose are situated toward the "individualist" end of the continuum compared to some of the other "collectivist" groups in the country! Ṣaul reports that all over Burkina Faso people almost invariably lend fallow land freely to anyone who wishes to cultivate it. Although borrowers give gifts as tokens of their appreciation, gifts that he says mark their status as borrowers, he shows that these gifts are not economic in nature—they are of low value. Such gifts are hardly ever negotiated or of any fixed amount, and borrowers never include them in reporting their production costs to the interviewers. Even strangers from other ethnic groups can ordinarily borrow as much land as they can use without any payment of rent. Ṣaul cites reports from various parts of Burkina Faso showing that one-fourth to one-third of the land in cultivation is borrowed land, including land under cultivation by both small-holders and large-scale modern farmers.

In the village setting, everywhere in Burkina Faso, it is extremely rare for land to be rented or sold, Şaul reports, and the rare sales that have occurred are of dubious validity—sales are indefinitely contestable by descendants of the seller. Even in towns, until quite recently Burkinabé have often shown little inclination to treat land as private property or as a commodity in any other respect, and domestic groups often persist in treating a compound in town as a commons to be used by members according to their current needs (Şaul 1988:267). Except in recent years in a couple of the largest cities, Burkinabé townspeople also continue to observe the traditional principle that everyone is entitled to have land to build a home, and as long as a home stands its occupants have the right to reside there. Like Moose, the villagers Şaul studied also organize agricultural production communally under the egis of an elder (with most adult members cultivating additional personal plots).

Moreover, both in towns and villages, this communal utilization of land holds up in conditions of scarcity and poverty, as well as when there is ample land:

> In the Mossi Plateau the indigenous response to increasing population density or to the expansion of the area under cultivation has generally been not privatization, but a sharing of the reduced production potential of the area in question. . . . In the areas where the agricultural potential has deteriorated relative to the population, the tendency has been to distribute the effects widely rather than to exclude whole sectors of the population from access to land. Members of established lineages without land use rights generally continued to be able to secure free land loans. . . . Possessing lineages loan land to those who do not have it. . . . The crucial consequence is that all household heads have access to farmland, regardless of whether they possess ancestral rights to it or not. . . . The farming operations of outsiders are also facilitated by the same conditions. (Şaul 1988:263–64)

Simply stated, land is not a commodity to be bought or sold, bargained for, or treated as any kind of capital investment. Land is just there, a Communal Sharing commons to be used by whoever needs it, limited only by "first come, first served" allocation and the custom that, in general, people may continue to use the land they are actively cultivating. This supports the conclusion of Margaret Mead's (1937:481) comparative study of a world sample of 13 cultures:

> It is not the actual supply of a desired good which decrees whether or not the members of a society will compete for it or cooperate and share it, but it is the way the structure of the society is built up that

determines whether individual members shall cooperate or shall
compete with one another. (Mead 1937:481–82)

In a critique of Marxist views, Godelier (1986b, Chapter 2) comes to the
same conclusion with reference to systems of ownership and the organization
of production (without any reference to this early work of Margaret Mead's
group). Subsequent work by Triandis and his colleagues has confirmed that
there are major cultural differences around the world between societies oriented toward collectivism and those oriented toward individualism, as well as
individual differences in the corresponding personality trait variable of allocentrism versus idiocentrism (CS and Null orientations, respectively;
Triandis, Vassiliou, and Nassiakou 1968; Triandis 1972, 1987; Triandis et al.
1988). Whether people are oriented to their membership in some collectivity
or to their personal selves as separate individuals is a function of the culture,
not of ecology or scarcity per se. Triandis's work also demonstrates that where
a given person or society is located on this dimension differs according to the
particular setting and domain of behavior in question: in one domain some
people will exhibit collectivism and other people individualism, while each
population will exhibit the opposite traits in another situation. Neither orientation is likely to be paramount across all domains. In other words, whatever
the context, selfish individualism is neither natural nor necessary.

In sum, Moose share labor, food, water, and land; they pool these resources
so that people take what they need and contribute what they have. This is not
to say that these domains are conflict free, but just that the work the Moose
do, the food they eat, the water they drink, and the land they farm are communal assets, belonging to groups as a whole, not merely to individuals. Transactions in labor, food, water, and land are organized as Communal Sharing:
When Moose distribute these resources, they do so without regard to the
amount each individual contributes, generally without even marking off distinct individual portions, without payment, and sometimes with relatively little consideration for rank or proportional equity. When Moose transmit food,
water, land, or labor from person to person it is without prices, and without
any negotiated, fixed, specified, or explicit quid pro quo. That is, for the most
part the Moose do not "exchange" labor, land and water or food in return for
something of equal value—people just help themselves and freely give what
they can to those in need. This is unquestionably CS.

As other chapters in Part IV indicate, there are other important modes of
exchange among Moose besides Communal Sharing. For one, they sell a small
proportion of all the goods they produce in local markets. And while there is
no labor market in the village, Moose do sell their labor in towns and abroad.
We have seen that there are elements of Equality Matching within the structure of work bees, and in the reciprocity principle that a person may stay away
from the bee of a neighbor who fails to attend his own bee. In the next chapter
we will consider what has been foreshadowed above, the importance of

Ranked Authority in the structure of labor and other domains. But overall it is evident that Communal Sharing is the preponderant mode of organization for labor, land, food and water.

The central concern of chapters of Part IV is the issue of whether people are naturally, fundamentally, and inevitably selfish individualists. The evidence of the first part of this chapter begins to resolve that issue. What sort of material welfare or utilities can Moose be maximizing as individuals if they communally share their four scarcest essential resources? If Communal Sharing were merely an expedient means to personal self-interest, then this self-interest would have to be defined in terms of some more fundamental purpose. But what deeper ulterior or superordinate purpose could Moose have than sustaining life itself? These are hungry, thirsty, tired, poor, often worried people: what would they put before food, water, labor and land? If they give and share these things generously, if their attitude is consistently one of kindness, "What's mine is yours"—if indeed they think of their food, water, labor and land not as "mine" but as "ours"—then where is the purported self-interested *rational* maximization of individual utilities? The common assumption of selfish individualistic materialism does not stand up to the ethnographic evidence. The ethnographic evidence does not even support the idea that people are cost/benefit calculators, much less maximizers.[25]

In this regard the Moose are representative of a great number of traditional societies, as is quite clear from the work of Marx (1973 [1857–8]), Malinowski (1961 [1922]), Mead (1961 [1937]), Firth (1965 [1938]), Polanyi (1957a [1944], 1957b, 1966, 1968), Sahlins (1965), Triandis (1972, 1987), and Godelier (1986b, Chapter 2). For example, Fortes (1945: 231–50; 1969:76–81, 337–340; 1970 [1963]; 1983), beginning with the neighboring and closely related Tallensi, shows that amity, altruism, and generosity (that is, CS) are characteristically implied and required in kinship relations. Fortes contrasts these kinship relations with either strictly balanced reciprocity (EM) or contracts and commercial transactions in commodities (MP). Within the inner lineage, Fortes says, equivalent returns are not demanded and goods or services received are not paid back one-for-one. Members of an extended family do not incur debts to one another for what they give each other. So there is nothing new or surprising in my descriptions of Moose society. But the implications of these common patterns of social relations have not been widely recognized. What they mean is simply that Market Pricing is only one of four forms of social relationships, and that there is nothing requiring any particular human social relations to be based on Market Pricing. Furthermore, there is nothing inevitable about individualistic maximization: selfishness is not inherent in the organism.

To reinforce this conclusion about Moose communality and their dedication of material resources to collective and often nonmaterial purposes, the next section describes what Moose do with much of their livestock and other resources—they give them away in funeral and sacrificial rituals.

## FUNERAL AND SACRIFICIAL OFFERINGS

> Conformément à la volonté des Pères, on se retrouvera le jour même
> du décès pour pleurer ensembles, parce que si la naissance entrâine
> une manifestation collective, la mort doit refléter aussi l'esprit du
> groupe; on a été heureux ensemble, on doit se supporter
> collectivement. (Pacere 1979:104)

> (In conformity with the will of the Fathers [ancestors], people meet the
> very day of the death to cry together, because if birth entails a
> collective display, death too must reflect the spirit of the group; having
> been happy together, people must support each other collectively.)

The Moose raise goats, sheep, and chickens, and indeed they tend to put
most of their surplus, if any, and much of the cash they save up from working
in the Ivory Coast, if any, into livestock. That makes sense in terms of economic motives: animals are individually owned and they reproduce, so they
represent a promising capital investment. As an investment, livestock provide
a kind of buffer or insurance against bad harvests or unexpected needs. They
are readily salable on the local market. But consider what Moose actually do
with most of the chickens and many of the goats and sheep they raise: they
sacrifice them or give them as offerings.

When an adult dies, the Yĩyõose (indigenous people of the earth) responsible for the burial together with the elders of the compound inquire into the
sociomoral nature of the death by slitting the throats of a number of chickens
(usually small chicks) provided by the kin of the deceased, and asking the
chickens questions about fault and moral responsibility for the death. They
read the answers by observing whether each chick dies on its back ("yes") or on
its breast ("no"). The number of chicks killed in this inquiry averages perhaps
six or eight. But there is no hesitation about killing them—it is extremely important to make moral sense of the death.

Later the deceased's close consanguineal and affinal kin offer up goats (in
the case of Yĩyõose and Sãaba deaths) or sheep (in the case of Nakomse deaths)
to the deceased and other ancestors (see Noaga 1978:53). More distantly related people offer up chickens. All the principal mourners and others who
have ties to the deceased also offer coins to the deceased. They make these
offerings as follows: The deceased is wrapped in blankets and mats, brought
out on a litter and laid in front of the compound. The men officiating at the
burial brush each animal against the ground near the deceased, naming the
giver. The animals are handed over to other Yĩyõose to hold for later, and people go to the grave. There the children and close friends of the deceased offer
up more coins, kola nuts, and tobacco, which the burial party collects. Later,
generally after dark, the Yĩyõose who have buried the deceased slaughter and
eat some of the animals. They divide up the rest of the animals and the coins,

tobacco and kola, and take them home. These offerings are theirs to keep. The donors get nothing back, and of course they are fully aware of what becomes of their offerings. At the funeral of an elder, 10 or more animals may be offered up, and twice as many chickens, as well as moderate but appreciable sums of money.

Why do the Moose make these offerings? What is the goal or manifest function of it for them? As an observer and a participant in many of these events, my understanding is that what the donor wants to do is to express a sense of solidarity with the deceased, to reconstitute a bond that death would otherwise break. These offerings are preceded by a meal that is "fed" to the deceased, with the people conducting the burial placing food in the hand of the deceased and bringing it up to the deceased's mouth. Moreover, the coins which people contribute are offered up to the corpse with the phrase, "[From] so-and-so, for you [familiar] to buy water to drink" (A Zaglaga, tɩ f ra koom n yũ). These offerings are a last act of sharing, an expression of concern, an act of kindness, a conclusion to the food-sharing relationship with a living person, and at the same time the initiation of such a relationship with an ancestor. Especially if the deceased is a lineage head and to some extent if he is head of a compound, or at least an old man or woman, he or she will henceforth receive sacrifices on a variety of occasions.

Since the Moose are among the poorest people in the world, the offering of a goat or sheep can be a considerable economic hardship, and even a chicken is a significant gift. The market price of a sheep or goat equals the value of about a month's labor, and a chicken is worth about two or three day's labor. But in this situation the goal of reconstituting the Communal Sharing relationship a final time is paramount. Of course, making these offerings is also a duty: its directive force derives from the fact that it is an obligation as well as a desire. But we should not let its obligatory character disguise the fact that on the whole the Moose are personally motivated to make the offering. Not every birthday, Christmas, or Hannukah gift comes from the bottom of your heart, no doubt—but some do, and most do in part. In any event, the directive force of this CS model of sharing, caring, and kindness (whether acting through "internalization" or "social pressure") drives the behavior. Generally, social pressure is redundant with internal desire (see Chapter 17).

In the dry season, some months after the death and burial ceremonies, Moose hold a funeral (kuure). Everyone attending the funeral in any formal capacity (there are also numerous unrelated attendees) makes a contribution to the presiding elders and receives a drink of red sorghum beer. There is no set amount for funeral contributions, one simply contributes what one has, but the range is about 25 to 100 CFA francs. The exchange rates during our field work were in the vicinity of 300 CFA per dollar, and the estimated per capita income in the country below $200. The total of the contributions— which is publicly announced—may come to several thousand CFA (although the amount of each individual's contribution is not marked or discussed). In addition, everyone with a connection to the bereaved pays a call on the principal mourners, giving each one another contribution in the 25 to 100 CFA range; callers again are offered a drink of beer. Later, during one phase of the ritual the elders and the bereaved toss coins to the drummers who are playing. Each of several drummers may receive as much as several hundred CFA. People generally seem to have little ready cash, and occasionally people do not attend a funeral—to which people like to go—because they have no money to give. So the amounts of money people contribute are by no means negligible. Life expectancy is low (around 35 to 40 years) and the death rate is high, so funerals are common events; everyone goes to many every year. People incur these expenses to express their solidarity with the bereaved and reinforce the CS relationship with them. The funeral contributions to the elders and the gifts to the bereaved, as well as the food and beer these people give to those who attend, mark and sustain a CS relationship that extends outside the lineage and the network of in-laws to the larger community within and beyond the village.

At a funeral the hosts provide food and beer for all their guests. There are two ritual meals for all the main participants, and simple hospitality food for everyone else—people do not bring their own food to a funeral. This food is a significant commitment in the commemorative funerals even more than in the mortuary rites, because scores of people may attend even a small funeral, while a thousand or more people attend a major one. Since the main events of either kind of funeral last for three days, and since people drink a great deal of beer, prodigious quantities of food and drink are often involved—perhaps something on the order of a thousand liters of beer. People (*reemba*—see below) of lineages that either have received or have been promised a wife from the deceased's lineage provide much of the beer, brewing it at home and coming to the funeral in long processions in which each woman carries a pot of beer on her head. The family of the deceased provides the food and some of the beer. Thus a funeral places an enormous material burden on Moose, who after all are extremely poor subsistence farmers. It is not uncommon for people to postpone a funeral somewhat beyond the appropriate time simply because they cannot get the resources together.

The motivations of Moose funeral hosts and their visitors are complex. In addition to reinforcing solidarity, people attend funerals partly to see their lovers (*rolba*, singular *rolle*) and friends from other villages, to drink, to dance and watch the dances, and to take a break from the drudgery of everyday life. But the hospitality Moose extend to visitors and the gifts visitors make to the bereaved are gestures of kindness, compassion, and solidarity—the motives for these transfers are the motives of Communal Sharing. A funeral is not a potlatch: it is not a cultural form whose point is to show off, try to outdo others, or vie for personal advantage. There are only two elements that involve economic and political motivations. First, at every major funeral (like any very large Moose gathering) a few small vendors come specifically to sell candy, kola nuts, and other small commodities. Second, the elders of the descendants of the indigenous people (*Yīyōose ninkeemba*) in attendance are said to engage in invisible magical battles, a sort of mystical combat. So they and in fact many other Yīyōose men come with their regalia of magic/medicine (*tum*) to protect themselves—and to attack other Yīyōose. These battles are merely for power, for prestige, for the joy of victory and the pleasure of being feared. (On the surface, however, generally all is courtesy, protocol, and accommodation.) With these two exceptions, nothing is "accomplished" at a funeral in any material or political sense. What a Moose funeral does is reinforce and sustain communal solidarity, at a major cost in material terms to many of the participants. Of course, the people in the burial party who take home the offerings and the freeloading acquaintances and strangers who attend a funeral "come out ahead." And I think that in fact drummers attend partly for the sake of the money they receive, judging by their eagerness to collect the coins tossed to them. But in the main the mourners, organizers, and visitors come together in an act of unity and solidarity. Material considerations impose significant constraints on when people can hold and attend funerals, but the principal purposes of the participants do not involve material (or political) motives.

In addition to funerals, Moose make sacrifices (*maando,* singular *maoongo*) on many other occasions. In these sacrifices they offer up libations of water, flavored flour water (*zom koom*), beer, chickens, and sometimes goats or sheep. Moose frequently sacrifice to address the sociomoral issues underlying illness and misfortune, according to the diagnoses given by diviners (*bagba,* singular *baga*). Moose also sacrifice to provide a safe and propitious sociomoral climate for precarious major undertakings like funeral ceremonies or travel to the Ivory Coast. Moose make promises to a variety of forces at various altars and other locations in order to propitiate the associated beings and obtain good fortune, especially to become pregnant and have their infants survive— as well as for protection from poisonous snakes and for general good fortune. In many kinds of promissory sacrifices, if individuals obtain what they request they return after (typically) three years and make sacrifices of thanksgiving, while renewing their request. Moose also make sacrifices to lift curses or to give thanks for curses that have killed transgressors. They conduct major community sacrifices in the annual ceremonies of *Kiuugu, Worbila, Tēndaoog Maoongo, Tangande.* And individuals make illicit sacrifices to obtain success over rivals for political office or over business competitors, to succeed and escape detection in their love affairs, and to gain protection from and vengeance against their enemies.

In making sacrifices, the officiant pours libations of water and beer, and offers up the blood of the sacrificed animal together with pieces of the animal's body and portions of the cooked meat of various organs. Those attending the ceremony then drink the beer and eat the roasted meat of the sacrificed animals, sometimes setting aside portions of beer and meat for important people who are absent. No one keeps track of how much beer each person drinks, although if the beer is divided up by drinking groups, the senior men get a larger portion, and they also get the largest share of the meat. At community sacrifices as well as in some sacrifices for the health of someone who is ill, and on other occasions, the people who have provided the beer or animals may not be present or get any share at all.

In addition to blood sacrifices, diviners also prescribe another kind of offering (*doose*, singular *doaaga*). Yarse and other Moslems perform only these non-bloody offerings (which do not include libations of beer), while other Moose perform both offerings and sacrifices. A person performing an offering sets out kola nuts, strips of cotton cloth, unspun cotton, thread, sour-dough bean cakes (*miisdu*), sesame, coins, cowrie shells, or whatever else the diviner prescribes. According to the diviner's prescription the offerer may leave the offerings at the intersection of two paths or elsewhere in the bush. He may call in someone to say a prayer over the offering; the diviner may specify a Moslem, especially one who is knowledgeable about prayers (*More*), or a mendicant Koranic student (*karembiiga*), or the young children of the neighborhood. Whoever says the prayers keeps the offering. Yarse and other Moslems make offerings at weddings and funerals, at which the hosts offer up one or more chickens, kola nuts, money, and other items, while everyone present contributes a few coins. After the prayers, they divide up the offering among those present; the chicken is roasted, carved into major parts, and distributed. (Participants may get more back than they contributed or less, largely as function of their seniority and the centrality of their role in the event.)

While there is a sense in which sacrifice and offering could be interpreted as expedient means to practical, material ends, such an account does not quite capture what is going on. A good harvest is not the causal result of being in the good graces of the Earth, it is a sign of its benevolence. Conversely, the ancestors do not directly cause misfortune—illness is an index of a disrupted or failed relationship with them. Moose take other, practical steps to cure the illness pharmaceutically: the remedy for the disease itself addresses the phenomenological symptoms causally. But the wrongdoing (*maan koaanga*) that illness or drought signifies must be redressed by a sacrifice. It is an act of expiation, of obeisance—an apology and a request for forgiveness. Moose pursue the causal and the sociomoral rectifications in parallel, as entirely separate and distinct courses of action. Similarly, when the village sacrifices for rain or a woman promises to sacrifice in three years if she bears a child who lives, the objective is to reinforce or create social relationships with other beings to whom the sacrifices are addressed. If these bonds with the Earth force and the ancestors are strong and solid, then good things will naturally come of it: the village will be secure, and the woman will safely give birth to a healthy baby. Feeding the forces to whom Moose address sacrifices and propitiating the beings to whom Moose address offerings are not so much causal means to practical material ends as they are social efforts to maintain solidarity and express loyalty to nonhuman social entities. The mechanisms Moose assume in sacrifice and offerings are the processes of social influence. The ends are social ends that subsume and incorporate practical concerns, but are not limited to them.

Sacrifices and offerings are not merely "superstitious" efforts to control the natural environment and protect material welfare, although there is a practical element in these acts. When Moose make sacrifices and offerings they hope to help assure rainfall, ward off lightning and damaging winds, avert epidemics and plagues, avoid strife, protect against witches and sorcerers, and resolve injuries and illnesses. But that does not mean we should interpret these religious acts as science-less technology. A sacrifice is more like inviting someone out to a meal than it is like setting a snare. An offering resembles a request more than it resembles making a brick. They are performative acts based on social-relational forms analogous to helping, thanking, apologizing, complimenting, praising, saluting, inviting, giving, promising, and pleading. The implicit mechanisms of sacrifice and offering are therefore social, not causal: they aim to establish social relationships or to restore equilibrium in social relationships with nonhuman beings. The Moose intention in sacrificing and offering is to exert social influence on these beings, not causal force. In these rituals Moose give obeisance and pay homage to superior beings, operating in an Authority Ranking mode. But above all they enact a desire for solidarity and unity with spiritual beings and harmony with natural forces. In sacrificial acts of communion Moose share their food and drink with nonhuman social beings, and in their offerings they make gifts to sustain or repair friendly social relations with nonhuman social beings. At the same time, the human participants in the sacrifice enact and reinforce their own Communal Sharing relations through the shared consumption of the sacrificial meat and beer. So the social relationships that sacrifice and offering sustain and restore are Communal Sharing and Authority Ranking.

Furthermore, sacrifice and nonbloody offerings are not MP activities. There are no prices for good fortune, no market for fertility or recovery from illness. Well-being is not a commodity to be obtained by shopping around and negotiating for the best deal. Sacrificers may implore, entreat, even (when addressing "fairies" [kĩnkirsi] for example) firmly demand, but they never bargain (barse) or negotiate as they do for commodities. Unlike any market vendor, Moose making a sacrifice or offering never extol the virtues of what they are offering up. Moreover, the Moose do not feel that the spirits and forces to whom they sacrifice owe them anything. Sacrifice is never a contract. When I asked Moose about the outcomes of sacrifices, they always treated the results as an unknown. Sacrificing is analogous to making a plea to a judge or a request to a dean—it is worth trying for what you need, but pleading is not causing. A sacrifice does not determine its outcome through an impersonal, material mechanism; rather, it is a social act involving both a desire for solidarity and an obeisant request for protection. That is, the sacrifice is both communion and tribute, based on Communal Sharing in association with Authority Ranking.[26]

Moose perform considerable numbers of sacrifices and offerings that consume substantial numbers of fowl and livestock and significant quantities of other items. While I have no quantitative data of my own to support my impression, I think that altogether Moose transfer considerably more chickens and more beer in sacrifices, nonbloody offerings, funeral offerings, courtship, and other gifts than they ever sell in the market. Additionally, Moose generally give a chicken to important visitors from outside the village; for example, I received a chicken from the chief of virtually every village I visited when reconnoitering for a field site, and often a second one from the village *tēngsoba* (custodian of the earth) as well. When Moose are courting a lineage for a bride (see the next chapter) they also give a chicken to the head of the lineage once a year at the *Kiuugu* festival. Aside from a few birds kept for breeding, Kaboré (1970:69; see her detailed breakdown cited by Pageard [1969:415]) estimates that the Moose of Surgu (Koudougou region) use three-fourths of the chickens they raise for funerals, sacrifices, traditional holidays, or for visiting gifts, while selling only one-fourth (see also Lallemand 1977:78). Furthermore, a major reason for selling something in the market is to obtain money to use for one of these noneconomic purposes, just as a great many of the purchases there (especially kola nuts, chickens, sesame, bean cakes, small pieces of cloth, and sprouted red sorghum) are destined for sacrifices, offerings, and gifts. So Moose Market Pricing transactions are often a means to noneconomic social and religious ends.

In sum, much of what little food and livestock Moose produce they sacrifice or offer up in collective (and sometimes individual) acts of obeisant communion. Rather than invest most of what they produce for material profit, Moose use their food and their livestock to feed and give drink to the dead, the ancestors, the Earth, the fairies, and the spirits that relate to humans. Moose generally make these sacrifices and offerings as food-sharing acts, eating with these forces and beings. The dead, the ancestors, the Earth, the fairies and the spirits are focal members of the community to which Moose belong, representing in many ways the unity, solidarity, and shared identity of the humans who sacrifice to them, and whom these beings and social forces look after. Sacrifices and offerings to them, like the collective meals that humans share on these and other occasions, are performative acts that mark, constitute, and sustain the sense of unity, wholeness, and oneness of the extended community.

There is only one plausible conclusion to draw from these observations about the purposes for which Moose use their scarcest resources: Moose are more concerned with sustaining and participating in Communal Sharing relationships than they are with furthering *rational* transactions in a Market Pricing mode. When Moose use what little they have to do this, they give witness of their basic motives, and their human character. Rather than calculating their personal material costs and benefits, rather than maximizing individual self-interest, Moose prefer to belong, to share, to enhance the solidarity and unity of the group. This Communal Sharing orientation extends beyond the sphere of manifest human beings to a world of social beings and forces with whom Moose seek Communal Sharing and Authority Ranking relationships.

Like Moose, many other people devote substantial portions of their production to social relational ends, both ceremonies involving gifts to other humans and religious transactions with nonhuman beings. Fortes (1945:240) comments on the importance of the religious and ceremonial uses that the nearby Tallensi make of their grain and livestock, and Hart (1982:148–49) cites reports of comparable patterns of noneconomic expenditures in the Maradi Valley of neighboring Niger and elsewhere. Firth (1965:344–47) describes equivalent uses of valuables in Tikopia (Polynesia), and Herskovits (1952, Chapter 20: The Service of the Supernatural) observes that religious activities represent a major form of consumption of goods in many traditional societies; Polanyi (1966:76–80) builds on Herskovits's Dahomean material and generalizes it. We have only to think of the cathedrals of medieval Europe, or of mosques and temples elsewhere in the world, to remind ourselves of the vast productive energies people in many societies have devoted to religious purposes. So the uses to which Moose put the fruits of their labor seem to be more or less representative of much of Africa and the rest of the traditional world, and the Moose orientation toward Communal Sharing probably represents a basic human proclivity.

In this chapter we have seen that Moose share communally the scarce resources that are critical for their survival. They generally do not conduct Market Pricing transactions in these resources: land, labor, water, and most cooked food do not have prices, and Moose do not transfer them as commodities on the basis of any kind of determinate exchange ratios. Nor do Moose individuals maximize their control over, acquisition, or utilization of these things. Most of the food and livestock Moose produce they share communally, offer up and consume together in food-sharing sacrifices, or give away as CS and AR gifts. They do not make *rati*onal Market Pricing choices among alternative selfish uses of their resources, they do not bargain to get an optimal rate of return on their costs. The ethnography refutes the assumption that calculatingly *rati*onal Market Pricing relations or individualistic materialism are inevitable or omnipresent human proclivities. Moose organize most of the allocation, transfer, use, and consumption of their most important material resources in a Communal Sharing mode, sometimes in conjunction with Authority Ranking. The next chapter will show that the same is true of Moose men's transactions in the most culturally valued "resource" in Moose society, wives.

# 12

# Transferring Women in Marriage: *Sharing, Not Self-Interested or Rational Exchange*

The last chapter dealt with Moose social orientations toward the four things that are most important to them materially for their subsistence, but what about the resources that are most important from the point of view of their cultural values? And what about the resources that contribute most to evolutionary fitness through natural selection? Presumably access to food, water, labor, and land are significant factors from an evolutionary point of view, and they are highly significant in Moose culture. But there is another "resource" that is still more important to male reproductive success and that Moose culture values more highly even than food: wives. If Moose men were to selfishly maximize anything, if there were anything they would commoditize so as to exchange on the basis of proportional, quid pro quo Market Pricing, then it should be women. Certainly the assumption in anthropology has been that men generally "exchange" daughters either in return for wives or for other valuable considerations like bride wealth. In this chapter we shall see what Moose do.

Moose have three principal alternative modes for transferring women in marriage. Before the colonial era, Moose men sometimes purchased women who had been captured in other regions and enslaved, conducting the transfer of wives through Market Pricing. These women then became wives with the same status as any other wife. Moose men have always given women to chiefs to honor them and show obeisance. Chiefs also give subjects wives as an act of noble benevolence and largesse. Furthermore, when giving wives in any manner, Moose typically transmit women from the head of one lineage to the head of another lineage, regardless of who the original giver is or who is the ultimate recipient of the wife. This is Authority Ranking. But Moose men typically give a wife as an expression of affection to someone who has been consistently kind, helpful and generous to them. While a man may receive a wife as a gesture of appreciation for a long series of gifts, courtesies, and offers of help, no amount of gift giving or assistance ever *entitles* a man to the *right* to receive a wife: wife giving is never obligatory, never negotiated, and never a determinately contingent quid pro quo. There is no bride price, and Moose do not exchange sisters or other women reciprocally; they never give a wife in return for a wife. For Moose, the transfer of women in marriage is an act of Communal Sharing.

In any given domain, one of the four elementary models for social relationships often predominates in terms of empirical prevalence, cultural preference, and motivational force. In Moose marriage, that model is Communal Sharing. But since one purpose of Part IV is to demonstrate the descriptive adequacy and explanatory power of the relational models theory as a total framework, and since Moose marriage draws on other models in addition to Communal Sharing, it is important to describe all the culturally defined forms of transferring women. Conversely, this concrete and fairly detailed account of the contrasts among the alternative forms of marriage will also serve to elucidate the distinctions among the four basic models. Thus this chapter illustrates what Chapter 7 asserts and the previous two chapters have already suggested: social relations in any domain are usually composed of a variety of acts oriented to each of the four basic models respectively. The chapter will portray the manner in which a major social activity, marriage, can be a composite built out of compounds of more than one mode of relationship, together with alternative forms based on other models and combinations of models.

For Moose men,[1] obtaining wives is a very high priority. The Moose are polygynous, so that a chief, custodian of the earth (*těngsoba*), wealthy man, elder or senior male often has three or four wives; a paramount chief (*kombere*) often has dozens of wives. Demographically, this works out because women marry at 17 or 19 (marriage at age 18 is inauspicious), while most village men do not acquire their first wife until they are in their late twenties or thirties; second and subsequent wives may come years later. Acquiring a first wife gives a man status and autonomy, which unmarried men lack. Moreover, one of the greatest desires of everyone, male and female, is to head a large family and leave many descendants. Moose treasure children. Hence men are extremely eager to obtain wives for their fertility above all (see Mangin 1916:30).[2] Economic considerations may also contribute to this desire, although I never heard the Moose talk about this: Since a husband controls the harvest from a field he cultivates together with his wife and children, marriage confers control over more grain, although young children naturally are an economic burden and not an immediate asset.

Men virtually never give up a wife willingly, although wives occasionally return to their natal families or run away with other men. There are only two situations in which a man ordinarily gives up a wife.[3] First, a man usually will abandon his wife immediately if she is found to be a witch (sõea)—that is, is killing lineage members and neighbors. (Usually his only alternative is to go into exile with her.) Second, a man of the chiefly clan (Nakomse) will divorce his wife if she has sexual relations with another man since it will henceforth be fatal for him to eat any food she cooks (Fiske n.d.). In both kinds of cases the women involved are immediately exiled and totally, irrevocably ostracized. Moose say that formerly they killed such women, but that they would be tried for murder in the modern courts if they did so now. But even a witch typically finds a new husband in another village before long, people saying that they did not "see" her accused and do not "know" that she is a witch. No woman of child-bearing age remains unmarried.

All this illustrates that obtaining wives is a paramount goal of Moose men (see Skinner 1960:20 on Moose in Nobere). But as Margaret Mead (1937:464–66) points out, a situation like this in which men want to marry but there is a shortage of women need not be culturally defined as competitive.

The Moose marriage system differs from what has been described in many other societies. Although there are minor forms involving elements of direct reciprocity (see Equality Matching, below), the predominant forms of marriage are not based on quid pro quo "exchange." Moose do not give wives in explicit return for any particular goods or services of any determinate amount. As mentioned above, there is no bride price.[4] Nor is there any dowry as such.[5] Nor do Moose engage in sister exchange.

There are some unsubstantiated statements in the literature to the effect that Moose marriage in general is structured as "reciprocal exchange," but they do not bear up on close examination. The underlying problem here and elsewhere in the literature seems to be that many authors have used the terms "exchange" and "reciprocity" very loosely in reference to any transfers of women between groups in which women or valuables pass in both directions at any time under any circumstances.[6] But the fact that transfers are sometimes bilateral (bidirectional) does not imply that they are balanced, symmetrically matched, or mutually contingent. In an early publication, for example, Izard-Héritier and Izard (1959:32–33) made the claim that marriage among the Yatênga Moose is based on "exchange," but they did not describe the process. Pageard (1969:98) also makes a passing reference to "reciprocity" as characterizing Moose marriage but without giving any details. Although Skinner, who did fieldwork in Nobere (in the south) and Ouagadougou, says nothing about formal structural reciprocity in his first report on Moose marriage (1960), later (1964a:22) he states that

> Most Mossi marriages were based on an exchange of women between
> two lineages linked by a long-term series of reciprocal exchanges of
> goods and services. . . . When a man from one lineage "made friends"
> with a member of another and rendered him a service or received a
> favor from him, their respective lineages were considered to be
> involved. The corporate nature of the lineage segment was
> acknowledged by all persons engaged in reciprocal relations. . . . When
> a man wished to give a daughter to a friend as a wife, he had to consult
> his Boodkasma [*buud kasma*— lineage head], who then gave the
> woman to the friend's Boodkasma. The latter accepted the woman as a
> wife for the lineage rather than for the man involved. (Skinner
> 1964a:22)

However, Skinner (1960, 1964a) gives no evidence and few details on "reciprocal exchange" as such, describing only the *pog suvre* among the chiefly clan
(Nakomse) of the Ouagadougou and Nobere regions. At least in Maane, *pog
suvre* means simply "giving wives," particularly when several are given at a
time in a ceremony (*suvbo*) to which recipients are asked to bring beer (the
root verb is *suv*. However, what Skinner describes under this rubric is the system specific to the giving of wives by the chiefly clan. In this system, when a
chief bestows a woman in marriage, he is entitled to the first daughter born of
the marriage, whom he may marry, pass on to a kinsman, or use to begin a new
cycle by bestowing the girl to another subject (see Delobsom [1930:6–7] and
Alexandre's [1953] definition of *suv* in the Ouagadougou dialect of Moore).

The system is hardly reciprocal, however; it is not symmetrical, since the
chief does not owe anyone a wife. The many wives his subjects give him are
tokens of fealty and honor, as Skinner observes, and the chief incurs no obligation to give wives to the particular lineages who give him wives. When he receives the first-born daughter of a woman he has bestowed, he has no obligation to give anything back in return. Nor does the chief *suv* women *in exchange
for* rights to their future daughters—this right is an absolute chiefly prerogative, not something the recipients agree to in order to gain a wife, or grant in
return for what they have received.[7] In fact, Moose say that the chief "owns"
(*soa*) all the people in his jurisdiction and, in principle, may take as wives
whichever women he wants (as Skinner also notes; see Authority Ranking,
below). Skinner (1960:20, 1964a:23) further states that most Moose marriages
are in fact based on "friendship" relations. In the context of Skinner's
(1964a:23) comment that, "commoners tended to be more generous to noble
friends than vice versa" and his references to asymmetry and generosity, the
term "reciprocal exchange" clearly does not mean Equality Matching or Market Pricing. Then what is the structure of Moose wife giving?

There are no moieties and no clans that are systematically related to each
other as wife givers[8] and wife receivers as such.[9] Indeed, Tait (1961:93–113)

describes patterns of transferring women in marriage among the Konkomba of Northern Ghana that resemble Moose practices, and observes that

> There is no system of prohibited marriages between clans nor does there seem to be any system of preferred marriages between clans. Apart from the rules prohibiting marriages between categories of kin the choice of a spouse appears to be random. (Tait 1961:100)

The Moose lineage (*buudu*) is exogamous, as is the "clan" (also *buudu*). As Pageard (1969:284–85) observes, the Moose prohibition against marriage with anyone with whom one has any known ancestor in common precludes any sustained "reciprocal" exchange of women. Lallemand (1977:156) states the exogamy rule in Bamtēnga (in the Koungoussi region of Yatēnga, 40 kilometers north of our field site) as prohibition against marriage within the patrilineage of either parent or the patrilineage of either grandmother. Hammond (1966:120–21, 142), in reference to Gourcy in Yatēnga only mentions a prohibition on marrying into the person's own sib (maximal lineage) and the patrilineage of his or her mother. All reports indicate that this prohibition may be breached if the link is very distant and only discovered after the marriage, but that the prohibition definitely covers kin of both parents.[10] Whatever the precise prohibitions, it is clear that any kind of long-sustained restricted bilateral reciprocity or regular cycle of generalized exchanges is ruled out.

What actually happens is that a Moose man may seek a wife from any unrelated lineage. He may meet a man his own age or older and start giving him gifts and extending him courtesies and help. Usually the wife-seeker's brothers and close kinsmen help him, and his friends often accompany or aid him. The wife-seekers treat the potential wife-giving elders with great deference, and make formal and informal gifts of chickens, money, beer, kola nuts, and tobacco, while providing labor on various occasions (see Mangin [1916:29] for the Koupela region, and Delobsom [1930:8] for Ouagadougou). In particular, the wife-seekers always come on *Kiuugu*, the annual feast and ritual day of chiefs, bringing a chicken, coins, and often kola nuts to the lineage head (*buud kasma*) and senior man of the neighborhood (*sak kasma*; typically the *buud kasma* and the *sak kasma* are the same person). The wife-seekers bring coins for other senior men, and generally something for the senior woman as well. When the courtship is directed at a junior man who is not himself the lineage head, the wife-seekers also bring a coin and/or kola nuts for him. If at any time an elder whom they are courting is ill, or is behind in his cultivating for any reason, the wife-seekers come, usually unasked, and cultivate for him. If they encounter him in the market, they buy him beer. If there is a funeral (*kʋʋre*) in the elder's lineage, the wife-seekers are sure to attend, greet the assembled elders, and make a courtesy gift of a few coins (as do other formal visitors). If the potential wife-givers are holding a cultivating bee (*sɩsoaaga*) or threshing bee (*zauga*), the wife-seekers make an effort to attend.

The idiom in which the wife-seekers most often offer such gifts and service is what we might call filial piety; they act as good sons or good friends. Such courtship is called *belōgo*, from the verb, *beleme*, to court. These terms seem to come from a root *bele*, to take care of, to please, flatter, humor, amuse, and keep happy, or to pretend, tease, mislead. A cognate verb, *belege*, and its gerund or noun form, *belegre*, refer to taking care of small children.[11] The flavor of this group of terms is indicated by the fact that Moose are extremely indulgent with young children, who are coddled and given whatever they want. Moose never let a child under about four cry—young children get their way about everything. The idea in both courtship and early child care is one of freely giving whatever is wanted, taking care of, fulfilling all needs, desires, and wishes, and in general pleasing and keeping the other person happy.[12]

Courtship of the wife-giving elders often goes on for many years, but the wife-seekers never state any reason for their kindnesses; they certainly never say that they are seeking a wife. Of course, this goal is understood by the recipients of the gifts and kindnesses, although often the recipients do not acknowledge the issue for some years. No matter how long courtship continues and how many gifts are given, the wife-seekers never establish any right to anything in return. Eventually, as an expression of affection and appreciation, the senior male may give the wife-seeking lineage a wife, but he is never under any obligation to do so. There is no explicit standard for how many years should have passed before a wife is given, for how many gifts should have been given, or how much labor service—and these in fact vary a great deal (see Delobsom 1930:8–9, 14–15).[13] Sometimes the lineage being courted never gives a wife, sometimes it takes 20 years, sometimes a few months, and sometimes people just give a wife to someone who has not courted them at all—someone just takes a liking to a man and gives him a wife. It happens fairly often that a man may start courtship, make a number of gifts, buy beer for an elder, come with a chicken and coins to visit him and pay respects to other elders and to the senior woman on *Kiuugu*—and then give up the effort after a while, without having received anything in return. If so, and no matter how long the man has been trying, he has no complaint and no claim, and normally gets nothing back.[14] However, in the long run, persistence usually bears fruit. Typically the first step is for the senior male of the wife-givers' lineage to state that he appreciates the attentions, respect, and kindnesses he has been receiving, but that regrettably he has nothing to give to express his appreciation.[15] Later the elder may praise the wife-seekers for their filial piety and tell them that if he gets a girl at some point, then he will give her to them.[16]

Ultimately, the wife-givers may call the wife-seekers and formally promise to give them a specific bride in appreciation for their respect and care. (This bestowal is called *pog-kūuni, pog-sιυυre*, or *riungu*). The bride so given is almost always a young girl, often between about age seven and twelve. Since a women does not actually "marry" (*kē yikaadm*—go to live with their husband) until age 17 (or frequently 19),[17] the courtship is far from over. From the time the girl is promised, however, the relation enters a new stage. The senior men of the wife-giving lineage are now in-laws (*reemdãmba*; the term is reciprocal in the first generation) to the wife-receivers. The wife-giving lineage continues to receive the same gifts and care they previously had, but they are henceforth also in a position to call their daughter's husband (*sida*) to do tasks for them, as they would a true child of their own. And, in fact, the wife-givers address their prospective son-in-law as *m biiga*, my child, and are addressed as *m ba*, my father.[18] So the wife-seekers may be called to help build a goat house, collect firewood for brewing ceremonial beer, or run an errand to a distant village. If there is a funeral in the wife-givers' lineage, the wife-givers call their daughters' husbands and prospective husbands to bring beer. This relation of service continues to a considerable degree even after the wife has actually gone to live with her husband. There are several named and prescribed ceremonies[19] that have to take place over the next few years before the wife can be brought home to her husband at another ceremony (*pog-peegre*). At most of these events the wife-seekers bring quantities of beer, kola nuts, tobacco, and money to the wife-givers. The wife-givers offer a major meal to the wife-seekers. Indeed, they are given far more than they can eat, and pass back much of the food to the wife-givers. Conversely, after the wife-seekers give the wife-givers the beer they have brought to them, the wife-givers give some of it back to them.

Virtually all of this courtship is patently constituted in terms of Communal Sharing, as is particularly clear from the sharing of food and labor and the gifts "freely given." There is never any negotiation (much less bargaining) between the two parties over the amount of money, gifts, or labor that the wife-seekers provide. The wife-seekers do check with their hosts in the wife-giving village, and sometimes directly with the elders they are courting, to make sure that they are following the local protocol, and especially to insure that they have not neglected anyone in the gifts they distribute. But there are no dealings about the amounts per se, nor are there any very precisely defined, fixed, or standard amounts to be given. Unlike all important Market Pricing transactions among the Moose involving deferred transfers on credit (*samde*), there are no outside witnesses (*kasetba*) to the transfers of courtship gifts.[20] Although—naturally—the participants have a sense of what is appropriate, the wife-givers never reject as inadequate the money and gifts the wife-seekers give informally or their ceremonial gifts at the rituals during the years between the wife's bestowal and her taking up residence with her husband's lineage. This contrasts with any kind of market transaction, in which Moose sellers commonly refuse to accept the offers that buyers initially make for a commodity. Also, it is unlike the typical practice in negotiating the price of a commodity under Market Pricing; in my experience, no wife-seeker ever cites or makes any comparison with the amount any other wife-seeker has given, even to the same wife-givers. And the Moose explicitly deny that marriage is a matter of *raabo* (purchase).[21] All of this indicates that the predominant frame in which Moose transfer women in marriage is based on Communal Sharing (with some elements of Authority Ranking), not Equality Matching or Market Pricing.

Further evidence for this comes from the fact that courtship gifts do not constitute a bride price or any other sort of quid pro quo. This is demonstrated, for example, by the fact that if a wife leaves her husband, even though everyone might acknowledge that she is at fault, traditionally her kin are not expected to return anything to her husband.[22] Pageard (1969:342–43) observes that the "old" tradition is that courtship gifts are not returned if the marriage is dissolved, writing that husbands who hold to the traditional Moose position reject both divorce and reimbursement.[23]

There is one element in premarriage ceremonies that bears a loose, superficial resemblance to market bargaining or haggling. At a number of rituals that take place after the bestowal of the bride, including the ceremony when the wife-seekers bring home their new bride (pog peegre), certain women among the wife-givers demand money from the wife-seekers. The women who make these demands include the bride's companions, playmates, and age-mates (redetaase, remetaase, and rogetaase—all three of these terms are used fairly interchangeably) and female younger siblings (yaopa, including father's brothers' daughters), and her "mothers" (marāmba, including mother's co-wives and father's brothers' wives, but excluding her own mother). They say that they want money because they are losing the young woman. The women are extremely obstinate in their demands, to the point of unreasonableness—especially the bride's age-mates and younger sisters, who try to steal the bicycles, hats, and other possessions of the wife-seekers and hold them for ransom. Hence the "negotiations" can go on for hours. The wife-to-be's younger siblings do all this as the joking partners, (rakuba), of the husband and his age-mates. The wife-seekers remain calm, polite, and patient throughout these trying ordeals—and in my experience they are very trying.

But this joking harassment is in no sense to be equated with bargaining over a commodity. In all their demands and their obstinacy, the mothers and sisters of the bride-to-be make absolutely no attempt to mention the qualities of the wife, or in any other way to treat the transaction as a negotiated exchange of anything for anything else. In fact, sometimes during this harassment the Moose explicitly contrast the event with the contractual commodity transactions of Market Pricing, saying that it is not buying (raabo). The norm is that the "mothers," being senior to the girls, should always get at least as much as the girls. Since the mothers come first and tend to be more reasonable, in principle this places a ceiling on how much the girls can expect. However, as an informant once said, these joking partners make their demands to be difficult and to aggravate, so they would not accept any initial offer, however large. The amounts given, though quite variable, are based on village tradition, not the assessment of any sort of "exchange value" of the wife.

Also, elders may take steps to intervene or direct the women and girls to control the amounts they demand. This contrasts with MP negotiations, where no one comments or intervenes between the buyer or seller while bargaining is in process (although people may have plenty of comments and advice after the fact). On one occasion the wife-seekers wanted to give far more than the elders had told the women and girls they could accept, so they re-turned what they were offered. The wife-seekers insisted on paying an unusu-ally large sum, and the problem was only resolved when they gave part of the money as a "separate" friendly side gift. Among other things, the wife-giving elders invoke the Equality Matching model to restrain importunate demands by their wives and daughters, reminding them that the time will come when their own lineage will be wife-seekers; if they torment the wife-seekers too much, they can expect to be tormented in return. If they are reasonable and forbearing, then others will be reasonable and forbearing to them. (But note that there is no implication that these wife-seekers will be wife-givers to *this* lineage later—only that they will get a reputation for obnoxiousness which will justify other wife-givers in being hard on them in turn.)

Observe, however, that the Equality Matching model is not applied to the transfer of the wives themselves from one lineage to another: the Moose do not "exchange" wives in any reciprocal sense. They construe the gift of a wife as an act of fondness, of paternal (or fraternal, see below) benevolence. The giving of a wife does not create an obligation to give a wife in return, and there is no evidence to suggest that wife exchange between lineages is generally re-ciprocal de facto. Sometimes a promised wife runs off with another man whom she prefers (*ruk sida n zoe*). This creates considerable embarrassment for the wife-givers if they have explicitly promised her to her husband; I believe that they would ultimately try to replace her with another girl. If a promised girl dies before the steps in the marriage process are completed, or a woman dies after she formally marries (*kẽ yikaadm*) and takes up residence with her husband, strictly speaking there is no obligation to replace her with another woman. But the wife-givers often do give another wife. Indeed, when a woman dies who has been happily married for some time, her husband's lin-eage formally expresses the hope that the wife-givers will give them another wife to replace her, and they report that often their wishes are eventually ful-filled.

Another well-defined custom in this pattern that contrasts with Equality Matching involves the wife-givers giving a second wife to the husband of the first. If her husband's lineage (and she herself) continues to be kind and helpful to her natal lineage, if the wife has been well looked after, and especially if, when she is an old woman, a son or another young man of her husband's lin-eage helps her with her cultivation and treats her well, her natal lineage may give her a wife, called a *yiri paga* ([from the first wife's] home wife), to pass on to her husband, who may optionally pass her on to a younger brother or a son by another wife. If this occurs, the gift of the new wife is construed as an ex-pression of appreciation and fondness, never as acquitting an absolute obliga-tion or as a quid pro quo.[24] So in fact, far from the bestowal of wives being a reciprocal quid pro quo in which women move in opposite directions to bal-ance each other, it is not unusual for wife-givers to keep giving more wives to the husbands of their sisters and daughters.

Like the giving of the wives themselves from one lineage to another, the collection of funds for the major gifts given by the wife-seekers in the years following the promise of a specific, named wife also entails Communal Sharing, this time within the wife-seeking lineage. On the morning before each formal visit to the wife-givers, the head of the wife-seeking compound invites his neighbors, lineage-mates, and other kin to come drink some of the beer. The visitors come and partake of the beer, and as they arrive they greet the elders and make a contribution to the funds which will be used for the gift to the wife-givers (see Mangin 1916:31). Like all such contributions (e.g., at funerals), any amount is acceptable, so long as one contributes something. The amount each individual actually gives is not ordinarily discussed or otherwise marked, although there is a general sense of how much people in various roles should contribute, and sometimes exceptionally generous gifts are noted. However, the principals would definitely remark on certain expected participants' failing to attend at all. What is important is the fact of participation, or nonparticipation, not the quantitative amount. Immediately afterwards, this money is pooled and allocated to the gift to be taken to the wife-givers, either as cash or as funds for the purchase of kola nuts. Or, if there were ample contributions, the principal wife-seeker might take some of the money to offset his other expenses related to the event.

In addition to these features of the acquisition of wives, there is another important way in which Moose marriage itself is based on Communal Sharing. The Moose not only pool their resources and efforts in seeking a wife, but the wife they receive is in an important sense a communal resource of the (sub)lineage as a whole.[25] Since courtship (*belōgo*) of wife-giving elders and parents frequently takes many years, a man very often begins the courtship without necessarily intending to marry any future wife himself. Sometimes a man has a specific husband in mind, perhaps a son, but I think that often a group of closely related men carry on the long process of courtship for quite some time without any clear idea or decision about exactly who will marry the woman eventually acquired. Even though one man may take the lead and assume the main financial burden, there is always close collaboration in courtship among the men of a compound. Frequently the courtship efforts are passed on from father to sons, or from an older brother departing for the Ivory Coast to his father and younger brothers. If the efforts bear fruit, the kinsmen of the man who initiated the courtship will send for him when it comes time for the bride to take up residence with him.

It is also common for a woman promised to an elder not to be assigned to a particular husband for some time after the formal bestowal; the elder may marry her himself, or pass her on to one of his juniors. In one instance that I followed closely the woman was brought home to the wife-seekers' compound and installed there without the compound head announcing for some weeks to whom he would give her.[26]

Furthermore, a man addresses the wives of his lineage-mates as *m paga*, my wife, while they all address him as *m sida*, my husband. The men of the lineage often refer to its wives as *tõnd pagba*, our wives, while the women may refer to *tõnd sidba*, our husbands (cf. Fortes [1969:109–110] on the Tallensi). In addition, the same woman usually is wife to two or three members of the lineage in succession. Since women first marry at age 17 or 19, while men ordinarily marry for the first time in their late 20s or later (and may marry subsequent wives at any age after that) many women are widowed and remarry. Widows have some choice about whom they marry, but it should always be within the lineage and ideally among the sons or younger brothers of the deceased. Thus in this additional sense, wives are attached to a lineage, not just married to an individual husband.

Pacere (1979:107–108), writing of his home village of Manéga (Zitēnga region, between Ouagadougou and Maane), captures the ethos of Moose marriage. He emphasizes that marriages are links between groups—bonds between communities, not between individuals. He then takes up the question that the "civilized world" asks of such marriages—what about the wishes of the couple themselves? He explains:

> On est toujours frappé par ce manque de volonté de la jeune fille et du jeune homme dans ce qui, pour le "monde civilisé," décide de leur avenir, de leur "bonheur;" cependant, il ne faudrait jamais oublier que l'individu est né dans un groupe et que, surtout, en atteignant l'âge du mariage, il a été tellement façonné par les idées du groupe que seuls les règles de ce groupe. . .lui sont bonnes; l'individu ne sait même pas qu'il a une volonté personnelle, donc surtout un bonheur personnel définissable en dehors de celui du groupe, des impératifs de celui-ci; vouloir en donner c'est lui imposer un bonheur qu'il ne connaît pas, c'est-à-dire qu'il ne pourra supporter parce qu'étant en définitive son malheur, le cloisonnant, l'isolant, lui simple particule, de l'intégralité, du groupe. . . .Le bonheur conjugal ne repose pas sur d'autre fondements, parce que le groupe, l'intérêt collectif, la nécessité de vivre en commun, fait partie de la définition de la conscience individuelle et de ses sollicitations. (Pacere 1979:108–109)

> (One is always struck by this lack of will [personal preference] in the girl and the young man concerning that which, for the "civilized world," decides their future, their happiness; however, it must not be forgotten that the individual is born into a group and, above all, that in reaching the age of marriage, he has been so thoroughly shaped by the ideas of the group that only the rules of this group. . .are good for him; the individual does not even know that he has a personal will, a fortiori a personal happiness apart from the group or its requirements; to wish these upon him is to impose on him a happiness that he does not

know, that he cannot bear because [such freedom and individuality] define his misery, cutting him off, isolating him as a mere particle from the wholeness, from the group. . . . Conjugal happiness is not based on any other foundation, because the group, the collective interest, the necessity for living together, constitute part of the definition of individual awareness [consciousness] and of its concerns.)

Evidently, Communal Sharing is the overwhelmingly predominant Moose mode of bestowing women in marriage. As Moose say, they give a daughter to a man when they like (*nonge*) him. A group gives a wife to another group as a gesture of affection and solidarity. From the evolutionary perspective of reproductive success and from the cultural perspective of the goal of having many children and siring many descendants, nothing is more important to Moose men than wives. So their Communal Sharing in wife seeking and wife bestowal displays their fundamental motives and values. Moose CS is not expedient conformity to social norms—it is not a covert strategy intended to advance ulterior selfish individual interests, nor is it based on *rat*ional calculations of the proportion of benefits to costs of this mode of transfer. What ulterior selfish individualistic Market Pricing ends could Moose possibly be pursuing by means of this Communal Sharing? Moose share communally because CS is an ultimate end in itself, they do it because it is an autonomous relational motive and a fundamental cultural value.

One of my purposes in Part IV is to show that Market Pricing is not the sole or necessarily predominant directive force in human social relations. My aims here also include illustrating how the four basic models illuminate Moose social relations, while demonstrating that the relational models are not simply our own ethnocentric Western impositions on an alien system of social thought. All these purposes will be served by describing other forms and aspects of wife giving that Moose structure in terms of Authority Ranking, Equality Matching, and even Market Pricing. While Communal Sharing predominates, in various ways the Moose do draw on all four fundamental models to transfer women in marriage. Examining how they use the other three models will be instructive in its own right. But it will also serve as a contrast to the core system: exploring the operation of AR, EM, and MP as alternatives to the Communal Sharing model for transferring women will make it clear just what the predominant Moose mode of marriage is not.

## Buying a Slave Wife

Until this century the outright purchase of a woman slave (*yempoaka*) was another common means of acquiring a wife. Such women (whom the Moose label as having been of Gurunsi ethnicity)[27] were typically captured as girls in raids and sold in slave markets, including a site marked by a still-standing tree

near the Maane market. We may presume that their purchase involved bargaining in which buyers and sellers made explicit comparisons with the alternatives available to them, with reference to the market prices of slaves according to their age, strength, health, beauty, and other features. Although such
women were acquired in a Market Pricing mode, their purchasers reportedly
treated them like any other wife, and they were not stigmatized (Paulme
[1940:107–108] describes a similar situation among the Dogon). Their children
reputedly were not, and in my observation are not today, distinguished from
other children of the same father, except that children of slaves lack the advantage of having a mother's brother (*yesba*) to turn to for help and support when
they need it. Similarly, the slave wife lacked the recourse of returning to her
father's home if mistreated by her husband: the Moose report that by adult-
hood such women generally did not know their home villages and would not
have been able to find their way home. When the French outlawed slavery, at
least a few of these women apparently did flee their husbands, however. Others remained, but none are alive today in the Habra area.[28]

While I do not know the details of how slaves were bought and sold, it seems
that they were purchased like other chattel and "owned" outright. Moose
wives, in quarreling with their husbands and demanding better treatment,
may ask the rhetorical question, "Did you buy me?!" (*Fo raa maam bi?!*). The
implication is that an ordinary wife, unlike a slave, may always return home if
she is seriously mistreated, with the potential support of her mother, father
and brothers.

Thus while the available evidence indicates that although slave wives were
apparently acquired like any other market commodity and were at some disadvantage due to the cutting of their kinship ties with their natal groups, they
were subject to the same authority under their husbands and other senior men
and women and in other respects were treated more or less like other wives. It
is important to stress that the acquisition of a wife by purchase does not imply
that the relationship between her and the lineage that purchased her is thereafter a purely material, economic relationship based on Market Pricing.
Kopytoff (1988) discusses the relatively low (estimated at 10 percent to 35 percent) desertion rate of slaves after the colonial abolition of slavery in West Africa. He cogently shows that the Western common sense view of slavery does
not apply to most African slavery, criticizing the model that

> reduces the slave to a Political Economic Man who maximizes the
> utilities of liberty and happiness and yearns for detachment from his
> social position. (Kopytoff 1988:489)

Kopytoff argues that for many or most African slaves, freedom—"autonomy
and detachment from binding social obligations"—was neither a meaningful
goal nor even a value as such. Since community membership, dependence on
elders, and some element of balanced reciprocity are the modal and the desired forms of social relationships in Africa, freed slaves did not seek freedom

from diffuse obligations, or individualistic "opportunity," or the freedom to negotiate and enter into voluntary contracts with others.

A purchased slave belongs to the purchasing group, but "belonging" is something people seek and perpetuate (although, given the option, presumably any slave would prefer to belong to her natal group as long as she retained effective potential membership in it). If abolition did not provide a given slave the effective alternative of rejoining her natal group because she no longer knew or was known in that group of kin and neighbors and had forgotten her natal language, if a freed slave's option was unfettered, unbound, unattached "freedom," then she would be likely to choose to stay on with her owners. "Owned" like any wife or subordinate whose owners owe her protection and responsible pastoral care, "bound" by mutual obligations like those of any kinsperson, "driven" by the existential, inalienable but unalterable fact of membership to feed and respond to the needs of its members, and "used" conversely like any member of the collectivity to support its collective needs, most women bought as slaves stayed on as wives and mothers, like any other. And, like other "free" women, some left their first husbands to seek new groups that would incorporate them and new husbands to own them.

Meillasoux's (1971:63–64) overview indicates that these Communal Sharing and Authority Ranking orientations toward domestic slavery were quite general in West Africa. The essence of West African slavery was generally not mere Market Pricing economic exploitation of slave labor (or sexual access). Slaves, like full members of a lineage, augmented the communal kinship group and, as dependent subordinates, the authority and rank of its leaders. Since my focus here is on the transfer of women in marriage, we need not dwell on this issue beyond drawing the conclusion that married women participated in pretty much the same Communal Sharing and Authority Ranking relations in their husbands' compounds regardless of how they were acquired. The point to make is simply that before abolition—and complete abolition came late to French West Africa—Moose men captured women and sold them to other men as commodities, so that men sometimes obtained wives by paying the Market Price for them. But as Moose themselves and any observer can see, the predominant communal form of transferring wives has virtually nothing in common with this buying and selling. Indeed, from inside the culture as well as from outside, this form of purchase serves as a clear contrast with the dominant mode of marriage.

## Giving Wives in Tribute and Largesse

One particular form of Moose marriage is based on the powers of the chiefs (Nanamse), and it is clearly a manifestation of Authority Ranking. When a chief gives a woman away in marriage who is not from his own lineage, he or his successor has the right to give away her first-born daughter.[29] Since this process tends to be self-replicating (barring the first woman's death, failure to bear a daughter, or flight from the region), it is an important component of a chief's power. One special form it takes is that a king (*riima*) or paramount chief (*kombere*) gives each page a wife at the end of his service.[30] A chief's subjects may also give him wives without his courting the lineage concerned, as an Authority Ranking act of fealty and obeisance. (Occasionally other people also receive wives "out of the blue" like this [see Pageard 1969:278], but it is uncommon.) This overall pattern of transferring women resembles the hierarchically centralized system of transferring goods that Polanyi (1966, 1968) calls "redistribution." In particular, subjects are obligated to give the chief women, whom he bestows on other subjects who are thereby beholden to him for their wives. These practices clearly are a form of Authority Ranking.

Beyond this special form, AR is also manifest in various aspects of the predominant type of Moose marriage. While the principal idiom of ordinary courtship (*belōgo*) of wife-givers is Communal Sharing, there is a major element of respectful deference as well. Courtship is a kind of filial piety, treating the potential wife-giver as a father with whom Moose have a relationship in which Authority Ranking predominates alongside elements of CS. Both the AR and CS aspects come out particularly in one variant of courtship in which a young man adopts the title of a chief or other high office holder (this is called *rike naam yʋʋre*). Courtship goes on as usual, but the idiom here is that of respectful identification with a great person. Moose assume a number of names, but sometimes men become generally known by this imitative chiefly name. It is flattering to a chief to have his title adopted by a young man, often one outside his jurisdiction, who is, in effect, offering obeisance. The admiring identification explicit in adopting a chiefly name is also a minor component in the ordinary courtship of lineage heads, in which a man voluntarily places himself in a subservient position under someone to whom he would not otherwise be subordinate. In other words, wife-seeking men seek out and create an AR relationship with potential wife-givers.

Moose emigrants practice a variant form of Authority Ranking wife-bestowal. According to Schildkrout (1978:90–91), Moose Muslims in Kumasi, Ghana—particularly the wealthy—frequently adopt the Hausa form of bestowal called *auren sadaka* in giving their daughters in marriage:

> A man demonstrates his status and his generosity by giving his
> daughter to a friend, a client, or occasionally to a relative and forgoes
> the marriage gift. . .customarily given by the bridegroom. (Schildkrout
> 1978:91)

Whatever its name and origins, this practice is certainly congruent with both the AR and CS aspects of traditional Moose marriage.[31]

The other major element of Authority Ranking in Moose marriage is displayed in the channels through which men transfer women from their natal lineage to the husband's lineage. Men *soa* (own, possess, control, are responsible for) their children, and a man *soa* his wife—indeed, as we saw above, all the adult men of the lineage collectively *soa* all their wives, and the head of the compound (*zak soba*) is the "owner of the compound." (The same verb is used as for material possessions and for the *tēngsoba*'s custodianship of the land.) So marriage is the transfer of control over a woman and responsibility for her from the wife-giving father and lineage elders to the wife-receiving lineage elders and husband. I believe that, in practice, daughters usually are given in marriage largely at the behest of their fathers, but women are always formally transmitted through the head of the lineage (*buud kasma*), who is at least the nominal bestower. Whether the wife-seekers directly court only the head of the lineage or focus their attentions primarily on a more junior man who is the father of a potential bride, the lineage head is the one who formally makes the gift. Indeed, it is one of the principal prerogatives of the head of the lineage to give (*siu*) its daughters, and the father may be merely an unobtrusive, unmarked participant in the bestowal ceremony.

Receiving the gift (that is, the promise) of a woman in marriage is a mirror image of the giving. Thus, while a girl may be designated to go to a particular junior man in the receiving lineage, she is received through a senior man of the lineage. The head of her own lineage gives her to the head of the receiving lineage, whether she is destined for the lineage head himself or for ultimate transmittal to another man. The girl being given in marriage is not ordinarily present at the event, and often the prospective groom is not there either (especially if he is a junior man), although generally most of the other men of both lineages witness the presentation. In many cases the head of the bestowing lineage gives a wife directly to a senior man, who has the option of marrying her himself, or passing her on to one of his lineage subordinates. Furthermore (as indicated in the discussion of courtship above), a father may begin courting several lineages when his sons are still young boys and any wife he gets he may pass on to his younger brothers or sons. So the bestowal and reception of a wife follows hierarchical Authority Ranking channels up the giving lineage and down the receiving lineage.

Finally, Authority Ranking relations among men determine the order in which they marry, and AR relations are more or less indirectly marked by the number of wives men have. Within the lineage, men first marry in their late twenties to mid thirties. This is not only a function of their increasing status as they grow older, but is the key transition in the acquisition of the more autonomous status of family head.[32] As a man grows older, and especially if he ultimately becomes head of the compound, he may acquire additional wives. The Nakomse (descendants of former chiefs and members of the clan eligible for chieftainship) also tend to have more wives than men of other clans, although this may be partly a function of relative wealth. Beyond this, the village chief (*naaba*) and custodian of the earth (*tēngsoba*) typically have more wives than their age-mates, as befits the two leading personages. Above them, the Paramount Chief (*Kombere*) of Maane reportedly has about 60 wives.[33]

In summary, Moose transfer women in marriage in much the same manner as they organize most important social activities: Communal Sharing is the model that governs the overall form, but Authority Ranking is integrated with it as a secondary model structuring some aspects of the process. As we saw above, Market Pricing used to be a definite but minor alternative that operated in a very circumscribed set of contexts. Thus in terms of the prevalence and overall predominance of the three models in Moose social relations, Communal Sharing comes first, Authority Ranking second, and Market Pricing last. Neither quid pro quo exchange nor any other manifestation of Equality Matching is salient in Moose marriage, but occasionally EM is visible. Since EM is so prominent in the wife-bestowal systems of so many other cultures, it is worth having a look at how it works among Moose when in fact it does operate.

## Egalitarian Reciprocity in Marriage

There is one recognized but relatively uncommon form of wife giving that appears to be structured in the form of an Equality Matching relationship. Two men may *yōk baando*, make a special vow of friendship. Or they may less formally but equally definitely become mutual friends, addressing each other as *m daoa* (my man) or *m zoa* (my friend). Often when they later have children each will give the other a daughter in marriage. If one of the men does not have a daughter, or does not yet have one, then in practice the exchange is unilateral, but sometimes they may conceive of it as a delayed balanced reciprocal exchange. Like virtually all Moose EM reciprocity, the reciprocity is not explicit—the quid pro quo is not stated. Moose say of such bilateral relations between peer friends, "If you have a daughter, you give her" (*F sã n tar biiga, f kõtalame*). This is the same formula which they use to describe friendship (*zoodo*) in general. The expectation is that you will give the other what he or she wants when you have it, and on another occasion when you need such a thing and the other has it, you will ask for it in turn.[34]

While giving a wife is a natural outgrowth of friendship, obtaining a wife is neither the explicit nor implicit motive underlying friendship in general. Moose sometimes make friends with the aim of acquiring a wife, but I am morally certain they sometimes make friends simply because they like each other. Friendship (*zoodo*) is an end in itself, an intrinsically rewarding form of interaction that Moose engage in to a large degree for its own sake.

There are some passing reports in the literature of what appear to be EM kinds of wife-bestowal among Moose, but often there is insufficient detail to determine the form unambiguously. Mangin (1916:28) describes Moose giving a girl in marriage to repay a monetary debt, or giving a girl in marriage to a healer who cures the father. Pageard also asserts (1969:280) that, "déguisé en acte d'amitié" (disguised as an act of friendship), the gift of a wife may "constitute" payment of a "debt," but neither writer gives any sources or provides details or description, discussion, or Moore terms for this practice. Mangin also mentions direct daughter-for-daughter exchange. According to Pageard (1966:116–17, 1969:280–81), while bestowal of a woman in marriage is generally an act of friendship freely given, Moose sometimes make reciprocal exchange of wives between one lineage (*buudu*) and another for two or three generations. He gives the Moore word *tekre* as the term used for these exchanges, the same term that Maane area Moose use in other one-for-one Equality Matching trades. Pageard reports observing such reciprocal gifts around Ouargaye (Yanga region), where it is the basic form of marriage, and in Yako, and he says that it is known in Ouagadougou. He also cites sources describing it in Manga and Taghalla (Kaya region). However, he provides no details on how it actually operates beyond saying that such reciprocal gifts can be "soit de simples gestes amicaux, soit au contraire de véritables conventions basée sur l'intérêt" (sometimes simple friendly gestures, or sometimes on the contrary true agreements/contracts based on self interest). The difficulty with this statement is that it confounds the very Communal Sharing and Equality Matching categories we are trying to discriminate here, and it is not clear where the European preconceptions of the acts in question leave off and the Moose conceptions begin. Later, when Pageard describes the obligations of the wife-receivers after a wife is bestowed (1969:292–93), he does not mention anything about reciprocal bestowal in the other direction—suggesting that perhaps the relationship is actually CS.

In Maane, we did not observe *tekre* in wife giving, nor did Moose explain marriages with reference to quid pro quo reciprocity. Indeed, informants specifically denied that marraige could be *tekre*. Altogether, it appears that one-for-one Equality Matching exchange of wives probably does exist among Moose in some regions, but it is a minor, uncommon form. However, Tait (1961:113) notes that "exchange marriages are a normal but not very frequent form of marriage" among the Konkomba to the south, and the marriage systems he describes as predominant are similar to the Communal Sharing practices of the Moose.[35]

While Moose marriage as a whole is only occasionally structured as Equality Matching, the EM model is involved in a few details of the courtship process. Going to make a gift, a wife-seeker always finds a peer to accompany him, as he would with any other sensitive or important task. Brothers, age-mates and friends of the groom always take the major, formal gifts that are presented to the wife-givers after the wife is promised, and they bring the wife home to her husband at the final stage. The prospective husband does not go himself on any of these formal visits. Reciprocally, a man will undertake the same duties for his brothers, age-mates, and friends. Indeed, the Moose observe EM in friendship, age-mate, and peer relationships in general. The EM model is also involved in the relationship of co-wives with their joint husband: the husband is expected to be impartial and fair toward each of his wives, balancing his gifts of money and skirt cloths to each. Jealousy arises when he goes too far in giving special treatment to a favorite wife (*pog rʋmde*) or a lover (*rolle*) to the neglect of equality (see Mason 1987).

Equality Matching also may come into play in the distribution of wives within the lineage (*buudu*), particularly within a minor lineage or compound (*zaka*). Within the compound there is some tendency to allocate wives to husbands in order of seniority; that is, according to Authority Ranking. But I believe—although I do not have definitive evidence on this point—that the decision on allocating a wife also involves EM considerations. Certainly among closely related men of roughly equal age, there appears to be a tendency to give a wife to those not yet married before giving a second wife to anyone. However, a man may sometimes seek and acquire a wife largely on his own courtship initiative and keep her for himself, or simply be given a wife by someone who takes a liking to him personally, thus resulting in inequalities. And a man who takes (*rʋke*) a woman without permission—invariably a woman promised to another man—and runs off with her will also keep her for himself. Nevertheless, there seems to be a general tendency to distribute wives equally among closely related men of the same age.

Ethnographic completeness requires a final note here about an illicit form of marriage, a kind of "elopement," in which a woman runs off with a man (*zoe n dɩk sida*) who is sometimes her lover (*rolle*). Generally this is not feasible unless the man lives far from the woman's father's and husband's lineages and either his identity and her whereabouts can be concealed from them, or he is totally beyond the reach of their social influence, or the couple flees to the Ivory Coast and remains there more or less indefinitely. However, this kind of illegitimate marriage reveals something important about basic Moose conceptions of wife bestowal: even if the man's identity is discovered, no one ordinarily thinks of seeking compensation of any sort. (Rarely, EM may perhaps be involved in the settlement of such a problem, if the wife-taking lineage replaces the stolen wife by giving the injured legitimate husband another wife—which could happen only if the *tẽese* curse is not in force.)

The penalties that people do invoke include the wife's lineage and the original husband's lineage both shunning everyone in the wife-stealer's village. Often they curse the man who has taken their wife on the *tẽese* (earth altar, protective and sanctioning spirit of a Yĩyõaaga lineage), so that the wife-stealer will die if he does not return her to her rightful husband. There are good reasons to believe that the Moose construction of this kind of transgression and their actions in addressing it are constituted within the framework of Communal Sharing, but to demonstrate this would require a detailed disection of *rigi* (exile, shunning) and *tẽese*, which I will not undertake here. It may also be that CS love is frequently the motivational basis for the man and woman running off together in the first place. So even this culturally defined breach of Moose norms supports the conclusion that CS predominates in men's giving and taking of women in marriage.

## Models and Motives in Moose Social Relations

Together, these observations demonstrate that Moose marriage is structured predominantly as Communal Sharing, with aspects and phases in which Authority Ranking and—formerly—Market Pricing are operative, and occasionally Equality Matching. Generally, Moose give a wife as a gesture of affection to someone who behaves like a good son or is a good friend. The wife-seekers and the potential wife-givers do not assess the value of most of the labor, food, and money involved in the early transactions setting up the CS relationship between them. Nor do they assess the qualitites of the woman who is given in marriage in comparison with the values of the things given to her lineage. When the two parties make comparisons with other marriages, the issues they discuss have nothing to do with the features of the wife involved, but are simply a matter of trying to do what is always done, to carry out the tradition correctly—not to compare alternatives or substitutes.

Generally there is no sense of quid pro quo: if "reciprocal exchange" means getting something of equal value in return to balance or pay for what one gives, then Moose marriage is not reciprocal exchange. Communal Sharing structures the overall form of most Moose marriages, but all the other models do organize delimited phases embedded in the process. The clearest example of this is the division and distribution (*puiibu*) in which gifts to the lineage as a whole are transmitted to their ultimate recipients (see Fiske 1985, 1990).

For the most part, however, Moose do not base even bilateral, "reciprocal" transfers of women on Equality Matching. A typical explanation by a reliable senior informant of a recent bride bestowal illustrates the Moose attitude:

> If someone does something nice for you, you do something nice for him/her. Are you going to let someone help you and then forget him? If someone fixes you up (takes care of your problem), you want to help him. . . . If someone takes his daughter and gives her to you, it is because he likes you. You will like him too. If you sire a child, you give it to him. If God gives his share here [a daughter], he [the friend] will receive it.

> {I ask about the recent bestowal of a bride.} Whenever Sida goes anywhere, he comes by here, greets us and sees how we are. His thing [bride to be] is here, so he too will receive. . . . It's become an in-law relationship. . . .

> {Is it like *tekre* (an even trade)?} It's not a trade. It's because of liking a person. If it were a trade we would not agree to it.

[He tries to make me see how it is:] If you were Moose, when we chat here, it's a friend. It's friendship (*boremdo*). It starts as friendship, then becomes in-lawship. [You think to yourself,] "I am happy, so what shall I give him?" So you take your daughter and give her to him. [He repeatedly explains the wife-giving relationship in terms of liking (*nonge*) someone. He explains that for at least three generations they have been giving wives to a particular lineage, and they previously had received wives from them.]

So even when Moose "exchange" women reciprocally (bilaterally), it is almost always out of friendship and affection. No one keeps score, no one owes anything or has any rights to receive a wife in return. What motivates Moose to give women in marriage is fond paternalistic benevolence. They give women out of friendship and appreciation, as an act of kindness toward men who have been courteous, helpful, generous, and selfless.

Some social theorists may be inclined to try to explain these practices as conformity to norms, or as cultural or social "structure," taking it for granted that the subjective motives of individual agents are egoistic. But what are "norms," structure, society, and culture, if not collectively shared evaluative models of and for human action? True, people may demand things of each other that they themselves would not choose to do if left alone. But there is no a priori reason to assume that sociability must be the product of normative structure. Ethnography may be an inadequate basis for making strong inferences about motives, but the ethnography constitutes good prima facie evidence. Shall we gainsay the manifest behavior and the accounts of the Moose and say that underneath all this they "actually" have selfish ulterior motives? Shall we insist that, despite the manifest Communal Sharing and Authority Ranking of the phenomenological forms, Moose are "actually" calculating cost/benefit ratios? What would these gratuitous presuppositions about covert motives add to our understanding of their social relations? Since there is little or nothing of greater importance to Moose men than wives (and the children they bear), what possible ulterior motives could they have in giving away what they care about most in return for mere kindness? That is, when senior men give away women to men who are like sons to them, what sort of material or utilitarian self-interest could be involved that would transcend the value of the women given away? There is no evidence at all to suggest that Moose really conceive of marriage as a market-like transaction conducted with reference to the exchange ratios of the "commodities" transferred—so why posit that they do?

Of course, it may be argued that men being courted have an interest in drawing out courtship so that it lasts as long as possible, that suitors are competing for a limited supply of wives whether they construe it that way or not, and that wife-givers may choose to give wives to the most generous suitors in order to maximize the gifts they receive. Quite possibly all this is true, although I know of no evidence that it is. But if women are more valuable than anything else, then why do Moose not barter women for women, quid pro quo? Why should the Moose give up women for various gifts, a little labor, and some money (in an amount the gift givers determine on their own), and get nothing important or enduring in return? They consume and share these gifts, so they cannot convert them into wives for themselves. Why do they not insist on receiving women, land, water, or livestock in return for women? If land and water are among their scarcest and most valued resources, then why do Moose simply give them away for the asking, even to utter strangers? If labor is the principal factor in production, then why do Moose pool and share it with less productive workers and spend so much energy trading work with each other? If food is scarce, why pool it with those who contribute little or nothing, and why offer hospitality to visitors, including strangers? If all people are at bottom selfish individualists, why do the Moose organize all these activities corporately, pooling and sharing communally what they value most?

Does their culture deny Moose any framework in which to express their material self-interest and give them no opportunity to maximize their true utilities directly? To accept this "normative" account is to admit that their cultural models have determinate directive force regarding their overt behavior, while continuing to assert that individual Moose would be selfish "if they could." Yet the Moose as a society and as individuals are strikingly attached to their culture—it is hard to imagine making any kind of plausible case for a major discrepancy between personality and culture among Moose. There is no support for this kind of "culture-distance" hypothesis. The motives of Moose agents, the structural forces of their society, and their cultural conceptions of their action appear to coincide. The strength and force of Moose adherence to their traditional culture is enormous, perhaps unsurpassed anywhere in the world. There are few "defectors" from Moose culture. On the contrary, Moose have maintained their culture strikingly intact and continue to carry on their traditions with extreme tenacity (see Pacere [1979] for a passionate defense of Moose culture). So there is no reason to believe that the phenomenology of Moose social relations is discrepant with their personal motives. Moose are committed and engaged in the social relationships in which they participate.

Quite simply, Moose ultimately care about solidarity, belonging, cohesiveness, and mutuality more than anything else. It is friendship, respect, loyalty and courtesy that really matter; if you have that kind of relationship with someone, then you want to be generous and beneficent to them. And you want to trust and depend on them. Even where we might expect to see individual self-interest come to the fore in litigation, it is by no means prominent. After four years on the bench trying Moose cases, the jurist Pageard (1969:21–22) introduces his two-volume compilation of Moose law by emphasizing their corporate orientation and the fact that for Moose, material goods are never ends in themselves, nor are they instruments of power.

Moose do not only—or even primarily—want personal wealth or individual prestige, they want to create and maintain relationships of kindness, of deference and responsibility, and of equality. They seek to participate in these social relationships because the relationships are intrinsically fulfilling in and of themselves—not in order to accomplish anything else by means of their engagement in the relationships. The social relationships as such, particularly Communal Sharing, are far more important than material goods, even among these, the poorest people in the world. As individuals, Moose do not maximize either material goods or the culturally focal good (and fitness constraint), women. They work together, eat together, drink together, give wives together, and take women in marriage together, as corporate groups, in a spirit of solidarity and unity.

# 13

## Authority Ranking:
## *Precedence and Deference*

Village communities [in Africa] are usually organized in lineages within
which relations of production are perceived as relations of personal
dependence between the elders and the junior members. They are
based on both direct and indirect control of the means of human
reproduction, in the last resort, subsistence and women. . . . Goods
circulate through a network of kinship, affinity, and clientage, through
prestation, redistribution, or gift exchange. Wealth, as an instrument of
social control, is a privilege of rank or birth. All other means of
acquiring wealth—through labour, specialization, or commerce—are
threats to the foundations of the community, whenever they favour
elements traditionally outside the power structure. The social
hierarchy and the authority system being linked to a mode of
prestatory and distributive circulation, goods acquire a social and
political content which makes it difficult to transform them into trade
commodities. . . . This system is incompatible with trade. (Meillassoux
1971:60–61)

In the previous chapter we saw that Authority Ranking is a significant secondary organizing principle in the bestowal of women in marriage among the
Moose. While it is less pervasive than Communal Sharing, even a cursory look
at Moose society shows that Authority Ranking is a widespread and important
model governing and motivating much of Moose social relations. In the first
section of this chapter, I will offer a very brief overview of the prominent place
of Authority Ranking relations in Moose society. However, it would be redundant to dwell on Authority Ranking at great length here, because Dim
Delobsom (1933), Skinner (1964a), Kawada (1979), and Izard (1985) have all

written books showing the importance of political structures in Moose society. But, since these writers demonstrate that Authority Ranking is very salient in Moose social relations, it behooves me to show why I think that Communal Sharing, not Authority Ranking, is the dominant form of social relationship. So the bulk of this chapter compares the relative force and prevalence of Authority Ranking and Communal Sharing in situations where there is a perceived choice or potential conflict between the two.

Authority Ranking is widespread in Moose society. Some relevant facts have already come out. We saw that the head of each communal corporate field and separate field group directs the labor and controls the grain produced. Similarly, the outcome of courtship (*belõgo*) is dependent on the personal will of the head of the lineage (*kasma*) and, secondarily, on that of the father of the girl who may eventually be given. On the receiving end, when people give a wife to the head of a lineage he has the unilateral power to either marry her or pass her on to one of his juniors. But there are numerous other Moose manifestations of the AR model.

Moose Authority is strictly rank-ordered. Thus a disputant who wants his case heard must take it to the immediately senior male, who in turn may take it on the disputant's behalf to the compound head. The head of the lineage will not hear a case unless it is brought through the head of the compound, and the village chief will not judge (*bʋ*) a case unless it is brought to him by the head of the relevant lineage. The paramount chief (*kombere*) will only hear cases presented by village chiefs or their emissaries. Everything has to go through the proper hierarchical channels. For example, important news and information is transmitted from the top down, just as we saw that the Moose give women in marriage up through the hierarchy of the giving lineage and then down through the hierarchy of the receiving lineage. The hierarchy extends beyond the living to the dead: the eldest male of the core lineage must conduct all sacrifices to the lineage ancestors at their lineage altar (*kʋmse*), and his invocation in such a sacrifice invokes the ancestors in strict reverse order, the most recent first. He addresses his ancestors asking the most recent to receive and transmit the sacrifice to his predecessor, and so on. Should the sacrificer leave out a name, the Moose say that the ancestors will punish him with death.

Moose constantly mark relative ranks in everyday life by terms of address and reference, by greeting postures and deferential postures in formal settings, by dress, by gaze, and by the speed and loudness of speech. Moose leaders have tremendous authority, authority that is, in principle, virtually unlimited within its traditional sphere of prerogatives. Indeed, as Weber (1978) shows in his discussions of charisma and traditional authority, the essence of personal authority is that the person who has it can give arbitrary commands, commands whose only grounds are that they are the will of the commander (see Fiske 1985). What is right is what the authority wills. A Moose chief is said to *soa* ("own," control, or have responsibility for) the people of the village, the head of the compound "owns" all the people in the compound, and a husband "owns" his wife and children. This means that in principle each of these people can command others to do things, without explanation or justification. In particular, rank confers control over the labor of others, including the overall direction of the communal cultivation of fields. Hierarchical superiors constantly send their inferiors (particularly but not exclusively children) on errands and the like. (Nevertheless, passive noncompliance is relatively common—the person sent to do something goes off, but does nothing.)

Ideally, a Moose authority can simply appropriate whatever of his people's possessions it pleases him to take, since all his subjects or dependents belong to him in the first place. Before the superordinate colonial powers imposed limitations on their indigenous subordinates, both paramount and village chiefs would sometimes simply expropriate their subjects' livestock or other possessions. It is said that this occasionally included taking the daughters of subjects to marry. As a minor contemporary example, our village Chief sent a boy to get a bench from us to seat visitors. Although Moose are generally quite careful to return borrowed property, the Chief never returned the bench. On another occasion the Chief saw a coil of rope in our compound, commented that he needed to make a bridle, and simply left with it. However, authority also entails proprietary responsibility for dependents, including the duty to protect dependents with the necessary sacrifices and ensure their safety from outside predation. Furthermore, people would flee a rapacious or tyrannical chief, compound head, or husband, and he would be left, abandoned, as "owner" of no one.

Moose not only exercise power and assert precedence, they place a very high value on it: they regard respect and deference, together with the responsible exercise of pastoral authority, as legitimate and necessary.[1] In the previous two chapters we saw that Communal Sharing is also a pervasive and very highly valued orientation in Moose social relations, so it is appropriate to consider how we can compare Authority Ranking with Communal Sharing in terms of their prevalence across social settings and their relative importance as cultural values and personal motives.

## PRIORITIES: THE CHOICE BETWEEN AUTHORITY AND COMMUNITY

In the domains we considered above—labor, food, water, ritual, sacrifice, and marriage—Communal Sharing is the predominant model, although it is often linked with Authority Ranking. In fact, people in many societies link Communal Sharing and Authority Ranking together in some domains, as Weber's

(1978 [1922]) analysis of his ideal type of *traditional authority* shows: he conflates the two modes in one ideal type that corresponds to a common combination of the two. But while AR and CS often co-occur, they are logically distinct. And, as Weber's delineation of charismatic authority demonstrates and many ethnographic examples attest, CS and AR frequently occur quite independently of each other. Furthermore, both CS and AR motives are at an equally high level in the human motivational hierarchy, in that they are independent of each other—neither is intrinsically a means to the other.

However, the major theme of Part IV is that in Moose culture Communal Sharing and Authority Ranking are not equally important in their ideological valuation, as normative obligations, or—for the most part—in their directive force as individual motives. While Moose are often oriented toward Authority Ranking, Communal Sharing is preferred and is more prevalent: Moose pursue goals involving power, authority, and rank less often and generally less forcefully than they pursue goals involving solidarity, collective identity, unity and food sharing. As we saw in Chapter 10, Equality Matching is also important in Moose society, though considerably less pervasive than either CS or AR. Market Pricing is the least powerful directive force in Moose social relations, and its manifestations are much more circumscribed, especially within the village setting.

What is the basis for these inferences about cultural preferences among the four basic models and about differential prevalence? Margaret Mead (1937:459–60) observes that to classify a social system as competitive, cooperative, or individualistic we need to examine the principal ends to which individuals and groups direct their action, together with the proportions of time and energy devoted to each kind of end.[2] Significantly, she notes that although it is difficult to do this kind of comparison quantitatively, all the participants in her book seminar were unanimous in their classifications of all thirteen cultures they studied. Independently of Mead (but citing Ruth Benedict's *Patterns of Culture*), Mary Douglas (1978) proposes a scheme for comparing cultures based on the relative importance of *grid* versus *group*, for which Gross and Rayner (1985) propose measurement scales that purport to operationalize the dimensions. However, Mead, Douglas, and Gross and Rayner are concerned only with categorizing entire cultures as wholes and do not address the somewhat more complex problem of ranking motives ordinally within a culture according to either prevalence or preference. Let us consider how that might be done.

To make statements about prevalence, one would ideally like to have a complete inventory of all the domains or settings in Moose social life, or a random sample of all social interactions. I do not have data of this type, so the reader will have to rely to some extent on my subjective impressions, but I hope I have already conveyed something of the pervasiveness of Communal Sharing in Moose life. In principle it would be possible to go through the list of domains of social action and thought outlined in Part II (see Table 1), showing that in all or most of these spheres of Moose social life, Communal Sharing predominates over the others. But rather than doing this or describing additional domains that Moose organize according to the CS model, I would now like to address the general issue of the comparative potency for Moose of CS and Authority Ranking motivation—which has the greater force? That is, when the two are alternatives, which prevails? Since the CS and AR orientations are the two most prevalent and the two closest both in relative prevalence and in relative value, it is worthwhile to compare Moose priorities between the two models. This analysis of the relative normative and motivational force of Communal Sharing and Authority Ranking is the topic of the remainder of this chapter. In the following chapter I will complement this by depicting the place of Market Pricing in Moose social relationships and the overall ranking of the MP model compared to the other three basic forms.

My goal here goes beyond understanding Moose society or showing that the three other social modes predominate over Market Pricing. I intend to explore the problem of how to assess (within a culture) the relative directive force of alternative models for social relationships. In Chapters 11 and 12, I argued that the Moose utilization of their most valuable "resources" in a Communal Sharing manner indicates that CS generally takes precedence over other models. The examples I offer in this and the next chapter will illustrate a second general strategy for within-culture analyses of the motivational strength and cultural valuation of alternative relational models. To show that Communal Sharing dominates or has greater directive force in a moral and motivational sense, the strategy that I adopt here is to analyze situations in which CS and Authority Ranking are more or less mutually exclusive so that there is a direct conflict or subjective choice between the two. Let us look at some such situations.

Dilemmas that require the Moose to choose between Communal Sharing and Authority Ranking seem to be very rare. As Fortes (1969, 1970) pointed out, for the most part prescriptive altruism (CS) is the essence of kinship, as well as the direct corollary of neighborhood, clanship, and ethnic bonds. As such, Communal Sharing usually is a kind of immanent fact—it is just given in the nature of people's social identity. Moose usually regard CS relationships as a product of birth (*rogm*), not something that can be chosen or negotiated. Similarly, there are few situations in which Authority Ranking is negotiable. Usually one's rank is objectively given and unalterable—ascribed. There is nothing one can do to acquire additional authority or prerogatives except to grow older. Rank is determined by relative age, gender, clan, and ethnicity. People of Euro-American culture (whatever their race, nationality, or ethnic origins) are accorded high rank; otherwise, older people outrank younger people and men outrank women. People usually know their ages relative to other people quite precisely (though not their absolute ages). There are few ambiguities about the obligations and ideals of Authority Ranking, the domain application rules are well delineated, and relative rank is usually unalterable. Since

Moose generally treat both sharing and ranking as unalterable brute facts, there is typically no choice to be made about when or how to apply either one. Hence Moose rarely perceive Communal Sharing and Authority Ranking as alternatives to choose between.

But sometimes there is room for negotiation about the intensity of Communal Sharing and its application to particular cases, since group membership—referred to as *buudu* (lineage at each level, clan, ethnicity, race, kind)—along with the motives and obligations it entails, is a shifter (Galaty 1982) whose meaning depends on how it is used. On the other side, authority depends on appointive office as well as on unalterable facts of birth: electors name the paramount chief, the paramount chief appoints village chiefs, and the chiefs at both levels select court officials. Occasionally there is even some uncertainty about relative ages. Competition for claims to office or ambiguity about relative rank may offer occasions in which pursuing the office (AR motivation) and maintaining communal solidarity with others (CS motivation) are to some degree incompatible. These occasions are relatively rare but worth examining. Let us look at the available cases.

### Succession to Office and Community Solidarity

The Yĩyõose are the people who claim descent from the original inhabitants of the land, and they have a special ritual relationship with the Earth and its associated powers. The head (*buud kasma*) of a Yĩyõose lineage is custodian of its ancestor altar (*Kumse*), the lineage's principal protective shrine (*tẽese*), and its mask, which is also a ritual object. The lineage head officiates at all its collective rituals, gives and receives on behalf of his lineage all women bestowed in marriage, and represents the lineage on formal occasions, including village-wide sacrifices, the chief's annual day (*Kiuugu*), or disputes brought before the chief. The lineage head also receives tributary gifts on a great many occasions. So the headship of a Yĩyõose lineage is in all respects an important office. A couple of years before we arrived in the village the head of one of the two Yĩyõose lineages in the village died. After his burial and later funeral, the lineage had to decide who should succeed to his office. Without exception, the eldest male in the lineage [3] becomes the lineage head. But three men over 70 each claimed to be the eldest. The reason for the ambiguity was that they were very close in age, and two of them had been raised by their maternal grandmothers (as is common) and had only returned to the village as adults. Small differences in relative age (less than a year or so) are of virtually no significance in any other situation. One of the men was already the head of a related lineage and holder of its sacred xylophone; many people felt that he could not logically be head of both lineages. But he persisted in his claims. Eventually the claim was resolved by divination, with one of the losers saying that "time would tell." By this he referred to the well-known fact that the ancestors would kill anyone who wrongfully usurped the office.[4] Evidently the dispute was the source of considerable tension.

The key fact of this case is that it did not result in fission of the lineage, or in a breakdown of the communal relationship the lineage represents. While neither of the unsuccessful claimants would attend most lineage rituals, both regularly sent young kinsmen as representatives, regularly made the requisite contributions to lineage sacrifices, and received their due shares of sacrificial beer and meat. They also gave and received wives through the man exercising the office of lineage head, and in general participated directly or indirectly in all the activities of the lineage. Neither disguised his bitterness or sense of injustice, but neither split the lineage—nor attempted to do so. If the Authority Ranking motives of the losers had been stronger than their Communal Sharing motives, they might have attempted to split off their dependents into an independent lineage that they would head. Or the dispute might have led to irreconcilable enmity, even violence. But in fact communal unity prevailed over Authority Ranking power-seeking ambitions.

Let us examine a similar situation among the Nakomse nobility of the village we studied. When a village chief dies in the Maane chiefdom, his successor is named by the Paramount Chief (*Kombere*). The eldest son of the previous village chief is the most likely candidate and the previous chief's eldest brother is another alternative, but the Paramount Chief may name anyone he pleases from among the Nakomse clan, the descendants of former chiefs. In principle, though not in current practice, he may even take someone from outside and place him at the head of the village. During the interregnum, which may last for two or more years after a village chief dies, the Paramount Chief receives gifts from all the contenders, who try to keep their aspirations secret. People do not publicly discuss what is going on, but the contenders' identities become known. When there are three or four or more chiefships to bestow, the Paramount Chief holds a ceremony and names the new chief of each village.

A few years before our arrival the Paramount Chief had named a man only about 30 years of age as chief of the village where we later resided. He was the youngest of 35 village chiefs in the region. In doing this the Paramount Chief passed over an older man who had expected to get the office and displayed extreme anger at not being appointed. He continued to be bitter but resigned about it. Yet he remained in the village, associated with the new chief in an appropriate way, and maintained a collaborative and respectful relationship with him as far as I could discover. As is sometimes the case, the three adjacent but separately walled compounds of their lineage maintained a social identity as a single *zaka* and continued to pool labor and resources in apparently normal ways. For example, all the men ate together in the yard outside the walled compounds. The women of each compound brought food out to the chief, who ate some and then passed it on to the group of other men a short distance away. Under the egis of the chief they sacrificed together like any lineage.

Such ritual and daily food-sharing is the prime constitutive enactment of Moose Communal Sharing.

My nearest neighbors and two of my best informants belonged to another Nakomse lineage that had previously held the Chiefship of the village through several successions, until the Paramount Chief shifted it some decades before to the lineage of the current Chief. My neighbors occasionally expressed some hard feelings about this to me in private, but they maintained perfectly proper relations with the Chief and his compound. They respected the Chief, cooperated amicably, were included in all the appropriate rituals and participated properly. (Like any independent lineage compound, they had their own separate grinding platform, farmed, and ate separately from the current chief's people.)

Shortly before our arrival in the village the *Yiraana* (religious leader cum "chief") who led the Yarse segment of our village died, and the next year the chief of a neighboring village died. (The offices were finally filled four or five years later, after we had left the village.) During the two years following these deaths, at least, I never detected or heard of any negative consequences from the competition on the solidarity of the Yarse. There may well have been tensions, possibly severe ones, and there may possibly have been social consequences of which I was unaware. But apparently in these cases, too, the struggle for power did not jeopardize the fundamental solidarity of the social groups involved, and their corporate unity certainly was unbroken. They pitched in energetically to dig a well together and cooperated in all kinds of joint rituals.

These chiefly offices are very important to all the aspirants, but nonetheless the Communal Sharing relations of the lineage neighborhoods involved seem to have been maintained. In no case did Authority Ranking motives give rise to even a potential split in the lineages or neighborhoods involved. Perhaps this should come as no surprise. After all, modern Western communities and nations rarely come apart over competition for power—"patriotism" and collective solidarity hold our societies together despite political struggles. But if power, authority, and rank were really the fundamental determinant forces shaping our social lives, then bitter factionalism and endless strife should be the social reality. Yet the manifest fact is that within communities on all levels up to the nation, the struggle for political power in modern states is generally tempered, moderated, and abated by a sense of common identity and solidarity. Of course, power-seeking sometimes does overcome the need for community, and both contemporary nations and many historical empires and kingdoms have been rent by struggles over succession. In the history of Moose emperors there have been intrigues, battles, and wars over succession to office. But at least in the village today the solidarity and shared identity of Communal Sharing relations appear to be stronger than any divisive antagonism that might be a product of belligerent Authority Ranking power struggles. Perhaps these few cases are atypical, and doubtless there was more strain than appeared on the surface. But the fact remains that the modal pattern is the maintenance of the communal group's integrity in the face of political intrigues and infighting. In part the divisive potential of political office-seeking is obviated by the fact that the Paramount Chief appoints people to the offices of village Chief and *Yiraana*; office-seekers do not compete for supporters and followers. Lineage headship is not appointive, however; yet there is no evidence of Moose lineages splitting over battles for succession.

Moose assiduously avoid appearing to usurp the proper sphere of any other person's authority or pretending to authority that they do not definitely have. As we saw above, they are very reluctant to reveal that they are seeking traditional office. One result is that when people actually do have ambitious Authority Ranking goals, they pursue them covertly, through the secret use of magic (*tum*). There are different kinds of amulets whose function is to help a person be appointed chief, or promoted foreman of a work team in the Ivory Coast, or get ahead in other ways.[5] These amulets are widely available and seem widely used, and Moose assume that office-seekers in particular use them assiduously. While the use of such amulets suggests that covert Authority Ranking motives are important, it is essential to stress that their use is covert because it is illicit. One reason that any overt power-seeking is illegitimate may be that Moose perceive overt competition for leadership as inconsistent with the undifferentiated solidarity and unity of the community. And the unity of the group comes first.

The conclusion that Communal Sharing has greater directive force than Authority Ranking among Moose is reinforced by the diffidence that Moose display about seeking office in such recently introduced institutions as the young men's work group and cooperative (*Jeunesse*). The villagers seem to model their participation in the youth coop with reference to the indigenous Equality Matching work groups of peers described above (in the last section of Chapter 10). In its modern form, however, the youth coop was set up along more Market Pricing lines by the agricultural extension agent of the governmental Regional Development Organization, which continues to monitor it. There is also an agricultural credit coop composed of adult men from Habra and surrounding villages, set up and supported by the Dutch ADRK. In both of these groups Moose typically display reluctance and embarrassment in offering themselves as candidates for election to office and to some extent in asserting authority in these roles. This discomfort reflects the extreme diffidence the Moose commonly exhibit in asserting any authority or claiming the prerogatives of rank unless they hold a major traditional office and are operating within a clearly defined traditional context, or else are elders dealing with their own dependents. Moose often reply to questions about group plans, decisions, or rituals with, "I don't know anything, I'm just a youngster; you'll have to ask the old men." Even the elders often answer this way! Such statements mean, among other things, "It's not up to me, I don't have any say or any choice in the matter, it's a question of tradition." In general, what Moose do collectively expresses who they are as a Communal Sharing corporation and not the personal will of particular leaders. Communality predominates over Authority Ranking.

## Use of Collective Grain Stores

The most common circumstance in which Authority Ranking might seem to be at odds with Communal Sharing is in a farming group leader's daily stewardship of communal labor and grain stocks. We saw above that Moose usually farm together as a communal group with their closest kin and wives. As I described, the group that farms together at the highest level cultivates a corporate field, while subgroups typically farm separate fields of their own in the very early morning and late afternoon. (The senior man may help his wives or younger brothers with their separate fields when he has time, and members of separate fields may also help each other.) The group of people farming together at either level plants, cultivates, and harvests in a Communal Sharing mode, but under the Authority Ranking direction of the senior man or woman in the group. This senior person makes decisions about when to plant, weed, and harvest, and controls the distribution of the grain harvested, and the senior person provides food for all the group's members during the cultivating season. But he is also free to dispose of the grain for personal ends, without discussing the matter or accounting to anyone else. In a sense, the harvest of the field is his own personal grain, and unlike most of his dependents, he has no other private store of grain. So there is a potential conflict between the senior person's personal "ownership" of the harvest in the framework of Authority Ranking and his or her stewardship of the grain as a trustee on behalf of the collectivity in the framework of Communal Sharing. Moose are cognizant of this issue, but surprisingly I do not recall and cannot locate in my field notes any disputes, gossip, or private recriminations about proprietors' failure to feed dependents. What this suggests is that villagers rarely perceive heads of cultivating groups as abusing their Authority Ranking control over the food to the detriment of their communal obligations. In part, this seems to reflect the fact that pastoral responsibility for the welfare of subordinates is an essential component of the Authority Ranking model, and failure to provide for dependents is a serious breach of the relationship. Moose authorities are trustees, not competitive entrepreneur-owners, ambitious status-seeking bosses, or power-hungry tyrants. Richards (1969 [1939]) is quite lucid in making the same point about why Bemba chiefs in Zambia lavishly feed guests, dependents, members of the court, and tributary workers:

> The whole of this system of distributing food is of course necessary to the chief if he is to make gardens and conduct tribal business through his councillors. But it is more than this. The giving of food, as in most African tribes, is an absolutely essential attribute of chieftainship, just as it is of authority in the village or household, and the successful

organization of supplies at the capital seems to be associated in the
Bemba mind with the security and well-being of the whole tribe itself.
This fact may be said to be symbolized by the institution of the sacred
kitchen (*kamitembo*) at the courts of the big chiefs [where the hearth
fire burns eternally]. (Richards 1969 [1939]:148)

Furthermore, Richards stresses that

The chief seems to have aimed at having just sufficient crops to put
him in a position of security, but not at increasing his supplies
indefinitely. To-day the big chiefs make proper gardens every two
years. . .and fill enormous granaries which they reckon to last for two
seasons or more. They definitely do not try to produce the maximum
amount of food possible each year, as the following table shows. It
appears that this was always the custom even when labour was easier
to get. (Richards 1969:215)

Bemba chiefs receive tribute in labor and kind, but Richards (1969:260–66)
points out that this does not constitute a rent conceived of as a fixed rate of
exchange. Instead, commoners give tribute in obeisant fealty, while chiefs provide the land their subjects need out of patriarchal—or perhaps pastoral—largesse.

Elias (1956:164–65) makes a similar point about the nature of African dominion, stressing that African political authorities hold the land in trust for the
people as a whole: "The African chief or king . . . enjoys only an administrative
right of supervisory oversight of the land for the benefit of the whole community." Despite working within a Marxist paradigm, Suret-Canale (1964:30–34)
reaches the same conclusion on the basis of his survey of the African literature. Rather than conflicting in this regard, Communal Sharing and Authority
Ranking may actually pull in the same direction. To the extent that a Moose
authority construes his subject-dependents as components of his extended
self, CS and AR will not conflict. To the extent that Moose perceive the two
to be at odds, it appears that once again Communal Sharing takes precedence.
This seems true quite generally in Africa. As Coquery-Vidrovitch (1969:75–76)
points out, precolonial African regimes, however despotic, almost never at-
tacked the communal basis of village agriculture.

## Allocation of Wives

A possible source of conflict between Communal Sharing and Authority
Ranking, and between both of these and Equality Matching, arises in the allocation of new wives. Rank is a determining factor, since older Moose men usually get wives before younger ones. The critical question is, who gets subsequent wives—does the lineage-neighborhood head (*sak kasma*) or compound

head take a second wife before giving one to a younger member of the lineage, or does he pass on women until every man has at least one?

Empirically, investigating this question is complicated by the fact that there are several other factors besides allocation through the lineage that affect the number of wives a man has. Men also have wives—typically former lovers (*rolba*)—whom they personally stole from other men in distant districts (or who were exiled from their first husband's village for witchcraft). Conversely, some Habra men have lost wives who ran away or were expelled for witchcraft, and some wives have died. When men die, their wives are inherited by younger lineage-mates, typically men within the same compound, generally younger brothers or sons of the deceased. Also, the initiative in different courtship efforts may be centered in either senior or junior men in the lineage and compound, although generally all members participate when needed. When a junior man has independently pursued the courtship more or less on his own, if the wife-givers give a daughter it will be to him personally, I believe.

So the distribution of wives reflects a variety of historical circumstances, not simply the decisions of the head (*kasma*) of the group concerned. An appreciable minority of wives were not transmitted through either the lineage head or the compound head or if they were so transmitted, he had no real possibility of deciding how to allocate them. It is also difficult to know how to weigh Moose norms about the appropriate age for men to marry. Does the fact that men first marry in their late twenties to mid thirties reflect the weight of male ranking and the consequent control of senior men over the allocation of wives? Or does it reflect ideas about maturity, responsibility, or the nature of procreation? The issue could be addressed, but I do not have the relevant data. Calculations of the number of wives married to different men is also complicated by the problem of whom to count as a "wife." Is a remarried widow in her fifties a "wife" (*paga*) or "mother" (*ma*)? There is some real ambiguity about these terms and these statuses for Moose, as well as for the analyst.

But given these complications, a look at the demographic statistics may still provide some indication of how Moose weigh AR and CS in the distribution of wives. Table 2 gives figures on the mean number of wives of husbands in different age brackets. It shows that men age 51 and over average slightly fewer wives than men of ages 41 to 50, and have approximately the same number of wives as men of ages 31 to 40, despite the fact that there is a considerable difference in authority rank over this age span.[6]

If we examine the pattern within each physical compound (*zaka*), we obtain congruent results, as Table 3 shows. This table compares the number of wives of the compound head and the number of wives of the other resident compound member who has the greatest number of wives. The compound head is as likely to have fewer wives than some other man in his compound (10 cases) as he is to have more (9 cases). There are three compounds where the compound head has at least two more wives than any other resident, and three in which another resident has at least two more wives than the compound head.

**Table 2** Mean Number of Wives by Husband's Age

| Age of Husband | Mean Number of Wives | Number of Men | Number of Wives |
|---|---|---|---|
| 51+ | 1.48 | 23 | 34 |
| 41–50 | 1.74 | 23 | 40 |
| 31–40 | 1.40 | 52 | 73 |
| 26–30 | .90 | 42 | 38 |
| 20–25 | .23 | 52 | 12 |
| Total | 1.03 | 192 | 197 |

NOTE: These figures are based on the total population of Habra, but exclude five women married to five young males who were aged 4, 12, 15, 17, and 19. Most of these were women past child-bearing who had chosen to be inherited by boy husbands. This is a way of remaining in the compound while retaining more autonomy than they would have had as wives of older men.

The distribution is quite symmetrical, suggesting that headship of a compound—Authority Ranking—plays little or no role in the preferential acquisition of wives.

The implication is that, while Authority Ranking plays a role in the distribution of wives, it does not outweigh Communal Sharing. This accords with the qualitative impression that compound heads are genuinely concerned with obtaining wives for their juniors. Men often begin courtship explicitly on behalf of sons who are still small children—or when the man beginning the courtship may be too old to have much chance of seeing the fruits of his efforts in his own lifetime. In sum, although seniority in age or rank gives precedence in acquiring wives, and although young men have to wait their turn,

**Table 3** Difference Between Number of Wives of Compound Head (*Zak Soba*) and Compound Resident with Greatest Number of Wives

*Difference in Number of Wives*
*(Wives of Compound Head Minus Wives of Resident with Greatest Number)*

| Compound Head Has More Wives | | Same | Another Compound Member Has More Wives | |
|---|---|---|---|---|
| 2 more | 1 more | 0 | 1 less | 2 less |
| 3 | 6 | 5 | 7 | 3 |

NOTE: A compound (*zaka*) is defined here as a geographic or architectural unit surrounded by a common wall. The calculations are based only on resident compound members with at least one wife. The figures shown exclude eight compounds in which there was only one married male resident, and one for which we do not have adequate data.

senior men do not monopolize women.[7] A compound head or lineage head does not use his control over land and labor to court exclusively for himself as an individual, and he does not use his control over the disposition of wives to retain for himself most of the wives given to the lineage as a collectivity. In principle, the possibility exists for elders to use their privilege of allocating wives to retain junior men in their coterie and thereby maintain their authority and status. But Moose lineage heads do not seem to "abuse" these powers very often. Indeed Moose lineages continue to court wives on behalf of long-absent migrants, calling them back when it is time for the new wife to take up residence with the migrant husband.

Above all else, Moose authorities are embodiments of the communal collectivity. Balima (n.d.) sums up in a description that unwittingly recapitulates Weber's (1978 [1922]) ideal type of *traditional authority*, writing that the Moogo Naaba ("Emperor") reigns, but custom governs:

> Le principe c'est que ses décisions ne sont pas prises selon sa volonté et moins encore selon sa fantaisie ou selon son bon plaisir. . . . Il est l'esclave de la loi, de la coutume ou ensemble des traditions séculaires dont le respect, aux dires des Anciens, a assuré la vie et la gloire du pays. Toute sa vie et réglée par la coutume. . . . Un chef est un modèle et un example. C'est sur lui que les communs se règlent. (Balima n.d.:24–25)

> (The principle is that his decisions are not made according to his will or still less according to his fantasy or his arbitrary whim. . . . He is the slave of the law, of custom or the collection of secular traditions respect for which, according to the Ancestors, has guaranteed the life and glory of the country. His whole life is regulated by custom. . . . A chief is a model and an example. It is on him that the collectivity [the common people] orders itself.)

In other words, the community comes first, and the personal decision-making authority of even the Emperor himself is subordinated to the communal welfare.

The comparisons in this chapter show that in the relatively exceptional cases where it is problematic which of the two models will apply, in Moose society Communal Sharing generally predominates over Authority Ranking. As we have already seen, Communal Sharing is far more prevalent. Indeed, the evidence I presented earlier indicates that the CS model pervades Moose social relationships. CS dominates in the organization of production and controls the distribution and transfer of critical resources. In Moose society, Authority Ranking is often incorporated into the overarching communal scheme of social relations in the form of an authority to whom people entrust their collective resources, typically a male elder or chief who acts on behalf of the communal group, directs it, and makes decisions for it. In these circumstances the pastoral responsibilities of the authority are usually congruent with the communal needs of the collectivity that he heads. Even power struggles rarely split Moose communal groups. There are a few tyrants and ambitious cut-throats among the Moose, as anywhere. But for the most part, Moose author-ities are shepherds, not ravenous wolves.

Moose society suggests that social relations based on rank and authority are neither more natural nor more fundamental than social relations based on communal solidarity and unity. Marx describes this fact with reference to pu-tative historical processes by which Authority Ranking might arise:

> It is of course very simple to imagine that some powerful, physically dominant individual, after first having caught the animal, then catches humans in order to have them catch animals; in a word, uses human beings as another naturally occurring condition for his reproduction (whereby his own labour reduces itself to ruling) like any other natural creature. But such a notion is stupid—correct as it may be from the standpoint of some particular given clan or commune—because it proceeds from the development of *isolated individuals*. But human beings become individuals only through the process of history. [The person] appears originally as a *species-being, clan being, herd animal. . . .* Exchange itself is a chief means of this individuation. (Marx 1973:496 [1857-8]—emphasis in the original)

We do not need to accept Marx's historical framework to recognize the basic truth of his dictum that the collective solidarity and identification with one's own kind of Communal Sharing is as fundamental and natural a form of human relations as either the individuation of Market Pricing or the hege-mony of Authority Ranking over others' labor. Contrary to Marx, the evidence we have reviewed indicates that Authority Ranking is intrinsic in human social nature—but this evidence also shows that Authority Ranking is no more natu-ral or inevitable a form of social relations than Communal Sharing, Equality Matching, or Market Pricing. Indeed for Moose, Communal Sharing has greater directive force than Authority Ranking. CS is more prevalent, and where they are alternatives, CS is a stronger motive and is valued more highly than Authority Ranking. This preference and priority of CS over AR is proba-bly true of many contexts in many African societies, although there are cer-tainly instances in all societies in which political struggles end in factionalism and fission. And in many of the world's societies, Authority Ranking may in-deed take precedence over Communal Sharing. It depends on the cultural im-plementation rules for applying and realizing the four models in the diverse domains of social life.

# 14

# Economic Rationality

This chapter describes and discusses the operation of Market Pricing in Moose society. Market Pricing is manifest as a culturally defined and traditional but highly circumscribed form of social relations. Moose organize few of their social relationships with reference to prices or rates of exchange. All men go to work as wage laborers in the Ivory Coast but they do so primarily because of their late age of marriage, the need to pay the family's head taxes, and severe scarcity of arable land—not out of an entrepreneurial desire to maximize their personal material gain. Even Moose businessmen and craftsmen are not apt to organize their operations like those of market enterprises or economic firms, often not calculating profits or accumulating capital and rarely choosing individual advancement over Communal Sharing. The distinguishing feature of Market Pricing is an orientation to socially significant ratios (prices, rates of exchange, interest rates, wages per unit of work, "utility") measured according to a multidimensional, intermodal standard of value that can be compared across all commodities in the market. (Such standards are multidimensional because they are measures that aggregate many value-relevant features in a single quantity.) Only in very limited contexts do Moose organize their social relations with reference to such a standard.

We have seen that Moose organize their social relations primarily within the framework of Communal Sharing, often in conjunction with Authority Ranking. Equality Matching is present but subsidiary. However, in certain restricted contexts Moose also operate in the framework of Market Pricing. Markets, the sale of commodities, and long-distance commercial expeditions have long existed in traditional forms. Furthermore, colonial practices—especially the annual per capita tax, obligatory planting of cash crops for export, and forced levees of laborers for plantations and public works—were explicitly designed to force people into the Market Pricing sphere, which formerly had

324

occupied a very circumscribed place in social relations (see Skinner 1965 and Pageard 1969:417, who cites Delobsom).

As Skinner (1962) describes in his classic article, markets as such are a well established element in the traditional culture, as indeed they are all over West Africa. Moose hold each market every three days. There are four major markets and two minor ones in the Maane district, for a population (in 1975) of about 30,000 people. People from outside the district also attend these markets, and Maane people may go to markets in other districts. The minor markets may be attended by only as few as perhaps 100 buyers and sellers, while the major markets attract crowds of thousands, especially in the dry season. Virtually everything Moose produce or make is available for sale in the markets, as well as manufactured and imported goods like bicycle parts, Western used clothing, sugar, cigarettes, matches, batteries, and—in the biggest regional markets and associated shops—lamps, metal pots, bicycles, "Dutch wax" cotton cloth, patent medicines, flour, corrugated metal roofing, bottled beer and soft drinks, and all sorts of other goods. Traditionally cowrie shells—*ligidi peelga*—were formerly used as currency; they had—and still have—important ritual uses as well. Now modern West African currency serves the monetary functions of cowrie shells. Prices are stated and calculated in units of *wakiri*, which equals five francs CFA. Moose often have little cash, so people commonly bring something to sell, take the money and spend it on whatever they came for, leaving with little or no currency in hand again. As Skinner (1962) points out, however, people often come to the market more for the social occasion than to buy or sell commodities (see Pageard 1969:414–15).

A person who wishes to sell (*koose*) something sits in the section of the market where commodities of that type are displayed and sets out his or her wares, typically grouped in piles according to their asking price (to fix an offering price is *saage*). Since a given type of commodity is sold by a set of adjacent people in a single area of the market, people can readily compare prices. Buyers ask for offering prices without incurring any commitment. A person who wants to buy (*ra*) something asks the seller what the offering price is, and the buyer may simply agree to buy at the offering price, especially if prices and qualities are quite uniform, or a long-term relationship exists between that seller and a regular customer (*raadga*). Commonly, however, the buyer says "*baraka*" (thanks, blessing, well-being—from the Arabic), refusing the offer, and the vendor typically reduces the asking price, sometimes substantially. The buyer then repeats "*baraka*," and the cycle may repeat itself a number of times. Or the buyer makes a counter offer, to which the seller responds, often by highlighting the qualities of the merchandise, or explaining that the season or other circumstances make it impossible to sell at a lower price. The buyer, in turn, may point out qualities rendering the commodity less valuable than the seller claims or, more politely and more effectively, describe other comparable purchases recently made or observed at a lower price.

In an effort to set a floor to the negotiations, the seller may point out (without being taken very seriously) how much effort was required to make or obtain the goods, or state the price that he or she supposedly paid for it wholesale. In the haggling, vendors often explicitly invoke the principle that they are entitled to some profit ( *yōodo*) for their work in making the item or a margin over what they paid for the commodity if they are reselling it, and they will refuse a bid, saying that they would make no profit at that price. A buyer may claim not to have sufficient funds, and so on, until the buyer and seller reach agreement or break off the negotiations. The vendor may make a final concession, saying that it is a special price "just for you" in particular, based on friendship. It is very bad form for either party not to go through with a transaction if the other agrees to a bid or an offer at any point. A price stated is a moral commitment. The term for this bargaining is *barsego* (from the verb *barse*, to repeatedly say "*baraka*"). Men are expected to bargain somewhat less forcefully than women, at least in minor purchases.

People also buy and sell things every day in the villages and fields and at the periphery of funerals and public ritual gatherings. Moose commonly sell kola nuts, chewing tobacco, candy, and beer in both market and village, as well as animals, mats, cloth, and the tools and pottery the Sāaba make. Basically, such transactions take the same form regardless of the location, except that in the village buyers may sometimes come and ask for a commodity not on display.

Other sellers and bystanders will not interfere with bargaining in progress. But after a market transaction is completed, observers may offer a critique to one participant, out of earshot of the other. Villagers commonly ask people returning from the market what price they paid, especially for novel commodities or items whose price varies considerably accordingly to quality or circumstances. In part, they ask for information in order to make comparisons and learn the state of the market. But they also are free with comments and criticism, chiding people who paid more than the normal market price for a commodity. In other contexts Moose usually avoid posing direct questions to each other and are typically extremely reluctant to reveal information about their social relations and activities. So the fact that people ask about prices freely— and get answers—distinguishes Market Pricing from other kinds of transfers and interactions. This exchange of information about prices is what maintains a relatively efficient market.

In a market transaction participants often are patently trying to maximize the ratio of what they receive over what they give up. Sellers are plainly trying to make a profit. There is no attempt to hide this, although there are some limits and rules of decorum. But almost any kind of strategy is acceptable in order to make a sale at a good price, including deception (see Noaga [1978] for descriptions of a variety of swindles perpetrated on travellers and strangers). For example, when avian cholera epidemics attack the poultry in a village, people quickly try to sell off their chickens, since the disease is extremely contagious and almost invariably fatal. No one wants to buy infected chickens, not least because they spread the epidemic. So sellers deny that there is any cholera in their village, even if the chicken being sold is on its last legs. Except among kin, in-laws, friends or neighbors, it is caveat emptor—let the buyer beware (cf. Fortes 1969:336 on the Tallensi). However, at the completion of the transaction people generally try to put a veneer of Communal Sharing on the interaction after the fact—as though they were uncomfortable at having acted so crassly. For the purchase of a commodity that is readily divisible (e.g., beer, peanuts, kola nuts, cloth strips, meat), a step at the close of the transaction adds this gloss of Communal Sharing: the seller gives the buyer a *lenga* (bonus, gift, extra), a small portion on top of what the buyer has paid for. Ordinarily the seller gives this bonus gift unasked, and determines how much it is: typically it represents a small fraction of the amount formally sold, but occasionally it is an appreciable addition. Generosity in giving such bonuses may lead to the buyer becoming a regular customer. If the seller neglects to add on a gift (*lembe*), the buyer may ask for it, and the seller would not refuse to give at least a token gift.

The fact that money changes hands in a transaction does not make it Market Pricing. I mentioned earlier that Moose lend money without interest: borrowers pay back exactly what they borrowed. There is another important class of situations in which people pay cash (*ligidi*) for something but do not bargain for it, and in which the transaction is not characterized as *raabo* (purchase). In particular, people often pay in cash for *tum* (medicine, magic), but the payment is *keoore*, remuneration or reimbursement. To pay in such a manner is *role*, to reciprocate, give back, give in return, reestablish equilibrium. It is common for people to give out a dose of medicine and ask that the recipient pay only if and when the medicine works. The remuneration in such a case might be a chicken. The Moose often say that *tum* will not work unless some money is given as return. Between friends or as an act of generosity, sometimes the reimbursement is reduced to a token payment. But for many kinds of *tum* there is a more or less fixed reimbursement that cannot be arbitrarily varied if the medicine is to function.[1] This is also generally the case when one obtains the recipe (*bulli*)—including "spells" or invocations—for concocting a *tum* together with the right to produce it oneself (in contrast to simply obtaining a limited quantity of the already compounded for *tum* immediate use). Another kind of transaction in which money changes hands is the reimbursement people pay in advance for divination (*bagre*). While there is a general understanding about the appropriate payment, usually a diviner will accept any reasonable amount. One friend and informant occasionally volunteered to divine for me and was not at all deterred when I had no money on me, nor did he apparently expect to be paid later.

It would be a mistake to confuse any of these reimbursement payments with Market Pricing transactions. There is never any discussion of what the items or services are worth, little or no comparison with alternative goods or services, and no bargaining over the amount to be paid. In other settings, outside the context of the transaction itself, people do discuss with each other who has good medicines and who is an insightful diviner. But they do not ask others how much they have paid for *tum* or divination, and do not comment on what kind of deal they got, as they regularly do with commodities bought in the framework of Market Pricing. Financial gain as well as status and reputation may be involved in some ways in the motivation of at least some diviners and providers of medicine, but the form of the social relationship does not reflect this. The specialist provides his expertise to help others, as a service. The reimbursement transactions themselves seem to take the form of Equality Matching, in which the recipient balances the value of what he or she receives, matching the thing given and compensating the giver so that they come out even. They are aiming at balance and equality, without regard to exchange ratios or profits.

In contrast, in Market Pricing transactions people are concerned with proportionality. Market Pricing is a framework whose operation is based on prices—ratios of exchange of commodities, by which any pair or set of commodities can be compared and evaluated according to a single metric. This metric is the ratio of money to quantity (as a function of the quality-relevant features). Prices make all MP commodities commensurable, so that people *rationally* decide among trade-offs between alternatives by comparing prices. Prices are thus rates, typically expressed in currency: CFA per kola nut, CFA per day of labor, CFA per hectare of land, CFA per CFA per year borrowed.

Moose structure very little of their interaction with reference to such price ratios. As indicated in Chapter 12, they never buy or rent land in the village and virtually never make interest-bearing loans. Nor do they ordinarily hire people to do agricultural work. In fact, work for pay is almost nonexistent in traditional settings in the area where we worked, except for bicycle and moped repairmen, tinsmiths, and indigo dyers.[2] All men go to the Ivory Coast and work on farms there, so Moose know that labor can be treated as a commodity. In the cities land is bought and sold and houses are commonly rented, so they probably know that land could be bought or rented. But in the village land is simply not a commodity and labor only very rarely is. People know what it is to work for money, they just do not do it in the village. There have been markets large and small throughout the area for centuries, and people are certainly used to the idea of buying and selling all the products they produce. Moose are accomplished at bargaining, familiar with credit, and knowledgeable about promissory contracts. Obviously Moose know how to interact according to Market Pricing. But what they overwhelmingly do is pool their labor, give out their land, share their food, and offer up much of their livestock and beer in sacrifice so as to create or maintain CS relations of identity, solidarity, and attachment. There is not much sign of "economic man" concerned with ratios of gains to losses or selfish individualists oriented toward maximizing personal profit.[3] However, two salient phenomena at first glance suggest that Market Pricing may have a major directive force in Moose social relations: emigration in search of wage labor, and the activities of some individuals who practice trades and crafts. The rest of this chapter is devoted to exploring the implications of these phenomena. Can we plausibly infer that Market Pricing motives and values generate these practices, or are alternative explanations more cogent?


## WHY MOOSE MEN MIGRATE TO WORK IN THE IVORY COAST[4]

There is one prominent phenomenon that *appears* to be an exception to the prevalence of Communal Sharing over Market Pricing. This is the universal exodus of Moose young men in search of wage labor. This obviously entails their working in a Market Pricing mode and might be interpreted as a maximization of individual self-interest. Let us see what we can discern about why they go.

Virtually all Moose men leave the village for periods of one to several years at a time to work in the Ivory Coast, or occasionally elsewhere (see Skinner 1965, Remy 1973:63–64, Schildkrout 1978). They generally return to visit from time to time, but the majority of men between 15 and 40 are absent from the village at any point in time (such a migrant is called a *kaoos weoogo*, a person who stays away for a long time). My calculations show that in 1979, 57 percent to 68 percent (depending on how the base population is calculated) of men whose estimated ages were between 15 and 40 were abroad, most of them working as wage laborers on plantations in the Ivory Coast.[5] Does this labor migration indicate that, outside the geographic context of the village itself, Moose are predominantly motivated by material economic self-interest? Is it evidence for an economic motivation that is covert within the traditional culture but emerges to become the dominant orientation of action when Moose are free of direct cultural constraints?

I have very little data of my own about the stated personal motives of Moose who emigrate. Regardless of the topic, Moose generally do not discuss their plans or the decisions they are considering and are even more reticent about answering direct questions. Men keep their departures a close secret from even their wives until the moment of leaving (although they may tell their mothers), in large part out of fear of witchcraft.[6] Furthermore, elders attempt to dissuade men from leaving (although they actually expect them to go), and young men are reluctant to confront their elders with plans of which they disapprove. So it is very difficult to discuss with men beforehand what factors enter into the decision to leave. But there are a number of sources of information in the literature from which we can infer motives.

Neither the villagers nor I know what has become of some of the long-absent emigrants, and among these there may indeed be some exceptionally entrepreneurial, achievement-oriented personalities. Without tracing these people, we are unable to determine their motives. Fortunately, however, in her study of Moose who have settled in Kumasi, Schildkrout (1978:43) briefly describes elderly informants' accounts of why they first left home. The main factors they mention are avoidance of the colonial forced labor levee and the imposition of taxation in a region where there was little or no local opportunity to earn money to pay the tax. Schildkrout says Moose emigrants often refer to the shame they suffered at "being tied up in the sun," apparently a reference to punishment for nonpayment of taxes. This suggests that these early emigrants were forced to leave rather than seeking to make their fortunes.

Schildkrout also describes the formidable social and economic barriers tending to inhibit migrants from returning to their natal villages. One of the barriers is their conversion to Islam and failure to keep up with sacrifices to the ancestors. However, the main reason has to do with their inability to bring back substantial gifts, because of difficulties with currency exchange, customs barriers, initially low wages, and later "capital investments" in land and urban housing with consequent low liquidity. As Noaga (1978) and Schildkrout (1978) both report, it is a great shame to return from abroad without generous gifts for one's father, mother, siblings, in-laws, the compound head, lineage head, and other village elders. Many migrants choose not to return at all rather than come back without suitable gifts (Kohler 1971:110, cited by Remy 1973:68; see also DuBois 1965:6–7). Attachments to home may initially be strong, and they may endure, but communication among illiterate villagers is infrequent and uninformative,[7] and the ties between permanent emigrants and their home villages can ultimately lapse.

Fiction provides another source of information about motives for emigration. In his novel *Le Retour au Village*, the Moose author Kollin Noaga (1978) describes the adventurous comings and goings of a young man from the village of Tema (near Boké), a village about 50 kilometers from our field site. Throughout his novel, Noaga describes his hero, Tinga Ouedraogo, as oriented toward CS and sometimes AR relations. Ouedraogo's economic motives are always subordinated to concerns about his family, his wives, and his social obligations toward the chief and toward his fellow-villagers. For example, Ouedraogo believes his natal family has suffered a series of horrible calamities. In order to return to help them, the hero hurriedly sells his coffee and cocoa plantation—the product of seven years labor, clearing, planting, and pruning the immature trees—for less than a quarter of what he estimates it is worth. With the money left over after a series of mishaps en route, like other labor migrants he buys a watch (purely for show), a new bicycle, elegant clothes for himself, presents for his family, and kola nuts for everyone else. After some days in the village he ultimately sells the watch, the bicycle, and many of the clothes to buy presents for other family members for whom he had not bought anything, since he had thought they were dead. He also uses this money to buy more kola nuts to give away and to pay for the ceremonies and gifts involved in his marriage to his first wife. This disposition of resources seems to be fairly typical of migrants returning from the Ivory Coast (see Remy 1973:67-72; Hyden 1980:161 cites similar practices in Tanzania).

To a large degree then, it may be the case that these labor migrants pursue their economic activities in order to fulfill their familial and marital roles. Their ultimate objective is probably not economic gain for its own sake but the material means to generous sharing, as well as the respectful payment of tribute to their superiors. It is notable that Noaga (1978) describes his hero, Tinga, as largely unaffected by his years as a wage laborer in the Ivory Coast. When Tinga visits his natal village he readily and happily returns to traditional Moose patterns of interaction. The novel ends with the hero's rejection of the impersonal, individualistic, and selfish commercial world of the Ivory Coast and his return to the village for good. Indeed it is very striking to observe how little Moose men are affected by their long sojourns abroad. Migrants frequently adopt Islamic names (among their several other names) and occasionally some elements of Moslem religion, and they purchase clothes, cassette radios, and bicycles. But their relationships with their fellow-villagers are surprisingly unchanged by their experience as migrants. With the partial exception of some veterans, Moose seem to bring back to the village very few of the habits or values of the modern world. They certainly show no sign of having adopted Market Pricing concerns or perspectives on human relations.

Remy (1973:66-67) reviews his own and others' research on migrants' motives for seeking work in the Ivory Coast, particularly Kohler's (1971) study among the western Moose. Kohler asked 300 returned migrants their principal reason for going abroad. Some 40 percent said they sought money to pay taxes, 20 percent just said "money," 11 percent said they were after clothes and other objects, 10 percent specified wanting a bicycle, and 8 percent said their reasons had to do with marriage, particularly seeking money to pay for expenses associated with obtaining a wife. Remy reports his own study in Nobere (south of Ouagadougou, near Manga), where 85 percent of former migrants cited "economic" reasons, including taxes, and 35 percent mentioned "social or psychological" factors. The Moose dislike answering questions and are extremely reluctant to reveal their motives and intentions. It is not clear from Remy's summary how the interviews were conducted, but it is doubtful that he was able to arrange for private interviews in a village setting, or that informants expected their answers to be confidential.

It is difficult to know what to make of such a survey. But earning money does come through as a factor. Evidently, at least some migrants want to earn money for conspicuous consumption but much more often paying taxes is the stated goal. Note that it is not only—and probably not even primarily—their own personal taxes they seek to pay: migrants are probably seeking money to contribute toward paying the taxes of the compound as a whole. In my own experience, a significant proportion of letters which villagers dictate to emigrant kin request money to pay the head tax. Remy gives other researchers' attributions of additional motives for Moose migration, including adventure and the lure of life abroad, family quarrels and the wish for independence, emulation of peers, and the prestige of sophisticated youths who have returned—although Moose themselves virtually never mention these considerations. Several other researchers have also suggested that migrants' motives involve a desire for consumer goods and the quest for enhanced social status among peers and young women.

It is important to reflect here on the core fact that the colonial powers, who regarded their colonial subjects as a pool of cheap labor, found that Moose (like most other West Africans) were generally quite uninterested in working for pay. The French colonial authorities ultimately resorted to corporal coercion, requiring people to plant cash crops and sell them to designated buyers, and instituting an annual head tax. They also commandeered labor for plantations and construction. Defaulters were pilloried or jailed. Nothing short of military force and constant coercion by colonial police would force Moose to sell their labor for money. All writers agree that the French imposition of the head tax in the absence of any local opportunities to earn money, together with a desire to avoid forced labor on public works and plantations, initiated the colonial phase of migration and sustained it thereafter.

A major factor that informants presume as understood and so do not mention, but which certainly contributes to labor migration, is the late age of marriage for Moose men. Men typically do not marry until their late 20s or early 30s, and an unmarried man (*rakoore*) has very little autonomy or standing in the village, being always at the beck and call of his elders and subject to their will. While bachelors are waiting their turn for a bride, there is little incentive to remain in the village. Given that most young men are abroad at any time, the few young men who do remain are burdened with all the errands and labor that would normally be distributed over them all. And who wants to stay behind when all one's friends and peers are going off to see the world, returning with Western clothes, radio-cassette players, new bicycles, and gifts for everyone?

## Necessity

Given that many of these factors are present, I think the heart of the matter is that Moose youths do not have any "choice" about whether to leave. No country in the world is significantly poorer than Burkina Faso, where villagers often are living at the margins of subsistence. The Moose plateau is one of the most densely populated regions in West Africa; in 1975 the region that was formerly the Département du Centre Nord, where Maane is located, had a population density of 29 people per square kilometer, while densities in other départements on the Moose plateau were still higher (Institut National 1979). Mooseland has suffered greatly from drought and overgrazing, so that water run-off and hence erosion have increased considerably and infiltration into the soil is very low. There is simply not enough arable land for everyone in the village to cultivate, and much of the land that is under cultivation is leached, compacted, underwatered, eroded, stony, and unproductive. Any given person may go to his mother's brother (*yesba*) to request land to cultivate for a period of years, but this can only redistribute the dense population in better correspondence with resources, not alleviate the regional problem. For those with poor or insufficient land who cannot get more in their own village or from their mother's brother, migration can be a material necessity. In general, younger men will tend to have less land and land of poorer quality than older men whether for corporate field or separate field, so their problem will be especially acute.

There is ample evidence of a local shortage of land. In the last three decades several compounds have moved out of the village where we worked to a bush settlement several kilometers away, a settlement that as yet does not have a fully distinct political or ritual identity.[8] Most of the people who have moved are Yarse, and they reportedly moved to the bush settlement as entire compounds or major segments of compounds. In 1980, the bush settlement residents made up 8.7 percent of the population of the village as defined for tax purposes. More recently—between 1975 and 1982—families representing another 12 percent of the population of the village of Habra have left to find land to farm in the less populated and better watered southern or western parts of Burkina Faso, and letters from the village indicate that this exodus has continued since we left the field in 1982. These people have left as groups of brothers with their wives and children, or as individual families. But the most mobile people are unmarried young men, and the precedent for their migration has now become an expectation. Unmarried young men have little standing in the community, and their CS ties to it are perhaps weaker than anyone else's. Their relationships (primarily in the form of Equality Matching) to their peers—age-mates, companions and old playmates—are among their strongest social bonds, and their peers all migrate. Young men have seen all their elder brothers and every other man before them go off to the Ivory Coast, so when they reach their late teens and their peers leave, they depart too. Very often they go with a neighbor, friend, or acquaintance who has been there before, and they go to join someone they know. In either case, their predecessors often introduce the newcomers to job opportunities and communities that the experienced migrant already knows.

The shortage of land is not the only material exigency Moose face. As we saw above, the villagers are subject to a severe shortage of water at the end of every dry season, so that they have to go five kilometers to get all the water they need for drinking, for cooking, and for watering their small stock—in a season when daytime temperatures in the shade are often over 110°F and the humidity is climbing. The shortage of water soon after the harvest limits construction and maintenance of houses, granaries, and compound walls. It is becoming increasingly difficult to obtain wood for roof poles, doors, granary supports, and posts for sun shelters used for storing donkey and cattle fodder. The kind of grass suitable for roof thatch is now in very short supply. Firewood for cooking, beer brewing, and cold-season heating is more and more difficult to obtain. In short, the physical necessities for even the minimal level subsistence at which Moose live are in very short supply. Hence the search for arable land and the fear of starvation, together with the shortage of water and these other subsistence burdens, may be sufficient to account for the exodus to the Ivory Coast without invoking Market Pricing social motives. For young men faced with the risk of not having enough to eat, seasonal difficulties in obtaining enough to drink, and very poor prospects of marrying soon or, once married, of supporting children, migration becomes a matter of assuring basic biological needs. However, migrants' return and reintegration into Moose society—into its communal relations in particular—is socially motivated. All Moose want to belong, to live together with their kin and participate in the collective life and sacrifices of the lineage.

Travel outside Mooseland apparently did not begin with the penetration of the Western Market Pricing system or modern transportation. Moose men have a tradition of making long trading journeys on foot in the dry season, carrying salt from the north and kola nuts from the south in head loads so heavy a man could not raise or lower them alone. Donkeys were also involved in this trade, both as beasts of burden and articles of commerce (see Ruelle 1904:691). Until this century Moose men, (particularly Nakomse on horseback) made slaving raids on their neighbors to the south and occasionally fought with neighboring chieftainships. Then, in the colonial era conscription of laborers forced to work on roads, construction projects, and plantations far from home, the military draft, the per capita head tax, together with peace and the safety of travel, increasing population pressures on deteriorating lands, drought, and the expansion of the market economies of first the Gold Coast (now Ghana) and then the Ivory Coast, combined with the tradition of dry-season trading journeys, accelerated labor migration to the point where it has become an established phase in the Moose male life cycle.

## Social Relations Away from Home

Once in the Ivory Coast, migrants must find jobs quickly, since they have very meager funds to subsist on, and virtually the only opportunities they find for supporting themselves are in the wage-labor economy, primarily as farm laborers (Remy 1973:65). Thus the fact that they work for pay—that their labor is structured in the form of Market Pricing—reflects the socioeconomic milieu in which they find themselves, not necessarily their own social motives, interests, or preferences. In contrast to the rural villages of the Moose plateau, the organization of labor in the Ivory Coast, including the agricultural sector, is dominated by Market Pricing. For Moose migrants, selling their labor in the market economy is virtually the only possibility open to them.[9]

As Polanyi (1957a) explains, the desire for food, clothing and shelter does not imply that people must organize their search for these necessities in a Market Pricing mode: the only opportunities the migrants find for subsistence in the Ivory Coast are in the Market Pricing economy. Were Moose to have the opportunity to work in some other mode (CS, or EM, or even AR) in the Ivory Coast, they presumably would prefer to do so. But their preferences are irrelevant to the form of social interaction they actually adopt, given the constraints they face. Hence in these circumstances we cannot make inferences about their social motives from the kinds of social relationships in which they actually engage.[10]

However, there are other ways to determine Moose migrants' preferred forms of social relations when they are away from the village. There are strong constraints on the form of migrants' relations with the indigenous people and on their place in the infrastructure of the Ivory Coast. But the material constraints on the possible forms of social relationships among the migrants themselves when they are away from the village may not be so severe. Hence the ways they choose to organize their social relations abroad may reveal their social orientations. Unfortunately, I am not aware of any extensive ethnographic work among Moose migrants in the Ivory Coast (although Remy [1973] reviews statistical data). So it is impossible to know in detail just how the Moose do organize social relationships among themselves and with other laborers in the Ivory Coast. But there are some hints that, given the opportunity, migrants may reconstitute social relations based on CS and other non-MP models.

For example, villagers sometimes are able to obtain small plots of land in the Ivory Coast for cocoa or coffee plantations. Holders of such plots may take turns living in the Ivory Coast developing the plantation, as a pair of my best informants wrote to tell me that they are now doing. This trading-off between peers and compound-mates appears to be a kind of EM. Remy (1973:33) cites four studies stating that foreign laborers in the Ivory Coast, particularly the Moose, commonly organize themselves as a team with a president who negotiates a contract with an employer and distributes the profit among the members. Remy cites Boutillier's (1960) description of these groups as composed of two to eight workers, usually belonging to the same ethnic group, chiefdom, or village, and led by the eldest member or the person with the greatest seniority. He also cites Dupire (1960) to the effect that employers find such teams assiduous and reliable, and prefer them to unattached individuals. Remy (1973:36–37) also cites Dupire's (1960:46–51) characterization of Moose laborers as extremely gregarious, with a tenacious social and sentimental attachment to their homeland, and as very slow to advance their careers. Moose consider their civilization to be distinctive and superior to that of their hosts. Dupire emphasizes the well-known esprit de corps of Moose laborers and their collective conservatism, noting that they live together around their eldest or most experienced member, help each other at work, eat together, and, more than any other immigrants, suffer from homesickness. Remy quotes Dupire as stressing

> qu'ils n'ont point acquis encore de mentalité économique et resteront même mal payés, chez un employeur qui les traite bien, tandis qu'ils abandonneront sur le champ une situation intéressante pour des motifs apparement bénins ou purement sentimentaux. (from Remy 1973:37n)

> (they have still not acquired any economic orientation [outlook, concern] and they will remain, even badly paid, with an employer who treats them well, while they will abandon on the spot a valuable position for motives that are apparently benign or purely sentimental.)

The research Remy (1973:85–94) reviews on Moose who leave their home-land and settle *in*side Burkina Faso indicates that such settlers set up new communities apart from their hosts, where they maintain traditional forms of social relationships much like those of their natal villages. This is also true of Moose labor migrants who seek out wage employment within Burkina Faso, including domestic service. So even what appears to a Euro-American to be a purely economic contract often turns out to be something else. Household servants take it for granted that their employers, as their AR superiors, are responsible for their welfare, including interceding for them with other au-thorities and providing financial assistance in every crisis. The relationship be-tween employer (*patron*) and servant also entails elements of Communal Shar-ing—some of which Euro-Americans are apt to misinterpret as theft when it involves sharing their food stores (see Richards 1969:150). Once again we see that while the nominal form imposed on the relationship by the labor market and the employer's expectations is MP, the predilections and presuppositions of the Moose participants involve other forms of social relationships.

Altogether, it seems likely that the Market Pricing motive is not the only one responsible for the exodus of migrants and is probably not their primary mo-tive. For the most part, Moose men migrate for non-Market Pricing reasons. They migrate because they want to match their peers (EM) and do what all Moose, including their closest friends and associates do (CS). They leave be-cause they need to find money to pay the taxes of everyone in the compound (CS). They used to leave because they feared conscription and forced labor, and some continue to leave because they wish to be out from under the con-trol of tyrannical elders. Or they go off in search of adventure. Above all, they seek work in the Ivory Coast because there is not enough arable land, not enough water, not enough fodder, and not enough wood, thatch, and wild game to sustain them at home. Having the fewest and weakest Communal Sharing and Authority Ranking ties with others and with Equality Matching bonds to peers pulling them along, these subsistence needs drive them to the better watered, more fertile, and less populated lands nearer the coast. The only opportunities they find there to sustain themselves are within the Market Pricing system. But neither individual ambition nor a concern with obtaining returns proportional to inputs explain what they do. Moose migrants do not go to the Ivory Coast in order to maximize their self-interest or because of any *rational* desire to sell their labor in the market.

Of course, Market Pricing does have a place in the constellation of Moose motives. In some contexts the Moose do calculate the material advantages of alternative courses of action, and choose according to their economic self-interest. Working as wage laborers, migrants are earning their livelihood on a *rational* basis, contracting to work under certain conditions, receiving pay in proportion to the number of days they work, and spending the money they earn on market commodities. Desire for status and for the means to conspicuous consumption plays a role in Moose migration to the Ivory Coast: young men want to display bicycles, cassette radios and new clothes to their peers and potential lovers (see Skinner 1965, Remy 1973, and Noaga 1978). But, like Moose everywhere, migrants' predominant concerns are with sharing, as well as deference and fairness. Notably, most migrants eventually choose to return to their natal villages, where, virtually unchanged by their experience, they resume their normal CS, AR, and EM relationships. In the cities and towns— where only 9 percent of Burkinabé live (Institut National 1979)—commerce is more extensive, but even the capital, Ouagadougou, is in many respects very village-like, preserving traditional values to an extraordinary degree (see Skinner 1974).

In sum, the core conclusion of this analysis of Moose migration is that, while migrants go to the Ivory Coast and work there in a Market Pricing mode, by itself this fact does not imply that they are driven first and foremost by MP motives. In general people may produce or exchange commodities in a *rational* (proportional) manner, attend to the rates of exchange we call prices, contract to perform jobs and live off their wages, all because this Market Pricing mode is the only structural possibility open to them. In order to determine peoples' true social motives, we have to examine their social relationships in detail and explore their motives in depth. As we shall see in the following section, this is as true of Moose entrepreneurs and craftsmen who stay in their homeland as it is of labor migrants.

It is sometimes thought that people must be materialistic, more or less *rational* economic maximizers because, after all, people are inevitably concerned with material needs for food, water, shelter, and other subsistence needs. But, as Polanyi repeatedly emphasizes (e.g., 1957a:46ff.), under ordinary circumstances people desire material goods for all kinds of social reasons and not primarily for their subsistence value. Moose labor migrants seek not just material subsistence but the means to contribute communally to the needs of their natal lineages, with whom they share much of what they earn.

Moreover, subsistence needs can be met in a variety of ways, of which Market Pricing is only one. The economic historian and anthropologist, Karl

Polanyi demonstrates this quite persuasively (Polanyi 1947, 1957a, 1957b, 1966; Polanyi, Arensberg, and Pearson 1957a; see also Sahlins 1965). Polanyi describes the diversity of "economies" in non-Western societies over a wide historical range, showing conclusively that the production and distribution of goods (and, we might add, the allocation of services) can be organized in a number of different ways, of which Market Pricing (as I am calling it) is only one (e.g., Polanyi et al. 1957a:239–42, 243ff.). Indeed, the MP system has typically played a very minor role in production and distribution in virtually all societies except in the West and in the modern era (e.g., Weber 1978 [1922]; Mead 1937; Firth 1965; Polanyi 1947, 1966; Sahlins 1965). In short, throughout history people have organized very few of their productive and distributive ("exchange") relations in the form of Market Pricing, and people's motives for seeking material goods often have little or nothing to do with MP.


## INDIVIDUAL PRODUCTION: THE CHOICE BETWEEN ACHIEVEMENT AND SHARING

If Market Pricing is not the primary motive impelling Moose to participate in the wage-labor economy of the Ivory Coast, then we should take a close look at other apparently "economic" activities of the Moose, especially the activities of craftsmen and traders. Are these people an exception to the rule that in Moose social relations Communal Sharing predominates over Market Pricing and other motives? Although the core and the productive foundation of the Moose economy is agriculture, Moose villagers also manufacture many kinds of traditional craft goods and engage in both traditional and modern service trades. While farming and the care of livestock are predominantly communal activities, individuals acting more or less on their own initiative—and sometimes working alone—conduct virtually all of this manufacturing and service work. Individuals autonomously sell the products they produce, and have personal control over the money they earn in this way.[11] A few villagers concentrate on trading or repair work to the point that farming becomes a secondary activity. Such craft and service activities apparently indicate the existence of economic individualism, especially since Moose sell these products and services in a predominantly Market Pricing mode. In any case, when Moose engage in these nonfarming, nonpastoral activities, pursuit of Market Pricing goals is to some degree mutually exclusive with pursuit of Communal Sharing goals. So in this section we will look into how Moose actually organize some of these nominally entrepreneurial activities, in order to determine their priorities.

All Moose villagers are farmers and small animal raisers, but everyone pursues other activities as well. All women spin cotton and most men weave some cotton cloth for their wives and children and for themselves. Any woman may mine and shape grind stones. Men weave mats and baskets of various kinds, and make unfired mud bricks. Some men are leather workers, making sacks to carry grain or water, amulets, hats, shoes and equestrian tack. Within the village there are some crafts that are associated with ethnic subgroups. Sāaba men are blacksmiths and forge virtually all of the hoes, axes, knives, spears, and arrows the villagers use, as well as tool handles, mortars and pestles, bowls, wooden doors, and locks and iron keys, while Sāaba women are potters. Some Sāaba are jewelers, making copper, brass, and iron bracelets and rings. The Yarse traditionally are more involved in commerce than other Moose ethnic subgroups, and often weave cotton cloth to sell.[12]

Moose use all these products themselves, and share them within subsections of the compound. But at times people also make such products in order to sell them when they need money for some specific purpose. The maker-seller owns the item and the proceeds from its sale (see Delobsom 1929:426). When the maker sells the goods, these activities profit the individual and contribute little to the group. So it is significant that I never heard anyone accused of taking time away from communal activities to pursue private manufacture of goods for sale. Like the separate fields individuals cultivate on their own, these crafts generally take second place to communal productive work like collective farming and livestock raising in the compound, and to community projects like digging wells and catchment basins.

Trade, craft, and service activities for pay ordinarily occupy only a very minor proportion of most people's time.[13] But where we did fieldwork, one village man is a trader in miscellaneous small manufactured goods, two brothers are tinsmiths and welders, and one man is a major kola nut wholesaler and retailer. All these men probably spent at least as much time in their nonfarm activities as they did in the fields.[14] These men begin to have incomes that must significantly exceed the value of the agricultural and craft production of any of their lineage-mates and compound-mates. Yet the village is not economically stratified in any manifest degree, which suggests that relatively wealthy people either share their wealth or do not engage in much conspicuous consumption. No one in the village maintains a markedly higher standard of living than anyone else. Differences are subtle, and for the most part relatively small. On the basis of habitation, dress, activity, or manner, a stranger would hardly be able to distinguish between the chief, or the wealthiest villager, and the poorest. People expect to be able to get help from their kin when they need it and are very reluctant to expose themselves to envy by the display of personal wealth.[15] However, "success" in nonfarm enterprises sometimes must require retention and reinvestment of "capital," rather than sharing the proceeds according to the needs and desires of compound members and other associates. So the choice for an "entrepreneur" is really between staying in the village and continuing to share resources, or leaving the village to achieve maximum retention of profits, capital accumulation, and increased wealth (see

Hammond [1966:106] on Gourcy in Yatēnga). Thus Moose traders and crafts-men may have to choose between Communal Sharing and Market Pricing. What do they do?

One welder did move out of the village to a small town 80 kilometers away and returned only infrequently. He explained to me that going a considerable distance away to pursue such an entrepreneurial activity considerably attenu-ates demands for sharing one's wealth, although kinsmen may still make the trip to ask for help if they are in great need. But leaving the village the way this man did is not the most common choice. The retail trader continued to live in the village and participate in its affairs, if somewhat less fully than others. The kola nut wholesaler remained in the community and was a mainstay of it, al-though a kinsman of the wholesaler who assisted him did move to a nearby town. All the kola retailers continued to reside in the village. This suggests that these people effectively tended to sacrifice personal achievement for commu-nity membership.

On a couple of occasions a close friend, the welder/tinsmith who lived in the village, discussed his finances with me in some detail. He was concerned that he was losing money, or at least not making any, and he had no idea of how to keep accounts and make the relevant calculations to find out. The welder had two or three helpers who worked with him sometimes and were in a sense apprentices in the trade, as he had been to his older brother. These helpers were age-mates, one of whom was a father's brother's son. They did the simpler jobs and assisted when needed. The welder did not pay these assis-tants a salary, nor a percentage of the profits. The money from all the jobs everyone did went into a single can. The welder purchased food at the market that they all ate together (they were too far from the village and too busy to return home to eat). At the end of the day the welder gave his apprentice assis-tants a portion of his earnings. The share he gave them was neither negotiated nor set in advance in either absolute or proportional terms, and the amount was not arrived at through any formal calculations. The welder simply gave them what he thought was appropriate, and the apprentices accepted it. In effect, even this trade was organized as a CS labor pool—under the egis of an AR leader who unobtrusively and loosely controlled the work when neces-sary—with individual contributions unmarked and the proceeds shared collec-tively. Furthermore, the welder was not setting prices by calculating his costs and adding on a proportional increment for profit. Besides his assistants, his major costs were for bottles of compressed acetylene, their transportation from the capital, and welding rod. But he had no idea what his per job or per day costs were for these items. He simply charged what he thought was a rea-sonable amount for each job, paid his assistants, and then waited to see if he had any money left to buy acetylene and welding rod when he needed them.

My welder/tinsmith friend is apparently typical of skilled tradesmen in West Africa. John Schiller (personal communication) reports that carpenters to the east in Fada N'Gourma were unaware of their material and labor costs.

When he helped them work out their accounts in conjunction with small business loans he made to them, he discovered that they made a profit on windows but lost money on every door they built. They simply charged a conventional price for each job that was unrelated to their actual costs or profits, which they never actually calculated. Silver (1981) reports (without giving precise details) modes of organizing work among Ashanti (Asanti) wood carvers outside Kumasi, Ghana, that resemble the way the village welder/tinsmith organized his workshop. Verdon (1979) makes similar observations on such apprentice workshops in Accra, Ghana. Using ethnographic material collected by Smutylo, Verdon concludes that

> a significant proportion of Accra apprentice workshops (and more generally East and West African ones) as represented in Smutylo's study cannot be identified in any fashion with enterprises, firms, or businesses. They are not based on wage labor, nor do they make any systematic reinvestment of their surplus or supranormal profits. (Verdon 1979:538)

Verdon notes that apprentices are not wage-labor "employees," that such workshops do not respond directly to supply and demand, and that it is the nature of apprenticeship that these workshops directly produce their own competitors. He emphasizes the structural differences between apprentice workshops and businesses, concluding that there is no reason to believe that such apprentice workshops will ever "evolve" into [*rational*, profit maximizing] "enterprises." So although these workshops sell products, by all the relevant criteria the internal organization of these workshops does not conform to Market Pricing.

Even when Moose sell specialized craft products, the mix of models they employ in the associated external transactions can be quite subtle. For example, Sãaba (Blacksmith) men make various kinds of hoes, axes, knives, and other iron tools. They sell these in a normal Market Pricing mode. But if a blade breaks or bends and requires repair—even in the midst of the cultivating season—Sãaba take time to make the necessary repairs (whether or not they made the particular blade themselves). But they do not set any price for making a repair, the two parties do not negotiate a fee, nor is there any fixed standard payment. Instead, the owner of the tool simply gives whatever he or she wants to (*a kõta būmb ning a sē n date bala*), and the Blacksmith accepts whatever is offered—grain, coins, or whatever—without discussion. These repair transactions clearly contrast with Market Pricing profit-making fee for service work. Furthermore, while Sãaba make and sell virtually all the wooden tool handles, utensils, doors, and the like that Moose use, they supply threshing flails without charge. Moose use these flails when they hold a threshing bee (*zauga*), so that the flails circulate around the village from bee to bee.[16]

All in all, despite the fact that Moose and other West Africans produce some craft products for sale, in this culture area Market Pricing is not the exclusive mode of organizing the division of labor and skill specialization, and in many contexts MP does not even predominate. Beginning in the precolonial era in West Africa, observers have long noted the lack of profit motive even in the purchase of many manufactured commodities, and they have noted the consequent lack of any meaningful or coherent price system (Meillassoux 1971:68). Of course, in itself the division of labor and skill specialization has nothing intrinsically to do with Market Pricing, as is evident in the complementary productive activities of men and women anywhere. Like the divisions of labor by gender in most cultures, Moose organize transactions within the family and the compound in the form of Authority Ranking or Communal Sharing. Women do not sell to men in their compound the vegetables and green leaves and spices they grow and collect; they prepare food with these condiments and give the food to their men. Men do not sell their services as builders or threshers to the women of the compound; they contribute their work without direct reimbursement or compensation. Men and women each do the gender-specific tasks that need to be done, without concern for the proportions or market exchange values of what they give and what they get, and without attempting to match or balance their tasks with the opposite sex.[17] Division of labor as such does not imply or require Market Pricing.

### Sharing the Wealth

Much of the money Moose do earn in individual craft and trade activities they share communally, just as they share the products of their communal agricultural labors. Even the most wealthy Moose townspeople in Burkina Faso typically maintain close ties with their natal villages, and return there regularly. Indeed, the natal villages of the few really wealthy Moose stand out, because these men have contributed large sums of money for the improvement of their home villages. This shows that when entrepreneurs do move out of the village, they usually maintain their membership in the communal collectivity, sharing the money they make. Similarly, when men go away to the Ivory Coast or elsewhere they usually send back money from time to time— and the few letters villagers send to them typically ask for money, especially if the harvest is bad. Kinsmen working abroad have always contributed a significant portion of the head taxes villagers paid. And, as we saw above, when migrants return from working in the Ivory Coast they bring back presents for their kinsmen, wives, and in-laws. Although migrants may save enough money to buy a cow or two when they return, they generally do not use the money they bring back to invest in private enterprises or otherwise turn into capital. Instead, migrants probably contribute the bulk of their savings to meet communal needs.

Within the village milieu it is virtually impossible to accumulate personal wealth because the obligation and the desire to share within the group takes precedence over individual "advancement," "success," or "achievement." As is true of many African societies, there is a general, diffuse, and limitless obligation—and a desire—to share any and all resources, especially among lineage-mates, but also more widely within the village, between in-laws, with parents and siblings, and with daughters and grandchildren.[18] This is more than just an abstract obligation. Particularly within the compound and above all within the subgroup that cultivates together, people really do pool their resources. That fact alone indicates the great directive force of Communal Sharing among Moose. The only acceptable excuse for not sharing, if asked, is that one does not have what is requested. Pacere (1979:112–13), an astute informant-observer, elegantly captures this sense of the priority of the community over the individual, writing that private property and individual differences in wealth are incompatible with the Moose ethos. Pacere sums up the fundamental collectivism of Moose social orientation that tends to preclude autonomous striving for personal success. He writes,

> Nous avons vu en effet que l'individu n'existe pas, et que tout se fait à l'intérieur du groupe dans la seule considération du groupe; cela donc interdit à l'individu de produire seul et de thésauriser quoi que se soit de "personnel" qui puisse le différencier d'un autre member du Mogho; la hiérarchisation possible ne se situe qu'au niveau constitutionnel; elle est impossible au niveau économique. (Pacere 1979:113)

> (We have seen in fact that the individual does not exist, and that everything is done inside the group, taking into account only the group; this thus prohibits the individual from producing alone and from hoarding anything "personal" which could differentiate him from another member of Moogo [Moose country, the total Moose community]; stratification is only possible at the constitutional [political] level; it is impossible at the economic level [as differences in personal wealth].)

When Moose do engage in Market Pricing activities, such interactions are highly segregated from the rest of their social life. Men and women buy kola nuts from members of their own compounds, or occasionally purchase an animal from a close kinsman, and it is not anomalous for a man to buy chewing tobacco from his wife. However, the vast bulk of buying and selling of commodities takes place in the market (raaga), a setting strikingly defined and delimited by time (every three days) and place (a location used just for this purpose). Work for pay is almost entirely limited to towns and foreign countries (all called weoogo—outside the village) or is arranged with members of other ethnic groups. Moose tend to exclude Market Pricing from the framework of normal day-to-day relations with kin, neighbors, and most other close associates.

In sum, while Market Pricing is a well-defined traditional form in Moose culture, it has only a minor place as a directive force in Moose society: MP is not a dominant motive or norm. The available evidence suggests that even for specialized crafts, trade, and other aspects of the division of labor among Moose, Market Pricing is frequently not the basic organizing principle. Although Moose sometimes engage in nominally entrepreneurial activities in which people trade, sell craft products, or do repairs for money, Market Pricing is often muted or absent and Communal Sharing, Authority Ranking, or Equality Matching modes may predominate. So the details of Moose nonagricultural production and exchange offer little support for the supposition that Moose tradesmen and craftsmen are *ratio*nal "economic men." Moose rarely orient even these trade and craft activities to exchange ratio prices alone, and rarely pursue the course of maximizing personal success at the expense of communal belonging.

As Chapter 9 indicated, the essence of Market Pricing is an orientation toward proportionality. When people operate in an MP mode, they concern themselves with prices or analogous ratios of exchange, with the ratio of benefits to costs, or with rates of return. Market Pricing per se does not entail maximization of expected returns, nor in fact do any of the other three basic models entail maximization. Indeed, maximization is not characteristic of any kind of motivation, social or nonsocial. Social motives in particular can be sated by participating in satisfying social relationships of the relevant type. It is not just that people "satisfice" because they face information-processing constraints (Simon 1956, 1965 [1947], 1981). People often find full satisfaction in finite social experiences. To the extent that people are chronically unsatisfied, they may appear to be maximizing because they are incessantly seeking more. But seeking satisfaction is not the same thing as seeking to maximize, as is easily demonstrated by showing that there is some finite level of "resources" or "rewards" at which people stop seeking more of the experience in question. Normally any hunger, any drive, can be sated under conditions that approximate the environment in which the drive evolved. Market Pricing is a social motive, and there is no a priori reason to assume that it is unslakable. The Moose show that even in one of the world's poorest, most agriculturally precarious societies, people typically seek social equilibrium, not material utility maximization.

Thus once again we see that the Market Pricing model alone is insufficient to explain Moose social organization and motivation. Market Pricing is one mode for organizing social relationships, but even in the nominally "economic" arena of wage-labor migration, trade, and craft production for sale, it does not account for many important orientations, processes, and structures. Only when we combine the Market Pricing model with the Communal Sharing, Authority Ranking, and Equality Matching models do we approach the goal of a comprehensive account of the full range of forms and directive forces generating Moose social relations.

However, my Moose ethnographic data on this topic are limited and my interpretations—though consonant with the inferences of other observers—are not beyond challenge. So we should seek confirmation for these inferences in what other ethnographers have reported about related societies in the Moose culture area. Hence, in the next chapter I will review relevant published material on four societies that are closely related to the Moose, and one far afield, all of which are well-documented by careful and perceptive ethnographers.

# 15

# Social Orientations
# in Neighboring Societies

**M**y claim is that Communal Sharing is the strongest directive force in
Moose social relations and Market Pricing is the weakest. If my characterization of the Moose is correct, are they unique? This characterization of
Moose motives, norms, and ideology would be reinforced and given broader
significance if it could be shown to be true of other societies in this culture
area. Review of the evidence about the Dogon north of Mooseland, the
Bambara to the west, and the Tallensi to the south shows that a Communal
Sharing orientation predominates in the social relations of all three of these
closely related neighboring peoples. The same is true of the Gouro of the Ivory
Coast and the Bemba of Zambia. Neither *rational* Market Pricing per se nor
selfish individualistic profit maximization is prominent in any of these three
societies. Both English and French ethnographers concur that in these cultures Market Pricing is almost always subordinate to Communal Sharing and
other social motives and norms. This indicates that the Communal Sharing
model is not an exogenous concept that I have ethnocentrically imposed on
the Moose. Communal Sharing actually informs the core of social relations in
many African cultures.

## DOGON OF MALI

North of Mooseland, in the Bandiagara cliffs of Mali, live the Dogon. Moose
tradition has it that the Dogon (called *Kibsi* in Moore) are descended from the
indigenous inhabitants of Mooseland. When the Nakomse horsemen conquered the resident populations, some stayed on and some fled. Those who
stayed are the ancestors of the Yīyōose ethnic subgroup, while those who took

refuge in the Bandiagara cliffs are the ancestors of the Kibsi/Dogon.[1] Given these connections, it is worthwhile to take a short look at the major forms of social relationships among the Dogon. Although the available ethnographic material does not always permit us to answer the questions we would like to ask, a review of the available material does show a number of salient similarities with Moose social relations.

In the first section of this chapter I will review evidence establishing that an emphasis on Communal Sharing characterizes Dogon social relations. Ethnographers report that, like Moose, Dogon only use Market Pricing to organize a very delimited sphere of transactions, a sphere that is neither focal nor particularly highly valued. The Dogon also resemble the Moose in their articulation of Authority Ranking with Communal Sharing and in their seemingly frequent implementation of the Equality Matching model. Altogether, the way the Dogon organize their social relationships with respect to land, labor, food, marriage, and the social and ritual utilization of resources is quite congruent with Moose modes of structuring these domains. However, Dogon appear to place somewhat less emphasis on Authority Ranking than Moose. Let us briefly review such details as are available.

## Marriage

Dogon transfer women in marriage using the a variant of the same Communal Sharing process that predominates in Moose marriage. Dogon marriage does not involve any kind of bride price (Desplagnes[2] 1907:201, 214, 224–25), and when a woman leaves her husband her lineage apparently does not incur any obligation to return the gifts the husband and his lineage have given them. In detailed accounts of Dogon marriage and divorce, no ethnographer mentions any obligations wife-givers owe to abandoned husbands, although all reports indicate that women often leave their husbands (Desplagnes 1907:213ff., 223; Paulme 1940:353, 410ff.; Dieterlen 1956). The lineage receiving a wife makes a number of gifts and the future husband, together with his age-mates, provides a considerable amount of labor to the wife-givers (Desplagnes 1907:216, 219; Paulme 1940:355, 359; Dieterlen 1956:138–40), but there is no indication that any of this is ever returnable. Dogon begin to court a girl's parents as soon as she is born, and while their son is still an uncircumcised infant (Desplagnes 1907:219; Paulme 1940:353, 356, 358–59; Dieterlen 1956:138). Age-mates work together, cultivating as a group for each of their future fathers-in-law in turn (Paulme 1940:363).

However, Dogon women often run off with a lover and marry him, apparently even more frequently than do Moose women. Although her parents have promised the woman to another man, and although she may have been properly married to him and lived with him, neither the parents nor the husband has any real recourse if she goes to live with a man of her own choosing. There is no indication that her lineage makes any sort of restitution to the abandoned husband. The new husband with whom she takes up residence has no major obligations with regard to his wife's parents or lineage (Desplagnes 1907:201, 215; Paulme 1940:361, 385–92, 412–16). As we saw among the Moose, the mere fact that wife-seekers give goods and provide services to pro-spective wife-givers does not indicate the existence of a bride price system. I take "bride price" to mean that the transfer of women in marriage (or control over women's fertility or the group membership of their offspring) is contin-gent on the exchange of a determinate quantity of goods and/or services, and that wife-receivers have an obligation to give certain things in order to obtain the right to a wife, while wife-givers have an obligation to provide a wife once they receive certain specifiable items. By this definition, Dogon apparently do not have a bride price system.

All this suggests that Dogon, like Moose, construe marriage as a benevolent act of Communal Sharing. Among Dogon there is no balanced quid pro quo exchange of wives. Ordinarily, Dogon marriage does not involve any negoti-ated compensation for the giving of a wife, and there is no conception of a market or exchange-ratio "price" for women. However, in exceptional cases Dogon—particularly old men who cannot hope to attract young women as lov-ers—purchase a wife from her parents. Interestingly, in the one such case Paulme describes, the girl ran away from her purchaser, who was unable to obtain even a partial return of what he had paid although he was a greatly feared sorcerer (Paulme 1940:375–76).

## Farming

The social organization of Dogon agriculture also closely resembles what we have seen among Moose—Communal Sharing complemented by Authority Ranking. If they have land they are unable to farm, Dogon lend it to any kin, neighbors, or in-laws who need it, without receiving any payment for the use of their land. As among Moose, a Dogon borrower may make a gift each year to acknowledge that the land belongs to the lender (Paulme 1940:100–101, 338). However, unlike Moose, individual Dogon may sell their land, although the lineage retains for some years the right to buy it back at the original sale price (Paulme 1940:101–105).

The Dogon work their major fields communally (Desplagnes 1907:209; Paulme 1940:148; cf. also Desplagnes 1907:340–41 on the Bambara, Bobo-Fing [Bwaba], and Senufo). At each of at least two levels the eldest man in the lineage segment directs communal labor, controls the distribution of the har-vest, and is custodian of the collective resources of the lineage segment (Paulme 1940:87–89).[3] This elder's wife, children, younger brothers, sons, and their wives cultivate a common field (like the Moose corporate field) four days out of five. The harvest of this field feeds the group that cultivates it during the rainy (farming) season (Desplagnes 1907:209; Paulme 1940:116, 148, 307, 340). On the fifth day, individual members or subgroups cultivate separate grain fields, and during the dry season the harvest of this separate field feeds the subgroup or individual who cultivates it (Paulme 1940:100–101, 148, 307, 337, 340). Women may personally plant and tend vegetables within the collective fields, and in the dry season individuals may grow vegetables in private plots, the harvest from which they are free to dispose of as they like. But husbands and wives often help each other with these personal gardens (Paulme 1940:143–44).

Like Moose, Dogon use much of the food they produce for communal social and ritual purposes, feeding guests and providing beer at funerals and sacrifices (Paulme 1940:149–50, 194). While Dogon own livestock individually, many sheep and goats and most roosters and hens end up being sacrificed in collective religious rituals, where they are roasted and jointly consumed. Dogon often use chicks and eggs for purification rites (Paulme 1940:341, 345). Thus Dogon structure the major processes of both production and consumption as Communal Sharing.

### Authority Ranking and Equality Matching

There are indications of the probable use of Equality Matching models in several domains of Dogon social life. Like Moose, Dogon loan money interest-free, the repayment being exactly equal to the amount lent.[4] Dogon distribute wives quite evenly, few men having more than one. Polygynous Dogon men sleep with each wife in turn for one night, and that wife cooks for her husband that day (Desplagnes 1907:208). Dogon work together to repair each of their houses and roofs (Paulme 1940:146), and youths work together with their age-set members, building a house for each in turn (Desplagnes 1907:215–16). Paulme mentions in passing what may be reciprocal cultivating arrangements like the Moose *sisoaaga*; Dogon harvest fonio collectively, beginning the first day with the field of the most senior male (1940:136, 161) and then harvesting each participant's grain on succeeding days.

The authority of Dogon lineage elders is rather limited and Authority Ranking appears to be less important among them than it is among Moose, but there are several indications of the existence of limited AR among the Dogon. Within a lineage segment, "brothers" marry in order of age, or get permission from their elders to marry out of seniority order (Desplagnes 1907:216). Paulme (1940:108) also states that Dogon distribute the proceeds from the sale of a captive beginning with the most senior member of a lineage segment and giving decreasing portions to each successive subordinate.

Overall, the accounts of Dogon economy and social life show that Market Pricing occupies a relatively small role in their culture, while Communal Sharing predominates. Yet Desplagnes (1907:339, 341, 343ff.) observes that compared to many other groups in the region, Dogon agriculture is more individualized and Dogon are more commercially oriented. For example, Paulme (1940:155) indicates that under certain circumstances a young landless man may work for another farmer and be paid with grain. Like Moose, Dogon sell baskets, cloth that they weave, and other artisanal products for personal profit (Paulme 1940:307).

But the predominance of Communal Sharing is patent. In concluding her account of the organization of production among Dogon, Paulme (1940:193–94) emphasizes the "social" nature of work. Tradition and social concerns, including concern for one's reputation and for the opinions of others, commonly take precedence over purely material considerations:

> Il apparaît clairement que l'intérêt personnel, entendu comme le souci de réaliser le maximum de gain possible avec le minimum de peine, n'est pas la seule force qui pousse l'homme au travail dans la société que nous étudions. Chaque individu est conduit, plus ou moins consciemment, d'une manière plus ou moins détournée, par le désir du bien-être, de la richesse et du prestige de la communauté tout entière. (Paulme 1940:194)

> (It is clearly apparent that personal interest, understood as the concern to realize the maximum possible return with the minimum effort, is not the only force which impels people to work in the society which we are studying. Each individual is led, more or less consciously, in a more or less indirect manner, by concern for the well-being, the wealth and the prestige of the community as a whole.)

This summary of the classical sources on the Dogon indicates that the Dogon emphasis on Communal Sharing resembles that of the Moose. This suggests that this orientation may be a feature of the culture area, and not unique to any one society. Let us briefly consider evidence from another neighboring group, the Bambara.

## BAMBARA ECONOMY AND KINSHIP IN MALI

In an investigation that is opportune for our concerns here, Lewis (1981) studied a Bambara (Bamana) village in central Mali. Lewis addresses the issue of the opposition between the individual economic interests of junior lineage members of the patrilineage as labor migrants on the one hand, compared to their ties to the lineage as a corporate group on the other hand. Since his material is so relevant to the issue of the relative weight of Communal Sharing and Market Pricing among these western near-neighbors of the Moose, I will discuss his report at some length.

Each Bambara compound pools labor and shares food, eating together the harvest of their collective fields. Comparing compounds, Lewis found that the ratio of grain produced per worker to number of dependents varied widely. This variability of production is possible, he observes, because of the sharing that takes place across compounds within the lineage. Lewis states that "inefficient" needy farmers draw on both "cooperative" lineage labor (Communal Sharing) and "exchange-labor" groups (apparently Equality Matching). Differences in productivity within the lineage "do not matter" to them, since their productive energy is seen as coming from a common ancestral life force. Indeed, individuals in the labor-sharing group are not praised for their individual contributions or marked or distinguished in any other way.[5]

Lewis reports that while many young Bambara men go the Ivory Coast to get laboring jobs, they generally return to the village to help with the weeding every year. They do this even though, as he shows, it is to their personal economic disadvantage to do so. Even when Bambara earn money, Lewis notes that they do not spend it in economically rational ways. In Mali there have long been material inducements to abandon participation in collective cultivation:

> The problem is not significantly different than it has been for
> hundreds of years: [a] male youth can find a better market-value return
> for his labor off the farm than he can on it. (Lewis 1981:54)

For example, although in the Ivory Coast young migrants earn much more than the wage rate obtaining in their homeland, they give up valuable wage-earning opportunities to return home and personally join in the weeding, [paying substantial travel expenses, I might add], rather than following the economically *rational* course of sending money home to hire someone to do the work. Yet Lewis finds no clear evidence that their returning to weed reliably increases the net agricultural productivity of their compounds. This suggests that it is not just the migrants' material contribution that matters to the compound, but their presence and personal participation, their sharing in the work alongside their kinsfolk.

The same Communal Sharing orientation emerges in Bambara marriage. Migrants who return with sufficient funds to pay their own bridewealth payments alone are discouraged from doing so. Apparently (Lewis is not clear on this point) the lineage insists on contributing to the bridewealth so that it comes from the corporate group as a whole, not just from the husband as an individual.

Yet against the overwhelming weight of his own data, Lewis (1981) gratuitously imputes selfish material motives to these migrants. Lewis offers security in old age as the goal that explains the Bambara villagers' choice of corporate lineage solidarity over either agricultural efficiency or the maximization of wage-labor earnings. He argues in effect that Bambara villagers trade short- and medium-term material self-interest for long-term economic well-being. He implies that such long-term economic well-being is based on secure membership in the lineage (CS), strong affinal ties to wives' nearby lineages (CS), together with actively maintained reciprocal labor relationships (EM). This explanation seems rather lame, for four reasons. *First,* Lewis does not provide any evidence for his speculation that either lineage membership and solidarity, or the ability to marry locally with the support of the lineage, would actually be reduced by a migrant's failure to return to help with the weeding. He describes the criticisms that would be leveled at men who failed to do their lineage or age-set duty, but offers no evidence that this would ultimately lead to others' refusing to share or reciprocate with them. On the contrary, Lewis (1981:54–55) himself indicates that kinship ties (CS) to the lineage are by their very nature absolute, irrevocable, and non-contingent—as are most kinship ties everywhere. It appears that Bambara would concur with the Moose proverb, "if you have your mother, you have flour [for the staple food]" (*f sǎ n tar f ma, f tara zom*). Or, as Warren and Mary capture the Communal Sharing idea in Robert Frost's (1969) poem about another culture, "The Death of the Hired Man,"

> "Home is the place where, when you have to go there,
> They have to take you in."
> "I should have called it
> Something you somehow haven't to deserve."

In just this sense, Bambara migrants who did not participate in the communal cultivation would still retain their full membership rights and privileges in the lineage.

The *second* reason for regarding Lewis's security hypothesis as implausible concerns Equality Matching within the age-set. Lewis describes kola nut fines that an absent member has to pay for missing work sessions, but typically the logic of such a relationship is that, once the fine is paid, the matter is finished. He never shows that failure to participate actually reduces later opportunities for reciprocal exchange.

*Third,* Lewis gives no evidence that the villagers themselves see their actions as motivated by considerations of old-age security or long-term insurance. Indeed, his self-interest interpretation is inconsistent with the accounts of the corporate solidarity values and the kinds of reasons he reports informants give for their own behavior. For example, Lewis states that the Bambara villagers say they resist ox-drawn plows in part because their use "interferes with the involvement of the compound labor unit in preparing the field" (Lewis 1981:69).[6] *Fourth,* Lewis fails to offer a material self-interest maximization account of the concentric circles of food sharing and labor pooling in compounds, lineages, and higher levels that he describes, or for the choice of corporate solidarity over individual efficiency and maximization in the organization of farm labor.

In short, like so many other Western social scientists, Lewis assumes Market Pricing motives without adducing any evidence for them. Does pooled production actually produce greater security in old age or at any other time? Lewis offers no reason to believe that individuals are sharing communally in order to maximize their personal advantage over the long run, or for that matter that they even could do so by sharing. The overwhelming impression conveyed by Lewis's descriptions is that the solidarity of the lineage, the pooling of labor and sharing of food, and the sense of belonging are desired for their own sake, not as means to ulterior ends. Let us grant that it must be important to these Bambara villagers to know that they will get help when they have more young children than they can support, to know that they will be taken care of in their old age, and to know that in general they can call on lineage-mates and in-laws when they are in need. But that is not to say that the villagers orient their actions primarily to selfish material ends, calculating the optimum level of help and generosity they must display in order to accomplish them. Communal Sharing is noncontingent—if you belong, you belong. So you share in the groups' resources regardless of how much you do or just what you do. And if you belong you try to participate and contribute to the collective work. But you do not participate as a means to the end of ensuring the maximum personal gain.

Lewis himself notes that future help in Communal Sharing lineage relationships is not contingent on how much or how little one has contributed in the past—it is given by virtue of the relationship as such. Consider a small child helping her mother cook dinner. Does she do this in order not to be thrown out of the house and abandoned to fend for herself? Is she motivated by long-run considerations like the prospect of getting her college tuition paid? Of course not—it never occurs to her that being fed and cared for is contingent on her helping with communal chores, because it is not contingent. Pooling labor, sharing food, and meeting each other's needs is intrinsic in Communal Sharing, from the mere fact of belonging. Phenomenologically, Bambara plainly structure their agricultural work as Communal Sharing, and this should be taken at face value—it does not reflect Market Pricing motives or values, but communal ones.

Other observers of the Moose, Dogon, and Bambara consistently report social orientations in these cultures consonant with my thesis that Communal Sharing is the predominant directive force structuring agricultural work and the exchange of women. All observers agree that, compared to other basic forms of social relations, Market Pricing is a minor motive and a lesser value and that MP operates only in a relatively restricted set of contexts in these societies.

## THE TALLENSI DEBATE: MORALITY AND MATERIALISM IN GHANA

Among the societies in this culture area, the Tallensi are probably the best described and most carefully analyzed. Moreover, there is a long-running debate about the relative weight among Tallensi of kinship solidarity (Communal Sharing) versus self-interested material economic motives (Market Pricing). The issue concerns whether the dominant, phenomenologically pervasive Communal Sharing kinship idiom represents the true motives and fundamental values of Tallensi individuals, or whether this idiom is merely the strategic veneer covering fundamentally selfish individualistic materialism. An account of this debate offers a review of the major themes of the ethnographic canvas of Part IV and a fitting conclusion to it.

The Tallensi are southern near-neighbors of the Moose in Ghana. They speak a language that is to a considerable extent mutually intelligible with the Moore language, and their society and culture resemble Moose society and culture in many other respects. In his classic analyses of the social organization of the Tallensi of Northern Ghana and in subsequent theoretical work, Fortes (1945, 1969 [1949], 1970) argues effectively that "Tale social structure is, fundamentally, kinship writ large" (Fortes 1969:340).

> The ideology of kinship is so dominant in Tale society, and the web of genealogical connexions so extensive, that no social relationships or events fall completely outside the orbit of kinship. . . . The concept of kinship is the primary category of Tale thought about the social relations of individuals and the structure of the society. (Fortes 1969:338–39)

In passages reminiscent of Pacere's (1979) account of the Moose ethos, cited above, Fortes (1969:343) concludes at the end of his ethnographic classic that at the level of the lineage, of the clan, and of the society as a whole, the individual's interests are submerged in and subordinated to the corporate group as a whole. He maintains that Tale kinship is fundamentally based on moral axioms, values, and religious ideas. Extending and clarifying this analysis, Fortes later states that

> Kinship relations, or rather the basic kinship norms, are commonly deemed to be binding *ab initio*, in their own right. Constraint is felt to be inherent in the elementary relations themselves. . . . In the experience of the actor, the elementary relations of kinship thus emerge as irreducible moral relations . . . in the sense that they are felt to be axiomatically binding and to stipulate the rule of amity as the basis of kinship behavior. (Fortes 1970:76)

In other words, kinship is felt to be inescapable, presupposed, and unproblematic. Fortes shows that in Tale society and in other cultures, kinship inherently involves a fundamental moral and affective premise of amity, solidarity, concern, trust, prescriptive altruism manifested in generosity, loving, and freely sharing. "Kinsfolk are expected to be loving, just, and generous to one another, and not to demand strictly equivalent returns of one another" (Fortes 1970:237). Kin should share "without putting a price on what they give" (p. 238). Kinship amity is opposed to bookkeeping, the deliberate calculations of reciprocity, and contrasted especially with commercial buying and selling in a market.

Leach (1950) criticizes the theoretical stance of Fortes's ethnographies, particularly his exclusion of the motivational force of economic self-interest. Worsley (1956) then reanalyzes the Fortes material, trying to show that self-interested considerations of material advantage really underlie the operation of Tale social relations, particularly the fissioning of compounds and the departure (and later return) of junior men with their wives and children.[7] Worsley makes a materialist argument that ecological (and unspecified "historical") factors together with the available technology shape the relations of production. Relations of production are the primary determinants of the kinship, religious, and political systems, Worsley maintains. The discussion continues with Bloch's (1973) similar secondary analysis attempting to explain what is going on in the kinship relations of the Tale and others in terms of long- and short-run balance. Bloch implicitly assumes that people are actually maximizing their material interests by trading off long- run and short-run reciprocities, comparing the "costs" and calculating what is most "efficient." Regarding kinship relations, he asserts that

> In fact of course it is reasonable to assume that in the very long term
> and on average the exchanges will be balanced but this is an observer's
> conclusion. The actor sees himself as forced into imbalanced
> relationships by morality. (Bloch 1973:76)

But this assertion is totally unjustified and quite without ethnographic support. Certainly there is no evidence in the actions of kin or in their public or private statements that the expectation of long-run balance enters into the Moose conception of kinship. And Bloch does not offer any evidence at all to indicate that Tallensi conceive of kinship as balanced reciprocity over any span of time. Moreover, Bloch's whole analysis misses Fortes's point that people in kinship relations do not do this sort of reckoning of benefits and costs, nor do they generally feel coerced into imbalance—balance is simply irrelevant to kinship. Nor is the behavior of Tale, Moose, or most other kinsfolk primarily oriented toward external sanctions. The solidarity, amity, and kindness of kinship relations is ordinarily axiomatic and natural to the participants, not felt as a constraint imposed on them.

Bloch (1973) and Pitt-Rivers (1973:96–97) do contribute to a clearer picture of Tallensi social relations by making much more salient than Fortes did the role of explicitly reciprocal relations (Equality Matching) in the organization of labor and other activities, as EM operates alongside collective labor structured in terms of Communal Sharing kinship.[8] Pitt-Rivers (1973) goes beyond Leach and Bloch, recognizing the existence of what we are calling Communal Sharing. In the context of this debate it is surprising that he takes CS for granted as an obvious fact that requires no further proof:

> A system of thought that takes the individual as its starting-point and
> assumes that he is motivated by self-interest, faces a difficulty in
> confronting the examples of behaviour that is not so motivated and this
> difficulty has given rise in western literature to theories of altruism, moral,
> religious and psychological. We need not here go into them, for the
> majority of the world's cultures do *not* share the individualism of the
> modern West and have no need to explain  what appears to them self
> evident: that the self is not the individual self alone, but includes,
> according to circumstances, those with whom the self is conceived as
> solidary, in the first place, his kin. (Pitt-Rivers 1973:90)[9]

After all these secondary reanalyses of Fortes's ethnographies, Hart (1978)
conducted his own fieldwork among the Tallensi, focusing on the social organization of production, particularly the agricultural basis of Tallensi society.
Hart is thus able to situate in historical perspective Fortes's account of Tale
society 30 years earlier, assessing Worsley's (1956) critique with the benefit of
new field observations on the impact of changing economic conditions. Hart's
reevaluation of Fortes's arguments makes it clear that Fortes did recognize the
role of ecological, economic, and other material factors in Tale lineage fission
but found that kinship ties dominate these pragmatic considerations.

> If Tallensi considered only their material interest, they would often
> stay where they were and reap the benefits of a virgin bush farm for
> much longer . . . Agnates [lineage-mates] are morally bound by the rules
> of the social system to stay together, but economic pressures
> sometimes force them to separate; later, however, they are reintegrated
> by the centripetal force of lineage solidarity backed by the ancestor cult
> independently of any material interests. (Hart 1978:201–202)

Hart reviews Fortes's case and concludes that Fortes was correct in his assessment of the forces at work in Taleland in the 1930's. Thirty years later
their population has doubled and, like the Moose, half of the adult men are
working away from Taleland. Hart notes that although there have been some
substantial changes in Tale economy, the traditional social and cultural forms
have proved surprisingly tenacious. He does not say precisely how much
change has taken place, but he concludes that

> It is because traditional links between land and labour, however
> diminished, have not been severed that Tallensi social ideology
> remains a considerable force even after 70 years of growing
> incorporation into the modern world system of political economy. In
> view of this evidence of attenuated conservatism, Fortes' insistence on
> the power of social tradition in the 1930s is certainly understandable
> and perhaps vindicated. (Hart 1978:213)[10]

In other words, subsequent fieldwork by an economic anthropologist with a very different theoretical perspective confirms Fortes's contention that the Communal Sharing orientation of Tale kinship is stronger than their Market Pricing materialistic motives.

Sahlins (1976) goes beyond any of these other analyses in formulating a more fundamental argument against the idea that cultural forms are governed by "objective" material advantage, *rational* self-interest, or utilitarian maximization formulated with reference to any universal means-ends calculus. Acknowledging that culture operates within broadly limiting ecological and material constraints, he argues effectively that it is cultural systems of meaning themselves that constitute value or "utility" in the first place. Sahlins interprets Fortes as saying that Tallensi interests (motives) and their social effects are a function of their particular culture. Thus demographic pressures and a shortage of land are one stimulus for compounds to fission and for a group of brothers born of the same mother to depart with their wives and children. But, Sahlins observes, the fact that fission results from these ecological factors is a product of the culturally defined system of land-holding, deference, and authority. The further fact, Sahlins argues, that it is Tale brothers born of the same mother, along with their wives and children, who depart and later return together (as a corporate CS group) is a consequence of the Tale kinship system, not mere ecology. He concludes that the validity of historical materialism is historically and culturally relative. It is only in modern entrepreneurial capitalist societies that a distinct sphere of rational utilitarian self-interested economic activity is the principal generator of cultural value for the system as a whole.[11] Unlike modern societies, Tallensi and other traditional cultures are not divided into structurally distinct economic, political, religious, family, intellectual, and educational spheres, Sahlins argues. In traditional societies these spheres are not structurally distinct, while social relations—and kinship in particular—are the primary source of value (and, I might add, motivation). Sahlins concurs with Fortes's conclusion that the moral force of kinship forms the core system of meaning enveloping all Tale activities and permeating all social relations in such societies. And kinship here means Communal Sharing.

The perspective on Tallensi society and culture that emerges from this debate is consonant with and strongly reinforces the account I have given of the organization of Moose production, distribution, consumption, marriage, and other social relations. In terms of the strength of Communal Sharing motives relative to Market Pricing motives, contemporary Maane Moose are perhaps even more "traditional" and "conservative" than contemporary Tallensi, Dogon, or Bambara. But in all four cultures CS predominates over other values and relational motives, and in all four societies CS remains the empirically prevalent form of social relationship.

Fortes (1970), Worsley (1956), and Hart (1978) all tend to assume that the world order based on Market Pricing must ultimately overwhelm and replace

Tallensi CS, AR, and probably EM relationships. Congruently, in Moose society over the last three generations the directive force of Market Pricing appears to have increased, largely due to ecological, demographic, and political circumstances. But at the same time the tenacity of Moose, Tallensi, Bambara (and probably Dogon) adherence to their traditional forms of social relations raises the issue of whether the triumph of Market Pricing really is inevitable. The questionable but widespread assumption these three authors make is that technological factors in local agriculture or constraints imposed by the existence of the world market economy necessarily require these peoples to abandon their traditional forms of social relationship in order to survive. But this axiom remains to be demonstrated, and perhaps cannot be demonstrated (cf. Hart 1982). As Moose are recognizing, given their precarious subsistence level and deteriorating environment, they do need to make some accommodations to the Market Pricing structure of the world economy. But whether adaptation to the objective world means replacing Communal Sharing with Market Pricing is not at all self-evident. Sahlins's (1976) analysis of the nature of value demonstrates that to a considerable degree human well-being is culturally constituted (and sociomorally oriented), not biologically or ecologically given.

The observations I have presented about the variety of forms of Moose social relations combines with the theoretical perspective developed earlier in this book to go beyond the terms in which the Tallensi debate has been formulated. We are no longer confined by the dichotomies of "moral" and "material" motives, or "kinship" and "economic self-interest." And we can now extend and formulate Sahlins's (1976) point more precisely. What must be added to Sahlins's argument is a recognition of the distinct and effective autonomous motive force of the desire to relate to other people in Communal Sharing, Authority Ranking, and Equality Matching relationships. Any particular social interaction may be oriented with reference to any of these motives and forms of social relations, and none is inevitably submerged in any of the others.

At the same time, all four of these models are moral, and usually jural, directive factors. They are partly endogenous, intrinsically rewarding forms of action, but they are also expectations which others hold as standards and uphold with sanctions. This means that individual motivation and social structure have to be considered together, since they are actually complementary aspects of the same fundamental models. Social structure is largely the product of the models people implement and the ways in which they implement them. People organize action and thought in a given domain as a function of their own motives and standards (derived from the basic relational models) together with their conceptions of the motives and standards of other relevant people. People may sometimes seek to apply a model when others do not expect it or disapprove of it, but there is no inherent or necessary conflict between personal desire and the social system. And the structural principles of the social system do not have a distinct status or origin independent of the shared social conceptions and standards that people apply to each other. It is gratuitous to assume, as many analysts do, that people's basic, natural motive is selfish Market Pricing, conflicting with a systemic "moral" principle of Communal Sharing. Both models operate concurrently as individual motives and moral obligations. It is also an analytic mistake to assume, as Worsley (1956) and others appear to have done, that MP is the dominant individual motive of human beings while CS is merely an epiphenomenal superstructure generated by the system of production in certain traditional societies. The system of production itself takes its form as the result of the particular social models people implement in productive labor, distribution, and consumption. As I believe Marx understood and Sahlins implies, the system of production has no existence independent of people's cultural conceptions of how it is appropriate and necessary to relate to each other in these activities.

The theory of the four fundamental relational models presented in this book provides an etic comparative framework that delineates the basic kinds of values any particular culture may apply to any given domain. Sahlins (1976) points out that it is culture that creates meaningful value, that what is "useful" or "functional" depends on the goals operating in each particular culture. Subsistence and physical comfort enter into these values, but do not determine them. Biology and ecology are not sufficient to account for the varied forms of human activities. We can reformulate this to say that each of the four basic types of social relationships is an end in itself; it is intrinsically rewarding to engage in a relationship of any of these types for its own sake. Given this, each culture provides implementation rules that delineate domains of activities, allocates these four types of social relationships to particular domains, and amplifies or attenuates the intrinsic satisfactions of engaging in each type of relationship.[12] As we saw in Chapter 7, none of these basic types of relationship can be realized without drawing on culturally provided parameter values required to realize each kind of generic model in a concrete interaction. In that sense each culture specifies the particular manifest goals of social action in any given context. Market Pricing is only one social motive, and it is no more (and no less) natural, basic, or inevitable than the other three. There is no way to say for sure, a priori, what the relative importance of MP will be in any given culture, or to which domains it will be applied, or how it will be implemented.[13]

The preeminent importance of Communal Sharing in Dogon, Bambara, and Tallensi society and the limited role of Market Pricing in all three societies indicate that Moose are by no means unique in this culture area. Reexamination of ethnographic materials on other societies would, I think, show that Moose, Dogon, Bambara, and Tallensi cannot be dismissed as exotic aberrations (see Mead 1937, Sahlins 1965, Polanyi 1957a). A very brief summary of two of the most influential classic monographs on production, distribution, and consumption in Africa demonstrates the predominance of CS, in conjunction with AR.

## GOURO OF THE IVORY COAST

Is this predominance of Communal Sharing over Market Pricing evident farther from the Voltaic culture area and in other environments, for example
among rice and cassava producers in the well-watered zone at the edge of the
rain forest? In the neighboring country of Ivory Coast, the patrilineal Gouro
straddle the boundary of the forest and the savanna. Meillassoux (1964) provides a rich account of Gouro society and economy, despite the limitations of
a six-month stay in the field without knowledge of the language. Gouro work
collectively in lineage groups on communal fields. People work the land together, and access to land is an automatic consequence of belonging to the
lineage and the village or having social ties to it (p. 258). People may always ask
for farm land from any other member of the village or any in-law, and will not
be refused. Gouro pay no rent and owe no gifts to someone who gives permission to cultivate land (pp. 260–61).

Just like Moose, an elder directs the cultivating group (and any subgroups),
each of which is composed of the elder's wives, children, sons, and younger
brothers and their wives and children. Often these permanent production
groups also incorporate other members who do not belong to the core lineage.
This group produces together, pools its harvest in a granary under the control
of the elder, and eats together, also feeding young children, invalids, and the
aged infirm who do not work. Often two or more production groups pool their
cooked food and eat together (p. 263). Like most Africans, Gouro consume
their meals in same-sex groups, eating commensally from shared bowls.

> Le repas collectif se trouve être l'aboutissement du processus de
> coopération agricole: le travail indistinct de chacun se retrouve dans un
> produit commun. Tous ont mêlé leur travail et tous participent au
> produit du travail de tous les autres. (Meillassoux 1964:125)
>
> (The collective meal turns out to be the conclusion of the process of
> agricultural cooperation: the undifferentiated work of each goes into a
> common product. All have mixed their work and all partake of the
> product of the work of all the others.)

Meillassoux shows how Gouro Communal Sharing in work and consumption—in conjunction with Authority Ranking—contrasts with the kind of division of labor that occurs in capitalist Market Pricing:

> Les travaux accomplis par chacun des membres de la communauté
> n'entraînent pour aucun d'eux la disposition d'une fraction distincte
> du produit, échangeable au sein de la communauté contres d'autres
> produits. Il n'y a pas de rémunération du travail. . . . La production de
> chacun est inextricablement liée à celle de tous et le produit global est
> consommé sous la forme d'une nourriture puisée dans un plat

commun. Les formes de la coopération ne permettent pas la comptabilisation de ce qui est dû à chaque producteur, elles ne permettent pas non plus l'application du principe, à chacun selon son travail . . . C'est par la centralisation des biens autour de l'aîné et leur redistribution sous son autorité que s'accomplit le cycle complet de la circulation. (Meillassoux 1964:187–88; see also pp. 172–73, 350)

(The work accomplished by each member of the community does not entail for any of them disposing of a distinct fraction of the product, exchangeable within the community against other products. There is no remuneration for the work. . . . The production of each is inextricably linked to that of all and the global product is consumed in the form of food eaten directly from a common plate. The forms of cooperation do not permit an accounting of what is due to each producer, nor do they permit the application of the principle, "to each according to his or her work". . . . It is by the centralization of goods around the elder and their redistribution under his authority that the cycle of circulation is completed.)

Meillassoux (1964:141, 188) observes that food goes to those in the group who need it. In the event of a bad harvest, the solidarity of kin and in-laws manifests itself in the transfer of food to those in need, without compensation (p. 263). Very little of the pooled harvest is ever sold, although the elder uses a part of it for social obligations to people outside the productive group.

La circulation des biens vivriers dans la communauté se fait donc sans échange, par transferts successifs et unilatéraux, d'abord des producteurs vers l'aîné, puis de celui-ci vers les membres du groupe. . . . Les récoltes sont stockées, jamais thésaurisées; prestations et redistributions se fondent dans une routine quotidienne et continue. (Meillassoux 1964:188–89)

(The circulation of food products in the community is thus accomplished without exchange, by successive unilateral transfers, first from the producers to the elder, then from him to the members of the group. . . . The harvests are stocked, never hoarded; contributions and redistributions merge in the continuity of daily routine.)

Meillassoux's account suggests that, as among Moose, Gouro elders rarely abuse their powers to the detriment of their dependents. They are trustees for the collectivity, directing its work and holding the harvest in trust for all.

Once in a long while an elder calls together a larger segment of the lineage, together with in-laws, neighbors, and friends to assist in a major agricultural effort (pp. 176–80). The hosting elder provides a major feast, and may give substantial gifts to in-laws who attend. Attendance at these infrequent events is not reciprocal; instead, they attest to the extension of Authority Ranking relations beyond the permanent cultivating groups.

In contrast, Meillassoux (1964) describes another system of agricultural aid that is reciprocal (pp. 182–85). The *klala* is an Equality Matching relationship among two or more people who take turns cultivating each other's fields together in rotation during the farming season. Such voluntary groups may contain up to 12 people, and each person may belong to more than one such group. Elders never belong to a *klala*, but dependents who cultivate with them may do their work in this way. Meillassoux (1964:98) also mentions another traditional manifestation of EM in one village, formerly divided into two hunting groups, in which each group gave the other half of its catch from collective hunts.

Individual Gouro also tend small coffee and cocoa plantations, largely for personal profit. But they traditionally regard such cash cropping as an unimportant secondary activity (p. 172), and Meillassoux gives no indication that this work detracts from communal cultivation. Gouro have long traded with people of the savanna and some of their other neighbors, and markets existed in the region well before the colonial epoch. They have always conducted much of this trade in the framework of Market Pricing. Nevertheless, within their own society Gouro produce and transfer craft goods in Communal Sharing modes even more than Moose do. In general, when an artisan produces something he turns it over to the elder or to the community as a whole (pp. 189–190). He receives no direct compensation, merely eating along with the other members of the production/consumption community. When an artisan produces for others, what an artisan receives for his work depends on the social relationship he has with the person for whom he makes the object:

> La contrepartie du travail fourni à l'étranger n'est pas basée sur la utilité de l'objet ou sur le temps passé à l'exécuter mais elle s'établit en fonction des liens qui unissent le producteur au bénéficiaire. On n'exige pas de contrepartie de celui que l'on appele son «frère» (*bwi*) ou «ceux avec qui on partage le repas», ni d'un comarade auquel on est lié par l'amitié.

> De parents lointains ou d'aînés du village et d'un autre lineage on attend un cadeau, poulet ou cabri, que représente la nourriture que l'on doit à qui travaille pour vous. Ce cadeau d'ailleurs est remis ensuite par l'artisan à celui dont il dépend, c'est-à-dire qui le nourrit. (Meillassoux 1964:190)

> (The compensation for work done for outsiders is not based on the utility of the object or on the time spent making it, but is established as a function of the bonds that unite the producer to the recipient. One does not insist on compensation from someone whom one calls "brother" or "those with whom one shares meals," nor from a friend to whom one is tied by friendship.

(From distant kin or village elders of other lineages one expects a present, chicken or kid, which represents the food that one owes to someone who works for you. Besides, the artisan then gives this gift to the person on whom he depends, that is, to the person who feeds him.)

Meillassoux (1964:191) makes it clear that within the framework of non-MP relationships, craft products do not have prices as such. Artisans produce them—when they make them at all—to accommodate people with whom they have significant social relationships. Furthermore, some important wooden goods, like looms, canoes, and mortars, are really communal property, freely used by all who need them.

On the other hand the elder of each productive group controls iron farm implements—they are neither private nor corporate property (p. 193). (The elder holds one implement for each dependent worker.) Indeed, elders have AR dominion over all iron, whether in the form of ingots or implements, and the possession of iron indexes their prestige. Gouro wealth is never investment capital in the MP sense, it is an index of rank and a medium of exerting authority. Elders use ingots and skirt cloths to make bride wealth payments to obtain wives for themselves and their dependents, giving these prestige goods only to other elders and only for such purposes. As Meillassoux (1964:218–20) explicates, bride-wealth payments are not a form of MP purchase: women are not treated in any respect as commodities, nor are many of the other entities people exchange. Within most spheres of social relationships, exchanges of iron, skirt cloths, livestock, tusks, guns, gunpowder, slaves are also traditionally limited to certain fixed combinations and specific equivalences, and certain other exchange combinations are excluded. The terms of such exchanges is such that no coherent "prices" can be attached to these items; they are not MP commodities (1964:267). More generally, Meillassoux shows that every other form of social relationship takes precedence over Market Pricing, so that people only exchange goods in an MP mode if they have no other preexisting social relationship (pp. 272–73, 350).

Meillassoux shows how colonization, the imposition of the head tax, forced labor, obligatory cultivation of cash crops, and subsequent depredations of the world market economy are disrupting many aspects of this system, and yet preserving much of it. At the time of his fieldwork 30 years ago, at least, the Communal Sharing and Authority Ranking orientations of the Gouro were very striking. As in the other four West African societies, Equality Matching and Market Pricing were manifest but clearly less prevalent, less culturally elaborated, and less valued.

## BEMBA OF ZAMBIA

Numerically and geographically, Bantu-speaking peoples represent by far the largest group of cultures in Africa. Do the patterns we have found in West Africa obtain among Bantu? All four of the cultures discussed here so far are patrilineal—what about matrilineal societies? Richards's (1969 [1939]) classic study of the matrilineal Bemba of Zambia provides the most detailed early description of the production, circulation, and consumption of goods in Africa. Here, almost 3,000 miles away from the West African cultures, we find another society in which Communal Sharing predominates over Market Pricing and other modes of relationship. Women farm collectively with their kin, and frequently men, too, farm joint fields (p. 384). Bemba also carry out some hunting, fishing, and public works projects communally (p. 384). Several households use a common granary, women sharing the cooking tasks, eating together out of the same pots, and feeding groups that eat together. Women will go hungry to feed their husbands and in-laws. All Bemba take pride in their generous hospitality, as well as sharing with kin 50 or more miles away (Richards 1969: 108–109, 135.)[14] If they are hungry, close kin may harvest one another's grain or root crops without asking (pp. 185–86). Kin and others may also demand grain from a person's granary (p. 189). This sharing is central to Bemba values, and is inculcated from infancy (p. 197):

> If the Bemba people share their meals and extend hospitality to a wider circle of relatives than we do, it is because from their earliest years they have never been able to consider food as something which could be procured, owned, and consumed by one individual alone. In childhood, or in subsequent dependent positions, it must be supplied by elders; throughout life it must be shared with contemporaries, and special delicacies such as meat and beer must be subject to older kinsmen's [AR] rights. Food is something over which relatives have rights, and conversely relatives are people who provide or take toll of one's food. The purely possessive [MP] attitude to property with all its concomitant virtues, such as thrift, foresight, or self-reliance, are not inculcated in the Bemba child and would probably unfit him for life in his society. The so-called communism of the Bantu, like any other form of distribution of material goods, is deeply rooted in a system of ideas, a common acceptance of particular laws of ownership and obligations to share and to give. (Richards 1969:199–200; abbreviations in brackets added)

In addition, Authority Ranking is clearly evident in the distribution of food. For example, a village headman (or any elder kinsman) may require people to contribute food to help him entertain (pp. 194, 253). Furthermore,

> To give with a flourish was the glory of chieftainship . . . Actual possession of great quantities of foodstuffs does not seem to have been a particularly cherished ambition of the Bemba. They valued a reputation for giving, not for having. . . . I never heard a chief boast to another about the size of his granaries, but often about the amount of food brought to him and distributed by him. (Richards 1969:214)

Richards (1969:145–47) also mentions an important tertiary mode of organizing work and consumption, *ukutumya* (working-bees), but she does not indicate whether they are organized according to an EM principle (as opposed to CS). She notes, however, that while this system is markedly inefficient and therefore economically irrational from the point of view of the host, it is motivationally important. People aim to produce enough grain every year to be able to brew beer for friends attending such events.

Regarding the lack of Market Pricing, Richards observes that the barter or sale of craft goods "is not subject to the ordinary laws of demand and supply, since once the sum for a basket or pot has been fixed at 3*d*. or 6*d*. there it will remain, however scarce the materials of which it is made" (p. 219). Although people occasionally exchange things on a quid pro quo basis (probably according to EM), in rational economic terms they often seem to lose on each exchange (p. 224). Moreover there is no generalized MP metric of value governing exchange:

> The traffic appears to consist of a series of isolated acts which have little reference to previous transactions of the kind, and are not governed by any recognized system of comparative values. . . . [In instances villagers reported] nothing like a regular schedule of prices or rates of exchange governed the transaction. (Richards 1969:223)

> To conclude, it can be said that the Bemba, owing to their particular environment and social organization, reckon to live by means of mutual support within their kinship groups, and only resort to the barter or sale of the goods they need sporadically, or on occasions of necessity. Then either temperament or their patterns of economic thought make them extraordinarily inept, according to European standards. Marketing, like any other form of economic activity, is evidently based on a system of values developed in earliest youth, and the trading instinct seems to be difficult to acquire by a people who have not been through such a training. (Richards 1969:226)

Richards then contrasts Bemba children who help out whenever asked—so long as they feel liked—to the neighboring Bisa, who are much more commercially oriented and prone to bargain, seeking to strike explicit deals when asked to help.

## Priorities and Motives

As Godelier (1986b) points out, in many societies with diverse technologies and systems of production, we can find some spheres in which people exhibit *rational* optimization based on calculations of alternative means and considerations of efficiency. But history shows that the realm of economic *rationality* and selfish maximization was typically devalued and narrowly circumscribed in the premodern West, and anthropology shows that this orientation obtains today in a great many societies. Like the Tiv whom Bohannan (1955) describes, many societies put the kinship ethics of Communal Sharing first, disdaining Market Pricing exchanges and disparaging the associated motives. The Trobriand Islanders value CS, AR, and EM, but disdain MP (Malinowski 1961:191). Another notable example is Marshall's (1961:242) description of the !Kung hunter-gatherers of the Kalahari in Botswana, who do not engage in "trade" (that is, direct exchange of commodities at rates antagonistically negotiated with respect to a known market rate) with each other: "they consider it undignified and avoid it because it is too likely to stir up bad feelings." Indeed Price (1975) shows that sharing is very common within bands in hunter-gathering societies. In his pioneering monograph Firth (1965 [1938]—see especially pp. 356–61) describes Tikopian society (Polynesia) as noncompetitive, not oriented toward maximizing, and not driven by supply and demand. Nor are such values limited to any particular system of production. In many regions of Africa there are also pastoral cultures notorious for their disdain of consumer goods, their disregard of profit considerations in animal husbandry, and their lack of interest in economic achievement more generally.

In fact, Polanyi (1947, 1957a, 1968; Polanyi, Arensberg, and Pearson 1957b) shows that most traditional societies, including those ancestral to our own, place Market Pricing at the bottom of their scale of values. Communal Sharing orientations and the negative valuation of Market Pricing are not limited to any particular region, ecological zone, or form of subsistence. Mead (1937) and her group describe six of the 16 cultures they studied as "cooperative" in regard to the dominant ethos and mode of distribution.[15] And Triandis (e.g., Triandis et al. 1988) shows that this "collectivist" orientation toward social relations is still quite widespread in the world—individualism is not the dominant orientation in all contemporary cultures (see also Price 1975; Cheal 1988). This orientation is prominent in prosperous nations as well as poor ones. Doi (1981 [1971]) and Lebra (1976) describe the group-focused, sociocentric "social relativism" of the Japanese, for example. Thus the Moose are by no means unique in their preference for Communal Sharing over Market Pricing. In many societies people organize their social life with reference to CS more frequently than they orient toward MP, they value CS relationships more highly than mere market interactions, and they tend to be moved by communal motives more strongly than by other motivations.[16]

The ethnological evidence is clear: we cannot take it for granted that humans as such are purely "economic" beings, treating objects and people as commodities. We cannot assume that people are ordinarily dominated by self-interest, or that they invariably govern their interactions with reference to utilitarian calculations so as to more or less "*rationally*" maximize their personal welfare, materially or otherwise. This is one kind of social motive, but there are other kinds as well. In any given domain in any particular society Communal Sharing, Authority Ranking, or Equality Matching may have greater directive force than Market Pricing. The motivations to share (CS), to respectfully defer or lead responsibly (AR), and to maintain egalitarian balance (EM) are essential elements of the basic human repertoire of social motives.

The two concluding chapters consider the psychosocial nature of these four fundamental motives, their autonomy with respect to each other, and their ontogenetic origins.

# Part V

# Human Nature
# and Society

## PREFACE TO PART V

There are two kinds of sociology distinguished by their starting point
and their global approach. In the first kind, one begins, as is natural for
modern scholars, by positing individual human beings, who are then
seen as living in society; sometimes one even attempts to show society
as arising from the interaction of individuals. In the other kind of
sociology, one starts from the fact that men are social beings, that is,
one takes society as a global fact irreducible to its parts—and here it is
not a matter of "Society" in the abstract but always of a particular,
concrete society with all its specific institutions and representations.
(Dumont 1986:1–2)

The truth is that our culture is permeated by nominalism, which grants
real existence only to individuals and not to relations, to elements and
not to sets [*ensembles*] of elements. Nominalism, in fact, is just another
name for individualism, or rather one of its facets. . . . Nominalism will
know only John, Peter, and Paul. But John, Peter, and Paul are men
only by virtue of the relations that exist between them. . . . In every
case the relations form a configuration, and these configurations vary
from . . . one milieu to another, but they do not vary as chalk does from
cheese, and we can try to see what they have in common at each level
of generalization. (Dumont 1986:11)

For communication within a research community, universal concepts
are required. Now, the recent development that emphasizes the
specific character of each culture destroys or weakens, sometimes no
doubt thoughtlessly, the universals which we have hitherto been
employing. It would therefore be useful to identify at least some sound
or sufficiently durable universals of anthropological discourse. . . . But
can we assert the presence in every culture of universal components?

369

For lack of substantial elements [universal components], these will be types of relations. (Dumont 1986:223–24)

The two concluding chapters consider what the relational-models theory implies about human nature and the nature of human society. In particular, this theory posits what Dumont advocates: universal types of relations and their cultural variations. The universal types never exist in "culture-free" form. They must be implemented in some specific, culturally formulated manner. Chapter 16 briefly discusses the implications of this polymorphous theory of social relations. It focuses on the consequences of the fundamental multiplicity, autonomy, and mutual irreducibility of social motives. In contrast to monistic theories that try to fit all human behavior into a single mold and assume a unitary goal for all human action, the relational-models theory posits a set of four distinct, autonomous orientations. All four social-relational motives are equally basic, equally "natural." Each orientation is independent, none is consistently subordinated to any of the others, and there appears to be no inclusive, hierarchically superior arbiter that mediates among them in a systematic way. As we have seen throughout the book, the four orientations may be concatenated in many combinations, but they are not necessarily integrated into any single overarching schema. They may simply coexist. Or they may interfere with each other. This implies that a society is not a functionally integrated system, since there is no unitary coordinating principle. In the end, how and when people implement each model depends on tradition, and tradition may be a haphazard assemblage. There is no theoretical reason why these cultural implementation rules have to be systematically integrated; how such rules actually do impinge on each other remains to be determined empirically.

Chapter 17, focusing on the sources of sociability, shows what the relational-models theory implies about human nature. The chapter begins by examining the concept of motivation, and then goes on to show how social motives and social rules have a common source in the elementary models. Duty and desire are not inherently opposed, and in fact tend to coincide. People are fundamentally sociable, because their most basic goals include social motives that can be fulfilled only by relating to other people in each of these four ways. Even Market Pricing is a culturally constituted, socially realized form of relationship. Market Pricing is not necessarily or typically a means to ulterior asocial ends: people frequently engage in MP for the sake of the MP relationship itself, to fulfill relational goals that can be satisfied only within such a social relationship. The sociable nature of Market Pricing (and the other basic models) is evident when we contrast such relations with the Asocial behavior of sociopathy, in which norms are merely means or impediments to selfish asocial goals. The same is true of Null interactions. On the other hand, studying the ontogenetic emergence of the four models in normal children has the potential to demonstrate the essential unity of motives, morals, and social comprehension. Preliminary observations suggest that children impose the models on their social relations by a process that we might call externalization.

# 16

# The Multiplicity
# of Fundamental
# Social Orientations

This short chapter poses a problem. In Part IV I have shown that Moose social orientations cannot be reduced to Market Pricing, or to any one motive. More generally, humans seem to have four basic social motives and evaluative standards, each of which is autonomous and not typically subsumed under any other. This polymorphic view of human social relations potentially challenges widespread conceptions of societies as functionally integrated systems, and of cultures as coherent systems of meaning. What, if anything, integrates these four directive forces?

## COMPARISONS, TRADE-OFFS, AND AGGREGATION

One of the major conclusions of this book is that in order to account for the full range of observable forms of social interaction, we need to use all four models. Each constitutes an elementary, autonomous orientation in its own right. Moose and others very commonly engage in Communal Sharing for the relationship itself, not as a means to an ulterior Market Pricing end. Similarly, participation in Authority Ranking and Equality Matching relationships is inherently rewarding and meaningful, each in its own terms. The same is true of Market Pricing relationships. Evidently there are four equally fundamental social orientations, none of them ordinarily derivative from any of the others, and none typically or necessarily subsumed as a means subordinate to any other.

If we accept the idea that people have four distinct, disparate social orientations, we have to address the question of how they are coordinated. In particular, the question arises as to how people handle incompatible, "competing," or mutually exclusive social motives or standards for action. There are cultural implementation rules that specify when and how each model should be applied (see Chapter 7). These implementation rules are historically transmitted, largely in the socialization of children. So the question is, do these implementation rules fit together in some larger pattern? Are they in some sense consistent and coherent?

The anthropological and historical evidence shows that, while most societies seem to use all of the models extensively, societies differ markedly in the relative prevalence of the models and in evaluative preferences among them. We can discern three kinds of rough ordinal rankings of predominance among the set of four basic orientations: We can compare the prevalence of the orientations, that is, the frequency with which people engage in social relations structured according to each model. Second, we can compare peoples' explanatory use of the models to understand their own behavior, the relative frequencies with which people explain or justify their behavior with reference to each model. Finally, we can compare "preferences" for the models, peoples' stated and implicit evaluations of each respective type of social orientation (although such rankings do not at all imply that there is any kind of simple or direct regulation of incompatible motives and standards). Although a society or an individual may have broad preferences for one orientation over another, this does not necessarily provide a consistent rule for deciding what model to implement in any particular ambiguous situation. People may organize their social relationships in one way more often than another without there existing any sort of orderly control mechanism arbitrating among the models when they are mutually exclusive or interfere with each other. Differences in prevalence among the four models in any given society do not imply that there is a straightforward, consistent, rule-governed "administrator" that can arbitrate among several mutually exclusive orientations when they all come into play at once. Appealing as it is to imagine some such highest level regulator, there is no particular a priori reason to believe that one exists. It may turn out that there is no simple answer to the question of how people coordinate these models, because there is only a long "list" of specific implementation rules without any simple, regular integrative mechanism. It seems reasonable to expect that the implementation rules mesh in some integrated fashion, but they may not. It is an empirical question for ethnographic and experimental investigation.

## Non-Commensurability: No Common Currency

Economic and utility models are based on the very strong assumption that all goals, motives, and standards of interest can be reduced to a single, typically unidimensional, metric: the price or utility of the entities in question. As long as there is a single metric by which the desirability of all possible states can be evaluated and compared, it is possible to assess end states and choose between them, to weigh the costs and benefits of all possible courses of action in the same scale, and to choose among them by simply selecting the alternative with the greatest net value (see Mead 1937:470, 480, 510). This assumption of a single universal currency in which all things can be evaluated is an extremely powerful but empirically exigent axiom. Bohannan's (1955) classic article on the separation of spheres of exchange in the ideology and practice of the Tiv of northern Nigeria shows how even material goods may be categorized into distinct classes of things that are not fully interconvertible (cf. Firth 1965:340–44 for an overview of the concept of spheres of exchange). Similarly, the ethnological evidence from the Moose research indicates that even within the Communal Sharing mode, money, land, labor, food, and wives are not directly interchangeable at any uniform or specifiable rate. Wives, village labor, and land do not have prices.

The axiom of a universal metric is even more problematic with regard to comparisons across the four fundamental types of social relationships. No evident common metric crosses the boundaries of these models. There is no set formula for converting authority and rank into money, no exchange rate that scales money with distributive equality, no orderly "market" for exchanging turn-taking balance for love and unity, no standard for making meaningful trade-offs between communal solidarity and authority. Solidarity, power, friendship, and wealth are not interconvertible in any simple or direct sense. As the Beatles said, "Money can't buy me love." Nor can you trade authority for true egalitarian fellowship. They are incommensurable. This is the point Walzer (1983) makes when he argues prescriptively as a philosopher about the distinctness of separate spheres of justice. The psychological research on individual Americans discussed in Chapter 5 also shows that social motivations cannot be directly compared in terms of their contribution to any single dominant, overarching need. Triandis et al. (1988) report, for example, that individualism and collectivism are orthogonal variables, which means that people do not trade off one kind of social goal against the other. They are independent motives, not mutually exclusive alternatives or supplementary options. Since the motives, the "utilities" of each type are distinct and incommensurable, there is no transcendent value that encompasses all four types of social motives.

This multiplicity of basic social motives and evaluative standards has far-reaching consequences. *Rationality* means that systematic calculation of the optimal means to an end, where the optimum is assessed by comparing the ratio of benefits to costs for all alternative means (Weber 1958 [1904–1906]; 1975 [1916, 1920–1921]; 1978 [1922]; see especially Rescher 1988). In this sense, the process of arbitrating among the four fundamental social motives is not *rational*. For it cannot be *rational* if *rationality* requires the evaluation of the "value" or desirability of states which must be compared in terms of a single universal measure of utility. The utility of equality cannot be consistently, reliably, or validly measured against the utility of love. Neither can be coherently measured against the utility of authority, or any of them against the utility of monetary profit.[1]

In consequence, "economic" models of human behavior are applicable only within the spheres of social action that people organize with reference to the Market Pricing model (see Godelier 1972 [1966]). Utilitarian *rationality* is limited to those spheres. The Market Pricing model of human social behavior can be appropriately applied only where the observer can show that there is a single common metric in which all relevant values are denominated. It does not operate at a metarelational level as an arbiter or selector of modes of relationship.

## Unsystematic "Systems"

> Systems need not be exhaustively interconnected to be systems. They may be densely interconnected or poorly, but which they are—how rightly [tightly?] integrated they are—is an empirical matter. To assert connections among modes of experiencing, as among any variables, it is necessary to find them (and find ways of finding them), not simply assume them. And as there are some rather compelling theoretical reasons for believing that a system which is both complex, as any culture is, and fully joined cannot function, the problem of cultural analysis is as much a matter of determining independences as interconnections, gulfs as well as bridges. (Geertz 1973c:407 [1966])

People have plans and goals, but they have many that often do not fit together very well. Moreover, only some of what people do is guided by consciously formulated or rational plans, and often the invocation of one model rather than another involves neither explicit "choice" nor manifest "decision making" (see Firth 1965:358 [1938]). The fact that sometimes people do in fact pursue one motivated social goal more or less to the exclusion of others does not imply that the process of selecting among motives is well organized or even orderly. A random number table provides an absolutely clear-cut basis for making a sequence of "decisions," but we would not describe it as rational, consistent, or implicitly structured. It remains to be determined whether cultural implementation rules have more coherence than a random number table. Surely they must be orderly to some degree, but the order needs to be recognized, described, and confirmed. Contrary to Fortes (e.g., 1966:342), Radcliffe-Brown (1965c), and many others, there is no clear evidence that social relations as a whole constitute an integrated or coherent system in Moose or any other society. On the contrary, the four models we have discussed above can be the sources of inconsistent, incompatible, opposing, even mutually exclusive rights, obligations, and sentiments. Yet they coexist within any given culture.

In his seminal classic of economic anthropology Firth (1965 [1938]:357-65) makes this point very clearly. In Tikopia (Polynesia), economic greed and self-interest (MP) coexist with a very strong system of chiefly authority (AR). These operate alongside "friendly borrowing" in which people borrow in times of scarcity and then at a time of plenty repay the loan with exactly the amount they received (EM). Similarly, a fisherman gives a share of his catch to some-one and later receives a corresponding gift of fish in return, or all the fisher-men in a canoe divide the catch from a fishing expedition into exactly equal shares. At other times, a Tikopian woman will plant taro seedlings or do other agricultural labor for a man who has no women in his household, and he may or may not give her taro at the harvest—either way it is all right (CS; pp. 293-94). Tikopians do not sell or rent land, and individual rights to use land coexist with the overarching system of "ownership" of all land by patrilineal kin groups, but at the same time anyone is free to plant crops on any vacant land without any need to ask permission; the cultivator gives the "owner" a stan-dard gift, regardless of the amount of land or yield (CS; pp. 58-59). As with Moose, all four of these disparate social orientations coexist without any par-ticular "conflict" among them.

As I have argued elsewhere (Fiske 1990), in Moose social relations consensus is far more common than conflict, clashes are relatively infrequent, and ambi-guity about how to structure a given social interaction is relatively uncom-mon—although all of these certainly occur. This reflects the comparative sta-bility of their culture together with a fairly high degree of agreement regarding the definition of events, persons, and interactions. Moose generally (but of course not always) agree about what is going on, and the relevant form of social relationship is rarely in doubt—although there may not be accord about the status of the relationship. For example, Moose co-wives may agree that in a given frame the necessary and proper mode of relating is Equality Matching, while they disagree vehemently about whether Equality Matching is actually being observed—and if not, to whose detriment.

My point is that Communal Sharing, Authority Ranking, Equality Match-ing, and Market Pricing coexist in any society and in individual psychology, but they are not necessarily highly integrated into a system at either the psy-chological or the societal level. Shweder (1979, see especially pp. 302-304) ar-gues that there is no good evidence for motivational integration within cul-tures. Accepting this—and, in particular, recognizing the autonomy of each of these four distinct kinds of individual motives—is the theoretical consequence we have to face if we acknowledge the idea that social action is not governed by any single paramount goal that integrates all action with reference to a sin-gle ultimate purpose. Neither in the society nor in the person can we continue to simply assume that there is a coherent, unitary social relational structure as such. Instead, within virtually any aggregation of people there are multiple disparate social structures, each the manifestation of different models and motives concatenated in distinctive ways. Whether and how the implementation of the models is functionally coordinated remains for us to determine.

The same issue arises with regard to the logical coherence of meaning and value in cultural "systems." The elementary models provide the four independent criteria for judging social relations. They are not necessarily reconcilable with reference to any meta-ethical principle. This gives rise to a kind of moral relativity, since there may be no superordinate ethical standard for choosing among a set of incompatible moral rules, any of which could equally well be applied to judge a given situation (Fiske 1990). The four elementary models also are the basis for understanding social life, but if there is no meta-cognitive standard of interpretation that incorporates and transcends them, then there is no unitary integrative principle. Thus the idea that a culture might be a fully coherent system of meanings and values is problematic. As Geertz (1973c) suggests, cultural analysis then must accept the possibility that cacophony is as important as harmony in most cultures.

## Nonmaximization

The most widely postulated form of integration of human behavior is maximization of utility. The economic model assumes that the coordination of the individual's behavior and the integration of behavior across individuals is the consequence of individual utility maximization in a free market.[2] But do people actually maximize? If this fundamental economic tenet cannot be sustained, then there is no obvious basis for systematic integration of social relations even within the sphere of Market Pricing.

As Godelier (1986b) stresses, the maximization axiom does not have to be associated with the other features of the Market Pricing framework. The usual economic model of human interaction stipulates that people compare alternative purchases, decide whether to buy or sell, and make other decisions within the framework of a market that is organized with reference to prices (generalized exchange ratios of commodities). But people could do all this without limitlessly maximizing their monetary profits or utility. In fact, observation suggests that people do not maximize in any absolute sense. Normal people never actually sacrifice everything for money. Of course, proponents of the economic model postulate that what people are maximizing is "utility," but this is a theoretical axiom, not an observable fact about the world. Very little evidence supports this axiom. Given any substantial, noncircular definition of utility, it is rarely possible to empirically substantiate even a quasi-rational intent to maximize anything significant.

Restricting ourselves for the moment to purely monetary or material pursuits, it is quite evident that people do not ordinarily maximize—people sometimes want to make a profit, earn money, and acquire goods, and they may be moderately *rational* and efficient in their efforts to do so. But most people do not seek limitless economic gain, and many people, like Moose, generally show little interest in profit at all. This is clearly evident in a variety of traditional societies, and can be quite striking when individuals from such societies interact with people whose ideology presumes Market Pricing. Among Euro-Americans in Africa and elsewhere in the third world, there is a widely known myth (recounted laughingly, with uneasy confusion) whose central figure is an exasperating, irrational "native" who comes out of the "bush" to work for a salary and then suddenly leaves for home when he has earned exactly enough money for the particular purpose that led him to seek the job in the first place (say, to pay a bride price). Offers to give the employee a raise and other material inducements fall on deaf ears—he has what he needs and sees no point in continuing. Money as such is of no interest to him apart from his needs in this one particular project. When he has earned enough for that, earning more seems pointless to him. This myth reflects the confusion of Euro-Americans who try to explain human behavior as if people were maximizing material gain.

In modern Western societies, the picture is complicated by the high value placed on Market Pricing behavior, along with the ideological belief that aggressively competitive economic profit-making is the natural and therefore proper activity of people (cf. Schwartz 1986), or indeed the measure of their grace and salvation (Weber 1958), or indicative of their value as people ("success"). This ideology may lead people to act as if they were economic maximizers, to present themselves as such, and to think they are doing so. Thinking they should have limitless ambitions and believing that deep down they really are ambitious, and moreover socialized to strive for standards of "success" that few people ever achieve in real life, people may live in a state of incessant striving. If the cultural ethos aims at being first, if "Winning isn't the most important thing, it's the only thing," if there is only one true winner in every race, and if the winner is judged only over the entire (unfinished) course of a life history, then most people will see themselves and everyone else as unsatisfied, and in some sense be unsatisfied. In that sense, maximization, striving without limit, becomes a more or less self-fulfilling ideology (again, see Schwartz 1986, as well as Wallach and Wallach 1983).

In these circumstances, or in extreme privation, it may be difficult to distinguish in practice between true maximization and chronic frustration of needs. If people are always below the level at which a given motive would be sated—are chronically frustrated in fulfilling a need—then they will appear to be pursuing that motive without limit. But even scarcity does not necessarily imply incessant striving. As we saw, Moose—among the very poorest people in the world—do not exhibit a calculating cost/benefit orientation to social life, much less relentless maximization of production. Although they are assiduous, hard-working farmers, they are not preoccupied with "efficiency" above all else, and they are definitely not profit-oriented "economizers" in any non-trivial sense.

No one who studies motives in any other organism reports any naturally occurring behavior that corresponds to an unfulfillable motive. Every motive can be satisfied, and in nature many often are. No animal wants food, water, salt, play and exploration, sleep, or even sex without limit. At a certain point (which in nature may rarely or quite commonly be reached, depending on the organism, the environment, and the drive) the animal makes less effort to obtain more of a given substance or activity, and some level can always be found where that entity is aversive—too much of a good thing. The same is true of the demand for any commodity ever studied by economists. Demand curves are always convex upwards, so that beyond a certain point, the marginal utility of any given entity decreases and typically becomes negative. Humans and other organisms generally have finite optimum levels (that are context and experience dependent) for anything they seek.

Similarly, there is no reason to believe that people generally maximize with respect to any social motive. Moose seek to participate in Communal Sharing relationships and strengthen these relationships, but that does not mean they do so without limit. People seek the friendship, camaraderie, fairness, and equality of Equality Matching, but participant observation does not reveal a calculating striving after the maximum number (or intensity) of such relationships. Authority Ranking is more complex, since for the most part it is ascribed as a function of ethnicity, gender, and age. When an office like that of village chief or leader of the Yarse is vacant, the pursuit of the office is covert, because Moose derogate overt ambition. No one admits to seeking office. What this means in part is that people do not "go for broke" in seeking office. They are loath to sacrifice Communal Sharing and Equality Matching relationships in the pursuit of power in an Authority Ranking relationship. So in social domains, too, people may be optimizers in some sense, but they are not maximizers.

The usual economic assumption is that what people maximize is their total utility function, aggregated across all needs, goals, and wants. However, as we saw in the previous section, both the psychological and the ethnographic evidence suggests that the four basic social motives and values are incommensurable. If indeed the four fundamental social orientations are not reducible to any common metric, and therefore could not be subject to *rational* trade-off or summation, then people cannot be maximizing any aggregation of them. Hence maximization of utility cannot comprehensively integrate either individual social behavior or social relations in a collectivity.

Even if the motives and values inherent in the four basic models were commensurable, this would not imply that people were maximizing across them. By the same token, systematic application of the four models would not ipso facto imply that the decision function was based on any kind of internally consistent or stable commensurability, much less maximization. Indeed, cultural implementation rules yield highly regular and predictable patterns of use of the models that probably do not reflect the maximization of anything. Ordered selection ("choice") among alternatives does not require or imply stable or consistent preferences. In fact, implementation rules seem to be formulated largely in terms of context, often ignoring anything resembling the "utility"of the social action for the people involved. In short, utility maximization is unlikely to operate to produce cultural coherence or social systematization, and what coherence and systematization we find need not be the result of any kind of maximization.

## TRADITION

I have argued that cultural implementation rules determine which models people apply and how and when they apply them. This is widely reflected in the data from participant observation. One often reads in ethnographies that people in non-Western cultures justify and explain their cultural enactments in terms of tradition. Usually the ethnographer says something to the effect of, "They can give no account of why they do such-and-such, merely saying that, 'It is our tradition'." Whereupon the ethnographer goes on and attempts to generate an explanation of the behavior in question as if "tradition" were inadequate to account for anything important. But I think we should take our informants seriously. They do organize their lives and their activities with reference to tradition. They are replicating and maintaining traditional cultural forms, and often no other explanation is adequate.

When I asked the Moose about the reasons for rituals and for basic patterns of social relations, their answer generally was, *Yaa tõnd rog m miki* (It is what we found/perceived at birth), or occasionally, *Yaa tõnd barãmba sẽ n maane* (It is what our fathers/ancestors did). The aphorism can be expanded: *Rog m miki, ki n basgo* (Come into the world and find, die and leave [leave behind for others to carry on]). Indeed, the invocations of sacrifices and the introductions to other rituals often begin with a statement, addressed to either the ancestors or to the participants and audience, of the following form:

*Yaa rog m miki. Yaa tõnd barãmba sẽ n maane, ti tõnd me maandame.*
*Tõnd rog m mik ed barãmba sẽ n mi n maan woto, ti tõnd me ket n maandalame.*

(It is born and found [tradition]. It is what our fathers/ancestors did, so we do it. We were born and found our fathers/ancestors habitually doing this, so we too continue to do it.)

Not everything is explained this way. Moose tend to justify their technology partly in terms of its efficacy, that is, as techniques that produce a given desired result. And some kinds of social interaction are explained in other ways.

For example the Moose typically account for their deference in Authority Ranking relations by saying that, *Tõnd zoeta bamba* (We are afraid of [run from] them.) But the predominant account that the Moose give for their actions is *rog m miki*—the tradition that they found at birth and perpetuate until they die and pass on to their descendants. Replicating the ancestors' ways, Moose constitute an enduring community, a sense of communal identity based on belonging to a continuous social whole that transcends personal birth and death. The core of their religion and a critical nexus in social relationships is sacrifice, the principal aim of which is to be one with the ancestors, the spirits of nature, and the Earth, to feed and be fed, in mutual dependence and nurturance. And Moose religion in particular is implicitly and explicitly grounded in the ways of the ancestors. As Weber (1975) and Piaget (1973) observed, one of the most fundamental and widespread forms of legitimation is in terms of the continuity of eternal traditions.

This form of legitimation in terms of continuity with the past, in terms of the perpetuation of "what has always been done," is prototypical of Communal Sharing. But as a rationale, Moose extend it to cover almost any social or cultural form that is brought into question. When the meaningfulness of social life is problematic, Moose ground it in tradition. In this sense and at this level, Moose are referring to their cultural implementation rules. They are saying that they are the bearers of their culture and instruments of their ancestry, so their purpose is to perpetuate the community into which they were born and which they hope to sustain through their descendants. The culture *is* tradition, the distinctive implementation rules of the community. Like many other peoples, Moose assert that their paramount goal in social relations is to maintain and reinforce their corporate solidarity, sharing communally among the living and with their dead progenitors, thereby perpetuating the immutable, immanent community of tradition. We ought to take their word for it.

At the end of Part II I suggested a number of directions in which the relational-models theory should be developed, foremost among them the study of the dynamic processes by which implementation rules change over time. The complementary problem for future research is the question of continuity and coherence posed here: If these four models are the elementary components of social lives, societies, and cultures, then are there any integrating principles for assembling them? Is any collection of pieces equally feasible? What are the constraints? Can any collection of implementation rules make a viable tradition? These are fundamental problems.

# 17

# Sources of Sociability

> One may speak of an impulse to sociability in man. To be sure, it is for the sake of special needs and interests that men unite in economic associations or blood fraternities, in cult societies or robber bands. But, above and beyond their special content, all these associations are accompanied by a feeling for, by a satisfaction in, the very fact that one is associated with others and that the solitariness of the individual is resolved into togetherness, a union with others. Of course, this feeling can, in individual cases, be nullified by contrary psychological factors; association can be felt as a mere burden, endured for the sake of our objective aims. But typically there is involved in all effective motives for association a feeling of the worth of association as such, a drive which presses toward this form of existence and often only later calls forth that objective content which carries the particular association along . . . The impulse to sociability distils, as it were, out of the realities of social life the pure essence of association, of the associative process as a value and a satisfaction. (Simmel 1971:128 [1911])

This final chapter argues against taking for granted the usual opposition between norms or structural principles on the one hand, and the motives of human agents on the other. It is typically assumed that people are inherently Asocial, or antisocial—that the fundamental interests of each actor are distinct, disparate, and often opposed to the interests of others. Socialization then is required to tame people so that they will submit to social rules; continued social pressures, norms, and sanctions are essential to maintain social control. The raw, natural human motivations are assumed to be inimical to social life, so it is only through "internalization" of externally imposed norms, together with sublimation or rechannelling of our dark and dangerous native instincts, that social life becomes possible—though precarious. But these assumptions seriously distort human nature. The "problem" of social order or social control becomes moot if humans have a number of fundamental natural proclivities toward sociability. Conflict between personal motives and normative obligations is not inevitable or pervasive. Motives, norms, and structural principles have common sources in the four elementary models, and tend to be in harmony. This can be seen by looking closely at individual ontogeny, where motives, awareness of, and commitment to social norms, and the relevant capacity to generate particular structures in social relationships probably emerge together. Humans are inherently sociable animals, and even the most seemingly autonomous individualism is culturally informed and socially realized.

## NORMS, STRUCTURAL PRINCIPLES, AND INDIVIDUAL MOTIVES

### What Are Motives?

Many anthropologists and sociologists would assume that the kind of ethnographic evidence presented in Part IV is informative about culture, norms, and the structural principles of society, but can tell us nothing about the personal motives of agents. The usual supposition is that people's motives are inherently selfish and competitive, that people make choices so as to covertly maximize their individual interests as they conceive them. Many students of society recognize that people exhibit the kinds of behavior I am calling Communal Sharing, Equality Matching, the pastoral protection of responsible authorities, and the respectful deference of subordinates. A few observers also acknowledge that people may orient to ratios of costs and benefits without, ipso facto, being patently selfish, competitive, or maximizing. But most theorists attribute such patterns of social action to norms or other socially imposed obligations, or more broadly to structural principles of the sociocultural system. In this modern version of Hobbes, norms, sanctions, and other kinds of macro "structure" are said to "control" individuals and generate organization where otherwise there would be anarchy and perhaps an overt (instead of merely covert) war of all against all. In contrast, the relational-models theory treats norms and other obligations, punishment and sanctions and susceptibility to them, the structures of social relations and institutions, and motives as diverse manifestations of the same elementary models. To understand what this means, let us examine the concept of motivation.

Consider how two important theorists, a psychologist and an anthropologist, define motivation. Gallistel (1980a, 1980b, 1981, 1985) analyzes the concept by linking it to the units and hierarchical organization of behavior. He concludes that motivated behavior is "goal-directed behavior whose functional cohesiveness is produced by the selective potentiating and depotentiating effects of neural and hormonal signals" (Gallistel 1980b:408). The crux of this definition is the idea that action is purposively organized by the activation of appropriate patterns of behavior and suppression of other patterns so as to bring about some end state. Although the level of analysis and the language used contrasts, this approach to motivation is entirely congruent with the one Geertz (1966:10–11) offers. Geertz describes a motivation as

> a persisting tendency, a chronic inclination to perform certain sorts of acts and experience certain sorts of feelings in certain sorts of situation, the 'sorts' being commonly very heterogeneous and rather ill-defined classes. (Geertz 1966:10)

He goes on to say that "motives are thus neither acts (i.e. intentional behaviors) nor feelings, but liabilities to perform particular classes of act or have particular classes of feeling" (Geertz 1966:11). He relates and contrasts motives with moods (which do not involve goals), writing that

> motives have a directional cast, they describe a certain overall course, gravitate toward certain, usually temporary, consummations. . . .
> Motivations are 'made meaningful' with reference to the ends toward which they are conceived to conduce. (Geertz 1966:12)

In these terms, the kinds of ethnographic evidence presented in Part IV and earlier are clearly relevant to making inferences about motives. Each of the basic types of social relationship we have considered involves a distinct kind of meaningful coherence in interaction, associated with distinctive relational goals. The goal in each case is to constitute and maintain a particular kind of interaction, while the coherence of the disparate acts undertaken toward this end—and the coherence of the associated emotions—derives from shared conceptions of what it is to relate to others in the framework of the particular type of relationship. For example, the "heterogeneous" class of actions that people who are communally motivated perform is just that class of actions which the actors conceive of as embodying Communal Sharing—making salient their solidarity and distinctive unity, eating together, helping and caring, being "close," making collective sacrifices.

The ethnographic account that I have presented suggests that Moose share their resources and pool their labor for the sake of the solidarity, unity, and "kindness" of the Communal Sharing relationship itself. Similarly, Moose exercise (and pursue) authority and give deferential obeisance for the sake of constituting Authority Ranking itself. The AR relationship is the state toward which the command and obedience, responsible authority, and loyal subservience of Authority Ranking are teleologically oriented. In parallel to these relationships, Moose take turns, reciprocate evenly, and match the work of others one-for-one because these are forms of Equality Matching; the EM relationship is the goal. In just the same way, *rationally* comparing alternatives and calculating the ratio of benefits to costs in a Market Pricing framework is inherently motivating.

By the definitions of Geertz and Gallistel, each of these four social orientations is a motivational goal, an alternative teleology for structuring human social relations.[1] Each is a tendency or potential to perform certain sets of actions (and to refrain from others) whose meaning and coherence derives from their contribution to the creation, maintenance, reinforcement, or repair of a particular form of relationship. But note that from this perspective motives are barely distinguishable from norms. As long as energy, fuel, or the power of movement was the implicit metaphor for motives, motives naturally seemed to be "in" the individual. Similarly, if the implicit metaphor for a norm (or a rule or structural principle) was a set of paths, boundaries, and obstacles, then norms were naturally conceived as external to the individual navigating such barriers. But the concept of motivation that Geertz and Gallistel propose is the idea of a goal-oriented functionally coordinated pattern of action. The goal and the coordinating principle of a motive do not have to be "in" the individual or "in" the milieu as such. They may inhere in an idea, a relational model. From this point of view, motive force and constraint are not opposed, they may be aspects of the same entity, the relational model. The intent and the structure, the goal and the means, are not intrinsically opposed. They may mesh or even merge.

## Duty and Desire

Does duty usually conflict with desire? Some recent accounts of social life offer a very expediential view of human behavior. These accounts describe people as playing a game, manipulating others by invoking rules just when it is in their self-interest to do so, interpreting the inherent ambiguities of what we are calling cultural implementation rules to their personal advantage, and generally using rules as resources in a calculating manner to secure power, material gain, or other personal utilities. A considerable amount of "role distance" is presumed. Social rules are thought to be imposed on people from the outside as "external" constraints.[2] In this account, people adhere to those rules it suits them to adopt as guises for their covert ends, sanctimoniously clothing their selfish motives in the garb of morality and law. There is an important grain of truth in this account; there obviously are occasions when duty and desire are opposed, and this conflict is of great practical and theoretical interest. But this approach presupposes a discrepancy between motives and norms that is probably not typical of most people in most situations in most societies. More often than most theorists suppose, duty and desire coincide. Furthermore, this account does not fully explain why people are susceptible to social sanctions per se (see Spiro 1961), or why people often undertake to punish others at some net cost to themselves.

In fact, people commonly adhere to the rules even when they know that no objective sanctions are operating. The classical account of this is that people often "feel obligated" to conform to social rules, so they may do so even when obligation conflicts with personal desire. The search for the source of this sense of objective binding obligation in social rules has been a core problem and indeed the major impetus for the creation of the sciences of society. This issue was a central concern of Rousseau, Hobbes, and Locke. Emile Durkheim (1965 [1912]) attempted to account for this sense of transcendent imperative in *The Elementary Forms of the Religious Life,* and Jean Piaget (1973 [1932]) later followed up Durkheim's work in *The Moral Judgment of the Child.* As the problem of legitimacy—the grounds for justifying political authority and other types of social organization—this issue was at the core of Max Weber's (1978 [1922]) seminal opus, *Economy and Society.* Both Durkheim and Piaget argued that the human sense of the obligatory nature of abstract moral principles derives from people's recognition of the intrinsic logic of social relationships. Weber's view was that each type of social organization is linked to a distinctive idea about how binding rules are constituted. Arising from diverse historical sources, Weber wrote, these legitimating ideas are necessary conditions for stable social order. Beginning with Freud, later psychological theories have focused on processes of "internalization," in which children acquire and retain some kind of motivating representation of a punitive external social world. What these theories have in common is that they depict motives as generally congruent with norms, since motives and norms are ultimately manifestations of social relationships.

The relational-models theory explains the congruence of social duty and social desire in terms of their common source. People use their collective repertoire of models for the construction, comprehension, criticism, and control of the social relationships they crave, and as their social conscience. The thesis of the relational-models theory is that in any given instance, people's social-relational cravings, construction, comprehension, criticism, control, and conscience are all usually driven by the same model. To extend Geertz (1966) along the lines developed above in Chapter 8, each elementary model is a motivated schema *for* constituting social relationships (a guide, plan, or recipe), and a model *of* what is happening in social relationships (that is, a model for understanding, a model that gives meaning to action). Furthermore, each model is a standard for reacting to, taking into account, judging, and intervening in social relationships, and conversely, for accommodating to (and anticipating) others' appropriate judgments of one's own relationships. The crux of the matter is that each model is simultaneously a goal that people actively seek to realize in their actions toward others, a standard by which they judge their own and their partners' behavior, and a recognized criterion for others' legitimate interventions. Third parties who are not immediate participants in a particular interaction are applying the model as a standard for assessing the interaction, demanding that participants conform to the relevant model even when the third party evaluator has little or no direct personal "interest" in the outcome. Participants expect this and recognize the legitimacy in principle of this use of the models as norms. So there need be no discrepancy between the assessment that outsiders impose and the person's own goals or standards.

All of these uses of a model in a given instance tend to coincide because ordinarily people are all using the same model to understand the interaction, to make sense of it in the first place. Once an interaction is consensually constituted as a relationship of a given type, the motivational, normative, and structural dimensions are potentially congruent. That is, if all the people involved in an interaction comprehend it in terms of the same model, then there will be harmony among participants' goals, their joint construction of a given social structure, the criticism and social controls people apply to it, and participants' conscientious susceptibility to others' critiques: all tend to correspond.

For example, in various contexts, to varying degrees and in culturally varied forms, Moose actively guide their own behavior in order to realize Equality Matching relationships. That is, they actively seek to distribute shares evenly, take turns, and reciprocate—these are personal goals toward which they orient. At the same time, Moose seek to get their partners in the relevant interactions to conform to the Equality Matching model by distributing shares fairly, taking turns, and reciprocating one-for-one. Meanwhile, other Moose attempt to prevail on the participants to guide their behavior in accordance with the Equality Matching model. The participants acknowledge that they are subject to this standard, and are hence susceptible to its invocation by either participants or third-party critics. Another example of congruence in the CS mode is Caudill's (1962) analysis of Japanese values and emotions. Caudill found that the dominant Japanese value orientation was collaterality, while the emotions manifested in responses to TAT cards reflected an emphasis on nonsexual sensual pleasures associated with the company of others, sympathetic care and concern for others in need, and harmonious marital relations.

In the context of any particular interaction, these aspects of each model do not necessarily coincide. Participants or observers may experience a conflict with other motives when they would like to implement a model not currently realized. There may also be discrepancies when different people are trying to apply different models to the situation. People may also be using inconsistent implementation rules, and in particular, may be at odds as to how a given model applies to them. This may result in conflict. But in most slowly changing, reasonably homogeneous traditional societies—and even in many modern ones—there is such implicit consensus about the cultural implementation rules that people rarely operate at cross-purposes.[3] To the extent that all concerned agree on what the relevant model is, then there is a binding social obligation which more or less coincides with a personal desire. People's sense that a model is binding reflects their recognition that, within the taken-for-granted terms of the given culture, the relevant model objectively just is the directive standard for action. Then the directive force of norms and motives typically coincide, and may be indistinguishable.

In the language of D'Andrade (1984), constitutive, directive, regulative, and interpretive (representational) social rules are inseparable, because they have the same source. They are simply manifestations of the same models from different perspectives. There is no intrinsic, necessary opposition between norms and motives. Social motives are relational models in the form of guides and goals for the actor in social relationships, while norms are the same models mutually applied as collective standards for relationships. When derived from the same model, the goal is the same whether it is used to generate action directly (a motive), or invoked to judge one's own or another's action (a norm), or recognized to acknowledge accountability to shared standards (conscience).


## The Motives of Groups: Levels of Analysis

There is a pervasive—not to say perverse—reductionist bias in the social sciences. In the West we often regard the individual organism as what is really real, while society is seen as an epiphenomenon. Particularly in psychology (but sometimes even in anthropology) the tangible person is thought to be the fundamental reality for scientific investigation, while social relationships, society, and culture are impalpable fictions. Hence even anthropologists are hesitant to acknowledge the emergent qualities of social and cultural realities, especially when it comes to motivation. But these prejudices are artifacts of our own culture, and need not, should not, limit our thought as restrictively as they have. Motivation—coordinated goal-directed action—is a property of culture-sharing collectivities as well as individuals. And the collective motivations to construct the basic types of social relationships are as fundamental as hunger, as real as thirst, as natural as nest building.

The coordinated teleological organization of action that we characterize as motivation may be a property of an individual, or it may emerge only at the level of a dyad, a group, or a whole society. In that sense motives are characteristics of higher order social entities. There is a tendency among anthropologists and other social scientists to consider culture as a set of symbols and meanings, which individuals manipulate according to their personal motivations. Culture supposedly provides the options, the tools, which people pick and choose among to accomplish their goals. This places the "ideas" and "rules" in the culture, and the goal-directed "purposes" in the individual. But cultures are comprised of teleological goals as well as meanings—there is "directive force" in culture (see D'Andrade 1990, in press). The fundamental models for social relations are purposeful. They generatively direct and coordinate the social relationships constituted by pairs and groups of people in just the same sense as a sexual drive, parental defense of offspring, or hunger generatively directs and coordinates the actions of an individual. At both levels what we observe is a goal or equilibrium state and some kind of feedback leading to the coordination and teleological modification of action so as to tend to bring about that end state.

Thus, in Communal Sharing the model directs toward continuous mutual sharing, kindness, and interdependent solidarity. However, even within the confines of the forms of Communal Sharing specific to Moose culture there are an infinite variety of ways of realizing—or working toward—that optimum state, dictated by histories, circumstances, disruptions, and opportunities. The Communal Sharing model specifies the goal, along with some of the basic mechanisms for pursuit of the goal. But the actual shape of the action that people collectively undertake in pusuit of that ideal is neither stereotyped nor fixed. Again, the goal of Equality Matching as exchange, for example, is a finite or reiterated correspondence between what each party gives and what each party takes. The model specifies the orientation and the cultural implementation rules provide the criteria for what constitutes balance, equality, evenness. Even so, reciprocity, turn taking, egalitarian distributive justice, and matching compensation can be implemented in an infinite variety of ways in any given culture; so the exact manner in which people achieve Equality Matching in a particular interaction is not fully specified. But the direction is given. When the model is operating to govern an interaction, the interactants collaboratively move toward their shared goal, and they correct deviations from it. The social relationship as such exhibits a kind of taxis or oriented movement, such that the mutual modulation of action is directed to the ideal. This taxis is not a property of the action of any one person alone, but emerges at the level of the social relationship, in the total sequence. It is the whole series of responses of all the participants in the relationship that shows this taxis. The pursuit of the model emerges from the directionality of the process, not just from any individual act or the sum of all the acts of any one person.

Motivated action is action that is functionally integrated, coordinated, systematic. Social relationships exhibit this feature on the level of the relationship as such, not just in the action of each participant. This complementarity of action is an essential feature of what constitutes a social relationship—the behavior of each person meshes with that of the other participants in a coherent way. Buying a commodity under Market Pricing requires both a buyer and a seller with a shared understanding of the framework in which they are operating. By itself, setting out piles of okra on a mat in a particular place on a particular day has no function. But when potential buyers regard okra as a commodity and have complementary expectations about market day and perceive this act as an offer to sell, a market is constituted. In the same way, there is no sense in removing hat and shoes, lying prone, and touching one's forehead to the ground if the person to whom this action is directed does not recognize it as obeisance and respond accordingly. Again, just sitting next to some food without eating is not the same act as waiting for an elder to offer up the first bite to his ancestors and then begin to eat before his juniors. However, one or more people waiting, combined with the other beginning first, mark a difference in rank, and together constitute deference when people share this understanding of the meaning of their joint actions. These acts (and others) fit together to constitute Authority Ranking, but the action of the participating individuals has no meaning in isolation from the expected responses of the others and their understanding of the intent of their counterparts. It is this coordinated, as well as purposeful, quality of action that identifies it as motivated, just as we recognize a predator's hunger in the coordinated set of bodily movements that together result in search, stalking, pursuit, capture, and consumption of prey. The difference is that the teleological coordination of social action is a property of two or more people acting together with reference to a shared model.

In the complex and extended pattern of action that is Moose courtship, the behavior of all the participants is coordinated with reference to an implicit shared understanding of how the relationship ought to be realized. For example, at certain events in the courtship process the wife-seekers bring beer to give to the wife-givers, and they give all they bring to their hosts. This makes sense, because they know that the wife-givers will divide up the beer and share it with them, giving back some of what they brought. They will get plenty to drink. At the same time as the wife-seekers are getting ready and proceeding on the trail to see them, the wife-givers are preparing a large and luxurious meal. Soon after the wife-seekers arrive, the wife-givers give them all the food, keeping none for themselves. The wife-seekers eat their fill, and give back what they cannot eat, so that the wife-givers have plenty to eat. Each of these actions by all these people on such occasions, and any step in the entire sequence of actions over the years of courtship, only makes sense because it complements the behavior of the other party, fitting together as linked, mutually presupposing components of the event. The coordination is achieved by the fact that everyone knows what the event is and how to enact it. They all use the same model to generate their own actions and to understand the actions of others. When someone acts in a manner that violates the movement toward the relational equilibrium or ideal, that person and others take corrective action (rebuke, retaliation, apology, compensation) to make the total series of actions move back toward the goal defined by the operative model. All of the action is teleologically oriented, coordinated, and integrated with reference to the particularly Moose implementation of Communal Sharing and the other models in the domain of marriage. Scores of people may coordinate their action in this way over a period of tens of years. This coordination and teleology of culturally shaped collective action define it as motivated. The complementarity and jointly goal-directed nature of the action are "emergent" characteristics of the dyad or higher order collectively, not of the individual participants acting alone.

From this perspective we can go beyond the theoretical stereotype of the motivated individual agent navigating his or her way through a maze of cultural constraints and choices. The functionally coordinated, purposively oriented character of action is the emergent product of the actions of many individuals collectively organizing their action with reference to shared relational models. The directional cast of the action and the feedback processes it entails are not characteristics of any one individual, they are features of the collectively shared, culture-specific realization of the models. So collective social action is motivated in much the same sense as the behavior of individuals. The relational goal is the same whether we call it a norm or a motive, whether we write of it as residing "in" the person or "in" the society.

## Intrinsically Social Motives

Even if we take a person-centered subjective perspective, seeing the world through the eyes of the individual actor, the contrast between norms and motives fades when we consider what the person is up to. The four basic motives that we have been discussing in this book are fundamentally social, relational motives in the sense that they would be inherently unfulfillable by a person who conceived herself to be alone, and they require other people not as objects, but as active partners in the construction of relationships. Even the motivation to command, control, lead, protect, and defend others requires subordinates, who defer, obey, give obeisance, show respect, loyally follow, and seek protection. At the same time, the complementary motivation to obey, submit, respect, and be protected cannot be fulfilled without relating to some being who is perceived as exercising authority in accordance with a jointly held model of Authority Ranking. (Of course, this alter, this partner in constituting a social relationship who plays the complementary role, may be an imputed social being like an ancestor or a god.) Similarly, one can only take turns, reciprocate, be just and fair with an (imputed) partner who has similar concerns (even if only an imaginary friend). It goes without saying that communal solidarity, belonging, sharing, generosity, love, and kindness cannot be enacted by a solitary actor. Each of these are social motives in that the model for their realization requires other social beings. The models cannot be implemented or the needs fulfilled without interacting with another social being, real or imagined.

People need to engage in social relationships. For example, Mead (1937:480, 486–97, 507, 510) repeatedly states that "cooperative" (Communal Sharing) relationships give all participants a uniquely strong sense of security. Deprived of membership in primary groups and in other secondary collectivities, people experience great distress. Indeed, Baumeister and Tice (1989) argue that fear of exclusion from social groups is the major cause of anxiety.

Moreover, when pairs or groups of people jointly construct social relations of each of these types, the relationships generally are mutually rewarding. Such social relationships are jointly constituted out of shared motives, and they fulfill shared needs. Of course, everyone involved may not find a given relationship equally fulfilling, or unequivocally satisfying: there certainly are dysfunctional and exploitive interactions. But in general people seek out and attempt to form relationships with others whose motives mesh, and social relationships tend to satisfy the motivations that underlie them just to the extent that the motives and models actually are shared. So the satisfaction of any person's social motives is generally achieved through the satisfaction of others' social motives. More precisely, social motives are fulfilled through the joint constitution of mutually rewarding relationships. In that sense, people are inherently sociable. If a person's goal is to engage in social relationships as such, the question of selfishness (or altruism, for that matter) does not arise—indeed with respect to such a motivation it doesn't make any sense. To illustrate the point that social interaction governed by the basic models is intrinsically sociable, and to show how it is culturally constituted, let us consider Market Pricing in particular.

## The Social and Cultural Nature of Market Pricing

Achievement seems to be definitely an ego value. It is the way in which the society provides for the expression of the self-maximating tendencies of the individual. In a society which disallows those self-maximating tendencies, achievement vanishes as an ego value, and achievement itself is likely to be minimized. . . . In the three competitive societies [studied by the group] . . . the culture provides a definite channel for this form of ego expression and it is not surprising to find strong ego development sought for and valued in all three of these societies. (Margaret Mead 1937:485–86)

The most basic conclusion which comes out of this research [is] that competitive and cooperative behavior on the part of individual members of a society is fundamentally conditioned by the total social emphasis of that society, that the goals for which individuals will work are culturally determined and are not the response of the organism to an external, culturally undefined situation, like a simple scarcity of food. (Mead 1937:16)

In one sense, Market Pricing is not "natural," in that it has no phylogenetic precedent as a form of social organization. No other organism has markets, uses money, engages in transactions or makes choices based on explicit prices, exchanges unlike commodities at set ratios, makes interest-bearing loans or investments, or seeks to accumulate inedible income-producing "capital." No other organism pays another for labor, or produces goods purely for exchange. Evolutionary models of natural selection notwithstanding, as far as can be determined no other organism makes rational cost/benefit utility calculations among novel social alternatives and systematically chooses the most efficient or the most profitable alternative. (Of course, evolved heuristics may tend to yield very rough approximations of such calculations—at least in situations that correspond closely to the environment to which the organism is adapted.) For one thing, efficiency and profit are defined by the comparison of differences and ratios, while there is no evidence that either in the wild or with any kind of training any of the Pongidae (apes) or Delphinidae (dolphins)—let alone other taxa—are capable of using such mathematical structures, at least in social relations (Premack 1976, Premack and Premack 1982, Matsuzawa 1985, Matsuzawa et al. 1986, Cheney and Seyfarth 1985). But cognitive capacity is only the raw material of Market Pricing: people need a culture through which to implement their social relations.

Far more than any other organism, humans relate to each other through the medium of their cultures. As Chapter 7 outlined, Market Pricing can be realized only in some particular, culturally defined manner: the cultural implementation rules have to be specified. There is considerable variation in the overall concern with Market Pricing in different domains of human activity, in different societies, and in different historical periods (see Marx and Engels 1906; Mead 1937; Polanyi 1957a, 1957b; Polanyi et al. 1957a; Kluckhohn and Strodtbeck 1973 [1961]; Sahlins 1965, 1976a; Triandis 1987; Triandis et al. 1988). But the role of culture is not simply a quantitative matter of degree. The contrast between Moose and, say, the United States exemplifies the importance of implementation rules that specify who sells what to whom, when, and where. With whom can you appropriately enter into market transactions? What are the settings in which Market Pricing is appropriate? What entities can appropriately be treated as commodities? Market Pricing can be implemented under virtually any particular specification of the implementation rules, but it cannot be implemented at all until the culture makes such specifications.

Beyond this variability in the cultural specification of times, places, substance, and participants, cultures also provide the necessary recipes for *how* to buy, sell, bargain, compete, be efficient, invest, and so forth. The culture defines what acts (statements, gestures, symbols) make a sale a sale, and not a gift, an offering of tribute, a trade, or a theft. Imagine that you have just moved into a village, and someone comes to you with a bowl of cooked food. Should you pay for it, or would the giver be mortally offended if you did? Should you reciprocate in kind, and if so when, and with what? Or is this a gesture of asymmetric respect, which should be accepted but not matched with anything comparable? A priori, there is no way of knowing the meaning of the food without knowing how this particular culture uses different sorts of transactions to mark different forms of social relationships.

As Austin (1962) has shown, many actions are performed by virtue of speech acts whose very utterance constitutes the action. The same is true of gestures and other symbolic actions. In Euro-American culture a slight movement or positioning of a finger at an auction may constitute a commitment to pay millions of dollars for the item on the block. Just what statements, gestures, symbolic displays, and other actions constitute offering for sale, making a bid, closing a sale, and so forth are culturally specified. Wearing certain clothing and being present in a certain neighborhood may, if culturally so defined, constitute an offer to sell sexual services (see the movie *Crocodile Dundee*). Among the Moose, saying *baraka* (blessing, well-being, thanks) after receiving a gift is an expression of appreciation, while saying it after hearing a bid constitutes the refusal to sell at that price. In the United States, signing your name to a slip of paper imprinted with a plastic card carrying your name, the name of a retailer and an amount of money constitutes a commitment to pay when billed by a third party, although the slip does not say this anywhere.

The cultural constitution of the Market Pricing model (like the other three basic models) entails setting parameters that must be specified before any MP transaction can take place: What is the currency—are these shells money? What are the prices—is a chicken worth a day's labor? What are the value-relevant features of commodities—is a red rooster worth more than a black one? One can enact only some particular, culturally constituted variant of Market Pricing, using the model with its parameters specified and its form elaborated according to some specific culture that is shared with the other participants in the social relationship.

Wittgenstein wrote about language games. Luce and Raiffa (1957) developed a tradition of mathematical analysis of competitive games, and subsequent social scientists have often used games as a metaphor for human relations. This metaphor highlights the inherently sociocultural nature of Market Pricing. Market Pricing as enacted in any given society is a culturally defined game with culture-specific rules, strategies, forms of deviation, purposes, and criteria for measuring success. Let us consider the modern Western competitive, self-interested, maximizing form of Market Pricing. Weber (1958), Veblen (1934 [1899]), Polanyi (1947), Sahlins (1976a), and others show that people commonly strive to acquire commodities for their social functions, not for the sake of the material or biological properties of the goods as objects. McClelland, Atkinson, and their associates (McClelland 1955, 1976; McClelland et al. 1953; Atkinson 1958; Atkinson and Feather 1966) add to these sociological observations the psychological insight that achievement motivation is specifically aroused by situations that the person regards as challenging. The need is to achieve success at tasks that measure general competence, determination, insight or knowledge, planning ability, skill at calculating risks, and other culturally valued talents. You can always win at bridge if you seek out poor enough opponents, and beat the electronic chess board if you set its skill level low enough. But it is no challenge, and there is little or no satisfaction in such "victories." The achievement motive research clearly shows that people high in need for achievement do not seek wealth, profit, high scores on tests, or victory in contests for their own sake but as indices of their social worth, as they assess this for themselves in cultural terms.

People do not engage in Market Pricing behavior only because they are self-interested, but also because they are socially interested. That is, the intrinsic motivation for Market Pricing social relationships is fulfilled by obtaining appropriate ratios in interactions with others (or against a culturally established standard that transitively indicates performance compared to others). When people are maximizing in a particular Market Pricing exchange, their goal is to get the lowest price for what they buy, when the seller wants as high a price as she can get. Or the goal may be to increase market share in a world where competitors are also trying to increase their market share. When the goal is to make a profit, people are calculating the risks and predicting the market, buying from others who are selling because they have made contrary predictions. When people are competing, their goal is to contest and win, succeeding over others to obtain culturally valued scarce rewards. All of these variant forms of MP are inherently social; the goal is always to relate to others according to some proportional standard.

Even in a noncompetitive culture, people are concerned about appearing to play the Market Pricing game competently. When one returns to the village from making a significant purchase in a Moose market, Moose inquire of the buyer, or the seller, at what price the transaction was made. Moose respond to these questions, and their interlocutors freely offer their critiques. (Asking questions about other peoples' activities, obtaining answers, and openly evaluating others' behavior are unusual in other Moose contexts.) A buyer who paid "too much" for a purchase, or a seller who got "too little," can be embarrassed to discover she struck a poor deal. Moose say to someone who was fooled or bested in bargaining, *a lubflame* (he threw you, knocked you down, fooled you, "put one over on you"). Bargainers haggle over prices partly, I think, to defend their *yʋʋre* (name, reputation) as much as anything else. Only a fool fails to inform herself about the going market price for commodities, or pays the initial asking price for a major purchase. It would be no defense against such an embarrassing show of incompetence to reply that "It was worth that to me" or "I sold it for the amount of money I needed." One informant told me ruefully about a bullock he raised for three years and sold for what he thought was quite a large sum of money, only to be told by a Nasaara (person of Euro-American culture) that, as he reported, *"Fo pa mi naaf koosgo ye"* (you don't know cattle selling); he could have made still more money.

In my own experience in Burkina Faso and elsewhere in Africa, bargaining is an enjoyable game. It is like playing chess, with good fellowship and joking mixed in. In the markets, I always bargained for the fun of it, for the sake of the contests, and sellers generally appeared to enjoy a good haggle too. This was notable in the profit-oriented sale of traditional art in the cities. Sometimes I would bargain intermittently about major purchases of traditional art over several days or even longer, and with some sellers I had a sense of a long-term contest, in which the challenge extended beyond any individual purchase to the entire series of transactions as a whole. The higher the stakes, the more exciting the challenge. Like other buyers and traders in my own and other cultures, it often happened that I got as much or more satisfaction out of striking a good deal, getting a bargain, as I did out of acquiring or possessing the item itself. I enjoyed not only the esthetic qualities of a piece of art, but the esthetic pleasure of looking back on an elegant piece of negotiation. The satisfaction of engaging in the Market Pricing relationship transcended the importance of the material transaction itself, which was merely the vehicle for the relationship.

Market Pricing need not involve bargaining or competition, and indeed competitive striving may be derogated. Cultures differ greatly in the extent to which they esteem or disdain Market Pricing in general, in the specific domains in which it is approved, as well as the domains in which self-interest, competition, and maximization are suitable. Where a culture values "achievement" highly, people will strive to "make the most of opportunities," "make something of themselves," and "get ahead." Where winning, outsmarting others, amassing individual wealth, and so forth are not valued, or are held in contempt, there is little drive to "succeed." The contexts in which people find such fulfillment are also quite specific. Observe that a Moose person who enjoys a sense of satisfaction at executing an advantageous Market Pricing transaction would not try to take advantage of his neighbor's need for land, his kinswoman's need for food, or a suitor's need for a wife. Seeking a profit in such transactions would be despicable if it were not senseless, and would provide no satisfaction. There would be no pleasure for a wife-giver in bargaining for money, labor, or gifts in Moose courtship. On the contrary, it would deprive him of the satisfactions of generosity. Moose do not try to thresh as fast as possible at a *zauga* (work bee), nor try to get ahead of the cultivating line at a *sisoaaga* bee—what would be the point? Far from being satisfying (or honorable), outdoing peers at a *zauga* or *sisoaaga* would be bizarre, pointless, and disgraceful. It is not that there is some kind of transcontextual pleasure in outsmarting others, exploiting opportunities, or maximizing returns in general. A villager with land to spare does not want to get the most he can in return for it. He does not want any compensation (except perhaps appreciation). He lends the land without even considering compensation just because neighborliness, belonging, solidarity, and sharing are gratifying as such. In this domain, the great pleasure that can be derived is the pleasure of meeting the other's need, and feeling a sense of unity and solidarity.

In sum, the satisfactions of competing, bargaining, and successful risk taking are context-bound—they are pleasures that can be realized only within the framework of particular kinds of Market Pricing relationships. Like interactions in the other three modes, Market Pricing activities are sociable because they are realizable only through the coordinated joint activity of more than one person enacting complementary components of the model: sellers and potential sellers, competitors, buyers and potential buyers, sellers of substitutes and alternatives, and so forth. A solipsist cannot engage in Market Pricing, for to act in this mode is to orient oneself with reference to the action and potential action of others. Even competition is not an action of autonomous individuals, but a relation between persons. More generally, the distinct satisfactions derivable from each kind of social relationship are intrinsic to the specific kind of relationship, and require such a relationship for their satisfaction. And at the same time, the pleasures of enacting any form of social relationship are attainable only by enacting it in some particular culturally formulated and therefore meaningful form.

## Nonessential Features of Market Pricing

In our own culture, we assume that when people operate in a Market Pricing mode they are individualistic, selfish, maximizing, and competitive. We also tend to assume that Market Pricing is associated with materialism, that it must involve free choice, and that the primary obligations entailed in Market Pricing are contractual. In fact, all of these are to some degree optional features of Market Pricing, controlled by implementation rules that may specify otherwise in other cultures. In a given cultural context, Market Pricing may involve any or none of these optional features. The characterizing feature of Market Pricing, remember, is an orientation toward ratios (e.g., prices, wages, interest, rates of return on investment, cost/benefit ratios, proportionate shares), with reference to which people organize and evaluate their interaction. Although historically in the West the myths of the autonomous individualist, competitive striving, freedom of choice, and voluntarily created social contracts are loosely associated with the idea of Market Pricing, there is no theoretically necessary connection among the concepts. It remains for further study to examine the question of whether and precisely how these ideas are linked in other cultures, but a moment's consideration reveals that there is no logically necessary or empirically invariable connection between any of these features and the core relational structure of the MP model (cf. Griesinger and Livingston 1973, MacCrimmon and Messick 1976, and Lowenstein, Thompson, and Bazerman 1989, who make some similar distinctions).

No one would doubt that Japanese businesses operate in a Market Pricing framework, but Japanese business is by no means *individualistic*. In general, Market Pricing sometimes operates between Japanese firms and often vis-à-vis non-Japanese firms, but not among individuals within firms (L. T. Doi 1962, Lebra 1976, Gallimore 1981, K. Doi 1982). The agent of Market Pricing is not necessarily the individual. Even when individuals are the primary interactants in MP, they need not be *selfish*. People may think in terms of ratios of benefits to costs or consider proportionate inputs without trying to benefit the self in preference to others. Research on equity demonstrates that people often seek due proportion in preference to personal gain: people want to be fair (Lerner

1974; Walster and Walster 1975; Deutsch 1975, 1985; Berkowitz and Walster 1976; Mikula 1980; Leventhal 1980; Bierhoff, Cohen, and Greenberg 1986; Kahneman, Knetsch, and Thaler 1986a, 1986b). Justice and egoism are equally compatible with MP.

Even when people are individualistic and selfishly oriented in a Market Pricing relationship, they need not be *competitive*. Competition means trying to outdo others, but participants in a Market Pricing interaction may not be concerned about whether they come out ahead of others. A person may seek a high benefit to cost ratio for himself alone without regard to how others fare, never comparing himself to anyone else at all. A person can compare rates of return on different investments or the expected utilities of alternative courses of action and choose high-yield options without taking into account whether he does better or worse than others. How often this occurs in any particular MP domain in any culture is a matter for empirical investigation. Analytically, Market Pricing need not be a race and people in such a relationship are not necessarily trying to win. Further, people participating in MP relationships may not be individualistic, selfish, or competitive. The manager of a marketing coop selling a scarce commodity may be operating with reference to cost/benefit ratios (or prices) and yet be collectivist, generously altruistic, and cooperative.

We have already seen in Chapter 16 why *maximization* is not a necessary feature of human sociability, so here it suffices to reiterate that Market Pricing in particular does not entail a maximizing attitude, or for that matter a concern with efficiency or even profit-seeking (see Godelier 1986b). People may even be selfish, individualistic, and competitive without endeavoring to maximize anything. Imagine a ruthless, jealous, greedy, but lazy robber. Or simply consider an entrepreneur who, when she has enough money, retires to make room for junior executives on their way up, devoting her time to fishing. The Western success ideology notwithstanding, when people get what they want, they often "coast," making little effort to get more. The whole of Part IV shows that the pursuit of *material goods*, even those necessary for subsistence, need not be organized in a Market Pricing mode. The work of Polanyi and the other anthropological and historical economists repeatedly cited above makes the same point. Conversely, MP relations do not always involve material concerns. Proportional representation in a decision-making body is MP, but it is not based on economic goods and services. Similarly, a *rational* assessment of the costs and benefits of a particular course of action—say, joining a club— may not focus on material things.

*Voluntarism* in social relations and freedom of choice in general are not necessary features of Market Pricing. People are often constrained to buy or sell products, including their own labor and their means of subsistence, without any choice of partners or terms of sale. Monopolies, company towns, sharecropping, and various conditions of debt may product such constraints. People may be required to buy goods and services (licenses, vaccinations, sewer hookups) without being given any choice in the matter. In addition, Market Pricing relations exist without *contractually-based obligations*. People often buy and sell without being bound by any contractual obligations before or after the event. And other kinds of obligations may operate within Market Pricing. Moose vendors have regular customers (*raadse*) who feel obligated to buy from them if possible, although they have not entered into any agreement to do so, and such noncontractual obligations are common in Western business dealings (Bradach and Eccles 1989).

Within the framework of Market Pricing, individualism, selfishness, competitiveness, maximization, free choice and contractualism can occur in various combinations. Some or none of them may obtain. Furthermore, any of the four models may be implemented with any of these features; they are by no means uniquely associated with Market Pricing. People may compete to make the most prestigious Equality Matching exchanges and have the most EM partners (Malinowski 1961 [1922], Mauss 1967 [1925]). People may make contracts of fealty, bonding themselves to Authority Ranking relationships. Without maximizing per se, people often attempt to augment their Communal Sharing relationships, making them include more aspects of the self or more people, more intense, or more frequent. Certainly people may be communally selfish if they ethnocentrically try to benefit the ingroup—the extended self— without regard to the welfare of outsiders (see Tajfel 1978, 1982). All of these are, in large part, culturally specified features of the basic models. Across the world's cultures, and even within our own, it is an empirical problem to determine the conditions under which these and other optional features tend to be associated with each of the models and the extent to which they actually co-occur in various permutations.

## The True Asocial (or Antisocial) Individualist

The implication of the relational-models theory is that there is no intrinsic reason why we should suppose with Thomas Hobbes that normal people are fundamentally selfish, inherently competitive, or individualistic by nature. These axioms in social theory are products of our ideology, not of deduction or observation. This is not the place to trace the history of Western conceptions of human nature, but it is worth noting that from classical times through the middle ages it was taken for granted that the true nature of humankind was social. It was assumed that if not otherwise perverted, people would realize their nature by playing their proper complementary roles as members in a coherent social system. Virtue lay in contributing to the interests of the state and society, in fulfilling a necessary social function (see MacIntyre 1981). And since at least Aristotle, virtue was thought to be natural in humans, even if people did not inevitably or invariably fulfill their better nature. The idea that people can exist outside of or prior to society, that the state of nature is a state of opposed interests and "the war of all against all," is a relatively modern

Western notion. Today people feel fettered by life in contemporary society, and so imagine that individualism is natural, while society enslaves (see Freud 1930).

Of course, people do not necessarily coordinate all of their behavior with others all of the time. As Margaret Mead (1937:15–16, 460–61, 467–69) observes, in some realms, "the individual strives toward his goal without reference to others" (p. 16). People may conduct some activities more or less independently, without any particular shared social orientation, without joint standards or understandings of the events. This is a Null orientation.[4] However, it is rather difficult to find examples of such Asocial behavior. Even defecation usually is a socially oriented activity. Among Moose, for example, children usually find a playmate to accompany them when they go out to defecate. Defecation is also social in that most adults take care to do it in private, since it is embarrassing to be observed. Similarly, most action that is Asocial in the immediate, narrow sense of the term is Asocial just because cultural implementation rules define it so. Thus for the most part it is the culture itself that determines the domains in which people act individualistically, by defining them as being of no concern to other people or to any collectivity. However, most human interaction with others is oriented with reference to one of the relational models. The goal that is immanent in the interaction is the joint construction of a relationship. Then motive and structure coincide; goals and obligations merge.

There is, however, one interesting case where intent and rule are uncoupled: sociopathy. The phenomenon of sociopathy also provides a natural contrast with all four basic forms of sociability, including Market Pricing behavior—even MP behavior that is selfish, individualistic, competitive, and maximizing. Sociopaths (formerly called psychopaths) are people who persistently operate in an Asocial mode.[5] Sociopaths lack a conscience. They do not care about others, they have no true compassion, compunction, or pity, and no true remorse when they harm others. They have no concern about others except as objects, and never form any enduring or meaningful bonds with others. Sociopaths treat others purely instrumentally, as means or obstacles to their own ends. They never make true commitments to others, although they may simulate social relationships effectively as long as it serves their Asocial purposes. They are often quite effective at doing so, manipulating others by acting as if they were relating to them humanely. But motivationally, their relationships are Null. For them, kindness, deference, and reciprocity are merely instrumental. Many sociopaths know very well the forms for Communal Sharing, Authority Ranking, and Equality Matching, and can fool others into believing that they are relating to them as kin, lover, or spouse, as a loyal subordinate or responsible superior, or as a friend. But they are merely con artists without morality, and readily abandon these pretenses at the slightest whim, or when it serves their ulterior purposes.

Significantly, sociopaths are unconcerned with social rewards and punishments per se. For example, disapproval or mild shocks that signal failure to adequately perform an experimental task provide no incentives for them, since sociopaths are unconcerned about creating, sustaining, or repairing the social relationships that their failures potentially impinge on. For a sociopath, there is no distinction between "punishment" in the S-R behaviorist learning theory sense of the term (pain) and "punishment" in the retributive sociomoral sense.

What sociopaths can teach us here is what people look like when they are truly Asocial. Sociopaths are not intrinsically entrepreneurs or achievers. They are not competitive, and they are far from being rational maximizers of their material interests or other utilities. Indeed, one striking feature of their behavior is its aimlessness, its pointless and sometimes self-defeating lability. Sociopaths can mimic Market Pricing relationships quite effectively, just as they mimic the other three modes of social relationships. They merely play at Market Pricing as if it were a silly game, which they abandon as arbitrarily as they picked it up. No one would mistake the biography of a sociopath for the biography of a person with high achievement motivation. They do not seem to have any consistent stable interest in achievement. Sociopaths lack long-term, single-minded purposiveness, consistent *rational* weighing of alternatives, calculated utilitarian undertaking of moderate risks with high expected payoffs, stable concern with efficient use of time and resources, interest in making a concerted effort to accomplish preset goals, desire to maximize returns on effort and resources expended, joy in bargaining and competing within the framework of agreed-upon rules, recognition of the validity of contracts and commitments, or even the satisfaction of coming out ahead in a fair contest. More generally, their aimless and inconsistent behavior reveals what people would be like without the social motivations of the relational models. In sociopaths, purposes and rules are disjunctive, individual intentions often conflict with structural constraints, motives are readily separable from morals, and desires are commonly opposed to externally imposed social obligations.

## THE ONTOGENETIC SOURCES OF SOCIAL MOTIVES

The theory that humans are fundamentally Asocial and that the basic human motives are opposed to social constraints (e.g., Freud 1962 [1923], 1930) assumes that young children must acquire their sociability from experience. It assumes that children's motives are inherently egoistic, and that they come to behave sociably as a consequence of their experience. In contrast, the relational-models theory implies that children are inherently sociable. Our theory implies that the elementary models are not imposed on children from the outside, but are endogenous motives, understandings, and standards that the child spontaneously attempts to impose on his social world. The child's task is to learn how to implement the elementary models in a manner appropriate to the particular culture in which he happens to find himself. If this is so, then we should see the motives, the moral standards, and the understandings of each model emerge together, more or less simultaneously. Because these first applications of the model are not the result of inductive learning from experience, the initial manifestations of the models should emerge more or less independently of social experience, and the child's first attempts to implement them should often be culturally incongruous.

Work on the ontogeny of social relations does indeed indicate that social motives are present very early in development. E. Pepitone (1980) reviews and augments the literature in social psychology (as well as quantitative research in anthropology) on the development of cooperation and competition in children (see also Scott 1967). She discusses a number of studies on competitive motives but notes (p. 94) that there is no comparable body of literature on motivation to cooperate. How do young children actually behave?

Even Moose four- and five-year-olds frequently organize their interactions with peers according to Equality Matching principles, even when they are totally unsupervised and engaged in activities which are of no concern to adults. For example, small groups of young boys hunt with slings for lizards and small birds. When they kill an animal they roast it, and then divide it up meticulously into equal shares. It requires some time and effort to divide a sparrow-size bird or tiny lizard into five shares such that all participants agree that they are indifferent as to which share they actually receive. Moose children operate in this mode despite the fact that the Moose do virtually no direct teaching in this or any other domain, and (unless someone gets into a fight) adults regard children's activities as of little interest or importance.

However, demonstrating that social motives are present in early childhood is not sufficient to establish that they have endogenous sources.[6] It is difficult to exclude categorically the possibility of any relevant sort of socialization as a factor in the initial emergence of sociability. But I would like to indicate here the kind of research that would bear on the issue, and illustrate the kind of evidence that, if systematically recorded from samples of children in diverse cultures, would support the thesis of endogenous social motives consistent with the elementary models. The data from two cases like this have little evidential weight in themselves, but the epistemological exercise will be valuable nevertheless.

## Observations of Two American Children

Let me describe two children of my acquaintance who may be representative of the phenomenon of interest: a sister (now ten years seven months) and brother (now six years ten months). I do not have field notes to check my memory, but I think almost anyone with intimate and extensive experience with children of this age will recognize and confirm the general outline of my descriptions. From the very beginning, both children were often very generous and eager to share. From their earliest semi-solid meals at around five months both frequently showed a great interest in sharing their food, spontaneously feeding others from their plates—something the girl, at least, had probably never seen done. They also had a strong desire to eat off their parents' plates at this age, even when they had seen that they had precisely the same food on their own plates. An informal survey of parents indicates that this early and apparently spontaneous desire for commensalism is quite widespread in American children, and Pepitone (1980:175-77) also mentions a number of studies that have observed sharing in young children. Blum (1987) also offers some elegant examples of concerned "responsiveness" to others in very young children. I take this to be incipient Communal Sharing motivation.

Around age three each child became very interested in size, age, and priority, as did their peers. There was a lot of "Me first!" and lots of talk about being older than others, which meant gaining prerogatives denied to those beneath them. They showed considerable concern about who was bigger than whom. The girl, in particular, was astonished, incredulous, and disconcerted to discover after a while that age, size, and power or status did not correspond very well among adults. She had assumed that bigger meant older, and that older meant higher in rank and authority. In many circumstances, at age three both children were still quite ready to share without prompting, and the girl was extremely solicitous of her infant brother and eager to care for him. But power and rank clearly appeared as a new, distinct, very salient issue at around three. In other words, each child exhibited a kind of nascent sensitivity to—and inclination to implement—Authority Ranking.

When each of them turned four they rather abruptly came into a "stage" in which concern with equality and justice dominated their thinking about social relations. Suddenly their overarching concern about social relationships became assuring that everything was "fair." This preoccupation had three aspects: turn taking, egalitarian distributive justice, and precise one-for-one in-kind reciprocity. Parents' and teachers' earlier efforts to recommend or impose taking turns had fallen on deaf, uncomprehending ears. Suddenly at this age each child suggested taking turns on his or her own initiative, and indeed they commonly preferred turn taking to monopolizing whatever opportunity was at issue. For example, the sister would initiate turn taking on her own, offering her playmates a turn without being asked. Taking turns sometimes seemed more important as a structure for its own sake than the activity itself. Each child applied this system to novel situations, and generally did it without prompting.

At the same age, each child became equally preoccupied with distributive justice. Whereas previously they had frequently shared communally on an open-ended "Here, have some," basis, without marking individual shares, now cookies and such had to be divided up into exactly equal portions. Sometimes they would divide up a favorite food into equal portions and share it with friends or family in preference to eating it all alone. Never mind that their parents might not want any cookies and might try to decline, they had to be divided and distributed equally. Each child commonly devoted considerable attention to getting the shares precisely matched. They did not know how to do division mathematically, had no concept of proportions, and did not calculate the shares in that way. Instead, they operationalized equality concretely, by directly matching shares one-for-one. At times this engagement in distributive justice amounted to an obsession.

Reciprocity also became a paramount goal at exactly this time. If someone did something nice for either child, the child insisted on doing just the same thing for the first person. If a parent sent one of them to her or his room, the child wanted to send the parent to his or her room in turn. If either child got something from someone, they often wanted to give back a precisely equivalent gift. They were quite explicit about all this, citing the first act or item in justification for even reciprocation. They also cited this rationale in demanding one-for-one reciprocation for many of their contributions to others. "I did such and such for you, now you have to do such and such for me." Their term for all this was "fair," a word they have each known and used occasionally before, but which at age four became a real and pressing value for them. Beginning at this age, fairness became their dominant goal in relating to people. They desperately wanted and expected everything to be fair.

Also at this age they were each shocked when anyone repudiated fairness as a relevant standard. For a while they often seemed simply unable to appreciate or even understand their parents' or teachers' insistence on "pulling rank" and exercising unilateral authority. Furthermore, beginning at age four equality was much more important to either of them than gain or maximization. For example, it substantially decreases the net happiness of a four-year-old to receive a gift if at the same time someone else in the family gets a different gift for which the four-year-old deems he has no counterpart. Indeed, one criterion for the existence of an EM motive is that, for example, a child would rather have two cookies, with everyone else getting two, than have four cookies, with everyone else getting five. At five and six, these two children, at least, would always choose two.

I take all this to be the spontaneous emergence of an endogenous model for Equality Matching. The girl insisted on many of these modes of acting toward other people without ever having seen any previous example from her parents. (Her brother had observed his sister engaging in many of them.) Some of the forms may possibly have come from peers or school or from parental instruction, but it is hard to see how either child's sudden, intense, and autonomous desire to achieve equality, evenly matched distributive justice, and balanced in-kind reciprocity in novel circumstances could have been a product of their experience.

Later the girl gradually moderated her preoccupation with egalitarian distributive justice, turn taking, and quid pro quo reciprocity. She continued to use this Equality Matching model in her social relationships, but it ceased to be the unique, salient, and dominant concern it had been when it first emerged. Instead it became one mode in her repertoire of alternative structures for organizing any particular interaction. In the following six years she has become increasingly sensitive to the contexts in which it is culturally appropriate to implement Equality Matching, Authority Ranking, and Communal Sharing respectively. As her brother nears his seventh birthday his preoccupation with Equality Matching too shows signs of moderating, but is still very salient.

It is notable that up until about her eighth birthday his sister manifested a total lack of interest in—or any understanding of—prices, profits, comparison shopping, or bargaining with reference to market prices. That is, she had no idea of what a given price meant with respect to alternative purchases, nor even its approximate magnitude with respect to, say, how many weekly allowances it represented. She was by no means lacking in general intelligence or age-appropriate mathematical ability; in fact she excelled in both. Yet when she sold lemonade she showed absolutely no concern with calculating costs (or with making a profit, much less maximizing it). However, she and her peers could readily divide up the money they made into equal parts by matching the shares coin for coin, and they were intent on doing so. She had no intuitive understanding of how to set prices or what was a reasonable price for something she wanted to buy, and it seemed difficult or impossible for her to grasp these concepts. In other words, she was incapable of using the Market Pricing model. This suggests to me that a characterization of their social motives before age eight in terms of economic rationality would be implausible. They simply showed no concern with such factors nor any understanding of the requisite MP concepts.

Shortly after her eighth birthday the girl rather suddenly became quite interested in money, in buying things, and in prices. She looked through catalogs, focusing on prices as much as on the items themselves. For the first time she saved money and planned ways of earning money to buy things. She began to recognize that spending money on one thing meant having less to spend on other things and made explicit choices, balancing the value to her of different commodities. She often considered what combinations of things she could purchase with a given amount of money, and how much it would cost to purchase a given combination of items. She now grasped the idea of making change. These were all new interests, perspectives, and ways of understanding, yet they did not correspond to any particular change in her social environment. She was not exposed to any new experiences or expectations that would account for this new orientation. It appeared that the Market Pricing model emerged from her, rather than being passively learned. Her brother as yet shows no signs of understanding, motivation, or moral concern related to Market Pricing.

## The Externalization of the Models

I have discussed these two cases here because I think they illustrate one kind of strong evidence that could be systematically collected to demonstrate the endogenous sources and concordance of motives and moral obligations. What conclusions could be drawn from observations of this sort if they were properly replicated in a large sample? The abrupt and apparently spontaneous emergence of the Equality Matching orientation, for example, and its almost indiscriminate application in heterogeneous contexts where it had not been elicited or reinforced, including novel ones where its use was culturally inappropriate, suggests that this is not simply the case of a rule imposed by society from "outside." Equality Matching necessarily develops into a culture-specific form which reflects what children have learned (but often never been taught) about the culturally specified values of parameters that the fundamental models leave open. But the fact that Equality Matching emerged when it did, with the urgency it did, with its diffuse focus and indiscriminate overgeneralization, suggests an endogenous source. The same is true of the other three models. Note that although parents and teachers often put a lot of pressure on young children to take turns and be fair, before age four children ignore these pressures. Then they suddenly insist on Equality Matching in contexts where no adult ever suggested it. Children in our culture are potentially exposed to a great deal of Market Pricing, yet they show no interest in it, no comprehension of it, and no desire to impose it on others during their first seven years. This looks more like externalization than internalization.

There is some U.S. research (including longitudinal studies) on children's concepts of how goods ought to be distributed that tends to confirm the idea that there is a regular ontogenetic sequence in which each of the four models predominates in turn (Damon 1975, 1977, 1980; Enright et al. 1984).[7] The youngest children tested (age four) tended to believe that people should get what they want; this is Damon's stage 0-A, corresponding to Communal Sharing. Later, at Damon's stage 0-B (Authority Ranking), children base distributions on such factors as relative age and size. Still older children in Damon's stage 1-A believe that everyone should receive exactly equal shares; this is clearly Equality Matching. Next, children come to stage 1-B, where they believe that what people get should be a function of how much they do or how hard they work; that is, they subscribe to Market Pricing. Damon's final two stages, 2-A and 2-B, appear to involve the use of combinations of the four models, which is what we would expect of children with a growing repertoire of social models and increasing competence in applying them in culturally appropriate implementations.

By itself, a shift in focus on one after another model among children in one culture says nothing about the sources of the models the children are applying. But if children are learning (either through instruction or imitation) the models from their culture, then the sequence should depend on the relative salience and comparative valuation of the models in each culture. Yet Enright et al. (1984) found identical sequences of distributive precepts in Sweden, where they argue that the predominant norm in distribution is "to each according to his or her needs," and in the U.S., where they argue that the distributive ethic "is one of competition and reward for initiative" (p. 1738). If the same sequence of apparently spontaneous orientations were manifest in many children in a variety of cultures, including cultures varying greatly in the modes of relationships that they value and inculcate, the case for externalization would be strong.

One likely basis for such invariance of sequence would be a maturationally induced progressive mastery of the increasingly complex, cumulatively-elaborated relational structures (the Guttman sequence of structures described in Chapter 9). This would be consistent with the relational-models theory, but cognitive maturation alone would not be sufficient to explain the motivational basis for the child's actively imposing the models on his or her social world. The cognitive capacity to utilize and understand each of the four forms of relationship seems to appear simultaneously with the drive to use them and the insistence that everyone adhere to them, which suggests a common endogenous source for cognition, motivation, and moral imperative. (Incidentally, it is conceivable that the ontogenetic sequence, CS, AR, EM, MP recapitulates a phylogenetic sequence of capacities for these social orientations.) The sudden onset of an age-specific "spontaneous" dispositional propensity to implement the models resembles one aspect of the critical period phenomenon in imprinting (see Hess 1973; also Ainsworth 1967; Bowlby 1969, 1988). This suggests that it would be worth investigating the question of whether the cultural implementation rules learned during the months immediately after the emergence of each model are uniquely stable, enduring, and resistant to change. In particular, are the first rules that the child learns about with whom it is appropriate to engage in each kind of relationship less labile than any such person-application rules learned later in life?

Abrupt, "spontaneous" emergence, initially diffuse and overgeneralized implementation, and invariant sequence would suggest endogenous sources for these models. Other kinds of evidence would help to establish conclusively that these four forms of social relations are motives. It is often taken to be characteristic of needs or motivations that there is some optimum level of fulfillment. Thus it would be important to show that people are more likely to seek out and structure social relationships of each type the longer they have been deprived of the opportunity to engage in them. It would also be important to show that the threshold level of eliciting behavior required to release each kind of social action decreases with increasing deprivation. On the other side, there should be evidence of satiation. The more people engage in a given type of social relationship in a given span of time, the less they should seek out social relationships of that type and the less they should tend to take the initiative to structure their relationships in that manner. It would be possible (though not easy) to design field and laboratory experiments to test such deprivation, satiation, and elicitation hypotheses about each form of social relations.

Any theory about the connections among patterns of social interaction, motives, social norms, sanctions and punishments, and culture is necessarily a theory about ontogeny and socialization. In contrast with social learning and psychoanalytic theory and with most theories of moral development, the relational-models theory posits that each of the four elementary models emerges spontaneously at a more or less fixed point in the course of ontogeny, independent of experience and of the other models. The child externalizes each of them in turn, trying to implement them in his or her social relations and gradually adapting them to the culture. In each case, the comprehension of the relational structure, the motive to relate in this way, and the moral imperative that obliges everyone to adhere to the model emerge together, as an integrated whole. None of the other theories predicts this close association among cognition, motives, and morality; none predicts just this kind of overgeneralization or independence of experience; and none predicts the appearance of just these modes of relationship in this specific sequence. These ontogenetic perspectives should be tested.


# A UNIFIED THEORY OF SOCIAL RELATIONS

This book proposes a framework for a unified theory of social relations. It suggests that the same relational structures govern the circulation of things in all kinds of transactions (exchange, distributions and contributions, justice); the organization of work; the social meaning of objects, land, and time; marriage systems in traditional societies and major forms of marriage and sexual relations in the industrial world; decision processes; social influence; group formation; group structure and norms; identity and self; social needs and motivations; moral judgment; political ideology and social legitimation; social emotions; aggression and social conflict; responses to transgression and misfortune; and possibly the psychology of religion and social ontogeny. The same four relational structures are evident in many diverse and historically unrelated cultures, at all levels of social organization. Once we recognize that the same basic structures organize so many domains of social thought and action, the only plausible explanation is psychological: people must always be using the same elementary models to generate, understand, coordinate, and judge most social relationships. There are four universal and fundamental models: Communal Sharing, Authority Ranking, Equality Matching, and Market Pricing.

The relational structure of each model can be precisely specified, and it turns out that the four models comprise an ordered set, each one in turn encompassing and elaborating on the preceding structure. Yet each structure is unique, because defining any new relation or operation changes the social meaning of the previously defined relations and operations. There is considerable latitude in the implementation of the models, and indeed the elementary models do not fully specify the form of any interaction. This gives rise to much of the diversity among cultures, and frequently to misunderstanding—or conflict—within and among cultures. We know very little yet about the rules for implementing the basic models, but they may be rather unsystematic and arbitrary, based on the more or less idiosyncratic historical processes that result in what each culture refers to as "tradition."

This relational-models theory construes human beings as inherently sociable. People seek to relate to others in each of the four basic modes. Participation in each kind of relationship is a principal end in itself. People understand their social life in terms of these four models, and they attempt to impose these relational structures on their social world. People want others to conform to the models. Consequently, conceptions of social relations, moral judgments, norms, and relational motives often coincide. We are social by nature and by culture.

# Epilogue to the Paperback Edition

Anthropologists, sociologists, social theorists, economists, social psychologists, cognitive scientists, and philosophers have all responded with great interest to this book. Moreover, in every case they have treated the book as if it came from their own paradigm, which confirms to me that we are all really working on the same questions. Reviewers have been so enthusiastic, yet so perceptive in their critiques, that there is no point in my responding to any of them in particular. However, I have learned a great deal from all these interlocutors, and in this brief epilogue I would like to mention an important gap in the theory and respond to a few of the questions people commonly ask when I give talks about this work. I will begin by mentioning some studies we have recently done to explore the manifestations of these models in everyday cognition, and conclude by pointing to some goals for the future.

Since the book was published, we have completed twenty-one studies to test hypotheses about eleven cognitive manifestations of the relational models. These studies have used nine different methods, primarily to explore people's everyday thought about their own social relationships. Eleven studies focused on naturally occurring errors in which people called someone by the wrong name, misremembered with whom they did something, or misdirected an action (Fiske, Haslam, and S. T. Fiske 1991; Fiske 1993a). We found that people making social errors exhibited a strong tendency to substitute a person with whom they related in the same mode as the intended person. This tendency was consistent across diverse U.S. populations, along with samples of Bengalis, Koreans, Chinese, and Vais from Liberia and Sierra Leone.

Two memory studies show that students and non-students use the relational models to remember their acquaintances; when asked to list everyone they know, people cluster their recall in runs of acquaintances with whom they relate according to each of the respective models (Fiske 1993b). Two studies show that Americans use the relational models to make sense of their suffering, and that Americans can accurately imagine how other Americans use the models to interpret misfortune. Two other studies show that both students and non-students in the U.S. use the relational models to classify their personal relationships, and to make similarity judgments among them (Haslam and Fiske 1992).

In two further studies Nick Haslam (1993) asked people to rate the typicality and plausibility of hypothetical relationships. He found that people's representations of relationships reflected discrete categories corresponding to the relational models; their cognition was not organized in terms of dimensions, interactional complementarity, or symmetry. In another study, Haslam confirmed that when people rate their relationships on a wide variety of identifying features, they use implicit categories corresponding to the relational models, rather than dimensional or prototype representations.

Our latest study asked people to report cases where they changed their minds about the person with whom they were going to interact. People tended to choose substitutes according to the model governing their relationships with both people. At the moment, we are studying long term patterns of social replacements.

The relational models theory was based on fieldwork, ethnographic comparison, and social theory, all of which tend to focus on institutional rules and collective practices. So it is striking to find strong confirmatory evidence for the models at the level of individual cognition.

When I wrote this book I half expected that readers would bring to my attention other models that operated in many domains of most cultures. No one has yet done so. The lack of counter-examples reinforces my contention that these models are elementary, and may be the only ones that have the defining features set out in Chapter 8 (see also Fiske 1991). However, there are certainly many other special-purpose models that do not meet these criteria, but that people in particular cultures use in limited contexts. The four relational models presumably do not govern castling in chess, throwing the bouquet at a wedding, or blowing sparks on Moose joking partners.

Several reviewers have taken me to task for over-emphasizing the harmonious functioning of social life. They are right: this book does not adequately deal with the coercive, exploitive, deceptive, discordant uses of the models. In this book I focus on interactions in which participants understand each other, agree about what models to use, and have mutually compatible motives. In a very discerning review article, Harriet Whitehead (1993) points out that interactants may—knowingly or unknowingly—use different models to generate a given aspect of their interaction, or to judge it. She also notes that people may impose a model on others, making them conform to a model which they would prefer not to follow. The generalization, as I see it, is that motivation, construction, coordination, evaluation, legitimation, and representation may be based on different models, or different implementations of the same model. This is true of each individual, as well as of the several interactants and members of the audience. We need to explore how this happens and to determine the consequences, if any, of various kinds of discordance. To do this, we may be able to build on Goffman's concept of role distance and Marx's concept of false consciousness, along with recent thinking about agency, hegemony and knowledge.

However, in considering this we should not fall back into the error of assuming that people engage in most social relationships as means to exogenous, non-social ends. Even in cases of discordant, deceptive, or coercive relationships, people's motives are often largely social in nature. That is, even when people are using discordant models, everyone involved is typically trying to create or modify Communal Sharing, Authority Ranking, Equality Matching, or Market Pricing relationships.

When people encounter this theory, certain questions repeatedly come up. Here are five of the most common questions, and my answers to them.

*Doesn't model X reduce to a special case of model Y?* People often try to collapse two models into one—but they don't agree about which two are equivalent! Sometimes people using the American folk model of "equality" conflate Communal Sharing and Equality Matching. People who see the world in hegemonic terms want to treat Equality Matching as merely a balance of power in Authority Ranking relations. People who think in terms of exchange see Equality Matching as a simplified, special case of Market Pricing. One person or another has argued for collapsing every one of the six pairs of the four models. I have set out many reasons for differentiating among the models, ranging from the phenomenological contrasts in diverse social domains (see Part II), to their distinct distributions and separate manifestations in many cultures (see Part IV), and the differences in their relational structures (see Chapter 8). Furthermore, we almost always find that each model has a separate, independent effect on the various cognitive processes we have studied.

*Why should we conceive of these models as discrete types rather than a dimensional continuum?* Different relations and operations are meaningful in each model, and each set of defined relations and operations represents a qualitative step to a different kind of structure (see Chapter 8). Either people attend to additive interval differences, as in Equality Matching and Market Pricing, or they don't, as in Authority Ranking and Communal Sharing. Either transitive order is socially important, as in AR, EM, and MP, or it is not, as in Communal Sharing. In Market Pricing relationships, ratios (defined in terms of the Archimedian and distributive principles) are meaningful, while ratios have no social significance in the other three models. Each model is a type of structure in which distinct properties and operations are defined, or are not defined. In this typological sense, the models are structurally quite distinct.

On the other hand, it would make perfectly good sense to sample some defined set of occurrences of some domain of social life, and observe how often

412                                        Epilogue to the Paperback Edition

some individual or some group implemented each model. We could differentiate persons or groups along a frequency scale by counting the number of times
in which a particular model appeared in the given domain(s). By extension, we
could represent the frequencies of use of all four models as positions in a four-
dimensional space. In that sense, we could derive a continuous spatial-dimen-
sional representation of the use of the models. It may be that we could also represent in this way people's evaluations of the relative importance or goodness of
the four models in defined domains.

*Can't the four models be derived from two underlying dimensions?* Many people get out paper and pencil and make an effort to place the four models in
quadrants defined by two axes or two binary alternatives, in the Parsonian tradition. As far as I know, no one who has experimented with this approach to the
models finds it satisfactory, and in any case there is no consensus on what axes
to try. In contrast, there are good reasons for ordering the models in terms of
increasing complexity. As explained in Chapter 8, the models form a kind of
Guttman scale in which each model encompasses the relations and operations
defined in the simpler ones, and adds new ones.

*Is the theory disprovable, or are these the only logical possibilities?* There are
many other logical possibilities and alternative theories about social life. There
are a number of competing theories that define putative elementary forms of
relationships (e.g., Foa, Converse, Tornblom, and Foa 1993; MacCrimmon
and Messick 1976; Parsons 1951). Any of these schemata *could* govern most
domains of social life in most cultures. But do they? There are innumerable
social rules and standards for relationships besides the four models. Here are a
few: *Place women on the left, men on the right. Value red things. Never work on
Sundays. Say, "check" when your move places your opponent's king in jeopardy.
Laugh at death.* None of these rules operate across most cultures, although in
principle they could. The relational models do, but it is not obvious, a priori,
that they have to.

Furthermore, the theory predicts that people use relational structures based
primarily on certain combinations of relational axioms and not others. Logically, it would be possible for people to use intransitive social rankings (with
loops in them), but Authority Ranking is defined as a transitive structure. How
do real social hierarchies actually work? Similarly, there are mathematical
groups defined by all the other properties of Market Pricing except the Archimedian axiom. In such a structure, some ratios are incomparable with some
others. People *could* organize markets in which the prices of some items could
not be compared with the prices of some others. It is an empirical question to
determine whether they do so.

We have also tested many cognitive predictions of the models that could easily have been falsified by the data. For example, social errors could be governed
only by the recency with which informants have interacted with each person,
or be based purely on the similarity of the sound of people's names. But we
have found these factors to be much less important than the concordance of

the relational models people use to interact with the people whom they confuse. People's explicit, linguistically marked relational categories (friend, boss, sister) could have accounted for all of their errors, but in fact the relational models taxonomy generally accounted for the errors better than this surface taxonomy. In short, the theory makes a great many strong, important non-obvious, refutable predictions.

*Why should there be only four elementary models?* We need to do a lot more work on this question, but a potential answer comes out of the mathematics of measurement structures, discussed in Chapter 8. There are apparently only five relational structures that have the optimal degree of homogeneity and uniqueness. Homogeneity and uniqueness identify the conditions under which the relational properties are the same for all of the elements everywhere in the structure, and the conditions under which the relational properties remain the same under permissible transformations. The cognitive simplicity and social flexibility of these structures may depend on the extent of homogeneity and uniqueness. If so, there may be very few simple but universally functional relational structures.

*How is this typology related to Talcott Parsons' pattern variables and system functions?* Parsons is the classical social theorist who is most conspicuously absent from my synthesis. I cannot see any connections between the relational models theory and his conception of four system functions (pattern maintenance, integration, goal-attainment, and adaptation). However, I have lately perceived an interesting link to the pattern variables he formulated (Parsons 1951, Parsons and Shils 1951). The pattern variables can be construed as meta-rules describing how implementation rules are formulated. *Universalism vs. particularism* concerns whether people implement a model in the same way with a large category of people, or implement the model in a way that is unique to a particular individual. *Achievement vs. ascription* is the distinction between implementation rules formulated in terms of how people act, compared to rules formulated in terms of other, less voluntary and less labile attributes of people. When interacting with a given person or set of persons, *specificity vs. diffuseness* is a matter of whether people implement the same model (or combination of models) in the same way across many domains, or use different implementations and different models in each domain. *Neutrality vs. affectivity* presupposes an asocial human nature, in which behavior that is social is inherently constrained and contrary to basic motives. However, without distorting Parsons' intent, we can also redefine this variable as a matter of the looseness of the implementation rules. Implementation rules can restrict and specify action, or they may be more open, allowing creativity, choice, and improvisation. Thus Parsons' pattern variables spell out many of the important abstract dimensions of the possible options for formulating any implementation rule.

There are a number of other questions to which I do not yet have clear answers. Why do people use specific models? Why are particular models prevalent around the world in certain kinds of domains, institutions, and social groups? Conversely, what accounts for the vast cultural differences in implementations of the models and in overall extent of use of each model? Why do people vary in their predilections for each model? When does each model work best, what are its functional limitations, and when does it fail? What happens when people implement models in ways that differ from their partners or that are inconsistent with society-wide implementation rules? What are the constraints on combining the models? How do individuals and groups change their uses of the models over various spans of time?

To answer these questions we need to develop a strategy for studying implementation rules and their changes. We will want to look at this ontogenetically and historically, as well as analyzing social "functions" and natural selection. Furthermore, we will want to observe how agents learn, represent, interpret, apply, communicate, and negotiate existing implementation rules and create new ones. It will be an exciting exploration.

In closing, I would like to step back and look at the ontological foundation of the relational models theory. Most previous ontological perspectives have treated psychological universals and cultural diversity as competitive accounts: the more universal behavior is, the less diverse it must be; and the more cultural, the less psychological. In contrast, the ontology of this theory posits that many universal psychological models have cultural realizations that are inherently diverse and unique. Such models strongly constrain action and orient people to attribute meaning to certain relational features. But these models are incomplete, indeterminate, and unanchored until they are informed by cultural specifications. People *must* use cultural implementation rules to generate any specific act, interaction, judgment, or social cognition. This ontological perspective can be applied to many other domains (cf. Fiske 1993c). It resolves the impasse between anthropologists' aversion to reductionism and psychologists' and evolutionary biologists' aversion to relativism.

This ontology implies that extensive and careful comparison of naturally-occurring behavior in diverse cultures is the epistemological requirement for distinguishing the cultural dimensions of behavior, thought, affect, and evaluation from their psychological components. It is not simply a matter of being able to generalize to other cultures: without examining multiple cultures you cannot understand culturally-mediated psychological mechanisms even in your own particular culture. Conversely, we cannot understand how people are constructing their cultural worlds until we discover the psychological tools they use.

# Notes

*Chapter 1*

Introduction

1. Barbara Fiske kindly informed me of this fact.


*Chapter 2*

The Framework

1. It is also worth noting that even Authority Ranking relationships that all participants regard as legitimate may be exploitive in some objective sense (for example,
see Llewelyn-Davies 1981).
2. If this distinction is still not absolutely clear, the discussions of rotating credit associations in the section Theoretical Roots in Chapter 2 and again the section Recursion in Chapter 7 provide a detailed demonstration of how Equality Matching differs from Market Pricing. There are many more illustrations of the differences
throughout the book.
3. I am indebted to Jonathan Baron in person and to Margaret Mead through her
writing (1961 [1937]) for making me see the importance of the Asocial orientation
and the Null case of individualistic behavior.
4. In addition, selfishness does not imply an intention to maximize anything: a person may look out for his or her own interests alone, yet desire to satisfy those selfish interests only in moderation.
5. In Saussure's (1983) terminology, the underlying model is the *langue*, while the
social interaction it generates is the *parole*.
6. Formerly spelled "Mossi," "Moshi," or "Mosi," this spelling follows the new or-
thography officially adopted in 1976 by the National Language Commission of
what is now Burkina Faso.
7. Weber offers a number of partially overlapping typologies of social orientations,
but this is the principal one in *Economy and Society* and elsewhere.
8. Susan Fiske thoughtfully brought this work to my attention.

9. If pure coercive force is involved, then this is not AR, but the hierarchies of authority in almost all organizations are based in part on actors' conceptions of how social relations *ought* to be organized: such systems of rank have at least some normative legitimacy. This aspect of Etzioni's approach is considered further in the section Social Influence in Chapter 4.

10. However, Blau assumes a self-interested individualism as the basis for all four of these modes, an MP reductionist position that I argue against in Part IV.

11. Ekeh (1974) perceptively compares and dissects Blau, Homans, and Lévi-Strauss.

12. For recent research on household production and distribution see Netting, Wilk, and Arnould (1984) and Wilk (1989).

13. Although he captures many nuances of the cultural meanings of different forms of transfer, Sahlins departs from Polanyi's typological approach in treating the degree of reciprocal balance as a continuum. Because he analyzes systems of exchange in terms of their material results, Sahlins sometimes does not fully address the issue of the actors' own implicit or explicit models (e.g., the contingent obligations they recognize). For example, he treats hard bargaining and warfare as differing only in degree of reciprocity. Despite the manifest qualitative differences for the actors, Sahlins does not clearly distinguish between communal sharing of resources and a system of compulsory tribute in which the chief uses some of the resources he collects to pay retainers, since both result in "pooling" and "redistribution" of resources. And Sahlins does not clearly distinguish between the subjective nature of subjects' obligation to give tribute and chiefs' responsibility to look after their subjects. Nevertheless, the ethnographic breadth of his knowledge and the perceptivity of his analysis make a very powerful combination.

14. See Bales 1958, 1970; Schutz 1958; Foa 1961; Lorr and McNair 1963; Triandis, Vassiliou, and Nassiakou 1968; Triandis 1972; Marwell and Hage 1970; Rosenberg and Sedlak 1972; Benjamin 1974; Wish 1976; Wish, Deutsch, and Kaplan 1976; Kiesler 1983; Wiggins and Broughton 1985; Triandis et al. 1988

15. Although she is otherwise very Durkheimian, for some reason Douglas does not discuss the obvious parallels between her dimensions and Durkheim's contrast between mechanical and organic solidarity.

16. But Douglas (1978:17) explicitly eschews any attempt to capture the controlling, commanding pole of AR relationships.

17. Among others, Talcott Parsons is particularly conspicuous by his absence from the list of major figures in social theory whose works are cited as the basis for the present synthesis. His influence on the present relational-models theory is significant, although indirect. Many of the modern authors cited here are using an implicitly Parsonian framework, and no work of social theory could be written today without being in some respects a response to Parsons. Indeed, one of the earliest roots of this work was my dissatisfaction with the Parsonian approach to social structure, norms, and individual motives. In fact, Parsons' synthesis clarified for me many of the major issues in this realm. But it is the fate of the most influential theorists to pass from explicit citation to adjectival allusion, and finally to being taken for granted as implicit presuppositions.

18. And our ethnopsychology may conceivably capture important facets of any social system—if this taxonomy were a distillation of Western folk models, that would not ipso facto make it inaccurate as a description of the essence of other societies. But for the most part I leave aside here the complex question of the links between

people's explicit, reflective, and systematic theories of social relations and the models that people actually use to generate social relations. The link is quite problematic, but I do not want to enter into a discussion of consciousness and false consciousness at this juncture.

*Chapter 3*

Things

1. Although I concur with their elegant analyses in other respects, Sahlins (1965) and to some extent Polanyi (1957a, 1966) do not make this aspect of chiefly redistribution clear.
2. Of course, this does not differentiate MP from any of the other models. The realization of each model is entirely dependent on the cultural specification of a number of kinds of implementation rules, spelled out in Chapter 7.
3. E.g., Mead 1961 [1937]; Evans-Pritchard 1951:124–45; Sussman 1953:152–56; Firth 1965 [1938]; Fortes 1970 [1963], 1983; Schneider 1980; for possible exceptions, see Cohen 1955, Turnbull 1972.
4. Thus treating all enemies as undifferentiated equivalents within the group and all members of one's own side as the same (it doesn't matter which of us was struck or who strikes the vengeance blow) in the CS mode, while qua groups, they interact in the EM mode.
5. See Fajans (1986) for additional ethnographic accounts illustrating diverse forms of non-MP exchange.
6. For example, Mikula (1977, 1980, and many earlier studies issued in German) conducts experiments varying the situation, the characteristics of the persons making the allocation, and the nature of their contributions. Stake (1983) studies the effects of gender and "motivation" (actually, experimenter's instructions) on reward distribution, while Tindale and Davis (1985) compare the allocations of individuals and groups hypothetically awarding either scholarship money or pay for work, showing the effects of the substantive content on the choice of a justice principle. Lerner (1975, 1977) explores the criteria people use in deciding how to treat third parties, especially victims. Deutsch (1975) considers the effects of different collective goals and the issue of participants' perceptions of the legitimacy of the principle used. Damon (1975, 1977, 1980) examines the ontogeny of justice concepts.
7. Part IV explores the issue of the existence of such metaprinciples, for which there is generally very little convincing evidence. Social justice norms are closely linked to morality and legitimation, discussed in another section below. See also the final section in Chapter 7 for more on social justice research.
8. Or nearly universal. Some hunter-gatherers exhibit very little AR, and there have been assertions that societies have existed in which concepts of legitimate AR command and deference were totally lacking (Miller 1955).
9. My own experience with children in the four-to-ten age range suggests that they actually prefer strict equality to many alternative distributions which would make none worse off and some substantially better off—equality per se is far more important than maximizing expected utility. I think this phenomenon is more robust than could be accounted for merely by children's inability to calculate expected

utilities accurately. It is worth considering under what conditions adults also prefer strict equality to, say, maximizing the welfare of the most disadvantaged.

10. Walzer (1983) advocates just this kind of autonomy among spheres of justice, arguing that it is illegitimate to transform any kind of social good into any other disparate kind of good. He makes this argument quite independently of the research
in economic anthropology that shows that in many societies people do demarcate
distinct spheres of exchange (e.g., Bohannan 1955). See also the section Morality,
Legitimation, Law and Ideology in Chapter 6.

11. The system of assessment may accord with one model (say, MP), collection and
enforcement another (say, AR), while the objective may be guided by quite another (say, the redistributive CS goal of sharing and providing for the needy).

12. My thanks to John Lucy for leading me to the key source here, Marx's *Grundrisse*.

13. The English translation of the crucial part of Marx's key work on the subject, the
*Grundrisse*, appeared in 1964, and the full translation in 1973, although a translation of a similar early analysis from *The German Ideology* had appeared in 1938.

14. Oddly, Durkheim himself makes only one trivial reference to Marx; apparently he
viewed his project as sufficiently distinct so as not to warrant relating his theory to
Marx's analysis of capitalism. When he wrote the first edition of *The Division of
Labor* (1893) he could not have read *The German Ideology* (manuscript written in
1845–6), the first pieces of which were not published until 1902 and 1921 and
which was not published in full until 1929, or the *Grundrisse* (manuscript written
in 1857–8), since it was not published until 1939. (Bibliographic details on Marx are
given in Rubel 1956.) Certainly Durkheim's methods, focusing on the preponderance of repressive or restitutive sanctions, did not require explicit recourse to
Marx, although they were all participants in the same socioeconomic discourse.
For an overview of the relations among the work of Marx, Durkheim, and Weber
see Giddens (1971)—although there appears to be no discussion anywhere in the
literature on the convergence in their three typologies of social forms. Tönnies's
(1988 [1887]) book would have been available to Durkheim (who was fluent in German), but he does not refer to it either.

15. See Marx's earlier description (1964b [1844]:123): "The workers on the estate are
not in the condition of day labourers, but are partly the property of the lord, as in
the case of serfs, and partly stand to him in relations of respect, subordination, and
duty. His relation to them is therefore directly political. . . . The lord does not try
to extract the maximum profit from his estate. He rather consumes what is there,
and tranquilly leaves the care of producing it to the serfs and tenant farmers. That
is the *aristocratic* condition of landownership which reflects a romantic *glory* upon
its lords." There could hardly be a more unambiguous description of the organization of labor in the form of Authority Ranking. This political role, Marx says, is
later transformed into one based on land as a commodity and a strictly material
relationship of cynically self-interested exploitation of workers (MP).

16. Erasmus (1956) does not cite Marx, Durkheim, Weber, or Piaget, nor is he cited by
Ricoeur, Sahlins, Blau, Etzioni, Udy, or social justice researchers; he does refer to
Polanyi's concept of redistribution. No English translations of Marx's *Grundrisse*
had been published in 1956.

17. Guillet (1980) argues that the persistence of these nonwage forms of labor is a consequence of capitalist exploitation under the world economic system.

*Chapter 4*

Choices

1. McCauley also induces that unanimous consensus often results from "promotional leadership," that is, from a strong leader's forceful early expression of his will. In our theory, this is clearly AR, a qualitatively different sort of phenomenon.

2. Sheeran is a Jesuit who became interested in the topic after discovering that the early Jesuits once followed a similar procedure called communal discernment.

3. As Sabini (n.d.) points out, another factor that subjects reported led them to obey the experimenter in the Milgram studies was fairness: subjects believed that the confederate had been assigned to his experimental role by a fair lottery (and hence that they could equally well have been in his place). This application of Equality Matching could have resulted in greater empathy, but instead subjects used it to justify their obedience. An additional factor is the MP contract—the subject has voluntarily chosen to participate, in return for compensation (although subjects were told they would still be compensated, regardless of when they left off). This illustrates the complex interplay that may obtain among the four models.

4. Clark McCauley suggested the second interpretation to me.

5. Another quasisocial influence mechanism that Cialdini also discusses, consistency, does not fit readily into our typology.

6. Although Etzioni's purposes and his inductively derived typology are clearly convergent with Udy's (1959, 1970) analysis of work, apparently neither is aware of the other.

7. A comment by Clark McCauley led me to work out this issue.

*Chapter 5*

Orientations

1. Although I will not draw on his sources here, Sahlins (1965) cites many valuable ethnographic examples of the uses of each of these models in generating sociable group relations.

2. Yet he acknowledges the importance of individual self-assertion: it is not a monistic theory.

3. Thanks again to John Lucy for leading me to reread Mead more closely.

4. Liminality is a state of transition, of being betwixt and between statuses, neither one nor the other. The concept comes from Van Gennep's analysis of rites of passage. Although Turner makes a convincing case that communitas is characteristic of such transitional states, he does not show that CS is limited to such liminal experiences.

5. Turner (1969:114, 128, 132) emphasizes the inclusive nature of communitas, and states that it is not based on an in–out, we–they contrast; yet the extreme marking and seclusion of initiates and the associated secrecy in the paradigmatic case of rites of passages seem to contradict this. Communitas (CS) merges participants, but often tends to exclude outsiders.

6. However, the otherwise elegant account that Meeker, Barlow, and Lipset develop of the links among food production, social relations, ideology, and self is weakened

by their failure to recognize the distinction between CS and EM relationships, both of which are prominent in this part of the world.

7. Interestingly, Tönnies used the organic analogy in describing Gemeinschaft, while calling Gesellschaft mechanical—the reverse of Durkheim's metaphor.

8. One superficial indication of this beyond what Mead discusses is the salience of "occupations" in American identity: A person may think of herself as an entrepreneur, a successful business executive, a broker, or a management trainee, as a banker, a salesperson, a welder, a professor, a farmer, as a union member or a student. That is, a core component of the American self is the person's economic role: how he earns his living.

9. In traditional cultures people often conceive of marriage in terms of men giving women in marriage to other men; although this may offend our modern Western sensibilities, it appears to represent the actors' points of view accurately, including that of the women who are exchanged.

10. The universal need for privacy in normal sexual relations may also represent the CS mechanism of exclusive, external boundary maintenance around the merged selves. Once again this suggests that CS tends to be a binary relation, in which the complement of communal unity is exclusionary separation.

11. Most of this work has proceeded independently of research in ethics and moral judgment, which I discuss in Chapter 6 below in the section Morality, Legitimation, Law, and Ideology.

12. Lévi-Strauss maintains that generalized exchange is ultimately only compatible with a preference for matrilateral marriage [in which men should marry their mothers' brothers' daughters], while a preferential rule for bilateral cross-cousin marriage is the expression of restricted exchange.

13. Each of these attitudes may occur within any of the three irreducible, necessary family relationships within the elementary unit of kinship: consanguinity between siblings, affinity between spouses, and descent between parent and child.

14. For incisive anthropological treatments of the relations between egalitarian norms entailing the exchange of equivalent or identical entities and the contrast with the asymmetrical complementarity of AR transactions, see Sahlins (1965) and earlier work; Forge (1972), and Godelier (1986a) (especially pp. 187–88).

15. Although fitness maximization through adaptation is an axiom for most biologists, the concept of natural selection does not imply any particular mechanism for organizing the various dimensions of adaptation. Nor has it been shown that human (or any other primate) social relationships actually can be explained in terms of (or reduced to) fitness maximization.

16. For more details on the early work on affiliation, see Boyatzis's (1973) review.

17. This work extends in various other directions. Davis (1983) identifies individual differences in dispositions to empathize, while Batson et al. (1981) study the relationship between empathy and altruistic motivation. Levine (1979) suggests that adolescents have an especially acute need for a basic sense of belonging and community membership, an observation Veroff and Veroff (1980) also make, among many others.

18. These are: (1) Obedience and respect for authority are the most important virtues children should learn; (8) Every person should have complete faith in some supernatural power whose decisions he obeys without question; (22) It is best to use some prewar authorities in Germany to keep order and prevent chaos; (23) What this country needs most, more than laws and political programs, is a few coura-

geous, tireless, devoted leaders in whom the people can put their faith; (26) People can be divided into two distinct classes: the weak and the strong; (27) There is hardly anything lower than a person who does not feel a great love, gratitude, and respect for his parents (Adorno et al. 1950:255–56).

19. Items 2, 13, 19, 21, 38 (Adorno et al. 1950:255–56).

20. Winter and McClelland each discuss various typologies of types of power, McClelland distinguishing among four types according to the sources and objects of power, which he relates to Freudian theory through Erikson's theory of stages of ego development. But these subtypes do not agree, and need not concern us here.

21. Perhaps motivated in part by a reductionist need to show that this motive is biologically "real," McClelland and Jemmot (1980) and McClelland, Alexander, and Marks (1982) produce evidence that inhibition of strong power motives may have adverse physiological consequences. For our purposes, it is sufficient that this motive have manifest social consequences, which the research of Winter and McClelland indeed demonstrates.

22. Rosaldo does not mention MP motives or related modes of interaction, perhaps because MP seems so self-evident and prosaic to a Western anthropologist.

23. In a comparative analysis of American and Japanese culture and personality, Doi also explores an important question which I will not be able to pursue more broadly here: what are the psychological consequences of the degree to which a basic social motivation is given explicit formulation and elaboration in the culture?

24. People may *amae* in relationships that also involve significant aspects of AR, but Doi is clear that *amae* has nothing to do with AR per se.

*Chapter 6*

Judgments

1. As indicated above in the section Transactions and especially in the work discussed there on social justice, the models are both procedural guides for ethical practices and, at the same time, systems of distributional standards for the outcome of transactions.

2. The *Hsiao Ching,* and Chinese philosophy in general, also incorporate strong elements of a Communal Sharing morality.

3. Fung (1947:21) identifies five traditional social relationships in China: sovereign: subject, father: son, elder brother: younger brother, husband: wife, friend: friend. Four of these are based on AR. In addition, the focus of Chinese religion is ancestor worship.

4. Rawls assumes that strict equality is not feasible, and that people would really prefer some compromise between strict equality and a utilitarian criterion of maximizing total aggregate welfare, so his scheme is a composite.

5. Walzer (1983) expounds this feature without linking it to egalitarian distribution per se.

6. See Elias (1956:88–90) on collective moral responsibility for compensation when one member of an African kin group harms someone from another group.

7. See O'Flaherty (1976) and Parkin (1985) for discussions of conceptions of evil in other cultural and religious traditions.

8. Even people who practice cannibalism attribute to uncivilized outsiders forms of cannibalism that they regard as abominable and aberrant–e.g., eating certain disgusting parts of the body, or eating strangers (Fitz John Porter Poole, personal communication).

9. Writing of Japanese concepts of kindness, compassion, pity and empathy, Lebra (1976:102) also refers in passing to another religious manifestion of Communal Sharing, referring to the Buddha as "the ultimate embodiment of unlimited benevolence."

10. Of course, socialization practices and in particular the kinds of social relationships a child experiences certainly shape, directly and indirectly, adult conceptions of gods and spirits (Whiting and Child 1953, Wright 1954, Lambert, Triandis, and Wolf 1959). But it is the basic models that are the ultimate source for adult conceptions, actions, and motivations oriented toward gods and spirits, not simply some kind of passive inductive learning. It seems to me that it is still an open question as to just how, and to what extent, early experiences other than direct observation and tutelage about the specific domain indirectly shape these "projective" systems through psychodynamic processes.

### Preface, Part III

1. Part III owes a great deal to Scott Weinstein, since it was in a series of exciting conversations with him that some of the ideas took their present form. Without his patient curiosity, enthusiasm, and demand for rigor many of the vague ideas I had would not have been forged in just the shape in which I express them here. The formalization at the end of Chapter 9, especially, was a collaborative effort that required his mathematical wisdom. Lila Gleitman, Michael Kelly, David Premack, John Sabini, and several graduate students then helped to temper and hone many of these ideas when they read an earlier draft of some of Part III in an interesting seminar we taught together on "rules." My thanks to all of them.

### Chapter 7

## Generativity and Cross-Cultural Variability in the Production of Social Relations

1. The discussion in this section was stimulated by issues raised by Richard Shweder in conversations and in various public talks where he has made the distinction between mandatory principles and discretionary features of moral systems. My aim here is to provide a systematic basis for this distinction.

2. Or "individualism," as opposed to the value of idiosyncratic self-expression that they call "individuality." Individuality is exemplified in permissive tolerance for eccentricity in a lineal or collateral system. Their contrast between individualism and individuality roughly corresponds to my distinction between Asocial and Null orientations.

3. The exception is that the chief outranks all his subjects, regardless of age.

4. The domain applicability rules, discussed above, determine what is relevant.

5. Cf. Chomsky (1981) and Roeper and Williams (1987) for the idea of parameter setting in language acquisition.

6. Lila Gleitman insightfully pointed out to me the importance of this issue.

7. Nick Haslam prompted me to address this unsolved issue explicitly.

8. That is, interaction may coincidentally conform to a model without being generated with reference to that model. Dissimulation is a different case entirely, of course, since it is definitely acting with reference to a model.

9. Mikula and Schwinger (1978) also offer some commonsense speculations about how task situations, interpersonal relations, and expectations about future interaction affect peoples' choice among the three justice principles when allocating rewards. They consider the consequences for people's interpersonal relations of their use of the different principles.

10. However, my ultimate goal for a social theory is to account for everyday social behavior, including garbled productions, partially formed actions, "errors," transgressions and responses to transgressions. In this respect, this is a theory of performance, not just competence—of social action, not just norms.

11. There is one other striking context in which people often fail to use matching models to generate relationships: in encounters across cultures.

*Chapter 8*

Defining Features of the Relational Models

1. Animals in a number of primate species modulate their actions and relationships with a second animal as a function of that animal's actions and relationships with a third animal (see Cheney, Seyfarth, and Smuts 1986 for an overview). But no one has yet looked to see whether a fourth animal would alter its behavior toward the first animal as a function of the first animal's modulating its relationship to the second animal.

2. Of course, there may be countervailing obligations and sentiments—friendship and loyalty to the transgressor, for example. But the jural pressure is still real, even when other factors outweigh it.

3. Although a major focus of Heider's theory was on the interdependencies among social relationships, almost all of the subsequent work building on Heider has focused on the interdependency among ideas or between ideas and actions, and in particular on consistency among attitudes.

4. Of course, there often are untoward consequences of being incompetent or acting in a way that is esthetically repellant. But they do not have the same sort of ramifications extending into the social network.

5. It would be culturally intelligible to repudiate someone by saying, "You never do X, Y, and Z: you're not my father!" Or, "He was never a father to me; he never did X, Y, and Z." Conversely, it would be equally coherent to say, "He was like a father to me—we always did X, Y, and Z."

6. War, of course, may be worse than anarchy. My purpose is simply to explain the observable regularity and structure in social interaction, not to recommend it.

7. Never mind that a considerable body of research demonstrates that trying to anticipate the market like this without insider information is actually futile.

8. Nevertheless, referring to the same model does not guarantee successful coordination: people may disagree on how to apply it.

9. They do not always fit together, as I pointed out earlier.

10. These terms were suggested by Edward Sapir (1927) and popularized by Pike (1954) on the analogy of the contrast between the phon*etic* analysis of the raw

sounds of a language (or at least the components of the sounds that are potentially available for linguistic use) and the phonemic analysis of the sound contrasts that are actually meaningful in the particular language under discussion.

11. Although I did not realize this until I had completed the separate analyses.

12. Other desires and appetites often overcome this concern with Equality Matching, of course—people have a multitude of motives.

13. The metaphor of incorporating norms into the self bears examination. Often, it is used as a facile "just so" story that amounts to nothing more than saying that (people assumed to be) selfish individualists behave as if they were subject to "external" (see Sabini and Silver 1987) sanctions, even when there are no objective sanctions operating. All such statements really mean is that people are sociable, and in fact not selfish individualists. Unless carefully explicated, the metaphor of "internalization" reveals nothing about the source or mechanism of human sociability.

14. The emotions of the person who imputes a transgression to herself or is imputed to have transgressed will differ from the emotions of those who are innocent victims or offended bystanders. There is much work to be done on the taxonomy and nature of moral emotions (are most "emotions" moral?), and I suspect we may find colloquial English and introspection both inadequate to accomplish the job.

15. "At least," because the genes shared because of the most direct kinship link are supplemented, in some cases substantially, by the average coefficient of relatedness in the population. This population average is a result of innumerable less direct kinship links, together with the effects of parallel selection.

16. I.e., you helped me three times, I helped you once, so how many do I owe you now? This is a subtraction problem.

17. There is a report of one language-trained chimpanzee capable of matching fractions of fruits with corresponding fractions of a cylinder of liquid (Premack 1983). This striking finding should be followed up.

18. This is Nick Haslam's phrasing (personal communication).

19. To the degree that a behaviorist and an economic account are logically parallel, differing largely in time scale, explaining the evolution of endogenous psychological structures requires hypothesizing analogous selective forces that would generate these relational structures. The difference between the two accounts is that if all people use only a few models in a great many domains in all cultures, a learning account has to show identical patterns of reinforcements in the lives of all children in each domain in every society—or else massive generalization. The nativist hypothesis allows for the possibility that the models evolved as a result of selective forces in one or two domains; once these social tools become available, people use them for many other purposes.

*Chapter 9*

## Semiotic Marking and Relational Structures

1. My taxonomy of the forms of marking social relationships is influenced by, but quite different from, Saussure's (1983).

2. See Goodenough (1944, 1965); Guttman (1944).

3. The axiomatization in this section was the product of collaborative work in which I was dependent on Scott Weinstein's mathematical insights and his patience in

explaining the relevant axioms. However, I am entirely responsible for any errors that may have resulted from my failure to grasp the principles involved. The text is mine, but often stimulated by or developed in conversation with Scott Weinstein.

4. Notice that for the case where R is the identity relation, (*) is just Leibniz's law of the indiscernibility of identicals (as opposed to the more controversial identity of indiscernibles). That is, things that are congruent with respect to a class of properties can not be distinguished by properties of that class.

5. This is not how Moose marriage ordinarily works, but it is a common enough system in many societies.

6. Binary operations like addition and multiplication transform two elements. Unary operations like taking the inverse of a number involve only one term: $^{-1}$ is the multiplicative inverse (e.g., $4^{-1} = 1/4$; $x \bullet y \bullet y^{-1} = x$), and $-$ is the additive inverse ($-(4) = -4$; $x + y + - y = x$).

7. In contrast, think about calculating time of day. Twenty-three hours after 10 in the morning is earlier than 10. This illustrates the fact that addition in some kinds of Abelian groups is not order preserving.

8. The multiplicative group cannot include zero, since dividing by zero is undefined. The notation "$C - \{0\}$" means "the set C with the element zero taken out."

9. The rate (of pay) itself could be represented as a set of geometrically similar rectangles (defined in terms of the proportion of their sides), or as the sine of an angle.

10. There is still the problem of horizontal décalage: people may have quite different capacities to apply an understanding in different domains. However, for a number of reasons one would expect children to master and manifest the relevant relations in the social domain before nonsocial domains, especially if the cognitive equipment has evolved through selection specifically for its adaptive social functions.

11. $12 \bullet 3 + 40 \bullet 3$ is undefined in relation to $3 \bullet (12 + 40)$; there is no reason why they have to be equal.

12. Economists sometimes analyze preferences in ordinal terms, because subjects are often unable to scale preferences reliably on a ratio scale. But when people cannot make meaningful practical decisions based on the ratios of their preferences, it probably indicates that the issue is not one that people naturally consider in MP terms. Experimenters should recognize that this incapacity (or unwillingness) implies that the experimental task as presented has no meaningful MP interpretation to the subjects. Regardless of how subjects rank preferences for various peculiar hypothetical outcomes in experiments, people set and pay real prices in the market every day, and prices are ratios. Indeed, every price is a ratio against all other MP commodities.

13. I am indebted to Donald W. Fiske and Frank Norman for leading me to these key references.

## Preface, Part IV

1. The concepts of experience-near and thick description are Geertz's (1984 [1974] and 1973b, respectively), although he has nominally different objectives for them.

2. I started work on Part III as a paper for the session on The Directive Force of Cultural Models at the 85th Annual Meeting of the American Anthropological Association in Philadelphia, December 4, 1986. The session was sponsored by the

Society for Psychological Anthropology, the American Ethnological Society, and the Society for Cultural Anthropology. I am indebted to Roy D'Andrade and Naomi Quinn, the organizers of the session, as well as to the participants, discussants, and the audience of the session for invaluable discussions and comments on my talk.

I conducted my fieldwork among the Moose jointly with Kathryn F. Mason, and she collected much of the data on which the work in Part III is ultimately based. Many of the ideas it contains were first worked out in discussions with her, and much of this book was written in time she generously gave me by taking on other joint responsibilities.

3. See Homans 1974 and earlier works, Blau (1964), Kelley and Thibaut (1978 and earlier works), Becker (1976, 1981), Ekeh (1974), and Walster, Walster, and Berscheid (1978).

4. See Fiske (1985) for a reanalysis and generalization of Weber's typology.

*Chapter 10*

## An Egalitarian Motive: The Goal of Even Matching

1. Cf. Delobsom (1929:425), who gives a capsule description of a *sısoaaga*; Pageard (1969:382–86) also discusses various sources on Moose *sısoaaga* bees and related practices; and Lewis (1981:69) makes a passing reference to similar practices in a Bambara village in Mali. Unless specifically attributed to other observers, all the ethnographic descriptions in this book are based directly on my own observations and/or those of Kathryn F. Mason, who has generously shared her notes and her knowledge with me. Where I am aware of other accounts that confirm our observations, I cite them in the form, "cf . . . ." or "see . . .".

2. A plate opposite p. 46 in Mangin (1916) shows such a line.

3. The exception is that men who have been promised or are courting for wives attend their in-laws' bees non-contingently; see Transferring Women in Marriage, below.

4. Pageard (1969:420) mentions another form of quasi-exchange, and Hammond (1966:94–95, 99–100) discusses comparable kinds of balanced reciprocity in Yatēnga. Skinner (1964b:81) cites material on similar sorts of cooperative work groups in other West African societies.

5. I encountered only one adult man who had never worked abroad, among dozens whom I questioned on this score.

6. See Skinner (1964b:81–85) on craft specialization and sale of crafts in West Africa more generally.

7. Indeed, the near absence of wage earners is typical of traditional societies (Herskovits 1952:110).

8. Cf. Pageard's (1969:385) citation of Yaméogo's unpublished (1961) account of a related practice near Koungoussi.

9. Leynaud (1966) describes other age-based work groups in Niger.

10. People will not participate in any formal event unless they receive an explicit invitation, however. A person who does not receive a direct personal invitation does not "know" about the event, and ignores it.

11. A small proportion of the total village labor is sold indirectly in the form of labor input to tangible commodities that enter the market.

## Chapter 11

## A Communal Solidarity Motive: The Goal of Sharing and Unity

1. See Fiske (1985) for a fuller description. See also Hammond (1966:76) on Gourcy in the Yatēnga region and Lallemand (1977:46–68) on Bamtēnga in the Koungoussi area.
2. Cf. Hammond (1966:87) on Gourcy in Yatēnga.
3. Including any foster children she has been given to raise.
4. Cf. Delobsom (1929:425). Such a field cultivated independently by a post-menopausal woman is called a *beoolgo*.
5. A *zaka* (plural *zakse*) is a walled area referred to in English as a compound (in French, *concession*) comprising at least one hut and yard for each adult, as well as animal huts and mud granaries. Ideally there is only one common entrance, opening onto a central courtyard (the *zaka* proper). All but the smallest *zakse* (compounds) are subdivided at one or more levels into nested units surrounded by their own walls, whose entrances open into the central yard or onto passageways to it. A *zaka* is also a social unit, made up of a group of closely related lineage-mates and their wives and headed by a senior male (*zak soba*) who is the proprietor of important ritual objects which protect the *zaka* (*Kumse, Tubo,* and—among the Yĩyõose and Sãaba—*Tẽese*; the Yarse, however, do not have these objects since they do not make animal sacrifices). The architectural *zaka* and the social *zaka* do not necessarily correspond; the social *zaka* unit may contain more than one distinct walled compound *zaka*.
6. See Tait (1961:197–98) for an account of similar patterns among the Konkomba of Northern Ghana. Schildkrout (1978:109) describes very extensive food sharing among Moose and other emigrants in Kumasi, Ghana.
7. Indeed, this leads to a "secondary" norm: it is not polite to appear when people are eating, or about to eat, and Moose avoid doing so. They are not so assiduous in observing the same etiquette regarding beer, however.
8. Kathryn F. Mason kindly provided me with most of these details of the organization of women's work. See Mason (1987) for more information and further analysis.
9. In the West, while production tends to be organized in the form of Market Pricing, in which individuals are paid for labor and compete for jobs with other individuals, consumption is largely organized with respect to families. U.S. family consumption generally takes a predominantly communal form, with the sharing of food, housing, recreation, and often transportation; earnings are often pooled. The extent and importance of familial Communal Sharing is not as widely appreciated as it should be in either U.S. ideology or social science. Of course in any family, domains other than consumption may be governed by other models (see Chapter 5, especially the section on Marriage), and many U.S. families use one of the other models to organize consumption.
10. Both of which they are likely to share communally to a greater or lesser extent with their age-mates or families.

11. Women do express concern that their husband may spend resources for his lover (*rolle*), but this may be a concern with Equality Matching, based on the standard that each woman should get an equal share.

12. Sometimes wives do run away, and young men may depart either for the Ivory Coast or to take up residence with a mother's brother when they feel that the senior male who "owns" them is not fulfilling his pastoral responsibilities. Probably this flight is usually the result of the leaver's perception of tyrannical or inattentive abuse of Authority Ranking standards.

13. See Firth (1965 [1938]) Chapters 7 and 8 for another example of a somewhat similar system of communal production among the Tikopia in Polynesia. Note that Udy finds that familial work groups commonly make use of Equality Matching reciprocal arrangements to supplement the labor of the core kin group.

14. For some reason Hyden (1980) equates the economy of affection to Polanyi's reciprocal model of exchange (EM), ignoring Polanyi's CS concept of householding.

15. I invented and had built a push cart that would hold three to five water-carrying pots (10–15 liters per pot), so that the youths we hired to haul our water could do so more easily. It proved to be a success, and all day long one person after another borrowed it. So I improved the design and eventually had a total of ten carts made, which we distributed to the various neighborhoods of the village when we left. In addition to reducing several fold the time and energy involved in carrying water, this had the unanticipated effect of transferring much of the water hauling from women to adolescent boys and girls, who were more willing and able to handle the carts and repair flat tires.

16. The disdain and disparagement are mutual.

17. The Yarse, who started their well during our fieldwork, were industrious, persistent, and successful well-diggers. The Sāaba undertook their well-digging after we left the village, and I have not heard what the outcome was. In any case, all along the Sāaba had been drawing most of their water from a well in an adjacent village that was much nearer to their neighborhood than the well of the village whose chief has nominal authority over them. This is the same well we all turned to when our village well went dry.

18. One particularly industrious man known for his strength (and independence) had at one time tried to dig a well on his own. It never reached water, and I believe another unsuccessful well had been the project of this man with a partner. But had the wells been successful, they would certainly have been open to all.

19. With the partial exception of a known witch—although there are several presumed witches who have been allowed to take up residence in the village.

20. On never treating land as a commodity, see Hammond (1966:77) on Gourcy in the Yatēnga region, Pageard (1969:391–93), and Kawada (1979:218) on Tēnkodogo. On freely giving land to whoever wants it, see Tauxier (1912:790), Şaul on Manga (1983:79, 94), and Hammond (1966:74–75). For similar practices among the Gourmantche to the south-east, cf. Remy (1967:37–39, 55–58). Corporate "ownership" of land is the mode in Africa, as Elias (1956:162–68), Suret-Canale (1964), and Coquery-Vidrovitch (1969) attest. (Of course, CS is not the only form of landholding in Africa.)

21. In principle, the ultimate proprietor of never cultivated land is the *tēngsoba*, the custodian of the earth, who is the ritual leader of the village (see Pageard 1969:394–98).

22. Otherwise, the only major exception is an area in the south of the Maane district, which is too far from water to be usable. Reportedly, Moose formerly shifted their cultivation so as to leave land fallow for some time every few years, but the population pressure in the Maane area now precludes this in most cases. Few people hold fallow land.

23. In the only land dispute I know of that occurred in the village during our two-year tenure, a Nakomse man tried to reclaim land he had apparently lent to the current cultivator's mother some decades ago. The case went ultimately to the Paramount Chief, who sent a representative to adjudicate on the spot. This representative divided the land between the disputants into two more or less equal portions. Even this dispute arose, I think, largely because of a boundary quarrel. The giver of the land accused the current cultivator of extending his planting into the area he, the giver, was continuing to use. But it is notable that the lender was unable to reclaim all of his land. Pageard (1969:393, 399, 400–405) discusses Moose customary law and tribunal rulings about such cases.

24. And elsewhere in the culture area: Fortes (1945:177–81, 240). For the context of land holding in Africa more generally, cf. Biebuyck (1964), and especially Deng (1988:362); cf. also Bohannan (1955:63) on Tiv.

25. Chapter 14 deals with another possible Market Pricing interpretation of Communal Sharing relations: the often gratuitous assumption that each person is better off as an individual in the long run if he or she pools work and resources with others. This is the "insurance against uncontrollable losses" interpretation of Communal Sharing. I show that this interpretation does not fit the evidence.

26. As stated, I am simply asserting this; the elucidation of Moose divination and sacrifice that would support my contention is still to come in a later work. Interestingly, Margaret Mead (1961 [1937]:492) suggests that it is typical of "cooperative" societies (essentially, ones emphasizing Communal Sharing) that their religious beliefs characterize the world as meaningful and comprehensible, and as susceptible to human pleading: "All these societies . . . have an ordered view of the universe. They conceive of a supernatural system which operates on its own rules and which man may propitiate and influence in an orderly way."

*Chapter 12*

Transferring Women in Marriage: Sharing, Not Self-Interested,
or *Rational* Exchange

1. This section describes things from the male point of view, which leaves out some important aspects of what is going on. However, it is a fact that in the Maane area at least marriage is predominantly a transfer of women arranged between and controlled by men. For Moose women's perspective on married life see Mason (1987, 1988).

2. Sexual access to women does not seem to be the primary motivation in seeking wives. For one thing, throughout most of their life span most Moose have lovers (*rolba*, singular *rolle*) who are other people's spouses (see Fiske n.d.). Although children belong to their biological father and thus men can father descendants by their lovers, siring children by other men's wives can be hazardous. So men want wives.

3. A man can divorce his wife by breaking and tossing out (*luki*) her water storage pot (*kõyūugu*), digging out (*viki*) her three hearth stones (*yega*; hearth is *yegre*), or by ripping out (*viki*) her grind stone (*neere*) from the grinding platform. These acts are irrevocable; if a man were to do any of these things and then, reconciled, take his wife back, either or both of them would die. The wife would also die if she failed to leave after her husband did any of these things.

4. Cf. Tauxier (1917:236–37); Delobsom (1930:14–15, 1933:181) on Goupana, Sao region, north of Ouagadougou; Marie-André (1938a:18, 1938b:98), Ouédraogo (1951:49); Skinner (1964a:84); Pageard (1969:342); and also Ruelle's (1904:686) comment that the only women who can be "sold" (*vendues*) are captives. Concerning other societies in the culture area, Rattray (1932:460) reported that neither the Mampruse nor the Dagomba pay bride price, although the other societies of northern Ghana, including the Tallensi, do so. This is of interest since the horsemen who conquered the indigenous inhabitants and became the Nakomse, the ruling clan of the Moose, are related to the Mampruse and Dagomba. Below we will also see that the Dogon, who are apparently an offshoot of the indigenous inhabitants of Mooseland, also do not have bride price.

5. However, the "mothers" of a bride do collect some money to give to her when she first departs for her husband's home.

6. Malinowski (1964 [1926]) and many others since have used the term "reciprocity" to cover any situation in which there are bilateral transfers, without making the kinds of distinctions that I am making in this book.

7. Cf. Kawada's (1979:305) similar point regarding the redistribution of consumable goods by chiefs in the Tenkodogo region.

8. There are no common Moore terms for "wife-seekers" or "potential wife-givers" as such, in part perhaps because before a wife is promised neither side explicitly acknowledges that a wife is being sought; I use these terms to make the exposition clear. Sometimes wife-givers refer to a wife-seeker to whom they have not yet given a wife (but have perhaps indicated that they appreciate the benefactions) as a *yel som soba* (good deed person), since he regularly does good deeds for them. In other forms of courtship based on friendship between peers, the men may address each other reciprocally as *m zoa*, my friend, or *m daoa*, my man (a term of friendship, not a general form of address to males). However, Moose also use all of these same terms, make gifts, and extend help and aid to people from whom they have no expectation of ever receiving a wife—people like me, for example. Later, if and when a bride is actually promised, each side addresses people in the other group as *m deemba* (my in-law).

9. However, once a lineage gives a wife to another, there are some tendencies toward continuing to give wives in the same direction. If a woman has been well treated and especially if her children have served their mother's natal lineage well, the woman's natal lineage may give her a wife to pass on to her husband or her children. Such a wife is a *yiri paga* (home wife; see Pageard [1966:119], Lallemand [1977:157], Mason [1987, 1988]). Also, when a woman dies, at the final stage of the funeral ceremonies long after her death (*ku wam peoogo*), the woman's husband's lineage solicits another woman to replace her.

10. Further references and implications of this are reviewed in Pageard (1966:112–23); see also Skinner (1964a:22) on Nobere and Ouagadougou.

11. In the Ouagadougou dialect, according to Alexandre (1953), *belem* means pleasing

and making happy, in the form of either courtship or baby care taking—the same word is used for both.

12. Compare with the *amae, amaeru* concepts Takeo Doi (1962, 1981) describes as central to Japanese culture and psychology.

13. In contrast to the Tallensi, whose set bride price Fortes (1949) states to be a bull and three cows.

14. Cf. Delobsom (1930:11), Izard-Héritier and Izard (1959:37), Skinner (1964a:84), Pageard (1969:280), and also the brief statement by Ruelle (1904:684).

15. E.g., *Fo maana neere. F yaa ni songo. Ed nongflame. La ed pa tar bũmb n kõ fo!*

16. For other descriptions of *belõgo* among the Moose in various regions see Delobsom (1933:174-76), (Ouagadougou region); Marie-André (1938a:18-19), Pageard (1969:279-80), Lallemand (1977:158-59), (Bamtēnga, Koungoussi region of Yatēnga), the novel by Ilboudo (1982:22-23), (Manga region) and Mangin (1916:29), (Tenkodogo and Koupela region).

17. Puberty occurs much later for the Moose than it does in the U.S. and Europe today, and even a girl of 17 may not be sexually mature. In that case, she would not go to her husband's home until age 19. Mothers often argue that their daughters are not yet mature, or simply insist that they need them at home, forcing postponement of the marriage until the bride is 19.

18. Moose actually address and refer to their own fathers and father's brothers as *m keema* (literally, my elder, elder brother), as long as the person being addressed or referred to has a living older kinsman.

19. *Pog-boole, pog-gesgo, be-puʋsm, pog-puʋsm, tom-yugri (tom-boko).*

20. For an excellent treatment of major Market Pricing transactions involving credit, witnesses, and the like see Pageard (1969:415-26); the contrast with courtship (*belõgo*) is complete and striking.

21. Except for the former practice of buying slaves (see below).

22. Cf. Tauxier (1912:564) and (1917:248) where he cites Vadier on the Yatēnga Moose; also Delobsom (1930:11).

23. However, Pageard indicates that contemporary tribunals have often held that such gifts do have to be reimbursed (1969:333, 340, 342), although this is not the custom among Moose Moslems (p. 355). Pageard (1969:295, 331) also cites Caboret (1964) to the effect that at least around Kombissiri, recent practice also involves reimbursement. Mangin (1921:29) states that if the "negotiations" are broken off before marriage, the wife-giving elder has to repay the gifts. However, on the same page he also writes that if a bride refuses to go to the man to whom her father gives her, the father does not have to return any of the money benevolently given (although he must repay any explicit loans). Later (p. 33) Mangin notes that in the event of dissolution of the marriage, nothing is returned to the husband.

24. Cf. Pageard (1969:280), who cites two unpublished papers on related practices in the regions of Saponé and Koudougou.

25. Cf. Skinner (1964a:21-23) on Nobere and Ouagadougou and Pacere (1979:107-108) on Manéga in Zitēnga.

26. Tait (1961:84, 96) describes similar practices among the Konkomba of Northern Ghana.

27. The Moose in all regions often refer to people to the south of themselves as Gurunsi, including people who call themselves Moose and speak the Moore language. These terms are ethnic "shifters" (cf. Galaty [1982] and Chapter 5 here).

Moose also sometimes captured or purchased male slaves, but male slaves did not marry and so are irrelevant to this discussion of the forms of marriage.

28. Tait (1961:163) mentions that in the period of his fieldwork, 1950–1954, the Konkomba of Northern Ghana "very occasionally" purchased wives from a neighboring society.

29. This system has been described by Delobsom (1933:164–69, 172), Marie-André (1938a:19–20), Skinner (1960, 1964a:42–43, 115, 170), Pageard (1969:277), Kawada (1979:218–19), and others. This is the only form of wife giving that has implications of further rights in the offspring of the women so given.

30. Such pages are sogõndãmba; they adopt women's clothing, hair styles, bracelets, and postures while serving the chief (cf. Skinner 1964a:43). Pageard (1969:281–82) describes a related institution called nokre, in which a young man puts himself at the disposal and under the protection of someone for a period of several years and receives a wife at the end of his service. He says this practice exists in many regions but is particularly widespread in the East. We did not observe nokre in Maane (nor, on the other hand, did we inquire about it as such).

31. Schildkrout also states that Kumasi Moose, who in many respects have adopted Hausa and Asante practices during their residence there, sometimes pay substantial bride prices.

32. Although there is no specific Moore term for married man or "head of household" as such.

33. Additionally, there are AR relations among all the wives in a compound and among the wives of one man, as a function of age, seniority of husband, and seniority of marriage to a given husband. A man's first wife is senior to the others and may direct them in some aspects of their work, as well as assume responsibility for new brides (see Mason 1987). The senior wife of the head of the lineage, the oldest wife in the lineage, and the senior wife of a compound each have specified roles in a number of lineage and compound rituals (on relations among co-wives, see also Mason 1988).

34. Cf. Hammond (1966:134–36) on Gourcy in Yatēnga and Tait (1961:216) on similar practices among the Konkomba of Northern Ghana.

35. In some other parts of the world, Equality Matching is the preferred basis for the transfer of women in marriage. Forge (1972) describes this in New Guinea, and Godelier (1986a:19–29) shows the difference between Equality Matching and other kinds of wife exchange.


*Chapter 13*

Authority Ranking: Precedence and Deference

1. Thus they are a counter example to Margaret Mead's (1937) finding that among the 13 societies her group studied, "will to power over persons" is absent in "cooperative" societies.

2. She also remarks that mechanisms of distribution of goods need not be correlated with the techniques by which goods are produced, citing the Maori as an example. In effect, this distinguishes the focal concern of Karl Marx from the focus of Karl Polanyi's analyses.

3. Excluding men descended from sisters' sons, although they may have been incorporated into the lineage in other respects.

4. However, the new office holder did survive—validating his claim—and both of these men are alive as I write this, about eleven years after the event. The holder of the sacred xylophone lineage headship has died, so the order of succession in the lineage is now unambiguous.

5. Two major kinds are *zu(g) sob n tuga* and *yud taaba tum*.

6. I have not computed statistical tests against a null hypothesis, since it is not clear what the appropriate null hypothesis might be. Moreover, these figures represent the total population of the village in question, but the village is not in any respect a random sample of the population of the region.

7. A paramount chief (*kombere*) may have dozens of wives, but I do not have data on what proportion of the wives he receives he redistributes to dependents and subjects.

*Chapter 14*

Economic Rationality

1. However, there is some room for flexibility. Thus, if the *keore* is nominally 333 *wakiri*, a friend may reduce it to 33 *wakiri*. Or a chicken may substitute for the goat that is required in principle. These variations and alternatives contrast categorically with price fluctuations based on market exchange ratios.

2. As outsiders, we ourselves hired people to haul water and do domestic chores. There were four boys whom we employed for child care and who were also friends. Interestingly enough, when I asked them to do a novel task, they sometimes did it and then asked with embarrassment whether it was *songre* ("help," which is either Equality Matching or Communal Sharing), because if not they could expect to be paid. Significantly, there is no common Moore term for paid labor as such.

3. Most "economic" theories conflate ratio pricing of commodities (MP) with selfish maximization. Therefore, in this chapter I will continue to treat the two as if they go together. But Chapters 16 and 17 show the distinction between Market Pricing per se and maximization, selfish or otherwise.

4. Regrettably, I did not devote very much attention to this issue while I was in the field. I have had to put together an account from information I picked up incidentally, and from the literature. So what follows has a rather less solid ethnographic foundation than the rest of this book.

5. This figure is based on the fiscal census (which is updated continually and checked by administrators who visit the village every two or three years), as corrected and amended for us, name by name, by the village *Naaba* (chief). By comparison, a map reporting the 1975 demographic census (Institut National 1979:23) indicates that census figures for the Maane district as a whole showed between 10 percent and 15 percent of the total male population absent for more than six months at the time of the census (December). If we add in the number of young men who have been gone less than six months, take into account the fact that about half the population is under 15 or over 40, and correct for what the Institut National calls a "strong underestimation" of emigrants, then it appears that the percentage of

young men absent from the village is roughly typical of the region. Other figures from this report (Institut National 1979:22) indicate that nationally 70 percent of the people absent over six months are men, and that 73 percent of the emigrant men are estimated to be between age 15 and 39.

6. If a witch knew of someone's impending departure, she could eat his "soul" (*suga*) before he left, and he would then die away from home some time later. Lacking his corpse in such an event, the villagers would be unable to interview the deceased to discover the circumstances of his death, and the witch would go undetected. Hence to let anyone, even someone in the same compound, know of one's plans makes one extremely vulnerable to witches who could kill without any deterrent fear of exposure. In addition, concealment of plans averts family pleas to stay. (Noaga [1978] and Ilboudo [1982] both describe—but do not explain—the secrecy surrounding departure from the village.)

7. I read many letters from emigrants abroad for the villagers and wrote many to emigrants on behalf of village kin and friends, serving as the principal scribe during the period of our fieldwork.

8. There may have been additional political factors contributing to their departure, but I do not have good information on this.

9. Remy (1973:8) estimates that one-fourth of the population of the Ivory Coast consists of immigrants, and if anything this may be a conservative estimate. Moose are probably a plurality of these immigrants, most of whom are temporary residents.

10. See Herskovits (1952:109–111) for a discussion of the issues involved in obtaining anthropological data about motives for working.

11. The communal digging of wells and catchment basins described above is an exception.

12. Among the Yīyōose, the head of each Bagba lineage is a diviner, while men (and, very rarely, women) from other Yīyōose lineages can also acquire the means of divination and learn to divine.

13. With the partial exception of beer brewing, Moose village women generally do not engage in commercial-scale market activities, although some women retail chewing tobacco in small quantities. Since there were no women in the village where we worked who brewed beer very frequently or on a large scale, I have no data on what happens when women become full-time brewers, for example. Nor do I have any data on the Deberse butchers who sell appreciable quantities of meat in the local market, or the Marense and Dapoore cloth dyers. I have only very limited data on the Yarse weavers in the village. In the future, these cases of craft and trade specialization need to be examined in detail with the issue of Market Pricing motives in mind.

14. A few other men retail kola nuts enough to reduce their farming activities slightly.

15. Remember that while migrants show off to some extent, they are equally conspicuous in their generosity.

16. Although I did not focus on smithing, I observed it often and knew several Sāaba well. The Sāaba of a compound all use a single forge. I believe that they often take turns using it day-by-day (EM?), and they commonly help each other out with projects that require more than one person (CS?). Boys pump the bellows for their elders (AR?). From my casual observations there is no sign of MP in the internal organization of the work within the Blacksmith community.

17. In some societies aspects of gender relations within the family are structured according to MP, of course, but this appears to be the exception.

18. As a result, much West African commerce is conducted by alien minorities who lack just these obligations and motives vis-a-vis the strangers with whom they trade (Meillassoux 1971:72, 82).

## Chapter 15

## Social Orientations in Neighboring Societies

1. Moose today identify some traditional wells as the work of the *Kibsi*, saying that the technology of their well construction is distinctive and inimitable. They believe that the *Kibsi* covered over other wells that have never been found. They also say that *Kibsi* occasionally come back secretly in the dead of night to make sacrifices at their old earth altars (*tēnkuga*). It is said that Moose travellers who reach the Bandiagara cliffs of Mali are queried about their natal villages, and that sometimes they encounter *Kibsi* who identify themselves as having come originally from that village.

2 Desplagnes (1907) focuses on the Dogon, whom he calls Habbés, but also discusses other societies to the south and west of the Dogon.

3. Debts that the head of a lineage segment contracts on behalf of the group are the collective responsibility of that lineage segment (Paulme 1940:113).

4. However, Dogon pay back loans of grain at the next harvest with double the amount lent, since, they point out, unlike money, grain can be planted and thus increase (Paulme 1940:115–16).

5. Bambara do not mark, compare, or assess individual contributions by holding any farming contests or competitions.

6. Compare my experience suggesting a more efficient way to dig water catchments, described at the end of the section, *Zauga: A Threshing Bee* in Chapter 10, and see Remy (1967).

7. However, even Worsley (1956:51) cites informants quoted by Fortes (1969 [1949]:72, 172), who describe the loss of a father or compound head as detrimental to their prospects for marriage and for agricultural security. This suggests that Tallensi authorities, like Moose leaders, tend to place their responsibility for the interests of their dependents above their own selfish interests.

8. Bloch (1973) and Pitt-Rivers (1973) both note that friendship relations, like kinship, also involve the amity of Communal Sharing.

9. Again, compare with the quotation from Pacere (1979) above.

10. Hart (1978:204) concurs with Bloch's gratuitous assumption about long-run balance, asserting that "the expectation of long-run equity (we might say, fair play) underlies the attachment of individuals to agnatic collectivities." But he gives no evidence at all to support this exogenous view of the Tale orientation toward kinship.

11. Cf. Polanyi (1957a [1944], 1957b) for the seminal development of this position.

12. Speaking thus of culture as if it were an active subject is merely convenient rhetorical shorthand—cultures do not do anything.

13. We will consider this issue in more detail below in Chapter 17.

14. The Bemba, like many other African societies, illustrate an interesting contrast with the U.S. in the implementation rules of CS: hospitable sharing of food does not involve conviviality or even conversation. The sharing of food (in contrast to beer) does not entail the sharing of thoughts.

15. The six cooperative societies are Zuni, Bathonga, Dakota, Samoa, and to a lesser degree Iroquois and Maori. Even the most "competitive" culture in Mead's sample, the Kwakiutl, stresses competition between groups, while each group prepares for it cooperatively and shares in the collective triumphs (or defeats).

16. For Americans, it is not clear that the empirical prevalence and ideological preference orderings of the four models agree, but Market Pricing may head both lists, followed by Equality Matching, Communal Sharing, and last (often negatively valued) Authority Ranking. However, Americans sometimes put Communal Sharing, in the form of selfless romantic love, commitment to family, gang, or platoon, and patriotic unity, ahead of all other values. Authority Ranking also tends to operate covertly in America, so that its prevalence greatly exceeds its valuation. As explanatory models for understanding social life, Americans use the basic models in about the same order. Market Pricing tends to be treated as the natural and proper orientation of human (social) behavior (see Schwartz 1986). However, Market Pricing and Equality Matching are not clearly distinguished in American ideology, where the two together often go under the rubric of "equality".

## Chapter 16

## The Multiplicity of Fundamental Social Orientations

1. The allocation of time does not necessarily reveal a consistent, coherent utility function, since we cannot assume that people regard time as a kind of currency in which all units are of equal "value." Nor does the mere fact of choosing indicate a common metric, since choices may be inconsistent (even arbitary).

2. Simon's (1981) concept of "satisficing" is not a fundamental exception. Basically it takes into account the cost of information and decision making, providing for maximization over the outcome inclusive of the information collection and decision making processes.

## Chapter 17

## Sources of Sociability

1. Just like any other motives (Gallistel 1980a, 1980b, 1981, 1985) these distinct social motives often operate in conjunction with each other to generate complex patterns of behavior. But the fact that people concatenate and combine the four models should not obscure the fact that they are analytically and psychologically distinct modes of relating to people. Each is motivationally autonomous, since the four relational goals are discrete.

2. For a cogent critique of the misleading metaphor of internal and external causes of behavior, see Sabini and Silver (1987).

3. Indeed, where people do not take the implementation rules for granted, the possibility exists for conflict between personal motives and cultural principles or norms. Then we ought to be able to detect that discrepancy in the overall pattern of action, and especially in systematic "desertion." No such pattern of wholesale permanent desertion from the cultural models (and the village framework in which they operate) is manifest among the Moose, or among most traditional societies. However, in some domains and in many particular instances in all cultures, and in

many domains in rapidly changing or multi-ethnic cultures, the implementation choice may indeed become apparent or at least implicit, and the negotiation over which model to apply and how to set the parameters may assume pivotal importance in people's daily lives.

4. As Mead notes (1937:16) and Chapter 2 mentions, it is important not to confuse this kind of solitary individualism with conflict or aggression. Nor does Asocial or Null behavior have anything to do with competition in the framework of Market Pricing.

5. My account here is based largely on Millon 1981, Cleckley 1988, Hare 1970, and McCord and McCord 1964.

6. Asserting that the models are endogenous in the child means that their source is not in the experience of the individual child. The implication is that the models have an evolutionary source, derived from the phylogenetic history of the species. Chapter 8 touches on this, but much more needs to be done.

7. I discovered this research only after having made these observations and written the preceding description, so the accounts are independent.

# References

Abu-Lughod, Lila. 1985. Honor and the Sentiments of Loss in a Bedouin Society. *American Ethnologist* 12:245–261.

Adamopoulos, John. 1984. The Differentiation of Social Behavior: Toward an Explanation of Universal Interpersonal Structures. *Journal of Cross-Cultural Psychology* 15:487–508.

Adams, J. Stacy. 1965. Inequity in Social Exchange. In Leonard Berkowitz, ed., *Advances in Experimental Social Psychology* 2. New York: Academic Press.

Adorno, T. W., Else Frenkel-Brunswik, Daniel J. Levinson, and R. Nevitt Sanford. 1950. *The Authoritarian Personality*. Studies in Prejudice series. New York: Harper and Row.

Ainsworth, Mary. 1967. *Infancy in Uganda*. Baltimore: Johns Hopkins University Press.

Alexandre, R. P. Gustave. 1953. *La Langue Möré, Tome II*. Dakar. Senegal: Mémoires de L'Institut Français D'Afrique Noire, No. 34.

Allen, V. L. 1975. Social Support for Non-Conformity. In Leonard Berkowitz, ed., *Advances in Experimental Social Psychology* 8. New York: Academic Press.

Allport, Floyd H. 1962. A Structuronomic Conception of Behavior: Individual and Collective. I. Structural Theory and the Master Problem of Social Psychology. *Journal of Abnormal and Social Psychology* 64:3–30.

Alper, Theodore M. 1985. A Note on Real Measurement Structures of Scale Type ($m$, $m + 1$). *Journal of Mathematical Psychology* 29:73–81.

American Psychiatric Association. 1987. *Diagnostic and Statistical Manual of Mental Disorders: DSM-III-R*. 3rd ed., revised. Washington, DC.

Anderson, Benedict R. O'Gorman. 1983. *Imagined Communities: Reflections on the Origin and Spread of Nationalism*. London: Verso.

Appadurai, Arjun, ed. 1986. *The Social Life of Things: Commodities in Cultural Perspective*. Cambridge and New York: Cambridge University Press.

Applebaum, Herbert. 1984. *Work in Non-Market and Transitional Societies*. SUNY series in the anthropology of work, June Nash, ed. Albany: State University of New York Press.

Ardner, Shirley. 1964. The Comparative Study of Rotating Credit Associations. *Journal of the Royal Anthropological Institute* 94:201–209.

Arendt, Hannah. 1977. *Eichmann in Jerusalem: A Report on the Banality of Evil.* Revised and enlarged edition. New York: Penguin Books.

Arens, William. 1979. *The Man-Eating Myth: Anthropology and Anthrophagy.* New York and Oxford: Oxford University Press.

Arnould, Eric J. 1984. Marketing and Social Reproduction in Zinder, Niger Republic. In Robert McC. Netting, Richard R. Wilk, and Eric J. Arnould, eds., *Households: Comparative and Historical Studies of the Domestic Group.* Berkeley: University of California Press.

Asad, Talal. 1972. Market Models, Class Structure and Consent: A Reconsideration of Swat Political Organization. *Man* (n.s.) 7:74–94.

Asch, Solomon E. 1955. Opinions and Social Pressure. *Scientific American* 193 (Offprint 450). Reprinted in Elliot Aronson, ed., *Readings About the Social Animal.* Fifth Edition. New York: W. H. Freeman.

———. 1956. Studies on Independence and Conformity: A Minority of One Against a Unanimous Majority. *Psychological Monographs* 70, Whole Number 416.

Athay, Michael, and John M. Darley. 1985. The Role of Power in Social Exchange Relationships. In Michael Frese and John Sabini, eds., *Goal Directed Behavior: The Concept of Action in Psychology.* Hillsdale, NJ: Erlbaum.

Atkinson, John W., ed. 1958. *Motives in Fantasy, Action, and Society.* Princeton: Van Nostrand.

Atkinson, John W., and N. T. Feather, eds. 1966. *A Theory of Achievement Motivation.* New York: Wiley.

Atkinson, John W., R. W. Heyns, and Joseph Veroff. 1954. The Effect of Experimental Arousal of the Affiliation Motive of Thematic Apperception. *Journal of Abnormal and Social Psychology* 49:277–288.

Austin, John L. 1961. A Plea for Excuses. In Max Black, ed., *Models and Metaphors.* Ithaca: Cornell University Press.

———. 1962. *How to Do Things with Words.* Oxford: Oxford University Press.

Austin, William, and Elaine Hatfield. 1980. Equity Theory, Power, and Social Justice. In Gerold Mikula, ed. *Justice and Social Interaction: Experimental and Theoretical Contributions from Psychological Research.* New York: Springer-Verlag. Bern: Hans Huber.

Axelrod, Robert, and William D. Hamilton. 1981. The Evolution of Cooperation. *Science* 211:1390–1396.

Axelrod, Robert, and Douglas Dion. 1988. The Further Evolution of Cooperation. *Science* 242:1385–1390.

Azzi, Assaad. 1988. *The Normative and Structural Bases of Conflict and Aggression between Ethno-Cultural Groups.* Ph.D. dissertation in the Department of Psychology, University of Pennsylvania.

Bailey, F. G. 1972. Conceptual Systems in the Study of Politics. In R. Antoun and I. Harik, eds., *Rural Politics and Social Change in the Middle East.* Bloomington: Indiana University Press.

Bakan, David. 1966. *The Duality Of Human Existence: Isolation and Communion in Modern Man.* Boston: Beacon Press.

Bales, Robert F. 1958. Task Roles in Problem-Solving Groups. In Eleanor E. Maccoby, Theodore M. Newcomb, and E. L. Hartley, eds., *Readings in Social Psychology.* New York: Holt.

———. 1970. *Personality and Interpersonal Behavior*. New York: Holt, Rinehart, and Winston.

Balima, Albert Salfo. n.d. (ca. 1969). *Genèse de la Haute Volta*. Ouagadougou: Presses Africaines.

Barth, Fredrick. 1959. *Political Leadership among the Swat Pathans*. London: Athlone Press.

Bascom, William R. 1942. The Principle of Seniority in the Social Structure of the Yoruba. *American Anthropologist* 14:37–46.

———. 1952. The *Esusu*: A Credit Institution of the Yoruba. *Journal of the Royal Anthropological Institute* 82:63–69.

Bates, Robert H. 1983. *Essays on the Political Economy of Rural Africa*. Berkeley and London: University of California Press.

———. 1989. *Beyond the Miracle of the Market*. New York and London: Cambridge University Press.

Bateson, Gregory. 1972a [1953]. Metalogue: About Games and Being Serious. Reprinted in Gregory Bateson, *Steps to an Ecology of Mind*. New York: Ballantine.

———. 1972b [1955]. A Theory of Play and Fantasy. Reprinted in Gregory Bateson, *Steps to an Ecology of Mind*. New York: Ballantine.

Batson, Daniel C. 1981. Is Empathic Emotion a Source of Altruistic Motivation? *Journal of Personality and Social Psychology*. 40:290–302.

Baumeister, Roy F., and Diane M. Tice. 1989. Anxiety and Social Exclusion. In press, *Journal of Social and Clinical Psychology*.

Becker, Gary S. 1976. *The Economic Approach to Human Behavior*. Chicago: University of Chicago Press.

———. 1981. *A Treatise on the Family*. Cambridge, MA: Harvard University Press.

Benjamin, Lorna Smith. 1974. Structural Analysis of Social Behavior. *Psychological Review* 81:392–425.

Benoit, Michel. 1982. *Oiseaux de Mil*: Les Mossi du Bwamu (Haute-Volta). Collection Mémoires No. 95. Éditions de L'Office de la Recherche Scientifique et Technique Outre-Mer.

Berger, Joseph, Bernard P. Cohen, and Morris Zelditch, Jr. 1972. Status Characteristics and Social Interaction. *American Sociological Review* 37:241–255.

Berkowitz, Leonard, and Elaine Walster, eds., 1976. *Equity Theory: Toward a General Theory of Social Interaction*. Advances in Experimental Social Psychology 9. New York: Academic Press.

Biebuyck, Daniel. 1964. Land Holding and Social Organization. In Melville J. Herskovitz and Mitchell Harwitz, eds., *Economic Transition in Africa*. Northwestern University African Studies, Number 12. Evanston, IL: Northwestern University Press.

Bierhoff, Hans Werner, Ronald L. Cohen, and Jerald Greenberg, eds. 1986. *Justice in Social Relations*. Critical Issues in Social Justice. New York and London: Plenum.

Bilu, Yoram. 1988. The Inner Limits of Communitas: A Covert Dimension of Pilgrimage Experience. *Ethos* 16:302–325.

Blau, Francine D., and Marianne A. Ferber. 1986. *The Economics of Women, Men, and Work*. Englewood Cliffs, NJ: Prentice-Hall.

Blau, Peter M. 1964. *Exchange and Power in Social Life*. New York: Wiley.

Bloch, Maurice. 1973. The Long Term and the Short Term: The Economic and Political Significance of the Morality of Kinship. In Jack Goody, ed., *The Character of Kinship.* Cambridge and New York: Cambridge University Press.

Blum, Lawrence. 1987. Particularity and Responsiveness. In Jerome Kagan and Sharon Lamb, eds., *The Emergence of Morality in Young Children.* Chicago and London: University of Chicago Press.

Boas, Franz. 1966 [1913-1914]. *Kwakiutl Ethnography.* Edited by Helen Codere. Chicago and London: University of Chicago Press.

Bohannan, Paul. 1955. Some Principles of Exchange and Investment among the Tiv. *American Anthropologist* 57:60-70.

Boulding, Kenneth E. 1953. *The Organizational Revolution: A Study in the Ethics of Economic Organization.* New York: Harper.

Bourdieu, Pierre. 1977. *Outline of a Theory of Practice.* Studies in Social Anthropology No. 16. Cambridge and New York: Cambridge University Press.

Boutillier, J. L. 1960. *Bougouanou, Côte d'Ivoire.* In *L'Homme d'Outre-Mer.* Editions Berger-Levrault. Cited in Remy 1973.

Bowlby, John. 1969. *Attachment and Loss, Volume 1. Attachment.* New York: Basic Books.

———. 1980. *Attachment and Loss, Volume 2. Loss: Sadness and Depression.* New York: Basic Books.

———. 1988. *A Secure Base: Parent-Child Attachment and Healthy Human Development.* New York: Basic Books.

Boyatzis, R. E. 1973. Affiliation Motivation. In David C. McClelland and R. S. Steele, eds., *Human Motivation: A Book of Readings.* Morristown, NJ: General Learning Corp.

Bradach, Jeffrey L., and Robert G. Eccles. 1989. Price, Authority, and Trust: From Ideal Types to Plural Forms. *Annual Review of Sociology* 15:97-118.

Brehm, Sharon, and Jack W. Brehm. 1981. *Psychological Reactance: A Theory of Freedom and Control.* Second Edition. New York: Academic Press.

Brown, Paula. 1951. Patterns of Authority in West Africa. *Africa* 21:261-278.

Brown, Roger. 1965. *Social Psychology.* New York: Free Press; London: Collier-Macmillan.

Brown, Roger. 1965. The Basic Dimensions of Interpersonal Relationship. Chapter 2 in Roger Brown, *Social Psychology* [First Edition]. New York:Free Press.

Brown, Roger, and A. Gilman. 1960. The Pronouns of Power and Solidarity. In Thomas A. Sebeok, ed., *Style in Language.* Cambridge: MIT Press.

Buber, Martin. 1987 [1923]. *I and Thou.* Ronald Gregor Smith, trans. New York: Collier-Macmillan.

Bulatao, James. 1964. The Manileño's Mainsprings. In Frank Lynch, ed., *Four Readings on Philippine Values.* Second Revised Edition. Institute of Philippine Culture Papers 2. Quezon City: Atenco de Manila University Press.

Bulman, Ronnie Janoff, and Camille B. Wortman. 1977. Attributions of Blame and Coping in the Real World: Severe Accident Victims React to Their Lot. *Journal of Personality and Social Psychology* 35:351-363.

Burgess, Ernest W., Harvey J. Locke, and Mary M. Thomas. 1971. *The Family: From Traditional to Companionship.* Fourth Edition. New York: Van Nostrand Reinhold.

Burling, Robbins. 1962. Maximization Theories and the Study of Economic Anthropology. *American Anthropologist* 64:802-821.

Buss, Arnold H. 1983. Social Rewards and Personality. *Journal of Personality and Social Psychology* 44:553–563.

———. 1986. *Social Behavior and Personality*. Hillsdale, NJ: Erlbaum.

Byrne, Richard W., and Andrew Whitten, eds. 1988. *Machiavellian Intelligence: Social Expertise and the Evolution of Intellect in Monkeys, Apes, and Humans*. Oxford and New York: Oxford University Press (Clarendon).

Caboret, Kouma Emilienne. 1964. *Les Conditions Juridique de la Femme Mossie*. Memoire de l'Institut des Hautes Études d'Outre Mer, Paris. Cited by Pageard 1969.

Caudill, William. 1962. Patterns of Emotion in Modern Japan. In Robert J. Smith and Richard K. Beardsley, eds., *Japanese Culture: Its Development and Characteristics*. Chicago: Aldine.

Cheal, David. 1988. *The Gift Economy*. London and New York: Routledge.

Cheney, Dorothy L., and Robert M. Seyfarth. 1985. Social and Non-Social Knowledge in Vervet Monkeys. *Philosophical Transactions of the Royal Society of London*. B 308:187–201.

———. 1986. The Recognition of Social Alliances among Vervet Monkeys. *Animal Behavior* 34:1722–1731.

———. 1990. Reconciliation and Redirected Aggression in Vervet Monkeys, *Circopithecus aethiops*. *Behavior*.

———. In press. The Representation of Social Relationships of Monkeys. Special issue of *Cognition*, edited by Charles R. Gallistel.

———. and Barbara Smuts. 1986. Social Relationships and Social Cognition in Nonhuman Primates. *Science* 234:1361–1366.

Chomsky, Noam. 1959. Review of *Verbal Behavior* by B. F. Skinner. *Language* 35:26–58.

———. 1981. *Lectures on Government and Binding*. Cinnaminson, NJ: Foris.

———. 1986. *Knowledge of Language: Its Nature, Origin, and Use*. New York and London: Praeger.

Cialdini, Robert B. 1988. *Influence: Science and Practice*. Second Edition. Glenview, IL: Scott, Foresman.

Clark, Margaret S. 1983. Some Implications of Close Social Bonds for Help-Seeking. In Bella M. DePaulo, Arie Nadler, and Jeffrey D. Fisher, eds., *New Directions in Helping, Volume 2: Help Seeking*. New York: Academic Press.

———. 1984a. A Distinction between Two Types of Relationships and Its Implications for Development. In J. C. Masters and K. Yarkin-Levin, eds., *Boundary Areas in Social and Developmental Psychology*. New York: Academic Press.

———. 1984b. Record Keeping in Two Types of Relationships. *Journal of Personality and Social Psychology* 47:549–557.

Clark, Margaret S., and Judson Mills. (1979). Interpersonal Attraction in Exchange and Communal Relationships. *Journal of Personality and Social Psychology* 37:12–24.

Clark, Margaret S., M.C. Powell, R. Ouellette, and S. Milberg. 1987. Recipient's Mood, Relationship Type, and Helping. *Journal of Personality and Social Psychology* 53:94–103.

Cleckley, Hervey M. 1988. *The Mask of Sanity*. Fifth Edition. St. Louis: C. V. Mosby.

Cohen, Yehudi A. 1955. Four Categories of Interpersonal Relationships in the Family and Community in a Jamaican Village. *Anthropological Quarterly* 28:121–147.

Commons, John R. 1957. *Legal Foundations of Capitalism*. Madison: University of Wisconsin Press.

Cook, Karen S. 1987. *Social Exchange Theory*. Newbury Park, CA: Sage.

Cooley, Charles Horton. 1922 [1902]. *Human Nature and the Social Order*. Revised Edition. New York: Charles Scribner's Sons.

———. 1962 [1909]. *Social Organization: A Study of the Larger Mind*. New York: Schocken Books.

Coquery-Vidrovitch, Catherine. 1969. Recherches sur un Mode de Production Africain. *La Pensée* 144:61–76.

Csikszentmihalyi, Mihaly, and Eugene Rochberg-Halton. 1981. *The Meaning of Things: Domestic Symbols and the Self*. Cambridge and New York: Cambridge University Press.

Damon, William. 1975. Early Conceptions of Positive Justice as Related to the Development of Logical Operations. *Child Development* 46:301–312.

———. 1977. *The Social World of the Child*. San Francisco: Jossey-Bass.

———. 1980. Patterns of Change in Children's Social Reasoning: A Two-Year Longitudinal Study. *Child Development* 51:1010–1017.

D'Andrade, Roy G. 1984. Cultural Meaning Systems. In Richard A. Shweder and Robert A. LeVine, eds., *CultureTheory: Essays on Mind, Self, and Emotion*. Cambridge and New York: Cambridge University Press.

———. 1990. Culture and Personality: A False Dichotomy. In David K. Jordon and Marc J. Swartz, eds., *Personality and the Cultural Construction of Society*. Tuscaloosa: University of Alabama Press.

———. In press. Schemas and Motivation. In Roy G. D'Andrade and Claudia Strauss, eds., *Human Motives and Cultural Models*. Cambridge and New York: Cambridge University Press.

Davis, Kingsley, and Wilbert F. Moore. 1945. Some Principles of Stratification. *American Sociological Review* 10:242–249. Reprinted in Edward O. Lauman, Paul M. Siegel, and Robert W. Hodge, eds., 1970, *The Logic of Social Hierarchies*. Chicago: Markham.

Davis, Mark H. 1983. Measuring Individual Differences in Empathy: Evidence for a Multidimensional Approach. *Journal of Personality and Social Psychology* 44:113–126.

Dawes, Robyn M. 1980. Social Dilemmas. *Annual Review of Psychology* 31:169–193.

Delobsom, A. A. Dim. 1929. Les "Nioniossé" de Goupana (1$^{er}$ article). *Outre Mer: Revue Générale de Colonisation*. Décembre 1929:419–446.

———. 1930. Les "Nioniossé" de Goupana (2$^e$ article). *Outre Mer: Revue Générale de Colonisation*. Janvier 1930:3–21.

———. 1933. *L'Empire du Mogho Naba: Coutumes des Mossi de la Haute Volta*. Paris: F. Loviton.

Deng, Francis Mading. 1988. Epilogue. In R. E. Downs and S. P. Reyna, eds., *Land and Society in Contemporary Africa*. Hanover, NH and London: University Press of New England for the University of New Hampshire.

De Soto, Clinton B., Marvin London, and Stephen Handel. 1965. Social Reasoning and Spatial Paralogic. *Journal of Personality and Social Psychology* 2:513–521.

Desplagnes, Lieutenant Louis. 1907. *Le Plateau Central Nigérien: Une Mission Archéologique et Ethnographique au Soudan Français*. Paris: Émile Larose.

Deutsch, Karl W. 1953. *Nationalism and Social Communication*. New York: Wiley.

Deutsch, Morton. 1975. Equity, Equality, and Need: What Determines Which Value Will Be Used as the Basis of Distributive Justice? *Journal of Social Issues* 31:137–149.

———. 1985. *Distributive Justice: A Social-Psychological Perspective*. New Haven: Yale University Press.

———. 1987. Experimental Studies of the Effects of Different Systems of Distributive Justice. In John C. Masters and William P. Smith, eds., *Social Comparison, Social Justice, and Relative Deprivation: Theoretical, Empirical, and Policy Perspectives*. Greenwood and Krauss series. Hillsdale, NJ: Erlbaum.

Diener, Edward. 1980. Deindividuation: The Absence of Self-Awareness and Self-Regulation in Group Members. In Paul B. Paulus, ed., *The Psychology of Group Influence*. Hillsdale, NJ: Erlbaum.

Dieterlen, Germaine. 1956. Parenté et Marriage chez les Dogon (Soudan Français). *Africa* 26:107–148.

Doi, Kiyoharu. 1982. A Two Dimension Theory of Achievement Motivation: Affiliative and Non-Affiliative. *Japanese Journal of Psychology* 52:344–350.

Doi, L. Takeo. 1962. Amae: A Key Concept for Understanding Japanese Personality Structure. In Robert J. Smith and Richard K. Beardsley, eds., *Japanese Culture: Its Development and Characteristics*. Chicago: Aldine. Reprinted in Robert A. LeVine, ed., 1974. *Culture and Personality: Contemporary Readings*. Chicago: Aldine.

———. 1981 [1971]. *The Anatomy of Dependence*. (Second Edition, but not labeled as such.) John Bester, trans. Tokyo, New York and San Francisco: Kodansha.

Douglas, Mary. 1978. *Cultural Bias*. Occasional Paper 35 of the Royal Anthropological Institute of Great Britain and Ireland, London.

DuBois, Victor D. 1965. Ahmadou's World: A Case Study of a Voltaic Immigrant to the Ivory Coast. *West Africa Series* 8(4). American Universities Field Staff.

Dumont, Louis. 1977. *From Mandeville to Marx: The Genesis and Triumph of Economic Ideology*. Chicago and London: University of Chicago Press.

———. 1986 [1983]. *Essays on Individualism: Modern Ideology in Anthropological Perspective*. Chicago and London: University of Chicago Press.

Dupire, M. 1960. *Planteurs Autochtones et Étrangers en Basse-Côte d'Ivoire Orientale*. In Études Éburnéennes, Volume 8. (Cited in Remy 1973.)

Durkheim, Emile. 1933 [1893, 1926]. *The Division of Labour in Society*. George Simpson, trans. New York: Free Press.

———. 1901. Deux Lois de L'Évolution Pénale. *L'Année Sociologique* 4 (1899–1900):65–95.

———. 1965 [1912]. *The Elementary Forms of the Religious Life*. Joseph Ward Swain, trans. New York: Free Press.

———. 1961 [1925]. *Moral Education: A Study in the Theory and Application of the Sociology of Education*. Everett K. Wilson and Herman Schnurer, trans., Everett K. Wilson, ed. New York: Free Press.

Dworkin, Gerald. 1985. Nuclear Intentions. *Ethics* 95:445–460.

Ekeh, Peter P. 1974. *Social Exchange Theory: The Two Traditions*. Cambridge, MA: Harvard University Press.

Elias, T. Olawale. 1956. *The Nature of African Customary Law*. Manchester: Manchester University Press.

Enright, Robert D., Åke Bjerstedt, William F. Enright, Victor M. Levy, Jr., Daniel K. Lapsley, Ray R. Buss, Michael Harwell, and Monica Zindler. 1984. Distributive

Justice Development: Cross-Cultural, Contextual, and Longitudinal Evaluations. *Child Development* 55:1737-1751.

Erasmus, Charles J. 1956. Cultural Structure and Process: The Occurrence and Disappearance of Reciprocal Farm Labor. *Southwestern Journal of Anthropology* 12:444-469.

Erikson, Eric H. 1980 [1959]. *Identity and the Life Cycle.* New York: Norton.

Etzioni, Amitai. 1975 [1961]. *A Comparative Analysis of Complex Organizations: On Power, Involvement, and Their Correlates.* Revised and Enlarged Edition. New York: Free Press; London: Collier Macmillan.

———. 1986. The Case for a Multiple-Utility Conception. *Economics and Philosophy* 2:159-183.

———. 1988. *The Moral Dimension: Toward a New Economics.* New York: Free Press; London: Collier Macmillan.

Evans-Pritchard, E. E. 1933. Zande Blood-Brotherhood. *Africa* 6:369-401.

———. 1937. *Witchcraft, Oracles, and Magic Among the Azande.* New York and Oxford: Oxford University Press.

———. 1951. *Kinship and Marriage Among the Nuer.* Oxford: Clarendon Press. Pp. 124-145, 152-156.

Fajans, Jane, organizer and chair. 1986. Beyond Exchange. Session at the 85th annual meeting of the American Anthropological Association, Philadelphia.

Festinger, Leon. 1954. A Theory of Social Comparison Processes. *Human Relations* 7:117-140.

Firth, Raymond. 1965 [1938]. *Primitive Polynesian Economy* (Second Edition). New York: Norton.

Firth, Raymond W., and Basil S. Yamey. 1964. *Capital, Saving and Credit in Peasant Societies: Studies from Asia, Oceania, the Caribbean and Middle America.* Chicago: Aldine.

Fiske, Alan P. 1985. *Making Up Society: Four Models for Constructing Social Relations among the Moose of Burkina Faso.* Ph.D. dissertation in the Committee on Human Development, Department of Behavioral Sciences, University of Chicago. (Not available through University Microfilms: contact author or Regenstein Library at the University of Chicago directly.)

———. 1990. Relativity Within Moose Culture: Four Incommensurable Models for Social Relationships. *Ethos* 18:180-204.

———. n.d. Taboo Combinations of Commensality and Sexuality Antithetical to Male Solidarity Among the Moose ("Mossi"). Manuscript under revision.

———. 1991. The Four Elementary Forms of Sociality: Framework for a Unified Theory of Social Relations. *Psychological Review* 99:689-723.

———. 1993a. Social Errors in Four Cultures: Evidence About Universal Forms of Social Relations. *Journal of Cross-Cultural Psychology,* forthcoming.

———. 1993b. Social Schemata for Remembering People: Relationships and Person Attributes that Affect Clustering in Free Recall of Acquaintances. Under review.

———.1993c. Why Should Psychologists Care About Culture? Forthcoming in Patrick Shrout and Susan Fiske, eds., *Personality Research, Methods and Theory: Festschrift for Donald Fiske.* Hillsdale, NJ: Lawrence Erlbaum.

Fiske, Alan P., and Jonathan Baron. n.d. Choosing among Models for Organizing Social Relations. Manuscript in preparation.

Fiske, Alan P., Nick Haslam, Kathryn Mason, and Susan Fiske. n.d. Confusing One Person with Another: What Errors Reveal about the Elementary Forms of Social Relations. Manuscript under revision.

Fiske, Alan P., Nick Haslam, and Susan T. Fiske 1991. Confusing One Person With Another: What Errors Reveal about the Elementary Forms of Social Relations. *Journal of Personality and Social Psychology* 60:656–674.

Fiske, Donald W., and Richard A. Shweder, eds., 1986. *Metatheory in Social Science: Pluralisms and Subjectivities.* Chicago: University of Chicago Press.

Fiske, Susan T., and Shelley E. Taylor. In press. *Social Cognition.* Second Edition. New York: McGraw Hill.

Foa, Uriel G. 1961. Convergences in the Analysis of the Structure of Interpersonal Behavior. *Psychological Review* 68:341–353.

Foa, Uriel G., and Edna B. Foa. 1974. *Societal Structures of the Mind.* Springfield, IL: Thomas.

Foa, Uriel G., John Converse, Jr., Kjell Y. Tornblom, and Edna B. Foa (eds.) 1993. *Resource Theory: Explorations and Applications.* San Diego: Academic Press.

Fodor, Eugene M., and Dana L. Farrow. 1979. The Power Motive as an Influence on Use of Power. *Journal of Personality and Social Psychology* 37:2091–2097.

Forge, Anthony. 1972. The Golden Fleece. *Man* (n.s.) 7:527–540.

Fortes, Meyer. 1945. *The Dynamics of Clanship among the Tallensi.* Oxford: Oxford University Press.

———. 1969 [1949]. *The Web of Kinship among the Tallensi: The Second Part of an Analysis of the Social Structure of a Trans-Volta Tribe.* Oosterhout N.B., The Netherlands: Anthropological Publications, and Oxford: Oxford University Press.

———. 1959. *Oedipus and Job in West African Religion.* Cambridge: Cambridge University Press.

———. 1965. Some Reflections on Ancestor Worship in Africa. In Meyer Fortes and Germain Dieterlen, eds., *African Systems of Thought.* Oxford: Oxford University Press. Reprinted in Meyer Fortes 1987, *Religion, Morality and the Person: Essays on Tallensi Religion.* Jack Goody, ed. Cambridge: Cambridge University Press.

———. 1970 [1963]. *Kinship and the Social Order, The Legacy of Lewis Henry Morgan.* Chicago: Aldine.

———. 1983. Rules and the Emergence of Society. Occasional paper No. 39. London: Royal Anthropological Institute of Great Britain and Ireland.

Foucault, Michel. 1977. *Discipline and Punish: The Birth of the Prison.* Alan Sheridan, trans. New York: Pantheon.

Frank, Robert H. 1988. *Passions Within Reason: The Strategic Role of the Emotions.* New York and London: Norton.

Freeman, Susan Tax. 1987. Egalitarian Structures in Iberian Social Systems: The Contexts of Turn-Taking in Town and Country. *American Ethnologist* 14:470–490.

French, Elizabeth G., and Irene Chadwick. 1956. Some Characteristics of Affiliation Motivation. *Journal of Abnormal and Social Psychology* 52:296–300.

French, John R. P., and Bertram Raven. 1959. The Bases of Social Power. In Dorwin Cartwright, ed., *Studies in Social Power.* Research Center for Group Dynamics, Institute for Social Research. Ann Arbor: University of Michigan Press.

Freud, Sigmund. 1955 [1893]. Studies on Hysteria. *The Standard Edition of the Complete Psychological Works* II. London: Hogarth.

———. 1959 [1921]. *Group Psychology and the Analysis of the Ego.* James Strachey, trans. New York: W. W. Norton.

———. 1962 [1923]. *The Ego and the Id.* Joan Riviere and James Strachey, trans. New York: W. W. Norton.

———. 1975 [1928]. *The Future of an Illusion.* James Strachey, trans. New York: Norton.

———. 1930. *Civilization and Its Discontents.* Joan Riviere, trans. New York: J. Cope and H. Smith.

———. 1967 [1937]. *Moses and Monotheism.* Katherine Jones, trans. New York: Vintage.

Fridlund, Alan J. 1989. The Sociality of Solitary Smiling: Potentiation by an Implicit Audience. Paper presented at the October annual convention of the Society for Psychophysiological Research, New Orleans.

———. 1990. Evolution and Facial Action in Reflex, Emotion, and Paralanguage. In P. K. Ackles, J. R. Jennings, and M. G. H. Coles, eds., *Advances in Psychophysiology* 4. London: Jessica Kingsley.

Friedman, Milton, with the assistance of Rose D. Friedman. 1982 [1962]. *Capitalism and Freedom.* Chicago: University of Chicago Press.

Friedman, Milton, and Rose D. Friedman. 1981. *Free to Choose: A Personal Statement.* New York: Avon.

Frost, Robert. 1969. *The Poetry of Robert Frost.* Edward Connery Lathem, ed. New York: Holt, Rinehart and Winston.

Fung, Yu-lan. 1947. *Short History of Chinese Philosophy.* New York: Free Press.

———. 1952. *A History of Chinese Philosophy. Volume 1: The Period of the Philosophers.* Derek Bodde, trans. Princeton: Princeton University Press.

Galaty, John G. 1982. Being "Maasai"; Being "People-of-Cattle": Ethnic Shifters in East Africa. *American Ethnologist* 9:1–20.

Gallimore, Ronald. 1981. Affiliation, Social Context, Industriousness, and Achievement. In Ruth H. Munroe, Robert L. Munroe, and Beatrice B. Whiting, eds., *Handbook of Cross-Cultural Human Development.* Garland Anthropology and Human Development Series. New York and London: Garland STPM.

Gallistel, Charles R. 1980a. *The Organization of Action: A New Synthesis.* Hillsdale, NJ: Erlbaum.

———. 1980b. From Muscles to Motivation. *American Scientist* 68:398–409.

———. 1981. Precis of Gallistel's *The Organization of Action,* and Matters of Principles: Responses to the Open Peer Commentary. *The Behavioral and Brain Sciences* 4:609–619, 639–650.

———. 1985. Motivation, Intention, and Emotion: Goal Directed Behavior from a Cognitive-Neuroethological Perspective. In Michael Frese and John Sabini, Eds., *Goal Directed Behavior: The Concept of Action in Psychology.* Hillsdale, NJ: Erlbaum.

———. 1990. *The Organization of Learning.* Cambridge, MA: MIT Press.

Gargan, Edward A. 1988. Across Chinese Countryside, The Watchword is Think Big. *New York Times* April 3. 1988, pp. 1, 14.

Geertz, Clifford. 1962. The Rotating Credit Association: A "Middle Rung" in Development. *Economic Development and Cultural Change* 10:241–263.

————. 1973a [1966]. Religion as a Cultural System. In Michael Banton, ed., *Anthropological Approaches to the Study of Religion*. Association of Social Anthropologist Monograph 3. London: Tavistock. Reprinted in Clifford Geertz, *The Interpretation of Cultures*. New York: Basic Books.

————. 1973b. Thick Description: Toward an Interpretive Theory of Culture. In Clifford Geertz, *The Interpretation of Cultures*. New York: Basic Books.

————. 1973c [1966]. Person, Time, and Conduct in Bali. In Clifford Geertz, *The Interpretation of Cultures*. New York: Basic Books.

————. 1984 [1974]. "From the Native's Point of View": On the Nature of Anthropological Understanding. *Bulletin of the American Academy of Arts and Sciences* 28(1). Reprinted in Richard A. Shweder and Robert A. LeVine, eds., *Culture Theory: Essays on Mind, Self, and Emotion*. Cambridge and New York: Cambridge University Press.

Gibbs, Jack P. 1981. *Norms, Deviance, and Social Control: Conceptual Matters*. New York: Elsevier.

Giddens, Anthony. 1971. *Capitalism and Modern Social Theory: An Analysis of the Writings of Marx, Durkheim and Max Weber*. Cambridge and New York: Cambridge University Press.

Gillan, Douglas J. 1981. Reasoning in the Chimpanzee: II. Transitive Inference. *Journal of Experimental Psychology: Animal Behavior Processes* 7:150–164.

Gillies, Eva. 1976. Causal Criteria in African Classifications of Disease. In J. B. Loudon, ed., *Social Anthropology and Medicine*. Association of Social Anthropologists Monograph 13. London and New York: Academic Press.

Gilligan, Carol. 1982. *In a Different Voice: Psychological Theory and Women's Development*. Cambridge, MA: Harvard University Press.

————. n.d. The Origins of Morality in Early Childhood. Working Paper No. 7, The Project on Interdependence, Fay House, Radcliffe College, 10 Garden Street, Cambridge, MA.

Gilligan, Carol, and Grant Wiggins. 1987. The Origins of Morality in Early Childhood Relationships. In Jerome Kagan and Sharon Lamb, eds., *The Emergence of Morality in Young Children*. Chicago and London: University of Chicago Press.

Godelier, Maurice. 1972 [1966]. *Rationality and Irrationality in Economics*. Brian Pearce, trans. New York and London: Monthly Review Press.

————. 1986a [1982]. *The Making of Great Men: Male Domination and Power among the New Guinea Baraguya*. Rupert Swyer, trans. Cambridge Studies in Social Anthropology 56. New York and London: Cambridge University Press. Paris: Editions de la Maison des Sciences de L'Homme.

————. 1986b [1984]. *The Mental and the Material: Thought, Economy and Society*. Martin Thom, trans. [London:] Verso (New Left Books).

Goode, William J. 1960. Norm Commitment and Conformity to Role-Status Obligations. *American Journal of Sociology* 66:246–258.

Gluckman, Max. 1955. *The Judicial Process among the Barotse of Northern Rhodesia*. Glencoe, IL: Free Press.

Golding, William. 1955. *Lord of the Flies*. New York: Capricorn.

Goodenough, Ward. 1944. A Technique for Scale Analysis. *Educational and Psychological Measurement* 4:179–190.

————. 1965. Rethinking 'Status' and 'Role': Toward a General Model of the Cultural Organization of Social Relationships. In Michael Banton, ed., *The Relevance of*

*Models to Social Anthropology.* Association of Social Anthropologists Monograph 1. London: Tavistock.

Goffman, Erving. 1971. *Relations in Public: Microstudies of the Public Order.* New York: Harper & Row.

———. 1974. *Frame Analysis: An Essay on the Organization of Experience.* Cambridge: Harvard University Press.

Gouldner, Alvin W. 1973a [1960]. The Norm of Reciprocity: A Preliminary Statement. *American Sociological Review* 25:161–178. Reprinted with revisions in Alvin W. Gouldner 1973, *For Sociology: Renewal and Critique in Sociology Today.* London: Allen Lane.

———. 1973b. The Importance of Something for Nothing. In Alvin W. Gouldner, *For Sociology: Renewal and Critique in Sociology Today.* London: Allen Lane.

Greenwood, Davydd. 1988. Egalitarianism or Solidarity in Basque Industrial Cooperatives: The FAGOR Group of Mondragón. In James G. Glanagan and Steve Rayner, eds., *Rules, Decisions, and Inequality.* Brookfield, VT and Aidershot, England: Avebury.

Griesinger, D. W., and J. W. Livingston, Jr. (1973). Toward a Model of Interpersonal Motivation in Experimental Games. *Behavioral Science* 18:173–188.

Gross, Jonathan L., and Steve Rayner. 1985. *Measuring Culture: A Paradigm for the Analysis of Social Organization.* New York: Columbia University Press.

Guhl, A. M. 1956. Social Order of Chickens. *Scientific American* 194 (February):42–46.

Guillet, David. 1980. Reciprocal Labor and Peripheral Capitalism in the Central Andes. *Ethnology* 19:151–167.

Guimera, Louis Mallart. 1978. Witchcraft Illness in the Evuzok Nosological System. *Culture, Medicine and Psychiatry* 2:373–396.

Gunderson, John G. and Margaret T. Singer. 1975. Defining Borderline Patients: An Overview. *American Journal of Psychiatry* 132:1–10.

Guttman, Louis. 1944. A Basis for Scaling Qualitative Data. *American Sociological Review* 9:139–150.

Hamilton, Virginia Lee. 1978. Who Is Responsible? Toward a Social Psychology of Responsibility Attribution. *Social Psychology* 41:316–328.

Hamilton, Virginia Lee, and Joseph Sanders. 1981. The Effects of Roles and Deeds on Responsibility Judgments: The Normative Structure of Wrongdoing. *Social Psychology Quarterly* 44:327–354.

Hamilton, William D. 1963. The Evolution of Altruistic Behavior. *American Naturalist* 97:354–356.

———. 1964. The Genetical Evolution of Social Behavior. *Journal of Theoretical Biology* 7:1–52.

———. 1971. Selection of Selfish and Altruistic Behavior in Some Extreme Models. In J. F. Eisenberg and Walter S. Dillon, eds., *Smithsonian Annual III—Man and Beast: Comparative Social Behavior.* Washington, DC: Smithsonian Institution Press.

Hammond, Peter B. 1966. *Yatênga: Technology in the Culture of a West African Kingdom.* New York: Free Press, and London: Collier-Macmillan.

Haney, Craig, Curtis Banks, and Philip Zimbardo. 1988 [1973]. A Study of Prisoners and Guards in a Simulated Prison. *Naval Research Reviews*, September 1973. Reprinted in Elliot Aronson, ed., *Readings About the Social Animal.* Fifth Edition. New York: W. H. Freeman.

Hardin, Garrett R. 1968. The Tragedy of the Commons. *Science* 162:1243–1248.

Hare, Robert D. 1970. *Psychopathy: Theory and Research.* New York: Wiley.

Harrell, Adrian M., and Michael J. Stahl. 1981. A Behavioral Decision Theory Approach for Measuring McClelland's Trichotomy of Needs. *Journal of Applied Psychology* 66:242–247.

Hart, Keith. 1978. The Economic Basis of Tallensi Social History in the Early Twentieth Century. *Research in Economic Anthropology* 1:185–216.

———. 1982. *The Political Economy of West African Agriculture.* Cambridge and New York: Cambridge University Press.

Hartocollis, Peter, ed. 1977. *Borderline Personality Disorders: The Concept, the Syndrome, the Patient.* New York: International Universities Press.

Haslam, Nick. 1993. Categories of Social Relationships. Ph.D. dissertation, Department of Psychology, University of Pennsylvania. (Manuscript under review for publication.)

Haslam, Nick, and Alan P. Fiske 1992. Implicit Relationship Prototypes: Investigating Five Theories of the Cognitive Organization of Social Relations. *Journal of Experimental Social Psychology* 28:441–474.

Haugerud, Angelique. 1989. Land Tenure and Agrarian Change in Kenya. *Africa* 59:61–90.

Haviland, John Beard. 1977. *Gossip, Reputation, and Knowledge in Zinacantan.* Chicago: University of Chicago Press.

Heider, Fritz. 1946. Attitudes and Cognitive Consistency. *Journal of Psychology* 21:107–112.

———. 1958. *The Psychology of Interpersonal Relations.* New York: Wiley.

Herskovits, Melville J. 1952. *Economic Anthropology: A Study of Comparative Economics.* New York: Alfred A. Knopf.

———. 1969 [1931–33]. The Best Friend in Dahomey. In Nancy Cunard, ed., *Negro Anthology.* New York: Negro Universities Press.

Hess, Echkard Heinrich. 1973. *Imprinting: Early Experience and the Developmental Psychobiology of Attachment.* New York: Van Nostrand Reinhold.

Hill, Craig A. 1987. Affiliation Motivation: People Who Need People . . . But in Different Ways. *Journal of Personality and Social Psychology* 52:1008–1018.

Ho, David Yau-Fai. 1982. Asian Concepts in Behavioral Science. *Psychologica: An International Journal of Psychology in the Orient* 25:228–235.

Ho, David, and Ling Yü Lee. 1974. Authoritarianism and Attitude Toward Filial Piety in Chinese Teachers. *Journal of Social Psychology* 92:305–306.

Hobbes, Thomas. 1958 [1651]. *Leviathan: Parts I and II.* The Library of Liberal Arts. Indianapolis: Bobbs-Merrill.

Hollnsteiner, Mary R. 1964. Reciprocity in the Lowland Philippines. In Frank Lynch, ed., *Four Readings on Philippine Values.* Second revised edition. Institute of Philippine Culture Papers 2. Quezon City: Atenco de Manila University Press.

Homans, George C. 1958. Social Behavior as Exchange. *American Journal of Sociology* 62:597–606. Bobbs-Merrill reprint #S-122.

———. 1974 [1961]. *Social Behavior: Its Elementary Forms.* Revised Edition. New York: Harcourt Brace Jovanovich.

Horowitz, Leonard M. 1979. On the Cognitive Structure of Interpersonal Problems Treated in Psychotherapy. *Journal of Consulting and Clinical Psychology* 47:5–15.

Horowitz, Leonard M., and John Vitkus. 1986. The Interpersonal Basis of Psychiatric Symptoms. *Clinical Psychology Review* 6:443–469.

Horton, Robin. 1967. African Traditional Thought and Western Science. *Africa* 37:50–71, 155–187.

Hostetler, John A. 1970. *Amish Society.* Revised Edition. Baltimore and London: The Johns Hopkins Press.

Howell, Richard W. 1973. Teasing Relationships. Module in Anthropology No. 46. Reading, MA: Addison-Wesley.

Humphrey, N. K. 1976. The Social Function of Intellect. In P. P. G. Bateson and R. A. Hinde, eds., *Growing Points in Ethology.* Cambridge and New York: Cambridge University Press.

Huston, Ted. L., ed. 1974. *Foundations of Interpersonal Attraction.* New York and London: Academic Press.

Hyden, Goran. 1980. *Beyond Ujamaa in Tanzania: Underdevelopment and an Uncaptured Peasantry.* Berkeley and Los Angeles: University of California Press.

Ilboudo, Pierre Claver. 1982. *Le Fils Aîné.* Ouagadougou: Presses Africaines. NOVEL.

Institut National de la Statistique et de la Démographie, Direction de la Recherche Démographique. 1979. *Principaux Resultats du Recensement de 1975.* Ouagadougou: Ministère du Plan et de la Cooperation.

Izard, Michel. 1985. *Gens de Pouvoir, Gens de la Terre: Les Institutions Politiques de L'Ancien Royaume du Yatēnga (Bassin de la Volta Blanche).* Cambridge and New York: Cambridge University Press; Paris: Editions de la Maison des Sciences de L'Homme.

Izard-Héritier, Françoise, and Michel Izard. 1959. *Les Mossi du Yatēnga: Étude de la Vie Économique et Sociale.* Bordeaux: Institut des Sciences Humaines Appliquées de L'Université de Bordeaux.

Jackson, Shirley. 1949. The Lottery. In Shirley Jackson, *The Lottery, or, The Adventures of James Harris.* New York: Farrar, Strauss.

Janis, Irving L. 1982 [1972]. *Groupthink.* Second Edition. Boston: Houghton Mifflin.

Janowitz, Morris. 1960. *The Professional Soldier.* Glencoe, IL: Free Press.

Kaboré, Lamoussa. 1970. L'Elevage de la Poule en Pays Mossi. *Notes et Documents Voltaique* 3(3):53–74. (Original 1961 E.N.A. mémoire de stage cited with detailed breakdown in Pageard 1969.)

Kahneman, Daniel, Jack L. Knetsch, and Richard H. Thaler. 1986a. Fairness and the Assumptions of Economics. *Journal of Business* 59:S285–S300.

———. 1986b. Fairness as a Constraint on Profit Seeking: Entitlements in the Market. *American Economic Review* 76:728–741.

Kahneman, Daniel, Paul Slovic, and Amos Tversky, eds., 1982. *Judgment Under Uncertainty: Heuristics and Biases.* Cambridge and New York: Cambridge University Press.

Kaut, C. R. 1961. Utang-la-laób: A System of Contractual Obligation among Tagalogs. *Southwestern Journal of Anthropology* 17:266–272.

Kavka, Gregory S. 1986. *Hobbesian Moral and Political Theory.* Studies in Moral, Political, and Legal Philosophy. Princeton, NJ: Princeton University Press.

———. 1987. *Moral Paradoxes of Nuclear Deterrence.* Cambridge and New York: Cambridge University Press.

Kawada, Junzo. 1979. *Gènese et Évolution du Système Politique des Mosi Méridionaux (Haute Volta).* Study of Languages and Cultures of Asia and Africa Monograph Series, Number 12 [Tokyo?].

Kelley, Harold. 1979. *Personal Relationships: Their Structures and Processes.* Hillsdale, NJ: Erlbaum.

Kelley, Harold, and John W. Thibaut. 1978. *Interpersonal Relations: A Theory of Interdependence.* New York: Wiley-Interscience.

Kennedy, John G. 1970. Bonds of Laughter among the Tarahumara Indians: Toward a Rethinking of Joking Relationship Theory. In Walter Goldschmidt and Harry Hoijer, eds., *The Social Anthropology of Latin America: Essays in Honor of Leon Beals.* Latin American Studies 14. Los Angeles: Latin American Center, University of California.

Kerlinger, Fred N. 1951. Decision-making in Japan. *Social Forces* 30:36–41.

Kiernan, J. P. 1982. The 'Problem of Evil' in the Context of Ancestral Intervention in the Affairs of the Living in Africa. *Man* 17:287–301.

Kiesler, Donald J. 1983. The 1982 Interpersonal Circle: A Taxonomy for Complementarity in Human Transactions. *Psychological Review* 90:185–214.

Kluckholn, Florence, and Fred Strodtbeck. 1973 [1961]. *Variations in Value Orientation.* Evanston, IL: Row, Peterson. Reprinted by Greenwood Press, Westport, CT.

Knight, Robert P. 1953. Borderline States. *Bulletin of the Menninger Clinic* 17:1–12.

Kohler, J. M. 1971. *Les Migrations des Mossi de l'Ouest.* Paris: L'Office de la Recherche Scientifique et Technique Outre-Mer. Cited in Remy 1973 and Schildkrout 1978.

Kohlberg, Lawrence. 1984. *The Psychology of Moral Development: The Nature and Validity of Moral Stages.* Essays on Moral Development 2. San Francisco: Harper and Row.

Kohlberg, Lawrence, Charles Levine, and Alexandra Hewer. 1983. *Moral Stages: A Current Formulation and a Response to Critics.* Contributions to Human Development 10. Basel and New York: Karger.

Komorita, S. S. 1984. The Role of Justice and Power in Reward Allocation. In G. M. Stephenson and J. H. Davis, eds., *Progress in Applied Social Psychology* 2. New York: Wiley.

Koopmans, Tjalling C. 1957. *Three Essays on the State of Economic Science.* New York: McGraw-Hill.

Kopytoff, Igor. 1988. The Cultural Context of African Abolition. In Suzanne Miers and Richard Roberts, eds., *The End of Slavery in Africa.* Madison and London: University of Wisconsin Press.

Kracke, Waud H. 1979. *Force and Persuasion: Leadership in an Amazonian Society.* Chicago: University of Chicago Press.

Kramer, Julian Y. 1974. *Self Help in Soweto.* University of Bergen Occasional Paper 12. New York: Lillian Barber Press.

Krech, David, Richard S. Crutchfield, and E. L. Ballachey. 1962. *Individual in Society.* New York: McGraw-Hill.

Krech, David, and Richard S. Crutchfield. 1965. *Elements of Psychology.* New York: Knopf.

Kropotkin, Peter. 1972 [1890, 1914]. *Mutual Aid: A Factor of Evolution.* Paul Avrich, ed. New York: New York University Press.

Kureshi, Afzal, and Bilquees Fatima. 1984. Power Motive among Student Leaders and Non-Leaders: Testing the Affective-Arousal Model. *Journal of Psychological Researches* 28:21–24.

Kurland, Jeffrey A., and Stephen J. Beckerman. 1985. Optimal Foraging and Hominid Evolution: Labor and Reciprocity. *American Anthropologist* 87:73–93.

Lallemand, Suzanne. 1977. *Une Famille Mossi. Recherches Voltaiques* 17. Paris: C.N.R.S., Ouagadougou: C.V.R.S.

Lambert, W. W., Leigh Triandis, and Margery Wolf. 1959. Some Correlates of Beliefs in the Malevolence and Benevolence of Supernatural Beings: A Cross-Cultural Study. *Journal of Abnormal and Social Psychology* 58:162–169.

Larimore, Victoria, director. 1985. *The Amish: Not to Be Modern*. Film produced by Victoria Larimore and Michael Taylor. New York: Film Makers Library. Shown on WHYY television.

van Lawick-Goodall, Hugo and Jane. 1970. *Innocent Killers*. Boston: Houghton Mifflin.

Leach, Edmund R. 1950. *The Web of Kinship Among the Tallensi* (Review). *Man* 50:21–22 (Item number 23).

Leach, Jerry W. and Edmund Leach, eds. 1983. *The Kula: New Perspectives on Massim Exchange*. Cambridge and New York: Cambridge University Press.

Leary, Timothy F. 1957. *Interpersonal Diagnosis of Personality: A Functional Theory and Methodology for Personality Evaluation*. New York: Ronald Cress.

Lebra, Takie Sugiyama. 1969. Reciprocity and the Asymmetric Principle: An Analytical Reappraisal of the Japanese Concept of On. *Psychologia* 12:129–138.

———. 1976. *Japanese Patterns of Behavior*. Honolulu: University Press of Hawaii.

Lerner, Melvin J. 1974. The Justice Motive: "Equity" and "Parity" among Children. *Journal of Personality and Social Psychology* 29:539–550.

———. 1975. The Justice Motive in Social Behavior: Introduction. *Journal of Social Issues* 31:1–19.

———. 1977. The Justice Motive: Some Hypotheses as to its Origin and Forms. *Journal of Personality* 45:1–52.

———. 1980. *The Belief in a Just World: A Fundamental Delusion*. New York: Plenum.

Lerner, Melvin J., and Sally C. Lerner, eds., 1981. *The Justice Motive in Social Behavior: Adapting to Times of Scarcity and Change*. New York: Plenum.

Lerner, Melvin J., and G. Mathews. 1967. Reactions to Suffering of Others Under Conditions of Indirect Responsibility. *Journal of Personality and Social Psychology* 5:319–325.

Leventhal, Gerald S. 1976a. The Distribution of Rewards and Resources in Groups and Organizations. In Leonard Berkowitz and Elaine Walster, eds., *Advances in Experimental Social Psychology* 9.

———. 1976b. Fairness in Social Relationships. In John W. Thibaut, J. T. Spence, and R. C. Carson, eds., *Contemporary Topics in Social Psychology*. Morristown, NJ: General Learning Press.

———. 1979. Effects of External Conflict on Resource Allocation and Fairness within Groups and Organizations. In William G. Austin and S. Worchel, eds., *The Social Psychology of Intergroup Relations*. Monterey, CA: Brooks/Cole.

———. 1980. What Should Be Done with Equity Theory? New Approaches to the Study of Fairness in Social Relationships. In Kenneth J. Gergen, Martin S. Greenberg, and Richard H. Willis, eds., *Social Exchange: Advances in Theory and Research*. New York and London: Plenum.

Leventhal, Gerald S., Jurgis Karuza, Jr., and William Rick Fry. 1980. Beyond Fairness; A Theory of Allocation Preferences. In Gerold Mikula, ed. *Justice and Social Interaction: Experimental and Theoretical Contributions from Psychological Research*. New York: Springer-Verlag. Bern: Hans Huber.

LeVine, Robert A., and Donald T. Campbell. 1972. *Ethnocentrism: Theories of Conflict, Ethnic Attitudes, and Group Behavior*. New York: Wiley.

Levine, Saul V. 1979. Adolescents, Believing and Belonging. *Adolescent Psychiatry.* 7:41–53.

Lévi-Strauss, Claude, 1967 [1945]. Structural Analysis in Linguistics and in Anthropology. In Lévi-Strauss, *Structural Anthropology.* Claire Jacobson and Brooke Grundfest Schoepf, trans. Garden City, NY: Doubleday (Anchor).

———. 1961 [1949]. *The Elementary Structures of Kinship.* Revised Edition. James H. Bell, John R. von Sturmer, and Rodney Needham, trans. Boston: Beacon.

———. 1966 [1962]. *The Savage Mind.* Chicago: University of Chicago Press.

Levy, Robert I. 1973. *Tahitians.* Chicago and London: University of Chicago Press.

———. 1985. Horror and Tragedy: The Wings and Center of the Moral Stage. *Ethos* 13:175–187.

Lewis, John Van D. 1981. Domestic Labor Intensity and the Incorporation of Malian Peasant Farmers into Localized Descent Groups. *American Ethnologist* 8:53–73.

Leynard, Emile. 1966. Fraternités d'Age et Sociétés de Culture dans la Haute-Vallée du Niger. *Cahiers d'Études Africaines* 62(21):41–68.

Liebrand, Wim B., and Godfried J. Van-Run. 1985. The Effects of Social Motives on Behavior in Social Dilemmas in Two Cultures. *Journal of Experimental Social Psychology* 21:86–102.

Llewelyn-Davies, Melissa. 1981. Women, Warriors, and Patriarchs. In Sherry B. Ortner and Harriet Whitehead, eds., *Sexual Meanings: The Cultural Construction of Gender and Sexuality.* Cambridge and New York: Cambridge University Press.

Lloyd-Bostock, Sally. 1983. Attributions of Cause and Responsibility as Social Phenomena. In Jos Jaspers, Frank D. Fincham, and Miles Hewstone, eds., *Attribution Theory and Research: Conceptual, Developmental and Social Dimensions.* European Monographs in Social Psychology. New York: Academic Press (European Association of Experimental Social Psychologists).

Locke, John. 1952 [1690]. *The Second Treatise of Government.* The Library of Liberal Arts. Indianapolis: Bobbs-Merrill.

Lorenz, Konrad. 1970 [1932–37]. A Consideration of Methods of Indentification of Species-Specific Instinctive Behavior Patterns in Birds; The Establishment of the Instinct Concept; Taxis and Instinctive Behavior in Egg-Rolling by the Greylag Goose. Reprinted in Konrad Lorenz, *Studies in Animal and Human Behaviour* I. Cambridge: Harvard University Press.

Lorr, M., and D. M. McNair. 1963. An Interpersonal Behavior Circle. *Journal of Abnormal and Social Psychology* 67:68–75.

Lowenstein, George F., Leigh Thompson, and Max Bazerman 1989. Social Utility and Decision Making in Interpersonal Contexts. *Journal of Personality and Social Psychology* 57:426–441.

Luce, Robert Duncan, and Howard Raiffa. 1957. *Games and Decisions: Introduction and Critical Survey.* A study of the Behavioral Models Project, Bureau of Applied Social Research, Columbia University. New York: Wiley.

Machiavelli, Niccolo. 1963 [1513]. *The Prince.* A. Robert Caponigri, trans. Chicago: Henry Regnery (Gateway).

MacCrimmon, K. R., and D. M. Messick. 1976. A Framework for Social Motives. *Behavioral Science* 21:86–100.

MacIntyre, Alisdair. 1981. *After Virtue.* Notre Dame: University of Notre Dame Press.

Macintyre, Martha. 1983. *The Kula: A Bibliography.* Cambridge and New York: Cambridge University Press.

Maine, Henry James Sumner. 1963 [1861]. *Ancient Law: Its Connection with the Early History of Society and its Relation to Modern Ideas*. Boston: Beacon Press.

Makower, Joel. 1988. *How to Buy a Used Car—How to Sell a Used Car*. New York: Tilden (Perigree).

Makra, Mary Lelia (translator), and Paul K. T. Sih (editor). 1961. *The Hsiao Ching*. Asian Institute Translations 2. New York: St. John's University Press.

Malinowski, Bronislaw. 1921. The Primitive Economics of the Trobriand Islanders. *Economic Journal* 31:1–16.

——. 1961 [1922]. *Argonauts of the Western Pacific: An Account of Native Enterprise and Adventure in the Archipelagoes of Melanesian New Guinea*. New York: Dutton.

——. 1964 [1926]. *Crime and Custom in Savage Society*. Patterson, NJ: Littlefield, Adams.

——. 1966 [1936]. *Coral Gardens and Their Magic: A Study of the Methods of Tilling the Soil and of Agricultural Rites in the Trobriand Islands*. Second Edition. London: Allen and Unwin.

Mangin, Pere Eugène. 1916. *Les Mossi, Essai sur les Us et Coutumes du Peuple Mossi au Soudan Occidental*. Reprinted from *Anthropos* 1914–1916. Vienna: Imprimerie des Méchitaristes. (Also reprinted 1921 Paris: Augustin Challamel.)

Mankoff. 1988. Cartoon on page 67 of the *New Yorker*, July 11, 1988.

Marie-André du Sacré Coeur, Soeur. 1938a. La Femme Mossi: Sa Situation Juridique. *L'Ethnographie* 35–36:15–33. (Société D'Ethnographie de Paris.)

——. 1938b. Situation Juridique de la Femme Indigène dans la Boucle du Niger. Congrès Internationale de L'Evolution Culturelle des Peuples Coloniaux: Rapports et Compte Rendu. Paris.

Marshall, Lorna. 1961. Sharing, Talking, and Giving: Relief of Social Tensions Among !Kung Bushmen. *Africa* 31:231–246.

Marshall, Mac. 1977. The Nature of Nurture. *American Ethnologist* 4:643–662.

Marwell, Gerald, and Jerald Hage. 1970. The Organization of Role-Relationships: A Systematic Description. *American Sociological Review* 35:884–900.

Marx, Karl. 1959 [1859]. *A Contribution to the Critique of Political Economy*. Excerpted in *Marx and Engels: Basic Writings on Politics and Philosophy*. Lewis S. Feuer, ed. Garden City, NY: Doubleday (Anchor).

——. 1964a. *Pre-Capitalist Economic Formations*. Jack Cohen, trans. Edited and with an Introduction by E. J. Hobsbawm. New York: International Publishers. (This is the key section from the *Grundrisse*, together with the relevant sections of *The German Ideology* [1845–6], and related letters.)

——. 1964b [1867–1881]. *Karl Marx: Selected Writings in Sociology and Social Philosophy*. T. B. Bottomore, trans. New York: McGraw-Hill.

——. 1970 [1859]. *A Contribution to the Critique of Political Economy*. S. W. Ryazanskaya, trans. Moscow: Progress Publishers.

——. 1971 [1857–58]. *The Grundrisse*. David McLellan, trans. New York: Harper and Row. [Selections, not the entire text.]

——. 1973 [1857–58]. *Grundrisse: Foundations of the Critique of Political Economy*. Martin Nicolaus, trans. New York: Random House.

Marx, Karl, and Frederick Engels. 1959 [1848]. *Manifesto of the Communist Party*. Excerpted in *Marx and Engels: Basic Writings on Politics and Philosophy*. Lewis S. Feuer, ed. Garden City, NY: Doubleday (Anchor).

————. 1906 [1867]. *Capital: A Critique of Political Economy.* Samuel Moore and Edward Aveling, trans. New York: Modern Library.

Maslow, A. H. 1943. The Authoritarian Personality Structure. *Journal of Social Psychology* 18:401–411.

Mason, Kathryn F. 1987. *A Woman's Place: The Articulation of Social Structure by Moose Co-Wives and Mothers.* Ph.D. dissertation in the Committee on Human Development, Department of Behavioral Sciences, University of Chicago.

————. 1988. Co-wife Relationships Can Be Amicable as well as Conflictual: The Case of the Moose of Burkina Faso. *Canadian Journal of African Studies* 22:615–624.

Matsuzawa, Tetsuro. 1985. Use of Numbers by a Chimpanzee. *Nature* 315(6014):57–59.

Matsuzawa, Tetsuro, T. Asano, K. Kubota, and K. Murofushi. 1986. Acquisition and Generalization of Numerical Labeling by a Chimpanzee. In David M. Taub and Frederick A. King, eds., *Current Perspectives in Primate Social Dynamics.* New York: Van Nostrand Reinhold.

Mauss, Marcel. 1967 [1925]. *The Gift: Forms and Functions of Exchange in Archaic Societies.* Ian Cunnison, trans. New York: Norton.

McAdams, Dan P. 1980. A Thematic Coding System for the Intimacy Motive. *Journal of Research in Personality* 14:413–432.

————. 1982. Experiences of Intimacy and Power: Relationships between Social Motives and Autobiographical Memory. *Journal of Personality and Social Psychology* 42:292–302.

————. 1984. Human Motives and Personal Relationships. In Valerian J. Derlega, ed., *Communication, Intimacy, and Close Relationships.* New York: Academic Press.

————. 1988. *Power, Intimacy, and the Life Story: Personological Inquiries into Identity.* New York: Guilford Press.

————. 1989. *Intimacy: The Need to be Close.* New York: Doubleday.

McAdams, Dan P., and Carol A. Constantian. 1983. Intimacy and Affiliation Motives in Daily Lives: An Experience Sampling Analysis. *Journal of Personality and Social Psychology* 45:851–861.

McAdams, Dan P., Sheila Healy, and Steven Krauss. 1984. Social Motives and Patterns of Friendship. *Journal of Personality and Social Psychology* 47:828–838.

McAdams, Dan P., and Joseph Powers. 1981. Themes of Intimacy in Behavior and Thought. *Journal of Personality and Social Psychology* 40:573–587.

McCauley, Clark R. 1989. The Nature of Social Influence in Groupthink: Compliance and Internalization. In press, *Journal of Personality and Social Psychology* 57(2).

McCay, Bonnie J., and James M. Acheson, eds. 1987. *The Question of the Commons: The Culture and Ecology of Communal Resources.* Tucson: University of Arizona Press.

McClelland, David C., ed. 1955. *Studies in Motivation.* New York: Appleton-Century-Crofts.

————. 1971 [1963]. The Achievement Motive in Economic Growth. In Bert F. Hoselitz and W. E. Moore, eds., *Industrialization and Society.* The Hague: Mouton, (UNESCO). Reprinted in William W. Lambert and Rita Weisbrod, eds., *Comparative Perspectives on Social Psychology.* Boston: Little, Brown.

————. 1975. *Power: The Inner Experience.* New York: Wiley, Halstead Division.

————. 1976 [1967]. *The Achieving Society.* New York: Wiley.

McClelland, David C., Charles Alexander, and Emile Marks. 1982. The Need for

Power, Stress, Immune Function, and Illness among Male Prisoners. *Journal of Abnormal Psychology* 91:61-70.

McClelland, David C., John W. Atkinson, R. A. Clark, and E. L. Lowell. 1953. *The Achievement Motive*. New York: Irvington.

McClelland, David C., W. N. Davis, R. Kalin, and E. Wanner. 1972. *The Drinking Man*. New York: Free Press.

McClelland, David C., and John B. Jemmott. 1980. Power Motivation, Stress, and Physical Illness. *Journal of Human Stress* 6:6-15.

McCord, William, and Joan McCord. 1964. *The Psychopath: An Essay on the Criminal Mind*. New York: Van Nostrand Reinhold.

McGonigle, Brendan O., and Margaret Chalmers. 1977. Are Monkeys Logical? *Nature* 267:694-696.

McMillan, Della. 1986. Distribution of Resources and Products in Mossi Households. In Art Hansen and Della McMillan, eds., *Food in Sub-Saharan Africa*. Boulder: Lynne Rienner.

Mead, George H. 1934 [1900, 1930]. *Mind, Self, and Society from the Standpoint of a Social Behaviorist*. Charles W. Morris, ed. Chicago and London: University of Chicago Press. [The relevant sections of Mead's lectures are also reprinted in *George Herbert Mead on Social Psychology: Selected Papers*. Anselm Strauss, ed. Heritage of Sociology Series. Chicago and London: University of Chicago Press.]

Mead, Margaret, ed. 1961 [1937]. *Cooperation and Competition among Primitive Peoples*. Boston: Beacon Press.

Meeker, Michael E., Kathleen Barlow, and David M. Lipset. 1986. Culture, Exchange, and Gender: Lessons from the Murik. *Cultural Anthropology* 1:6-73.

Meillassoux, Claude. 1964. *Anthropologie Économique des Gouro de Côte D'Ivoire: De L'Économie de Subsistance à L'Agriculture Commerciale*. École Pratique des Hautes Études—Sorbonne, VIᵉ Section: Sciences Économiques et Sociales. Le Monde D'Outre-Mer Passé et Présent: Première Série, Études XXVII. Paris and La Haye: Mouton.

———. 1971. English Introduction. In Claude Meillassoux, ed., *The Development of Indigenous Trade and Markets in West Africa*. London: Oxford University Press (International African Institute).

———. 1981 [1975]. *Maidens, Meal and Money: Capitalism and the Domestic Economy*. Cambridge and New York: Cambridge University Press.

Mikula, Gerold. 1977. Considerations of Justice in Allocation Situations. Graz, Austria: Berichte aus dem Institut für Psychologie der Universität Graz.

———. 1980. On the Role of Justice in Allocation Decisions. In Gerold Mikula, ed., *Justice and Social Interaction: Experimental and Theoretical Contributions from Psychological Research*. New York: Springer-Verlag. Bern: Hans Huber.

Mikula, Gerold, and Thomas Schwinger. 1978. Intermember Relations and Reward Allocation. In Herman Brandstätter, James H. Davis, and Heinz Schuler, eds., *Dynamics of Group Decisions*. Sage Focus Editions 5. Beverly Hills and London: Sage.

Milgram, Stanley. 1974. *Obedience to Authority: An Experimental View*. New York: Harper Colophon (Harper and Row).

Miller, Walter B. 1955. Two Concepts of Authority. *American Anthropologist* 57:271-289.

Millon, Theodore. 1981. *Disorders of Personality: DSM-III: Axis II.* New York: Wiley (Interscience).

Mills, Judson, and Margaret S. Clark. 1982. Exchange and Communal Relationships. In Ladd Wheeler, ed., *Review of Personality and Social Psychology* 3. Beverly Hills: Sage.

———. 1986. Communications that Should Lead to Perceived Exploitation in Communal and Exchange Relationships. *Journal of Social and Clinical Psychology* 4:225–234.

Mitchell, J. Clyde. 1965. The Meaning of Misfortune for Urban Africans. In Meyer Fortes and Germaine Dieterlin, eds., *African Systems of Thought.* London: International African Institute.

Mitchell, William E. 1988. The Defeat of Hierarchy: Gambling as Exchange in a Sepik Society. *American Ethnologist* 15:638–657.

Morgan, Lewis Henry. 1877. *Ancient Society, or, Researches in the Line of Human Progress from Savagery through Barbarism to Civilization.* Chicago: Kerr.

Morgan, William R., and Jack Sawyer. 1967. Bargaining, Expectations, and the Preference for Equality over Equity. *Journal of Personality and Social Psychology* 6:139–149.

Morris, William, ed. 1970. *The American Heritage Dictionary of the English Language.* Boston: Houghton Mifflin.

Morsbach, H., and W. J. Tyler. 1987. A Japanese Emotion: *Amae.* In Rom Haré, ed., *The Social Construction of Emotions.* New York: Basil Blackwell.

Much, Nancy C., and Richard A. Shweder. 1978. Speaking of Rules: The Analysis of Culture in Breach. *New Directions for Child Development* 2:19–39.

Murray, Henry A. 1938. *Explorations in Personality.* New York and Oxford: Oxford University Press.

Narens, Louis, 1981a. A General Theory of Ratio Scalability with Remarks about the Measurement-Theoretic Concept of Meaningfulness. *Theory and Decision* 13:1–70.

———. 1981b. On the Scales of Measurement. *Journal of Mathematical Psychology* 24:249–275.

Narens, Louis, and R. Duncan Luce. 1986. Measurement: The Theory of Numerical Assignments. *Psychological Bulletin* 99:166–180.

Nemeroff, Carol J. 1988. *Contagion and the Transfer of Essence in Adult Thinking in the United States.* Ph.D. dissertation in the Psychology Department, University of Pennsylvania.

Netting, Robert McC., Richard R. Wilk, and Eric J. Arnould, eds. 1984. *Households: Comparative and Historical Studies of the Domestic Group.* Berkeley and London: University of California Press.

Neuman, F. L. 1950. Approaches to the Study of Political Power. *Political Science Quarterly* 65:161–180.

Niebuhr, Reinhold. 1953. Coercion, Self-Interest, and Love. In Kenneth E. Boulding 1953, *The Organizational Revolution: A Study in the Ethics of Economic Organization.* New York: Harper.

Noaga, Kollin. 1978. *Le Retour au Village* (Novel). Issy les Moulineaux, France: Les Classiques Africains, No. 716. (Editions Saint Paul).

Noddings, Nel. 1984. *Caring: A Feminine Approach to Ethics and Moral Education.* Berkeley: University of California Press.

Nozick, Robert. 1975. *Anarchy, State, and Utopia*. Oxford: Blackwell.

O'Flaherty, Wendy D. 1976. *The Orgins of Evil in Hindu Mythology*. Berkeley: University of California Press.

O'Malley, Michael N., and Glena Schubarth. 1984. Fairness and Appeasement: Achievement and Affiliation Motives in Interpersonal Relations. *Social Psychology Quarterly* 47:364–371.

Orne, Martin T. 1962. On the Social Psychology of the Psychological Experiment, With Particular Reference to Demand Characteristics and Their Implications. *American Psychologist* 17:776–783.

———. 1969. Demand Characteristics and the Concept of Quasi-Controls. In Robert Rosenthal and Ralph L. Rosnow, eds., *Artifact in Behavioral Research*. Social Psychology series. New York and London: Academic Press.

Orne, Martin T., and Frederick J. Evans. 1965. Social Control in the Psychology Experiment: Antisocial Behavior and Hypnosis. *Journal of Personality and Social Psychology* 1:189–200.

Ortner, Sherry B. 1984. Theory in Anthropology since the Sixties. *Comparative Studies in Society and History* 26:126–166.

Ouédraogo, Joseph. 1951. La Polygamie en Pays Mossi. *Notes Africaines* 50(April):46–52.

Pacere, Titinga Frédéric. 1979. *Ainsi On A Assiné tous les Mossé: Essai-Témoinage*. Sherbrooke, Québec: Éditions Naaman.

Packer, C. 1977. Reciprocal Altruism in *Papio anubis*. *Nature* 265:441–3.

———. 1979. Male Dominance and Reproductive Activity in *Papio anubis*. *Animal Behavior* 27:37–45.

Pageard, Robert. 1966. Contribution à L'Étude de L'Exogamiee dans la Société Mossie Traditionnelle. *Journal de la Société des Africanistes* 36: 109–140.

———. 1969. *Le Droit Privé des Mossi: Tradition et Évolution*. *Recherches Voltaiques* 10, 11. Paris: C.N.R.S., Ouagadougou: C.V.R.S.

Palmer, H. 1988. Deeming Everyone Selfish. *International Journal of Moral and Social Studies* 3:113–125.

Pandya, Vishvajit. 1988. Displacing and Replacing Process in Andamanese Places: Political Economy of Smells. Manuscript of paper; an earlier version was delivered at the session Beyond Exchange at the 85th annual meeting of the American Anthropological Association, Philadelphia, 1986.

Parkin, David, ed. 1985. *The Anthropology of Evil*. New York: Basil Blackwell.

Parsons, Anne. 1969. *Belief, Magic, and Anomie: Essays in Psychological Anthropology*. New York: Free Press. London: Collier-Macmillan. (See Part I—Family Dynamics.)

Parsons, Talcott. 1949. *The Structure of Social Action*. New York: Free Press.

Parsons, Talcott 1951. The Social System. New York: Free Press.

Parsons, Talcott, and Edward A. Shils, eds. 1951. *Toward a General Theory of Action*. Cambridge: Harvard University Press.

Pastore, Nicholas. 1952. The Role of Arbitrariness in the Frustration–Aggression Hypothesis. *Journal of Abnormal and Social Psychology* 47:728–731.

Paulme, Denise. 1940. *Organization Sociale des Dogons (Soudan Français)*. Institut de Droit Comparé, Études de Sociologie et D'Ethnologie Juridiques 32. Paris: F. Loviton (Éditions Domat-Montchrestien).

Pepitone, Emmy A. 1980. *Children in Cooperation and Competition: Toward A Developmental Social Psychology*. Lexington, MA and Toronto: Lexington Books (D. C. Heath).

Peristiany, Jean G., ed. 1966 *Honour and Shame: The Values of Mediterranean Society*. Chicago: University of Chicago Press.

Peters, Pauline E. 1989. Rational Choice, Agency and Meanings: Notes Toward a Critique of Bates. Paper presented in a session on the "Rational Man in Africa" approach of Robert Bates at the African Studies meetings, Atlanta.

Pfeiffer, John. 1986. Democracy by Design: No Longer Can a Man or Woman's Worth Be Measured in Square Feet of Office Space. *Science 86* 7(2):18–19.

Piaget, Jean. 1973 [1932]. *Le Jugement Moral Chez L'Enfant*. Bibliothèque de Philosophie Contemporaine. Paris: Presses Universitaries de France. Translated by Marjorie Gabain 1965 as *The Moral Judgment of the Child*. New York: Free Press.

——. 1965. [1941–1951]. *Études Sociologiques*. Geneva: Librarie Droz.

Pike, Kenneth. 1954. *Language in Relation to a Unified Theory of the Structure of Human Behavior*. Volume 1. Glendale: Summer Institute of Linguistics.

Pittman, Thane S., and Jack F. Heller. 1987. Social Motivation. In *Annual Review of Psychology* 38, Mark R. Rosenzweig and Lyman W. Porter, eds.

Pitt-Rivers, Julian. 1973. The Kith and the Kin. In Jack Goody, ed., *The Character of Kinship*. Cambridge and New York: Cambridge University Press.

Polanyi, Karl. 1947. Our Obsolete Market Mentality. *Commentary* 3:109–117. Reprinted in George Dalton, ed., *Primitive, Archaic, and Modern Economies—Essays of Karl Polanyi*. 1968. Garden City, NY: Anchor.

——. 1957a [1944]. *The Great Transformation: The Political and Economic Origins of Our Time*. New York: Rinehart.

——. 1957b. The Economy as Instituted Process. In Polanyi et al., *Trade and Market in the Early Empires: Economies in History and Theory*. Glencoe, IL: Free Press.

——. 1977 [1957]. The Semantics of Money-Uses. *Explorations*. October 1957. Reprinted in Janet L. Dolgin, David S. Kemnitzer, and David M. Schneider, eds., *Symbolic Anthropology: A Reader in the Study of Symbols and Meanings*. New York: Columbia University Press.

——. 1966. *Dahomey and the Slave Trade: An Analysis of an Archaic Economy*. (In collaboration with Abraham Rotstein). American Ethnological Society Monograph 42. Seattle and Washington: University of Washington Press.

——. 1968. *Primitive, Archaic, and Modern Economies—Essays of Karl Polanyi*. George Dalton, ed. Garden City, NY: Anchor.

Polanyi, Karl, Conrad M. Arensberg, and Harry W. Pearson. 1957a. The Place of Economics in Societies. In Polanyi et al., *Trade and Market in the Early Empires: Economies in History and Theory*. Glencoe, IL: Free Press.

——. eds. 1957b. *Trade and Market in the Early Empires: Economies in History and Theory*. Glencoe, IL: Free Press.

Pollet, E., and G. Winter. 1968. L'Organization Sociale du Travail Agricole des Soninke (Dyahunu, Mali), *Cahiers d'Études Africains* 32:509–534.

Premack, David. 1976. *Intelligence in Ape and Man*. Hillsdale, NJ: Erlbaum.

——. 1983. The Codes of Man and Beasts. *The Behavioral and Brain Sciences* 6:125–167.

Premack, David, and Ann Premack. 1982. *The Mind of an Ape*. New York: Norton.

Price, John. 1975. Sharing: The Integration of Intimate Economies. *Anthropologica* 17:3–27.

Prus, Robert. 1985. Price-Selling as Social Activity: Defining Price, Value, and Profit in the Marketplace. *Urban Life* 14:59–93.

Quinn, Naomi. 1978. Do Mfantse Fish Sellers Estimate Probabilities in Their Heads? *American Ethnologist* 5:206–226.

Radcliffe-Brown, A. R. 1965a [1940]. On Joking Relationshiops. In A. R. Radcliffe-Brown, *Structure and Function in Primitive Society: Essays and Addresses*. New York: Free Press.

———. 1965b [1949]. A Further Note on Joking Relationships. In A. R. Radcliffe-Brown, *Structure and Function in Primitive Society: Essays and Addresses*. New York: Free Press.

———. 1965c. *Structure and Function in Primitive Society: Essays and Addresses*. New York: Free Press.

Rattray, Capt. Robert S. 1932. *The Tribes of the Ashanti Hinterland*. Volume II. Oxford: Oxford University Press.

Rawls, John. 1971. *A Theory of Justice*. Cambridge, MA: Belknap (Harvard University Press).

Razran, G. H. S. 1938. Conditioning Away Social Bias by the Lunchroom Technique. *Psychological Bulletin* 35:693.

———. 1940. Conditioned Response Changes in Rating and Appraising Sociopolitical Slogans. *Psychological Bulletin* 37:481.

Read, K. E. 1959. Leadership and Consensus in a New Guinea Society. *American Anthropologist* 61:425–36.

Redfield, Robert. 1955. *The Little Community: Viewpoints for the Study of a Human Whole*. Chicago and London: University of Chicago Press.

Reis, Harry T. 1987. The Nature of the Justice Motive. In John C. Masters and William P. Smith, eds., *Social Comparison, Social Justice, and Relative Deprivation: Theoretical, Empirical, and Policy Perspectives*. (Greenwood and Krauss series) Hillsdale, NJ: Erlbaum.

Remy, Gérard. 1967. *Yobri: Etude Géographique du Terroir d'un Village Gourmantché de Haute Volta*. Atlas des Structures Agraires au Sud du Sahara, 1. Maison des Sciences de l'Homme. Paris, The Hague: Mouton.

———. 1973. *Les Migrations de Travail et les Movements de Colonizations Mossi: Recueil Bibliographique*. Travaux et Documents de L'Office de la Recherche Scientifique et Technnique Outre-Mer, No. 20. Paris.

Rescher, Nicholas. 1988. *Rationality: A Philosophical Inquiry into the Nature and Rationale of Reason*. Oxford: Clarendon Press.

Rey, Pierre-Phillippe. 1975. The Lineage Mode of Production. *Critique of Anthropology* 3:27–39.

Richards, Audrey I. 1969 [1939]. *Land, Labor and Diet in Northern Rhodesia: An Economic Study of the Bemba Tribe*. London: Oxford University Press for the International African Institute.

Ricoeur, Paul. 1967. *The Symbolism of Evil*. Emerson Buchanan, trans. Boston: Beacon Press.

Roeper, Tom, and Edwin Williams, eds. 1987. *Parameter Setting*. Norwell, MA: Kluver Academic; also published in Holland Reidel.

Rosaldo, Michelle Z. 1980. *Knowledge and Passion: Ilongot Notions of Self and Social Life*. Cambridge and New York: Cambridge University Press.

Rosenberg, S., and A. Sedlak. 1972. Structural Representations of Implicit Personality Theory. In Leonard Berkowitz, ed., *Advances in Experimental Social Psychology* 6. New York: Academic Press.

Rosenthal, Robert. 1969. Interpersonal Expectations: Effects of the Experimenter's Hypothesis. In Robert Rosenthal and Ralph L. Rosnow, eds., *Artifact in Behavioral Research*. Social Psychology series. New York and London: Academic Press.

Rozin, Paul, Maureen Markwith, and Clark McCauley n.d. Inter-relations between Physical and Moral Aspects of Illness: The Case of AIDS. Manuscript submitted.

Rubel, Maximilien. 1956. *Bibliographie des Oeuvres de Karl Marx*. Paris: Librarie Marcel Rivière et Cie.

Ruelle, E., 1904. Notes Anthropologiques, Ethnographiques et Sociologiques sur Quelques Populations Noires du 2e Territoire Militaire de L'Afrique Occidentale Française (Suite et fin). *L'Anthropologie* (Paris) 15:657–703.

Ryan, William. 1971. *Blaming the Victim*. New York: Vantage Books.

Ryle, Gilbert. 1949. *The Concept of Mind*. London: Hutchinson.

Sabini, John. In press. *Social Psychology*. New York: Norton.

Sabini, John, and Maury Silver. 1982. *Moralities of Everyday Life*. Oxford and New York: Oxford University Press. Especially chapters on Anger and Envy.

———. 1987. Internal and External Causes of Behavior. *International Journal of Moral and Social Studies* 2:11–23.

Sade, Donald Stone. 1967. Determinants of Dominance in a Group of Free-Ranging Rhesus Monkeys. In Stuart A. Altmann, ed., *Social Communication Among Primates*. Chicago: University of Chicago Press.

Sahlins, Marshall. 1965. On the Sociology of Primitive Exchange. In Michael Banton, ed., *The Relevance of Models for Social Anthropology*. Association of Social Anthropologists, Monograph 1. London: Tavistock. Reprinted in Marshall Sahlins 1972, *Stone Age Economics*. New York: Aldine.

———. 1968. *Tribesmen*. Englewood Cliffs, NJ: Prentice-Hall.

———. 1976a. *Culture and Practical Reason.* Chicago: University of Chicago Press.

———. 1976b. *The Use and Abuse of Biology: An Anthropological Critique of Sociobiology*. Ann Arbor: University of Michigan Press.

Salisbury, Richard F. 1973. Economic Anthropology. *Annual Review of Anthropology* 2.

Sampson, Edward E. 1963. Status Congruence and Cognitive Consistency. *Sociometry* 26:146–162.

———. 1969. Studies of Status Congruence. In Leonard Berkowitz, ed., *Advances in Experimental Social Psychology* 4. New York: Academic Press.

———. 1975. On Justice as Equality. *Journal of Social Issues* 31:111–136.

———. 1988. The Debate on Individualism: Indigenous Psychologies of the Individual and Their Role in Personal and Societal Functioning. *American Psychologist* 43:15–22.

Sandel, Michael J. 1982. *Liberalism and the Limits of Justice*. Cambridge and New York: Cambridge University Press.

Sapir, Edward. 1927. Anthropology and Sociology. In W. F. Ogburn and A. Goldenweiser, eds., *The Social Sciences and Their Interrelation*. Boston: Houghton Mifflin.

Şaul, Mahir. 1983. Work Parties, Wages, and Accumulation in a Voltaic Village. *American Ethnologist* 10:77–96.

————. 1988. Money and Land Tenure as Factors in Farm Size Differentiation in Burkina Faso. In R. E. Downs and S. P. Reyna, eds., *Land and Society in Contemporary Africa*. Hanover, NH and London: University Press of New England for the University of New Hampshire.

Saussure, Ferdinand de. 1983. *Course in General Linguistics*. Edited by Charles Bally and Albert Sechehaye, with the collaboration of Albert Riedlinger; translated and annotated by Roy Harris. London: Duckworth.

Schachter, Stanley. 1959. *The Psychology of Affiliation: Experiemental Studies of the Sources of Gregariousness*. Stanford Studies in Psychology 1. Stanford: Stanford University Press.

Schieffelin, Edward L. 1976. *The Sorrow of the Lonely and the Burning of the Dancers*. New York: St. Martin's Press.

Schildkrout, Enid. 1978. *People of the Zongo: The Transformation of Ethnic Identities in Ghana*. Cambridge Studies in Social Anthropology 20. Cambridge and New York: Cambridge University Press.

Schneider, David M. 1980. *American Kinship: A Cultural Account*. Second Edition. Chicago: University of Chicago Press.

Schneider, Harold K. 1974. *Economic Man: The Anthropology of Economics*. New York: Free Press.

Schutz, William C. 1958. *FIRO: A Three-Dimensional Theory of Interpersonal Behavior*. New York: Rinehart.

Schwartz, Barry. 1986. *The Battle for Human Nature: Science, Morality, and Modern Life*. New York: Norton.

Schwimmer, Eric G. 1983. *Exchange in the Social Structure of the Orokaiva: Traditional and Emergent Ideologies in the Northern District of Papua*. New York: St. Martin's Press.

Schwinger, Thomas. 1980. Just Allocation of Goods: Decisions among Three Principles. In Gerold Mikula, ed., *Justice and Social Interaction: Experimental and Theoretical Contributions from Psychological Research*. New York: Springer-Verlag. Bern: Hans Huber.

————. 1986. The Need Principle of Distributive Justice. In Hans Werner Bierhoff, Ronald L. Cohen, and Jerald Greenberg, eds., *Justice in Social Relations*. Critical Issues in Social Justice Series. New York and London: Plenum.

Scott, J. P. 1967. The Development of Social Motivation. In David Levine, ed., *Nebraska Symposium on Motivation*. Lincoln, NE: University of Nebraska Press.

Seyfarth, Robert M., and Dorothy L. Cheney. 1984. Grooming, Alliances and Reciprocal Altruism in Vervet Monkeys. *Nature* 308:541–543.

Sheeran, Michael J. 1983. *Beyond Majority Rule: Voteless Decisions in the Religious Society of Friends*. Philadelphia: Philadelphia Yearly Meeting of the Religious Society of Friends.

Sherif, Muzafer, and Carolyn W. Sherif. 1964. *Reference Groups: Exploration into Conformity and Deviation of Adolescents*. New York: Harper and Row.

Sherif, Muzafer et al. 1988 [1961]. *Intergroup Conflict and Cooperation: The Robbers Cave Experiment*. Middletown, CT: Wesleyan University Press; Scranton, PA: Distributed by Harper and Row.

Sherman, Jacqueline R. 1984. *Grain Markets and the Marketing Behavior of Farmers: A Case Study of Manga, Upper Volta*. Ann Arbor, MI: Center for Research on Economic Development.

Shipley, T. E., and Joseph Veroff. 1952. A Projective Measure of Need for Achievement. *Journal of Experiemental Social Psychology* 43:349–356.

Shweder, Richard A. 1979. Rethinking Culture and Personality Theory, Part II: A Critical Examination of Two More Classical Postulates. *Ethos* 7:279–311.

Shweder, Richard A., Manamohan Mahapatra, and Joan G. Miller. 1987. Culture and Moral Development. In Jerome Kagan and Sharon Lamb, eds., *The Emergence of Morality in Young Children*. Chicago: University of Chicago Press.

Silver, Harry R. 1981. Carving Up the Profits: Apprenticeship and Structural Flexibility in a Contemporary African Craft Market. *American Ethnologist* 8:41–52.

Simmel, Georg. 1971 [1911]. Sociability. In *Georg Simmel on Individuality and Social Forms*. Donald N. Levine, ed. Chicago and London: University of Chicago Press.

Simon, Herbert A. 1956. Rational Choice and the Structure of the Environment. *Psychological Review* 63:129–137.

———. 1965 [1947]. *Administrative Behavior: A Study of Decision-Making Processes in Administrative Organization*. Second Edition. New York: Macmillan.

———. 1981. *The Sciences of the Artificial*. Second Edition. Cambridge, MA: MIT Press.

Skinner, Elliott P. 1960. The Mossi "Pogsioure." *Man* 60:20–23.

———. 1962. Trade and Markets among the Mossi People. In Paul Bohannan and George Dalton, eds., *Markets in Africa*. Evanston: Northwestern University Press.

———. 1964a. *The Mossi of the Upper Volta: The Political Development of a Sudanese People*. Stanford: Stanford University Press.

———. 1964b. West African Economic Systems. In Melville J. Herskovitz and Mitchell Harwitz, eds., *Economic Transition in Africa*. Northwestern University African Studies, Number 12. Evanston, IL: Northwestern University Press.

———. 1965. Labor Migrations among the Mossi of Upper Volta. In Hilda Kuper, ed., *Urbanization and Migration in West Africa*. Berkeley: University of California Press.

———. 1974. *African Urban Life: The Transformation of Ouagadougou*. Princeton, NJ: Princeton University Press.

Smith, Adam. 1976a [1759]. *The Theory of Moral Sentiments*. D. D. Raphael and A. L. Macfie, eds. Oxford: Clarendon Press.

———. 1976b [1776]. *An Inquiry into the Nature and Causes of the Wealth of Nations*. Glasgow Edition of the Works and Correspondence of Adam Smith, Volume 2. General editors R. H. Campbell and A. S. Skinner; textual editor W. B. Todd. Oxford: Clarendon Press.

Soloff, Paul H., and James W. Milward. 1983. Developmental Histories of Borderline Patients. *Comprehensive Psychiatry* 6:574–588.

Spiro, Melford E. 1961. Social Systems, Personality, and Functional Analysis. In Bert Kaplan, ed., *Studying Personality Cross-Culturally*. New York: Harper and Row. Reprinted in Benjamin Kilbourne and L. L. Langness, eds., 1987, *Culture and Human Nature: Theoretical Papers of Melford E. Spiro*. Chicago and London: University of Chicago Press.

Stapelton, J., and R. Bright. 1976. *Equal Marriage*. New York: Harper and Row.

Stake, Jayne E. 1983. Factors in Reward Distribution: Allocator Motive, Gender, and Protestant Ethic Endorsement. *Journal of Personality and Social Psychology* 44:410–418.

Stevens, S. S. 1946. On the Theory of Scales of Measurement. *Science* 103:677–680.

———. 1951. Mathematics, Measurement, and Psychophysics. In *Handbook of Experimental Psychology*, S. S. Stevens, ed. New York: Wiley.

———. 1958. Measurement and Man. *Science* 127:383–389.

Stine, Wm. Wren. 1989. Interobserver Relational Agreement. *Psychological Bulletin* 106:341–347.

Suppes, Patrick, David H. Krantz, R. Duncan Luce, and Amos Tversky. 1989. *Foundations of Measurement, Volume II: Geometrical, Threshold, and Probabilistic Representations*. New York: Academic Press.

Suret-Canale, Jean. 1964. Les Sociétés Traditionelles en Afrique Tropicale et le Concept de Mode de Production Asiatique. *La Pensée* 117:21–42.

Sussman, Marvin B. 1953. The Help Pattern in the Middle Class Family. *American Sociological Review* 18:22–27.

Tait, David. 1961. *The Konkomba of Northern Ghana*. Jack Goody, ed. Published for the International African Institute and the University of Ghana. London, Ibadan, Accra: Oxford University Press.

Tajfel, Henri. 1978. *Differentiation between Social Groups: Studies in the Social Psychology of Inter-Group Relations*. London: Academic Press.

———. ed., 1982. *Social Identity and Intergroup Relations*. European Studies in Social Psychology. Cambridge and New York: Cambridge University Press; Paris: Editions de la Maison des Sciences de l'Homme.

Tauxier, L. 1912. *Le Noir du Soudan: Pays Mossi et Gourounsi*. Paris: Émile Larose.

———. 1917. *Le Noir de Yatēnga*. Paris: Émile Larose.

Taylor, Charles E., and Michael T. McGuire. 1988. Introduction: Reciprocal Altruism: 15 Years Later. *Ethology and Sociobiology* 9:67–72.

Therborn, Göran. 1980. *The Ideology of Power and the Power of Ideology*. New York: Verso.

Thibaut, John W., and Harold H. Kelley. 1959. *The Social Psychology of Groups*. New York: Wiley.

Tindale, R. Scott, and James H. Davis. 1985. Individual and Group Reward Allocation Decisions in Two Situational Contexts: Effects of Relative Need and Performance. *Journal of Personality and Social Psychology* 48:1148–1161.

Tönnies, Ferdinand. 1988 [1887, 1935]. *Community and Society (Gemeinschaft und Gesellschaft)*. Charles P. Loomis, trans.; with an introduction by John Samples. New Brunswick and Oxford: Transaction Books.

Triandis, Harry C. 1972. *The Analysis of Subjective Culture*. New York: Wiley-Interscience.

———. 1987. Collectivism vs. Individualism: A Reconceptualization of a Basic Concept in Cross-Cultural Psychology. In C. Bagley and G. K. Verma, eds., *Personality, Cognition and Values: Cross-Cultural Perspectives of Childhood and Adolescence*. London: Macmillan.

Triandis, Harry C., V. Vassiliou, and M. Nassiakou. 1968. Three Cross-Cultural Studies of Subjective Culture. *Journal of Personality and Social Psychology* 8, Monograph Supplement (No. 4, part 2).

Triandis, Harry C., Robert Bontempo, Marcelo J. Villareal, Masaaki Asai, and Nydia Lucca. 1988. Individualism and Collectivism: Cross-Cultural Perspective on Self-Ingroup Relationships. *Journal of Personality and Social Psychology* 54:323–338.

Trivers, Robert L. 1971. The Evolution of Reciprocal Altruism. *The Quarterly Review of Biology* 46:35–57.

———. 1974. Parent-Offspring Conflict. *American Zoologist* 14:249–264.

Trosset, Carol. 1988. Welsh Communitas as Ideological Practice. *Ethos* 16:167–180.

Turiel, Elliot. 1983. *The Development of Social Knowledge: Morality and Convention.* Cambridge and New York: Cambridge University Press.

Turnbull, Colin M. 1972. *The Mountain People.* New York: Simon and Schuster.

Turner, Victor. 1969. *The Ritual Process: Structure and Anti-Structure.* London: Routledge and Kegan Paul.

———. 1973. The Center Out There: Pilgrim's Goal. *History of Religions* 12(3):191–230.

———. 1975. *Revelation and Divination in Ndembu Ritual.* Ithaca and London: Cornell University Press.

Udy, Stanley H. 1959. *Organization of Work: A Comparative Analysis of Production Among Nonindustrial Peoples.* New Haven: Human Relations Area Files Press.

———. 1970. *Work in Traditional and Modern Society.* Englewood Cliffs, NJ: Prentice-Hall.

Uleman, James S. A. 1972. The Need for Influence: Development and Validation of a Measure, and Comparison with the Need for Power. *Genetic Psychology Monographs* 85:157–214.

Ulman, Richard B., and David W. Abse. 1983. The Group Psychology of Mass Madness: Jonestown. *Political Psychology* 4:637–661.

United States Office of Strategic Services. 1948. *Assessment of Men.* By the OSS Assessment Staff. New York: Rinehart.

Veblen, Thorstein. 1934 [1899, 1918]. *The Theory of the Leisure Class: An Economic Study of Institutions.* New York: Modern Library.

Vélez-Ibañez, Carlos. 1983. *Bonds of Mutual Trust: The Cultural Systems of Rotating Credit Associations among Urban Mexicans and Chicanos.* New Brunswick, NJ: Rutgers University Press.

Verdon, Michel 1979. African Apprentice Workshops: A Case of Ethnocentric Reductionism. *American Ethnologist* 6:531–542.

Veroff, Joseph. 1957. Development and Validation of a Projective Measure of Power Motivation. *Journal of Abnormal and Social Psychology* 54:1–8.

Veroff, Joseph, and Joanne B. Veroff. 1972. Reconsideration of a Measure of Power Motivation. *Psychological Bulletin* 17:59–69.

———. 1980. *Social Incentives: A Life-Span Developmental Approach.* New York: Academic Press.

Vlastos, Gregory. 1962. Justice and Equality. In Richard B. Brandt, ed., *Social Justice.* Englewood Cliffs, NJ: Prentice-Hall (Spectrum).

Wade, Ted D. 1978. Status and Hierarchy in Nonhuman Primate Societies. In P. P. G. Bateson and Peter H. Klopfer, eds., *Perspectives in Ethology, Volume 3: Social Behavior.* New York: Plenum.

Wallach, Michael A., and Lise Wallach. 1983. *Psychology's Sanction for Selfishness: The Error of Egoism in Theory and Therapy.* San Francisco: W. H. Freeman.

Walster, Elaine, Ellen Berscheid, and G. William Walster. 1973. New Directions in Equity Research. *Journal of Personality and Social Psychology* 25:151–176.

Walster, Elaine, and G. William Walster. 1975. Equity and Social Justice. *Journal of Social Issues* 31:21–43.

Walster, Elaine, G. William Walster, and Ellen Berscheid, in collaboration with William

Austin, Jane Traupmann, Mary K. Utne. 1978. *Equity: Theory and Research*. Boston: Allyn and Bacon.

Walters, Richard H., and Ross D. Parke. 1964. Social Motivation, Dependency, and Susceptibility to Social Influence. In Leonard Berkowitz, ed., *Advances in Experimental Social Psychology* 1. New York and London: Academic Press.

Walzer, Michael. 1983. *Spheres of Justice: A Defense of Pluralism and Equality*. New York: Basic Books

Watsuji, Tetsuro. 1962. Rinrigaku [Ethics]. Part 1 of Watsuji Tetsuro Zenshū [Collected Works of Watsuji Tetsuro], Volume 10. Y. Abe, ed. Tokyo: Iwanami.

Weber, Max. 1958 [1904–1906]. *The Protestant Ethic and the Spirit of Capitalism*. Talcott Parsons, trans. New York: Charles Schribner's Sons.

———. 1975 [1916, 1920–21]. The Social Psychology of the World Religions. In Hans H. Gerth and C. Wright Mills, eds. and trans., *From Max Weber: Essays in Sociology*. New York and Oxford: Oxford University Press.

———. 1978 [1922]. *Economy and Society*. Gunther Roth and Claus Wittich, trans. Berkeley: University of California Press.

Wellar, Robert. 1986. Discussion paper at the SPA, AES and SCA sponsored session on The Directive Force of Cultural Models at the American Anthropological Association Meetings, Philadelphia, 4 December 1986.

Welsch, Roger L., ed. 1981. *Mister, You Got Yourself a Horse: Tales of Old-Time Horse Trading*. Lincoln and London: University of Nebraska Press.

Westen, Drew. 1984. Cultural Materialism: Food for Thought or Bum Steer? *Current Anthropology* 25:639–653.

Whiting, John W. M., and Irvin L. Child. 1953. *Child Training and Personality: A Cross-Cultural Study*. New Haven and London: Yale University Press.

White, Geoffrey M. 1980. Conceptual Universals in Interpersonal Language. *American Anthropologist* 82:759–781.

White, Geoffrey M., and Chavivum Prachuabmoh. 1983. The Cognitive Organization of Ethnic Images. *Ethos* 11:2–32.

Whitehead, Harriet. 1993. Morals, Models, and Motives in a Different Light: A Rumination on Alan Fiske's *Structures of Social Life*. *Ethos*, forthcoming.

Whorf, Benjamin Lee. 1956 [1941, 1950]. *Language, Thought, and Reality*. John B. Carroll, ed. Cambridge, MA: MIT Press. Chapters on The Relation of Habitual Thought and Behavior to Language [1941], and An American Indian Model of the Universe [1950].

Wiggins, Jerry S., and Ross Broughton. 1985. The Interpersonal Circle: A Structural Model for the Integration of Personality Research. In Robert Hogan and Warren Jones, eds., *Perspectives in Personality* 1. Greenwich, CT and London: JAI Press.

Wilk, Richard R., ed. 1989. *The Household Economy: Reconsidering the Domestic Mode of Production*. Boulder and London: Westview Press.

Wilson, Edward O. 1971. *The Insect Societies*. Cambridge, MA: Belknap Press of Harvard University Press.

Winter, David G. 1973. *The Power Motive*. New York: Free Press; London: Collier Macmillan.

Wish, Myron. 1976. Comparisons among Multidimensional Structures of Interpersonal Relations. *Multivariate Behavioral Research* 11:297–324.

Wish, Myron, Morton Deutsch, and Susan B. Kaplan. 1976. Perceived Dimensions of Interpersonal Relations. *Journal of Personality and Social Psychology*. 33:409–420.

Wong, David B. 1984. *Moral Relativity*. Berkeley: University of California Press.

Wood, Beatrice. 1985. Proximity and Hierarchy: Orthogonal Dimensions of Family Interconnectedness. *Family Process* 24:487–507.

Worsley, Peter M. 1956. The Kinship System of the Tallensi: A Revaluation. *Journal of the Royal Anthropological Institute* 86:37–75.

Wright, George O. 1954. Projection and Displacement: A Cross-Cultural Study of Folk Tale Aggression. *Journal of Abnormal and Social Psychology* 49:523–528.

# Index

Abelian group, 217
  definition, 215
Abse, 132
Absolute measurement, 229
Abstract symbolic representation, 205, 206
Abu-Lughod, 92
Accessibility to abstract self-reflective analysis, 205–206
Accessibility to verbal report, 206–206
Accounts, small business, 340
Accra, 341
Acheson, 60
Achievement, 34, 338–345, 391, 400
Achievement motivation, 106–110, 393, 394, 400
Acquisition of cultural implementation rules, 381–408
Adamopoulos, 36
Adams, 57, 59
Addition, whether order-preserving, 425
Additive identity, definition, 215
Adorno, 103–104, 421
ADRK (Moose development organization), 247, 270, 317
Affection (social dimension), 36; see also economy of affection
Affiliation (social dimension), 36
Affiliative motives, 100–102, 420
Africa (in general), 65, 116, 117, 124–127, 128, 133, 149, 237; see also specific cultures and nations
  other cultures in Voltaic region, 346–367
Agency, 30, 411
Agentic mode, 94

Aggregation of the models, 371–379
Aggression, 56, 112, 130–135, 410
Agreeable (social dimension), 36
Agriculture, 244–247, 258–285; see also bees; collective fields; separate fields
  Bambara, 350–353
  Bemba, 364
  Dogon, 348–349
  Gouro, 360–347
  relation to self, social relations, and ideology, 413
AIDS, 125
Ainsworth, 186, 406
Alexander, 421
Alexandre, 289, 430
Alienative recruitment, 79
Allen, 78
Allocation of wives, 319–322
Allocentrism, 276
Allport, 76
Alper, 229
Altruism, 116, 195, 196, 277, 313, 354, 391, 420
Amae (Japanese dependence motive), 112, 113, 421, 431
Amaeru (Japanese dependence), 112, 113, 119, 125, 128
Amazon, 114
Ambitious (social dimension), 36
American Psychiatric Association, 135
Amish, 83, 121
Amity, 354
Amulets, 317
Anarchism, ideology, 117

Anarchy, 283, 423
Ancestors, 282, 284, 310, 314, 315
Ancient mode of production, 65
Andaman Islands, 60
Anderson, 19
Andes, 68
Antagonistic (social dimension), 36
Anthropological perspectives on exchange,
    53–57
Anti-Semitism, 103, 104
Antisocial personality, 135, 398–400
Antisymmetry, definition, 213
Antitheses of the four models, 122, 191–192
Anxiety, 390
Apes, 392
'Apet (Ilongot EM jealousy), 112
Appadurai, 69, 143
Apprentice workshops, 340–341
Arapesh, 38
Archimedean ordered fields, 222–223, 226,
    228, 229, 411, 412
    definition, 218
Ardner, 29, 153
Arendt, 123, 132
Arens, 122
Arensberg, 32, 238, 239, 338, 366
Aristotle, 398
Arnould, 268, 416
Artisans, 338–345, 365, 426, 434
    Dogon, 349–350
    Gouro, 362–363
Asad, 14, 237
Asante: see Ashanti
Asch, 76, 78
Ascription and acquisition of roles, 145–147, 413
Ashanti, 69, 140, 341, 432
Asia, 117, 149
Asiatic mode of production, 64
Asocial orientation, definition, 19–20, 410; see
    also sociopathy
Assertive (social dimensions), 36
Associative property, 215
Athay, 32, 97
Atkinson, 101, 107, 111, 393
Austin, 57, 58, 392
Australia, 87
Australian aboriginals, 69
Authoritarian personality, 103–104
Authority, influence, 78
Authority Ranking, definition, 14, 213–215
Autism, 135
Autonomy (social dimension), 36
Avoidant personality disorder, 135

Axelrod, 89, 123
Axiomatic definitions of the four relational
    structures, 210–223
Azzi, 58

Bachiga, 38
Bagba, 428
Bailey, 37
Bakan, 85, 91, 94
Balance, 171, 355, 417
Bales, 36, 416
Balima, 322
Ballachey, 76
Bambara (Bamana), 236, 246, 348, 350–353,
    426, 435
Bamtēnga, 290, 421, 431
Bandiagara, 346–350, 435
Banks, C., 130
Bargaining: see haggling
Barlow, 87, 92, 413
Baron, 123, 134, 160, 164, 197, 415
Barsego (Moose bargaining); see haggling
Barth, 237
Bascom, 29, 54, 153
Bates, 237
Bateson, 166
Bathonga, 436
Batson, 420
Baumeister, 190, 390
Bazerman, 110, 257, 396
Beatles, 373
Becker, 89, 93, 229, 238, 249, 271, 426
Beckerman, 89, 197
Bedouins, 124
Bees (work parties), 244–259, 341, 365, 395,
    426, 435
Behaviorism, 424
Belōgo (Moose courtship); see courtship
Bemba, 236, 318, 319, 363–365, 435
Benedict, 312
Bengal, 86
Benin, 285
Benjamin, 410
Beolgo (Moose separate field); 260–264, 318,
    348, 349, 427
Beret (Ilongot EM distributive justice), 112
Berger, 58
Berkowitz, 59, 397
Berscheid, 57, 59, 271, 426
Betang (Ilongot AR deference attitude), 112
Biebuyck, 429
Bierhoff, 58, 397
Binary operations, definition, 425

Bisa, 250, 274, 275
Blacksmiths; see Sāaba
Blau, F., 93
Blau, P., 31, 32, 36, 77, 137, 163, 416, 426
Bloch, 355, 435
Blum, 116, 117, 402
Boas, 30
Bobo, 87, 274, 275
  Bobo-Fing, 348
Bohannon, 56, 366, 373, 418, 423
Bootzin, 77
Borrowing, 247
  Dogon, 435
  Tikopia, 375
Botswana, 366
Boulding, 79, 118
Bounce-back device, 132
Boundaries, 419
  Boundary maintenance, 420
Bourdieu, 238
Boutillier, 335
Bowlby, 71, 92, 186, 190, 406
Boyatzis, 420
Bradach, 398
Brazil, 130
Brehm, J., 77
Brehm, S., 77
Bride price (bridewealth), 287, 292, 430, 431
  Bambara, 351
  Gouro, 363
Bright, 93
Broughton, 416
Brown, P., 117
Brown, R., 37, 104, 107–108, 171
Buber, 30, 86, 91, 103
Buddha, 422
Bulatao, 117
Bulman, 126
Burgess, 93
Burial societies, 62
Burkina Faso: see Bobo; Moose; specific
  regions and towns
Burling 237, 271
Business (social dimension), 36
Buss, 100
Buying a slave wife, 297–299
Bwaba, 348
Byrne, 196, 197

Caboret, 425
Calculative recruitment, 79
Calculus of costs and benefits, 232–233,
  355–366, 391

Calvinism, 108
Campbell, 61
Cannibalism, 416
Capital reinvestment, 338–345
Capitalism, 65
Cash crops, 264–265
  Gouro, 362
Categorical scale, 209, 229
Caudill, 113, 386
Causation, 282
Central Africa, 86
Chadwick, 101
Chain of command, 75
Chalmers, 196
Characterization of the four models, qualita-
  tive, 13–19
Charisma, 103, 310
Charismatic legitimation of authority, 26–27,
  75, 312
Cheal, 366
Cheney, 196, 197, 205, 392, 423
Chiefship of village, 315–317
Child, I., 422
China, 70, 103, 117, 134, 421
Choice between achievement and sharing,
  338–345
Chomsky, 187, 416
Cialdini, 77, 79, 419
Civetas, 120
Clark, 30, 31, 36, 62, 77, 102, 165
Cleckley, 99, 135, 431
Clinical implications of the models, 134–135
Coefficient of relatedness r, 424
Coercion and force, 19, 79, 410, 416
Cognition, 406, 409, 410
Cognitive consistency, 171
Cohen, 58, 397, 417
Coherent systems of meaning, 371–380
Cold (social dimension), 36
Collateral orientation, 144–145, 386
Collective field, 260–264
Collective grain stores, 318, 319
Collective responsibility, 415
Collectivist orientation, 276, 366, 373
Colonial period, 332
Combinations of four models, 21–23,
  155–168; see also syntax
Commensual consumption, 259–277, 361,
  402; see also food sharing
Commensurability of the four models,
  372–374
Commitment, 78, 399
Common metric, lack of, 372–374

Commons, 60–61, 79, 270; see also land sharing
Communial cultivation, 259–277
Communal discernment, 419
Communal relationships (Mills and Clark theory), 30
Communal Sharing, definition, 13, 211–213
Communion, 30, 85, 94
Communitas, 85–86, 103, 419
Community, 116
Commutative principle, 223, 225
    definition, 215
Companionship, form of family, 94
Comparisons, 371–379
Compassion, 399
Competence, 423, 425
Competition, 18, 77, 219, 232, 233, 236, 341, 366, 382, 396–398, 400, 401, 436, 437
Competitive (social dimension), 36
Competitive societies, 38, 312, 391
Complementarity of social interaction, 21, 181–184, 388–394; see also jointly constituting a social relationship
Complexity, how generated, 150–155
Compliance, 31, 73, 79, 80
Composition of social forms, 155–168
Compound (Moose social unit), 427
Comprehension of social relationships, 385
Compunction, 399
Concrete operational representation, 205–206
Conformity, 76
Confucius, 117
Confusing one person with another, 137, 409
Congress, U.S., 75
Congruence of motives and norms, 385–386, 410–411; see also directive force
Congruence with respect to a collection of properties, 212, 425
Connected, definition, 214
Conscience, 385, 399; see also morality and moral judgment
Consensus about cultural implementation rules, 386, 410–411
Consistency, influence mechanism, 419
Consistency of implementation rules, 371–380, 410–411
Constantian, 102
Constitution of groups, 82–98
Constitutive functions of models, 387
Constitutive parameters, 147–148; see also parameter setting
Constitutive taboos, 191, 192
Construction of emergent entities, 175–177
Construction of social relationships, 385, 410

Consumption: see food sharing
Context-bound satisfactions of Market Pricing, 395, 396
Contract law, 90, 119
Contracts and contractual obligations, 18, 28, 78, 231, 236–237, 396–398
Contractual recruitment, 34
Contribution, 60–63
Control (social dimension), 36
Control of social relationships, 385
Cook, 77
Cooley, 76, 84, 85, 100
Cooperation, 401
Cooperative (social dimension), 36
Cooperative societies, 38, 268, 312, 366, 390, 391, 429, 432, 436
Coordination of use of four models, 166, 181–184, 371–380, 410–411, 423
Coquery-Vidrovitch, 65, 319, 428
Corporate fields, 318, 348–349
Correspondence between mental representations and the preferred cultural mode of marking, 206
Cost/benefit ratios, 232, 306
Courtship, 290–294, 300–301, 310, 389, 430, 431
Crafts and craftsmen: see artisans
Craving for social relationships, 385; see also motivation
Credit, 247, 431
Criterion for identifying relationships, 18
Critical period, 406
Criticism for identifying relationships, 18
Critical period, 406
Criticism of social relationships, 385
Cross dressing, 432
Cross-cultural understanding, 187–189
Cross-cousin marriage, 420
Crutchfield, 36, 76
Csikszentmihalyi, 69
Cultivating bee, 244–245
Cultural constitition of social relations, 177–179, 414
Cultural implementation rules; see implementation rules, see also parameter setting
Cultural meanings, 177–184
Cultural translation, 188, 189
Cultural variability, how generated, 142–150, 414
Culture-distance, 307, 411
Custodial labor recruitment, 34–35, 68

D'Andrade, 177, 179, 189, 237, 240, 258, 387, 426

Dagomba, 430
Dahomey, 285
Dakota, 436
Damon, 405, 417
Dapoore, 434
Darley, 32, 97
Davis, J., 417
Davis, K., 32, 97
Davis, M., 420
Dawes, 61, 98, 197
De Soto, 196, 205
Death, 278–281
"Death of the Hired Man," 352
Deberse, 434
Decision function, 378
Decision making, 3–5, 73–76, 144, 145
Decision theory, 249
Deference motivation, 103
Defilement, 28
Deindividuation, 130
Delobsom, 262, 263, 289, 290, 291, 309, 325, 339, 426, 427, 430, 431, 432
*Delphinidae* (dolphins), 392
Demand curves, 378
Demand effects, 77
Deng, 429
Dependent personality disorder, 135
Depression, 135
Deprivation, 406
Desertion, 436
Desire and duty, 370, 384–387, 410–411
Desire to punish others for violations, 192–193
Desplagnes, 347, 348, 349, 350, 435
Deutsch, K., 79
Deutsch, M., 165, 397, 416, 417
Development, child: *see* externalization; socialization
Devoted (social dimension), 36
Dictatorial (social dimension), 36
Diener, 130
Dierterlen, 347–350
Differences that make a social difference, 207–210
Diggers, 117
Dimensional analysis of social relationships, 35–37, 411–412
Dion, 89, 123
Directive force of the four models, 179–180, 240, 279, 312, 328, 343, 344, 353, 358, 371, 386, 387; *see also* motivation
Discord, 130–133
Discrete interval scale, 229
Discretionary features, 416; *see also* implementation rules; parameter setting

Dissimulation, 423
Distribution, 7, 8, 34, 60–63, 110
Distributive principle, 223, 227–228
    definition, 217
Divination, 278, 281–282, 327–328, 434
Division of labor, 239, 342
Divorce, 424
Docile (social dimension), 36
Dogon, 236, 298, 346–350, 435
Doi, K., 109, 111, 396
Doi, L. T., 74, 84, 101, 109, 112, 113, 117, 119, 125, 128, 134, 366, 396, 421
Dolphins, 392
Domain application rules, 142–145; *see also* implementation rules; parameter setting
Dominance (social dimension), 36
Dominance hierarchies, 196
Dominance motivation, 103
Douglas, 37, 38, 87, 123, 137, 312, 416
Dowry, 430
DuBois, 330
Dumont, 118, 239, 369, 370
Dupire, 335
Durkheim, 26, 28, 30, 36, 51, 63, 66, 67, 84, 91, 96, 120, 128, 137, 163, 166, 167, 192, 239, 385, 416, 418
Duty and desire, 370, 410–411
Dworkin, 132
Dysfunction, 134–135
Dysthymic disorder, 135

Earth, Moose ritual force, 282, 284
East Africa, 87
Eating: *see* food sharing
Eccles, 398
Economic activities, 338–345
Economic alternatives, 249–257
Economic self-interest: *see* self-interest
Economic theory, 198, 232, 237, 240, 271, 350–353, 376–379, 404, 433
Economy of affection, 268
Egalitarian reciprocity in marriage, 302–304
Egoism: *see* self-interest
Ekeh, 416, 426
Elias, 271, 319, 415, 422
Elopement, 304–305
Embu, 273
Emergent qualities of social and cultural realities, 387–390
Emic, definition, 423
Emigration: *see* Ghana; Ivory Coast, migration
Emotions, 189–190, 424; *see also* Ilongot; Japan
Empathy, 420

Empirical differences that make a social difference, 207–210
Enactive representation/marking, 26, 204
Endogenous source of models, 405
Ends, 238, 382–383; see also motivation; rationality
Enemies, 417
Engels, 35, 63–66, 69, 90, 120, 167, 239, 392
Enright, 405, 406
Ensembled individualism, 84
Entrepreneurs, 338–345
Equal (social dimension), 36
Equal-quantity trades, 248–249
Equality as distributive principle, 35, 165
Equality Matching, definition, 14, 215–216
Equality motivation, 110–111
Equity as distributive principle, 35, 110, 165
Equity theory, 59, 237, 396
Equivalence relation, 178–179, 211–213, 220, 224
  definition, 211
Erasmus, 36, 63, 67–68, 137, 163, 168, 418
Erikson, 421
Errors, social, 137, 409
Eskimo, 38
Ethicization, 28
Ethnocentrism, 61, 103, 104
Ethnopsychology, 416
Etic, definition, 423
Etzioni, 31, 79, 92, 167, 229, 238, 416, 419
Europe, 69, 117, 140
Evans, 77
Evans-Pritchard, 54, 124, 125, 127, 417
Evil, 121, 415
Evolutionary biology, 195–199, 391, 406
Exchange, 31–33, 53–57, 231, 237, 416
  equivalents vs. identicals, 96
Exchange relationship (Mills and Clark theory), 30
Exclusion, 419–420
Experience-near, 425
Exploitation, 415, 418
External, 424
External constraints, 384
Externalization of the models, 370, 381–400, 404–408
Extra, Moose market bonus, 327
F-scale, 103
Fada N'Gourma, 340
Fajans, 417
False consciousness, 417
Familial labor recruitment, 34, 68
Family (social dimension), 36

Farming: see agriculture
Farrow, 105
Father, 178
Fatima, 105
Feather, 107, 111, 393
Ferber, 93
Festinger, 76
Festive labor, 67–68; see also bees
Feudal ownership or estate property, 64
Feudal relationship, 27
Feurbach, 86
Fieldwork, 188–189
Filial piety, 103
Finer than, definition, 212
Fire fighting example, 3–12
Firth, 29, 33, 153, 236, 277, 285, 338, 366, 373, 374, 417, 428
Fiske, Al., 13, 29, 62, 93, 116, 120, 122, 123, 134, 137, 143, 160, 164, 170, 173, 175, 191, 197, 228, 288, 305, 310, 375, 376, 409, 410, 414, 426, 427, 429
Fiske, B., 415
Fiske, D., ix, 425
Fiske, S., 21, 181, 409, 415
Fissioning of compounds, 356–357
  Tallensi, 355
Foa, E., 36, 53, 100, 412, 416
Foa, U., 36, 53, 100, 412, 416
Focal taboos, 122, 191–192
Fodor, 105
Folk models, 410
Folk-urban continuum, 120
Food sharing, 263–268, 292, 421, 435
  Bemba, 364
  Gouro, 360, 361
Forge, A., 17, 18, 29, 256, 257, 420, 432
Formal (social dimension), 36
Forms of address, 37
Fortes, 116, 117, 125, 236, 277, 285, 296, 313, 327, 354–357, 374, 417, 429, 431, 435
Foucault, 192
Fox Indians, 73, 76, 160, 411
Frank, 87, 116, 131, 197, 238
Franklin, 72
Freedom of choice, 18, 233, 298–298, 396–398
Freeman, 55
French, E., 101
French, J., 58
Freud, 88, 89, 92, 128, 164, 385, 399, 400, 421
Fridlund, 19, 189, 190
Friedman, M., 98, 118
Friendliness (social dimension), 36

Friendship, 116, 302–303, 429
Frost, R., 352
Fry, 164
Fulani, 253, 267, 269
Functional integration of societies, 166–167, 371–380
Funerals, 278–281, 430
Fung, 117, 421

Gahuku-Gama, 244
Galaty, 87, 314, 431
Gallimore, 101, 109, 111, 114, 396
Gallistel, 189, 225, 258, 382, 384, 436
Galloping horses, 243–244
Game theory, 237, 393, 412
Gandhi, 117
Gargan, 70
Geertz, 18, 29, 124, 153, 177, 179, 181, 189, 374, 376, 383, 384, 385, 425
Gemeinschaft, 28, 83, 84, 86, 90, 414
Generality, 199–200
Generalized (indirect) exchange, 95, 420
Germanic production, 65
Germans, 66, 107
Gesellschaft, 28, 90, 420
Ghana, 206, 290, 300, 334, 341, 353–359, 427, 431, 432
Gibbs, 170
Giddens, 412
Gillan, 196
Gillies, 124, 127
Gilligan, 85, 87, 116
Gilman, 37
Giri (Japanese obligatory gratitude), 54, 55
Giving wives in tribute and largesse, 299–302
Gleitman, 422
Gluckman, 119
Goals, 382, 383
Godelier, 150, 202, 203, 276, 277, 365, 374, 376, 397, 420, 432
Gods, 416; see also religion
Goffman, 166, 411
Golding, 187
Goode, 170
Goodenough, 424
Gouldner, 33, 77, 96, 97
Goupana, 430
Gourcy, 290, 340, 427, 428, 432
Gourmantche, 428
Gouro, 236, 360–363
Grain stores, collective, 318, 319
Grammar: see language analogy; syntax
Gratitude, 97

Greece, 117, 129
Greenberg, 58, 397
Grid (Douglas theory), 37, 312
Griesinger, 396
Gross, J., 37, 312
Gross participation, 34
Group (Douglas theory), 37, 87, 312
Groups, constitution of, 82–99
Groupthink, 73
Grundrisse, 64
Guhl, 89
Guillet, 35, 68, 137, 163, 418
Guimera, 124, 125, 127
Gunderson, 135
Gurunsi, 87, 297, 425
Guttman, 424
Guttman scale of the four structures, 210, 224–226, 229, 406, 412

Habbés: see Dogon
Hage, 36, 416
Haggling, 325–326
Hamilton, V., 37, 89, 119
Hamilton, W., 52, 123, 195, 196
Hammond, 252, 253, 259, 273, 290, 339, 340, 426, 427, 428, 432
Handel, 196, 205
Haney, 130
Hardin. 60, 61, 98, 270
Hare, 99, 135, 437
Harm, 130–133
Harmful (social dimension), 36
Harrell, 106, 111
Hart, 285, 356, 357, 358, 435
Hartocollis, 135
Haslam, 423, 424
Hatfield, 57, 58
Haugerud, 273
Hausa, 268, 300, 432
Haviland, 124
Hawaii, 69, 101, 109, 114
Head of household, 432
Healy, 102
Heider, 39, 86, 171, 172, 423
Heller, 100
Helpful (social dimension), 36
Hero-worship, 76
Herskovits, 54, 285, 426, 434
Hess, 406
Heteromorphic reciprocity, 96
Heteronomy, 26–27, 121
Hewer, 121, 123, 190
Heyns, 101

Hierarchy, 94
Hill, C., 102
Histrionic personality disorder, 135
Ho, 103, 114, 117, 169
Hobbes, 89, 237, 238, 382, 385, 398
Hollnsteiner, 29, 97
Homans, 77, 89, 410, 420
Homeomorphic reciprocity, 96
Homestead Act, 70
Homogeneity (the extent to which all elements
    have the same properties), 229, 413
Horizontal décalage, 425
Horowitz, 134
Horse, 233–244
Horton, 124, 128, 181
Hostetler, 83, 121
Hostile (social dimension), 36
Householding, 32, 416
Howell, 138
*Hsiao Ching* (Chinese philosophy), 117, 421
Hull, C., 237
Human nature, 238
Humphrey, 197
Hunter-gatherers, 411
Huston, 87
Hyden, 268, 331
Hyper-social malfunctions, 135
Hypo-social malfunctions, 135

Iconic representation, 204
Ideal-logical coherence of cultures, 166–167,
    371–380, 410–411
Identity, social, 82–98, 414; *see also* self
Identity, definition as a formal relation, 212
Ideology and ideological legitimation, 26–28,
    115–124, 149, 150, 312, 355–359,
    410–411, 419, 436, *see also* values
Idiocentrism, 276
Ifugao, 38
Ilboudo, 431, 434
Ilongot, 112
Imagoes, 88
Imitation, 78
Implementation rules, 23, 24, 142–150,
    188–189, 233, 240, 266, 323, 359, 370,
    371–380, 384, 392, 393, 399, 405, 406,
    413, 414, 417, 435, 436, *see also* parame-
    ter setting
Incest taboo, 95
Inclusive fitness, 195–196
Inconsistent orientations, co-existence of,
    374–376, 410–411
India, 105, 117

Indiscernibility of identicals, 425
Individual production, 338–345
Individual prominence (social dimension), 36
Individual self-interest: *see* self-interest
Individualism, 18, 20, 219, 233, 236, 237, 238,
    240, 276, 307, 323, 331, 338–345,
    354–359, 364, 366, 369, 373, 396–398,
    415, 416, 422, 424, 437
Individualistic value orientation, 38, 144–145
Individualistic societies, 312
Individuality, 38, 298, 381–408, 424
Indulgent (social dimension), 36
Infuence, 31, 76–81, 282
Informal (social dimension), 36
Information exchange, 326, 329, 394, 426, 434
Inherent sociability of human nature,
    400–407, 411
Innateness hypothesis, 424, 437; *see also* exter-
    nalization; language analogy
Institut National, 332, 337
Institution, form of family, 93
Institutions, 158–159
Instrumentality, 399; *see also* means and ends
Integration of modes, 371–380, 410–411
Intensity of social relationships, 30, 37
Interconnections, 374
Interdependence (social dimension), 36
Interdependence of relationships, 170–175; *see
    also* ramifications of transgression
Interest theory, 237, 387; *see also* economic
    theory; self-interest
Intérieur, 343
Internal, 424
Internality, 384
Internalization, 73, 80, 381–408, 424; *see also*
    externalization; implementation rules;
    parameter setting
Interpretive functions of models, 387; *see also*
    models of
Interval scale, 209, 229
Intervening in social relationships, 385; *see
    also* ramifications of transgression
Intimacy (social dimension), 36
Intimacy motivation, 88, 101–103
Intrinsically social motives, 390
Invariance of relational structure under spe-
    cific transformations, 208, 413
Invariant sequence of externalizationb of the
    four models, 406
Invisible hand, 62, 98
Iroquois, 436
Islam: *see* Moslems
Italy, 128

Ivory Coast, 68, 236, 251, 261, 278, 281, 295, 304, 317, 324, 328, 329–338, 342, 351, 360–363, 428, 434
Izard, 288, 309, 431
Izard-Héritier, 288, 425
I-Thou, 30, 91, 103
I-It, 30

Jackson, 132
Janis, 73
Janowitz, 79
Japan, 54, 55, 74, 101, 109, 113, 114, 117, 127–129, 134, 220, 366, 386, 396, 421, 422, 431
Jealousy, 185, 186
Jemmott, 421
*Jeunesse* (Moose youth group), 246, 247, 253–254, 317
Job (Biblical character), 194
Jointly constituting a social relationship, 388–390, 410–411; *see also* complementarity of social interaction
Joking relations, 138, 293
Jonestown, 132
Jural feature, 170–176
Justice, 8, 9, 35, 57, 58, 59, 165, 418, 421, 423
Justice motivation, 110

Kaboré, 284
Kahneman, 232, 397
Kalahari, 182, 366
Kaluli, 55, 56, 132
Kaplan, 410
Karuza, 164
Kaut, 114
Kavka, 132, 238
Kawada, 246, 265, 309, 428, 430, 432
Kaya, 262, 303
Kelley, 89, 426
Kelly, 422
Kennedy, 138
Kenya, 273
*Keore* (Moose EM reimbursement), 327–328, 433
Kerlinger, 74
Kibsi; *see* Dogon
Kiernan, 124, 125
Kiesler, 416
Kin selection, 195–196
Kinesthetic marking/representation, 26, 204
*Kĩnkirsi* (Moose fairies), 283–284
Kinship, 116, 277, 313, 352, 355, 356, 357, 358, 366, 424

*Kiuugu* festival, 246
Kluckhorn, 38, 72, 143, 144, 145, 392
Knetsch, 397
Knowledge, 410–411, 425
Kohlberg, 121, 123, 163, 190
Kohler, 330, 331
*Kombere* (Moose paramount chief), 315–316, 433
Kombissiri, 425
Komorita, 97, 165
Konkomba, 290, 303, 427, 431–432
Koopmans, 98
Kopytoff, 298
Koudougou, 284, 431
Koungoussi, 290, 426, 427, 431
Koupela, 290, 431
Kracke, 114
Kramer, 29, 62, 153
Krause, 102
Krech, 36, 76
Kropotkin, 84, 117
Kula, 16–17, 30, 53–54, 398
Kumasi, 300, 330, 341, 427, 433
Kung, 150, 182, 366
Kureshi, 105
Kurland, 89, 197
*Kürwille*, 90
Kwakiutl, 436

Labor migration, 236, 261; *see also* Ivory Coast; migration; Remy; Schildkrout
Labor; *see* work
Lallemand, 284, 427, 430, 431
Lambert, 422
Land sharing, 69, 271–276, 418, 428
Land shortage, 333
Land use, Tikopia, 375
Language analogy, 3, 25, 165, 166, 180, 187–189, 199, 203, 224, 422, 424; *see also* competence; externalization; implementation rules; learnability; overgeneralization; parameter setting; recognition; shifters; syntax
*Langue*, 138, 415
Larimore, 83, 121
Law, 115–124
Lawick-Goodall, H., 196
Lawick-Goodall, J., 196
Lazy (social dimension), 36
Leach, E., 355
Leach, J., 53
Leach, L., 53
Learnability, 188; *see also* socialization

Learning theory, 237
Leary, 37
Lebra, 54, 55, 84, 97, 113, 114, 115, 127, 128, 366, 396, 422
Lee, 103, 117
Legitimacy of punishment, 193–194
Legitimation, 115–124, 379, 385, 410
Lending, 247
  Dogon, 435
  Tikopia, 375
Lenga (Moose market bonus), 327
Lerner, 110, 124, 397, 417
Levels of analysis, 22, 23, 387–390
Leventhal, 61, 164, 165, 397
Lévi-Strauss, 54, 59, 87, 95, 96, 136, 146, 175, 244, 416, 420
LeVine, 61, 121, 123, 190, 420
Levy, 190
Lewis, 246, 350–353, 426
Leynaud, 426
Liebrand, 109
Liget (Ilongot EM jealousy motivation), 112
Liking, 78, 86–87
Liminality, 85–86, 419
Limited time, 77
Lineage, 427; see also zaka
Lineal value-orientation, 144, 145
Linear ordering, 196, 213, 214, 215, 221, 223, 412
  definition, 214
Linear quasi-ordering respecting E, definition, 214
Linguistic representation, 206
Links among relationships, 21, 170–176; see also ramifications of transgression
Links between people and things, 68–71
Lipset, 87, 92, 419
Livingston, 396
Llewelyn-Davis, 67, 117, 415
Lloyd-Bostock, 124
Loans: see lending
Locke, 89, 93, 385
Logic of social relationships, 385
Logical coherence of cultures, 166–167, 371–380, 410–411
London, M., 196, 205
Lorenz, 129
Lorr, 416
Lottery, 132, 419
Lovers, 304
  Dogon, 347–348
Lowenstein, 110, 257, 396
Luce, 98, 209, 229, 393

Lucy, 418, 419
Lunchroom effect, 78

Maasai, 67, 87
MacCrimmon, 396, 412
Machiavelli, 117
MacIntyre, A., 398
Macintyre, M., 53, 54
Magic, 317, 327–328, 433
Maine, H., 90, 119, 120, 137, 163, 166
Making sense of social reality, 180–181; see also models of
Makower, 56
Makra, 117
Malfunctioning of models, 135, 414
Mali, 246, 346–353, 426, 435
Malinowski, 16, 17, 30, 32, 33, 54, 69, 96, 150, 228, 239, 256, 277, 366, 398, 430
Mampruse, 430
Mandatory principles, 422; see also relational structures
Manéga, 296, 431
Manga, 250, 251, 252, 265, 303, 331, 428, 431
Mangin, 287, 290, 295, 302, 303, 428, 431
Manipulations of indexical tokens, 205
Mankoff, 93
Manufacturing, 338–345
Maori, 38, 432, 436
Maradi Valley, 285
Marense, 252, 434
Marginal utility, 378
Marie-André, 430, 431, 432
Market exchange (Polanyi's theory), 33
Market Pricing
  definitions, 15, 217–219
  nonessential features, 15–16, 18, 20, 396–398
Market women, 434
Markets, 325–327
Marking of the models and social relationships, 148–149, 203–207, 392
Marks, 421
Markwith, 125
Marriage, 92–95, 142, 287–308, 425, 429–432
  Bambara, 351
  Dogon, 347, 348
  late age for Moose men, 332
Marshall, L., 52, 54, 116, 150, 159, 182, 366
Marshall, M., 54
Marwell, 36, 410
Marx, 35, 53, 63–66, 68, 69, 90, 96, 120, 137, 163, 166, 167, 239, 277, 323, 359, 392, 411, 418, 432

Masai: *see* Maasai
Mason, 26, 69, 426, 427, 429, 430, 432
Massed labor, 254
Material subsistence needs, 18, 219
Materialism, 232, 237, 285, 324–367, 376, 377, 396–398
Mathews, 124
Matrilateral marriage, 414
Matsuzawa, 392
Mauss, 33, 51, 54, 69, 87, 96, 97, 398
Maximization, 18, 219, 232, 233, 249–257, 277, 286, 298, 319, 324–367, 376–379, 382, 391, 396–398, 400, 403, 404, 415, 417, 418, 420, 433, 436
McAdams, 88, 101–102, 106, 111
McCauley, 73, 125, 419
McCay, 60
McClelland, 105, 106, 107, 109, 111, 393, 421
McCord, J., 99, 135, 437
McCord, W., 99, 135, 437
McGonigle, 196
McGuire, 197
McMillan, 262, 264–265, 273
McNair, 416
Mead, G. H., 85, 86, 88, 89, 91, 92
Mead, M., 38, 268, 275, 276, 277, 288, 312, 338, 359, 366, 373, 390, 391, 392, 399, 415, 417, 429, 432, 436, 437
Meanings, cultural, 177–184
Means ane ends, 238, 371–380; *see also* instrumentality
Measurement theory, 209, 229–230, 413
Mechanical solidarity, 28, 239, 416
Medicine, 327, 328
Mediterranean, 131
Meeker, 87, 92, 413
Meillassoux, 54, 96, 154, 236, 249, 299, 309, 342, 360–363, 435
Melanesia, 16, 17, 18, 53, 54
Messick, 396, 412
Meta-cognitive standard of interpretation, lack of, 376
Mfantse, 206
Migration, labor, 322, 329–338, 350–353, 355, 356, 433, 434; *see also* Ivory Coast; Remy; Schildkrout
Mikula, 57, 165, 397, 417, 423
Milgram, 76, 77, 132, 419
Miller, 73, 76, 160, 417
Millon, 135, 437
Mills, 30, 31, 36, 165
Milward, 135
Misfortune, 9–11, 28, 124–129

Mitchell, W., 33
Mitchell, J., 124
Mo Tzu, 117
Models and motives in Moose social relations, 305–308
Models for, 385, 410–411
Models of, 385, 410–411
Money, 325, 327
 neither necessary nor sufficient for Market Pricing, 327–328, 433
Monistic theories, 370
Moogo Naaba, 322
Moore language, 32, 97
Moose, 24, 26, 27, 29, 37, 55, 58, 62, 64, 66, 67, 68, 69, 70, 71, 75, 87–88, 93, 109, 111, 122, 123, 125, 128, 129, 143, 146, 147, 148, 149, 151, 172, 175, 177, 180, 182, 192, 204, 205, 206, 208, 212, 213, 214, 217, 231–347, 352, 355, 357–358, 362, 371, 373, 374, 375, 377, 378, 379–380, 383, 386, 389, 392–395, 398, 399, 401, 426, 427, 429, 430, 431, 432, 434, 435, 436; *see also* specific ethnic subgroups (clans); specific regions and towns
Moral development, 407
Moral recruitment, 79
Morality and moral judgment, 5, 6, 26, 27, 28, 115–124, 406, 410
Morgan, L., 120
Morgan, W., 61, 110
Mormons, 143–145
Morris, 14
Morsbach, 112
Moslems, 282, 300, 330, 331, 431; *see also* Yarse
Motivation, 99–114, 189, 190, 235, 237, 239, 240, 249–259, 266–269, 277, 280, 297, 305–308, 311–329, 338–354, 359–371, 380, 381, 387, 400–408, 410–411, 434, 436; *see also* achievement motivation, initimacy motivation, power motivation integration within cultures, 375; of groups, 387–390
 of nonwestern people, 111–114
Motor regularities, 121
Much, 123
Murray, 100–103, 106–108, 110–113
Muslims, *see* Moslems
Mutual aid (Kropotkin theory), 84
Mutual contingency among relationships, 170–176; *see also* ramifications of transgression
Mutual respect and cooperation, 26–27

Mutually presupposing components of social relationships, 387–390, 410–411

Naive folk social psychology, 39
Nakomse, 87, 244, 273–274, 278, 288–289, 301, 315–316, 334, 346, 429
Narcissistic personality disorder, 135
Narens, 209, 229
Nassiakou, 276, 310
Natural selection of the four models, 195–199, 391, 414, 420
Navaho, 143, 144, 145
Nazis, 132
Necessity, 332, 333, 334
Need, 35, 165
Need for achievement: see achievement motivation
Need for affection, 106
Need for control, 106
Need for inclusion, 106
Nemeroff, 69, 125
Netting, 416
Neuman, 79
New Guinea, 17, 18, 38, 55, 56, 132, 256, 257, 432
Niebuhr, 79, 97
Nietzsche, 117
Niger, 285, 426
Nigeria, 56, 271, 366, 373
Noaga, 278, 326, 330, 331, 337, 434
Nobere, 288, 331, 430, 431
Noddings, 116
Nokre (MOose bride labor), 432
Nominal scale, 209
Nominalism, 369
Non-farm enterprise, 338–345
Nonessential features of Market Pricing: see Market Pricing; see also implementation rules; parameter setting
Nonmaximization, 376–379
Norm of benefience or goodness, 96
Norm of reciprocity, 96
Norman, 425
Normative feature, 170–175
Norms, 95–99, 240, 381–408
Norms, structural principles, and individual motives, 382–400, 410–411; see also duty and desire
Nozick, 98, 118
Null orientation, definition, 19–20
Nurturance motives, 100–101; see also amae
N-fold sum, definition, 218

Obligation, 385

Observations of two American children, 401–404
Occupations, 420
Oceania, 87
Offerings, 282
Office and proprietorship, 34
Office example of structures, 220–223
O'Flaherty, 421
Ojibwa, 38
O'Malley, 61, 109
On (Japanese reciprocity), 54, 55
Ongees, 60
Ontogenetic sources of social motives, 185, 187, 224, 225, 370, 381–408; see also externalization; socialization
Operation of the four models, 20–25
Optimization, 377, 378–379
Optional features of Market Pricing; see Market Pricing; see also implementation rules, parameter setting
Order preserving, 225
definition, 216, 218
Ordered Abelian group, 221–223
definition, 216
Ordered fields, 225
definition, 218
Ordinal scale, 209, 229
Organic solidarity, 28, 67, 90, 239, 416
organic analogy, 420
Organizations, 158, 159
Orientations to objects, 144–145
Orne, 77
Ortner, 237
Ouagadougou, 288, 289, 290, 303, 430, 431
Ouargaye, 303
Ouédraogo, 430
Overgeneralization, 404–406; see also implementation rules; language analogy

Pacere, 278, 296, 307, 343, 354, 431, 435
Packer, 196, 197
Pageard, 231, 247, 252, 272, 284, 288, 290, 293, 300, 302, 303, 307, 325, 426, 428, 429, 430, 431, 432
Paid work: see wage labor
Palmer, 238
Pandya, 60
Parameter setting, 359, 392, 393, 422, 436; see also implementation rules
Paramount Chief, 315–316
Paranoid disorder, 135
Pareto optimum, 98
Parity, 110
Park, 100

Parkin, 421
*Parole*, 138, 415
Parsons, A., 129
Parsons, T., 18, 412, 413, 416
Partial ordering, definition, 213–214
Pastore, 130–131
Pathan, 237
Patriarchal power, 27, 64
Patrimonial relationship, 27
Paulme, 298, 347, 348, 349, 350, 435
Pearson, 32, 238, 239, 338, 366
Pepitone, 401, 402
Performance, 416; *see also* language analogy
Peristiany, 131
Personal relations between individuals,
    156–157
Personal success, 344
Personality disorders, 135; *see also* sociopathy;
    other specific disorders
Peters, 238
Pfeiffer, 220, 221
Philadelphia, 62
Philippines, 38, 114, 117
Phylogeny: *see* evolutionary biology
Piaget, 26–30, 36, 70, 92, 120–124, 137, 163,
    190, 192, 205, 380, 385
Pike, 423
Pilgrims, 86
Pittman, 100
Pitt-Rivers, 355, 356, 429
*Pog-sivvre* (Moose wife giving), 289, 291
Polanyi, 32, 33, 36, 53, 59, 63, 68, 109, 120,
    159, 236, 238, 239, 277, 285, 300, 335,
    337, 338, 359, 366, 392, 393, 397, 416,
    417, 432, 435
Politeness, 57
Political economy, 237, 346–367
Political ideology, 5–6; *see also* ideology
Political labor recruitment, 35
Pollet, 268
Polymorphic view of human social relations,
    371–380
Polynesia, 285, 366, 375, 428
*Pongidae* (apes), 392
Poole, 422
Pooling (Polanyi's theory), 416
Pooling food: *see* food sharing
Pooling work: *see* work; *see also* familial labor
    recruitment
Power, 14, 19, 32, 58, 103–106, 239
    motivation, 104, 105
    social dimensions, 36, 411
Powers, 102
Prachuambmoh, 36

Practice, 237
Preference, 296, 425
Prejudice, 103
Premack, A., 392
Premack, D., 205, 392, 422, 424
Preoperational representation, 205–206
Prescriptive altruism, 354; *see also* kinship
Prestige goods, Gouro, 363
Prevalence of four models, 372
Price, J., 32, 209, 366
Prices, 373, 425, 433; *see also* rationality
Primary groups, 84
Priorities among four models, 365–367, 372
    the choice between authority and commu-
    nity, 311–323
Prisoners' dilemma, 98
Production (Marx's analysis), 64–65
Production organizations, 33–34; *see also* Udy;
    specific forms of labor recruitment
Profit, 247, 326, 342, 377, 418
    profit making, 239
    profit seeking, 231
"Projective test" of four models, 186–187
Pronouns, 37
Propositional representation, 205–206
Proximity, 94
Prus, 53
Psychoanalytic theory, 407
Psychological reality and features of the four
    models, 184–195, 409–410
Psychopathy, 135, 398–400
Puberty, 425
Punishment, 11, 26, 27, 28, 90, 126, 190–195,
    240, 381, 384, 400, 424; *see also* ramifica-
    tions of transgression; rectification
Purposes: *see* motivation
Puugo (collective field), 260–264, 318–319

Quadratic form of models, 21, 170–176; *see
    also* mutual contingency among relation-
    ships; ramifications of transgression
Quakers, 4, 74, 76, 80, 129
Quarrelsome (social dimension), 36
Quasi-ordering respecting an equivalence rela-
    tion, definition, 213
Quinn, 206, 420

r, coefficient of relatedness, 424
Radcliffe-Brown, 95, 138, 374
Raiffa, 98, 393
*Rakuba* (Moose joking partner), 138, 293
Ramifications of transgressions, 21, 170–176;
    *see also* mutual contingency among rela-
    tionships

Rancorous (social dimension), 36
Rank order, 178
Rates of exchange, 324; *see also* rationality
Ratio scale, 209, 229
Rational-legal legitimation, 26–27
*Rationality*, 231–240, 249, 253, 256, 277, 284,
    285, 324–350, 353–367, 373, 376–379,
    394, 397, 400, 404
Ratios, 412, 424
Rattray, 430
Raven, B., 58
Rawls, 52, 61, 118, 119, 421
Rayner, 37, 312
Razran, 78
Reactance, 77
Read, K., 244
Reagan, 132
Reciprocal labor recruitment, 34, 67–68
Reciprocity and reciprocal exchange, 33,
    51–60, 78, 95, 416
Recognition of structures in novel cultures,
    187–189
Recognition of the legitimacy of punishment,
    193–194; *see also* sanctions
Recruitment, 31
Rectifications, 11, 192
Recursion, 150–155
Redfield, 120
Redistribution, 32, 68, 361, 364, 416–418, 430,
    433
Redress, 11, 192
Reductionist bias in the social sciences, 387,
    414
Regulation (social dimension), 36
Regulative functions of models, 387
Reimbursement, 327, 328
Reinvestment of capital, 339
Relational structures, 26, 203–230
Relations, 369
Relations among relationships, 170–176
Religion, 127–129, 278–285; *see also* gods; sac-
    rifice
Religious Society of Friends, 74, 76
Remorse, 399
Remuneration, 79, 327, 328
Remy, 250, 329, 330, 331, 334, 336, 337, 428,
    434, 435
Repair work, 338–345
Representations of the models, 148–149,
    202–210
Rescher, 373
Respect the identity relations, definition, 213,
    214
Responsibility, 37

Restricted (direct) exchange, 95, 420
Rey, 66
Richards, 319, 319, 364, 365
Ricoeur, 26, 27, 28, 29, 36, 121, 124, 125, 137,
    163, 166, 190
Rites of passage, 413
Rivalry, 76
Rochberg-Halton, 69
Roeper, 422
Roles, 145–147, 327–329
    Role-distance, 384, 411
Rosaldo, 112, 415
Rosenberg, 410
Rosenthal, 77
Rotating credit associations, 152–154, 415
Rousseau, 385
Rozin, 125
Rubel, 412
Ruelle, 334, 430, 431
Rules, 387
Running away with a wife, 304–305
Ryan, 124
Ryle, 204, 205

Sāaba, 87, 251, 270, 274, 278, 339, 341, 427,
    428, 434
Sabini, 77, 78, 80, 130, 132, 190, 419, 422, 424,
    436
Sacrifice, 278–285, 310
Sade, 89
Sadistic (social dimension), 36
Sahlins, 20, 32–33, 36, 53, 69, 138, 163, 196,
    236, 239, 268, 277, 338, 357, 359, 392,
    393, 416, 417, 419, 420
Salisbury, 109
Salvation Cult, Japan, 127, 128
Samoa, 436
Sampson, 59, 84, 89, 143
Sanctions: *see* punishment
Sandel, 118
Sanders, 37, 119
Sao, 430
Sapir, 423
Saponé, 431
Satiation, 344, 377, 378, 406
Satisficing, 436
Saul, 168, 250, 274–275, 428
Saussure, 415, 424
Sawyer, 61, 110
Scale types, 207–210
Scandinavia, 221
Scarce resources, 77, 235, 271, 275, 276, 285
Schachter, 101
Schieffelin, 55, 56, 69, 132, 182

Schildkrout, 300, 329, 330, 427, 432
Schiller, 340
Schizoid personality disorder, 135
Schneider, D., 178, 411
Schneider, H., 237, 271
Schubarth, 61, 109
Schutz, 106, 416
Schwartz, 239, 377, 436
Schwimmer, 54
Schwinger, 57, 134, 165, 423
Scott, 401
Secrecy: see information exchange
Sedlak, 416
Segregation of Market Pricing activities from village life, 343
Selection of models, 163–166
Self, 82–99, 323, 356, 419, 420
Self-interest or selfishness, 18, 20, 116, 219, 232–233, 236–240, 238, 277, 285–286, 297, 306–307, 329–338, 350, 351–359, 366, 375, 381–410, 418, 424, 433, 435
Self-reflective consciousness, 224
Semiotic codes, 148–149, 203–207
Sensorimotor rules and rituals, 26, 204
Senufo, 348
Separate field, 260–264, 318, 348, 349, 427
Service work, 338–345
Sets of roles, 157–158
Sexual relations, 94, 138, 420, 429
Seyfarth, 196, 197, 205, 392, 423
Shared motives, 390
Sharing food: see food sharing
Sharing land: see land sharing
Sharing the wealth, 342–343
Sharing water; see water sharing
Sheeran, 74, 80, 419
Sherif, C., 61, 86
Sherif, M., 61, 86
Sherman, 265
Shifters, 314, 431
Shipley, 101
Shweder, ix, 123, 375, 422
Sih, 117
Silimiisi, 87
Silver, 80, 131, 190, 341, 424, 436
Similarity, 78
Simmel, 381
Simon, 232, 344, 436
Sin, 28
Singer, 135
Sisoaaga (Moose cultivating bee), 244–246, 395, 426
Sisters' sons, 427
Siuure (Moose wife giving), 289, 291

Skilled trades, 340–342
Skinner, 55, 56, 249, 254, 288, 289, 309, 325, 329, 337, 426, 430, 431, 432
Slaves, 65, 297–299, 431, 432
Slovic, 232
Smith, 62, 98, 99, 237
Smuts, 196, 423
Smutylo, 341
Sociability (social dimension), 36
Social and cultural nature of Market Pricing, 391–396
Social attraction, 31
Social contracts: see contracts and contractual obligations
Social control, 381
Social dilemmas, 61
Social errors, 137, 409
Social exchange: see exchange
Social functions of commodities, 393
Social identity: see identity, see also self
Social influence: see influence
Social justice: see justice
Social learning theory, 407
Social order, 381–408
Social organization of Moose abroad, 334–338
Social proof, 78
Social relationship, definition, 19, 21
Social rewards and punishments, 399–400; see also sociopathy
Social structure, 358
Social system functions of four models, 95–99
Socialization, 126, 240, 365, 366, 381–400, 407–408, 422; see also externalization; implementation rules; sociopathy
Societas, 120
Societies, 159–163
Society of Friends, 4, 80, 129
Socioemotional (social dimension), 36
Sociological features of the four models, 170–176
Sociopathy, 126, 135, 398–400
Sogōndāmba (Moose pages), 432
Solidarity (social dimension), 36
Soloff, 135
South America, 67
Southeast Asia, 87
Soviet Union, 134
Soweto, 62
Spanish-Americans, 143–145
Spatial structure of relationships, 35–37, 411–412
Spatiotemporal representations, 204–206
Spheres of exchange, 373, 418
Spheres of justice, 418

Spirit of capitalism, 107
Spirits, 422
Spiro, 193, 384
Spontaneous emergence of the four models in
    ontogeny, 400–407
Spontaneous generation of the four structures,
    186–187
St. Francis, 86
Stahl, 106, 111
Stake, 411
Standards for judging relationships, 385
Stapleton, 93
Status law, 90, 119
Stevens, 208
Stewardship, 309–323
Stine, 277, 229
Strategic interaction, 384, 410–411
Stratification, 343
Strictly economic exchange, 32
Strodtbeck, 38, 72, 143–145, 392
Structural principles of the social system, 358,
    381–408
Structures of relationships, 36, 203–230
Subjectivity, 416
Sublimation, 381
Submission (social dimension), 36
Subordination (social dimension), 36
Subservient (social dimension), 36
Subsistence, 337, 338
Success, 338–345, 377
Succession to office and community solidarity,
    314, 318
Succorance motives, 100, 101; see also amae
Superordinate ethical standard, lack of, 376
Superordination (social dimension), 36
Suppes, 229
Sucret-Canale, 65, 319, 428
Susceptibility to sanctions, 384
Sussman, 417
Swat, 237
Sweden, 406
Switching among modes, 166, 410–411
Symbolic normative rewards, 79
Synchronized work, 245–247
Syntax, 6, 28, 138, 167, 380; see also language
    analogy
System of production, 359
Systematic properties of societies, 371–380,
    410–411
Systems theory, 374–376

Taa (Moose language EM root), 37
Table 1 (manifestations and features of four
    elementary relational models ), 42–49

Table 2 (mean number of wives by husband's
    age), 321
Table 3 (difference between number of wives
    of compound head and compound resi-
    dent with greatest number of wives), 321
Tacitus, 66
Tagalog, 114
Taghalla, 303
Tait, 289, 290, 303, 427, 431, 432
Tajfel, 61, 86, 398
Tallensi, 236, 253, 277, 285, 296, 327,
    353–357, 431, 435
    morality and materialism debate, 353–359
Tanzania, 331
Task-oriented (social dimension), 36
Tasmania, 130
Tatemae (Japanese consensus), 74
Tauxier, 252, 428, 430, 431
Taxes, 331, 342
Taylor, 21, 181, 197
Tēese (Moose lineage Earth force), 304
Tekre (Moose even-quantity trade), 249–249,
    303
Telelogical coordination, 387–390
Tema, 330
Tēnkodogo, 246, 265, 428, 430, 431
Texans, 143, 144, 145
Thaler, 397
The German Ideology, 64
Theoretical roots and conceptual convergence,
    25–39
Therborn, 149
Thibaut, 89, 426
Thick description, 425
Things, meaning of, 68–71
Thomas, 93
Thompson, 110, 257, 396
Threshing bee, 245–247
Tice, 190, 390
Tum (Moose magic/medicine), 317, 327, 328,
    433
Tikopia, 285, 366, 375, 428
Time, 70–72
Tindale, 417
Tithing, 62, 63
Tit-for-tat, 89
Tiv, 56, 366, 373, 429
To (Moore language EM root), 37
Tönnies, 28, 36, 69, 83, 84, 86, 90, 418, 420
Trading (social dimension), 36
Trade-offs, 371–379
Traders, 338–345
Trading in contracts and markets, 154, 155
Tradition, 379–380

Traditional legitimation of authority, 26, 310, 312, 322
Tragedy of the commons, 98
Transformation of EM to AR, 97
Transformations of structures that preserve the defining relations and operations, 208, 413
Trangressions, 11, 21, 190–195
  ramifications of, 170–176
Transitivity, 196, 412
Transvestites, 426
Triandis, 276, 277, 366, 373, 392, 416, 422
Tribal or clan ownership, 64
Tribute, 299–302
Trivers, 91, 116, 131, 196, 197
Trobriand Islanders, 16–17, 150, 366
Trosset, 86
True asocial individualist, 398–400
Trust, 231
Trusteeship, 309–323, 361–429
Turiel, 92
Turkey, 107
Turnbull, 411
Turner, 85–86, 103, 128, 138, 163, 419
Tversky, 232
Tyler, 112

Udy, 33–36, 55, 63, 66–68, 134, 137, 163, 168, 257, 268, 419, 428
Uleman, 105
Ulman, 132
Unary operations, definitions, 419
Understanding social relations, 180–181, 188–189
Unequal (social dimension), 36, 411
Unified theory of social relations, 407–408
Uniqueness (redundancy under transformations), 229, 413
Unit relations, 86–87
United Nations, 23, 75
Universal currency, lack of, 372–374
U.S. Office of Strategic Services, 187
Use of collective grain stores, 318–319
Uses and consequences of axiomatic formalization, 223–230
Utang-la-loób (Tagalog EM obligation), 114
Utility, 232, 237, 307, 324, 373, 376–379, 400, 436
  function, 378
  maximization, 238–240

Vadier, 425
Vaisnavas, 86
Values, 240, 353–359, 365, 381, 436

Van Gennep, 419
Van-Run, 109
Variability, how generated, 142–150, 414
Vassiliou, 276, 410
Veblen, 69, 76, 108, 393
Veil of ignorance, 61, 118
Vélez-Ibaněez, 29, 153
Verdon, 341
Veroff, Joanne, 105, 420
Veroff, Joseph, 101, 104–105, 420
Virtue, 398
Vitkus, 134
Voluntary choice, 18, 233, 236–237, 396–398
Voluntary labor recruitment, 34

Wade, 89, 196
Wage labor, 236, 250–257, 341, 433; see also Ghana; Ivory Coast; migration
Wallach, L., 238, 377
Wallach, M., 238, 377
Walster, E., 57, 59, 271, 397, 426
Walster, G., 57, 59, 271, 397, 426
Walters, 100
Walzer, 373, 418, 421
War, 417
War of all against all, 382, 399
Warm (social dimension), 36
Water sharing, 269–271
Watsuji, 115
Weber, 26–30, 36, 58, 70, 72, 75–77, 82, 86, 103, 107, 108, 119, 120, 124, 137, 163, 166, 167, 239, 249, 310–310, 322, 338, 373, 377, 380, 385, 393, 415, 418, 426
Weinstein, 140, 210–223, 422, 424
Wel (Kaluli EM reciprocity), 55–56
Wellar, 238
Welsch, 56
Wesenwille, 83
West, 64
West Africa, 68, 236, 249, 299, 325, 340–341, 426, 435, see also Bambara; Dogon; Ghana; Gouro; Ivory Coast; Moose; Tallensi
Western, 238
Western Moose, 331
White, 36
Whiten, 196, 197
Whiting, 416
Whitehead, 410
Whorf, 71
Wife giving, 235, 286–308
Wife-givers, 430
Wife-seekers, 430
Wiggins, 116, 410

Wilk, 416
Williams, 422
Wilson, 196
Winning, 377
Winter, 105, 106, 268, 421
Winterbottom, 107
Wish, 36, 410
Witches, 288, 428
Wittgenstein, 393
Wolf, 422
Wong. 117
Wood, B., 134
Work, 6, 7, 31, 33–35, 63–68, 144, 259-262,
    419, 433, see also artisans; bees; farming;
    pooling work; production organizations;
    synchronized work; wage labor; work par-
    ties; work organizations
    Gouro, 361
Work organizations, 34
Work parties, 244–259
World economic market system, 358, 418
Worsley, 355, 356, 357, 359, 435
Wortman, 126
Wright, 422

Yadse, 87; see also Gourcy; Yātēnga

Yako, 303
Yaméogo, 426
Yamey, 29, 153
Yanga, 303
Yarse, 87, 270, 271, 282, 316, 333, 339, 427,
    428, 434
Yātēnga, 259, 284, 290, 340, 426, 427, 428,
    431, 432
Yiraana (Yarse leader), 316
Yiri Paga (Moose follow-up wife), 294
Yîyōose, 87, 244, 270, 273, 278, 281, 314, 346,
    427, 434
Youth group, 317

Zauga (Moose threshing bee), 245, 246, 247,
    395, 435
Zaka (Moose compound), definition, 421
Zambia, 236, 318, 319, 363, 364, 435
Zelditch, 58
Zero, 425
Zimbardo, 130
Zinder, 268
Zitēnga, 296, 431
Zunis, 143–145, 436